essi

Guillem Balagué is a key member of Sky Sport's Spanish football team, appearing regularly on live match coverage and on the weekly round-up show, *Revista de La Liga*. He is also the UK correspondent for *AS*, the Madrid-based Spanish sports newspaper, and *El Larguero*, Spain's most popular sports radio show, attracting some 1.5 million listeners. His work appears regularly in *twentyfour7* magazine, *Bleacher Report* and *Champions* magazine, where he writes a regular column on international football. He wrote the bestselling *A Season on the Brink*, an insider's account of Liverpool's 2004–05 Champions League-winning campaign, and the acclaimed biography *Pep Guardiola: Another Way of Winning*, published in 2012.

@GuillemBalague

By Guillem Balagué

A Season on the Brink
Pep Guardiola: Another Way of Winning
Messi

Messi

Guillem Balague

FOREWORD BY
ALEJANDRO SABELLA

An Orion paperback

First published in Great Britain in 2013
by Orion
This paperback edition published in 2014
by Orion Books Ltd,
Orion House, 5 Upper St Martin's Lane,
London WC2H 9EA

An Hachette UK company

1 3 5 7 9 10 8 6 4 2

Copyright © Guillem Balagué 2013

Project director: Maribel Herruzo
Translation: Peter Lockyer and Marc Joss

The right of Guillem Balagué to be identified as the
author of this work has been asserted by him in accordance
with the Copyright, Designs and Patents Act 1988.

The author and publisher are grateful to Miguel Ruiz
for permission to reproduce all the photographs
except 1, 2, 3 and 19 (Press Association).

A CIP catalogue record for this book is available
from the British Library.

ISBN 978-1-4091-4660-5

Printed and bound in Great Britain by
CPI Group (UK) Ltd, Croydon, CR0 4YY

The Orion Publishing Group's policy is to use papers that
are natural, renewable and recyclable products and
made from wood grown in sustainable forests. The logging
and manufacturing processes are expected to conform to
the environmental regulations of the country of origin.

www.orionbooks.co.uk

To my dad, who has started reading again
To my mum, who is the strongest person I know
To Maribel, my good fairy

Contents

Part Three: At the Peak

Foreword

by Alejandro Sabella

I was appointed national team manager after the Copa América in Argentina. The national side had been eliminated despite not losing a game: they drew twice and beat Costa Rica in the group phase, then drew with Uruguay in the quarter-finals, before losing on penalties. When a team with players of this quality and strength plays in a tournament of that nature, we all find it frustrating if they don't end up as champions. Even when, as happened in this case, they do not lose a single game.

It is normal for the players to have a heightened sense of expectation at the beginning of a new era, with a new coach. We were coming at a low ebb, having failed to progress further in the Copa América. I felt there were conflicting feelings – despite the disappointment, we were sufficiently motivated to move forward with renewed optimism.

The first time I spoke to Leo was in Barcelona. It was in 2011, soon after my appointment. I set out to meet all the players who were playing for sides in Europe. My first stop was Portugal, followed by Barcelona. I didn't know Leo personally, but I wanted to speak to him and to Javier [Mascherano], whom I had met before and who was the captain, to suggest that Leo should wear the armband of the national side. The main purpose of my trip was to introduce myself and to get to know the players, especially those I didn't know, such as Leo, but the question of the team captaincy was important to me. I considered it essential for everyone to know Leo was the leader and that he would lead in his own natural manner. It was vital that he should be recognised as such by the players.

The three of us met, and afterwards I went to Italy, leaving them to discuss it among themselves and to give me their answer. I think it was Javier who rang me to say yes, Leo would be the captain.

After that meeting we met again in India to play one of the national team's first games, a friendly against Venezuela, and later against Nigeria in Bangladesh. But if one match symbolised the new era, it was surely the one against Colombia in the South American qualifiers for the Brazil World Cup 2014. We went through a difficult moment in Barranquilla where, fortunately, the lads were able to turn around a match played in suffocating heat. We were losing 1–0 after a goal from Dorlan Pabón that went in off Mascherano. Fortunately Messi equalised before Agüero made it 2–1 near the end.

As I often say, in football there are defining games, matches that provide the lift you need, the push required to get you going along this new road. I think that game was perhaps the beginning, because after that we started to build a close-knit group and, when a group is close, they get results, are happy playing together and achieve so much more. It is the perfect way, the only way, to overcome your weaknesses.

I am asked if that match defined not only the national team, but Leo himself, since it was from that match onwards that he began to be perceived differently in Argentina. It was certainly the start of a change of perception but there was another one as important, on 29 February, the day we played Switzerland away. That was such a wonderful performance. The day Leo scored a hat-trick. It was his first hat-trick for his country. He had done it for Barcelona countless times, but that was his first one in the blue and white of Argentina. Later in the same year he scored three more goals against Brazil… But, yes, that game against Colombia was, from both a footballing and coaching point of view, the confidence boost we needed.

What I can say is that Leo is a very calm person. He possesses natural leadership as a result of the enormous level of ability he has attained, and what is more, his leadership is accepted by everyone.

I like to give all footballers freedom, and that includes Leo. They live with enough pressure as it is, and I prefer to let them move around freely. The captaincy brings with it greater responsibility, but Leo knows this and has accepted it, and it is helping him to mature and grow. And that is also good for his team-mates.

His team talks and private discussions remain in-house, but I can say that there is undoubtedly a generally happier vibe within the group, a sense of calm that goes beyond work and the job. There is a relaxed and happy atmosphere. It is crucial.

And there you have the mixture you need for Messi to show what he is capable of. Leo has to feel comfortable, and first and foremost he needs to be free. He needs the flexibility to know that he can do whatever is necessary on the pitch at any given moment. In truth, I only discuss the bare minimum with him, merely what is necessary. I don't want to put any extra pressure on him, because the footballers already know the importance of the games, and of their individual contributions to the side.

When you talk about Messi, you need to talk about his development, because, as they say, the hard bit isn't about getting there, it's about staying there. So winning four consecutive Ballon d'Ors is a sign of great progress. Obviously just winning one Ballon d'Or is hard enough, but to win four on the trot is proof positive of just how far he has evolved as a player. During the past few years he has grown to maturity and has developed extraordinary skills that have served to make him increasingly better as a player. It is difficult to maintain, let alone exceed that level of excellence, but somehow he has achieved it.

I am sure that taking over the captaincy of Argentina has served him well in that process. It is necessary to get the confidence of everybody around you to grow as a person and as a player.

The year 2012 was a great one for Leo with the national side, a result of the maturity he has gained as he has grown older. When they say that a footballer has reached his peak, what are you supposed to do? Leave him to his own devices? It is important, for my part, that education and direction continue. No player is ever too good to receive constructive advice and direction.

To illustrate his immense attributes as a player you need only look at the opening match of the 2013–14 league campaign against Levante that Barcelona won 7–0. When Leo goes in to steal the ball he does it with conviction and determination until he succeeds in his objective, as he demonstrated in that game: he stole it and it became the third goal. I have even seen him score headers as if he were a natural. What he is, in fact, is one of those extraordinary players who only gets better, as difficult as that is.

Barcelona chose to play him in the centre, a ploy we copied in the national side, simply because it worked so well for them. Leo gets more of the ball in that area, and the more he gets the ball the better it is for everyone else. As he is mature, confident, intelligent, he cannot be marginalised on the sides. And with Higuaín and Agüero opening up the spaces for him, and with Di María operating on the wing, Leo can decide from his position in the centre where to take the game. It is clear that with these players Leo has become more powerful, and vice versa.

So that everything works out well, I ask all of the players to make that little extra effort to win the ball back, to help those at the back, to sacrifice themselves more. And Leo has to defend wherever he may be in the play and within the possibilities opened up to him. No one asks him to perform miracles, but the main thing about Leo, and others in the side, is what they do with the ball. This is where Leo's work bears fruit.

Normally the best players in the world play in the world's best sides, and they are the ones who have the longest seasons and play the most games. Naturally this sets them apart. What is important is that they get to that stage, at their peak, at the World Cup. Some achieve it, some do not. Now we have a team that is playing well, that gives an appearance of solidity and looks like a team; that is what they showed in a friendly against Italy on 14 August 2013. But the fact of the matter is that any team in which Messi plays is never going to be the same team without him. We have to try to get rid of the notion that we cannot achieve victory without Messi. That obviously affects morale, and on that day, despite Leo's absence, we played a great game. There is no doubt though – yes, we can survive without him. But he is irreplaceable. And no, there is no contradiction in what I am saying.

Messi is our symbol, our standard-bearer. An extraordinary player who plays in an extraordinary team. Maybe the greatest player of all time.

Introduction

Where's Leo?

That was the question on everyone's lips in Leo's classroom at the Juan Mantovani Middle School. His school was situated in the district of Las Heras in the south of the Argentinian city of Rosario, close to his home. Leo had missed a week of school and, apart from brief illnesses, he rarely did that. His desk stood empty, and at playtime, when someone got a ball out, the game seemed even more confusing. There is no football pitch at the Juan Mantovani and there are always too many kids for the small, cramped playground. It did not encourage spacious, expansive games and, with Leo absent, even less so. It had been some days since he had been seen.

It was September, three months before the end of the academic year which in Argentina begins in December. Exams were set around that time and Leo couldn't be present. Someone asked on his behalf if he could do his exams on another day or if he could be given work while he was away.

No, sorry.

Has Leo come in today?

His team-mates at Rosario club Newell's Old Boys (NOB) where he played in the lower ranks were asking the same question. He'd missed a number of training sessions at the Malvinas training academy, and he wasn't he around for the match at the weekend either. 'Hepatitis,' said someone at the club. 'He's got hepatitis.' Ah, that'll be it. Nobody really knew what it was, but it sounded terrible, something that if you caught it meant that you certainly couldn't play football. 'Yes, the Maestro has hepatitis.' That'll be it.

The Maestro. Messi had at other times also been *el Piqui* (Titch) at school, but was 'the Maestro' to his adolescent peers (as others among them were 'Clark Kent', 'the Galician', 'the Greyhound', 'the Korean' because of his haircut): no one had Christian names and surnames in Argentinian football. And that's how the official squad list was written. Name, date of birth, height and nickname: 'the Mouse', 'the Bitumen', 'the Short One' …

Where has Leo gone?

Adrián Coria looked after this diverse group, Leo's first 11-a-side trainer, but he too knew nothing of the boy's whereabouts. Strange to disappear in September. And more than strange, a problem: winning without Leo would be much harder. Someone telephoned Quique Dominguez, his previous coach at Newell: 'No idea, I don't know where he is.' But he assumed that something was happening: he was always a reliable boy but when he had gone for a trial at River Plate just over a year earlier he hadn't said anything then either. Had River finally taken him on? Someone said he had hepatitis.

The Messi family got a phone call some days before. 'Come now, bring the boy.' They had waited so long for this day, and now, suddenly, everything was happening in a rush. They had to prepare to go to Europe.

Newell's were not told. Not a single coach, technical director or player in the club knew what was going on. Neither Leo nor his dad, Jorge, always looking after the kid's career, wanted to tell anybody. It was not difficult to keep their own counsel: they are both discreet, equally reserved. Cast in the same mould.

With a sense of premonition the Rosario newspaper *La Capital* devoted an entire page to the youngster. The first one. It was 3 September 2000. 'A Very Special Little Leper' read the headline, 'Leper' a sobriquet shared by all his team-mates at the club that had once, in the 1920s, played a charity match to raise money for a leper clinic. And on one side a smiling Leo, head tilted, wearing an NOB shirt. He will always be a Leper, a passionate supporter of Newell's, the club that was 'everything' to him in his youth, where he had just won the title in his team's age group, a source of pride to him. And with his quiet voice (it was difficult to get the boy to smile for the camera), he shared with the journalist interviewing him some of his dreams. He wanted to be a PE teacher. And to play in the first division, naturally.

And get into the Argentine national youth team. It was a long way away, but yes, of course, to get into the national side, a dream. He liked chicken. His favourite book? Errr ... the Bible. The first thing that came into his head. He isn't one for reading books. If he hadn't been a footballer what other sport would he have chosen? Do I have to answer that? I don't know, handball maybe. But, yes, he saw himself as a PE teacher. It was the only class at school that he enjoyed. He could be a PE teacher.

It was the newspaper supplement devoted to the *rojinegros* (the red and blacks, the colour of the NOB shirt). The text began: 'Lionel Messi is a player from the tenth division and is the '*enganche*' [player 'in the hole', playmaker] of the team. As a boy, not only is he one of the finest prospects from the Leprosa Academy, he also has a tremendous future ahead of him, because, despite his size, he manages to go past one, two players, dribble, score, but above all he enjoys himself on the ball'. *Gambetear* (to dribble), *enganche*, the words, the concepts, all very Argentinian. Leo was not the cover star of edition 97 of that supplement. That was left to Claudio Paris of the first team who had decided a few days earlier to stay with the club.

A black and white photocopy of the article made its way across the Atlantic.

Jorge and his son Leo, and the friend who was travelling with them to Ezeiza airport, discussed the article as they made their way from Rosario to Buenos Aires. The journey of three and a bit hours seemed longer than that as they travelled along a straight, boring road featuring little else but valleys and traffic signs. Leo gazed out of the window from the back seat.

It was 17 September 2000. A Sunday.

From Ezeiza, with the knowledge only of those closest to them and the school principal, they left for Barcelona.

A 24-hour journey lay ahead of them.

'[The first journey] was good because it was a completely new experience for me. I'd never flown before, never undertaken such a long journey and I enjoyed it all, until the aeroplane started to move about a bit ...' (Leo Messi in *Revista Barça*).

Memories can play tricks on you. In truth the flight experienced a lot of turbulence. When the first meal was served Leo didn't eat, sleeping instead, stretched out over three seats. In his short trousers, with his skinny little legs. He felt nauseous, his stomach was churning. He slept fitfully, and felt sick.

Years later, and with great frequency, he would feel the same nausea before running onto the pitch and would sometimes ask himself if that feeling of sickness he had experienced on that flight really had been caused only by turbulence.

The party arrived in Barcelona at midday on Monday, 18 September, seven months after taping a home video that demonstrated in some eyes that Messi was the new Maradona, and in others, more familiar, closer to him, that his was a natural talent that could help him make it as a footballer, if everything went according to plan.

Someone brought Messi a kilo of oranges and some tennis balls. They asked him to practise with them for a week. Seven days later they recorded the VHS tape which showed him making 113 touches with an orange. With the tennis ball it was easier: 140 *jueguitos*, as they say in Argentina, 140 kick-ups.

There was a table tennis ball lying around. 'Give it to Leo.' They gave it to him. Twenty-nine touches in a row. You try it. See if you can reach three. This Leo had an advantage over you: he spent all day, every day, with the ball. Between games, during the game, at home, in the school yard. Every blessed day.

Eight years later, Mastercard released an advertisement using some of those same images. You can see it on YouTube.

And since February, when the video was recorded, the Messi family would ask themselves, 'When are we going? Where are we going? Are we going?' It became the daily topic, one discussed both with uncertainty and a hint of excitement.

The video, along with others taken at the Malvinas pitch showing Leo in his Newell's shirt performing his slalom-like runs and dribbles, landed on the desk of Josep María Minguella, a well-known players' agent with a lot of influence at Barcelona. And a member of the Catalan club as well. He wasn't too sure at first; the age and distant location of the youngster put doubts in his mind, and he would not be the only one. In the end, though, months later, convinced partly by the spectacular technical skills Leo showed on the tape, partly by the insistence of colleagues who had faith in the boy's future, he decided to put all his weight behind the project and persuaded Barcelona to give him a trial.

Just before Real Madrid made their own initial move to try to sign him.

From his office Minguella called Argentina to tell the Messis to get their things together and come to Barcelona as soon as they could. 'Bring the boy.' Leo was about to fly for the first time.

And to cross the Atlantic for the first time.

Out of the aeroplane and into a humid Barcelona towards the end of summer stepped a 13-year-old Argentinian boy with talented feet and a suitcase. With the dream of succeeding, against new rivals and with new companions, at a big club far, far away from home.

Those who saw him for the first time, so small, thought that Barcelona had made a terrible mistake. All this effort for … this? How was someone so small ever going to become a good footballer?!

'I started to follow Barcelona at the time of Ronaldo and shortly afterwards came the opportunity to come here. At that time, to tell you the truth, I was very excited, and very keen to come here, to see what everything was like, because I was seeing it from a long way away. But when I got here I didn't know how difficult it was going to be' (Leo in *Revista Barça*).

It wasn't Lionel Messi who arrived in Barcelona that day. It was just an excited kid.

Dave Sudbury's song 'The King of Rome' says that when you live in a dump like the West End of Derby you can't live out your dreams. 'I know that,' says someone who wants to challenge destiny. 'A man can crawl around or he can learn to fly/And when you live 'round here/The ground seems awful near.' In Rosario in 2000, it was harder than ever to learn how to fly.

Newell's rejected the chance of helping the Messi family who needed a great deal of money to pay for the hormone injections that Leo so badly needed to help him grow. Had they paid for them, the young Leo would never have left Argentina.

Nobody knew of anyone who had crossed the Atlantic so young in search of their footballing fortune: 13-year-olds certainly didn't leave Argentina, nor was it usual for European clubs to sign foreign players of such a tender age. No one had ever had such an opportunity so early. Back at Las Heras nobody had the faintest idea what was going on. Leo has hepatitis. Yes? That'll be it ...

In Barcelona, Minguella had been told that if Barcelona were prepared to meet the cost of the expensive growth hormone treatment and his father got a job, thus fulfilling the necessary regulations for the transfer of the youngster, Leo would come to them. There were calls to Real Madrid and Atlético de Madrid but nothing concrete emerged. 'In any case, if Barça show interest, better with Barça' was the rationale of all those who had worked to seal the transfer.

Josep María Minguella: Most of us involved in this were not used to dealing with such young players. For example, I came into contact with Pep Guardiola, or he with me, when he [Pep] was 20 years old, so I became his first agent at the time he was coming into the first team. All the machinery that is now in place for players of 12, 13, and 14 years old was not there at the time. So when our contacts in Argentina spoke to us about a youngster who was different, my first reaction was, right, what are we going to do with a boy of this age? I doubted it at first but in the end they insisted so much I started to take it seriously. I received a video, the one where he picks the ball up practically from his own goalmouth and dribbles it past about a thousand people and scores and yes ... he struck me as something different. A few months later I spoke with the president Joan Gaspart and Anton Parera [sporting director] and Charly Rexach [technical director and adviser to the president].

Charly Rexach: Playing tennis one day, Minguella told me he knew of a boy who was a phenomenon ... a bit similar to Maradona. But I've heard that many times ... and then later he told me he was in Argentina. I thought, 'ah, a youngster about eighteen or nineteen years old'. Then Minguella told me he was 13 years old. I said, 'are you mad, or what? Do you think I'm going to put myself there ... No way, no way.'

Joaquim Rifé: I was the director of the academy at Barcelona. And I eventually got offered the boy. Charly Rexach was the technical director of Barcelona and obviously centred more on the first team. What happened was that Charly Rexach is a good friend of Josep María Minguella who was the one who introduced the lad to FC Barcelona, so he listened to what he had to say about the kid.

Charly Rexach: There's a process here. If they say to me that there's a kid, for example, in Zaragoza who is a phenomenon, I ask, who is he, where does he play, and where do I have to go to watch him? Then I send two or three people to study him and then if one of them says yes, and the other no, I go myself and have the casting vote. Later you have to try to find him a place in the team and a number of other things. Another possibility is that an ex-Barcelona player, let's say, Rivaldo, says to me, 'listen, there's a twelve- or thirteen-year-old boy in Brazil who is a fantastic footballer'. I will take notice immediately, because [when] it's someone like Rivaldo who is telling you this, you take it into account. If someone else tells me I will suspend judgement on it for the time being. But even if Rivaldo says, go and see him, I will say no. Let's do it the other way around. If he's so small and he's coming from so far away ... send him to me here, we'll keep him for fifteen days so the coaches at the academy can study him at their leisure. And if in the first few days he is a bit nervous, he'll get over it. Imagine if we go all the way to Argentina or wherever and the lad becomes ill, or can't play or whatever. He has to be very good for us to skip the rules and regulations.

Josep María Minguella: The parents and the boy were going to leave Argentina anyway, come what may. If they had been unable to stay in Barcelona, they would have tried other clubs. I told Charly that he was following a course of treatment that the clubs in his country were not paying for and that Barcelona would have to make themselves responsible for this treatment.

Charly Rexach: So Minguella, who I trust very much, said to me: there's a bloke they tell me is a phenomenon. So how do we do it?

And so since Minguella had received the video that displayed Leo's keepy-uppy and dribbling skills, the months passed by that way – oh, I don't know, maybe he is too far, he is too young ... That was the confusing message that reached the family from Barcelona. Months of uncertainty for the Messi family who asked what had happened to that tape, the interest and the contacts? What was going to happen to Leo? What should they tell him?

Charly Rexach: So I said to Minguella that I was not prepared to travel so far to see a boy of twelve ... Had he been eighteen or twenty ... Anyway, that's when I told him that by Easter, or Christmas, or whenever, we had to find a date for the boy to come over with his parents and stay here for fifteen days.

Rifé: I told Rexach that I had organised a game so he could watch the boy.

Gaspart, Parera, Rifé, Minguella, Rexach ... Barcelona royalty to deal with a 13-year-old boy coming from Argentina. Heavyweights. And the significance of the presence of these 'fathers' to the young boy did not go unnoticed by the academy trainers who would be responsible for judging and training him for the next two crucial weeks.

Rodolfo Borrell: I remember that one day in the office, someone, I can't remember who, gave me two black and white, double-sided photocopies, an article from an Argentinian newspaper that talked about Messi. And they told me that this boy was coming over for a trial. I have been looking for these photocopies, I'm sure that they are at my parents' home, I should find them. And I remember it because it was the first time I heard the word *gambeta*, dribbling, and the word *enganche*, which is a very Argentinian word used to describe the player who plays just behind the striker. They told me that the youngster was going to be in my group because he was born in 1987. I have always said that the reason I trained Messi first is only because I was responsible for the training of that under-14 side. I'm sure you have heard that there are 10,000 trainers who claimed to be the first to coach him. No?

Waiting for them at Prat airport in Barcelona was Juan Mateo from Minguella's office, who took them to the north of Barcelona where the agent was based. In the lift the Messis crossed paths with Txiki Beguiristain, the future sporting director of Barcelona and someone close to Minguella. 'We're from Argentina,' one of them dared to say. And Txiki, ruffling Leo's hair said, 'This boy must be good, he is small.'

After talking with the Catalan agent, Jorge and Leo made their way to the Hotel Plaza. It was not Barcelona who paid the expenses for this trip: they never did. Minguella, who knew the owner of the hotel situated in the Plaza España, arranged for the Messis to stay in room 546 of the hotel. With views. From the window they could see the halls of the Barcelona Exhibition Centre, and away in the distance the National Palace and the Montjuïc fountain that lit up at night in a blaze of colour to the sound of synchronised music. Closer were the towers that flanked the Avenida Reina Maria Cristina, erected for the Universal Exhibition of 1929. And in the foreground the fountain of the Plaza España, a classical allegory of the country with sculptures that symbolise the rivers that flow into the three seas that wash the shores of the Iberian Peninsula.

Leo Messi left his suitcases in the room. The young footballer was feeling a little better but still weak after the bumpy flight. Even so, Rifé had let Jorge know that he wanted to see Leo train. Today. At six o'clock. He had to go.

Rodolfo Borrel would be his first trainer at FC Barcelona.

Rodo, now director of the Liverpool FC academy, was for the 2000–01 season in charge of the *Infantiles* A side that would later become historic. Cesc Fàbregas, Gerard Piqué, Marc Pedraza, Marc Valiente, Víctor Vázquez, Toni Calvo, Sito Riera, Rafael Blázquez ... One of the best junior sides that Barcelona have ever had, and now they were adding to it with a player who'd arrived with something of a reputation of his own.

That Monday afternoon those in charge of the academy (Quimet Rifét, Quique Costas, Juan Manuel Asensi, the coaches Rodolfo Borrell, Xavi Llorenç and Albert Benaiges) met on pitches two and three next to the Mini Stadium, one with grass and the other with artificial turf, to follow the progress of the group and especially the new boy.

Charly Rexach was not present, having gone to Australia to watch the games at the Sydney Olympic football tournament that was packed with well-known young players (among them Tamudo, Xavi, Puyol, Zamorano, Suazo, Mboma, Lauren and Eto'o). But in truth the matter of a young Argentinian boy did not require his presence: his prime responsibility lay with making decisions about the first team, not the academy. If down in that cauldron of talented youth they could all agree, then the boy recommended by Minguella would be signed. If not, he wouldn't. Charly had arranged the trial; for the time being he didn't have to do much else.

Messi felt calm as he made his way to his first day of training. Still a bit nauseous after the exertions of the journey, but he was there because this was what he had wanted and what he had fantasised about. He had a week at most (he had to go back to school) to demonstrate what he could do with the ball. That was the easy part.

Imagine never having seen the Camp Nou or the Mini Stadium. Leo hadn't.

Arriving at the pitches adjacent to the Mini, a Camp Nou in miniature, 'the Flea' hesitated before entering the dressing rooms. He felt embarrassed walking in by himself. His shyness (no, he is not shy, he is reserved) is extreme. He started to get changed outside the locker room and ended up doing so inside, away from the rest of the group. In a corner with no one nearby. Standing up. Tense.

Imagine never having seen Lionel Messi. Like that group of players of the same age, or those coaches who had only briefly heard of him.

'He's so small,' said the youngsters. Rodo was in the dressing room. 'Sit down, young man,' he said to Leo. The kid hadn't said hello when he entered. Or, the noise he made when he came in did not sound like a greeting; it didn't seem like a friendly hello.

For Cesc, for Piqué, who were also getting changed, the Argentinian was just another kid coming for a trial with Barcelona. They were rarely foreigners, but occasionally one or two were. A few new boys every month. Rodo approached the group while Leo was changing in the corner. 'Be careful with him, he's very small, don't break him.'

Piqué: In that first week, Leo was isolated, very isolated. If there was a group of people talking or having a laugh, he was on the bench, right at the end, very reluctant. Quiet. Introverted.

Cesc: So many new players came that we didn't attach any importance to it, but I remember his first day perfectly well.

The young players were giving him mocking looks. Messi was bandaging his ankles.

Piqué: He was very short, he hardly said a word and no one could have imagined what was going to happen.

He measured one metre and forty-eight centimetres – four foot ten and a quarter inches.

Cesc: He had longish hair, and spoke soft, quiet Argentinian so you could hardly hear him. In fact, he hardly spoke at all. He was a noodle. We thought, this bloke is a waste of space. ...

That was the general consensus.

One of Borrell's assistants was worried. He saw how he was putting on bandages and asked him if he was injured. No, no, it's an Argentinian custom. To prevent sprains.

Leo said nothing.

The jokes kept coming from the group of 12- and 13-year-old boys. 'The bloke's a midget.'

Messi ran onto the pitch next to Piqué, who looked twice his size. Leo came up to his waist.

Jorge was in the stands and heard what was being said. 'He's very small, he's too small.'

The group began to warm up. Always with the ball. Firstly, it was all about controlling the ball. One touch, two, three ... ten, eleven, twelve ... 'He's not dropping the ball,' said one of the spectators. Twenty, twenty-one ...

Cesc: When he started to touch the ball we saw that he was different from the rest of the boys who came for trials.

Gradually Rodolfo Borrell set up some one on ones and shots on goal. And when Leo got it ... problems.

Cesc: First, he made me look like a complete fool and stuck it in. And as a young player I had a special talent in defensive one against one situations. Now I'd lost it. I used to steal the ball with ease, I don't know how I did it. Anyway, he made me look so stupid you wouldn't believe it. Okay, the first time you're not expecting it, you're a bit too relaxed. But he did it to me again and again.

Messi was dazzling, with his dribbling, his finishing, his

consistency. The youngsters entertained themselves watching the new boy's moves. He had won the group's respect. From that moment on, anyone who called him 'the midget' did so with admiration, even affection.

From the stands you could hear: 'Oh, wow. This is something else.'

Leo travelled to the Mini and the pitches adjacent to it by underground from the Plaza España. Four stops on the Green line to Les Corts. As there wasn't training every day, with his father and one of Jorge's or Minguella's colleagues they passed the time strolling beside the port, with an occasional visit to a museum, although he didn't spend a lot of time in them – they didn't make a great impression on the kid. The tourist bus took them to the Sagrada Familia, to the port, the zoo. He would tour the Old City. Tuesday was a free day. Monday, Wednesday and Thursday he was part of the group and joined them in the drills on the clay court. Friday they would concentrate more on tactics and he took a less active role. The weekend was also free for him; naturally he couldn't play official games yet.

It was still sunny in September, the heat less fierce than in August and better for walking at any time of the day. So the Argentinian group would travel to Sitges, spending mornings on the beach, and took in a football match, his first visit to the Camp Nou. The first Saturday of his stay he saw Barcelona play there. The opponents, Racing Santander. Patrick Kluivert scored a brace, Marc Overmars the third. The men of Llorenç Serra Ferrer, not the most popular of Barcelona coaches, won 3–1. Leo took a photo from the stands. The stadium was enormous but the crowd made little noise.

They wanted to go to the Barcelona–Milan group stage Champions League match on 26 September. They couldn't get tickets. The Italians won 2–0.

The rest of the time Leo was never far away from a ball. They played head tennis in the hotel bedroom and he would take the ball out onto the terrace to weave past imaginary opponents, to play keepy-uppy, to caress it. Television filled the remaining gaps.

Lionel did not say much; he wasn't timid so much as introverted, charming to any adults who approached him, monosyllabic to his team-mates in those first days. Off the pitch there was a lot of killing time waiting for the return from Sydney of Charly Rexach because no one would give the nod to confirm his signing.

On the pitch he was something else. Next to his new team-mates he didn't seem like that timid boy who the day before was quietly eating a pizza, or a hamburger or a plate of pasta. Or just walking, lost in his own thoughts.

When he was alone in his room, or just before going to sleep, by the light of his bedside lamp he would take out a thick pen syringe and inject whatever leg needed injecting that day.

And the same routine the following day. Touches of the ball, a visit to the city, pizza, training in the afternoon. An injection.

'Leo, do what you know. Get the ball, don't pass to anyone, and head for goal.' Jorge Messi's advice was about exploiting the very talents that had brought him to Barcelona, but also a natural reaction to Borrell's insistence, as a Barcelona trainer, that they should play one- and two-touch football. 'We have to come with our own game, show you as you are.' If he knew one thing, it was how to dribble. While the rest of the group passed the ball around and obediently kept to their space, Messi offered something else.

And so it went on. Day after day. He trained with the Junior A group, and at the end of training would play a game with the Junior B side. His father would watch him from the stands or leaning on the fence that separated the two pitches.

One day he scored five goals and hit the post twice.

He played for himself but did so with such conviction, with such talent, that it wasn't worth trying to correct him. 'One touch, Leo,' shouted Rodo, but he was really reminding the rest of the group. 'One, or, at the most, two touches.' It didn't matter what he was told. Leo played as he had always done, with little touches, with speed, with flow, dribbling right and left. A ball player more than a footballer – and there is a huge difference.

Another day he scored six goals.

Jorge wasn't sure if the pressure was good or bad for his son. At some point a friend of Minguella suggested to him that he should reward Leo's goals with presents. If there was a rucksack that he liked, some football boots, he would be given them in exchange for goals, let's say five. His father wasn't sure it was going to work and preferred not to interfere. But the challenge motivated Leo. He scored four but one shot crashed against the woodwork and appeared to go in. No, no, it didn't go in, he was told. Leo went crazy – it *did* go in! There was a complete set of sportswear at stake. A heated discussion followed. He eventually got the present.

After the first week, the former Barcelona player Migueli, who was working in the youth ranks of the club, came round and asked: 'Who's the boy who has come from Argentina for a trial?' Leo, who was training, was pointed out to him. 'The little feller there, the one in the middle of the pitch.' He looked at him. He had a ball on top of his left foot. He was awaiting instructions. 'I don't have to see him play football; just by the way he is standing you can see he is a good footballer.' Just like that. Nothing more.

He'd hit the nail on the head.

It was late, around eight o'clock in the evening. Migueli continued watching the session. 'What are these people doing that they haven't signed him yet? This boy is the closest thing I have seen to Maradona.' And he should know. Migueli, a former centre-back, played with Diego at Barcelona.

But the days were passing and no one was saying anything to Jorge. Nor to Leo. They were waiting for a decision from Rifé and the return of Rexach, who was still away.

But they had to get back to Argentina; they had already lost too many schooldays. Jorge insisted that they could not be away for more than a week. It was now the eighth day.

Something wasn't right.

There is one thing in the Messi mythology that has been misinterpreted. It's said that some of the Barcelona coaches were not convinced of his talent, uncertain about signing him, would say one thing to his face and another behind his back. Their names are mentioned *sotto voce* because some of them are still at the club. Others have developed successful careers away from the Camp Nou that might be damaged if this was to be revealed. Rexach's interpretation of the situation further confuses the issue. 'There was your typical guy who would say: well, he's too small, the sort of bloke that should play indoor football, a table football player … the usual stuff!'

But in truth, the trial was going well. More than well; it was also decisive. Just five minutes at one of the training sessions was enough to show his talent. From a coaching point of view, Charly Rexach's appearance at pitch two or three to watch Messi was hardly necessary either. He had no need to make the casting vote.

But in the end Rexach had to be convened and the Messis had to delay their return to Argentina – the first team director should not have been involved in such decisions, but no one, it seemed, was prepared to take responsibility for the possible failure (or even, in the best case scenario, the success) of signing up a 13-year-old Argentinian boy.

How on earth do you explain the doubts?

To begin with, the involvement of such club heavyweights (Rexach, in spirit at least, Minguella, Anton Parera, Rifé) in the potential transfer of a child footballer was proof that this was something special, something unusual. Leo was protected from above and, with so many important names on the case, something was definitely going on. Or at least that's how it was seen by those looking on from the sidelines. The matter became the talk of the town during those weeks and created great expectations. Rodolfo Borrell's colleagues spent whatever time they could taking a look at him. The debate was not so much about his talent but how to harness his individuality to the club's own established and collective game plan.

But this heavyweight interest was not the oddest thing.

In 2000, the very idea of bringing over a youngster from Argentina seemed like lunacy. It simply wasn't done.

Leo's talents were obvious for all to see. An anonymous source at the club who saw him during those two weeks described Leo as *las ostia en patinete*, which means 'the dog's bollocks' (but translates more or less as 'something that moves like lightning'): 'he did then' – that source continues – 'the same as he does now, but in miniature'. It would be an injustice to history to suggest that the reason they might not have wanted him was because he was too small. There was something else.

These days it is considered quite normal to bring a youngster of whatever age to a club from anywhere in the world, and the battles to sign children as young as eight years old are well documented. But in 2000 they were breaking new ground. Five years earlier, the signing of an *Infantile* (12–13 years old) from Mataró, Granollers, Santpedor (towns less than an hour from Barcelona) was considered to be bringing them a long way. The Cadetes (14–15 years old) came from all over Spain.

And now they were talking about taking on a young Argentinian lad who had arrived, aged just 13 ... hold on a minute!

Many studies have been carried out on the subject, and at that time the general idea was that, no matter how good a player might be at that age, no one could guarantee that he would make it into the first team. Or even end up as a professional footballer. 'To take him away from his family, his country, his friends, all of that, to put him in a situation where there are no guarantees. Of course, now he has become the best player in the world and it has become a wonderful story but ...' so says another witness to that most unusual of arrivals. It would not be the youth football coaches who would decide his future, but they talked among themselves about the possible dangers of the situation; the club had been reticent even about signing players from distant parts of Spain, taking them from their home environment, their school. The normal thing, the logical thing – it was said – was that Leo should be treated the same. Oriol Tort, one of the most renowned scouts, the leader and ideologist of the Barcelona academy, has always claimed that the preferred age for a player to join La Masía is 15 or 16. That's how things were in 2000.

So was it, as legend has it, lack of awareness among the coaches, or a sensible reluctance on their part because they knew the effect that uprooting the boy would have on his family?

For example: Andrés Iniesta. As a youngster (12 years old, 1996) he took part in the National Tournament of Brunete with teams from the Spanish first division, La Liga. As always happens in tournaments of importance, the clubs sent various scouts. The best players on this occasion were, first, Iniesta from Albacete, and second, Jorge Troiteiro from Mérida, at that time both La Liga clubs. There was no prize for second place, but the debate centred around which one of the two was better. Barcelona took note, spoke with Iniesta's family, worked out the contractual details with the player before deciding that he should remain at home and that they would monitor his progress from a distance. The idea was to bring him to La

Masía two or three years later when he had reached the age of Cadete.

Troiteiro's father was not prepared to take defeat sitting down, so he set out by car from Mérida, in Extremadura in western Spain, across the country to the offices of Barcelona; his son was going to be a footballer – no question about it. He knew that the club had had positive reports about the boy and the idea of Barcelona appealed to the family. So, either they signed him now or he would go to Madrid or to Valencia, or wherever. Barcelona had told the family about the effect on the boy's schooling, the upheaval, the relocating, but his father persisted. It was his son and he was going to get him into a big club.

Barcelona, despite their initial objections, yielded to the pressure because the youngster, an extremely skilful left-winger, had a lot of talent, something that he would soon show at the lower levels. But there was no boy of that age at La Masía; in fact there was only one under the age of 16. So what did Barcelona do? They called Iniesta, also from La Mancha, to come to Barcelona to keep Troiteiro company so that he would not be lonely.

Jorge Troiteiro was eventually thrown out of La Masía for indiscipline. Iniesta, who spent a lot of the time crying in his room in the farmhouse in which the players from outside Barcelona lived, would years later score the goal that earned Spain its first World Cup.

There are fears, doubts, promises and today also a methodology in Barcelona's famous academy, but still there is no guarantee of success.

Someone asked Leo after eight days of training if he still thought it was a good idea to sign for Barcelona? That person was Rodo Borrell. Leo said yes, he liked the training methods, in Rosario it was all much more physical and here most of the work was done with the ball, which pleased him. He was enjoying it. And he could see how massive the club was. And the challenge.

He wanted to stay.

Ten days after the Messis' arrival at Barcelona, there was little more to see of the city. No more to know about him as a footballer. Everything was done. He had taken nearly two weeks off school and that had never been part of the plan. It was clear that any club would have wanted Leo, but this was a unique experience for Barcelona and no one wanted to take the risk: they had to wait for Charly.

Jorge was ready to return home. 'Stay one more day, Rexach will be back on Monday,' he was told.

The president's adviser finally arrived from Sydney and met up with Rifé. There were a number of issues on the table, among them the matter of the Argentinian boy. 'Play him in an older group, two years older. I want to see how it unfolds when he plays with the bigger boys,' said Rexach.

Charly Rexach: I got involved so as to give my casting vote, because if those under me had said 'let's sign him' then I wouldn't have come down.

The final trial was set to take place on 2 October. At six in the evening. Instead of the clay surface where he had played most of the time, this would take place on pitch three, the artificial surface located behind the bowling alley. Facing the Mini Stadium.

The moment had come. There was no going back. The following day Leo and Jorge were to return to Argentina. Leo, all one metre forty-eight centimetres of him, was to face youngsters two years older than him.

Migueli came to see him. And Rifé, of course. And Quique Costas, Xavi Llorenç, Albert Benaiges, and also Rodolfo Borrell who had had him in his team for the last ten days. They sat on the substitutes' bench.

The game started. And Charly Rexach still hadn't arrived.

He was coming late after a lunch. Recently back from Australia, he was between time zones.

Two minutes later, Charly climbs up the steps leading to the pitch.

Charly Rexach: I did the usual; walked about a bit, and stopped when I saw him get the ball.

Rexach comes through the door, passes the corner flag and goes behind the goal.

Charly Rexach: He was easy to spot, because he was tiny, quite a sight, no?

Messi gets the ball in the centre of the pitch and starts to dribble towards whoever stands in his way.

Jorge Messi: Carlos [Charly] came in and Leo made a move.

Charly Rexach: Like I said; I went behind the goal, and kept walking ...

Leo dribbles past two, rounds the goalkeeper. Scores.

Jorge Messi: Great play. Goal!

It was their only goal of a game that Leo's team ended up losing 2–1.

Rexach gets to the substitutes' bench – not the first but the second – where all the coaches have gathered.

Charly Rexach: It took me seven or eight minutes to complete the lap. I went to sit down on the bench, and ...

Ten minutes after he had arrived, Charly Rexach left pitch number three. He had sat down for a couple of minutes on the youth coaches' bench, turned around and gone out again the way he had come in.

All that waiting. And he hardly saw a thing!

Jorge Messi thought Rexach had not given Leo the attention he deserved after the journey, the days of waiting. Had Charly noticed the couple of things that Messi did? Jorge was asking himself. Surely that was enough to keep him at the club. Hopefully.

At the end of the game, Leo said nothing. Always quiet, he just listened.

Part One

In Rosario

1

'Pass It, Leo!'
But He Never Did

Every Sunday: last one is a rotten egg!

Without fail, Leo would arrive at his grandmother Celia's house and there, on a small concrete patch in front of the house, would play rondos (toros, or, in English, piggy in the middle) with his brothers Rodrigo and Matías, though in those days it wasn't called rondos. Or they would play foot tennis. Then his cousins would arrive, Maxi and Emanuel. A third cousin, Bruno, would also be born to Claudio and Marcela, Leo's aunt and uncle, some years later.

Two rocks served as goalposts. The first to score six goals. So the game began.

Leo's grandmother and her daughters, Celia and Marcela, busied themselves in the kitchen preparing pasta with a rich sauce. The husbands, Jorge and Claudio, and his grandfather, Antonio, chatted animatedly on the sofa in the small, narrow, dining room, or on the doorstep, ears and eyes ever alert for the children at play. Look at that touch, notice how Emanuel dribbles with the ball, Leo as small as he is and how difficult it is to get the ball off him ...

'Good, Maxi, good, shouted Jorge, who had played in the lower ranks of Newell's Old Boys until called up for military service.

Time to eat! The children drifted in, hungry but reluctant to leave the game.

Hands had to be washed before everyone sat around the table of that humble two-bedroom house that no one ever wanted to leave, and that served as a meeting point for hundreds of Sundays for brothers-in-law Claudio and Jorge, sisters Celia and Marcela, and *for the cousins who always wanted to play football. Sometimes the sofa doubled as a bed for one of the grandchildren, whichever one insisted on staying over on that particular day. They adored their grandmother Celia and it wasn't just because of the delicious pasta, or the rice, every scrap of which was finished off. Celia was one of those grandmothers who could never say no to her grandchildren.*

Food was eaten in a rush. Everything was delicious, but with the ball tucked under an arm, the five youngsters, still savouring the taste of dulce de leche *(milk candy), headed off to the square in the Bajada part of town.*

And it was there that they would finish what they had started, or start another game of first to six. Once more, giving it their all. Four hours non-stop; sometimes more.

There were never uneven games. Sometimes the bigger boys, Rodrigo, born in 1980, Maxi, in 1984, and Matías, in 1982, would challenge the smaller boys, Leo born in 1987 and Emanuel, in 1988, who was a good goalkeeper. The kicks they received were shared evenly, far more rough and tumble than in the younger football matches. Much more. Leo and Emanuel were at the receiving end from the older frustrated ones. Especially Leo. 'Matías, careful, man!' Jorge would shout.

And Leo would run around like a headless chicken after the ball, and then, when he got it, he would refuse to let it go. With veins bulging, his face redder than a tomato – that is how his uncle Claudio remembers him. And watch out if he lost. He would start to cry and throw a tantrum, hitting out at anyone who dared try to console him. He had to carry on until he won.

'Always ending badly, always fighting. Even if we won, my brother would annoy me because he knew I would get angry. It always ended badly, with me crying and furious.' So said Leo to the Argentinian magazine El Gráfico.

Often the clashes were between neighbourhoods. The Sunday matches they played in the little square next to grandma's house were open to anyone. And the Messi/Cuccittini team never lost. Matías explains: 'At first they didn't want to play against us because Leo was so small, and so was Emanuel, and they ended up congratulating him. Leo was nine years old and he was playing against eighteen- and nineteen-year-old kids and they couldn't stop him.'

Is it any wonder that at least a couple of footballers emerged from this rich mix of talent?

Rodrigo was signed by the Newell's younger section at the age of 11, having previously played – as had all the Messis – for Grandoli. He was a central attacker with a great ability to score, fast and skilful. He was selected for his age group for Rosario in intercity meetings. Leo told the story of his brother's early football retirement in Corriere della Sera: 'Yes, he was very good. Sadly he had a car accident where he fractured his tibia and fibia, and in those days if something like that happened to you that was the end of your career.' That, and perhaps he lacked the tenacity needed to become a professional. His passion, he discovered, lay in the kitchen. He wanted to be a chef.

Matías was a defender in Newell's lower ranks for a year before deciding not to carry on. But he returned to football years later, and his last club was Club Atlético Empalme Central who competed in the Rosario Regional league and where he played until he was 27 years old.

Maximiliano, one metre sixty-five tall, and the eldest of Marcela and Claudio's three sons, scores regularly for the Brazilian side Esport Clube Vitoria in the Serie A Brazilian championship, having been in Argentina (with San Lorenzo de Almagro), Paraguay, Mexico and also the Brazilian club Flamengo. In his first training session with his first Paraguayan team, Libertad, he fractured his skull. But he is stubborn. And came back to football. The day after the premature birth of his daughter Valentina, who spent her first few days in an incubator, he scored for Fla. The same evening Messi hit a hat trick for Barcelona against Valencia and dedicated the three goals to Valen.

Emanuel, from Rosario, like all of them, inseparable from Leo as a child and with whom he shared time at Grandoli, started as a goalkeeper and spent a year at Newell's before making the step to Europe. Now he is a left-sided midfielder. He arrived in Germany in 2008 to play in the reserves of the TSV 1860 Munich side, and the following year made it into the first team. He was also at Girona in the Spanish second division. Now one metre seventy-seven tall, he plays for Club Olimpia in the Paraguayan first division. One day he would like to play for the Ñuls (as

Argentinians refer to Newell's Old Boys) with Maxi and Leo.

Bruno was born in 1996 and missed out on the early street con-tests, although he enjoyed many other street matches with other youngsters, and was one of the great prospects from the Rosario-based club Renato Cesarini that produced Fernando Redondo and Santi Solari, the son of one of the club's founders. He looks and plays very much like Leo: the way he runs, his touch on the ball, even the way he celebrates his goals. But you have to be careful with comparisons. Today on his Twitter and Facebook accounts he writes: 'Life is not the same without football' (February 2012). He left it all behind him but now he is trying once again to climb aboard the high-speed train that is football.

Leo left for Barcelona aged just 13 and so the meals he shared with his cousins became less frequent. And the football matches naturally became a thing of the past. The boys were growing up, life was separating them. But some of the child remained in all of them, as it does in all of us.

Celia, Leo's grandmother, died when he was 10.

A river, the meandering Paraná, the Monumento Nacional a la Bandera, the National Flag Memorial, two great clubs. And its people. Above all, its people. This for the visitor is Rosario.

What sort of place is Rosario?

Rosario is 300 kilometres from the capital Buenos Aires, about three hours via a road that runs arrow-straight, cutting through an enormous valley with little between the two cities. Far from the madding crowd, seemingly isolated, a proud little city (the people are not from the province of Santa Fe, they claim, they are Rosari-nos) and their local derby is *Lepers* vs *Scoundrels*, Newell's Old Boys vs Rosario Central, half of the city's inhabitants plus one against the other half plus one, 'the most passionate game of all', according to anyone you ask, even though many prefer to forget that sometimes passions become confused and turn to violence.

Leo is a *leproso* (leper). Newell's are referred to as such because a century ago both they and Rosario Central were invited to take part in a charity match in aid of a leprosy clinic. Newell's accepted, Rosario Central did not. Since that day the NOB rivals have been called *canallas* (scoundrels).

Arriving from Buenos Aires via the motorway, you have to take the exit to the ring road, a large C flanked on the right by an area comprising tin shacks boasting the colours of Rosario Central that tell you that you are entering the city of the *canallas*. This is soon confirmed – as is the very opposite: no, no, 'this is the city of the *leprosos*' you can read on other walls, daubed in the red and black of Newell's Old Boys. The statistics and the graffiti disagree with each other. These tin shacks, home to so many families on the out-skirts of Rosario, have windows with views over the motorway. The areas around here are poor, with dirt floors, where people ride around on motorcycles without crash helmets; old motorcycles, but not vintage ones. Later, the poverty disappears to be replaced by factories and other large buildings. Every driver seems to be admir-ing the scenery or taking note of something because none of them seem to be paying attention to road signs or markings. Either that, or perhaps as some Argentinians say, traffic signs are put up merely to hinder your progress.

Before you come to the end of the motorway, you begin to see the outline of an attractive city, with skyscrapers of varying size; the road becomes tree-lined and all of a sudden you espy a gigantic modern factory complete with those labyrinthine tubes on the out-side that add a strange industrial beauty to the landscape. The plant is fed by the Paraná River, and this is the first sight of this crucial river artery, bringing with it its fertile alluvial soil, an age-old source of wealth. And after the trees and the factory, then you enter the city through a new park before two-storey houses begin to dot the land-scape on both sides. The ring road turns into a great avenue flanked by the outline of a city, tall, stately, old.

It was from Rosario, the gateway to the pampas, a village mas-querading as a city, that Che Guevara, the singer Fito Páez, the car-toonist and writer Roberto 'el Negro' Fontanarrosa and football greats Marcelo Bielsa and César Luis Menotti emerged to chal-lenge the establishment; and where thousands upon thousands of European immigrants landed. And it was also here that other iconic Argentinian symbols were born: here where the blue and white flag of Argentina was hoisted for the first time, created in 1812 to distin-guish them from the Spanish troops they were fighting.

On the way to the centre of town is Independence Park, described by the journalist Eduardo van der Kooy as 'where the city starts to define its own style and personality. From the park starts the elegant Boulevard Orono which looks like a Parisian postcard. Buried in this mass of mature trees and natural foliage is Newell's stadium.' The streets become narrow and at the crossroads – of which there are many – you're never sure who has right of way: it seems to be the first person to get there. The white walls have turned grey and the cafés have high ceilings, large picture windows and small tables. Inside the cafés many of the men pass the time looking at the pretty girls, while the ladies, including the older ones among them, enjoy admiring the physiques of the young guys, all of whom look fit enough to be footballers.

Everyone says that the most beautiful women in Argentina come from Rosario; there's that irresistible mix of Serbian and Italian genes that combine to create blonde-haired beauties with olive skins and light coloured eyes. The good food contributes to the overall healthy and lustrous complexions of the inhabitants. Rosario is one of the most productive agricultural regions in the country, surrounded by fields producing cereals and soya oil. The young grow fit and strong.

There are not many football shirts in evidence, neither those of Central or Newell's or of the national side, although there are football pitches everywhere, sometimes every two blocks. There are five or six leagues and many of the footballers play in more than one: finish one game, pick up your motorbike and then go and play another in a different league. In Rosario, anyone who isn't a footballer is an organiser, trainer, referee or whatever. Women included.

'It's different from other cities because of its unique passion for football,' says Gerardo 'Tata' Martino, former Newell's manager and now at Barcelona. 'The area near the city is a conveyor belt of players, a football factory that produces the talents that are central to the objective of Rosario's footballing dreams. They are what we describe around here as "well-fed" youngsters with an enormous passion for football. That's why the Rosario academy is so important and has created such great stars as Valdano, Batistuta and an interminable list in which Lionel Messi is the icing on the cake.'

He could also have named Mario Kempes, Abel Baldo, Roberto Sensini, Mauricio Pochettino and many more. Indeed, ten of the regular players in Alejandro Sabella's squad for the qualifying stages of the 2014 World Cup are from Rosario, including Javier Mascherano, Ever Banega, Ángel di Maria, Ezequiel Lavezzi, Maxi Rodríguez, Ignacio Scocco, Ezequiel Garay ... and, of course, Leo.

It was in Rosario that 'the Church of Maradona' was formed (half in jest one would imagine), devoted to Diego, whom they consider to be the greatest player in history and in whose honour they have a quasi-religious ceremony every year on 30 October, his birthday, that parodies the Catholic tradition of the country. Maradona had a brief spell at Newell's in 1993. Leo went to his debut in the black and red shirt.

Football is life in Rosario, and life is football. And to that end the spirit of the city is appropriately reflected in one goal in particular, according to *The Guinness Book of Records* the most celebrated one in history. It happened on 19 December 1971 in a match played in suffocating heat in Buenos Aires between Newell's and Central. It was the semi-finals of the National Championship and the only time the two clubs had faced each other in the country's capital. Neither side was able to find the opposition's net in a match that was taken up with the battle to win control. Then, 13 minutes from time, there was a foul close to the Newell's penalty area. Aldo Pedro Poy, the Rosario Central striker, made his way into the area. As he did so he called out to one of the cameramen – what was it? A premonition? A prediction? Call it what you will – 'Get your cameras ready, this one's going in.' And so it happened. Poy, jostling with his marker, before getting away from him, soaring into the air with his body arched, his arms extended. Goal. A flying header. So what if the ball had brushed the stomach of central defender DiRienzo, wrong-footing the goalkeeper. Goal, a definitive one, too: the eternal rival had been knocked out in the semi-finals. Central went on to win the final, the first title the *canallas* had won in their history, but not as celebrated as Poy's diving header. The ambitiously titled Organización Canalla for Latin America has for the past three decades met every 19 December on the pitch at the Central stadium: on this day someone crosses the ball and Poy re-enacts his diving header. Lately, however, the problem, as Poy himself says, is not so much making the dive, but 'getting up again after it'.

This is Rosario. This is football. Messi did not rise out of nothing. Neither did Alfredo Di Stéfano or Diego Armando Maradona. Perhaps it's not about an Argentinian gene, but one thing for certain is that the three were born in a country where every day football takes you to the bigger glory (the fame, the money) or the smaller one (the recognition of all your neighbours).

But as Martino says in the magazine *Panenka*, this excellent raw material and passion that is found in the streets of Rosario has to be channelled in one way or another: 'To this end the work of Jorge Griffa has been vital. A man who, after retiring as player, was quite clear about what he wanted. He had no ambitions to become the manager of a team in the Primera, but rather the creator of players and he never betrayed his original ideas. From the mid-seventies, and for 20 years thereafter, he left an indelible mark on Newell's Old Boys. Later he went on to become youth coach at Boca, but always with the same idea; to be a forger of players. Griffa has a great talent in this area and a clinical eye for spotting talent. Even to the extent of enlisting assistants. Marcelo Bielsa was one of his assistants in the glory years. He crossed the country from end to end, not just Rosario and the surrounding areas, searching, always searching, for hidden gems. Bielsa travelled thousands of kilometres in his tiny Fiat 147 in this tireless mission that bore so much fruit for the "*Leprosos*". His hard work was rewarded. Newell's were champions in 1988 with José Yudica and in 1991 and 1992 with Marcelo Bielsa as first team coaches.' Griffa also spotted the talent of Messi at a crucial moment in what had been, till then, a brief footballing career.

You breathe football everywhere in Rosario, but, curiously, the air doesn't smell of Messi. There are hardly any photos, or pictures, nor even advertisements depicting Leo. Everybody has a story about 'the Flea' but the Santaferina city does not seem to want to gloat. It's almost as if it is considered vulgar to have his face posted everywhere. Or perhaps they have just decided to respect his low profile.

But for Leo, Rosario is everything. When you ask him what his favourite memories are, he is in no doubt. 'My home, my neighbourhood, where I was born.'

The Messis lived for decades in a small house on the Calle Lavalleja, located in a suburb some four kilometres south-east of the centre of Rosario, known by some as La Bajada or Las Heras. To others it remains nameless; it is just home. It is a typical low-rise community where front doors are left ajar. *Cumbia* music, chatter and laughter emanate from within. Kids play in the streets. Traffic is rare. Time seems to stand still in Bajada. In this sleepy working-class area, at number 525 on the narrow Calle Estado de Israel, is the house Jorge Messi built with his own hands.

His father, Eusebio, was a builder by profession and Jorge quickly learned to do everything. The two Messis used the weekends to lay brick upon brick on a 300-square-metre plot of land bought by the family. It was at that time single-storey, a similar size to all the other houses in the street, with a backyard to play in. One wall faced the house of Cintia Arellano, who was the same age as Leo and his best friend. Today the road surface has been improved, as has the street lighting and the drains. The house has a second floor, a fence (the only one in the street) and a security camera, but almost always remains closed.

This is where Jorge Messi, Celia Cuccittini and their four children lived in the early years. It was, remembers Leo in *Corriere della Sera*, 'Small. A kitchen, living room, two bedrooms. In one bedroom my mum and dad slept and in the other me and my brothers.'

This, then, was Leo's street, just 200 metres from an uneven piece of fenced-off land covered with rough, wild grass where football was played; next to it, the kiosk where Matías worked when Leo was already in Barcelona, is still there, right next to the house where Matías lived and that he later gave to a relative. Go to the top of the street and there you will see Grandoli. Grandmother Celia lived around here and a little further up were the cousins. And close by are the paternal grandparents, Rosa María and Eusebio Messi Baro, who, at 86, and years after retiring, still gets up every morning to open the humble bakery he installed in a room in the house that they have lived in for the past 50 years.

Everything starts and finishes in that neighbourhood. The family unit is the fertile ground on which the Messis and the Cuccittinis were raised. Leo is devoted to his parents, his brother, his cousins, his uncles. To his mother, above all to his mother: he has a tattoo of her face on his back. 'He did it without saying anything to anyone. He came around one day and showed us. We almost fainted with the shock. We didn't have a clue that he was going to do this. But it's his body and there's nothing we can say to him,' his father said in Sique Rodríguez's book *Educados para ganar* ('Educated to Win') in which the parents of the best-known graduates from FC Barcelona's La Masía give their side of the story.

From here also come Leo's best friends whom he still sees whenever time permits. For Messi, Rosario, La Bajada, or whatever you want to call it, represents his childhood, 'a man's true homeland' as the poet Rilke would say. The place where he wants to return (where he returns constantly), the place he has never left; the place he has recreated for himself in Barcelona to make everything easier.

That's why he returns home to his family whenever he can. It is to Rosario that he escapes when there is a sufficiently long break at any time in the summer, or at Christmas. You don't see him in the neighbourhood so much now, not since he bought a larger property on the outskirts of the city, but at other times he has been seen cycling there. Sometimes he travels around neighbouring regions, as in the summer of 2013 when he was seen in a supermarket pushing a trolleyful of muffins, wine and breadsticks; he was spending the day in Gualeguaychú, in the south-east of Entre Rios, a sleepy town where, despite the cap he was wearing, he was easily recognised and asked to pose for photos. He's had to get used to being photographed in the street. He never has any protection.

He even has a long-term girlfriend from his home town. Antonella Roccuzzo, is, like Leo, from Rosario, and is the cousin of his best friend, Lucas Scaglia, who plays for Deportivo Cali in Colombia. He has known her since she was five and today she is the mother of his son, Thiago. But things could have worked out differently. Antonella and Leo stopped seeing each other for a while, when he was just another boy trying to attract her attention and she was a cute little girl who wasn't interested. Leo went to Barcelona and, on a trip back home for the holidays, the romance blossomed.

Make a note of this: Roccuzzo, Scaglia; Leo is a Messi and his mother's maiden name is Cuccittini. The family are grandchildren and great-grandchildren of Italian immigrants who came to Rosario from Recanati and Ancona, in the Marche region of Italy. Lionel also has Spanish blood. Rosario attracted Europeans, mainly the

Spanish and Italians who made up half the population in the first decades as the city grew. One of Leo's great-grandmothers, Rosa Mateu i Gese, came from Blancafort de Tragó de Noguera, an area in the Pyrenees near Lleida, and emigrated to Argentina as a child. Crossing the Atlantic she met a man from Bellcaire d'Urgell, José Pérez Solé. When you leave home, new relationships are strong and long-lasting; they are the life raft of the immigrant. This is the real New World, the foundation of a new life. Rosa and José supported each other throughout the transition to a new beginning in a foreign land. They eventually married in Argentina and had three children, one of whom was Rosa María, wife of Eusebio Messi, the parents of Jorge Messi.

Recently, *Corriere della Sera* carried out an interesting exercise with Leo, reminding him of the Messi family roots.

- They were from Recanati, like Giacomo Leopardi.
- Who was he?
- A great poet: *Sempre caro mi fu quest'ermo colle / e questa siepe, che da tanta parte / dell'ultimo orizzonte il guardo esclude.*
- I've never heard of him. I'm sorry.
- Maybe you've heard of the Virgin of Loreto. It's close.
- No. I'm sorry. Where is it?
- Le Marche. Central Italy. Have you never been curious to go and see where your grandparents came from?
- No. I think my father knows the place. He has been there and has seen our relatives. Maybe one day I'll go as well.
- Have you at least seen the 'Hotel of Immigrants' in Buenos Aires? It's where most of the Italians who first arrived in the country based themselves.
- No, I don't know it.

Then the journalist showed him some old black and white photographs of those who'd gone in search of their fortune on the Pampas. 'Stern-looking women with shawls and long, black skirts. Skinny, barefoot children. Enormous casseroles for food. The men in dark jackets, white shirts and felt hats. The eyes gazing into the void of the unknown, the kind of look that ought to be described in the lyrics of a melancholy song.'

Leo looked at them with some curiosity, but little else.

For Leo, everything starts and finishes in Rosario.

The Messi/Pérez family settled in Las Heras. Close by lived the Cuccittini Olivera parents of Celia, who were also of Italian descent. In the neighbourhood the spark of love between Jorge and Celia was struck and they wasted little time: aged just 15 and 13, they realised what was happening and didn't fight it. Five years later, when Jorge returned from his military service, they married.

Soon they were planning to go and live in Australia. Would an Australian Leo have been a footballer, or a footballing star? We'll return to that later, but as it turned out the Messis preferred to carry on living in their parents' neighbourhood. Celia worked for years in a workshop producing magnetic coils for industrial use and, like everyone else in the migrant community, Jorge was prepared to do any job that would provide an income – whether it be making screws in a metal workshop from six in the morning or as a door-to-door collector of monthly medical insurance premiums. But he knew that to better himself, to guarantee a future for his family, he had to work hard. He didn't make it as a footballer after four years at the Newell's Old Boys' academy, so he started to study in the evening, from five until nine, after he had finished work, to become a chemical engineer. It took him eight years to finish the course. He was 22 years old and had his priorities in order: his efforts reaped their reward.

Jorge joined Acindar, one of the main pressed-steel production plants in Argentina, in 1980, the year his first son, Rodrigo, was born. To get to the factory in Villa Constitución, some 50 kilometres from Rosario, he had to catch a works bus. Competition was encouraged and Jorge rose swiftly in the company, finally becoming manager. His salary made keeping a family of three no hardship. Or, rather, four: Matías arrived in 1982. 'My father,' says the second Messi/Cuccittini, 'was a worker, we never wanted for anything, but he was always, as now, humble. We always worked for a better life, my old man, my old mum ... and all of the brothers were able to study in the best schools. We wanted for nothing.'

Theirs was a house in which food was always good and never wasted, always a good reference point: Leo corroborates this, telling *Corriere della Sera*, 'we eat Argentine or Italian cooking: spaghetti, ravioli, chorizo sausages ... My passion is for beef "milanesa".

My mother makes it like nobody else. Exceptional. Normal or with sauce, tomato and cheese on top. Ours was a modest family, but we weren't poor. Honestly, we wanted for nothing.'

There is a common misconception about the origin of most Argentinian footballers: the overwhelming majority come from that section that would be classified as middle class, that in Europe would be known as working class, but not lower class or poor. The same as the Messis, in fact. There are not many examples of footballers who have emerged from poverty to become successes in Argentinian football. At least, that is, not since Diego Maradona was born in the slums of Fiorito to the south of Buenos Aires.

The truth is that the poor rarely get to trial for football clubs, sometimes because of lack of contacts, or sometimes of resources, that prevent them from going to training, buying kit, being properly fed or getting into a football school with all its corresponding costs: without this last step hardly any of them become professionals. And those from the lower classes that do manage to get into a club are not accustomed to having continuity and perseverance in their lives because of the absence of a family structure, and because they live in villages and communities where discipline and sacrifice are not encouraged, where drugs are a distraction. Few professional footballers therefore emerge from poverty. There are some, like René Houseman (World Cup 1978), Maradona (even though he never went hungry), Carlos Tévez, perhaps Ezequiel Lavezzi or Chipi Barijho, a player with Carlos Bianchi's Boca of 2000 who these days dedicates himself to giving back to football what it gave to him: taking kids from the street, feeding them and training them at Bajo Flores. But very few others.

Argentinian footballers are, in the main, middle class, a section of society that experienced great difficulties in the last decade of the twentieth century when inflation caused the peso to lose value daily. Argentina stopped growing.

The future looked bleak.

The face of Argentina in the eighties was changing. The Falklands War of 1982, the military reclamation of the islands occupied by Great Britain, was intended to distract attention from the continual and progressive failure of the economic policy of the military *junta* then running the country. Social tension was palpable and infla-tion unstoppable. Argentinians were dying and their hopes with them. But the military failure united indignation that was finally converted into the definitive action that would finally overthrow the regime. In December 1983, democracy returned.

Four years later, the country was on the brink of civil war follow-ing the rise of a group of young army officers known as the *Carapin-tadas* ('Painted Faces'), under the leadership of Colonel Aldo Rico. The army could not take any more humiliation and resolved to put an end to judicial processes against the military regime that sought to prosecute them for violations against human rights. Even though Argentinians took to the streets to defend democracy, and despite national strikes across the country, including in Rosario, President Raul Alfonsín bowed to pressure and finally passed the Due Obe-dience Law that exempted military personnel below the rank of colonel from responsibility for crimes such as forced disappearance, illegal detention, torture and murder. The Argentinian government was covering their recent past with a very thick coat of paint.

Up to 15 explosive devices caused chaos in various cities between 1984 and 1985, including Villa Constitución, close to the factory where Jorge Messi was working: this was the soundtrack of out-raged Argentinians unwilling to accept the obligation to forget the dark past, or to submit to military blackmail. In the following months the streets of cities and towns throughout the country were filled with protestors demanding higher salaries and a fairer eco-nomic policy.

On 24 June 1987, in the middle of an economic and political crisis and almost a year to the day since Maradona had lifted the World Cup in Mexico, and on the fifty-second anniversary of the death of composer and actor Carlos Gardel, Lionel Andrés Messi was born.

After a scare.

Doctors feared that they might have to induce the birth with forceps because they diagnosed a foetal distress. Jorge feared the consequences for the baby who was ultimately born naturally, even though he was a little redder than usual and had one bent ear. 'No, no, it won't be for ever, wait and see; tomorrow it will be all right,' the parents were told by gynaecologist Norberto Odetto.

The third son of the 27-year-old Celia Cuccittini and 29-year-old Jorge came into the world at the Italian Clinic in Rosario, weighing in at 3.6 kilograms and measuring 47 centimetres.

Leo. Leonel? That's what the parents decided to name the baby. But it was not Lionel Ritchie who inspired the name, despite popular legend, even though the singer, much admired in the Messi household, was then at the height of his fame.

Jorge made his way to the register office, having agreed with Celia that Leonel was to be the infant's name. Sounded nice, but not quite right, he thought. On arrival he asked for a list of other names he could use: he didn't want his child to be called Leo. The list included Lionel, which was the name in English. He liked that, so Lionel would be entered in the records. There was a row at home because (in the name of God, Jorge!) that was not what was decided! It was a fleeting row, but a row none the less. As it was, fate was to get its own back on Jorge for today the whole world knows his son as Leo. Fortunately for his father, in Argentina that becomes Lio.

Leo started to walk at nine months and was often found chasing a ball that his brothers had left around in the house. Just days after getting himself up on two feet for the first time, the child dared to go out into the street. The front door was often left open, cars seldom passed. That, remember, was the type of neighbourhood they lived in.

As he tottered out, a bike went past and knocked him over.

Leo cried, naturally, but it seemed that he hadn't been hurt. As he slept, the boy made little noises. His arm was swollen. Indeed, more than that. A cracked ulna of the left forearm was the hospital's diagnosis. The first sign of a weak body. And also of an extraordinary resistance to pain.

For his first birthday he received his first NOB shirt. The whole family are '*leprosos*'.

Except for the most rebellious one, Matías: he was Central, of course.

The new Messi/Cuccuttini was already playing with the ball with his brothers, a child more fascinated by watching football than he was cartoons, and who on his third birthday received as a present a ball with a pattern of red diamonds. 'Look after him!' shouted his mother when he went out, aged just four, for a kickabout with the older boys. 'My mother let me go out to play football, but as I was younger than the others she was always there on the sidelines to see if I started to cry. This influenced me a lot,' Leo told the Colombian magazine *Soho*.

The following will be familiar to many, especially those who grew up wanting to be footballers, and, more especially by those who actually made it.

In bed, Leo did not sleep well without a ball, if he couldn't feel it close by, normally at his feet. And he was in despair when they took it off him when he went to bed. For him a football was like bread at meal times, an ever-present. When his mother sent Leo to do some shopping, the ball went him. If not, then he didn't go. And if he didn't have one handy he made do with rolled up bags or football stockings, whatever he could find. 'Leo left the house with a ball, lived with the ball, and slept with the ball. He only wanted the ball,' remembered Rodrigo Messi in a video played during the gala presentation of the 2012 Balon d'Or. Jorge insists that he used to do other things with his friends – he went out on his bike, played marbles or PlayStation with his neighbours, watched television. He was a normal boy, his dad repeats. But as Jorge also admitted in the German magazine *Kicker*, 'since I can remember, always close to a ball'.

Jorge, who himself showed promise as a central midfielder in the lower ranks of NOB, admitted to Ramiro Martín in his book *Messi: Un genio en la escuala del futbol* ('Messi: A Genius in the School of Football') that one day Leo surprised everyone.

'It was during a *rondo* that we were doing with all my sons in the street … My son Rodrigo had the ball at his feet and Leo was in the middle chasing it. In a flash he threw himself at the feet of his brother and took it off him. We all looked at each other, surprised. No one had told him how to do this. It came naturally.'

From that moment all eyes were on the boy and his talent. The plaudits fell on the child who felt happy at their happiness, happy with himself. And, like all youngsters he wanted more: more of the ball, which meant more attention, more enjoyment. In *El Gráfico*, Jorge remembers that 'at four years of age we real-ised that he was different. He did little plays and the ball slept on the point of his boot. We couldn't believe it. A bit older, he played with his two brothers who had seven and five years on him and he used to dance around them. It's a gift, something he was born with.'

That small child, that quiet boy, who would spend his time either at home or at his Aunt Marcela's, 'who only liked football' as remembers his friend and neighbour Cintia Arellano, soon began to attract attention in the narrow Calle Estado de Israel. Cintia's house – she is a month and a half older than Leo – was next to the Messis' house in La Bajada. They shared the same first school years, and he sat next to her in the classroom or behind her if there was an exam. With Cintia, *el Piqui* ('Titch') spoke more. ('That's what they called him. One day a boy shouted out, "Come here, Titch" and the name stuck,' remembers his best friend, today a qualified psychologist and teacher of children with learning difficulties.) Cintia was the one that would go to his house and persuade him to go to school. The one who would sometimes explain to others what he was trying to say. The one who would pass him the crib sheets, the little notes, either on a ruler or a rubber. The one who wrote on the small pieces of paper that she passed to Leo during his exams. The one who brought him his afternoon snacks. The one who told him, you're going to be sorry if you don't learn things now, and the one who heard him reply, yes, I'll regret it, but I can't do it. The one who explained his absence if he skipped class one day, which occasionally happened. The one who told the little white lie that she was his cousin.

She was the one who learned of the fact that he was injecting himself with hormones when, on one trip at the end of the term, Leo's mother asked Cintia's mother, who was travelling with the kids, to make sure that he was injecting himself every night.

'Lionel was small, and always went around here barefoot and played with the ball,' says another neighbour, Ruben Manicabale. 'Many times we used to get mad at him, grab him and throw him to the ground, but he used to get up and carry on playing.'

A member of the Quiroga family, neighbours across the street, remembered that 'the kids didn't play all day with the ball, but he did. They all left and he carried on by himself by the gate. My mother scolded him many times because it was late and he carried on with the ball.'

'When he played sometimes he would be hit, fall and cry, but he soon stopped and carried on running. You could see he was different: the skill he had, the speed ...' remembers Cintia.

It's said that Rodrigo was the first person to call him 'the Flea'. In truth no one in the neighbourhood gave him that name. The family believe that it was a Mexican football commentator who, years later, gave him the nickname. They are talking about Enrique Bermúdez, considered one of the most prestigious voices in the Castilian language, a champion of pure entertainment, a narrator of what Jorge Valdano describes as 'the most important of the least important'. The 'dog' Bermúdez – that's how he's known – was a rocker, hippy, singer and film extra, before becoming a narrator and a creator of hundreds of nicknames (Adolfo Ríos became 'Christ's Archer', Rafael Márquez 'the Kaiser of Zamora' and David Beckham 'Blue Shoes' because of the Smurf-coloured boots he wore) and of the outlandish description of the footballing style of Barcelona's Pep Guardiola's : 'yours, mine, have it, lend it, caress it, kiss it, give it to me'. But Bermúdez never claimed to be the creator of the nickname. Whoever it was still remains anonymous.

In any case it was clear that Leo had something special. 'He is a shining light sent by God. You know when someone says, "he will make it, he will"? He was a footballer from the day he was born,' says Claudia, Cintia's mother, who sometimes baby-sat the young Leo.

'He played with a number five ball, so big that he could have hit it anywhere and yet he controlled it perfectly,' remembers his brother Matías. 'It was something beautiful, you had to see it, and whoever saw it for the first time would go back to see it.'

The ball, with a diameter that reached up to his knee, seemed stuck to his left foot, never too far away, small touches that enabled him to keep control, light strikes with the side of his boot, the ball always on the ground to avoid the possibility of a failure of technique that would cause the ball to bounce off his knee or his shin and run away from him to where the older boys could get it back.

He had extraordinary co-ordination, a stature that helped him control the ball and natural speed. He challenged the older boys and he shone. Was this a divine gift or natural talent? There'll be time to discuss that later.

What's more (his face redder than a tomato), he was a great competitor. Or, rather, very competitive. Or better still: he had a brave character, and did not like losing. Behind the silences, there was a boy. He would often come home with a box full of marbles that he had won in the street. He counted them and if there were ever any missing he would go wild.

Celia, his mother: When he was small, at home he was very naughty. We used to play cards and no one wanted to play with him because we knew that sooner or later he would cheat.

Jorge Messi: He did not want to lose at anything.

Celia: If he didn't win he would toss all the cards away. He did not want to go to school, he would say no, he did not want to go.

Leo (to *El Gráfico*): Once I had a fight with my cousin in his house, my grandmother was there as well. Everyone ended up against me, they threw me out and wouldn't let me in. So then I started throwing stones at the gate and kicking it.

Celia: When I left him at the gate, he began throwing stones at me, saying he would not be coming back at midday, he would pepper the house with stones, and so I would go out and say to him, 'I'm going to tell your father!' And he just scoffed at it. He was very spoilt … he had a very strong personality, which I guess he has got from the both of us, but a bit more from me. He is a person who says what he feels, both good and bad, because he doesn't try to hide his annoyance or his joy. From his father he got his sense of responsibility and he is very fair.

That is what his parents were trying to convey in a documentary for *Informe Robinson* (fronted by the former Liverpool player Michael Robinson) of Canal + Spain: you cannot hide fierceness; if you have it, you have it, and sometimes, just occasionally, he would bare his teeth.

The small pitch at Grandoli Football Club is surrounded by the Soviet-style concrete blocks of a dormitory town, a humble neighbourhood on the fringes of the city. Some say it is a hard and dangerous place. If you look closely between the buildings you can see the boats that go down river to the port of Rosario. The pitch is of earth with strips of green along the sides which mark the touchlines. The tall blocks seem like giants to the small players, who are indeed very small: children of five, six and seven years old and some older ones up to 12. A gate, a blend of turquoise and rust, flanks the entrance while a fence around the pitch stops the balls. There's a sign that reads, 'Clean your boots here'. The stand only has three rows of seats, and in the second row the parents of some of the children and grandmother Celia are seated. She has led little Leo by the hand to watch her grandson Matías. Rodrigo, who has also worn the red and white shirt of Grandoli, now plays for the juniors at Newell's.

Leo is intermittently kicking a ball against the wall.

The group is taken by Salvador Ricardo Aparicio, a thin, calm man who has spent four decades involved with formative football. On that day there was one player missing so the generation of '86 could play the usual 7 vs 7 game. It happens sometimes. Salvador waited to see if one more turned up.

'Put him on, put him on,' says the grandmother, referring to the little five-year-old who in those days was not yet known as 'the Flea'.

'He's too small, woman. He could get hurt,' answers Aparicio.

'Put him on, put him on,' insists Celia.

'OK, I will, I will. But if you see that he is crying or he is scared, take him off. Open the gate and take him off.'

And so the coach puts him on even though he is a year younger than the rest at a time when such age differences are very noticeable.

Out comes the little shrimp. The ball, when it comes to him for the first time, looks bigger than he does.

And what happens next just had to happen. The usual thing.

The ball comes to his right foot. Leo looks at it and it goes way past him. The boy doesn't move.

Aparicio raises his eyebrows. It's what he'd been expecting.

Leo receives another pass. This time the ball comes to his left foot: to tell the truth it hits him on the leg. But he takes two steps, accommodates the ball, brings it under control. And with little touches he starts a diagonal run across this vast obstacle course, dribbling past anyone who gets in his way.

'Kick it, kick it!' shouts Aparicio. 'Pass it, pass it, Leo!'

Grandmother smiles.

Leo doesn't pass it.

He's very small. But from then on there was no way the coach was going to take him off. 'He played like he'd been doing it all his life, him against the other thirteen,' Salvador remembered much later on. That year he played the rest of the matches with the 1986 Grandoli side. And won titles.

Messi doesn't remember anything from that day. His grandmother told him he scored two goals.

Leo wanted to play, of course, be it in the square, in the street, on his own, with his cousins and with Rodrigo and Matías, but, like any other kid, he wanted to do so with a kit, a team shirt, with a side like his brothers played in. And so at the age of five and after that day of surprises under the watchful eye of Celia, his smiling grandmother, in fact even before his first day at primary school, he began playing every week in what is called baby-football (seven-a-side, for those aged between 5 and 12) at the Grandoli club in the neighbourhood where he was born, located at number 4700 Laferrere Street, an institution founded in February 1980 by a group of local fathers hoping to form a competition for children from the area.

Take a look at this video: youtu.be/ojUNSUW6DHg

Leo is five years old. He is already demonstrating the same ease of dribbling and change of pace that he does today. The same joyous celebrations. The same diminutive stature compared to the others.

El Piqui gets the ball and looks for a gap, driving, dribbling. All his opponents follow him. So do his team-mates. If he can't get in one way, he keeps the ball. He searches on the other flank, teammates and opponents all around him. You have to understand that in Argentina it is considered vulgar to score – it is much better to create, assist and link and to leave your opponents in your wake. For that very reason many thought that there was little about this extraordinary player that needed putting right. Rarely would the cry of 'Pass it, Leo' be heard again. At any given moment, the way would open up, Leo would launch the ball close to the post, far from the goalkeeper. Goal.

There are those who like to say, probably to provoke you, that you need to see if Messi is capable of playing on a freezing Wednesday night in winter at, say, a rain-soaked Stoke. They need to look at the slopes, the stones, the small pieces of glass on the uneven football pitch on which he played for his first team, Grandoli's pitch, which is provided by the local authority and can only be used at night because by day it is used by a school. The lighting was also poor.

From the age of two, Lionel and his maternal grandmother, Celia, walked the 15 blocks that separate the Messis' house from his first club, Leo holding onto her arm as he struggled to keep up with her. Tucked under his arm was the ball he'd been given as a present. They were off to see Rodrigo and Matías. Later, just Matías. Finally now in the team of boys a year older than him, he took the same route to training on Mondays, Wednesdays and Fridays. Games were played on Saturdays.

'She was too good. She lived for us, the grandchildren. She would put up with all our whims, the cousins used to fight to be allowed to sleep at her house. I don't know whether my grandmother understood football but it was she who took us to play. She was my first fan at training, at the games. Her cries of encouragement were always with me,' Leo told *El Mundo Deportivo* in a rare moment of personal reflection.

Celia did not watch football on television, nor would you find her at the Newell's stadium. For her, football was where her grandchildren played. And for the grandchildren, life revolved around their grandmother, a definitive point of reference for this matriarchal unit of Italian origin in which mutual respect and family support formed the cornerstone. If Leo is asked to define some of the best moments of his life, his illuminating answer will be 'the birth of each one of my nephews'. That was asked, mind you, before the birth of his own son.

Leo and his grandmother walked from home to Grandoli and back again, and when he started school Grandma would collect him there at five o'clock in the afternoon, they would have a refreshing drink, and then, along with Matías, go off to training. 'The fact is that it was a beautiful period in our lives, we really enjoyed Leo because as a kid he was already showing what he was made of.

My grandmother died later, but everything started with her,' says Matías Messi.

'Pass it to Lionel, pass it to the little feller. He can score goals,' she would shout. Grandma knew about football.

And because of her roots – she had more Latin blood in her than the others – she was less able to control her emotions, showing her hand more often than not. Like every club in the world Grandoli has its eternal rivals, opponents who go back to the beginning of time; sometimes it seems even earlier. These are the games that they just cannot lose. Playing Alice was one of those. Hard, physical encounters that would sometimes end up with fathers exchanging words and the occasional slap. At one of these matches that got out of hand, Celia struck one of the Alice supporters over the head with a bottle. 'Stop messing around,' she screeched. No great harm was caused. That day, needless to say, Grandoli won.

Shortly afterwards, it was discovered that Celia had Alzheimer's.

The journalist Toni Frieros reveals this in his early biography of Messi, *Messi: El Tesoro del Barça* ('Messi: The Treasure of Barcelona'): 'Celia gradually began to lose her memory, to have speech difficulties and to confuse people, so for the last months of her life the family watched helplessly as her vitality was slowly consumed by a degenerative and incurable disease. For Leo, it was like losing a part of himself.'

It was like watching a living death.

Leo's grandmother died on 4 May 1998, shortly before his eleventh birthday.

Celia never saw him play at the top or at Barcelona.

'For everyone it was a huge loss and all of us without exception felt such great pain. To this day I still get emotional remembering Leo grabbing onto the coffin, weeping uncontrollably,' recalls his Aunt Marcela.

'It was a dreadful blow,' says Leo now.

Since then, when he celebrates every goal Messi looks to the sky and points to the heavens. 'I think about her a lot and I dedicate my goals to her. I would like her to be here but she left before she could see me triumph. This is what makes me most angry,' he confessed to *El Mundo Deportivo* in 2009.

'The poor woman, she never saw him triumph but she was the

catalyst,' says Alberto Arellano, father of Cintia and neighbour of the Messis.

'When he was forging his career, he always told me that at night he spoke to his grandmother and asked for her help,' remembers Leo's mother. 'It's a shame that today she cannot see him. Who knows whether from up there or from wherever she may be, she can see what he has become and is happy for the grandson she loved so much.'

Leo believes in God, even though he is not a practising Christian, like all the other Messis. But he owes gratitude to his grandmother for accompanying him in the formative years of his life. And because, surely, she is still with him. The only time he didn't raise his fingers first in salute to his grandmother after scoring was just after his son Thiago was born, when a thumb went into his mouth. But after that one instance he would once again acknowledge Celia in the usual way.

Leo left his neighbourhood for the first time at the age of 11. It was a Saturday in spring. He caught the bus with his friend Diego Vallejos, who is, incidentally, the brother of Matías's wife. He was from the same neighbourhood. The two youngsters made their way half an hour out of town to Villa Gobernador Gálvez, in the south of the city.

To visit his grandmother's grave.

Leo was at Grandoli from the age of five to almost seven. In that team of '87 he wore the number 10 and his cousin Emanuel was the goalkeeper. Two things in particular kept repeating themselves during this period: they won practically everything that was going and, well, Lionel always had the ball.

Each practice, each game, was the most important ever, and before every practice, every game (and each one was the most important of all), Leo prepared in the minutest detail and without any assistance from anyone. First the boots, cleaned with water then a cloth and a brush. Then the ankles were bandaged. He was like a professional, small and deadly serious.

Salvador Aparicio was his first trainer and in his sessions he made them jog, then asked them to loosen up a bit and then introduced the ball. In those days the entire enterprise consisted, really, of playing, playing and playing.

Salvador, 'Don Apa', had a wonderful story – he was not the man who discovered him, rather the conduit for an unstoppable talent. The former railway worker who died of a brain fissure in 2009, aged 79 (according to some people, you could hear the air escaping from his head), never presumed to be any more than that: 'I didn't discover him. But I was the first person to put him on the pitch. I am proud of that.'

Don Apa, like hundreds of anonymous trainers and technical directors, convinced dozens of children from the neighbourhood, aged between 4 and 12, to come off the streets for a while and spend time with Grandoli where they would learn a certain order and happiness. His are the videos of a Leo, small and going at full pelt in his red and white shirt, dribbling around defenders, getting the ball in his own box and taking it into the opposition's, scoring, then collecting the ball from the net to put it back on the centre spot to start all over again.

'He scored six or seven goals every game. He positioned himself in the middle of the pitch and waited for the goalkeeper to kick the ball. The goalie kicked the ball, one of his team-mates would stop it, he would then take it off him and set off on a dribble. It was something supernatural.' This is how Don Apa, in various interviews, remembered Leo. 'When we went to a pitch, people would crowd in to see him. When he got the ball, he owned it. It was incredible, they couldn't stop him. Against Amanecer he scored one of those goals like you see in the adverts. I remember it well: he dribbled past everybody, goalkeeper included. How did he play? Like he plays now, with freedom. He was a serious boy, he always put himself beside his grandmother, he was quiet. He never protested. If they whacked him, sometimes he would cry but he would always pick himself up and carry on running.

'Every time I see him play I start to cry. When I see the Maradona-type goal he scored, the one he got against Getafe, I remember when he was little, so little ...'

David Treves, who replaced Don Apa, is today president of Grandoli. He proudly displays the trophies won by the club and the team photos. Messi is the one wearing the shirt that is too big for him. 'It was very rare for a boy of his age to do all this,' confirms Treves. 'It was said that we had the next Maradona. The best footballer in the world began here, and his first football shirt was ours.'

'He would get the ball and the move would finish with a goal. He made the difference even if they kicked him. This is how it is: if you're small and you play well, they break you.' So recalls Gonzalo Diaz who played with Leo during the time he was at Grandoli, and naturally won everything.

Matías Messi finds it easy to put into words those days when he himself had dreams of becoming a footballer. And he, like all the Messis and all the other anonymous spectators, believed they were witnessing something special. 'Very often there were problems because of this, because he played so well. So well, in fact, that some coaches of the other boys sent their team out to bring him down – if they couldn't get the ball off him by fair means, they'd get it in other ways. It was something that you had to see to believe. There were even players on the other team who would applaud some of his moves. "What are you doing?" the rival fans would ask.'

Sometimes it seems that many of those recollections reflect the Lionel Messi of today rather than those of the little boy who played good football; certainly a tireless scorer of goals but, at the time, a footballer of individual brilliance rather than a team player, and there is a big difference. They do not speak of a child, rather of a child who has become the greatest footballer in the world. It isn't the same thing. It is easy, with hindsight, to idolise those who succeed. And for this reason it's difficult to find anybody who would dare to add a qualifying 'but'.

Anyway, at Grandoli there were many others who showed promise. 'I have seen several who could have been like Messi but they did not have the perseverance in training,' says Gonzalo Diaz.

Ah, perseverance. Without it, you cannot be a footballer.

Jorge Messi also dreamed of becoming a footballer, but after four years at the NOB academy, just as a player starts to blossom, when the first team beckons, Jorge left to do his military service, and on his return he married. When Jorge was 29, the age when most footballers reach their peak, Leo was born.

Jorge has always had very fixed ideas, but he teaches by example rather than by word. His philosophy is simple: work hard, be persistent, show humility and you can achieve your goals. Maybe that is why Leo is not seduced by the celebrity culture, is not dazzled by those great names in neon lights. In any case for Jorge, as with the overwhelming majority of the Argentine people of his generation football was the inevitable and irresistible face of Maradona, videos of whom Jorge treasured and played frequently to his sons.

Leo's father therefore passed down to his sons an appreciation of the one man who rose above the rest to lead his side, who caressed the ball as he was looking for the next pass, and who had the power in his feet to create a symphony of answers. For Lionel, and for many of his generation, that type of player could be seen in the shape of Pablo Aimar, the ex-River player. Lionel has said many times he did not have any football idols as a kid, but he liked to see Aimar. Is it true that he had no heroes? Don't we all have some point of reference? When he was asked at the age of 12 to name his idol, he said he had two: 'My father and my godfather, Claudio.' In that same interview he confessed he considered humility the greatest of all virtues. Something with which his father would agree.

Leo, like his brothers, shared his father's passion for football. Jorge is a reserved man, even a little distant at times, and also a decent central midfielder, as little Leo would see when Dad played games with his workmates at the Acindar factory. He understood football, a game he loved. The Messis came down every weekend to Grandoli to watch Matías and Lionel play, and one day a club director asked Jorge if he would take charge of the kids born in 1987. He thus became Leo's second coach. 'We were part of the Alfi league, one of the independent competitions that play in Rosario and the municipality. There were different categories up to 12 years old, and the youngsters always played on a seven-a-side pitch,' Jorge told Toni Frieros.

He trained three times a week with simple, individual exercises, always with the ball to improve technique, and the occasional tactical exercise which the youngsters learned quickly, like little sponges, eager and delighted to soak up Jorge's instructions. Leo never did any specific work, he never spent his afternoons passing the ball with his right foot, or dribbling around stones with his weaker leg. His father never asked him to. He simply played and Jorge endeavoured to respect that free spirit in the weekly training sessions.

It was 1994. Leo was six years old.

Jorge Messi's side never lost a game in his only year as their trainer. 'We won the league and all the tournaments we entered, even the friendlies. Maybe it's a bit crude to say this, but the side caused a sensation because of the high standard it reached and in that team Leo shone out like a beacon,' he has told the Argentinian press. 'In this team – and I don't want to overdo it – practically everything that is good he did. The goals, the dangerous situations, the one player who made the difference was him, the one who excelled was him. OK, I'm his father, he is my son, and I'm not saying it for that reason, but because that's how it was,' he told the magazine *Kicker*.

The journalist interviewing him followed a line of questioning that might seem banal but is none the less fascinating: 'Lionel, the footballer: who did he take more notice of, Jorge Messi the trainer or the father?' Jorge answered: 'He was always very disciplined in his play, always obedient and did what was asked of him. He always took notice of what I said to him as a trainer. Even today he is like this. Like when Frank Rijkaard at Barcelona put him on the right. He always complied with what the coach asked of him, he always played where he asked him to, it didn't matter who it was. And he never complained. That's how it always was.'

'In life there are three elements: mission, vision and values,' adds the prestigious Argentinian sports psychologist Liliana Grabín. 'The legacy you inherit from a father is the way he walks the path, the values he transmits. Leo carries with him the strong personality of his mother and the calmness, tolerance and forbearance of his father: a strange combination; ying-yang, I suppose. But he also passed onto him humility, self-sacrifice and tenacity.'

But the son is also the result of his father's vision. Jorge once said that to hear your name being chanted is the greatest thing that can happen to a human being. If this is your dream, then you pass it on. Jorge had a vision. When he saw Leo play and understood that he had talent, his attitude was that of a proud father who wanted his son to stand out from his peers. A son always wants to please his father, and will always try to continue pleasing him. The vision, the attitude. All this marks the journey. Jorge lit the way: you *can* be a footballer.

'The family had the values, the vision is the future, and the mission is the playing of football. Jorge had vision, the family had vision. Obviously he had a talent, and the mother and the father had the vision to continue the path that allowed him to explore and develop his talent,' explains Grabín.

Afterwards, Jorge, in his role as trainer, adviser and even as manager, helped Leo negotiate the road. A dad *and* a manager, then. He gave him very little praise in comparison to the universal adulation he received; rather, he gave him perspective. And, when necessary, he reminded him of the values that he considered ideals. At all times he kept his son's feet firmly on the ground, particularly when it looked as though too much success might distract him and lead him to lose sight of the bigger picture, which would happen, as we shall see.

Jorge, therefore, has from the start been father, guide, mirror, mentor, counter-balance, Leo's hero. The man he has to follow, occasionally rebel against, but the one who has to be recognised as his companion along the road. Someone in whom Leo places absolute trust and unshakeable faith.

It was Jorge who decided that they had reached the end of the road with Grandoli. The whole family went to watch matches involving Matías and Leo, but on one occasion he was unable to pay the two pesos' admission. He asked them if, just this once, they would waive the admission fee. They said no.

Leo played that afternoon, but it was the last time he wore the Grandoli shirt.

Teacher Mónica Dómina has her recollections. She had Leo in her class at Las Heras school between the ages of six and eight, in the first, second, third and fourth grade, the first years of primary education.

'... the thing is he was a very quiet boy. Unfortunately you always remember those who misbehave, those who bring you problems. But he was quiet, polite, and sometimes very introverted with feelings that he did not want to show. He was a protected child, because with his classmates like Cintia, they bonded together, they went into the same grade and she was like his mother, she was twice as tall as him because he was very, very small, he looked like a kid in kindergarten. And he had such a cheerful little face ... the same as it is now. You feel like hugging him! And back then, even more so. Back then the teacher was like a second mother. It isn't the same feelings that the teachers have nowadays … yes, these young girls haven't got the same maternal instinct. We used to do it a different way, I would sit him on my knee, look after him, and now these things don't happen. And he was one of those who was like a baby, a little baby, you felt like picking him up and sitting him with you and chatting to him.

'He was very easygoing, but he hardly spoke at all. But one thing that I do remember very well: I tried to get him to speak. I did this in the free time and during special lessons when we were doing stuff like drawing. That's when I had him close to me, but he wouldn't say anything. Only "yes, no", he wouldn't say anything else. But when I asked him questions about stuff in my field, like maths or comprehension, he would answer and that set my mind at ease.

'Generally Leo sat in the first row in the classroom, but he was very shy, and it was difficult for him to take part in class, he did his work but didn't take his class by storm. He was doing well, doing what work he had to pass tests and always handed work in on time.

'We, the teachers, tried to help him and he did what he could; but it was not that he was incapable. No. It was that he didn't want to, because he had another interest, all he wanted was the ball.

'He was a normal boy, but not excellent. He was responsible, he did his work as well as he could. He did not study a lot. In the seventh grade he got a good report. The head teacher let a newspaper take a photograph of the book in which the marks were recorded and there you could see all of the marks. He was one of the best in PE, and did well in handiwork and music. In comprehension and mathematics, he did just enough, seven, that was a pass grade, so he was so-so.

'But my first image of him is playing with the football in the schoolyard, taking the ball from way back and dribbling with it. Even though they didn't always have a ball, sometimes they made one up with whatever they could, like socks that they had stuck together in a ball, or plastic bags, or even with Silly Putty. With whatever they could find they played in the yard.

'But normally there was a ball. The PE teacher had a cupboard they would go to, to fetch it, or sometimes they would bring one from home. They knew if the PE teacher was there or not, and if he wasn't, some other teacher would look after the ball in between lessons.

'All those years ago, you would lend them a ball. Now you don't lend them one. Nowadays they use the ball to hit their mate over the head. The number of students in those days didn't make any difference, there could be 100 of us but we would all get on. They took care of each other. Therefore the boys were allowed to play football.

'All his friends looked upon him as a kind of leader, they put him in the centre of the class photo, they all loved him, loved him. They waited for him, "let's go and play!" They admired him because he shone. He would run from one side to another and no one could catch him; he was a flea, a toy doll; he enjoyed himself and brought enjoyment to others.

'He never played pranks, but those eyes told you that here was a boy who did as he pleased. I think that the family ... I always wanted to ask his mother what he was like at home because he behaved very well at school so as not to lose the chance of playing football. Because in the classroom he was very quiet, but when the bell went he would run outside with everyone following behind him.

'You could see them all in the large multi-purpose room, with the two goals and all those youngsters desperate to play. Playtime was a football championship.

'Before, classes went like this: 40 minutes, a playtime of 15 minutes, 40 minutes, a playtime. But now lessons last one hour, and then a 15-minute break. They would play in that long break. That's when they would have time to play. They were like mini-matches, maybe they would play the first half in the first break and the other half in the second break.

'So he would go out for that quarter of an hour along with the other boys and he was like another person and even if it was seven against seven, or all against all, he would get the ball and his game consisted of taking them all up and down the pitch. Because this wasn't about playing football, it was about dribbling ... He was already practising in ... what do you call it? ... a small football school. And so many of the children that were with him were also in football schools.

'I always said that when his mother came with all his trophies and stopped at the classroom door, proud as any mother would be, he did not want his mother to come in, he didn't want to talk about what he had done. Or, rather, from an early age, he didn't want to show that side of himself, he played because he liked playing, he had passion, just like now ... He wasn't going to show that he was the best because it was something he had inside. He always wanted to be treated just like any other boy, he did not want to stand out. And now he is exactly the same.

'An angel. But an angel as a person. I always meet his mother at the supermarket nearby, because his mother doesn't go around the city saying, "I am Messi's mother." She goes around like any other woman, modestly dressed, nothing vain, because I know the mothers of other footballers, and well, some are full of "I aaaammmmm the moooother ooof" ... She is a lady, uncomplicated and good, and so is he. He doesn't go around telling people, "I have so many millions" ... no. He lives his simple life, as simply as possible, I suppose. Because that's how he was. Neither did he go around boasting about whether he scored a lot of goals or whether he hadn't, because there are many boys that would say, "Did you see that, Miss? Me, me ..." but him, nothing of the sort. The family, the mother, that's how they showed him and that's how they gave him the house rules, and that's why at school he was very quiet, very introverted.

Little Leo did not have to walk far to his school at Las Heras. As soon as he hit the street with the ball glued to his feet, he headed for the wall that surrounded the army barracks, and crossed the fields before coming out into Buenos Aires Street, just where it meets Juan Hernández Square. The little school, painted white, with touches of green, with its barred windows, occupies one side of the unkempt square with its trees and benches and paving slabs from which grass sprouts. It is one of those rare schools with well-behaved children, much like the neighbourhood itself, not like the usual Rosario schools with rowdy kids. Mónica Dómina would probably disagree. The most valuable thing is not the building, but the culture and ethos that radiate from it. When the child enters the school he already knows about the level of behaviour expected, the values that he has to learn or maintain once there: the importance of belonging to the neighbourhood, of learning to improve, the need for collective effort. A genuinely good state school, then.

The yard that leads to the classroom, with an arch framing the entrance and a tree in the centre, was so small it was barely big enough for keepy-uppy or even to play with just one goal. For that reason the boys preferred to resort to an area that today has many uses.

'There is a multi-purpose room where school assemblies take place, but at that time, when Leo was here, it did not exist: it was all just a small field, lots of space for kids to run around or for games to take place.' So says Diana Torreto, who taught Leo when he was six years old and who often stumbles over her words emotionally as she recalls 'the Flea's' time here. 'We would go into that small field with all the children. And something that I remember very well, and it makes me laugh even to this day, is that all of them ran after the ball and none of them managed to get it from him and they would come up to me and moan, "miss, he won't pass the ball". They couldn't take it off him!

'He was a very happy boy,' continues Miss Torreto. 'Introverted, yes, but happy. He was always smiling. And he had a lot of friends. He was very popular with his peers. With a family that were always there for him, that always asked about what he was doing at school because at home he was quite naughty and his mother used to ask how he was here.'

There was, then, the Leo with the ball, the Leo at home and the Leo at school. One Leo in the classroom and another one outside, free, in the schoolyard, competing. The conversation continues with Diana:

- Where does this need for his family, his school and his peers to protect him come from?
- He generates that, this need to always keep an eye on him, look after him, that's why he had so many friends, I guess. His mates were very fond of him. When he was demonstrating the great skill he had with the ball, they admired him, leadership qualities emanated from him. Not sure he knew about it, but the others saw that in him – a contradiction because at the same time in the classroom he was quiet. But where he went his mates followed him. He organised the game and he took them to an activity that he loved, the playing of football.
- This is extraordinary, this leap from introversion to leadership …

- Yes, he was two different children.
- And if Leo had not been a Messi and had not made it as a professional, where would he be now?
- I think he would be with his family. Maybe he would have made his own family, as he now has, and of which we are very proud and we hope that one day he will bring his son Thiago to see the school that he attended. That is what all of us teachers hope for. I think that, yes, he would be surrounded by all his family ...

... I get emotional when I talk about him.

'93, six years old, the year of the birth of María Sol ... bad at adapting to school environment, hygiene practices, effort shown, manual expression, music, writing and physics.

'94, under the tutelage of Mónica Dómina. Bad at adapting to the school environment, creativity and effort shown.

'95, eight years old ... spectacular progress. Very good at mathematics. Very good at creative writing, good at oral expression. Not a single bad report. Cintia helped him a lot. 'An extension of himself, always together,' says Dómina. Ten in PE, very good behaviour.' (Extract from Toni Frieros, Messi: El Tesoro del Barça.)

Leo was protected by both adults and children. Because he was small. Because he was good with the ball. Because he was a good kid. Because he was a son, or a friend's son. For that cheeky smile. Because he was reserved; not shy, but introverted, guarded, even. No one crossed him, no one gave him any aggravation. At least not at school, he had won them all over. It is easier to grow as a person, as a footballer, even, with all that protection giving you a safety net.

All children go through a testing time at school that has nothing to do with studying. The mob will bully them, it always happens. Childhood can be cruel. When it's your turn, make sure you come out of it well. Leo played well with a ball and this drew people to him and helped him to be respected, loved, needed and protected. He was small and conscious of his size, but the rest of the playground ignored this difference because he never failed to impress those who played alongside him, those who watched him as he played. So he was never bullied. There were fights to be on his team because with him on your side you were sure to win. And better to win rather than lose the yard games, because the defeats had to be put up with for the rest of the day. Even when there were boys missing in the older grades' teams, they would invite him to play for them so that he could help them become champions. And Leo obliged, leading with his silence and his game. Just as now: more by his actions than by his words.

But it couldn't all be football; the teachers could not allow that passion for the ball, for the playground match, to take over the pupils' lives to the point where it was impossible to make them understand that playtime had ended. The teachers' challenge with Leo was to disengage him from the game. And distancing him from the ball, from this invisible but oh so tangible connection, was a daily struggle.

– Today the teachers cite Messi as an example of ...?

The question is directed at Cristina Castañeira, the new head teacher at Las Heras school, who did not know Leo and who views the phenomenon that was Leo's presence from a certain distance and with some surprise.

– I don't know, I don't know ... just about everyone who comes to this school knows about Leo, they all know he used to be here. I don't know if it's explicit but it's here all the time. Now I'm in charge, I'm going to see if we can create a Messi corner, with all the cuttings. There's nothing anywhere.
– Is that good for the students; to create his own special corner?
– I don't know, but so many things get done in his name ...
– ... so you feel that something should be done that can serve as an example, a motivation ...
– What do I know ... we have ... the Argentine culture allows these situations of ... we are very much of...
– Legend, myth ...
– Yes, yes, of course, the success of Messi is not going to be on the curriculum, but it would be good to have something so that when people come from outside we could always be ready to show them things. Or to him if one day he comes back here, because he

has been to the school before. I have been in this profession for 30 years and I always follow school procedure. This seems like I am departing from procedure, but, anyway, it doesn't matter. You don't have to be that strict. I don't think they'll applaud me for it, but that isn't the idea; the idea is that there should be a Messi corner that will serve as a reminder of him.

– Leo, the public Leo, represents a series of commendable values.

– Of course, above all, because he is a person of whom one can be proud. Messi has those values inside him that one would like to instil in others.

– An Argentinian friend of mine, a footballer, told me that the government should get hold of Messi once a month and get him to say 'Brush your teeth', and then suddenly all the country would brush them, or 'behave yourselves at school', and then suddenly the whole country would change. I don't know if it could come to that ...

– Yes, it could ...

When Leo's grandmother took him for training with Grandoli after school, they would have crossed the fields of the old quarter that will probably in the future become – who knows? – some kind of business park or maybe – now that the council has loaned the land to the Messi family – pitches created so as to train young footballers who share Leo's dreams.

If there was no training he would meet up to play with friends from the neighbourhood, friends like Diego Vallejos: 'We often did things together, there was always some new trick to learn, something to try or something to do. We weren't really mischievous – sometimes we would wreck flowerbeds with the ball, or use gates as goals ... We played with an air pistol ... we did a lot of things. Coming out of his house, on the left-hand side about 200 metres down, there is an open space: this was the Camp Nou of Argentina. This is where he took his first steps in football. Where we used to have our kickabouts, where we ran, where we hid ... it was our place.'

At Fragotti's, a nearby store, Leo would use the iron door to do one-twos to prevent his friends stealing the ball from him. It was an age where neither time nor clearly marked out lines existed, and few limitations were put on them other than those set by their school or parents.

'We cut the wire fences [that surrounded the old quarter] to be able to play and time and again were chased out by some of the military people because we weren't supposed to be there,' recalls another neighbour, Walter Barrera. 'But the thing was that this field was perfect for us to play football because it had a wonderful grass surface that no one ever walked on and was great to play on. Sometimes they took us by surprise while we were playing and took us indoors where they had a type of cell. But nothing happened: they would take you in through one door and then let you out through another; more than anything it was just to scare us.'

Leo spent his primary school years in Las Heras before starting his secondary education, at the age of 13, at Juan Mantovani Middle School on the Avenida Uriburu, also close to home, only to leave it just four months later: in his mind, his future was away from all that he knew. At Juan Mantovani he did not have his inseparable soulmate, Cintia, at his side; some of the things closest to him were beginning to change.

Leo is the benefactor not of that school, but of his first one at Las Heras: over the past decade he has donated the equivalent of two years of the total school budget. And he visited the school in 2005. One of the teachers had a son who had played football with him and made the most of that contact by inviting him along for the school's anniversary. They were putting on an event and Leo turned up. He wasn't as well known then as he is now, but he still made their day. And one afternoon two years later, towards the evening, he returned again, this time to see his cousin, Bruno Biancucchi. It was a surprise visit and he arrived with his head down, quiet, hiding behind Bruno's mother, his Aunt Marcela. He was dying of embarrassment.

Suddenly something switched on in his head. He began to connect with the other children, to talk to them. He went around all the classrooms, kissing people, signing autographs and allowing himself to be photographed. Three memorable hours for both students and parents in a school where, except perhaps for the playground breaks, hardly anything ever seems to happen.

A boy from the first year, no more than five years old, said to a friend of more or less the same age and size, wearing the same little shorts and with the same little school smock: 'Pinch me.'

2

Waiting for Leo

A true story (with scenes and imaginary meetings set in two acts). Characters (see Appendix for full list of characters).

We hear from Leo's team-mates, coaches and technical directors during his years at Newell's, some of his opponents, neighbours and others who have played a part in his life. They speak with a touching devotion, but also of time tinged with melancholy. This is what can happen when genius touches your life.

There are plenty of names and they all have huge relevance – this is, after all, their story as well as Leo's. But allow your imagination to be suspended while you read this. You don't have to remember who is who, or who says what. In a way, they all symbolise a single character who represents all those that accompanied him in Rosario. So if you get lost in the maelstrom of names, just latch onto the hand of the kid who couldn't grow.

The action takes place in Rosario, in the late nineties, the last years of a forward-looking Argentina. The first act is set in a cafeteria at Malvinas, the training centre for youth teams of Newell's.

ACT ONE

Scene One

Voices can be heard off. The set is lit by a single light.

– Where's Leo?
– He's got hepatitis, so they say.
– Ah.

The scene goes dark and the words SIX YEARS EARLIER appear. On the wall of the set, the following video is projected:

http://www.youtube.com/watch?v=9GFeiJEGjUo

It shows a five-year-old Messi who collects the ball and controls it. He doesn't pass it, but searches out the route to goal. He dribbles past opponents moving from side to side, until he can hit an accurate shot away from the goalkeeper. And he scores. He turns and runs back into his own half, with the minimum of gestures. Taking little steps. Waiting for the game to restart. Later, his side kicks off and the first touch is to Messi who heads for goal, dribbling once again past whoever crosses his path. The ball is almost as high as his knees.

It is a game played at the Malvinas, a name with particular connotations and where the Newell's Old Boys youngsters play seven-a-side, also called 'baby' football. The simple sports centre is divided into two parts by Vera Mújica Avenue and the best cared-for pitch is pitch number one – it has a stand and hosts most of the games. Such as the one in the video.

Walking from Leo's home was impossible, it was too far, so someone always had to bring him – his father, mother, the father of a team-mate perhaps, and often he would arrive in a white Renault 12 that belonged to the father of his friend Agustin, a car that would be driven down Uriburu Avenue until it reached Boulevard Orono, and then up, crossing Independence Park (where the Newell's stadium was located) up to Pellegrini Avenue. You had to turn left before arriving at Francia and two blocks further you turned left again, by Zeballos Street. The main gate was at number 3185. Inside is a mural with all the names of the players who have made it into the first team. Leo's name isn't there yet.

Between the entrance and the goal of pitch one there are two small buildings: the café, with tables and chairs, and the office area. There's always something going on around here: fathers sitting around with coffee or beer talking football, their sons kitted out in their NOB shirts, people going in and out, older men who used to be at the club and who now come by to see what's happening, friends of the fathers ...

In the Malvinas cafeteria, while keeping an eye on the children as they play on the adjacent field, a group of friends chat as they sit at round tables with a beer or a coffee. It is mid-afternoon. Some time ago, someone removed the Malvinas sign that hung in the entrance and now we see it in a corner, abandoned, its corner rusting. Painted on the wall at the back of the set, a building of two floors. The ground floor has a door that leads to offices with random papers strewn about, the odd trophy on the floor and others on a shelf. On the second floor there is a door, which, strangely leads nowhere. Nobody can explain this. Maybe the money ran out and there wasn't enough left to put in a staircase. Hardly anyone goes up to the second floor, the club's office is on the first one. On the edge of the set, between the actors and the audience, are some goal nets.

Gabriel Digerolamo (coach, NOB): The day they brought him to me I said, 'well, this is something totally different from what one would expect, no?'

Ernesto Vecchio (coach, NOB): He had a spectacular technique; no one taught him that, he was born with it.

Gabriel Digerolamo: You never expected that something so diminutive could make such an explosive impact. He was someone who thought about what he was going to do, and then did it: he went from right to left, from left to right, through the centre, moving deep, and always with the goal in his mind, always there, inside his head.

Ernesto Vecchio: Before he even got to Newell's the whole of Rosario was talking about the talent of a young boy who played for Abanderado Grandoli.

Diego Rovira (No. 9 with the juniors at NOB): I had arrived at Newell's halfway through 1998. My first training session was at the Bella Vista site, where the first team train. We played a friendly against Renato Cesarini. We won 7–0, something like that. Three of the goals were scored by a tiny, extremely quick and skilful little feller. I didn't know anyone, but he was the first to catch my attention. It was Leo.

Rosario was getting to know Leo because he was starring in the inter-school tournaments, like the popular Alfi league. Here you would meet technical directors, scouts, trainers with eyes sharpened by years of watching coaching sessions and 'baby' football matches. Rodrigo and Matías were in the junior ranks of NOB and it was Rodrigo who suggested that Leo was ready to play for Newell's in preliminary tournaments at the start of the Rosario season. So at the beginning of 1994, at the age of six years and seven months, he played for a few weeks with a number of the Newell's youth teams, afternoon and evening.

Roberto Mensi (director of NOB): At the time of picking a player, primarily what you have in mind are his technical qualities, then his physical attributes and finally you take a look at the home life of the boy.

Quique Domínguez (coach, NOB): At Newell's there was a philosophy, driven by Jorge Bernardo Griffa, a former player with Atlético de Madrid: Newell's has to have the best players, we cannot allow ourselves the luxury of losing a great talent. So I would take my car and stop and wait five minutes watching a kids' game and, if there was something that grabbed my attention, I would get out of the car, get to the side of the pitch and ask, 'are you the mother?', 'yes', 'has your boy signed for any club?', and if he had, I would say, 'wouldn't he like to play for Newell's?' We would steal them before they could be stolen from us. By way of natural selection really, Leo always played alongside the best players in the area.

Gabriel Digerolamo: Claudio Vivas came to see me, the one who was assistant to Marcelo Bielsa, and said, 'You are going to have a boy here who is out of this world.' He played three or four games with my team, and with other coaches at the club, like Walter Lucero, a few others.

Quique Domínguez: When it came to comparing Leo with his rivals in terms of quality the gap was vast, and I mean vast. Up against a defender, eight out of ten times Leo would do exactly what he wanted; the defender got it right and *almost* recovered the ball once and lost possession on the other occasion. The difference was enormous. Today, Leo seems still to be a superior player compared to the rest, but the rest are now players from Real Madrid, from Serie A in Italy, from the Premiership in England ...

Gabriel Digerolamo: At the end of the preliminary tournament we asked Leo if he wanted to play for us.

Ernesto Vecchio: After watching him play, we spoke to the parents and reached an agreement. He joined Newell's. All the Messis are Newell's fans.

Except for Matías. As we know, he supports Rosario Central.

And so it was that on 21 March 1994, just shy of his seventh birthday, he was signed up by the club he supported. A Leo who measured one metre 22 centimetres in height (that's just over four feet), arrived at Ñuls where, three months earlier, Diego Armando Maradona, who was preparing himself for the 1994 World Cup, had played his last game during his brief stay with the Rosario club.

Jorge Valdano (ex-NOB player): [Newell's] has a very good football school in a city that clearly has an overwhelming connection with football, being in an area that is just one huge football pitch.

Quique Domínguez: I encouraged them to do what they did best and then subtly polished it, that's how I made my reputation in the schooling of football. I never shouted, or threatened, or scolded, or humiliated, or applied pressure, as my father did with my brothers and me. So if you make a big cock-up, I want you to understand what you have done and not to repeat it, not because you're frightened, but because you understand what you did wrong.

Gerardo Grighini (ex-junior player with NOB): We had all seven- and eight-year-olds and we played on the seven-a-side pitch and did the usual kids' training: a bit of speed work, keepy-uppy and technique. But at that time the most important thing was to learn to play the ball with your feet, to domesticate the ball. We trained Tuesday, Thursday and Friday, and played Saturday and Sunday.

Quique Domínguez: Yes, we did the typical training sessions about passing and stopping the ball. Once, one of the coaches asked his pupils how many ways of touching the ball a player had. And they answered: ten, fifteen, twelve. Well, there are in fact almost two hundred. You can even stop it with your back. So, now then, how many ways are there of passing the ball? You see, what we were trying to do at the football school is teach the kids all these things: how to pass the ball, how to stop it, how to imagine the play, to be aware that to reach the goal it is not always the best idea to look for a long pass ...

Gerardo Grighini: We had fun, above all, because we were a group of friends, we were not at school, or at work, where nobody spoke to each other, no way; we were a group of mates. In fact, I couldn't wait to get out of school, get something to eat and then go to training.

Quique Domínguez: We also showed them situations that could occur in a game. And sometimes we encouraged competition: we showed them what we call here *loco* (crazy), and what is known at Barcelona as *rondo* (piggy in the middle), although there were always arguments because no one wanted to go in the middle. Somehow we created an environment that encouraged craftiness, even though, it has to be said, the Argentinians have sometimes gone too far down that road, as was demonstrated by Maradona's handball goal. But in those games, in practice, you needed cunning.

There are six categories at the Malvinas for kids aged 6 to 12, and even though now they still have some 300 children, it is said that there have been occasions when there were 800 under the control of Newell's. From these earth pitches (now grass on the pitch one) have come Bielsa, Sensini, Balbo, Batistuta, Valdano, Pochettino, Solari. And this is just one of the schools scattered throughout Argentina. Thousands of youngsters sign up for them, the assured route to the top. But normally, after just a couple of years, here too is where, for many of them, their footballing dreams come to an end.

Jorge Valdano: I left my home and found myself on a football pitch that measured 1,000 square kilometres: a vast plain, interrupted only by the odd cow or an occasional tree, with everything else a football pitch. And a well-fed area, which is also important, because there are other, more deprived, areas where the problem of nutrition does not favour the rise of great footballers.

There is passion, sentiment, hope and frustration in Rosario. And you learn about football, but, above all you gain friends, you understand about the meaning of community, and you create narratives for your life that will be with you for ever. Argentina creates its social image around the ball. They play for their lives: and even if ultimately that isn't true, that's the feeling you're left with – it is a place to win and to learn how to win, and that attitude helps kids improve. Football at this age is pure, old, real and unrepeatable even though market forces are threatening it, even though some of the legendary technical directors (such as Griffa) did not make footballers to sell but, rather, to grow as more rounded individuals.

Quique Domínguez: The way of competing is also very important, because it is no fun having four goals stuck past you, it's obviously much more fun to score them. But above all, you have to show that at the end of the game it is just a game – the kids have to shake hands, congratulate the winners, even if you have lost 10–0. Or if you have won, you have to congratulate the losing side: and if they don't want to shake hands, no problem. We turn round and go home. Sometimes it will be us who will not feel like doing it …

Jorge Valdano: Jorge Griffa was the guru of football development in Argentina and Newell's followed his ideas, which placed their academy at the top of the scale.

Quique Domínguez: And from Newell's Leo took technique, craft and his winning attitude. What I always said to my lads was: we go onto the field, we are winning 1–0, we look for the 2–0, we look for the 3–0, 4–0 … and so on unless the ref decides to stop the game. There was a time here when we won 10–0, 15–0 and, of course, the matches used to get to a point when the boys from the other side, maybe after the tenth goal, did not want to play any more; then they put a limit of 6–0. At 6–0 the game would he halted.

Jorge Valdano: But in a way it all ended when Griffa packed up. In recent years some terrible abuse has taken place. For example, the *Barras Bravas* (football's ultra supporters) were the owners of the youth players. This alone tells you about the moral bank-ruptcy that overtook the club, something that has thankfully been remedied under new management.

Ernesto Vecchio: It's possible that the standard of 'baby' football has gone down a bit, but this is because of the change in society. There are boys whose fathers can't bring them because they are unable to pay. That's it. Also the children of today are different. They are more rebellious. Answer back. Don't listen. Before, they were more manageable, now they are more difficult. Another thing that has an effect is that there are not so many new fields available. We lack pitches. Today technology affects children who prefer to be with their computer, PlayStation, the internet and they are not so interested in doing sport. Unfortunately.

Scene Two

Onto the darkened set a video is projected where you can see the eight-year-old Messi scores with both feet, he hardly gives the ball to anyone, shows his competitive spirit when they hit him. When he is knocked over, he stops at first and then carries on. Even in this he isn't like the rest. And then, in the fifth minute, comes a typically Rosarian moment: Messi and the rest of the side, who have just won the game, receive instructions from their coach to go and console their beaten opponents. Leo runs to a young rival lying on the ground rueing his team's defeat. Of course he is doing what he has been told by the coach, but nobody ordered him to run to the player. Nor to get down on his knees. Nor embrace the rival lying on the floor. At this age there is no hypocrisy, none of this can be forced. Many would call this football in its purest state.

The characters look over the newspaper Olé. *One of them starts to read in a loud voice: 'Lionel Messi is quite sure in his own mind that his future does not lie as a coach. He cannot see himself giving instructions from the bench. However, when he starts to talk about football, his references all finish at the same place, always stressing the main traits: a side that always attacks, a high defensive line, a great deal of pressure high up the pitch to force the opposition to play long, and goals. Lots of goals. Pep's Barcelona? No: the Machine of '87, an unbeatable side that joined the ranks of Newell's*

Infantiles: Leguizamón, Pecce, Gianantonio, Casanova, Scaglia, González, Giménez, Ruani, Mazzia, Bravo, Miró among others.'

Gerardo Grighini: I think the name 'Machine of '87' came much later. I don't remember anyone calling us that.

Diego Rovira: Newell's side of '87. Quique's side. Quique Domínguez, the father of Seba, the one who plays at Velez, the central defender. In goal was Juan Cruz Leguizamón, who is now at Central Córdoba. At number 5 played Lucas Scaglia, a monster. They called him 'Pulpo' (the octopus). These days he is at Once Caldas, in Colombia. Rosso is today at Brescia, Grighini, you have played in Italy. Leandro Giménez, who afterwards went to River, and another Leandro: Benítez. And Leo, Roncaglia and me. 'The Newell's '87 side was invincible,' people used to say. We won everything in 1999 and nearly everything in 2000. This is how the games went: 8–0, 7–2, we lost count.

Gerardo Grighini: In Rosario they talked a lot about this group because we had Leo, Juan Cruz (Leguizamón), Lucas (Scaglia) … they were very good players. We started on small pitches, seven-a-side. Leo on his own would score three or four.

Diego Rovira: That forward line was tremendous. Leo number 10. At 7, Roncaglia, yes, Roncaglia. Very fast, hit in some great crosses, I remember. Add there Bergessio. What a guy, what a player Bergessio. And up front with the number 9, me.

The same person as before (it could be anyone) begins to recite again in a loud voice, another paragraph from the Olé *article: 'The team functioned with the collective solidarity of a colony of worker ants. That's how they maximised their potential. And Leo at just eight years of age was already the distinctive feature, the driving force of a well-oiled machine.'*

Diego Rovira: In 1999 we played three tournaments and won them all: I even remember winning all the matches too, like 45 of them, 15 per tournament, madness; all of them, well, except for one: against Central. They were the only side that could give us a game, although in the return we walloped them, 4–0. They never got close to our goal that day, it was rare that any side got close to our goal.

Quique Domínguez: From Argentina, Leo took the natural technique of the Latin American, like Neymar, like Ronaldinho,
Riquelme ... the way to position the body to accommodate the
ball, to control it, to direct it. From Newell's he took the winning
mentality.

Leandro Benítez (ex-junior player at NOB): He was a sensation, we'd
arrive at the pitch and our opponents would say, 'I wouldn't give
you two pesos for him', but when he got the ball he skinned them.

Diego Rovira: One time it occurred to one of Quique's assistants
that it would be a good idea to compete against each other to
motivate us. The Newell's of the first half against the Newell's of
the second. At half-time we were winning 3–0. Perfect. And in the
second half? Four? So then the Newell's second team won 4–3. It
was a laugh. With Leo, playing football was a laugh.

Ernesto Vecchio: He was a marvel. He was clever, he had a good
short touch, he would leave the ball dead, he played for his team-
mates. Once on pitch one at the Malvinas, the goalkeeper gave
him the ball and he went from one goal to another to score a
stupendous goal. You didn't have to show him anything. What
can you show a Maradona or a Pelé? The only thing that a coach
could do is correct some little details.

Juan Cruz Leguizamón (ex-junior player at NOB): In Europe he
became famous for that goal he scored against Getafe, but for us
that was normal, we saw him score goals like that as a matter of
course.

Diego Rovira: Leo, every time I see him ... I smile thinking about
the crazy things that he does. He's a monster. Like the five goals
he scored against Bayer Leverkusen: who else would think of
scoring five in a match, let alone in the Champions League? And
just how does he do it? That's exactly how it was at Newell's.
Less acceleration, less explosion, but the same.

Quique Domínguez: He had fantastic co-ordination for someone
of his age. For Leo it's like the ball forms part of his body. If it
comes high and he has to use his head to control it, he uses his
cheek because he knows that is the best way to cushion it. Perhaps another boy will put his forehead first because he knows it's
a harder part of his body and more used to taking a hit. Why?
Because Leo is different.

Gabriel Digerolamo: Technically he was gifted like no boy I have ever seen. He was so good that a lot of times I changed his position so he could adapt to all aspects of playing on the pitch. On one occasion I played him as sweeper, and, yes, it looked like he had been playing there all his life.

Quique Domínguez: I often say that I don't know who learned more from whom. Leo from us or us from Leo.

Adrián Coria (coach, NOB): 'You don't coach your team when Leo's playing', they used to tell me.

Diego Rovira: Leo would take on a couple of players and left me one on one. It was always like that. I had to get myself prepared, stopped on the last line of our opponents, and ready: one on one, guaranteed. The other trick we did was the long ball if things got complicated, which they rarely did. Leguizamón, the goalkeeper, would look for me. 'Bring it down for me,' Leo would shout. Can you imagine. I was a head taller than my rivals. Easy.

Juan Cruz Leguizamón: At one of the tournaments, if we became champions the organisers were going to give us each a bicycle. We got to the final but we started the match without Leo, he just didn't arrive ... and we finished the first half 1–0 down. Where was he? He got there late because he'd been locked in the bathroom at home and had to break the glass in the window to get out! He got in there in time for the second half and we ended up winning 3–1 ... with three goals from Leo. But like I said, millions of games. There were many things we lived together, a whole childhood.

Bruno Milanesio (ex-junior player at NOB): I remember telling my grandmother, who saw me crestfallen, that Leo had sprained his ankle and wouldn't be able to play the following day. My grandma is a healer and she asked me the name of the boy. 'Leo, Leo Messi,' I told her. She never told me what she had done, nor did I want to tell Leo that my grandmother had ... well, that she'd healed him ... but the following day Leo got up as if nothing had happened, with the swelling on the ankle gone. He played and we came out champions. Years later I was at my grandmother's house, and on television there was Messi playing for Barcelona. 'Grandma, do you remember him?' I asked her. When she answered, 'not in the slightest', I reminded her. Now when she sees Messi on television she smiles and boasts: 'That boy ... I healed that boy once.'

Gerardo Grighini: At that time we did not have to work for the team, not much anyway. It was simple: we just needed to give him the ball and that was it. Game over. He might lose it once or twice, but the third and fourth time he'd score two goals. Guaranteed.

Ángel Ruani (father of ex-NOB player 'Luli' Ruani): Maybe people nowadays don't believe it, but Leo scored about 100 goals per season in all the games we played. If we bear in mind that he came to Newell's in 1994 and left in 2000, we are talking about more than 500 goals throughout his time with the *Infantiles*, which is totally outrageous.

Adrián Coria: Perhaps he was not aware of it at the time, but in a way it is an advantage to be small – you control the ball better, you're more agile and faster than the rest.

Quique Domínguez: He passed the ball, but wouldn't just push it to you, but, rather, lift it up, bounce it up on his toes a couple of times before passing, that kind of thing. Leo is football in its purest sense. Not obsessed with the money, no, football for the fun of it.

Gerardo Grighini: On the Newell's pitch, the directors would ask him to do some keepy-uppy before the game or at half-time. On one occasion, in Mar del Plata, he did keepy-uppies before the game, and fans would throw money at him, coins. Fifteen minutes would go by and he still hadn't lost control of the ball. In Peru, I think he got up to 1,200 touches. He was nine years old at the time.

Franco Casanova (ex-junior player at NOB): At the farewell of the legendary Newell's player and current Barcelona manager Gerardo Martino in the summer of 1996, the Newell's boys did a lap of honour at half-time. They had been crowned champions. Suddenly they stopped in the middle of the pitch and pushed Leo into the centre circle. The stands raised the roof. 'Marado, Marado!!' screamed the crowd as Leo practised his keepy-uppies.

Nestor Rozín (former director of NOB): For every 100 touches, sometimes he got an ice cream and I think he made 1,100 touches and they gave him 10 ice creams.

Gerardo Grighini: At 11, we went from seven-a-side to 11-a-side. Sometimes both, Saturday the sevens, and Sundays, 11s. To get used to it. And against 11 he stood out even more, he had more pitch, more space. He was fast. Very fast. He got through gaps he didn't fit into. It was incredible.

Adrián Coria: I played him just behind the strikers, either in a free role or, as it is known, the *enganche* in a 4-3-1-2 formation.

Quique Domínguez: His opponents tried to hide the effect he had on them, but would eye him up and down with a bit of fear. He generated something inexplicable for a kid of 10 or 11 years old.

Diego Rovira: The conversations between the opposing defenders were wonderful:

- We can't stop this kid.
- No.
- So what we going to do?
- How should I know? Didn't you just say that he can't be stopped?

They were right. Once at a training session one of the coaches played me at the back.

- 'Mama, they made me play at the back and on top of that I had to mark Leo.' You should have heard me that night. 'Mum, I couldn't even grab him by the shirt. And I wasn't about to start kicking Leo.'

My poor mother. She remembers it to this day

- Enough Leo, stop fucking about, stop running – I kept saying to him, while he was pissing himself with laughter. He's fun is Leo. Funny.

Quique Domínguez: We were playing against Morning Star and their trainer came up to me and asked me if I would take Lionel off at half-time, and of course I said no, because Leo and the goalkeeper, Leguizamón, I never took off.

Gerardo Grighini: Once he performed five flick-overs against one player. The player threw himself to the ground and grabbed his feet! Five flick-overs, one after the other. On top of that he was 1.40 metres, while the other boy was 1.70. That's how he enjoyed himself. He didn't do it to brag … no, no, no. There was never any lip, none of that, never. In the Rosario league, Oriental, Rio Negro ... they are teams from the neighbourhood that like to play it rough, dish it out, and no ... they bitched at him, said things to him, and he said nothing. He just showed everything with his football.

Quique Domínguez: I have seen games in the lower levels of Argentinian football that are pitched battles. It is okay if you dribble past me, but next time I'll have you, I'll get sent off but you won't be doing that to me again. That happens a lot here. And that's what they would have done to Leo had he stayed here any longer. One of the few instructions that I gave him was to release the ball quickly, because when he had control of the ball, defenders did all kinds to stop him. And the kids, sometimes from instructions given to them by their elders, or sometimes off their own backs, if they couldn't stop him and he went past you, then past you, then past you again ... they would elbow him, kick him from behind. So I told him 'make sure you get rid of the ball earlier'. But for him the way he played, which is the way you see now, keeping the ball was only natural. And, by the way, he had a very good eye to see when they were coming in to hit him. So often they couldn't even come close.

Adrián Coria: On the contrary, that rough treatment lit a spark in him; the more they went for him the more he fronted them up.

Ángel Ruani: On one occasion, on the Adiur pitch, we, the parents, were really angry and we asked Gabriel, the coach, to take him off because they would not stop kicking him. On another game, at the home of Velez Sarsfield, they put in a very hard tackle, he fell awkwardly and injured his arm. His mother and my wife took him to hospital.

Quique Domínguez: For Leo, the ones who protected him were the referees. Because he didn't kick anybody, didn't protest, or grab players' shirts, or taunt his opponents ... so when they bombarded him, he generated a need to protect him – he was tiny, with a tiny face, mischievous with a smile ... and 100 per cent skilful but with a tremendous work ethic. He was the player who ran the most.

Gerardo Grighini: Leo was also very strong. Lots of people would throw themselves at him to try to bring him down, but he was strong, he took it. He fell, he got up, he fell again, and he got up again. Incredible. If any of us fell, we stayed down. And probably started to complain. But not him, he fell and still carried on with the ball. I don't know where that comes from, one in a million must come out like that.

Quique Domínguez: He never complained, despite the fact that ... while the other boys were waiting to be handed their shirts, Leo was the only one who would turn away to remove his shirt, away from everybody's sight, and put on the red and black number 10. I thought it was because he was embarrassed. The time I did see him, I was stunned – he hardly had a ribcage, it was caved in, looking at his chest was scary. One time he fell and broke and dislocated his wrist, bone problems, he was very fragile; but I never saw him wince, or make any show of pain. He didn't play the following games, in a competition we used to call the mini-World Cup, but on the first day of the tournament we saw he was carrying a small bag. Intrigued to find out what he had in it, I asked one of the mothers of the other players. She said he had brought his boots and his shin pads with him ... So he could play, and he still had 15 days to go with his plaster cast. He said. 'I know if Quique needs me, he'll put me on.' No way!! And then one day, during that competition, I asked him as a bit of a joke if he felt like playing in the second half, plaster still on, and he said yes, but no way would I play him like that. He was a fragile little boy from the outside, but inside he was very strong.

Leo Messi once said, 'The last time I felt pressure, was as a footballer with NOB when I was eight years old. From then, I come on to enjoy myself ...' He was at that time 23 and had played in two Champions League finals, two World Cups, and cup finals. Never mind those – he left behind the real pressure on a pitch in Rosario.

Gazzo (journalist): Rosario Central and Newell's were playing in the final of the tournament named after my radio programme, *Baby Gol*. The game finished 2–2, and in the penalties that followed the kids got to a score of 22–22. At this point the Rosario Central player took his kick and missed. Everything rested on Leo's feet. If he scored, the tournament would be Newell's.

Quique Domínguez: Once they asked me what was the greatest characteristic that I saw in Leo, and I said his naturalness. Everything, from the moment he greets you, even though he seems reserved, is natural. At 12, he would finish a game and used to go to the house of his friend, Antonella's cousin, Lucas, and there he would stay for the weekend. Sometime on Thursdays, after training, he would go to Lucas's house. For a while, he used to spend most of his free time at Lucas's! Needless to say, his now wife didn't give him the time of day. Now he is living with and has a son with the woman he has loved all his life. He did not need to put on a lavish wedding, nothing of the sort. I observe that things with Leo occur naturally, it is all a natural progression. Argentina, the national team, has started to play well naturally, because they engage, get in line behind Leo. My mother died three years ago and she said to me, 'the difference between a dictator and a leader: a dictator imposes himself, a leader is someone you follow, you choose'. And Leo, without shouting, without making any fuss, is one of those who is followed. When he scored a goal in 'baby' football everyone went to congratulate him, but when others scored he also went to hug them. And we're talking about a Leo Messi who was 12 years old and already in Rosario as much an idol, a star, and a footballing giant at junior level, as he is in the world today. And a 12-year-old does not normally have to handle such risks, or such pressure. For him, scoring those goals, running and dribbling with the ball that way, it was all natural.

Gazzo: The tournament was Newell's. Leo scored. The winning penalty.

In January 1996, Leo's team played in the International Friendship Cup tournament, in Lima. It was his first trip abroad. He was nine years old. Messi surprised everyone with his ability to control the ball with technique and balance. Even at that age he had already tamed it. Of course, they won the competition. They gave them the trophy in the shape of a dolphin. But he suffered in order to play in the first match.

Gabriel Digerolamo: When we got to the airport the parents of some of the children of the Peruvian side were there. We were shared out and each family took charge of one of the boys, a bit like a lucky dip.

Kevin Méndez (son of the family that put Leo up): One night he had some barbecued chicken and it made him ill. The next day, he could hardly move and the following day it was his game.

Gabriel Digerolamo: Leo was practically in tears, sick and with symptoms of dehydration.

Kevin Méndez: So when Leo got to the pitch, he fainted and the trainer said, 'you play the game and I'll take Leo to hospital'. Hearing that, he regained his composure.

Gabriel Digerolamo: We gave him an isotonic drink and within half an hour he was on the pitch doing keepy-uppies.

Kevin Méndez: He drank a Gatorade and asked to play. Newell's won 10–0, and he scored eight goals, just in case there was any doubt that he was the best. Before he left he gave me his shirt.

William Méndez (Kevin's father): At a supper we asked him and another boy from there what their objective was. We are Argentinian: where we go, we win, and then we go home.

Gerardo Grighini: On the pitch he would pout if we lost, the few times we did lose; he did not like losing one little bit, always wanted to win, to the point that sometimes there would be arguments, even sometimes on the pitch. If we were losing, he would convert his anger into a way of winning games – he would pick up the ball and make sure we left the pitch having won. I remember that happening on various occasions.

Adrián Coria: He had a lot of pride.

Gerardo Grighini: One of the things I remember most was a tournament we played in the countryside. We went to Pujato and after 10 or 15 minutes we were 2–0 down. Leo got nervous, very nervous. With just eight or nine minutes left, he scored three goals. Just like that. The other day I was watching a game that Barcelona were losing and I said: 'Son of a bitch, you're getting upset!' I recognised the face! Just like before! And then, just like before with three or four minutes remaining he stole the ball and found himself facing the keeper and almost saying: 'Fuck it, I will sort it.' He would kill me or anybody if he lost, he would be unbearable!

Adrián Coria: He had to put his seal on it. It hurt him when he lost. In the kickabouts he liked to pick the teams. Every footballer who reaches the top has that thirst to succeed, that thirst for glory.

Gerardo Grighini: We lost a championship – in the Arteaga tournament, which is like a mini-World Cup that you play when you are
11 – and it was my fault. We beat everyone, 8–0, 9–1 and so on.
We got to the semi-finals where we played against a team selected
from the Ardyti league, which is a local league in Rosario with
eight or nine teams. The match started, their goalkeeper cleared
it upfield – I was playing central defender at the time – but he hit
it further than I thought, and I touched it on with my head into
the path of the opposing forward who was running behind me.
He scored … They then put 11 men behind the ball and it became
impossible. We lost 1–0 in the semi-final. Leo was furious. Can
you imagine? He didn't speak to me for two or three days. No
way, he did not like losing. No way, no way.

Quique Domínguez: In the '87 team, also called the '87 A, I got
the impression that Mazzia, another forward who sometimes
played with Leo, was a bit of an individualist. I never knew him
well enough to say that he would have been competition in the
long run for Leo, but he certainly could have competed with
him in things like technique, control. But I had to prioritise the
team. It's like an apple, and perhaps this is not the best comparison, like the bruised apple in the basket. What I was looking
for was for Leo to take all the weight of the team and this kid,
Mazzia, to do the same but in another category. So I moved him
to '87 B so that if he grew and looked like he could overtake
Leo, then that really becomes a problem for the two of them to
sort out the following year as they would meet up again on the
11-a-side pitch. At that stage, football is more cold-blooded,
it's hard, nobody greets each other, childhood is over. And the
fathers are not there to protect you and what is more if a father
did poke his nose in, he would get dirty looks. Natural selection – whoever survives reaches the next level. Leo did survive,
Mazzia didn't.

Gerardo Grighini: The forwards finished every game fighting with
Leo, because he wanted to score more goals, and they wanted to
score more goals … He loves having the ball, and if he could he
would play with two balls, one for him and one for the rest – if I
put myself inside his head, as to what he was like then, when he
was with us … it's like this, that's how it was. We were given an

instruction by the coaches that made us feel bad: Adrián Coria told us that Leo could do what he wanted, and we became jealous! 'Why him, and not us?' we would ask. Give it him, he would say, so he could do what he wanted. It was the easiest option.

Quique Domínguez: At Malvinas, we were always, 'hi Leo, how's it going?', a hug, a kiss, a handshake. To him and to all the kids. And when he finished training he never wanted to leave. And this pleased me very much. At times the mosquitoes would eat us alive, and the fathers would gather in small groups; at other times it would be the middle of the night, damp and misty. And he just wanted more football

Claudio Vivas (coach, NOB): When we played in a neighbourhood tournament he would come to Malvinas. Behind pitch one there's a *quincho* (a little open outdoor shelter, often used for barbecues) and, next to it, some tables where people eat, chat, drink. 'But, Leo, you can't play here, there are people eating, you're going to break something …' He would be told all that, but no reaction. As soon as the game finished he would carry on playing, you couldn't stop him. Or he would ask his father to take him across to the two earth pitches opposite so he could continue playing with friends.

Adrián Coria: Ball against the wall, and again, and again … they used to say to him: 'we love this wall, we look after it, we paint it, we try to avoid getting it dirty, you know? Calm down, you will be playing soon, take a breather', and him: bang, bang, bang. Another coach said to me, 'there's no way of stopping this boy, he spends all day playing and he wants to play when the sun has gone down. And with no lights. When everybody is asleep.'

Ernesto Vecchio: And if he was ill, the same. One day he was at the Adiur pitch, after he had been ill, but wanted to come on anyway. I had him sitting on the bench, we were losing 1–0, and there were five minutes remaining, so I asked him if he wanted to play. As soon as he said yes, I said to him, 'good, go out there and win me the game'. Needless to say, we won.

Claudio Vivas: He likes football, watching and playing. His family lived close to the Central Córdoba stadium and I used to go and see my brother-in-law who played for them. And I saw Leo often there. Central Córdoba is like an Alavés or an Eibar, a team of the district, a second, third division team.

Quique Domínguez: And so ... there have been players in the academy who have been phenomenal, out of this world, and have found themselves stuck in the lower divisions and have not made it. Leo, at 12, was already a player out of this world and continued being so. That is so hard to achieve. Life has gifted me the chance to have been able to coach three fantastic players at that young age: Maxi Rodríguez, 'Billy' Rodas and Leo Messi. Of the three the one who had incredible potential was Billy.

Ernesto Vecchio: His parents were always with him. You could always spot his father behind the goal. He never said a word, nor did he mix a lot with the other fathers.

Quique Domínguez: Leo was the son of all the other fathers and the brother of all the other kids. And not just in my team, in any other team he had been in. Leo's mother would be the type to stay with a group, but normally Jorge, his dad, would be on his own, standing to one side.

Ernesto Vecchio: We went to the Cantolao tournament. In the 1987 team, we had Leo. And in the 1986 team, Gustavo 'Billy' Rodas, who later became famous for having made his first division debut at 16. But, well ...they had different personalities. Sadly, I look at where Rodas is now, I think playing in Peru, and it is sad to think that he had some extraordinary talent and could have made it to the highest level.

Quique Domínguez: I say that my great attribute – and I will always boast about this – is to have protected and developed what the players have brought along naturally. Leo, it's like, how can I put this ... like a work of art but with a famous provenance, that cannot fail to succeed, impossible. Because there are footballers, and we have the example of our greatest ever idol in the past, Diego, who are brought down by drink, parties, an inflated ego, disagreements ... Leo is not one of those.

Scene Three

On a dark set a video is projected.

http://www.youtube.com/watch?v=youtu.be/I2rpU8AIkNO

He is ten years old. His team-mates are looking for him. He is the one wearing the red and black number 10; the number covers the whole of his back. With one touch he controls the ball before sending it away from the goalie. He doesn't blast it, rather, places it in. Then he passes the ball from outside the area and gets into the box to receive it back from his team-mate. Just as he's done so many times before. And since. Later, straight from the kick-off, he dribbles past one, then another and a third and as he gets to the edge of the area gets away a shot. This time it's saved by the goalkeeper. A 'brick' passed to him becomes a ball again once it is touched by his left foot, he opens his body up and scores with a cross shot. He scores another goal from a free kick, one with his right foot, one with his left. After stealing the ball, after dribbling past several players, after lobbing the goalkeeper. He rushes to embrace his teammates. At the final whistle, the humbled opponents approach him to ask for a photo. Or to ask him to do some keepy-uppies. Everyone stops to watch as he reaches 100-plus touches.

Quique Domínguez: We used to warm up with the ball around the pitch, so when they played they would recognise what they had in front of them as a ball, not a brick. You know what I mean? Sometimes Leo would be in charge of the warm-up. I would do the paperwork, they would sign it and I would say to Leo, 'take them out', and Leo would trot up to the pitch. If Leo moved his leg this way, they'd all move it that way. They went down to the ground, Leo with his knee like this, and everybody did the same. But it wasn't something I imposed on them, or that he told them to do; it was because he was the one they wanted to copy, a model to follow, it was natural. The image I have is of a mother duck with her ducklings following her.

Gerardo Grighini: We did not have a single leader. There were about 16 of us in the group, and quite a few of us made decisions. Leo, of course, and I also had a strong voice in the group, Leandro

Benítez ... Lucas, Leo's cousin, maybe not so much, he probably
followed the three of us. There was another one, Juan, who also
wanted to lead, but when you're kids you sometimes clash and
... well, he was not allowed to lead. Leo was not an all-powerful
leader, imposing his ideas, but, rather, someone who was the best
at football and had to be followed.

Adrián Coria: He used to listen to the coach's instructions. He was
respectful. He took it in. He never said, 'I play the ball', never
said, 'I'm the best'. His team-mates loved him. But ... he did not
like exercises. He loved the ball. And only I had to punish him
in training. I'm not an ogre or a sergeant major, but I've always
liked seriousness. We were doing a *rondo* when he started touching and playing with the ball. I called out to him once, twice, but
he ignored me. In the end I said to him: 'Give me the ball, get
changed and go home.' Ten minutes later I saw him with his bag
on his back leaning against the wall, looking at the pitch. I was
sad and it hurt me to see him like that. 'You left without giving
me a kiss,' I shouted at him. He came back, kissed me, and I sent
him back into the dressing room to get ready for training again.
He was a shy boy, but stubborn, and that was the only time I had
to speak that way to him.

Quique Domínguez: Do you see those players who try to do a one-
two, and although what comes back to them is more like a brick
than a ball they carry on running? Leo did that. A lot of them
would have stopped halfway if they didn't get it back the way
they wanted.

Ernesto Vecchio: One very sunny Saturday afternoon at the Malvinas, we came up against Pablo VI. He received the ball from the
goalkeeper, and accelerated from our area, going past players and
around the rival goalie, who, in the act of trying to stop him, fell
and twisted his ankle. The boy let out a cry of pain, which Leo
obviously heard, and, instead of putting the ball into an empty
net, stopped, turned back and not only went to help him but also
got the referee's attention so that the goalie could receive treatment. That stuck with me.

Quique Domínguez: And, what's more, he was discreet. He didn't
shout, he wasn't too effusive. Even when playing a prank. Once
Newell's gave us a pre-match training club jersey, all red with

some white on the sides, and Leo comes up to me and says: 'what are you doing dressed as a Father Christmas? You look like one.' I guess my girth was a bit out of control then and that didn't help! Cheeky boy!

Diego Rovira: At that time we'd got into the habit of having our afternoon snack at my house. Scaglia, Benítez, Leo and me. We'd get together to play Nintendo. How we laughed. While my mother was preparing our snacks, we got ourselves ready: we would open the drawers of the wardrobe in my bedroom and put on the European football shirts that I had. My father is a doctor; he would travel to conferences, that sort of thing, and he would always bring me back a shirt: Barcelona, Manchester United, Real Madrid. I never used them, I just had them as souvenirs. Two drawers full of shirts. And before we played Nintendo, we would each pick one. Grighini, for example, would put on the Real Madrid shirt. Leo, the Barcelona one. The one they brought out in their centenary, the one that is half scarlet and half blue. Rivaldo's shirt. He would always do the same thing: arrive at my house and go looking for the Barcelona shirt. Leo in one of my shirts, so funny – it looked like he'd put on a nightshirt.

– Right, I'm having that – he said to me afterwards, after everyone had put the shirts back where they belonged, in my drawer. Not Leo:
– Go on, give it to me.

He asked me with a smile on his face.

– Yes?

It was my only Barcelona shirt. As if I was going to give it to him!

Gerardo Grighini: He says that he is a Newell's fan, but when we were kids, he was a River fan. I was a fan of River, Lucas of Newell's and Leandro, Boca. Leo was fanatical about Aimar, who at the time was playing at River, and we used to watch his matches and became fans of River. We spent a lot of time together. We used to stay in a *pensión* at the weekends when we had to play.

Nestor Rozín: To improve the boys' performance we had a *pensión*, where boys from outside could come. To make sure they ate and slept well.

Gerardo Grighini: Leo, the little squirrel, would sleep in the very top bunk, he'd sleep on the third bed up. We enjoyed ourselves, we had a common purpose: to have a good time. At that time, a bottle of Coca-Cola cost 1.25 pesos. It was 2000, the year of the Arteaga mini-World Cup, and we had spent something like 20 days living together in the *pensión*. It had rained the night before, and we wanted some Coca-Cola, but no one had a peso on them. That was the time when car windscreen cleaners, standing at the traffic lights, waiting for the red, first appeared in Argentina. So we said, 'Shall we go and clean windscreens?' 'Go on,' we said. 'At least we'll get a bit of loose change.' Leo decided to cover him-self in mud, mud that he got from the ditch beside the road, and as people were leaving the supermarket, he would ask, 'a coin, lady?' and she would give him two pesos. 'A small coin, lady?' So it was one and a half pesos, two pesos ... 56 Coca-Colas we bought that day!! In future, when I have children I will tell them that I was a friend, that I played, that I shared all sorts of experi-ences with the best in the world.

Quique Domínguez: I said to my son (Argentinian international) Sebastián, that when he made his debut, even if it was with Boca (my heart is with River), I would give him my Ford Sierra. That same day, because it was all so emotional, I arrived late for training and, after the session, I came out of the dressing room and real-ised that I did not have the keys for the Sierra that I had promised my son. Worried, I returned to the dressing room, but I could not find them, and there I was met by all the boys sitting in a group together with Leo in the middle pretending to drive and making a noise as if he was accelerating, with the keys to the Sierra in his hand. 'Looking for these, Father Christmas?' asked Leo.

Gerardo Grighini: In those days, because we were so young, we could not go to the discotheque. So what we did was arrange meetings between friends and invite along the girls from our class. For example, if it was my birthday I would invite all my football team-mates and my school friends to my house, and we would try to match up. And Lucas's three cousins were always invited. Antonella – Leo's wife; Carla – the youngest; and Paula, the eldest. And Leo always, but *always* – I'm telling you, he was 10, maybe 11 – always in love with Antonella, always, always.

The truth is at that time it wasn't mutual. I suppose afterwards Lucas did his stuff and they got to know each other better ... At the parties when we were together Leo was shy, reserved ... we used to say to him: 'Go for it, Leo, go for it! Why don't you fool around like the rest of us. When you play football, you are a little braver, mate!' But he was shy, he stayed sitting down. Mischievous? We were placid kids. That was the type of mischief we got up to, going out and begging for money, but nothing else. More often than not we'd meet up at someone's house and play PlayStation. Or at Lucas's. Lucas's house had two five-a-side football pitches and we would get together and play football there.

Gerardo Grighini: It was obvious to me that Leandro Benítez, Lucas and Leo all had the necessary qualities to play in the first division. What I never imagined was that Leo would go on to become the best in the world. 'What do you dream of?' we would ask each other; we would always talk about this. 'Getting into the first division' was always his answer. His dream was to play for Newell's. Later things happened, and he ended up at Barcelona, but I don't think it will be more than five years before he returns to Newell's. When he is 30 I think he will come back. Once he has won the World Cup – God willing, we'll win the next one coming up – he will feel he has really made it. And he'll come home. That is what I think anyway.

Ernesto Vecchio: I always said that he had a huge future, and I wasn't wrong. I would have loved it if Rodas had got there as well, Depetris, kids with superb technique. But anyway ...

Adrián Coria: I had to spend some time watching those who were about to start playing on the 11-a-side pitches. Leo had growth problems. No one could raise the money that was needed for the treatment he needed. I used to say to Pepeto (Roberto Puppo, the junior technical director at Newell's), 'you have influence and contacts, why don't you try to help him? When Leo becomes better than Diego he will return the favour.' I think the money we're talking about for the injections was about 900 pesos per month. Fortunately I have witnesses who can confirm that I was pressing his case, that I thought he could be as big as Diego. Sometimes I mention it to Tata Martino and to other important footballing friends. He was going to make it for sure.

ACT TWO

Scene One

On a dark stage the following video is projected, an Adidas advert featuring the voice of Leo.

http://www.youtube.com/watch?v=7U2k1EqZp68

'When I was 11 years old they discovered that I had a growth hormone deficiency and I had to start treatment to help me to grow naturally. Every night I had to stick a needle into my legs, night after night after night, every day of the week, and this over a period of three years.

'I was so small, that I was an 11-year-old with the measurements of a child of eight or nine, or even less, and this was noticeable on the football pitch and in the street with my friends.

'They said that when I went onto the pitch, or when I went to school, or at lunch time, I was always the smallest of all, very different from the rest. It was like this until I finished the treatment and I then started to grow properly.

'I think being smaller than the rest allowed me to be a bit quicker and more agile, and that helped me when it came to playing football.

'What I have learned from this experience is that what at first seemed all bad, and ugly, has turned into something very positive and I have been able to achieve a great deal, and I got here with a lot of hard work and a lot of effort.

The image projected onto a large screen shows two little legs in short trousers, a little container that looks like a pencil box but in fact it holds a syringe. He puts the syringe together, as we explain later in this act. Then he injects his leg. The video goes dark. The light comes back on again. He repeats the procedure: two legs, one case, an injection for the other leg. Meanwhile we hear the voice of an Argentinian boy reading extracts from the following interviews:

Leo Messi in *El Gráfico*: 'I was a bit smaller than the rest, but on the pitch you didn't notice it. The people who saw me injecting myself were surprised and felt ill. It didn't worry me and it didn't hurt. Wherever I went I took the syringe with me in its case and put it straight into the fridge, if I went to a friend's house, for example. I would then take it out and put it straight into my quadriceps. Every night it was like this. One day one leg; the next day, the other one.'

Lights back onstage, but the shadows are deep. For those sitting around the tables in the Malvinas, it is now quite late. A few remain drinking a last beer.

Nestor Rozín: When he went from seven-a-side to 11, we noticed the difference, because Newell's were known for bringing on players from the countryside, well-built and well-fed, and he was small.

Gerardo Grighini: He would administer them [the injections] as if it was perfectly normal. He never explained to me what they were for. He carried with him a little box like a freezer, cold, and inside he would have little bottles of liquid, and it was like a type of pencil with a little needle, and he had a hole where he put the little bottle, and then he'd stick the syringe in his leg. Week after week, every day. Before going to sleep. Seven days in one leg, seven days in the other. And he did it quite naturally, just like that, sorted! When he'd finished it he took out the needle; it's not as if he looked at us so we could ask him about it, no. When we were all at the *pensión* (there were about 16 of us, about 11 years old), can you imagine seeing that ... But we didn't laugh about it, or talk about it, nothing.

Juan Cruz Leguizamón: You looked at his legs and they were full of little punctures, but we weren't sure what they were. We were kids and at that age we took no notice. The only thing that interested us was playing.

Matías Messi (Leo's brother): Yes, to tell you the truth it was a bit difficult for all the family; we brothers didn't feel it so much because we were so young, but the family did.

Gerardo Grighini: What's taken him to the level he's now reached is his talent – no question – and his self-belief. I don't think just anyone has the mental strength when they're only 10 or 11 to say: 'I'm going to do this, because it's got to help me in the future.' Alone, sticking in the needle, giving himself an injection before going to bed. He knew that in the future it would help him fulfil his dream of playing in the first division.

Lucas Scaglia (Leo's best friend, footballer): He never cried about the injections.

Scene Two

The Messi family decided to consult a specialist because they saw that, at the age of 10, Leo was not as big as the other children. Medical tests were scheduled.

We see on stage a consulting room in an old house. It was one that the father of Dr Diego Schwarzstein had lent him some years back. It's on the first floor which is reached via an elegant, wooden staircase similar to those built a hundred years ago. It's a small room, measuring three square metres. Just outside the consulting room there's a small waiting area. We see Dr Schwarzstein in his white coat, looking for papers in the drawer of his medium-sized writing desk. He starts to talk and to tell old stories.

... so, I was told, 'we definitely have someone who is the best, a phenomenon, but he needs to grow'. Every now and then, when the medical staff at Newell's see something at the club that attracts their attention, something that needs the involvement of an endocrinologist, they would call me and say: 'we would like you to see this patient.' And so it was that Leo and his mother found themselves in my consulting room.

In truth, I remember some of the things, and others I only remembered afterwards, because as you can imagine I have had to tell his medical story many times in answer to questions, and also because I was curious. It was my birthday when he came to see me for the first time. A coincidence, 31 January 1997 if I remember correctly. He came with his mum and ... I explained to him a bit just as I explain to all the boys: that doctors cannot help everybody who wants to grow; we can only help those who have a growth problem that stops them growing normally. So, I said, there is no treatment or medicine to grow. We try and find out if there are problems that are stopping growth or making it difficult. And when we detect these problems, that is when we can help. So, anyway, I suggested we did some tests.

A child who is the size he is supposed to be because that's what his genes have dictated can be happy or otherwise, but medicine is not going to change the situation.

I explain this to them because sometimes patients expect the doctor to give them a magic pill, something that's going to allow them to play in the NBA [National Basketball Association]. And that doesn't exist. I explain this to them so they don't build up any false hopes, and then I begin my investigation. What sticks in my mind about Leo is he was a very introverted, reserved boy. I don't know whether the word is shy or reserved. He didn't really strike me as being shy, I think he is the introverted type. By shy, I mean someone who can feel inhibited or a bit detached. I don't believe that Leo was ever that; rather, he was reserved, careful. He had to be opened up before he would trust you.

But as he loved football so much, as do I, we very quickly broke the ice by talking about football; who was his idol, who he liked, where he played and so on. And very quickly we established a good relationship. And soon I realised there was only one thing that mattered to him – he wanted to be a footballer.

When I explained to him that what I had to do was a quite aggressive, somewhat uncomfortable examination, I thought he might become nervous but he said to me: 'I want to play football.' What concerned him was that he should grow enough to be able to become a footballer.

Anyway the diagnosis is a bit tiresome, but we got there relatively quickly, considering. At the end of the 1990s, we did not have certain biochemical diagnostic technology, so everything took a bit longer and sometimes in Argentina it's hard work trying to get the National Health to authorise this type of investigation. If the investigations show there is indeed a lack of growth hormone, you then have to carry out new tests, called confirmation tests, to be absolutely certain of your diagnosis. What's more, one of the elements we use for diagnosis is the speed of growth, and the only way we can do this is by measuring someone today and then measuring them again a few months later. So, as a result, this is generally a diagnosis that takes at least three or four months, or in the case of Leo, if I'm not mistaken, six.

And, indeed, what he lacked was a hormone. You can genetically engineer exactly what was lacking and inject it under the skin once a day. The treatment consisted of putting into his body an organism that he was missing. He didn't produce this organism naturally, so it had to be taken externally. And the treatment is expensive, $1,500 a month, more or less.

You have to inject yourself, I told him.

The doctor takes a small case out of his cupboard that he opens while he is talking.

And how did he react? I don't remember. What I'm suggesting is that he reacted just like anyone would have done in the circumstances, because I don't remember anything unusual.

It's a pen, that, instead of having ink, has a growth hormone, and instead of having a nib has a needle. So, first I load the dose, it has a regulator, he pricks himself, the needle can be hidden, it's well hidden, and he injects himself. Normally I would give the first one in my surgery, or, rather, I help them, and I supervise them until they learn how to do it on their own. They can put it in the thigh, they can put it in the abdomen, they can put it in the arm. It's very similar to insulin; you've seen people injecting themselves with insulin. It's very similar; every individual selects the area they feel most comfortable injecting themselves, where it hurts less. And, well, Leo apparently preferred to inject himself in the legs rather than anywhere else.

When I give them to my patients, I say: stay calm, this doesn't hurt at all. So they ask you: really? It doesn't hurt? And I say, if I inject you while you're looking somewhere else, you probably won't even know that I'm doing it. A mosquito bite hurts more. It's an injection using needles that you can hardly see. They are needles that are changed every day, they never break, they're very short. These days they measure no more than three millimetres.

These are patients you see more or less regularly. During the diagnostic stage, I probably saw him four or five times in six months. After that I probably saw him every three months. So you develop a relationship and you start talking about other things. Because the key was football, we both liked football and he played for Newell's and I am a Newell's supporter. I used to ask him: how's it going? Who's training you? Do you watch the first team train? Stuff like that, but after a while you begin to develop a relationship that goes beyond the technical, the medical side of the patient. So, I carry on asking him, how's it going? What are you doing? And one day he comes with his father and you ask him how his mother is, and the next time he comes with his mother and you ask him how his father is, and so on. Then he'd tell me, my father hasn't come because he's doing this or that. You go on chatting, building a relationship. That's my style anyway.

And he would keep saying, 'What I want is to play football.'

I would always try to explain to him, or to other patients, that the treatment had nothing to do with whether or not he would become a footballer; it was about growing. In fact, if I'd wanted to become a taxi driver I would have had to receive the same treatment, unless of course I wanted to be a very short taxi driver ... The difference is that being very, very short, you could still have been a taxi driver, but it would be very difficult to become a footballer, but it isn't just the treatment that helps you make it. Or, rather, the interaction between the treatment and football is more indirect. The treatment helps you grow, and growing would help him with football, and he was clear in his own mind that this was the road he wanted to go down.

I don't remember seeing him cry. In my consulting room? No, I don't recall ever seeing Leo cry. What's more, I'm convinced that if you ask him directly what his worst moments were, when he suffered most, what hurt him the most, I don't believe for a minute that he even remembers his treatment. I don't recall that the treatment was especially traumatic for him. Clearly, for all youngsters, when you tell them they have a problem, and that it will be resolved by using injections it has two effects. First, they are pleased when you tell them the problem is easily solvable. Or if not easily, at least solvable. And then this difficulty with growing will disappear and they will grow normally, and they will conquer the limitations that it puts on them. This makes them happy. But when you tell them that the solution is to stick an injection into themselves for the next two thousand days, or ... I don't know ... three, four, years, they don't fancy it much. But I don't remember that his reaction was to cry. Of course when you say to him, yes: you're going to have to inject yourself, he didn't like it at all. But then, who would?

If you notice, the players ... it's rare to find a player like Cristiano Ronaldo who is talented and big. Generally, the talented players are small. In Argentina, Orteguita, who played at Valencia, or Maradona, or Neymar, as well, they are not big players. I think for the type of game they played, the dribbles they make, they need to have a fairly low centre of gravity and for reasons of mobility ... it helps to be small, no? But, that said, is the talent Leo has for playing on the ball what makes him what he is now?

The doctor continues arranging the papers on his office desk. He takes off his white coat. The consultation is coming to an end.

To put it another way, Leo's treatment has no influence whatsoever on his emotional development. But what is clear, and I tell you this also as a small person (I am short, I measure 5'7" and I was short as a child as well), at times it means you are at a disadvantage. With your friends who are taller. It is common for children to get into fights, and I'm not talking about Messi here, I'm talking in general. With kids it's easy to get into a fight over the silliest things, and if you're small you cop it. If you're tall it's easier to get ahead. And with girls, exactly the same: the girls like taller blokes. When you're small, very small, it is not easy. In truth, with Leo it was pathological: he lacked a hormone. He was below what was considered to be the normal, which can lead to certain personality traits, a certain inhibition, insecurity. In other words, when the body permits ... or at least doesn't put limitations on you ... your personality will develop normally. But if a person is already introverted then lack of stature will only add to feelings of insecurity.

Is it doping? The growth hormone has been used as a supplement by adults who do not need it, with the objective of gaining a sporting advantage. But you have to differentiate between growth hormone treatment for an adult who doesn't need it, who is looking for a physical benefit – and they are high doses and can have very negative side-effects – and the treatment of a physical deficiency in a young boy. The first thing to say is that Leo was a nine-year-old boy and I don't think he could ever have imagined this scenario. What's more, if you could ask him: when you were nine, 10, 11, what did you dream about? I don't believe he dreamt about this, being the best in the world. I think that this would have exceeded any dream. Look, when I was a boy, I dreamt about wearing the number 9 Newell's shirt. I would come on with five minutes remaining, and score the winning goal that won us the league. I dreamt that they gave me the number 9 shirt for Argentina and I scored the winning goal in the last minute of the World Cup final. But if you achieve this, you have to say it exceeds your dream. The treatment he received is not the reason why he managed to achieve his dream. He was a nine-year-old boy who loved football, just like 99 per cent of nine-year-olds in Argentina. Imagine for a minute that today at Newell's they give one hundred boys aged between 8 and 10 the same treatment – they would have a hundred Messis! And that's not even taking into account a place like La Masía in Barcelona, which has an economic capacity far in excess of ours, and probably also junior divisions superior to ours. They would now be manufacturing with growth hormone some 10 or 12 Messis every year!

I have a young child, and when I was giving Leo this treatment in 1997, my son was three. If giving this treatment to a boy can turn him into the best player in the world, I would have given it to my son, not to Leo.

What's more, if I remember correctly, the treatment was interrupted when Leo was 15, or was almost 15. Already in Barcelona. It's said that growth like his puts a strain on the body, muscular problems like those he suffered as an adolescent, but that has nothing to do with it because in truth every child with a hormone deficiency is growing less than he should. And when the treatment replaces the deficiency, and the child no longer has a shortage of this particular hormone, he starts to grow normally, at the same rate as his peers. Do you understand?

That explains why it is not doping: because whoever has this hormone deficiency is at a disadvantage to everyone else. Making up for this deficiency with a hormone that he is lacking simply means that while he is no longer at a disadvantage he doesn't have an advantage either. To put it another way, he gains something by adding the hormone but not compared with his peers who already have it naturally.

It was certainly an expensive treatment. The charity that Jorge created and his National Health were very good over a long period. What happened is that this country fell apart in 2000 and 2001, and the whole welfare system broke down, and in many cases such treatment was interrupted, generating a great deal of uncertainty. This country went up in flames. But perhaps at that time Newell's could have done more.

I never saw him play in a Newell's shirt. I hope I shall one day. I have watched him on television. I have seen him play live in the

Argentina shirt. Maybe one day I will see him in the red and black.
I hope so: back in the days when he had doubts about becoming a
footballer, I said to him: 'stay calm, and you can dedicate a goal to
me. I will tell you where I am, where I'm sitting and you will come
to me and you will dedicate a goal to me.' And when I see him, I tell
him: 'you owe me that goal.' Ha! In a Newell's shirt, at the Coloso,
our ground.

*The doctor switches off all the lights but one, and stands in front
of a door that leads to a small exit. He puts on his hat; doctors
should always wear hats.*

At one time he used to look at me as if to say, 'this is the doctor
who will help me to grow' and would probably look up to me. I must
have been a strong presence to him. But today I am the one in awe
of him. I'm the one who says 'he is the best footballer in the world'.

(A child's voice is heard): Will I grow?

You're going to be taller than Maradona. I don't know if you're
going to be better, but you'll be taller.

That's exactly what I said to him.

Scene Three

*The voice of an Argentinian radio commentator, maybe that of
Gazzo, is heard, talking about 'baby' football at Newell's. On the
wall in large letters, at first individually and finally all together, the
following words appear:*

At the age of 10, in the first month of 1997, Leo measured 1.27
metres. Delayed growth.

By the time he was 11, he measured 1.32 metres, and
weighed 30 kilos.

At 12 years old, Leo measured 1.48 metres and weighed 39
kilos.

Today he is 1.69 metres, two centimetres taller than Maradona.

*A family of three boys and a girl, the youngest, gather with their
mother and father around a small table in a little dining room and
talk among themselves. The father dominates, though everyone contributes.*

On one of those cumbersome televisions that still existed in 2000 there are images of an Argentina in crisis.

Suddenly all the lights apart from one go out. The only one that remains on is pointed at the father of the family who turns to the audience and answers questions put to him in a deep voice with a German accent. What follows is an interview that Jorge Messi gave to the magazine Kicker.

Kicker: You had a lot of concerns, fear and uncertainty.

Jorge Messi: Well, after all, I had my work at Acindar and things were good there. It was the era of *uno a uno* (one peso the equivalent of a dollar) and my salary of 1,600 pesos a month wasn't bad. Except that the treatment cost 900, more than half what I earned. And my social benefits only covered the treatment for two years which meant the third year was very difficult.

Kicker: And he needed at least one more, as the endocrinologist Diego Schwarzstein, in charge of the treatment, explained.

Jorge Messi: Yes, and it is not true when people say that, in any case, the state took care of it. The state never called me and I never asked them for anything. Perhaps if I had managed to speak to some high-up people ... But I was just an ordinary citizen, no one knew me.

Kicker: You've said once 'I wouldn't be able to do this again today'.

Jorge Messi: It was a risk, even though at work they were willing to wait for me and see how things turned out in Spain. But all these comings and goings, the uncertainty and everything, it wasn't easy at all.

Kicker: And what did they say [when you went to talk to River]?

Jorge Messi: When we got back to Newell's they said, 'we will pay for the treatment, don't worry.' But nothing happened, we talked about it again, it was like I was begging, they gave me 300 pesos and never any more. But it was not Newell's as an institution that let us down, it was the people who were in charge of it at that time.

Kicker: In a nutshell: if an Argentinian club had paid for the treatment, Lionel would not have left Argentina?

Jorge Messi: If they had paid, naturally he would have stayed at Newell's.

Kicker: And what did Leo say?

Jorge Messi: He was keen to go.

Lights go off.

Scene Four

Sergio Levinsky, author, sociologist and journalist, addresses the audience on a stage where images of Argentina in 1999, 2000 and 2001 are projected onto a backdrop behind him: we see youngsters playing football, grandfathers demanding their money from closed banks, angry fans, all sorts of images related to the subjects Sergio is addressing.

As Sandra Commisso and Carlos Benítez say in their book *La infancia hecha pelota* ('Childhood Made Football'): 'It's one thing to have a boy who likes football, and who also plays well, and something very different to create a star, with all that it signifies.' It is no coincidence the year that the book first appeared, nor is the fact that the prologue is written by the late humorist and genius Robert Fontanarrosa, one of the greatest storytellers of real-life Argentina, who was born, like Lionel Messi, in Rosario.

The book is divided into seven chapters and at the end contains tips on how to organise and conduct a junior training session, how to avoid making errors and how to develop the appropriate fitness for every child, while exploring the idea that football has become a business even with children, pressured by parents, coaches and agents, so the game stops being a pleasure and becomes a quasi-professional obligation.

In his prologue, Fontanarrosa writes with some justification, 'no one has the right to frustrate the dreams of a kid'. But the book asks whether it is ethical that a child, not yet 10 years old, should bear the burden of being the breadwinner of the family by playing football.

For many years now, but especially in the twenty-first century, the socio-economic frustration of a vast sector of the Argentinian population (an estimated quarter of the 40 million people, according to the last national population census held in 2011) has led them to pursue a career in football as their only route to salvation.

How did we get to this? On one side, it has to be understood that from 1999 to 2001 Argentina lived through the last years of an economic plan that had lasted for a quarter of a century; a plan perpetrated by financial oligarchs and supported by the Church. This followed a bloody *coup d'état* that resulted in the disappearance of a total of 30,000 people, from 24 March 1976 onwards.

The economic plan involved borrowing money from North American banks at very high rates of interest, just as the rest of South America did. The country ended up in such debt that it was effectively bankrupt, while increasing rates of interest meant the country was being monitored by organisations like the International Monetary Fund (IMF).

Eventually, in the last week of 2001, Fernando de la Rua's centre-left alliance government fell. The Argentinian people, shaken by years of fiscal incompetence, demanded that they should all step down, with the result that the country had no fewer than five different heads of government in a week. Then, at the beginning of 2002, the ruling class opted to put in charge, unelected, the powerful Peronist Eduardo Duhalde.

Thus the country was trapped between the '*corralito*' and the '*corralón*'.

Before the crisis, the large foreign banks had withdrawn all their funds from the country so that it was now impossible to withdraw dollars, the preferred currency of the Argentinian people (they did not trust the peso); and to make matters worse, they placed a superlow limit on the amount of money that could be withdrawn, when the cash machines were not working (the *corralito*).

While this chaos ensued, a bank holiday was announced and at a time when there was parity between the dollar and the peso. But when, a few days later, the banks reopened, the dollar cost three times more. Suddenly, many people found that the value of their savings had been cut by two-thirds and there was nothing they could do about it (the *corralón*).

In other words, in a white-collar attack the banks had robbed the people. This led to mass demonstrations outside the banks (which remained shut), pensioners smashing the windows with hammers and sticks, and of course all confidence in the Argentinian banking system evaporated.

Around this time, without the circulation of money in the system, the government implemented a policy of printing 'painted papers'. These were vouchers that in different provinces had different names (the Patacones, Lecor, Lecop or Tucumano dollar); they were quoted lower than the peso, and some businesses announced in their windows that they accepted many of these vouchers, as well as dollars, pesos, reales and all types of credit cards. Many still remember Duhalde's hollow promise that those who had dollars in their accounts 'would receive dollars', as well as those who had pesos 'would receive pesos'.

It was during this period at the beginning of the twenty-first century, at the time of the worst institutional crisis Argentina has ever experienced, that football, as a business, having already been established as the people's sport of choice, came to the fore.

The triumphs of Argentinian teams during these years represented some of the few successes in life that could be enjoyed by every member of the failed classes, beaten down daily by life's trials. For many, the only hope during this period of unrest was the possibility that a member of the family might make it as a professional footballer and 'rescue' the rest of the family from financial disaster. A slang saying much repeated at the time was, 'yo soy yo y mi tío de América' or 'I am me and my uncle from America'. Argentinians were helped by those fortunate enough to succeed and earn money abroad.

It was certainly incredible listening to fans in the stands in first division games, where large numbers of unemployed or desperate people would scream 'loser, loser' at a player solely because he had been unsuccessful in Europe, although you have to bear in mind what this represented symbolically. In the Nineties, we were all complicit in planting seeds of avarice in our children. President Carlos Menem's message that with power comes licence to live a life without scruples became a fashionable ideology that ended up being transferred to football, and manifested itself at games. In 2000 we looked on passively as young professionals played, while tolerating the frenzied abuse coming from their parents during training and at matches, being chased by labels like Nike etc. trying to sign them up for their first contracts, the appearance of agents hoping to discover future talents and the arrogant posturing of very young players, confused by the whole debacle.

And that's why there were incidences in 'baby' football of fathers hitting coaches and referees, clubs stealing players, games that needed a police presence and bosses who took advantage of family anxiety.

In this context it became commonplace for children or youngsters, often sponsored by large organisations, to become the family breadwinners. This depended to a large extent on the amount of pressure applied by their elders.

A few of those kids had the good fortune to team up with some excellent coaches whose first concern was for their welfare. One of those was Carlos Timoteo Griguol, creator of the dominant Ferro Carril Oeste in the Eighties and the Gimnasia and Esgrima la Plate in the Nineties. 'He advised us that with the first big money we earned we should buy our house, and he used to go crazy if he saw us with the latest model of car,' some of the former players often claim. Griguol was also a pioneer in that he insisted, as a condition of playing in the team, that players obtained good grades in their studies, something quite unusual. Quique Domínguez and Ernesto Vecchio were also among those coaches who showed such care and sensitivity.

At the beginning of the Eighties, Diego Maradona was the prime example of one of those youngsters who ended up maintaining a huge family. His team Argentinos Juniors bought him a house so that he could get away from the *villa miseria* (shantytown) of Lanús. In his rented house in Barcelona, where he moved in 1982, he lived with his fiancée Claudia, and a large number of friends. He also sent a lot of money home to his family on a regular basis.

In this context we consider the Messi family in 2000 faced with the dilemma of Lionel's hormone deficiency. Without enough money to pay for treatment it was clear that his size would remain inadequate. They had complete faith in his ability but when Newell's wouldn't pay for it, they took matters into their own hands; like thousands of other families in the country, they realised it was worth the risk to ensure that their son would go as far as he could in the sport he loved.

And that's how the Messis, determinedly, rationally and with a great deal of spiritual strength, decided to set out on a great adventure.

Scene Five

The beginning of the twenty-first century saw the start of a period of exile for Argentinian footballers whereby they crossed the Atlantic in search of their dreams. The crisis accentuated the process that saw football schools throughout the country become breeding grounds of talent. Footballers were being converted into assets and in many cases the principal income of clubs, institutions that often worked hand in hand with exploitative directors and bosses. And so the footballing exile from the country became the norm and continued to grow throughout the first decade of the century. Between 2009 and 2010, Argentina exported almost 2,000 footballers, more than Brazil, historically the number-one seller of footballers.

We are in a high-ceilinged café. People are sitting around a table drinking coffee. In the corner there is a television set circa 2000 featuring the same animated family conversation we saw earlier, but without sound. On one side is a large glass window. Outside it is raining.

Dr Schwarzstein (endocrinologist): Throughout this period Argentina became an expulsive country. In fact between 2000 to 2003 the number of Argentinians arriving in Spain to work soared dramatically.

Liliana Grabín (sports psychologist): We were really 'thrown out' of the country. Even my daughter left, went to the USA. It was a total debacle.

Sergio Levinsky (sociologist): Jorge Messi worked for Acindar, a state-owned company. And as the country was in such a state, workers worried about their future. Considering all that and seeing that Leo had talent to make it as a footballer, I think his dad put a lot of faith in him.

Liliana Grabín: What the Messis did represented a huge challenge. They challenged what was on offer to them, the road most people took. Instead, they said: 'I can build somewhere else with new and better hope for the future.' The number of people who said: 'I won't move from here, I am scared, staying is safer' ... Many people left, however, and with their vision of the future, with their abilities and talent, they managed to succeed. Not everybody can do that.

Sergio Levinsky: There were three levels of 'expulsion' of Argentinians in the last few years. Firstly, the Night of the Long Truncheons

(1966), where mostly scientists left the country, also referred to as the 'Milstein', a name derived from that of César Milstein, who was awarded the Nobel Prize in Medicine in 1984. He lived in London and when the government offered to allow him to return it was too late for him. The second generation of exiles, mostly political, took place during the military dictatorship in 1976. The journalist Ernesto Ekaizer, for instance. And the third one, the one we are talking about, of 2000–2001, the economic migration, included the Messis.

Liliana Grabín: Argentina expels people about every 10 to 15 years. The land to which our grandparents came to try to make their fortunes is today, definitively, a land of expulsion with two or three generations having gone through bad governments that have made many want to return to Europe.

Federico Vairo (supervisor at the River Plate trial): I used to go looking for young players and there are many in Rosario. A friend took me to see Messi. I thought he was very small. His father told me that he would like me to see him; he was nearly 12 and I had a trial for 16-year-olds. I told him that, but his father said his son was used to playing with older boys.

Eduardo Abrahamian (former director of River, now deceased): It was 2000. Messi was 12 years old and his parents brought him to River along with another boy called Giménez, with whom he doubled up in attack at Newell's. The first day I saw him I was amazed, and I called Delem, who is the technical director of the juniors to come and see him, too.

Leandro Giménez (ex-player): We came to the trial together. We travelled in a car with Federico Vairo, and our parents separately in Jorge's (Messi's father's) car. We were very tense. We were having a trial with River! I was so nervous that I even left my boots at home. Fortunately my old man was coming a bit later so he brought them for me. We were shocked from the outset when we heard how the fitness coach was shouting at the River players. 'These idiots are coming to take your places, so make sure you kill them.'

On the television screen the Informe Robinson *programme about Messi is being shown. Someone shouts, 'look, it's Jorge Messi'. The rest turn to the screen and listen to Jorge.*

Jorge Messi (on *Informe Robinson*): He put himself in a line of footballers who were there for the trial and the coaches looked at him, and, seeing how small he was, they said to him, go over there. At the back. The boys started to come on for their trial and he was the last one and they would not call him. I was by the wire fence and I said to him, 'make sure they put you on, because the trial is about to finish'. But absolutely nothing happened until the person in charge of the trial turned around, looked at him and said, 'where do you play?' And he said, 'behind the striker' (*enganche*). And he answered, 'okay, on you go, play'. Just like that, without making a big deal of it. Two minutes went by, three, until he received the ball and when he got the ball he did two or three things that for us were normal, things he always did.

Leandro Giménez: When he came on in his first move he nutmegged this central defender who was about two metres tall. And in his second he did it again.

Jorge Messi: And the person in charge looked at him like this [surprised face], and said, 'who's his father?' So I turned around and said 'I am'. He said, 'we want him, eh!' He'd touched the ball twice! Just because he did a couple of dribbles and then smacked it at goal and forced the keeper into making a save. They asked me if I could bring him to River and I said, 'No ... the truth is that he is at Newell's, but if you take charge of things and speak to Newell's about bringing him here and sort out the move, no problem.' He said. 'No, because they are going to ask us for money, and this, and that.' Anyway, it all eventually came to a sudden halt.

Leandro Giménez: Abrahamian asked us to return on Tuesday. That day he put us both on. We played against a group of boys who were also there for trials ...

Federico Vairo: After ten minutes I called him over. Leo thought I was going to tell him off because he was going around everyone, but I said to him: 'Don't give the ball to anyone, and if you see me in your way, go around me as well.'

Leandro Giménez: We won about 15–0. Leo scored about ten goals. Abrahamian announced that they wanted to sign us.

Federico Vairo: The way he played, little Messi guaranteed himself a chance of becoming a River Plate player. But the youth football department thought he was very small. Also, we had to find accommodation for him, something we didn't do for the juniors.

Leandro Giménez: Before we went back to Rosario, before we knew if we were going to become River players or not, Messi was worried: he was 12 and only guys of 13 onwards were allowed at River's accommodation. 'Could I stay with you?' he asked me. We had already decided that if I came to Buenos Aires to be a River footballer I would live with my grandparents. But he had no one in the capital. I told him that he could come and live with me. Once in the car, though, we argued: Vairo was in the front with his assistant, and in the back Messi, another boy from Rosario and me. I don't know the name of that other guy and I've never seen him since. Neither Leo nor I wanted to sit in the middle but he managed to sit by the window. I was really cross. I said to him, 'Fine, sit by the window, but find your own house in Buenos Aires.' So Leo looked at the other boy, and even though he didn't know him, he asked him, 'I'll stay with you in Buenos Aires then?' Days later, I changed my mind about what I'd said, but Messi never showed up. I found out through my father, who had spoken to Jorge, that Leo would not be coming to River. They wouldn't say why.

Federico Vairo: I persisted [with the youth football department] and they told me that River tried so many youngsters that if we lost this one it wouldn't be a big deal. I told them that he was different, a mixture of Sivori and Maradona, but they took no notice. I think the situation arose because a group of ex-River players had interests at the Renato Cesarini club, and they took on a lot of their players, not so much those from Newell's. I think that is why Messi didn't stay.

Jorge Messi took Leo to the trial to put pressure on Newell's who had promised to take care of the cost of his treatment. He had to go and pick the money up dozens of times, and of the 900 pesos that he needed, they gave him 400. It was humiliating. So he decided to go to Buenos Aires, to see what would happen, to see what Newell's would say. It is not true, as it has been reported, that 'Pipita' Higuaín was involved with those trials that took place on the outer pitches of the Monumental.

So when the directors of Newell's found out that they had travelled to the capital, the director, Almirón, in charge at the time of 'Baby' football at the Malvinas, went to the Messis' house along with a coach. They came to ask Jorge not to take him away from Newell's, that they would handle the cost of his treatment, and that this time they meant it. So the Messis returned to the Malvinas, once again in search, night after night, of what they had been promised. Sometimes they couldn't get hold of Almirón, at other times he did not have the money on him. Why do we have to put up with this? the Messi family wondered.

Scene Six

Only a small table and a telephone are visible. From the left side of the stage the father of the family we have been seeing, first on set, then on the television, appears again. He looks as if he's been hit by a bombshell: he has finally realised he cannot escape his family's predicament. His son, the footballer, the talented one, cannot carry on playing in his own country.

He has spent weeks talking with his wife, Celia, and with his sons, but no decision has yet been reached. The dream of leaving has a dual purpose, to help Leo and to improve their lives, now that the country's economic crisis has drastically reduced their income. He has been dreading the final decision, meal after meal, discussion after discussion. But it is becoming inevitable: all roads are taking the Messis away from home. If someone was prepared to bear the cost of Leo's treatment, if someone would look after him, treat him with kindness, then this would be the club for which he would play his next games, spend his next years. There is talk of Italy (but he never had a trial with Como, as one particularly imaginative director of the Italian club has claimed). 'Should we go to Italy?' The possibility was discussed.

After the trial with River, some intermediaries connected to the prestigious Catalan agent Josep María Minguella, very close to Barcelona, got in touch with the father.

Jorge looks at their business card.

And picks up the phone.

3

Goodbye, Leo

'**W**ho's that?' asked Charly Rexach when he arrived after a lei-
surely post-prandial stroll to the benches where the various Barcelona academy trainers were following the game. It was a rhetorical
question. The youngster with the ball stuck to his feet, with superior speed and dribbling prowess had to be the Argentinian who
was being tried out against taller and older boys. Migueli and Rifé
answered Charly in unison without taking their eyes off the pitch:
'Messi.'

– Fuckin' hell, we've got to sign him – now!

Charly wanted to sign him immediately: 'He's been here for fifteen
days, and that's fourteen more than necessary. If a Martian had
passed by and watched him, he'd have seen that he was something
special.' It was 2 October 2000.

Jorge and Leo returned to Argentina the following day. 'Don't
worry, we'll sort everything out and you can come back when the
season begins. Or before,' Charly promised.

But Leo was a foreigner so was ineligible for national competitions.

And as small as a table football player.

And just 13 years old.

And Barcelona had to find his father work in accordance with
FIFA regulations.

And at that time the first team, which was not doing well, was the
main priority of an unstable institution.

And they had to give him a better contract than juniors would normally get.

And 'when and if he's a superstar, we won't be here,' said one director.

And…hardly anyone was prepared to take the chance. That was it.

'Do you really think he's worth the aggravation, Charly?'

That was the question asked by club president, Joan Gaspart.

Meanwhile, weeks later, in Rosario they were still waiting for an answer.

Waiting for it was the young man who was once again playing for Newell's junior side.

Waiting for it, too, was his father, unsure about his work situation.

Waiting for it was a family, unsure about whether to pack their bags and quit the country, their friends, their school, their lives. Or not.

A month went by.

And with the decision made that this youngster's precocious talent should be allowed to flourish in the perfect setting, wherever that might be, hours turned into days and days into weeks as everyone marked time …and waited.

Another month went by. It was now December.

They were taking the piss. Didn't they like him? Hadn't they made a promise? Things like emails and faxes were not used as often as they are today. The telephone seldom rang.

And so it was that Barcelona received an ultimatum: either something was signed right now, or the boy would seek his future elsewhere. In Italy. There was an attractive offer on the table from AC Milan. At Atlético de Madrid. Or at Real Madrid, where, just months earlier, the club had launched a rasping and painful attack on the Barcelona soul with the capture of the Catalans' captain, Luis Figo. It had left a festering wound. The Real sporting director, Jorge Valdano, was keeping an eye on the matter.

Rexach insisted to everyone that it was worth signing him, and everything else would be dealt with as it happened. Charly looked for the answers to convince the doubters. 'We are taking the matter seriously, tell Jorge,' was the message Rexach sent to the Messis. But it wasn't enough.

'Fancy a game of doubles, Charly?' The offer came from Josep María Minguella, the Catalan agent famous for bringing Maradona to Barcelona, close to the board, a club member, and the man that had borne the cost of the Messis' trip when they came for the trial. The two of them often met at the Pompeya tennis club run by the agent himself, and, as sometimes happened, Horacio Gaggioli, from Minguella's office, the Messis' guide during their visit to the city, also put his name down.

It was 14 December, ten weeks after Leo and Jorge's visit to Barcelona.

After the game they had a beer. And as afternoon turned to early evening, and as the men gazed over the club's courts, it was Minguella who raised the subject. 'Charly, we ought to call the family; we keep telling them yes, that everything's all right, but we still haven't got anything concrete, we ought to sign a contract or something.'

Horacio insisted, 'Charly, we've come this far. You are the technical director of the club, you need to commit to the signing of Leo today. And if not, leave it, that's fine, you go your way and we go ours, that's it.'

The Messis did not want a repeat of what had happened to them with River, promises not worth the paper they were written on. They had reached the point of no return. Barcelona was on the point of losing Leo.

And an impatient Charly, who understands little of protocol, said: 'Let's see, pass me a piece of paper.'

– Waiter, a pen and paper.

The waiter had a ballpoint pen but no paper. The club's offices were closed.

– Here then.

He pulled a paper napkin from one of those small metal containers they put on bar tables.

– So you can see that we are serious about this, said Rexach.

'In Barcelona on 14 December 2000 in the presence of Messrs Minguella and Horacio [Gaggioli] Carles Rexach, technical director of FCB, commits to the signing, regardless of some opinions to the con-

trary, of Lionel Messi, as long as the figures previously agreed are respected.'

That was it. That's what Minguella thought. So did Horacio, who had the napkin formally authorised by a notary before locking it away in a safe. And so did Rexach, who is one of those people who make quick decisions. In football and in life. It was about a gentleman's agreement made between friends. As in the old days, when a handshake was gospel.

For some, it is the most important document in the recent history of Barcelona FC.

For others, Rexach, for example, it is a piece of paper with no real importance but one signed to placate Jorge and Leo, one that a few years later would become the subject of the most oft-repeated anecdote in the story of the Argentinian's signing. Rexach would, to the whole world, from then on become known as the man who signed Messi.

The Messis have never seen that piece of paper.

But just what were Barcelona doing reaching agreements signed on a paper napkin?

'When a player does well, everybody has something to say: I said that, I predicted that, it was down to me ... And when it goes wrong, no one takes responsibility for anything.' So says Charly Rexach, one of the most familiar figures at a club he joined as a 12-year-old and with whom he has had a contractual arrangement for more than four decades, as a player, assistant to Johan Cruyff, coach or right-hand man to various presidents. Charly cannot find any report on Leo written by himself, not that he is bothered. 'I didn't do one, I simply told them how good he was.'

Jorge Messi gives Rexach's contribution much more relevance. He never got to know Rexach in those first few months, but he has always admitted that if Leo is playing for Barcelona today it is for two reasons: the insistence of Charly, and because Leo and him preferred to stay in Barcelona when his elder daughter had to go back to Argentina as she was unable to adapt.

Jorge and Charly know each other now. They met, by coincidence, at the 2011 European Cup final at Wembley. As big as the stadium is, Rexach found himself sitting in the stands next to Jorge.

'Sometimes I get embarrassed when I hear some of the things I hear, when they come up to me and say I discovered Messi. It doesn't make me cross, but I think, fuck me, all those years playing football and now I'm only going to be remembered for discovering Messi, when, as I've said many times, Messi discovered himself. And I was saying this to his father.' Jorge laughed, listening to Charly as he kept repeating, 'what courage from the boy, what courage from you, but especially from the boy!'

'What *cojones* [balls] is what I say. Messi's triumph was his, and his alone,' Rexach insists.

But before the celebrations, the successes, there was more to pay. So it was in December 2000, at a time when Jorge and Rexach still did not know each other, that the phone rang in the Messi house. 'Charly has signed a piece of paper,' Jorge was told. The napkin was enough to placate the Messis even though they were a bit surprised to hear that something like this had been used, especially by a club that had always boasted about its clear junior football philosophy and solid structure. In truth, Barcelona were entering unknown territory. Now it was time to give the agreement shape, with all its variables, promises and more than one unpleasant surprise.

In January, Newell's wanted to register Leo with the Argentine Federation because, and this is key, 'the Flea' was not yet registered to the Rosario club. Argentinian clubs do not request this licence until the footballer has reached the age of 13 or 14. Had NOB taken this step, the matter would have become complicated: the Rosario club could have insisted on a transfer fee. The confirmation of the deal was, therefore, a matter of urgency.

Barcelona had to agree to the Messis' requests, which were accepted by Rexach: a house for the family, travel costs and a job for Jorge Messi, partly because he had to leave Acindar, and partly to fulfil the requirements of FIFA, who forbid the international transfer of minors under the age of 18 unless they are accompanied by their parents.

Leo was not going to live at La Masía where the youngsters from outside Barcelona were based and where a safety net is created by fellow exiles. Another rare, unheard-of demand. 'From the first moment, his parents – and I can understand this – wanted to live with him and look after their son from close by. There was no other player who said: I'm coming with all my family, and I'm going to install myself in Barcelona ...' says Joan Gaspart, the club president who gave the final go-ahead for the signing, although no one gives him credit for this. This is but one of the many small dramas that exist in the world of football: his image as vice-president over a period of 22 years and of president without any title wins over two and a half years, during which the institution that is Barcelona suffered a severe identity crisis, left him stripped of all recognition.

In the first team, the unpopular Louis Van Gaal made enemies of anyone who doubted him. The Dutchman, who never knew how to explain his projects, was none the less key to the progress of the club for his work behind closed doors, for his courageous implementation of his methods, for his gamble on the academy and for his insistence on positional play from which so many trainers after him would benefit. To many Louis was charmless, and he did not always make the best of signings: Juan Román Riquelme never fitted in, nor did Javier Saviola, and there were many more. It was a turbulent time in the history of FC Barcelona, an era described by Jorge Valdano as one of 'historic urgency' to return to better times: Madrid won everything with Luis Figo as their star, signed from Barcelona in the summer of 2000. 'I have brought a lot of players here who haven't worked out: Giovanni, Rochemback. When a player fails, it is the president's fault, even though the president doesn't make the signing, but merely takes the advice of coaches, the ones who make the decisions. When a signing doesn't work out, the coaches disappear,' says Gaspart.

The information received about Leo was clear: 'An excellent ability to dribble, super-fast with the ball at his feet, low centre of gravity that gives him great balance on the move, skilful, electric, powerful for his age, with good powers of recovery – he can do eight to ten sprints every game – likes to try for goal often, a goalscorer, intelligent and mentally fast, occasionally a bit too greedy, although in his case this is a virtue because of his directness, intuition and versatility in any attacking position.' With just one snag: 'he is very small, but he is undergoing growth hormone treatment.'

Another expense for Barcelona, the treatment.

The boy did not come cheap. That's what the president told Joaquim Rifé, the director of the junior football academy. The budget for the academy at that time was around €13 million and that was tight, every age group had an amount allotted to it and Messi broke the budget. That was one of the main reasons for the heated exchanges before and after the paper-napkin saga, the highs, the lows, the tension. 'Why so many meetings?' asked Rifé. Rexach supported him. Probably because they served to delay making a decision. Jorge Messi told Rifé, 'my son is going to be a great foot-baller for Barcelona and will work out very cheap for you'.

In those meetings between coaches and the board, the president would insist that he was not about to start thinking about a 13-year-old boy; what he had to do was sign two or three players to beat Madrid. No one could have imagined that, three years later, Leo would be making his debut for the first team. 'If you sign him, you will be making a mark for the future,' urged Rexach. It was a power-ful argument that tends both to impress and seduce most directors.

Gaspart, however, explains it another way. 'Charly was close to me, the president, he was the man I trusted, because he's a bloke who understands football and footballers. We met at the club, in my office, as we did regularly. We didn't just talk about Messi, we talked about various things and at some point Charly told me there was an exceptional player who we could not let escape. "This is very simple – whatever you say, goes," I said. He said, "Are you in agreement about setting up special accommodation for him?" I said, "Do you think he is something out of the ordinary?" "Yes." "Well, go ahead".'

Some of the coaches advised against the signing, but, more than any, it was certain members of the board who did not want him. The director of the youth system, Joan Lacueva, was possibly the only one on the board who strongly supported the signing. He trusted in Rexach so he started to build what Charly described as a 'made-to-measure suit' for Leo, a sort of legal support for that contractual napkin.

On his return from Barcelona, Leo played for the Newell's tenth team (another name for the juniors aged between 12 and 13) under the direction of Adrián Coria, who now works with Tata Martino as Barcelona's match analyst. He won the Apertura (or Opening, a league competition even though it only includes the first half of the calendar) of the tenth division and ended up being the leading goalscorer.

Most of those around 'the Flea' could not have imagined what was going to happen, but some of them knew something was afoot. Rosario businessman Néstor Casal remembers one day, while having a meal with Jorge Messi, Leo's dad told him that, after a great performance by his son, he was approached by someone who said he was a representative of Barcelona and that he wanted to speak to him. That day, Jorge kept the man's visiting card.

A little later father said to son. 'Hey! Can you believe it? You'd be making the same journey as Maradona! Imagine that you go to Barcelona and you come back later and finish your career at Newell's!'

The dream was close.

Quique Domínguez:
In October 2000 I was waiting for the kids to arrive and I saw Jorge Messi, who always distanced himself from the others, approaching. I greeted him: 'Hello, Jorge, how are you?' and I remember his exact words, and how surprised I was when he said, 'enjoy these next two months because I'm taking him away'. 'Where are you taking him? You're not taking him anywhere!' I said. 'Yes, I'm taking him away,' he repeated. 'Anyway,' I said jokingly, 'as long as you're not taking him to Central (because that really would be a betrayal) then that's fine.' When training had finished I looked for him to ask more about it but he had already left. The following Saturday we were playing away. I saw Jorge and I stopped him: 'What did you say to me the other day about taking Leo away?' 'Yes,' he told me, 'I'm taking him away. For the last two years we've been paying the cost of his treatment with the health cover I have with Acindar and with the help of ASIMRA [the Association of Supervisors of the Metalworking Industry], but as I have no health cover any more, they have stopped paying, and I can't afford it any longer.' 'Is that why you're taking him away?' And he said to me, 'No, I went to speak with Pupo and he told me there was no budget for this.' Pupo was the technical director of the juniors at Newell's. 'Pupo said this?' I asked. 'And what did you say?' 'That if it was like that, I'd take him away, and he said to me: whatever you decide.'

Sometimes decisions are taken about certain issues for reasons that don't appear obvious but are important none the less. In Rosario, people were talking: Pupo and Jorge never seemed to have got on. It all started with Rodrigo, Leo's older brother and a number 8 of some quality, who had missed the chance to play for one of the sides that the Argentine Federation put together occasionally when the club made an error. He was transferred to Central Córdoba against his wishes – he would no longer play for his beloved Newell's again. Two dreams ruined. Why was Pupo not more supportive of the Messis? Perhaps he was unwilling to take the pressure put on him for Leo to stay? Sometimes those in charge think they know more than anybody else. But it isn't always like that. Some people will not accept being told what to do. That might well have been the reason, but no one is really sure.

'Newell's sent Rodrigo to a club at the arse end of nowhere, with a completely different training regime,' Domínguez says now. 'I got the impression that Pupo made it a personal issue when he told Jorge there was no money for the treatment. When people at Newell's found out he had said there was no budget they could not believe it: he's a moron! A madman! they would say.'

Jorge had spent six months weighing up all the options, whether or not it was worth changing their entire life, and spoke to every member of his family. One day he sat all of them around the dining-room table. Rodrigo was 20, Matías, 18, Leo, 13. María Sol was five. He was looking for everyone's approval before giving his answer to Barcelona. Italy was still an option, but Spain created fewer doubts, was more appealing: since Leo had heard from Barça he hadn't thought of any other club. He asked them one by one, including the little girl. There were many things that had to be discussed, not just Leo.

It wasn't only that he had enough talent to triumph with the backing of an institution that offered the biggest guarantees and better financial arrangements. Other things had to be taken into consideration: the Messis wanted Rodrigo to continue playing football. At the time Central Córdoba were fighting for promotion to the first division, and Jorge believed he had enough ability to earn his living as a footballer in Spain. Plus, Matías and María Sol would grow up in a country that appeared more steady, with greater chances for the future than those offered by their own country. They were talking of GOING TO EUROPE, in capital letters, something that many wanted to do but didn't have the chance to.

Leo had said around that time to Rodrigo that he wanted to win the Ballon d'Or. 'Without this crazy willingness to give it everything and to progress, his supreme talent would have been pointless,' his brother says today. No one in the family wanted to impede his progress.

Yes or no?

Yes, they'd go. Yes. Everyone would go to Barcelona. No balls, no glory!!

That is, if a final agreement actually came from Barcelona.

On 8 January 2001 a decisive step was taken. At a dinner in the Catalan capital attended by Joan Lacueva and Rifé, the club finalised the contract details: the player would earn 100 million pesetas a year (€600,000) as well as receive payments for image rights, another new concept for a junior players' contract. In addition, they would pay the Messi family money to rent an apartment and about seven million pesetas (€42,000) in annual wages for Jorge – he was going to work for Barna Porters, a company owned by Barcelona which supplied security staff for the club.

As soon as Messi signed the contract, the club would start paying for the hormonal treatment that, it was calculated, would increase his height to 1.67 metres. He ended up reaching 1.69 metres.

Seven days later, Charly Rexach was writing an official letter, complete with club seal, to Jorge Messi pledging to honour everything that had been agreed with his representatives in Barcelona. Three days after that, Joan Lacueva sent another letter confirming the financial agreement.

With 'yes' from Barcelona and 'yes' from the Messi family, nothing could stop the agreement going ahead. Surely Rosario was to be a thing of the past. But there was one thing left to do.

Jorge and a friend walked 75 kilometres to give thanks for the conclusion of the negotiations at the Shrine of the Virgin of St Nicolas. They left at five in the morning and took 14 hours to make the journey. A barefoot Leo joined them for the last 800 metres. They returned by car. With a big bottle of water. Dead from the heat and the exertion.

On 15 February 2001, after weeks of preparation and tension, a rush to get passports, travel authorisation and suitcases, the Messis began their journey to Barcelona.

'Leo disappeared from Newell's at the end of the championship,' Quique Domínguez remembers. 'Ernesto Bocha, one of the coaches, called me and asked about Leo, but I didn't know where he was. Nobody knew anything, I swear, nobody knew a thing! I told him that they'd called me asking for Leo, but that I didn't have the faintest idea what had happened to him. And he said, he's not in Rosario any more, because I have spoken to members of his family and friends and nobody knows where they are, but they are not at home. Four, five months go by and Ernesto calls me and says: "guess where Leo is? In Barcelona." And automatically I thought of Barcelona in Ecuador, the closest one, because I couldn't get my head around the idea that he had travelled to the European one. For us, Europe still remains a faraway place, distant, and not just physically. Then he cleared it up for me: "no, Barcelona, Spain." "Seriously?" "What's he doing there?" He told me, "he's going to FC Barcelona and they're going to pay for the treatment."

'Hey, brilliant, I said, much better. This made me very happy, very happy. We knew where he had landed, we knew that he wasn't at a club that was going to use him, as is the norm in football – they give you a contract and then they use you. Barcelona are light years away from us. Barcelona are the kind of club that gives you everything, but then don't use you: "you have your beliefs, your dreams, your way of doing things, we will pay for your treatment, we will protect you." That is what he was going to get. We were told that they had also given work to the father; but they probably said to him, "well, work out later if you will actually go to work or not". Both parties planted and watered the tree and now they both share the benefits. Thank God he landed where he did.

'I assume,' insists Quique Domínguez, 'that the Newell's president would have said, "How? Leo Messi played for Newell's? Let's go and ask Pupo. Pupo! Was it you? Yes? Get out then! How could you let a player like that go?" It wasn't that he, Pupo, didn't see him. Pupo used to watch the training sessions! He was the technical director of the youth set-up. He was the one who decided where players went, not the coach; it was he who decided. The president had enough with the first division, I am sure he didn't know Leo.'

Many in Rosario repeat the story that, actually, the president of Newell's, Eduardo López, did nothing to stop the departure of Lionel either. 'No problem, Messi can go. We keep the best one: Gustavo Rodas.' Rodas made his debut at 16 for Newell's, wore the number 10 with the Under-17 national team and was champion of the South American tournament in Bolivia. He was called up by Argentina again but did not join them. He couldn't settle at NOB and tried his fortune at Tiro Federer, El Porvenir, Cúcuta (very modest semi-amateur clubs) and moved to Peru, where he played for Bolognesi and León de Huánuco. Nobody knows where he is now. Perhaps Rodas could have filled the void left by Leo in terms of talent, but, since when has too much talent been a problem?

Eduardo van der Kooy, journalist and co-author of *Cien años de vida en rojo y negro* ('A Hundred Years in Red and Black') with Rafael Bielsa, the brother of the well-known coach Marcelo, goes further: 'Leo left Newell's because the mafia that controlled the club during that era did not believe that something so great, so brilliant, could be contained within a physique so small. He left because they abandoned him when his body needed both spiritual and material assistance. But Newell's still consider him theirs and Leo feels that it is his club. Oh, that he could return, albeit with grey hair.'

Newell's is a historical institution traditionally nourished by its junior ranks, in whom they take great pride. But they are also exporters, a club that sells those academy players they look after with so much care. In 1988, NOB finished as champions, having produced every player who started that season, every substitute and all the coaches, the only time this has happened in the history of Argentinian football. 'And from that point on, a process of fourteen years of destruction began, a personal project that had the help of the judiciary and other parts of society that permitted one man to destroy the club.' That is how one well-known, but on this occasion anonymous, Rosarian refers to Eduardo López, the then president of Newell's and head of gambling syndicates in Rosario, with casinos and other businesses, some of which brought him to the attention of the police. Others talk about more direct responsibility: for example, Sergio Almirón, former Newell's left-winger, 1986 World Cup winner and sporting director during that era. When Jorge called him looking for help, he was either unavailable or the appointment would be cancelled at the last minute, or he would give him 40 pesos for a treatment that cost twenty-five times that amount. And this only when Almirón was feeling generous. Another member of the Argentinian club who never supported Leo.

The presidential elections of 2008 allowed a change at the helm of the club. López stood twice, winning once and losing fourteen years later. In between, he arranged for elections to be suspended, for the lists of candidates to be challenged, or for the justice department to fail to authorise the voting. Since 2008 the club has tried to return to the way it once was: in 2013 Newell's became champions again, with Tata Martino in charge, just before he went to Barcelona.

When Celia, Leo's mother, declared in 2010, 'I speak for myself, not my husband: for me, Newell's doesn't exist', she was referring to the old Newell's. The current board is very close to Jorge and to Leo, so much so that the Messis have even invested, so it is said, in a new gymnasium for the Sports City and a number of other projects. There are some who can see Jorge as a club director and Leo wearing the red and black shirt. One day.

Leo's departure has left scars, as Wright Thompson explained on a website. ' For years he [Ernesto Vecchio] resented his former player. Something happened here at this school, a bit of magic, and Vecchio played a role. Many people did. There should be some acknowledgment. Instead, they're known as the short-sighted fools who let a legend walk away. The former Newell's team official in charge of Messi's growth hormone payments still carries around receipts, which seem like forgeries, trying to prove that he didn't make the dumbest decision in the history of professional sports.'

And Leo? When he was asked in 2009 how he felt about Newell's, he chose to be diplomatic. 'Angry, no, because I'm not like that. I have a lot of love for the club. I went to the pitch as a small boy and dreamed of being on it one day.'

*

So there it is. In Rosario, Leo had been surrounded by the people who valued him, who protected him, people who encouraged him and who helped him grow. All of them wanted to see him come out on top. All bar a few at the place where he played, his club. 'When we found out that the club was not going to pay for his treatment, we were very sad,' remembers Cintia Arellano. 'When the boys from the neighbourhood said their goodbyes, I was with him. He hugged me and said, don't cry, don't cry.'

People who knew him well wanted to give him a send-off. They were leaving, surely never to return. We're staying here, said his friends, his family. You're very brave. Good luck to you.

'We left the neighbourhood, Las Heras, and all our friends, all our people, came out to say their goodbyes,' Leo told Cristina Cubero in the Catalan newspaper *El Mundo Deportivo* in 2005. 'They were all in the street. The whole family was going, my parents Jorge and Celia and my brothers Rodrigo, Matías and my little sister María Sol who at that time was five years old. That day we were so sad that my brother Matías and I cried, we cried a lot. It was a very gloomy journey; we missed our family, my uncles, everybody.'

Today, more than a decade later, he remembers the trip as if it were a dream, but at the time it was terrible – they were going to what seemed like the other side of the world, with the sound of his very roots being torn up playing in his ears. It happens with every departure, and it is a powerful echo.

'He left, and from one day to the next we knew nothing about him,' remembers Gerardo Grighini. 'Maybe his neighbours knew. He is a very reserved person, not someone who finds out about something and has to go and tell everybody. And probably his father, his mother, told him, don't say anything. What's more, he had gone to River Plate, he had been at River for a week and later on he went to Barcelona. We didn't know anything about River or the trial at Barcelona either; we found out about it afterwards when he was in Spain.'

'I went to greet him at his hotel when he came with the national team to Rosario to play Brazil, but he couldn't come down to reception,' Vecchio remembers. 'His parents came down, and I spoke to them for quite a while. The only thing I managed was to say hello to him when he was sitting in a group. He saw me and smiled ... I cherish that memory.'

Ángel Ruani, the father of 'Luli', Leo's friend, recalls the following: 'The last time I saw him was with my son and a few friends on New Year's Eve 2005 when they came home at about five in the morning. They woke me up to wish me Happy New Year. Big-hearted, no?'

And Nestor Rozín: 'You keep in your heart, in your mind, the good things that he did, and the day I have to go, maybe one or two will know in their minds and in their hearts that I helped him a bit.'

'I had not seen him for a while and we met at the Copa América in Venezuela, in 2007. He came up to greet me. That was rewarding, he was the same kid I had in the ninth and tenth teams. He came over and gave me a hug ... You should remember this: he's the same person I knew when he was a nipper.' This is Adrián Coria, who, as assistant to Martino with the Paraguayan national side in the 2010 World Cup in South Africa, saw him again after that affectionate meeting. Coria was walking onto the training pitch just as Argentina were leaving. From a distance, Leo saw him, took off his top and gave it to him. Adrián has put it in his office in Rosario.

The boy Leandro Giménez, who had a trial with Leo at River, never saw Leo in person again after he left Argentina. Nor has he spoken to him. 'He gave me his telephone number when he went to Barcelona, but I never called him. I don't know why. Before the last World Cup I left him a message on Facebook. I told him that he was a source of pride for all Argentinians. He was grateful for all the messages he received. But I also got a Like from him,' he smiles. Today, aged 24, Giménez lives in Buenos Aires and works with a foreign trade company. He doesn't want to play any more, except with his friends on Saturdays. He ended his footballing career a disillusioned man.

Grighini, who spent six years in Italy, went to see an Inter–Barcelona game but did not ask Leo for a ticket. Or a shirt. Earlier, he had seen him at an airport, 'but he wasn't yet famous. At that time, as we had distanced ourselves from each other and we didn't communicate on a day-to-day basis, he was that shy boy once again. He would answer: "yes, no, it's going well, what do you know, Barcelona ..." I'm talking about when he was 16 and had only just started to play. For me we would have to speak on a daily basis or maybe after a few hours together everything would click again and we could go back to "you remember when ..." and all the anecdotes. But at the beginning, if you hadn't seen him for a while, he was reserved, distant. But of course he is an idol to me. For me the matter of a shirt is different, I'm not interested, I'm more interested in sharing a meal, or going out for a bit.

'I went to England, to Everton, in June 2005,' Grighini continues. 'But after that I had a bit of bad luck: I had a very bad car accident, we hit two lorries. I only fractured my fibula but my friend, the player Julio González, was travelling with me and could have lost his life. He had multiple fractures and they amputated his left arm. He returned to playing a bit later, how cool is that! Later I tore my cruciate ligaments, three times in a row, and I was out of the game for three and a half years. I came out all right but destiny and life mark you and if they tell you that football is not for you, then you have to follow your life in another direction.'

And Diego Rovira: 'I had to tell my parents, so I did, after supper. In fact, it wasn't so much me coming up with any big news – I just confirmed what they guessed all along. Mum, Dad, I am leaving football. That was March 2011. Yes, I am quitting. They had supported me, bankrolled me. My dad said something very obvious: it is a shame, son. And it really was. He knew how hard I had tried, he was the one who had watched me in hundreds of games, with Leo at Newell's ... they still call me the number 9 who played with Leo.'

It's very difficult to make it in football.

The last farewell, that of Quique Domínguez: 'A while ago we played a qualifier for the 2014 World Cup, Argentina–Uruguay in Mendoza and Chile–Argentina in Chile. My eldest son Sebastián, Maxi Rodríguez ("the Beast") and Leo were called up. The three of them in the same squad! And now they were going to meet. Maxi had to leave the squad because of an injury and return to Rosario and my son Sebastián said to me: "the Beast is coming back, look for him because he's got something for you. I don't know what it is, but he told me to warn you because he has a present." It had been more than 20 years since I had last coached the Beast, and 13 since I had trained Leo. Maxi brought me a shirt. Signed by both of them, by Leo, by himself. There are people who say to me, "How ungrateful, you never hear from them." No, things happen naturally when you feel them. And that day they thought it was a good idea to send me a shirt. I am very thankful.

'I feel,' Domínguez says, 'one drop of sweat, only one, from every game that Leo plays is mine, it tells me that I have something to do with Leo's life, but I don't ask for anything back, I don't ring him, I don't need all that. I saw him one day on television on a programme that honoured him, I was there and I said hi to him. But if Leo closes his eyes and you ask him, "remember the people who passed through your life" … roll of drums … Quique Domínguez will be there, briefly, in passing … this to me has a much greater value than any shirt …

'No, I am no longer coach.'

Is that Leo Messi, the one talked about by Domínguez, or Grighini or Rovira, the real one? Or are they seeing the Leo they want to see? With this Argentinian fascination for the Messiah, for the one who has the gift, the special one, it becomes difficult to separate image from reality, especially when the country was and still is in turmoil. It is in times of crisis when the need for heroes intensifies.

This stage of his life was coming to a close for Leo, but it never totally ended for those who had been close to him. He stayed with them, in their minds and hearts.

Jorge, by the way, never collected his final pay cheque from Acindar.

Part Two

In Barcelona

1

Landing in Barcelona. Well, in Rosario. That is, in Barcelona

On the flight from Rosario to Buenos Aires, Lionel Messi cried non-stop. As though he was never going to return. Silent tears. His face twisted, the teardrops streaming down his face. Until he breathed in and let out the deep sigh of a lost boy. That's how he cried on the 50-minute journey to the federal capital.

It was 15 February 2001. After landing at Ezciza airport and before boarding the plane to Barcelona, conversations took place around the table to take their mind off the coming events, and Leo calmed down. En route to Spain, in between bouts of nausea caused by the turbulence, he fell asleep, and bit by bit, with every mile further away from home, in the words of Jorge Luis Borges, 'the sea worked its magic, the sadness of absence would come later'.

The Messi/Cuccittini family arrived in Barcelona on a cold mid-afternoon, and took a taxi to the Hotel Rally in the Travessera de les Corts, opposite the Camp Nou. The club had summoned them a few days later for a meeting with the aim of getting all the contracts signed, although, strangely, nobody had so far offered to meet the cost of the treatment that Leo had started in Rosario.

Eventually, director Joan Lacueva agreed to stump up €2,000 of his own money so he could take the first doses he needed.

And so they spent 15 days in a hotel room and at training, feeding a passion and trying to put some order into the chaos of a new life.

On 1 March 2001, at a table in the hotel restaurant under the watchful eye of Lacueva, the young Leo Messi signed his first two-year contract with Barcelona. In insisting that all the bureaucracy was sorted out and ensuring that Messi finally became a Barcelona player, Lacueva was derided by many of his fellow directors. They were convinced it was all a waste of money. Time, however, would reward him for his efforts, and those of Rexach, Rifé and Minguella.

But the matter didn't end there: one director – who prefers to remain anonymous – was furious to discover that agreement had been reached without the approval of the board. Without any consultation. How could a young boy cost the club so much money!? He not only refused to sign the document, despite the fact that it had already been signed by both side's lawyers and a vice-president; in a fit of rage he also tore up the document.

None the less, the club confirmed the contract.

'When I hear someone say "I signed this guy or that guy ..." it's a lie; you signed no one, Barça signed,' says ex-president Joan Gaspart in charge of the club at the time. 'Did you pay for it, out of your pocket? You didn't, did you? So it was Barcelona who signed him. You may have been the intermediary at the time ... but you signed no one. And they say that Messi's contract was signed on a napkin. Well, no actually. It's a funny story, a good anecdote, but Messi's contract was signed by the then vice-president of Barcelona, Francisco Closa. And he signed it because I authorised it.'

The most difficult part was still to come – how Messi would adapt. Barcelona had found a flat for the family on Gran Via Carles III, near the Camp Nou, and the Messi/ Cuccittinis moved in at the beginning of March, two weeks after their arrival. It was a large apartment, with four bedrooms, two bathrooms, a kitchen and a balcony that led to an internal area where there was a communal swimming pool adjoining another building, trees and tranquillity. Lionel could get up 15 minutes before training and still arrive at the ground on time. That way he could sleep a little longer. The concierge of the building – as revealed by Luis Martín of the newspaper *El País*, a journalist well known for asking those kinds of questions that no one else thinks about – did not realise for five years that the guy who greeted him every morning played for Barcelona. 'It's amazing, no? It's just that I don't really do football. I don't like it,' he told Martín.

In Rosario people from all over the province would come to see him. In Barcelona not even his concierge knew who he was.

And right from the start, everything went pear-shaped. Did he really want to be a footballer? Let's see what he was made of. A rocky road lay ahead.

'I did not understand a word. They all spoke in Catalan!' A few years after his arrival, Leo looked back at his first days with Barcelona with a mixture of excitement and irritation. As happens with every new kid in a group of kids, Messi felt shy and apprehensive about jumping into conversations, but he was received with a lesser degree of understanding than people would admit now. During the first training games he did not get much of the ball, team-mates were not particularly encouraging, he felt a complete outsider. Even as a 13-year-old he understood there was a price to pay to be accepted – he was there, potentially, to replace one of the friends of those playing.

Leo was told by some of his team-mates that one of the coaches who was checking on his level in the first weeks had told some of the kids to go in hard on him; he didn't want him to stay at Barcelona. He was, Messi explained later on in the Argentinian TV show *Sin Cassette*, the same coach who 'asked me to play one-touch, not to dribble too much. But to be honest I didn't take much notice of what he said, I used to do what came naturally to me.'

It is the same story the world over. Once the door is open, when it is confirmed that you are staying with the group, then you're accepted, the attitude of your team-mates changes. But Messi never forgot those early weeks when he was made conscious of his outsider status. He felt he had earned his place in the club.

As a foreigner, Leo was unable to play official matches with the *Infantiles* A side, the team that corresponded to his age group. He only had permission to play in the Catalan regional league and in friendlies, and what's more, Rodolfo Borrell, the team's coach, preferred to use him sparingly, in keeping with the unwritten law of not changing an unbeaten side during a season that was well underway, with youngsters performing at a high level and who had already become league champions with seven games still to play.

In any case the physical fragility of this Argentinian footballer was so obvious that in training sessions Borrell instructed his players to tread carefully with him. 'Please don't kick him,' he asked his defenders when Leo came out to train, the first to step onto the pitch. 'He's so fast, and so slight that you could injure him.' He might have looked like nothing but he was difficult to stop. He kept looking for the second dribble, the third, travelling at speed. Cesc Fàbregas couldn't get the ball off him during one of those afternoons where Leo was showing off his stuff. He gave him a good kicking. 'Cesc, please, calm down, he's only just got here, that's not the idea.' The next time Rodo urged the players to be careful. To the amusement of everyone Piqué shouted, 'How can we be careful? We can't even get close to him!'

'He was incredible, he picked the ball up and just started to dribble past everyone, that's how he used to spend each session, dribbling past everyone and scoring goals, it didn't matter against who,' remembers Víctor Vázquez, who played with him for a few years in the lower ranks. 'We hadn't seen anything like it before because we were more of a passing side; he just got the ball and went. We said among ourselves that he was more of an individualist, but that was at the beginning. We soon realised that we should have been delighted to have a player such as him in our team.'

Bored of winning by six-, seven-, eight-goal margins, Borrell wanted his squad to play one of the tournaments against older teams so that his players would 'feel the heat'. Barcelona accepted his suggestion and sent them to the Pontinha tournament in Portugal where they would come up against Portuguese opponents, a French side and one from Germany, with youngsters two years older than that historic generation that included Piqué, Cesc, Vázquez, Marc Pedraza, Rafael Blázquez and the recently arrived Messi, who was able to play because this was not an official competition. They finished third out of eight and Leo felt comfortable.

Another test passed.

Without the international transfer papers that Newell's still hadn't sent, he received a provisional licence from the Catalan Federation on 6 March, and the club, conscious of the strength of Borrell's *Infantiles* A team, decided that Leo would play more regularly if he went down to the *Infantiles* B side of Xavi Llorens, the only time in 'the Flea's' career that he was the oldest boy in the group.

At Newell's he even took the warm-up sessions while the coach was otherwise occupied; at Barcelona, he was not yet completely in his comfort zone.

But despite the fact that the situation was a new one for the club and complicated for the new arrival, no one doubted his talent. He trained with Llorens four times a week, from six to nine in the evening. He arrived a little before six, collected the kit that the club had got ready for him, changed and trained. And he was never in any hurry to go home afterwards.

Where are you from? Where do you play? the kids would ask him in his first training sessions with the *Infantiles* B side. He was a year older than them but physically still much smaller. '*Enganche*,' he'd reply. No one was quite sure what that meant; it was a very Argentinian expression. But, at the end of the first week, a boy approached Llorens to ask what was becoming a rhetorical question: 'Is he going to play for us for long?' The boy wanted it to be a positive answer, but it wasn't to be – the coach preferred to sidestep the question. Surely Leo was too good for that level.

'I well remember one match we played in training,' says the *Infantiles* B trainer. 'There was a corner against our side, and he put himself on the edge of the area to defend, as he'd been told to do. The ball fell to him, he started heading towards the opposing goal, going the length of the pitch, the one we call number three, opposite the Mini Stadium, passing one, two players – they'd all been attacking up the other end so there weren't many. He got to the opposition's area, took two more steps and then did what Maradona had done that day against Red Star: disguised his shot by sticking in a little dink, a lob. Unbelievable. He scored and went back to the centre circle as if nothing had happened. And you'd look at him and think … bloody hell! He walked back without looking towards the bench, straight down the middle of the pitch, hugging his teammates. When players do something like that, they look at the bench to catch your eye, to see if they've done well or not. Not him, he just did it his way. It's a small thing that I will always remember. As if nothing had happened.'

A bit later, Xavi Llorens wrote a report that Joaquim Rifé had asked for, confirming that the quiet, 1.47-metre-tall Leo was a 'little Maradona', small in stature but with supreme speed and skill.

Leo made his debut in an official match in a Barcelona shirt, with the number 9 on his back, at Amposta's ground, in the Catalan regional league in which he was eligible to play. He scored one of *Infantiles* B's three goals and naturally he was selected for the next match, against Ebre Escola Deportiva. It would be played on 21 April.

The teams had breakfast together on the day of the game and their photographs were taken on the pitch. Marc Baiges, the opposing number 10, placed himself for the photo behind Leo's slender frame. In fact, the star of that side was not Leo, who had only just arrived, but Mendy, a goalscorer with great physical presence.

The game kicked off. That was the good news.

In playing what was his second official match for the *Infantiles* (aged 12–13 years), he fulfilled the requirements of the Spanish Federation that would now allow him to play in the national category, too, a rule that youth coach Albert Benaiges discovered almost by accident: further proof of just how unaware and unprepared Barcelona were for what Leo was bringing. If, as a foreigner he had not played in those two games, he would have been obliged to jump from the next category, the Cadetes (aged 14–15 years), directly to Barcelona B in the second division without being allowed to participate in the two intermediary stages Barcelona academy footballers tend to play in to ensure their careful progression through the ranks.

By being unaware about the obligation for foreign players to play at least two games in the *Infantiles*, the club had inadvertently affected the career of other footballers. Leo was kept on the right road by Benaiges' chance discovery, but Gilberto, a Brazilian youngster, was not so lucky. Having not played at *Infantiles* level and so having the normal progression through the ranks blocked, the club decided to loan him out. But he did not adapt to being sidetracked and finished off playing in minor leagues after leaving Barcelona. Sometimes the margins between success and failure are very narrow.

Now for the bad news.

Seconds after the start of the game, the ball came out to Leo on the left wing and he lost control of it. From the throw-in, Baiges, the kid who'd stood behind Messi in the team photo, shaped to boot the ball upfield, only for the young Argentinian to put his leg in the way. Result? A fracture of the left fibula. The first major injury of his career, and one that prevented him from playing for two months. 'Are you saying that I broke it? Mother of God!' exclaimed Baiges years later when the magazine *Libero* told him what had happened that day. 'It's not that I didn't know that I'd broken Messi's leg, it's that I didn't know that I'd broken anybody's leg.' In fact, it wasn't even a foul.

'He got injured in front of the bench,' remembers Xavi Llorens. 'We noticed that something serious had happened and so we sent him to hospital to have it checked. He twisted in pain at first, but soon calmed down. He said he had hurt himself, but wasn't moaning or anything. His father was at the hospital with him. I couldn't go at that point because we had to finish the game. One of the directors went with him. And the boy asked, "What have I got? Will I be out for long?" When a footballer is injured he thinks, "tomorrow I want to go and run, and now I can't. In a few days I have a game, and now I can't play …" That is all he had on his mind.'

Messi had to wear a plaster on his leg. He would occasionally go to training on crutches, but his trainer noticed a surprising strength in the 13-year-old: 'We didn't have to encourage him, you saw that he was strong.' Those closest to him, though, remember him being 'fucked'. His little sister María Sol didn't need to be told about how difficult it was to take Leo from training, away from the ball. Some afternoons when the day was dragging, without saying a word she would hold Leo's hand.

Then, in June, a week after coming back, he suffered ligament strain to his left ankle. Going downstairs! Three more weeks without playing. His body wasn't just small, it was fragile. By the end of that unfortunate period, four months after he had arrived in Barcelona, Leo had played only two official games and one friendly tournament.

The Messi/Cuccittini family spent the summer of that short and irregular first season back in Rosario. Celia had travelled home earlier to be with her sister, Marcela, who needed a kidney operation.

But something had changed; a light had gone out during those first months in Spain. It was not clear if Leo, now 14, would return to his new club; if he would decide to stay at home or return to Barcelona with his family after that summer.

*

It has been said somewhere that, even before the family left Rosario, Jorge spoke to his mother's cousin who lived in Lleida, 76 miles from Barcelona, seeking support. In fact, they met many months later when they were already established and living in Spain. They had set out on their voyage of discovery without a safety net, without even life jackets, without any family support other than what the five of them living together in the apartment on Gran Via Carles III gave each other.

All this, and the fear of shipwreck, brought them closer in those first months in Barcelona: they shared free time together, meals, disappointments. Leo wanted to discover the sea and they would all walk there together. 'We'd go to the beach. I lived in a city with a river, without the sea, so the beach for us was very attractive. It was cold, that made it a bit sad, but I liked it,' Messi told Cristina Cubero in *El Mundo Deportivo* in 2005.

Jorge tried to ensure that the setbacks did not affect the harmony of the family unit, but Leo couldn't play football, the main reason they were there. And Barcelona were not paying what they promised, nor were they rushing through the necessary paperwork. You could already discern a certain sloppiness, a lack of urgency, following the September trial, and now that everything had been signed and sealed, certain doubts were beginning to surface, evidence of a lack of care even. Furthermore, Jorge's employment situation had not been sorted out, and he ended up writing a letter to the president, Joan Gaspart, explaining how abandoned they felt. 'My situation and that of my family is desperate. I have made all the necessary economic provisions up to the current month, at which time the signed agreements between us should have taken effect, and today I find myself without notice of any new payments and without anyone to speak to and advise me as to what actions I should take.' This desperate letter had been written on 9 July 2001 and published much later in *El Gráfico*.

The list of grievances was becoming long and heavy. The Messis felt deceived. Not so much by the club as an institution, but, rather, by those who had promised to take care of the family, and that included some of the player's representatives. Leo was FC Barcelona's principal, or more accurately, sole concern: they wanted him at school, at training, to make sure he ate properly, and to supervise his physical and hormonal development. Leo and his father were the only members of the family with an NIE (*Número de Identidad de Extranjero*, an identification number required by non-Spanish nationals in Spain). For this reason, Rodrigo was unable to carry on playing football, María Sol ended up in a state school where she suffered a certain amount of discrimination because she was foreign and Matías, who had left his girlfriend back in Rosario, felt lonely and displaced. The fabric of family life was slowly coming apart at the seams.

With the first team repeatedly trying unsuccessfully to win titles, as a consequence the entire club was in the doldrums, and Leo Messi was seen by those both inside and outside the club as something of an experiment. Let's see what comes of it was the thinking. He was just a number, perhaps a good financial investment. But it was becoming obvious that the Barcelona board lacked experience, astuteness or an understanding of how to handle their Argentinian.

Meanwhile Leo attended classes, as did all the young *blaugranas*, at the Lleó XIII school. He didn't enjoy it and as a result did not get good marks. He wasn't lazy, just a bit uninterested and, like many, would open a book at a particular page that would remain before his glazed eyes, unread, until the end of the lesson. He attended, but wasn't there, complied – but that was it: he knew that it was all part of becoming a professional footballer. And so he did it. Albeit reluctantly.

Sometimes the school bus that picked the boys up at the gates of La Masía left without him. Training, yes. Resting, yes. And the PlayStation, any time of the day. Anything else: not a great deal. He had completed the first year of his secondary schooling in Rosario but, in Barcelona, he left his studies two courses short of a possible transition to university. He still excelled in gymnastics, but his childhood dream of becoming a PE teacher was soon abandoned. Celia would have liked him to work harder, in case a career in football failed to materialise, but Leo's lack of attention in school, a source of many a family discussion, was readily forgiven. When he rose to the Barcelona B side in 2004, aged just 17, he did not have much time to attend lessons, what with all the training and so many hours in the gym dedicated to putting on muscle. He had the perfect excuse. No more school, then; it lost its appeal when the objective of becoming a professional seemed even closer.

But there was something else that made it a bit less attractive. In Barcelona, at the Lleó XIII, he was 'different' – he was from abroad, had an accent, different customs, was quiet, and had growth problems; he was a figure of ridicule. He couldn't overcome that just by showing off his footballing skills so as to win the appreciation and unconditional respect of everyone, as had happened in Las Heras, because in the Catalan school there were others, his team-mates, who were just as good.

So he had to toughen up quickly. In public, Leo had become even more reserved than he had ever been in Argentina, with the attitude of a much older boy, serious, taciturn. He preferred to listen, remain seated, watching. Surrounded by older people, away from the ball, he didn't seem like a normal boy, rather someone who had switched off. His father says that he is more responsible than he is himself, his mother that he has a strong but quiet personality. All true, but Leo was, above all, a boy in exile.

In Rosario he had lived the healthy, if fantasy-filled life of a child. Dreaming of getting onto an 11-a-side pitch and playing. Getting into the first division with Newell's. Like his brothers and his father, he wanted to be a footballer. Later on came the training, the matches, including the important issue of the 11-a-side game urged on by the coaches, together with an obligation to behave responsibly; and the perennial question, 'you want to be a professional footballer, right?' At the age of 12 he had to answer categorically because the chance of emigrating had arisen. And football was no longer just a game.

Suddenly everything became black or white. Yes or no? Did he want to be a professional footballer? He would do whatever was necessary to achieve it. He didn't mind going abroad. Even at that early age he had to get it right; 'yes' was the only answer, he could not get it wrong. This wasn't pressure put upon him by his mentors, but failure had potentially disastrous consequences for the family. His father had left his job, his mother had said goodbye to her family, his brothers had left their friends behind. And if it didn't work out, what then? Many children of that age have felt such pressure that their progress has become permanently stifled.

There's a seed, one planted almost always subconsciously, which germinates in the minds of these youngsters. Leo had been heard saying, from the time that he was playing with the *Infantiles*, that he would one day play in the first division. At 11 he'd told his brother Rodrigo that he wanted to win the Ballon d'Or. This was no longer the innocent dream of a seven- or eight-year-old boy; it was effectively a refusal to allow the remotest possibility to enter his head that he would *not* achieve his objectives, that it would all end in disaster.

This happens to the majority of boys who take the step from playing for fun to playing because they want to earn their living from it. But especially to those who leave everything behind them: failure is not an option. If failure was ever to be considered (and it never would be), their whole world would fall apart. Leo and many other 12-, 13-, 14-year-old boys tell themselves every day of every week, with all the certainty of an adult, that everything is going to come good. And the reality is that things, particularly at that level of expectation, rarely do.

This extraordinary mindset doesn't just reject the possibility of failure, but is also accompanied by the suppression of emotion. You become desensitised.

Leo Messi arrived in Barcelona at the height of *Pujolismo*, a political programme begun by Jordi Pujol, the president of Catalonia, in 1980. Embraced by the Catalan middle classes, the Church and the intelligentsia, it still exists today. As an ideology it sought to create a Catalan ideal that would bring social cohesion to the Catalan nation in the post-Franco period.

One of the first directives was to restore a national holiday, to be held annually on 11 September. This date, seared into the minds of Catalan nationalists, recalls the nation's defeat by Spanish Bourbon troops in 1714 and the suppression of Catalan identity. It was clearly chosen to play on that sense of exclusion and victimisation that is so much a part of the conservative nationalist ideology that has become so popular. Harnessing and promoting feelings of discrimination by the central government based in Madrid (with justification, both historically and to the present day) has been the hallmark of 'Pujolism' and its political offshoot, CiU. This has often led to misperceptions internationally, as many observers confuse Catalonia with the conservative nationalistic ideology that claims to speak in its name. Quite intentionally 'Pujolism' perverts and occludes the fact that there are many ways to be a 'Catalan', and all of them are legitimate.

None the less a programme of positive discrimination took root as the regional administration bowed to Pujol's fantasy and implemented a number of radical reforms that further fed public sentiment. The most far-reaching was the imposition of the Catalan language in all state schools. This had its origin in the doctrine espoused by the pedagogue Alexander Gili, who taught that students should not be separated by language, and was based on his teaching experience in Quebec and the USA. His philosophy would eventually be enshrined in the 1983 Language Policy Act.

FC Barcelona became central to the policies of *Pujolismo*. Viewed by many as the Catalan national team, it was used by politicians to foment and export nationalistic sentiment, while at the same time integrating recent arrivals to Catalonia in such a way that they would 'become' Catalans. Nationalism used FC Barcelona and the club bowed to the pressure. The result of this was, and still is, the perverse notion that to be a true Catalan you must support Barcelona.

In Barcelona in the spring of 2001 having the surname Messi carried no weight whatsoever – the family was just one more group of South American immigrants. They had arrived from Rosario with only four months remaining in the school year, and Leo's sister María Sol had to integrate quickly into the state education system that would require her to learn a completely new language. The delay in payments and Barcelona's inflexibility meant that she was unable to put her name down for a private school where the language barrier would have been non-existent or dealt with differently.

She was approaching her sixth birthday.

State schools have an obligation to welcome and support new pupils, but most of the teaching is in Catalan. Castilian Spanish is introduced gradually. How an immigrant child adapts depends on many factors: the origin and social background of the other pupils, the percentage of other immigrant children (low in the case of the school that María Sol attended) and, of course, the willingness of the pupil to learn and adapt quickly. Maybe María Sol was just unlucky in the school that her parents were obliged to choose for her, but in general there is a certain conflict within Catalonian society that, while encouraging national pride, often discriminates both socially and economically against those who do not speak Catalan. The *sudaca* (a pejorative term used to refer to those of Latin American origin – the English equivalent would be 'spic') never receives the same kindness and acceptance as someone from white northern Europe. Schools made and do make a conscious effort to eliminate discrimination but in the street, at the shops, in the neighbourhood, the spectre of xenophobia hovers.

The Messi/Cuccittinis felt alienated, like 'bugs from another well' as they say in Argentina. So explained Sique Rodríguez in his book about the parents of footballers at La Masía in which Jorge Messi said, 'It was a very hard change. The customs, the idiosyncrasies, the values, the food … everything was different. We had to start from scratch. Practically from zero. Even the language was different. We had to adapt to Catalan.'

Argentinians are proud people, respectful of their roots and keen to maintain them. Perhaps no one had thought to give them a small potted history on Catalonia. Maybe they would have identified and empathised with a region that had suffered discrimination and suppression and was now attempting to assert itself by promoting its own language. Argentinians are no strangers to oppression. The fact is though that integration into this baffling new society was taking much longer than anticipated. In addition to the emotional upheaval and the perennial financial problems, FC Barcelona's perceived and continuing lack of sensitivity towards any number of issues meant that family suppers at the flat on Gran Via Carles III were becoming increasingly tense.

As matters continued to worsen, María Sol celebrated her sixth birthday. The family made a brave effort to make her day special, but it was clear that the child was unhappy, as the realisation dawned on her young mind that the world could be a hostile and unforgiving place. Both Celia and Jorge agonised to see her cry when she had to go to school. Seeking reassurance, Celia attended a parents' evening at the school and, asking if it would be possible during the meeting for the teachers to speak in Castilian, was told bluntly, 'Wait until the end and we'll explain it all to you.' They were reaching their limit, or so it seemed. Leo remembered that period in an interview with the Argentinian magazine *Para ti* in July 2005. '[María Sol] did not adapt either to the school, or to Catalan.'

Years later, in 2009, 'the Flea' did an interview with the Argentinian television station TVR. He was asked how he was getting on with learning Catalan. Messi admitted having difficulties initially but said he thought that he'd learned enough at school. 'Now it's easy,' he said. The presenter asked him to say, 'Good night, I am Lionel Messi' in Catalan, and Lionel, feeling under scrutiny, challenged and out of his comfort zone said, '*Bona nit ... y*'. The audience laughed at his inability to finish the phrase.

Curiously, the first public political statement made by Leo Messi was an honest defence of Catalan. On 6 December 2012, he did a show with his sponsor, Turkish Airlines, the company having appointed him one of their international ambassadors. The show was presented by this author. As often happens at such events, rules and boundaries were established between Leo's press chief and the representative of Barcelona's media department prior to questions from the press. No one counted on the fact that one of the journalists present would ask about the changes that the Minister of Education, José Ignacio Wert, was seeking to introduce in his Education Act, considered in Catalonia as an attack on the Catalan language. In this matter, FC Barcelona had issued a communication vindicating the use of Catalan in the educational system. 'The Catalan language and its teaching in schools forms part of our identity and is a key element for social cohesion and the harmony of our people.'

On hearing the question, I looked at Leo's head of press and Barcelona's representative. They looked at each other from a distance. They had a couple of seconds to react before Messi answered. I got a nod from Leo's media man. Go ahead, let him talk. Leo, an expert in dodging all manner of questions, had not prepared a reply. He said that since he had arrived in Catalunya he had, 'grown, studied and learned in Catalan' and that he had never had 'any problem' with it because, 'the more languages a boy knows, the better for him'. An answer considered exemplary by all those around him.

Nevertheless, eleven years earlier, the strong sense of remoteness and the general sense of alienation from this new culture, meant that half the Messi family wanted to go back to Argentina (and stay).

So, as has been seen, at the end of a difficult season Leo and family returned to Rosario for the summer. When they met at the house in Las Heras, there was no avoiding the big issue: María Sol was going to stay in Argentina. Nobody wanted to see her cry any more. Leo had to decide what he wanted to do next.

Jorge Messi recalls it in *Informe Robinson*: 'One day I asked Leo: "well, what do you want to do? Because the decision is yours, if you want to come back to Argentina, then we'll come back".' Jorge offered his son his unconditional love, his total support. The objective was clear: Leo wanted to be a footballer and Jorge wanted the consequences of his decision, whatever they may be, to be seen not as a defeat, but as another step towards the finishing line and a happy ending. Leo must have known that there were no guarantees that he would triumph. Not one. But he found himself at a crossroads and, having just reached 14, had to make a decision: either they all returned to Argentina or the family split.

'Leo looked at me,' continued Jorge, 'and then said: "No, I want to stay, I want to play football in Barcelona and want to play in the first division for Barcelona". That was Leo's decision, it was his decision: nobody forced him into anything. That's why I stayed with him. Celia stayed in Rosario with the children.'

The Messi/Cuccittinis were going to part company.

They wanted to believe it would only be a brief separation. They must have imagined that they would get together again before long. When you are aware that things are transient, you undoubtedly develop a greater mental strength. The Italian grandparents of Jorge and Celia knew that they were leaving their families for ever, that they were abandoning Europe, never to return. The Argentinian families who emigrated to Europe at the beginning of this century parted knowing that they would do everything possible to be reunited with their loved ones. And the Messi/Cuccittinis were clear that they were going to manage it somehow. You have to try to understand the thought process that led them to decide to separate: people like this have a different vision from most of us. Who would be separated from their wife or husband and three of their children, in order that another one of their offspring might make a success of himself in a sport that devours dreams?

Jorge admitted on *Informe Robinson* that his wife would have preferred for them all to come home and that, in Barcelona, 'for the children, it was as if they had changed ship and wanted to return. The truth is that several negative factors conspired to come together at a very critical time.'

Remember the Italian origin of the family in which everything revolves around *la mamma*. Leo was about to be motherless, with only his twice yearly visits and contact via telephone and the internet. Jorge stayed in Barcelona to look after Leo. Rodrigo would join them a few months later, but for the time being there was just father and son in the four-bedroom flat on Gran Via Carles III.

Leo adores his mother but his father is the one who tells him yes or no. The relationship is different to most as he also manages his affairs. He is a father who is a manager, a manager who is a father, with all that that entails. But Leo will never forget that the one who sacrificed his life was his old man.

Celia, Rodrigo, Matías and María Sol were going back to live in Rosario. Returning to Rosario? It was better to think, as Napoleon had at Waterloo, that they were not retreating but merely advancing in another direction. Was Rosario the point of arrival or the point of departure? Whatever it was, back in Las Heras they began to feel at home again.

'Both of us boys had girlfriends and we stayed in Argentina,' remembered Matías in the *Informe Robinson* programme. 'In that we were conscious of the fact ... that we were leaving him alone ... While he always says that the family is the most important thing he has, that we always helped him, that might be true; but at that moment, I, particularly, from my point of view, think that I left him on his own, you know? That's why I don't like to remember that time too much ...' And his last words come out falteringly. Put yourself in Matías's shoes for a moment: he had also been left, without a father figure and without a brother whom he adored.

Rodrigo was equally sincere: 'We didn't adapt very well. It was a problem, we were united but one person did something and the others did nothing. Therefore we all suffered in different ways. Unfortunately we ended up parting, but we're always coming and going. We travelled twice a year.'

Rodrigo's dream, his idea of becoming a professional footballer abandoned partly because of the lack of opportunity but also because of the lack of ambition needed to succeed, was to become a chef. He returned to Barcelona with his girlfriend Florencia to help his dad, Jorge, and Leo and enrolled on a cookery course. Ultimately his presence in the city would bring great familial comfort to Leo. Subsequently, Rodrigo sometimes seemed like the father and Leo one of his sons. Confusingly, the roles had changed.

Jorge Messi has admitted that if he had to make the decision all over again, to relive the whole story, he would never have let the family split up.

Around this time, Messi was on the point of going to Real Madrid.

In that same summer of 2001, Barcelona had a new general manager, Javier Pérez Farguell. In August, with Messi returning from Rosario fit and ready for the new season, Barça complained, this time via the players' status committee at FIFA, that Leo's transfer documents had still not arrived from Newell's, and without them his chances of playing would be seriously impeded. Meanwhile, Farguell glanced over Leo's first contract, drawn up some months earlier, and was perplexed to note that he had been guaranteed 100 million pesetas per season, an excessive amount for a youngster who could not be fully used yet. The decision had not been his and he now saw fit to rescind it.

A new contract for a lesser amount was renegotiated: the club would instead pay 20 million pesetas per season (€120,000). To be fair, Barcelona had been stung in the past, paying huge wages to young players, especially to Haruna Babangdida, who made his first-team debut at only 15 and was loaned to Terrassa in the second division four years later, where he was lost to elite football, and to the winger Nano, both of whom earned the same wages as a player with Barcelona B. The club was understandably reluctant to make the same mistakes twice. It was explained to Jorge Messi that there was a salary cap for the youngsters in the academy and they could not go above those limits. No salary caps or limits had been mentioned in previous negotiations.

Several meetings ensued as they tried to reach an agreement but it was not possible to bridge the gap between the old contract and the new. The club proposed gathering together all those responsible for bringing Leo over, sitting them round a table with all the directors and thrashing the matter out. These comprised Minguella, Joan Lacueva, Jaume Rodríguez from Barça's Human Resources department, Joaquim Rifé, the players' liaison Carles Naval, managing director Anton Parera and agents and lawyers. Inevitably they reached an impasse, as both sides refused to compromise. One of the directors could not understand why Jorge and Leo would not accept the club's offer and asked, 'Who does he think he is, Maradona? Let's close this now and he can go back to Argentina.'

That single statement sums up the attitude of some of the club members and illustrates perfectly the apparent lack of care and urgency over the previous few months. The Messi side looked on, appalled. The club clearly had no appreciation of the sacrifices the family had made. It seemed senseless now to continue betting everything on one card.

Negotiations seemed to have broken down irretrievably.

At the other end of a phone was Jorge Valdano, then sporting director of Real Madrid who confirmed that the 'Whites' would be prepared to pay 20 million pesetas a season, and maybe more. But he didn't want to go to war with Barcelona. If the player wanted to come along as a free agent, he would be welcome.

There was no official offer from Real Madrid, but neither was one needed; everyone knew the conditions. 'I think we'll go to Madrid,' someone in the room was heard to mutter.

Finally arms were twisted and a deal was struck, but in the process relationships were broken. Jorge Messi found out that there were some people whom he had trusted who had deceived him, a revelation that would have dire consequences. Writer Roberto Martínez says in his book *Barçargentinos*: 'Jorge Messi, sick and tired of waiting for communication from the club that never arrived, firstly asked for the situation surrounding Leo and his family to be resolved quickly. When he saw he wasn't getting any response he met with the new general manager to discuss whether he would be staying at Barcelona or returning to Buenos Aires. He got a shock. Pérez Farguell told him that some of those who had organised Leo's trip from Rosario were asking Barcelona for an enormous sum of money and the club could not pay this amount for a boy of 12. Surprised, Leo's father explained that all he was interested in was a job, somewhere to live with his family and the payment of Leo's treatment.'

Leo's representatives had told Jorge that Leo would earn 100 million pesetas a year and Jorge himself would have a paid job. The first never happened, and the second took months to be confirmed. Jorge found out that there were issues about commissions that led to a breakdown in trust that would never be repaired. From then on, Leo's father took charge of all his son's affairs, a decision that led to legal proceedings brought by one of the now redundant intermediaries, still ongoing, and which have already, on two occasions, been judged in favour of the Messis.

'So Pérez Farguell,' continues Roberto Martínez 'agreed to the family claim and formalised a new agreement. Jorge Messi reveals that "in reality the sum of €3,900 a month was for a job for me. Also Lionel received a variable sum dependent upon when he played and whether or not he won or drew. And the amount went up or down according to what level he played at."' The new contract was signed on 5 December 2001, nine months after the first one. So Leo, still without the international transfer documents, would, in an unprecedented move, receive a wage as if he was a Barcelona B player and Jorge also got a loan to do some building work on their flat in Barcelona, an ingenious way of compensating the family.

Finally everything off the pitch seemed resolved. There was no need to return Valdano's call.

In *El Gráfico*, years later, Leo explained how he felt as a 14-year-old when he was left alone with his father in Barcelona. 'When I left, I cried a lot, I cried for everything that I was leaving in Argentina, but at the same time I had a dream and I knew it was for the better.' Sometimes he hid quietly in his bedroom. 'I locked myself in my room and cried. I didn't want my father to see me.'

The youngsters at Barcelona used to go through the same routine that they still follow to this day: a bus would pick them up at the gates of La Masía, they'd go to school, eat together and then train, and then a few of them would rest in their rooms while the majority would be at the country house opposite the stadium, a home to hundreds of kids before the new Masía was inaugurated in 2011. Leo would sometimes go from school to home to eat something his father had cooked for him, watch television for a while, play on his PlayStation, or take a nap and then walk to training. Usually alone.

As the years passed he felt more comfortable with his team-mates and ended up having breakfast at La Masía; there, instead of going to school, he would benefit from the help from a teacher who would assist him and other players, who, because of match journeys or the hours of training, or more likely through lack of enthusiasm, did not make a habit of attending the Lleó XIII school. Nonetheless there were still many free hours to kill.

After half of his family had gone back to Argentina, the time when Leo did not have a ball at his feet began to drag. Jorge did what he could to entertain him. He would challenge his son on the PlayStation and they would often leave the apartment and stroll to El Corte Inglés or to Les Corts, the residential and commercial district crossed by the long Avenida Diagonal. No pitches there, or many parks either, on which to improvise a game of football. Jorge became his companion around the city, a playmate in any games, a temporary substitute for his friends, his moral support and the backbone of Leo's life in Barcelona. At the stage when most boys in their mid-teens are looking for any excuse to rebel against their parents, Leo, a 'boy-man', a kid with the responsibilities and experiences of a grown-up, found protection under his father's wing.

When things like that happen, when a father is obliged to take on the role of both father and mother, a confusion of identities can occur within a boy that can stunt his natural growth and maturity: yet another of the sacrifices that many aspiring professional footballers are obliged to make. When these roles become fudged, there is only one thing that stops an identity crisis and that is to focus on just why you have done what you've done. That, and the unconditional love of those who surround the child, is the cord that binds everything together and makes sense of it all.

Jorge, in his self-imposed role of single parent, aimed to rear Leo with a firm set of principles, not least a respect for authority and a clear appreciation of his roots. In this he has been successful. The problem for any single parent, coping with the breakup of the family unit, is to avoid over-protection. And yet over-protection is inevitable as they attempt to ward off accusations that the child is not being sufficiently well cared-for.

But when he says to his son, 'don't forget those who ask you for an autograph have spent hours waiting for you', as he has had to on some occasions, is it the manager or the father talking? In the worst of cases, when the father is unable to clearly separate the two roles, a situation can arise that is recognised by many sports psychologists: at the time when the father is playing the role of manager, the son is an orphan. And he looks for a father figure elsewhere. It's even worse, say the experts, to be an orphan with a father alive – when the father is still around, the child can become a resentful orphan. And at that point the father gets the feeling that he has no control over his own life, that he is in tow. And when someone has no control over their own lives, say the experts, they feel the need to control everything else that is around them.

And how does a footballer cope with this situation? At the end of the day he is the one responsible for the family upheaval. All successful players are not just aware of their sacrifices, but also feel an infinite debt of gratitude for everything their fathers, mothers, brothers, sisters have done, because without their efforts they would not have got to where they have. But there's more: at the same time they also carry a large feeling of guilt because they have broken the lives of those closest to them. So the son, to compensate, buys houses for the parents; he becomes a provider. And in the process the bricks and mortar serve as tangible evidence that effectively their lives have been turned around.

And, finally, what about the brothers? The ambivalence continues: wonderful, most think, we wouldn't live like this were it not for you, brother. But on the other hand, maybe you'll never know, but you have squashed our lives, everything in our lives has always centred around you. Who would want to be the brother of Lionel Messi or Cristiano Ronaldo?

Maybe it is because of these difficulties of dealing with a broken family that Jorge admitted he would not have split up the family. But out of all this came one advantage, as he told the magazine *Kicker*: 'The luck came at the time when the "one for one" state financial policy between the peso and the dollar was changed. When my wife and my other children returned to Argentina and I stayed with Leo in Barcelona, we lived in Barcelona on just half my Spanish salary, and the other half I was able to send to Argentina. It meant that shortly after the devaluation my wife and children could live well on the half we sent. That really was lucky.'

Back home, Matías showed his mother how to use the webcam so she was able to keep in touch with Leo, who in any case chatted to her every day on the internet and telephoned her every three days. Celia never failed to cry whenever she spoke to her son. And whenever she saw him on television.

Claudio Vivas, the former assistant to Marcelo Bielsa at Athletic de Bilbao and another Argentinian involved in the world of football, reflected upon the subject of absence and distance: 'Everything is a sacrifice. Those who know you most intimately know whether or not things are going well; in truth socially and economically things are good for us, but bad from the sentimental side of things. I know what Leo's mother or father feel because, on the one hand it's nice to be here, in Europe, but there are sacrifices that have to be made.'

Curiously where evidence of all this is seen the least is on the training ground, where players tend to hide any perceived weaknesses. The reason for this behaviour is perhaps best explained by the English player Joey Barton in the magazine *Football 24/7*: 'It's the same every Saturday before players take to the pitch. When they're in the hotel room or at home a couple of hours before kick-off, that's what's going through their minds. Most players, not all players, but a lot will be feeling vulnerable. Because no one wants to play badly, everyone wants to do well … and it's a sign of weakness to show it. But what I learnt, certainly from my own trials and tribulations as a human-being, was that actually it's not. It's actually a great strength to say "do you know what? I feel a little bit nervous and a little bit vulnerable." Once you voice that to your peers and it's out there, it almost dissipates it. Some people's retort to it is to shout and get loud: "I'm not nervous. I don't care. Blah, blah, blah." I can see that and say "but yeah, you are".'

If you look at Leo's first interviews in Spain in public, you see a young man, excited and mature for his age. When he was only 14, the Catalan television station TV3 visited him in his flat on Gran Via Carles III to interview him about his arrival, his first steps at the club, and he handled it like a veteran. Yes, he said, he was well, comfortable and calm. They asked him who his favourite Argentinian player was and he said, 'I would like to play with Aimar.' Javier Saviola was at Barcelona at that time and he had the good sense to add, 'but I like Saviola very much as well'. Leo has done many such carefully considered interviews. No sign of the stress the family was going through.

Neither the players nor the trainers at La Masía knew that Leo cried at night alone in his bedroom. 'It seemed like he was managing everything quite well,' remembers Alex García, one of his academy coaches. 'I think he was very clear about one thing: he knew what he'd done: "I have been separated from my mother and my brothers because I want to be a footballer; I don't know how far I'll get, or how long I'll last, but I know that I want it." He knew that would require sacrifices and cause suffering. I asked him how he was, because after all he was so far away from his family, and he said to me: "well, my mother is coming now with my brothers."' No room for weakness in public.

But the kid gave away clues: after spending three hours training, if you count the time getting there, changing, warm-up, exercises and shower afterwards, Leo always wanted to stay on the pitch a bit longer.

For a young footballer, someone who has not yet made it to the first team, this is what loneliness is: six o'clock on a Sunday afternoon, already dark if it's winter, a few hours after the morning game, in your house, a long way from home. The rest of the evening stretches before you. No one to go out with, nowhere to go anyway, tucked up in bed after supper, with only the sound of the television or, in the case of Leo, his father's 'goodnight' ... hard, very hard.

Sometimes Leo avoided those long afternoons by taking a long time over lunch in one of several Argentinian restaurants. Or sharing a new Xbox with a team-mate from one of the youth teams or an Argentinian friend from another club. He watched Argentinian television, followed the Argentinian league. His favourite films were the Argentinian *El hijo de la novia* ('The Son of the Bride') and *Nueve reinas* ('Nine Queens'); his favourite actor fellow country-man Ricardo Darín. Leo never lost his Argentinian accent, or the customs of his country. He ended up recreating a sort of Rosario in Barcelona. 'I have always said that he is the most Argentinian footballer from Argentina that I have ever known,' said Cristina Cubero, who was very close to him during his first, tentative steps in Spain.

But, in reality, shutting yourself off from the alien world around you is the only way of preserving your identity. People always say that integration in a strange new society is the best way forward for any newcomer, but in doing so you deny yourself and all you hold dear – you die just a little. The footballer from South America, with a few notable exceptions, feels obliged to come to Europe to earn money and gain prestige, but normally returns to his roots at the end of his career. He wants, like everyone else, to die at home.

Leo is not your typical Argentinian (a subject that will be considered later in the book) but he is certainly very Argentinian. If an Argentinian wanted to describe himself it would probably be in this way: an expansive Italian who speaks Spanish, thinks like a Frenchman and would love to be an Englishman (the very words overheard in a bar in Rosario), but Leo is simply a reserved individual who adores Argentina. His talent with the ball helped him to adapt well (it is much easier to be accepted in a foreign country when you're good at what you do), but in his fight, consciously or otherwise, to preserve his identity he relied on the support of his environment (his family), on Barcelona, who, despite espousing the Catalan language, never forced him to speak it, and also on the Argentinian community in Barcelona, a group that welcomes all new arrivals and which shares Leo's pride in their customs, accent and food.

'The Flea' often visited an Argentinian restaurant, Las Cuartetas, in Carrer de Santaló, the first one he discovered. He enjoyed it so much he went there frequently and he was almost always the last to leave. On another occasion when out strolling he came across another Argentinian restaurant in Hostalrich, a town not far from Barcelona. He enjoyed that, too, and went there several times. 'How about going to Hostalrich?' was another way of saying, 'Let's go and spend some time in Little Argentina.'

At this stage, Barcelona had asked him to have breakfast regularly at La Masía, which he and the others were given as part of the endocrinological work carried out by the club relating to the players' diet. At the same time the club doctor, Josep Borrell, decided to gradually wind down the growth hormone treatment Messi had been receiving. At the age of 14, a controlled diet and a suitable physical fitness programme would, in the doctor's opinion, help him to reach his maximum height without further hormone treatment. 'In Spain he grew in a way that you wouldn't believe,' remembered Jorge Messi in *El Gráfico*. In fact, he grew 29 centimetres in as many months. But he often swapped his diet for the restaurants of his Argentinian friends who would feed him up with gigantic Scaloppe Milanese with potatoes, and milk pudding to finish.

After a few months in Rosario, Leo's brother Rodrigo returned permanently to Barcelona with Florencia, now his wife, and their baby son, Agustín, who Leo spent hours looking after. In 2005 he told Cristina Cubero: 'I am always with them. While my sister-in-law makes dinner, I am with the boy. It's always me who puts him to bed at night. At first I used to sing him lullabies, but my brother, my sister-in-law and even the baby would laugh, so now what I do is walk around the house with little Agustín in my arms, but not singing, just walking. And he's soon fast asleep. One day, I'll have children too ...' His brother worked as a chef at the Hotel Rally and at El Corte Inglés, and was even in touch with Ferran Adrià, the legendary chef-owner of El Bulli, who had a workshop in Barcelona. He could have worked with Adrià, but preferred to look after his brother.

Leo relied on others to look out for him as protectors. Pablo Zabaleta was one such person. Zabaleta was captain of the Argentinian Under 20 side with which Leo played his first international matches and they sealed their friendship when the wing-back played for RCD Espanyol of Barcelona. He willingly took Leo under his wing, extricating him from restaurants when he started to become recognised, advising him, guiding him and helping him steer clear of dubious company.

Leo bought a dog, Facha, a boxer he used to take for walks around Castelldefels. Another companion.

Oscar Unari, another friend of Leo's, who today plays for Almería, shared many confidences. 'If there's one thing that he won't talk about, one thing that hurt him, it's his uprooting. It happened to me. I'm from a small town, much smaller than Rosario, with 15,000 inhabitants, and as a thirteen-year-old I started to go around on my own, without a father, or a mother, to find my life in Buenos Aires. From a town of 15,000 to a concrete jungle.'

Javier Mascherano, like so many others, knows the feeling. 'I have heard Leo say that when he was younger he went through phases, after training, when he would return to his room and say "I can't take any more". It's logical, it happened to me, even though I wasn't so far away. When I was thirteen or fourteen, I also left my home in Rosario in search of my dreams in Buenos Aires: you have the uncertainty of not knowing what's going to happen, if you're really wasting your time or not. You think, "I'm here and perhaps I'm missing out on the chance to live a whole host of things, and I don't know if tomorrow what's to come will be worth it or not." Life is beautiful now … when things work out. You go in search of your dream, the important thing is to try. Why resist when you feel bad? It's obvious. Leo's life is playing football, where he feels happiest, when he goes out to train, when he touches the ball … In truth what motivates us is our passion for this sport. So we have to resist the temptation to give up.'

'You despair, you cry,' says Pedro the Barcelona winger who left the Canary Islands to join La Masía when he was 16 years old. 'It's hard, because you don't have anyone, let's says "close", to tell your problems to. Yes, you have people, a lot of people who work at the club, team-mates who can help you, but at this time you need someone closer, your family, your parents. And when you have them on the telephone it's difficult to tell them all this type of stuff, it's all much colder. And on top of that you don't gel with the other boys of your age who are not footballers, because you are no longer involved with the things that interest them. For us everything happens very quickly. Footballers have fiancées from a very young age, they have children quickly, they mature earlier and live life at an unusual speed and intensity.'

'I always say that we blow our own trumpets too much writing books about Leo, Piqué, Fàbregas ...' says the coach Rodolfo Borrell. 'Those are fantastic stories but they are the exception. You hear many traumatic tales of footballers who at the age of twelve leave home only to return at seventeen having failed at school, at football, with a family in disarray, and a five-year absence during which time they may well also have lost their friends.'

Leo went through much physical and psychological pain before becoming the very best at what he does. You need that strength in football in order to reach the finishing line, and you need the ability to make sacrifices. And perseverance.

But it was many years before he stopped crying after speaking on the telephone to his mum.

2

Making His Way

Rodolfo Borrell, his first coach at Barcelona:

If he was suffering we didn't really notice. All we, as coaches, saw was a lad enjoying the sheer thrill of playing. Perhaps, with hindsight, that was the only time he was enjoying himself. He was always outstanding but, unusually for such a young player, he bore on his shoulders a huge weight of responsibility. This is an enormous burden for a young lad of 13, and the pressure could have broken him, but for Leo it had the opposite effect. He had utter conviction that he would make it, and that belief, a total belief in his destiny, enabled him to cope and overcome whatever trials he faced.

Additionally, he had extraordinary passion. I've never seen a player with such zeal. He was desperate to train, to run around the field, to do whatever was asked of him. And when we finished training he would ask if he could take free kicks. The others had left, and he still wanted to carry on! On his day off he'd suddenly appear, watch other teams and I swear that if we asked him to join, he would have! It was his day off, for God's sake! Every other player enjoyed their rest day, went to the cinema or met with friends, whatever. But not Leo. Maybe that was his idea of rest and recreation. To play football. Maybe he had nothing else to do.

I vividly remember a particular occasion when I'd gone to the gym at the Mini Stadium, just before his team was about to start a training session. I was no longer his coach as he'd left the Infantiles level a year or two before. Like all the other coaches I spent hours there watching, chatting and learning about the up-and-coming players. That is, after all, part of our role in the club. To observe. As it happened it was one of the days when the kids were allowed to spend some time in the gym. His coach at that time had not arrived and the scene is imprinted on my memory. There were Víctor Vázquez, Piqué and I can't remember who else, stretched out on a mat, throwing a tennis ball between them, and Messi, the bastard, working on his own. As if the coach was there. I'm not suggesting that the exercises were right, maybe he was doing the wrong kind of work, but I remember that, it was unusual.

A few hours later I met him opposite the Mini Stadium, and I stopped him and said, 'with your attitude you may or may not make it to the first team. But you'll certainly become a professional, because what you have, that passion, is not normal.'

I can't remember if he answered or not.

Leo is being interviewed on the Catalan television channel TV3. His first months at Barcelona had been far from successful. He could, at first, only play friendlies. And he got injured in the second official match with the *Infantiles* B side. He returned to Rosario to recover and get his career back on track before going back to Barcelona to start all over again. In the new season, he was playing more regularly and scoring.

Interviewer: We're now going to talk with Leo Messi, one of the players from the lower ranks of the club, who scored twice in the recent game. Last season he could hardly play at all because he had an injury. I suppose you're happy to be able to return to play with your team-mates and score goals?

Messi (his voice has not yet broken – he's still a boy): Yes, last season I played just one game and after just a few minutes of the second I was injured, but now I'm back and …very happy.

Interviewer: Last season you weren't able to really develop and enjoy playing for your new team. Just so our viewers know who you are, you come from Newell's Old Boys.

Messi: Yes, Newell's Old Boys from Rosario, Argentina.

Interviewer: Newell's has produced some great players. Mauricio Pochettino is just one who comes to mind. He's now with PSG and once played for Espanyol.

Messi: Sensini and Batistuta came from there too, a lot of great players have come from there.

Interviewer: For those who don't know you, you play number 10, a classic Argentinian number 10, an '*enganche*' as they say in your country, how would you describe yourself as a footballer?

Messi (looking away, hesitantly): Err... well, I don't know, it's not for me to describe myself.

Interviewer: But what is clear is that you play behind the frontmen, in the middle of the pitch, with more freedom of movement to take advantage of your characteristics.

Messi: Yes.

Interviewer: And this season. What is your objective? Consolidate with Barça? Get the form and the rhythm that you had in Argentina that perhaps you haven't been able to find here yet?

Messi: Yes, it's still missing, after my injury I still need to find my rhythm.

Interviewer: So these are the words of Leo Messi, one of the future stars, one of the great prospects of Barcelona FC.

Leo, it should be added, always struggled to explain what made him what he is.

Season 2001–02: Taking off

Recovered from his injuries, Leo began the 2001–02 season with the Junior B side coached by Albert Benaiges. The boys of '87, a historic generation of players from La Masía that included, among others, Cesc Fàbregas and Gerard Piqué, shared a dressing room for two and a half seasons. This team, usually playing the 3-4-3 instilled in them at the academy, deserves special mention as representative of one of the greatest generations ever to have come out of La Masía. At the start of the season, a typical line-up might be:

Dani Plancheria; Marc Valiente, Piqué, Carlos Algar; Cesc, Rafa Blázquez, Robert Giribert, Marc Pedraza; Toni Calvo, Víctor Vázquez and Juanjo Clausi.

And Messi?

Leo's transfer issues still hadn't been resolved and he was still ineligible for national competitions, so he was to be in and out of Benaiges' team, and when he did play he was placed wide on the left. 'He loved playing as an *enganche*, between the lines and enjoyed coming inside,' recalls the Junior B coach. 'We put him wide because for the system we played it suited us better. But he had a tendency to come in between the lines, where he really wanted to be. He knew that with a couple of mazy runs, he would find himself in front of goal.' Leo, therefore, took some time to fit in and adapt to the discipline. Marc Pedraza played in the *enganche* role behind Víctor Vázquez, and only when he left for Espanyol did the position go to Cesc and, sometimes to Leo. 'He was a very quiet, calm boy, but you could read a lot from his expressions. Even when you saw him with his team-mates, he seemed quite forlorn, that's the truth,' recalls Benaiges.

The Junior category was divided into two parts: Junior A (17-year-olds) played in a league with Junior B of Espanyol, and the Junior B (16-year olds) of Espanyol had the A of Barcelona as rival. It was a tacit agreement between the two big Catalan clubs so that the A sides could share the titles between them. The generation of '87 therefore found themselves competing for the league against the Espanyol Junior A side, in other words against boys a year older than them, some of whom went on to play in La Liga, players like Sergio Sanchez, today at Málaga, and Marc Torrejón (now at Racing Santander).

But for the first time in the history of the Catalan competition, a Junior B side became champions against an A side: in the twenty-third game of the season, seven games before the end, in the Damm stadium, the *culés* of '87 won the league. In their last match against their city neighbours, Cesc, Piqué and Rafael Blázquez (another pearl of the Barcelona academy whose career was blighted by a terrible car accident) all scored to earn a comfortable 3–0 win. The Junior B side also won the Catalonia Cup, and, in fact, just about every title on offer apart from the Nike Cup, where they went down in the semi-finals against Atlético de Madrid.

The league win against Espanyol coincided with a change on the coaches' bench where Benaiges handed over to a former Barcelona player who had finished his playing career at a modest club, Gramenet: Tito Vilanova had suffered a knee injury that stopped him from performing at the right level and he had been promised a team from the academy when he retired. At the start of 2002, halfway through the season, he began his work as a coach, at the same time, coincidentally, as the arrival of a communiqué from FIFA finally declaring in favour of Barcelona in their dispute with Newell's, still reluctant to agree to Leo's transfer without compensation from the Spanish club: FIFA agreed that a 13-year-old child should have the chance to be a professional footballer if he so desired.

Messi was enrolled into the Spanish Football Federation on 15 February. At last, one year after his arrival in Barcelona, nothing could prevent him from playing any game, in any competition. One less hurdle to jump.

'Boys,' said a serious Vilanova to his young charges at the end of the following day's training session. 'We have a new player with us.' They all looked at each other; there was no new face ... 'Leo Messi. Leo is our signing.' The group, to a man, cheered, applauded and congratulated the young Argentinian.

The 17th of February, Can Vidalet Stadium. Opponents, Esplugues de Llobregat. Messi starts the game on the bench. He comes on in the second half to make his debut in the national championship. He scores three goals. Final result, 1–14.

Tito began to use him as a number 9, in the middle. His first time ever in the position of false number 9, an elusive role between the lines that would make him difficult to target. Cesc, who usually played in front of the defence at number 4, moved to being the organiser behind Messi.

It has sometimes been said that the real star of that generation was Víctor Vázquez, a young man brimming with quality and goal-scoring talent who finished up playing in the first team in a match against Rubin Kazan, alongside Leo. He got injured, though, and sadly never wore the Barcelona shirt again.

'In the 3-4-3, before Tito, Leo played wide, but with the new coach Leo and I began to play as striker or in the hole just behind; bit by bit we developed an understanding,' explained Vázquez. 'We worked well together. If we needed more speed up front, we'd put Messi as striker because he was the fastest, and you could pass the ball to him. If in another game the defenders were more aggressive, I'd be up front and Messi would play behind. And Cesc behind both of us! Mad!'

'Tito was the first to play Leo in a particular position on a regular basis,' remembers Charly Rexach. 'Tito came to tell me that he had a bloke in his team who was gifted, a phenomenon. "Oh, yes, I know who you mean," I said. People sometimes think a well co-ordinated team happens by accident, but that one was full of very good players and Tito knew a lot about football. And it was his tactically intelligent brain as a footballer that he brought to coaching. From then on things really began to motor for Leo. When Messi was small he was entertaining to watch because he scored more goals than the rest, because he would go around three or four players, and also because he would sometimes overegg the pudding. And we thought, when he grows we'll tell him to stop milking it and pass the ball more. But you had to let him grow his way. And Tito was the first to make him go into a game, with a footballing plan, a tactic. And Barcelona generally have one advantage: they are better than other teams, so they can play as they wish. So you can try players in different positions, experiment a bit more.'

'Tito would talk to us about all the other sides as if they were excellent,' explains Junior player Julio de Dios to Jordi Gil in his biography of Cesc, *Descubriendo a Cesc Fàbregas* ('Discovering Cesc Fàbregas'). 'He would have all the data relating to all of the other Juniors: if a forward had so many goals, or if this player was fast or had a particular technique. Speaking to us like this about our opponents meant that we were always on our toes and motivated. He gave us just enough information to make sure we weren't overconfident, but at the same time he drove us mad with the blackboard and his strategy. None the less we beat them all!'

Tito Vilanova knew that he had something special on his hands: he loved Piqué's leadership qualities and the quality and competitiveness of Cesc. And Blázquez, and Vázquez, and defender Marc Valiente. But Leo had something else. 'I never saw a boy as demanding of himself as he was,' says the former Barcelona coach. 'Sometimes he would play a fantastic game but would then leave the pitch angry with himself because he thought he could have done better.' That's how practically all of them were in that Junior B side, but Leo pushed himself to the limit.

After that game at Can Vidalet, Leo played six more matches and celebrated winning the league, his first title with Barcelona.

'You looked forward and you saw Messi,' remembers Víctor Vázquez, who has continued with his career at Bruges. 'And you said, "fuck me, mate, I know we're going to do something good here". And you also had Cesc behind you, and you said, "something's going to happen, you're going to pass the ball, Cesc is going to give you a good pass back, you're going to combine well together and it's going to finish up a goal". We were so much better than any other side. Never have I seen a team as superior as we were at the lower levels. Sometimes at walking pace we would win 10–0 and the gaffer used to say: "hey, do some running!" And we used to answer him: "What have we got to run for?" It's just that it wasn't necessary, you passed the ball, and in three or four passes you were where you wanted to be.'

'They were an extraordinary group, with some very competitive players, true winners. At just fifteen or sixteen years old they had the maturity of people of twenty-two or twenty-three,' says coach Alex García, who inherited the group from Tito the following year. 'Everyone knew that Messi, Piqué and Cesc were different. They were the mainstays of the team and they accepted it. It's easy to say now with hindsight, but the fact is you could see that no other team had players of this quality.' Cesc is honest: 'In any case, if at that moment they had told us that one day all three of us would form part of the Barcelona first team, the three of us would have said that that was impossible. Perhaps one or two, but three?'

'I said to Leo one day that I could quite happily sit down on the bench and leave him to enjoy his football; the truth is that I saw a Maradona in him,' recognises Tito.

'Leo had qualities that were totally different from ours,' recalls Cesc. 'And as much as they say that I was good, or that Piqué was this, or whoever was that … the truth is that we all had characteristics very similar to all the others. We were better, because we were better, but we didn't have anything markedly different; he, though, had qualities that set him apart. You know he's going to go to your left, but he still goes past you. You see it a thousand times on television and you say "how is it that they don't get the ball off him and he always goes to the left?" Even knowing and anticipating that you still can't. Seriously, I'm telling you, he is gifted.'

'I was the director of the Villarreal football school.' This is Juan Carlos Garrido, the former boss of the Castellon club. 'Our paths would cross when he played against my sides and I remember that he used to win games on his own. There was a tremendous difference between him and the rest of the players. The first time I saw him was at a summer tournament organised by Villarreal: for 14-year-olds. The final of this tournament was between Barça and Villarreal. Half-time arrived and Villarreal was winning 1–0 I think, and then Messi came on in the second half. The game finished 1–3. Messi scored all three goals. It was like a revolution, something extraordinary.'

The president, Joan Gaspart, would occasionally spend Saturday mornings by the pitches next to the Camp Nou, watching whatever match happened to be going on, either by himself or accompanied by Charly Rexach. 'I never said "that number 10 is one of a kind and is going to be the best player in the world". I never said it. That he was very good, yes, but no more. I never said it, and it never entered my head that he would get to where he has got. But he got the ball and he would do things differently from the rest. And it was strange because he was a very shy young man, but when you saw him on the field he was the leader of the pack. And, what's more, he liked to milk it. If he could dribble round three, better than two. He was fast and there was something "hard-nosed" about him – he wouldn't run away from the physical battle, wouldn't get scared after a tackle. He was one of those types of boys who leaves a great impression on you.'

That youth team trained, like the majority of the sides in the academy, on the pitches next to the Mini Stadium, about 500 metres from the Camp Nou and the space next to La Masía where the senior players trained. Rarely did their paths cross, however, even though three of them were Leo's fellow countrymen: Juan Román Riquelme, Roberto Bonano and Javier Saviola.

Riquelme had tremendous quality, an attacking midfielder who dictated the pace of the game, albeit sometimes with a certain coldness. But he played at the Camp Nou. With the big boys. And with the national side. Juan Román was, then, in Leo's eyes, one of the greats. When their paths did cross, at barbecues organised by Minguella at his home in Barcelona, for instance, Leo would somehow become even smaller and he would stare at him with his head bowed, eyes like saucers, the top of his head just reaching Riquelme's chin – with the apparent awe of a penitent in the presence of his god. For their part, Saviola and Bonano would stop and ask him how things were going and from time to time invite him for an ice cream and chat for a while. When Leo needed them, following a stroke of bad luck the following season, they were there for him.

FC Barcelona's first team was, a year after the departure of Luis Figo and Pep Guardiola, suffering from lack of leadership. The money that came in from the sale of the Portuguese midfielder had been spent badly on players who failed to make the grade (Emmanuel Petit, Marc Overmars, Alfonso Pérez, Gerard López), and others who made little impact, like Riquelme and Saviola. Carlos Rexach, on the sidelines, never really managed to convince the fans, and the team, with Rivaldo and Kluivert as its stars, were left the wrong side of the title doors, finishing fourth in the league and ending up as Champions League semi-finalists, having lost to Madrid. The institutional crisis, with Joan Gaspart receiving little support from the faithful, would eventually translate into five years without a single league title.

In those early days, Leo still changed in a corner of the dressing room, away from the rest. His team-mates kept their distance, not knowing what to say to him or how to draw him out. There seemed to be an invisible, protective wall around him.

During breaks in training, Leo would have a drink of water by himself, a ball tucked under his arm or resting by his feet. Always near. He entertained himself with little touches on the ball while the others talked about their plans for the day, or about school, or about their girlfriends.

He was the first to shower, when there was no one else in the dressing room. Or the last. But normally he'd get there first, change in five minutes and then rush to meet his father who was usually waiting for him outside. His team-mates thought he didn't want to shower with them at the same time, that he was wary of them. Too wary.

Sometimes he said goodbye, sometimes he didn't. Usually it was a raise of the hand, and a quiet 'see you tomorrow'.

It wouldn't be long before the veterans in the group approached the new boy from Argentina.

Unsurprisingly, Gerard Piqué was the first to approach him. A typical practical joker, he hid his clothes while he was showering, moving them to another hook. Leo returned with a towel around his waist and couldn't find his things. He became nervous, agitated. Five or six of the boys began laughing but they quickly returned his clothes before things got out of hand. 'Where are you from? What brings you to these parts?' asked Piqué. 'You can talk to us, nothing's going to happen to you, we won't bite.'

'Sorry, I'm just quiet,' replied Leo.

Piqué had opened the door for him. From that moment on he spoke more. But not much more.

'We thought he was a mute,' says Cesc, laughing.

'Messi is very shy, and I think he always will be, even though he is a bit better now. He is very respectful of people. There are those who say it's because he is the best player in the world, as if he is super-important and has an inflated opinion of himself. But I think that this is more the case with players like Cristiano Ronaldo. Not Leo, though. He's more of an "I don't feel comfortable here, I wonder what this person is going to say to me" type of person.' This is how Víctor Vázquez, who tried to discover if they shared any common interests, remembers it: 'We tried to get him united with the group but he was more "no, I don't fancy it, I'd rather go home". He was the type of boy who just wanted to be with his family. He wasn't like the rest of us. We could spend an afternoon laughing and joking, or at the cinema, or at El Corte Inglés, or just hanging out in the neighbourhood where anything could happen.'

Leo did not live at La Masía, so he missed the nightly goings-on on the second floor where the bedrooms were situated and where the boys met to study. Or, rather, where they were meant to study. Sometimes someone would turn off the lights. Then some unfortunate, usually Piqué, whose cheekiness had done more than enough to deserve it, would get slapped on the back of the head. It was all done in fun and Piqué enjoyed it and laughed along with the rest of them. But that wasn't Leo's scene.

'He was very shy,' the full-back Oriol Palencia recalled in Jordi Gil's book. 'He went out, played, and nothing else. He wasn't one of those types that puts himself in the forefront and says things like "come on, give more to the team, we need to work harder, come on guys" or stuff like that. He was much more in the background, but playing he was in a completely different class. In the *Infantiles* A group it was a bit more difficult for him because his physical short-comings were more noticeable. He was very good, fast, skilful. But shorter. And as he responded to the physical conditioning, at Junior level he was explosive. But a whole year went by before he opened his mouth, or so it seemed. It was when we went to play a couple of tournaments with the Junior B side that he really opened up.'

His family insist that Leo is not shy, he's just reserved. This is worth reiterating because the difference is crucial and it is some-thing he learned at home, a code of behaviour instilled in him in Argentina: he would speak, if necessary, on the pitch, respect the group and take on whatever role was assigned him. No more. His attitude was extreme, but in many ways also reflected his immigrant status. He was, after all, a stranger in a strange land.

The consequences and effects on any youngsters forced to leave their country and adapt to a strange new environment are too numerous to mention. One constant, though, is their ability to mature faster than their indigenous peers. Threatened by an alien culture and maybe a new and baffling language, they feel vulner-able and, like any creature plucked from its natural habitat, quickly develop survival skills that often show themselves in a lack of trust, at least until new friendships are forged. Often the best form of self-protection is the simplest. Merge into the background. Offer no threat. And, if you're lucky enough to have them with you, enjoy the protection of a loving family.

The pressures heaped on young footballers aiming for the top make them age before their time, as they miss out on the natural develop-mental and emotional growth of childhood. They are entering a cut-throat, adult world and are suddenly exposed to a level of pressure that many 30-year-olds would find daunting. Even more so for the young migrant footballer. The child remains, though, locked inside the man-child, and every so often his plaintive cry can be heard...

This makes them complex, and for many people hard to under-stand. And sometimes it creates instability.

'Leo is smart, he knows when he has to be good, when to joke, when to be serious,' explains Cesc. 'I notice these things a lot. Many of us here are, at times, out of control, loose cannons who say things without thinking ... but Leo is very smart, he knows how to handle himself, how to pick the right moment. We know how he is on the pitch, but in his house, or in the dressing room, he always knows what he has to do and when he has to do it.'

But an immigrant boy is still a boy.

And it's that young boy we see when he gets cross at being substituted, or when he collides with an opponent or a team-mate. Nobody's perfect. Can we accept it? These conflicts come from the child within, the child in all of us. Both family and club wanted to make the most of this part of his character: if it didn't exist, an essence of who Leo was, the pleasure of playing, would be gone, would be lost. Those close to him believe that if he retains the characteristics of a child, he will continue to get pleasure from playing; that without them he will simply be a footballing automaton.

And because part of Leo is still a child, he cries. Not only the tears of someone who misses his mother or his brothers, private tears. Also, the tears that flow after losing a match.

'I saw him cry after one game, I think it was against Espanyol,' remembers Víctor Vázquez. 'We lost at their ground when we were playing in the league. We were in the Junior A side, and that particular game wasn't a decisive result, because we ended up winning the league anyway. We had some chances towards the end, me as well as him, that we missed loads of chances lost, their goalkeeper stopped everything.'

They were 15 years old. Víctor and Leo entered the dressing room together, Leo with his head bowed. He sat down, Víctor next to him. Messi covered his face with his shirt, just as he did when he missed that penalty against Chelsea in the semi-final of the Champions League in April 2012. 'I thought, he's missed a lot of chances, he hasn't played badly but I guess he is upset. Later I put my arm around his shoulder and asked him: "Anything wrong?" And when I saw he wasn't talking I pulled his shirt a bit. He was crying. "Fuck me," I thought. He really felt it. He didn't cry loudly, like many people do. His eyes looked watery, and tears were falling. There was such anxiety. And he said to me, "I'm sorry, I couldn't score, I feel really bad, I couldn't help you win." And me as well, fucked, thinking: "holy shit, we couldn't score any goals and the chances are that now we're going to lose the league because of this one stupid game." He was crying with rage. And, of course, despite what I was thinking, I was trying to console him by saying, "don't worry, we're going to win the league".'

They showered and Víctor carried on talking to him, and he promised him that they would win the next game. A joke or two. We'll stick three past our next rivals. We'll win next week, wait and see. We go now and have something to eat with the family and everything will be forgotten, believe me. And Leo said, 'Okay, maybe, but I'm so upset because I couldn't score, because we lost.'

In the next game Leo scored a hat-trick.

There were four games left until the end of the season, and after the defeat they were six points behind Espanyol. But their Catalan rivals lost two games and Barça won all theirs. And Víctor and Leo remembered that tearful day. He was the first to say, 'See how everything can change?'

One of the trials of the man-child is the growing realisation that he is not the centre of the universe and that in the future things will not be exactly as they are now. The reference points in life – home, family, friends – begin to shift as the wider world and new experiences start to encroach. The sooner this lesson is learned and embraced, the better for the individual's emotional growth.

When Leo went to Italy with Barcelona's Junior A side everything started to make sense and he began to integrate himself into the group. He became one of them, rather than an outsider. As a consequence, the world became a slightly bigger place.

Víctor Vázquez tells the story: 'Messi had gone back to Argentina following a serious injury with the *Infantiles* and when he returned everything was, if not exactly new to him, almost. He was practically starting from scratch. When we went to Italy, to Pisa, for a Junior tournament, we were put up in a hotel that was a bit like a summer camp. Here we spent twenty-four hours a day with him and we started to joke about with him, so he would become more confident.'

That Junior side of Tito Vilanova's was invited to compete for the Maestrelli trophy in Pisa, and Leo at 14, wearing the number 14 shirt, finished up as top goalscorer and player of the tournament that Barcelona won by beating Parma 2–0 in the final. Messi also won the virtual league on the PlayStation.

'I remember that Piqué, the first or the second day, took all Leo's things out of his room, his PlayStation, his clothes, his bed even, everything – and left his room completely empty. We hid it all somewhere else.' Vázquez smiles mischievously as he recalls the event. 'Poor Messi. After eating he went up for a rest, for a siesta, and we all trooped up silently behind him without him noticing, and he arrived at the room, and stared. He became serious, his eyes like dinner plates, and he started to cry. But really crying, the poor lad. Throwing himself on the ground: they've stolen everything, I haven't got anything, no phone, no PlayStation, nothing ... And Piqué, laughing, recording it on his phone, and all his stuff hidden in another room. We told him what we'd done, but not until a few hours later, and a team-mate had to take him to another room to rest. He was so wound up. Piqué is a real practical joker, and we laughed a lot that day, poor lad.'

But from that moment everything changed. Leo wanted to be part of the group dynamic, he knew them all a bit and he knew they were a healthy, competitive group and that they respected him – in the sometimes strange world of football, being the target of a joke is a good thing, a sign of respect, of belonging. 'Well, Leo never let himself go totally, because he isn't the sort of person to let himself go, and didn't get involved the way Piqué or Cesc or even I did,' says Vázquez. 'But he laughed more, he was more integrated, he participated more. You might have been eating and he'd play a joke on you like hide your fork or your glass of water. And we spent a lot of time playing on the PlayStation. I've never played as much PlayStation as I did during that tournament, we were playing all hours. We had loads of free time and it was all PlayStation tournaments, PlayStation tournaments, and he always won. And I mean, *always*. We played for a bit of money, nothing huge, probably about €10 or 15, always joking with him. I used to say to him: "Fucking hell, this fucking dwarf wins everything, the lot." We tried to get him off the PlayStation, and beat him, on something called Golden Goal. We put on a game that would last for an hour and whenever someone let in a goal that person would drop out and someone else take over. Messi played for three hours without a break ... and there was us, sick to death of him!'

Víctor Vázquez and Toni Calvo, two of Leo's best friends in Barcelona were the first people to call him *enano* – dwarf. 'And Leo, to get his own back, would speak to us in Argentinian slang. We didn't understand a word,' Calvo says. An insult is an insult if it is taken as one, and Leo knew that it was not said with any malice, and that to reject the nickname would have been to show disrespect to the group and a sign of weakness.

'We saw a completely different Leo on that trip,' says Cesc. 'I don't know if we made him feel more comfortable, but we certainly paid more attention to him. It's that sometimes, when you see such an introverted boy, it does something to you, you don't want him to think that he's not part of everything, but nor do you want him to think he deserves special attention. You have to measure what you do. We were adolescents, we used to hold little parties ... without drinking alcohol or anything ... but anyway ... Leo opened up ... imagine just how much he opened up that everyone remembers that trip ... He was still introverted, but something good happened in Italy.'

At Barcelona airport, the left-sided midfielder Robert Giribert had to ask for something from someone he didn't know. He couldn't pluck up the courage. Off his own bat, Leo got up and asked on his behalf. The boys looked at each other.

Back in Barcelona, Leo's flat was transformed into the meeting place for the next round of PlayStation.

As often happens, the passage of time created a certain order and unity in the team. Every player started to become more comfortable in his role, and every role was defined by the shared experience and growing interaction between the team members, by the common cause. The team were beginning to gel. The generation of '87 spent two and a half years together before the departure of Piqué and Cesc, and during that time Leo went from being an unknown to a valuable member of the team, although there were still minor hurdles to be overcome. In the eyes of his team-mates he was both strong and fragile at the same time. There were many in Rosario who would have done anything for him, those who wanted to sit him on their lap and look after him; his grandmother, the girlfriend from school, his mates from the schoolyard who followed his lead and always wanted him in the centre of the photograph, the coaches who asked the referees to look after him, and the referees who didn't have to be asked.

But in Spain, a combination of a changing physique, his reserved personality, undeniable talent, the self-belief that he would go far and his footballing style were contradictions that often confused the rest of the group and created mixed feelings among them. 'Just leave him alone, he can look after himself,' said some of his team-mates, all of whom were vying with him to achieve their own dreams of first team football. 'You have to look after him,' others said. The feeling that he needed protection was no longer unanimous now that he was beginning to grow, but there were still some who cared and who recognised his vulnerability.

Leo and the rest of the gang moved from Tito's Junior team to Junior A, managed by Alex García. From that season 2002–03 everybody remembers a youth *clásico*, a Barcelona–Damm played on one of the pitches near the Mini Stadium. Barcelona were winning 6–0, but Leo was still looking for one on ones attacking from the left. And wham! They whacked him, then again, and again. In the Cadete category, more than one of the boys had had a growth spurt and all of a sudden looked twice as big as the rest. Messi still looked small. 'They gave him such a kicking, I tell you,' Víctor Vázquez says today, closing his eyes almost as if he was the one receiving it. 'It was inhuman. But the bloke got up, and got up again, and again, and the kicks he was getting were heavy. That day they were killing him. I remember Alex got off the bench to protest: we were all protesting. There was a brawl.'

'Piqué came to blows defending him. He was sent off,' says Cesc. 'Piqué jumped in at the first opportunity, he would come running from the back, and at one metre eighty, who was going to argue with him! Anyway, he'd stop and say to them "don't kick him like that, he's not doing any harm, he's just making sure everyone enjoys the game; if you can't stop him, well, then don't stop him".' 'Piqué was the boss,' Messi has often said.

'If the referee isn't going to protect you, then I will,' Alex García told Leo as he subbed him. 'The Flea' was furious, not because they were kicking him badly, but because he wanted to carry on playing. 'The normal reaction,' Víctor Vázquez says, 'is to think, "they're kicking me because I'm very good and they can't stop me, but anyway, probably best if they take me off". But not him, he wanted to carry on playing, he probably thought, "put me on the other wing, I don't care, but let me play". And we were winning 6–0, remember!'

'Some of us saw him as defenceless,' remembers Vázquez. 'He was good with his head, for his height, with a spectacular left foot, dribbling, speed ... he played well, he was a good person, a good friend, nobody wanted any harm to come to him ... in fact you had to help him, you felt bad if you didn't. How can you not help a person who's looking at you, albeit out of the corner of their eye, as if to say "please, help me, I need you to help me, because I need to adapt to this level of football because I want to be here and I want to succeed here"? So your heart takes over from your head and you say: I've got to give him a hand.'

Víctor Vázquez saw him administering his hormone treatment at his home on Gran Via Carles III. By now they were meeting at Leo's to play on the PlayStation and sometimes his father would interrupt them. 'It's time for your injection.' Leo would leave the room, he'd go to the kitchen or the bathroom and inject himself. Again. As time passed, Leo opened up to Víctor and told him that he didn't like doing it. 'Víctor, I hate this, I hate it, but I have to do it. If I don't I'm going to end up a dwarf.'

'On the one hand we were working hard at the club to ensure that Leo would grow normally, so his physique would match his natural skill,' explains Alex García. 'But on the other we were praying that Piqué wouldn't grow any taller.' At the age of 14 the central defender already measured one metre ninety. A few centimetres more, the club thought, and perhaps his footballing days would be over.

In any case, Barcelona decided to stop Leo's hormone treatment when he was 14. The following year, he measured one metre sixty-two and weighed 55 kilos. But he still couldn't finish games well. 'I lack resistance, speed. And, yes, I get tired from time to time,' he said in an interview in 2002. He participated in a voluntary individual physical fitness programme designed by the club that was being overseen by a physiologist, a sports doctor and a physical trainer. Gerard Piqué and, on occasions, Javier Saviola, also took part in the programme.

The idea, as Toni Frieros explains in his biography of Messi, consisted of individual training to suit his own muscle structure. The final report, written in June 2002 after analysing 44 gym sessions,

was, in Messi's case, ambiguous: 'He is the player who has participated the least in this study. He has missed 12 sessions because of
problems caused by the Christmas holidays and because of illness.
When he has been able to work he has done so always in the shadow
of his team-mates, correctly but without showing any initiative.'

Behind the apparent fragility of the Argentinian lay a personality
prepared to fight for his place in the football jungle. 'I don't see him
as a weak bloke ... well, perhaps he is a bloke people feel they need
to protect because they are close to him, I understand that,' admits
Cesc. 'Leo may well be introverted, may well be timid, perhaps he
doesn't say much, but Leo has got *collons* [the Catalan word for
cojones]. What Fàbregas is saying is that he never felt the need to
come to blows in his defence, because Leo could, when necessary,
demonstrate a steely resolve that showed his inner strength. One
minute an opponent would be attempting to kick the hell out of him
and all of a sudden Leo would come up with a spectacular dribble
and the attacker would be left floundering! And that is much worse
for the victim. Yes, Cesc believed Leo could look after himself all
right.

In one Junior game, Messi performed a *sombrero* on a defender,
a little touch that flicked the ball over his opponent, only for the
player to catch the ball, whispering under his breath, 'you little bastard', something that goes against all the rules. 'I'm a bastard? I'm a
bastard?' Leo screamed and he had to be calmed down. That particular gene, the one that, at the age of three, caused him to throw the
cards away when he lost playing with his family, has never left him.

Again, with the passing of time, protection gradually developed
into respect. Leo learned where he stood with his group and in the
club, and continued to win their confidence. And they knew, as
footballers, that they couldn't put the boot in training because they
could not afford to lose the one player who was helping them win
games. 'It wasn't like at the beginning when Cesc wanted to kill
him because he realised he couldn't stop him,' Vázquez analyses. 'He
began to be the Leo Messi we know today, the bloke who scores you
fifty goals a season, and you'd better look after him. He had won
the respect of everyone.'

'The loneliness he suffered was something we only became aware
of much later,' Cesc recognises. 'We knew he was a boy who lived

with his father and who missed his family a great deal. We knew that because the coaches told us, not because he told us. At that time we were at the stage where football either went well for you or it didn't. So we were all too preoccupied trying to make the grade. We didn't have the time or the inclination to be too aware of what Leo was doing or was going through.

'I know he spent hours on messenger, on the internet, and didn't do much on the studying front ...' But did he go to school? 'Yes, yes, he went. I don't know if he just painted or did drawings, but he went ...' Cesc jokes about this, but for Leo and many of his team-mates school would soon become an intolerable nuisance.

'He was with us at La Masía school,' says Víctor Vázquez. 'But half the time he never turned up because he didn't like studying. Mind you, none of us did!' The nine o'clock bus that would take them to the Lleó XIII school on Avenida Tibidabo would arrive and more than once neither Víctor nor Leo was aboard. The fact is they found school boring. 'We'd get there and we'd put on our music, or talk, or play with our mobiles, sometimes joke with the girls, there were girls from tennis and basketball clubs. We'd flick little balls of paper, jokey notes ... and if Leo was there we'd try to include him, but Leo was always very shy, he always stuck himself in the corner. I'd go with him and say: "right, let's do such and such." Or we'd play noughts and crosses, or some other game, while they would be trying to teach us. The teacher would see us and say: "right! You two. Sit apart from the rest, and do what you want but stop taking the piss!"' Víctor laughs. 'So we'd put on our music, open a book to make it look like we were studying, just in case one of the school directors came in, and that was that. But we weren't bad kids. We didn't want to study, but we didn't disrupt the class. Only the teacher!'

Oriol Palencia explained to Jordi Gil in his biography of Cesc, how Cesc and others passed the time at the Lleó XIII school: 'When the teacher turned to face the board, we would get toilet paper and begin to shake it about as if it was a "white hankie" protest at the Camp Nou and start screaming "off, off". At other times we would send a remote control car around the classroom ... And Cesc wasn't on his own with these pranks, he was the gentler one to be honest, though he was certainly no shrinking violet. Piqué on the other hand had a crueller streak with his jokes. He'd tease his elders, they'd whack him and he'd laugh. Cesc was more the type who would hide your boot, niggle you, but Piqué was much cockier.'

'Messi is one of the reasons why I came back to Barcelona,' says Cesc, who returned to the *blaugrana* after eight years in London with Arsenal. What he means is that he wanted to relive those happy times, those laughs, those jokes, 'the best years of my life', as he has occasionally described them. Leo, on the other hand, simply remembers this period as a necessary preamble that would lead him, inevitably, to his final objective.

Season 2002–03: Continuity

Barcelona's first team continued its barren run. Manager Louis Van Gaal got rid of three pillars of the club, Rivaldo, Abelardo and Sergi, but was unable to sign the players he really wanted. The team was not responding to the coach. He was dismissed in January, with Barcelona languishing in thirteenth place. Radomir Antić was brought in to try to save the day, but they ended up finishing sixth in the league, the worst finish in fifteen years. Neither did they get past the quarter-finals of the Champions League. The mistaken decision to recall the Dutchman, one that failed to please the fans, hastened the departure of Joan Gaspart, who resigned at the beginning of 2003. The club remained in the hands of a board of directors who organised elections for the summer, the results of which would bring a breath of fresh air and, more crucially, youth to the club. The era of Joan Laporta and Sandro Rosell was about to begin. And of Ronaldinho.

Meanwhile, though, the soundtrack at the Camp Nou was one of frustrated and angry whistles, and the general image from the stands was of a sea of white hankies being waved. Further down, on the dirt and grass pitches where the Barcelona 15-year-olds played, Alex García's Junior A side were creating something magical, also ephemeral, something that was to come to an end much sooner than anyone expected.

This was a typical starting eleven, usually playing in a 3-4-3 formation:

Plancheria; Valiente, Piqué, Palencia; Cesc, Giribet, Julio De Dios,

Messi; Juanjo Clausi, Frank Songo'o and Víctor Vázquez.

'According to their ID cards, and judging by the pranks they got up to, the group comprised fifteen- or sixteen-year-olds, but they might have been ten years older when it came to training and the matches they played,' Alex García explains. 'They were boys with the mentality of professionals and during training you had to put the brakes on them, they were that competitive. Such rivalries in short matches, those four against four games, five against five! Incredible, I had to stop them. And later, in games, they would never settle for a 3–0 win. If they could, they'd win 4–0 or 10–0. And if there was a penalty to be taken, four players would chase after the ball. An argument would ensue.' Alex García would referee from the sidelines.

'With all due respect to their opponents, they competed against each other during the week, so that the day of the game felt like a training session to them,' concludes García.

García had Messi for an entire season, the only coach in lower-grade football who can boast that, a season that saw Leo complete the campaign without any major interruptions and one in which he played every game (the only one who did), and scored 36 goals, five more than centre-forward Víctor Vázquez: it was a season that would provide the runway from which the Argentinian's career would take off.

Leo was a boy 'very young, small for his age, with a lot of hair, a long mane, very quiet, very formal. He spoke very little. But he listened. And I knew that he listened because he put into practice what we talked about in the dressing rooms, in the coaching sessions.' So remembers Alex García who had often seen him play under Tito Vilanova. But if he had any doubt about his ability, Leo excelled himself against a powerful Damm side. The game was his: he scored the first goal, an individual effort that included a nutmeg on one of the defenders, and also scored the goal that made it 0–3. 'I saw the potential of the boy then,' García recalls.

Leo considered himself a *mediapunta* (a midfielder who plays just behind the main striker). 'He didn't like staying on the wing, he told me that he would, but every chance he got he would cut inside. It's normal, you can't put the brakes on talent. What happened is that I used to mess him about a bit and make him play in various places;

I wanted him to get used to playing in different positions, I did with Cesc as well, Víctor Vázquez ... I never saw a better pairing than Víctor and Leo, it was tremendous.'

Leo was now fully aware of the level he had reached, of how important he was to the side and, perhaps more importantly, the possibilities that now lay ahead for him. 'I remember one particular match that we had to play at the Europa pitch. The championship was at stake,' continues Alex García. 'It was midweek because the previous match had been called off due to rain. I got there and explained to them that it was important to win this game because then we'd have the chance to win the league. Leo came up to me and I said "stay calm". And he said to me, "don't worry, Gaffer, I'll soon sort this out". Within ten minutes he'd scored three goals. Just like that, bam, bam, bam. I think we won 7–1. He was fifteen years old and filled with a belief in his own abilities.'

That Junior side did not miss out on a single title. They won the lot: the league, Championship of Spain and also of Catalonia, in the now famous *partido de la máscara* ('final of the mask').

Those who remember the game still get goose bumps when they recall it.

On one of the auxiliary pitches beside the Mini Stadium, it's the last game of the season, Barcelona vs Espanyol, and there's maximum rivalry between the two sides that have battled out a league that had already been won by the culés.

Barcelona's Junior A side is winning 1–0.

Long ball. Messi goes for it and jumps as he tries to control it. The Espanyol defender runs across, aiming to cut him off, eyes fixed on the ball.

Messi turns. His face smashes into the defender.

The sound can be heard at the other end of the field. Leo tumbles to the ground, arms outstretched.

And there he lies – perfectly still. He briefly loses consciousness.

The other players run over to see what has happened to him, nobody dares touch him. There's blood. It's running down his nose.

His father comes racing out of the stand, anxious. He opens the gate to the pitch. He steps onto the grass.

And Leo doesn't move. Eyes wide open, calm. He's conscious again. His focus is blurred and he's confused. What happened?

The doctor arrives.

Some of the boys move to one side, nervous: they're not the only ones. His father looks at him closely, he wants to know what's wrong with him.

Leo gets up, calmly. They gather him up, but no, he wants to walk.

You have a fractured cheekbone, they tell him.

They take him to the FIATC hospital on the Diagonal. Diagnosis confirmed: fracture of the right cheekbone. He stays under observation for 24 hours. Leo asks his team-mates the result of the game: 3–1, they tell him, we won. He tells them he will try to be back for the final of the Catalonia Cup that is to be played the following week.

He says he wants to play in the final.

Leo visits the group two days later. His cheek is swathed in protective bandaging.

'How are you?' they ask him.

'I'm good, everything's fine. They are saying eight weeks out but I think it'll be less than that. They're telling me that I could play with a mask, you know I don't like being injured.'

'But do you feel okay?'

'Yes, yes, I was very frightened, but everything's okay.'

The fear is, above all, of missing a run of important matches. Particularly now that everything is starting to go so well.

He doesn't even mention the pain. His pain threshold walks the same road as his tolerance for frustration and, in the case of Leo, is very high indeed. The optimist views problems as challenges to be overcome. The pessimist foresees disaster. Leo is part of the first group – he just sees success and triumph, whatever the odds.

But it looks, for now, as if Messi will not be playing. The other players are worried: the final without Leo!

Saviola hears about the injury and sends him a shirt and his best wishes for a quick recovery. Messi, still only a Junior, has never forgotten this gesture from 'the Rabbit'.

Barcelona's captain, Carles Puyol, had suffered a similar setback at the beginning of the season following a collision with Frank de Boer. His specialist made him a plastic protector that was still with the club's medical department. Messi could play, they told him, on the strict condition that he wore the mask. There was still a risk, even with that protection, because another collision could have serious repercussions that might necessitate surgery.

Alex García spoke to Leo before deciding whether or not he would play.

'You know the conditions for you to play. The doctor's told me, "don't even think about playing without the mask".'

'Yes, Gaffer, don't worry.'

'You know that I'm going to have to take you off if you don't do as I say. We're risking your cheekbone here. In all honesty, you should rest. If you're injured again you're going to end up in the operating theatre.'

'No, don't worry yourself.'

Seven days after the injury the same teams met again in the final played at the Via Ferrea, at the Cornella Stadium. Leo starts. The plastic protector is a little big on him and he regularly tries to adjust it. It's irritating him.

The game gets under way.

After seven minutes, he picks up the ball on the wing and begins to move with it. As he is running he adjusts his mask. He loses the ball and appears irritated.

'Alex, Leo isn't comfortable with the mask, it seems as if he can't see properly,' Ángel Palomo, the player liaison, tells the coach.

'Gaffer, I can't see anything,' Leo confirms a bit later.

Alex speaks to him from the bench:

'Listen, Leo, remember what the doctor told you.'

He picks up the ball again, removes the mask and, holding it in his hand, goes past one player, then another. He loses the ball.

He runs to the side and throws the mask to the bench.

'Don't worry, Gaffer, nothing's going to happen.'

He receives a pass from Frank Songo'o and scores. Soon after, he shows some individual skill and puts a shot past the advancing keeper. Goal. Two goals in ten minutes and, with a 3–0 lead at the interval, Alex García, fearful of tempting fate further, insists that he should be substituted. 'Yes, Gaffer, I'm off now, I am off.' But he's still disappointed: he wants to carry on playing. Víctor Vázquez and Piqué, who is later sent off following a confrontation with

Espanyol coach Ramón Guerrero, score. The game finishes 4-1.

'At the partido de la máscara, *I found out that Messi understood football not only as a game but also as a collective effort that bases its laws on the respect you ought to have for your peers, your coach, and the sport, too. The effort he put into that match showed me that he was willing to do anything for us and him to win,' says Alex García.*

Although the international scouting system was far less developed and universal than it is today, it would have been impossible for the generation of '87 not to have attracted admiring glances from foreign clubs. So it was that during the 2002–03 season the Cadete A side was followed closely by Arsenal who were looking to sign not just Cesc Fàbregas, but also Gerard Piqué and Leo Messi.

It all began with a game in Lloret de Mar against Parma. On that day Piqué didn't play, but the rest of the gang, who had already won the game, did. Arsenal's representative in Spain, Francis Cagigao was astonished: he had just witnessed something very different, and quite extraordinary, namely the control of Cesc and the talent of Leo. He spent that day, and many more, fruitlessly searching for the Argentinian's agent. He came back to see Alex García's side in the MIC tournament at Easter. While Barcelona were battling against a new rival, Cagigao was speaking on the telephone. 'If only I could find someone who works with the Argentinian youngster ...' As he put the phone down one of Leo's representatives in Spain, Horacio Gaggioli, who had overheard the conversation, approached him. 'I believe you're looking for me.'

That night Francis had dinner with the agent and expressed an interest in Messi, an interest that culminated in an offer being passed to the boy's father, Jorge. From that moment the lines of communication between Arsenal and the Messis were open. Cesc and Piqué were also targets.

Cagigao's report was unequivocal. Messi was a 'little flea' aged 15 with extraordinary qualities, although he still didn't possess the power that he would later add to his game. He was intelligent with an extraordinary capacity for finishing. There were some doubts because of his lack of height, but they were easily outweighed by the quality of his playing.

Cagigao was one of the few, indeed, probably the only, European club scouts at these tournaments, so the offer from Arsenal was Leo's first from a foreign club since he had arrived at Barcelona. The Messis listened to what Arsenal had to say but they were not about to have their heads turned. Obstacles were apparent in any potential agreement. The English club could not offer a flat for the family, and there would be difficulty obtaining a work permit. Bit by bit points of mutual interest evaporated until the offer lay dead in the water. But they left Jorge with a message: 'Any time you encounter problems, remember, our club wants him.'

In any case, Arsenal had managed to secure the signings of Piqué and Cesc. Well, almost. Piqué travelled to London to see their training facilities, everything was agreed and confirmed, only for a legal matter to delay the process: he was not yet old enough to sign and Arsenal suggested that they should make a verbal agreement that would be confirmed in a year's time, when he was 16. The same agreement that they worked out with Cesc. Piqué (or, to be precise, his agents) said no.

With the Catalonia championship in the bag, there only remained one barrier for the completion of a perfect season: the championship of Spain. Cesc knew that they were going to be his last games, that at 15 he was going to abandon the club of his life, his city, his people.

Alex García saw him crestfallen: 'I asked him if he had some kind of personal problem, if it was a family matter. He told me that it had nothing to do with that, that he had had an offer from Arsenal and he was probably going to be leaving.' He felt that with Xavi and Iniesta blocking his path, he had to go somewhere else to see whether or not he was good enough for this game.

'Arsenal carried out negotiations in secret, although the deal did get as far as the head of junior football, Quimet Rifé,' remembers Albert Benaiges. 'But at that time there were many changes going on and there was a sort of power vacuum within the club caused by the change of board, just before the arrival of Joan Laporta. Arsenal ended up signing him.'

Cadete A also won the Spanish championship after beating Espanyol, Albacete, Atlético de Madrid and Athletic de Bilbao in the final. Messi was unable to play because of some bureaucratic problem:

the federation had listed him as 'assimilated' or, put another way, not Spanish, and non-nationals were not allowed in that competition despite having been allowed to compete in the league. Cesc, slotted into Leo's position, was the best player of the competition. Piqué, Cesc and Leo would not be together on a pitch again until a summer night in 2011.

In September 2003 Cesc left Barcelona. In October the same year, with a new board in place, Barcelona signed Messi until 2012, with a buyout clause of €30 million, which would increase to €80 million if he got into the Barcelona B squad, and €150 million should he get into the first team.

'It was during that time that I felt most alone,' remembers Víctor Vázquez. 'Cesc, Piqué, Songo'o were leaving. I went up into the Junior A, as did Messi, although he swiftly jumped into the Barça C side, where he played three or four games before moving up to the Barça B. His progression was much faster than the rest, it was spectacular. I stayed, on my own, well, not alone of course, there were the other team members, but the four I wanted to be with were no longer there. Thank God we carried on winning everything. It was still a good team. They had gone but I stayed, flying the flag for them! It was the best time of my career, we enjoyed ourselves, like children. Well, we were children, really.

'I'm going to call my son Leo. It pleases me to give him that name. Not Leonel, not Leonardo, but Leo.' Leo Vázquez.

Season 2003–04: Four levels in a year

'Barça Dying for This Kid' was the headline on the front page of the leading Argentinian newspaper *El Gráfico* in August 2003. Underneath it said: 'He's Argentinian and he's destroying them all in the lower ranks. He left Newell's at the age of 13, before dazzling Carles Rexach. He's only 16 but they can already see him in the Barcelona first team and they are already comparing him with Maradona. Messi is pure *potrero* (an Argentinian word which loosely means "footballer developed on uneven pitches"): left-footed, skilful and a goalscorer.'

Diego Borinsky, journalist:

On 18 November 2003 the newspaper El Mundo Deportivo, *a huge Spanish sports paper, published its first big story dedicated to Lionel Messi, at that time an emerging talent. The headline was 'Star of the Future'. The photo accompanying the article: Leo playing infinite keepy-uppy with an orange that just wouldn't fall to the ground in a hushed and expectant Camp Nou. It is an honour for me to have done that interview with Leo and to have defended the way it was published and appeared on the newsstands that day. Various voices had been raised saying that they thought it was an exaggeration. From then, until today, Lionel Messi, Leo as he prefers to be called, hasn't stopped surprising the world with his touches and dribbles. The orange, his co-star at that time, now rests in a hermetically sealed jar.*

The journalist Roberto Martínez does indeed, to this day, keep the now famous orange preserved in a hermetically sealed jar.

Joan Laporta was liberal with his smiles and hugs, à la Kennedy, as he entered his first weeks in charge of the club. Emerging from two decades of an obsolete and antiquated management style, it needed a complete overhaul, not least with regard to its finances. By June 2003 radical changes had been implemented: it modernised its image, restructured its finances and completely overhauled the infrastructure. It also 'Catalanised' its message and recycled the squad. Within two years Barcelona had turned itself into one of the most recognised and admired clubs in the world.

Laporta was the engine that drove through these changes, with the support of the God-like Johan Cruyff in the background and sporting vice-president, Sandro Rosell, who used his Brazilian contacts to bring in, first, Ronaldinho and then later a host of Brazilian footballers of class and personality. In that first season they brought in Ricardo Quaresma, Rafa Márquez, Gio van Bronckhorst and halfway through the season, Edgar Davids, who stabilised a strong, attacking line-up. Director of football Txiki Beguiristain and coach Frank Rijkaard made up the rest of the management line-up with a brief to get the very best out of a group of young and hungry footballers.

After a poor start, Rijkaard took his side to second place in a league won by Rafa Bénitez's Valencia. Ronaldinho scored 25 goals in all competitions, although his influence was probably felt more off the pitch than on. His hypnotic effect on the fans, entranced by his huge smile and the surfing motion he used to make with his right hand, soon rekindled a new feeling among Barça supporters, once again proud of their team.

Sandro Rosell was also in charge of changing the staff at the academy. Joan Colomer replaced Quim Rifé in charge of the youth set-up and his was the voice that would tell of the spectacular progress of a young Argentinian boy whom Rosell already knew from when he had worked with Nike, the first big brand to sponsor him.

That season began for Leo in June with the side for 16-year-olds that was coached by his fellow countryman Guillermo Hoyos, also a Newell's fan and recently arrived at the club. Hoyos had never seen him close up. In their first day together, the training was light but Leo shone with the ball. After five minutes, Hoyos was staggered. 'He was great!'

What would happen that season was something that had never been seen before at the Barcelona academy.

The Youth B side travelled to Japan to take part in the fourth edition of the Toyota International Youth Under 17 Football Championship. Their first opponents were the Dutch side Feyenoord. 'We were losing by a goal to nil after a quarter of an hour,' explains Hoyos in Toni Frieros's book. 'It was difficult for the team to get into the game ... I saw that Leo was angry on the pitch, he started to ask for the ball and with half an hour played he did something astonishing, dribbling past four defenders and the goalkeeper before putting in the killer pass to Songo'o.' Four games later, Leo was voted player of the tournament. Just as he was in the next tournament held in Sitges. And in the one at Sant Vicenç de Montalt. And at San Giorgio della Richinvelda in Italy. In that last one, the under-16 side scored 35 goals in five games of just 45 minutes' duration. The only thing they conceded was one corner. But Leo missed a penalty in an earlier phase. 'The goalkeeper will be able to say that he once saved a penalty taken by the best player in the world,' says Guillermo Hoyos. There was another one in the final against Juventus. Leo demanded the ball. He scored. He practised penalties at training at

The smallest one is Leo (second row, l to r, fifth), age four with the children's football team Grandoli. Behind him is coach Salvador Aparicio.

Age five (front row, l to r, second). Jorge, his dad, with the blue coat, was his coach for a season with Grandoli.

The great 87 generation. And the Game of the Mask.

The day of the debut with the first team, against Porto (16 October 2003).
Yes, he was a bit lost.

Then he got onto the pitch and came to life.

Ronaldinho adopted Messi as his 'brother'.

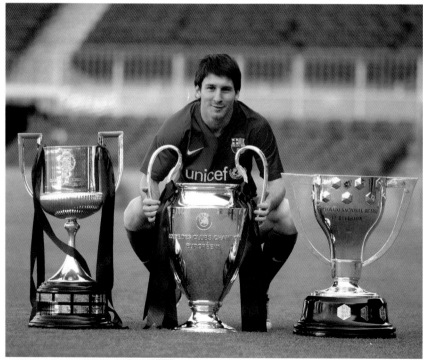

An extraordinary season. In 2009, Barcelona won everything.

The winning goal of the FIFA Club World Cup, 2009, in extra time. A very hard game.

Six titles out of six. The perfect year for Barcelona and Leo.

First Ballon d'Or, 2009. With his mum Celia, and his dad Jorge.
The road to that point was arduous.

When Messi was 13, his mum had to leave Barcelona to look after the other half of the family who could not adapt to life in Barcelona. She is the centre of his world. Here he celebrates her birthday after yet another goal.

Messi cried the day Barcelona lost
against Sevilla in the Cup . . . after
having won every single title in
the first year and a half with Pep.
Every defeat is a little death.

After Ronaldinho left, the
Catalans looked after Leo
They knew he was going
to make them better, to
help them win

the request of Hoyos. It would serve him in good stead at a crucial stage in his career the following summer.

The coach, who identified Leo as a natural leader, although very quiet, gave him the captain's armband. For a few games. 'I'm choked up, Ángel, this kid is just like Diego.' Ángel Alcolea was Hoyos's assistant. And Diego ... there's only one Diego. In the pre-season with the Youth B, Leo lost just one game, against Real Madrid.

And it was at that moment that Pere Gratacós dispensed with one of the unwritten rules of the club in order to acquire the whirlwind that was Messi. His meeting with Leo was accidental but the consequences of it would be overwhelming.

Pere was the coach of the Barcelona B side that played in Spain's Division Two B, three levels of the academy above the under-16s. Between the two were the under-17s, Barcelona C and then Gratacós's side, the first one with professional contracts. In the pre-season, around about August, they shared a training pitch in the annexe of the Mini Stadium with the youth team. 'Barça B took half of the pitch and the rest of it was shared out among two other teams,' he recalled. 'While my assistants were preparing what we were going to do, I was watching the youngsters, in particular Guillermo Hoyos's team. And I saw a player taking part in a short football match. He was fast, electric, very active, he would get hold of the ball, dribble with it, score.'

Leo had an extra gear compared to the rest of the group but what really impressed Gratacós was his speed in the first few metres and his efficiency.

'Our training started and I said to my people that I was going to watch these players for a bit longer and that I'd be along later. That day Leo scored a number of goals. When he finished I said to my assistant, Arseni Comas: "I have seen a player with the Juniors who I think is going to have to train with us." And he said, "from what team?" And I said, "I think he's from the under-16 side", and he said to me "are you mad?" So I said to him, "Arseni, he is better than some of the players we have in Barça B at the moment. Follow him for a week and when you've finished, we'll speak and decide." At the end of that week he came up to me and said: "Pere, you know what? I think you're right, he should train with us."'

Gratacós and Comas went off to speak to director of the youth set-up, Josep Colomer. They wanted him for the Barcelona B side. In that particular Junior side there were a couple of other players who were also outstanding, and Gratacós suggested that they should move up too, 'more than anything to disguise Leo's rise'. They were Oriol Riera and Jordi Gómez. 'Are you nuts?' Colomer asked them, but eventually he approved the decision, albeit with doubts over Leo's physique and his ability to adapt at the new level, but nonetheless aware of his considerable progress. Just two months after coming under the control of Guillermo Hoyos, the 16-year-old Leo began to combine sporadic training sessions with Barcelona's second team with playing and training for the Junior A side of Juan Carlos Rojo.

'They quickly put Leo and me in the Junior A side,' said Gerard Piqué. 'Cesc had just left for Arsenal. At this age it's usual for you to spend a season in the under-16 side, but Leo and I went into the under-17s with footballers a year older than us and we were a gang! Chechu Rojo was our coach, and in December they found out that I was going to Manchester so they dropped me back to the under-16 side again. But I went to see the Messi team, and in the Copa del Rey matches, Leo won the games single-handedly. I remember one match against Osasuna and it was a "Leo against the world" type of game and you need to remember that this was a side that had a lot of quality.'

Messi scored 18 goals in 11 games for the under-17s, one of them a memorably precise left-foot strike from the centre of the pitch that went in over the Betis goalkeeper in the final of a friendly tournament.

Barcelona C had problems – they'd won just one of their 15 games, and were lying bottom of their division group – and so Gratacós and Colomer decided he should play for the C team to get experience – his third team that season. 'We'd seen him train and play with the Juniors,' remembers Pep Boada, coach of the C team, Barcelona's third side. 'We thought he could give us something and that's exactly how it turned out. We were going through a difficult period. The third division is a very hard and tricky division and we were a team full of very young kids. He arrived like a breath of fresh air, and the truth is he helped us a lot both as a group and individually. We were struggling at the bottom of the division and

Messi reactivated us; he had an extra gear from everybody else.'
First game, against Europa: victory for Barcelona C, 3–1.

Leo scored five goals in ten games for that side, including two
in four minutes to turn around a game against Gramenet that they
were losing. The C side emerged from their crisis.

He played in a Spanish Cup round for the same side against
Sevilla. The job of marking a Messi brimming with confidence fell
to Sevilla's right-back: Leo scored three goals in eight minutes. The
defender would never forget that morning. His name? Sergio Ramos.

Messi continued to make great leaps forward, always positive
and never complaining. 'He loved football so much that it was difficult for him to say no to anyone, no matter who the side was,' says
Boada. 'He needed to become stronger, but none the less he made
us more competitive. When Messi had the ball it was a revelation.
The other boys were enthralled and wanted to copy his style and
technique. That creates a lot of competition, which was very positive for the group.'

'My first memory of Leo would have been about 2003,' recalls
Ferran Soriano, at that time recently appointed the club's financial
vice-president and an emerging heavyweight on the new board. 'My
first conversation about him was with director of football Txiki
Beguiristain: we wanted to find a way of facilitating his continued
growth. To start with we had put him in a side with bigger boys that
would test him more. I remember on one occasion he had scored
five goals in a game and we said to Txiki, we can't go on like this.
We had to push him more.'

But he continued to be physically weak, and, despite the fact that
he was going up the levels, his physical appearance continued to be
a problem. Unless ... 'What we wanted was to build him up,' says
Gratacós, 'so that when he went out onto the pitch against men of
thirty-two, thirty-three, he would have sufficient body mass not to
be pushed around. We said: let's treat him on a physical level. Let
him train the same as everyone else, but with more physical work.
But no weights. He may have used them occasionally, but very little.
We were talking about physical exercise.'

Having stopped taking hormone injections when he was fourteen, Leo needed to feel confident that his footballing progression,
now well advanced, would run parallel with his body growth. That

same season, even before the intervention of Gratacós, Leo and his father had frequently gone to a piece of waste ground close to the Hotel Juan Carlos (not far from their flat) and the Camp Nou to try out a physical regime, based on speed and stamina, initiated by Guillermo Hoyos. When he started training regularly with the Barcelona B of Gratacós, he focused on power and speed, aiming to increase the muscle mass in his legs and to strengthen his lower body. Later he would ask Ronaldinho's personal trainer to complement this work, hoping to reduce the negative effects that such a rigorous exercise programme could have on a young boy. And when he wasn't working, he was resting, crucial so that the benefits of the physical exertion should not go to waste: he had a siesta every day. On the sofa if he was at home.

So it was that Leo, in a demanding but carefully monitored way, gradually grew.

'We'd been training for some months,' recalls Gratacós. 'Normally in the sessions I would put him on the right-hand side. Every Tuesday I would get together with Frank Rijkaard and we'd talk a bit about everything. Frank was insisting on replicating everything in the B side that existed in the first team. Ronaldinho would play on the left despite being right-footed, while Giuly was on the right. Leo would do what Ronnie did but on the right; being left-footed, with his mazy runs from far out into the danger areas, he would come inside and shoot at goal or confront the defence. Sometimes I would put three youth players (Paco Montañes, Oriol Riera and Leo) in those three positions in the attack; it was a way of helping them develop.'

At first when they asked him to train with the B team, four years older than himself, Leo felt out of his comfort zone, displaced. The players' kit is kept in a cupboard inside the dressing room and everyone has to get their own. Leo, surrounded by new faces, could not shake off his shyness, and head bowed, would collect his things and find a place to change. None of this was helped by his slightly confused situation: he was a Barcelona player, but not from any particular side. These were exciting times because he was going through the stages at breakneck speed, but they were also perplexing times.

The day of his Barcelona B debut drew closer. Inevitably. But, before that, a surprise, and a present.

Sunday, 9 November 2003

Leo Messi scores a hat-trick for Juan Carlos Rojo's side against Granollers.

Tuesday, 11 November 2003

Pere Gratacós meets up with Frank Rijkaard, who has now been at the club for seven months. The Dutchman both needed and actively sought out the opinion of those in charge of the academy. They talked about the youth set-up, the players.

– Who've you got this week? asked Frank.
– We're playing Novelda.
– Well, Pere, I hope it doesn't mess your plans up too much but they've given me a friendly against Porto on the same day that you're playing, and I've got everyone with their national teams.

Barcelona had been invited to participate in the inauguration of the new Porto stadium, built in time for the European Championships that were being played in Portugal the following year.

– Take whoever you want. Including a couple of youngsters who are being integrated into our squad, although they are only Juniors. Oriol Riera and Leo Messi, an Argentinian boy. It would be good if you could take them as well.
– Oriol and Messi?
– Yes.
– Where do they play?
– Messi, you can put him anywhere on the pitch.
– Sure?
– Take them and next week we'll meet and you can tell me about it.
– Okay, perfect.

Saturday, 15 November 2003

'I'm writing to you now to give you some really good news just as you asked me to. Are you sitting down? ON SUNDAY I HAVE BEEN CALLED UP FOR THE FIRST TEAM FOR A FRIENDLY

*AGAINST PORTO OF PORTUGAL. THIS INFORMATION IS
GOING TO COST YOU. GET MY PRESENT READY. HAHAHA.
Well, I hope you're still alive after this piece of news. I love you very
much. Pray for me and wish me luck. Ciao, a kiss.'*

Email from Leo Messi to a friend telling him of his call-up to the squad.

That morning the first team, or what was left of it, trained with
some of the B team players who were to travel to Porto the next day.
Leo Messi had been called up too but trained with the under-17 side
that morning. That night, he had trouble sleeping. He kept turning
over in his mind that this was the night before a possible debut for
the FC Barcelona first team. He imagined the drive to the airport,
wondered who would cross paths with him in the corridors on the
way to the plane, who would sit with him. He pictured himself sitting on the bench at the Porto stadium. Being called up to warm up.
Making his debut. Even for just a minute or two. Then he fell asleep.

Sunday, 16 November 2003

At Prat airport, Frank met the boys from the B team who were joining the squad and also the four Juniors Jordi Gómez, Oriol Riera,
Xavier Ginard and Leo Messi, who had now played for his fifth
team in one season, something unheard of at the club. The press
photographers took a couple of pictures of the squad, the serious
looks on the faces of the youngest members disguising their enthusiasm very well; so well in fact that they seemed totally unabashed.
In truth they were a bundle of nerves on their first ever trip with
the big boys. But the press were actually at the airport that day to
record the return of Ronaldinho from Brazil, where he had played
two games for his country and whose arrival coincided with the
departure of his team-mates to Portugal.

The boys went around everywhere together. Conversation was
limited.

- I think I was the last person to know I was going to Porto, said
  Xavier Ginard, the goalkeeper.
- My father told me on Thursday night, said Leo. Colomer had
  told him that it was likely that they would take me to Porto but

it wasn't certain. And later they confirmed it and my father told me on Thursday night. I didn't breathe a word to anyone.
- Well, it appeared in the paper, that's how I found out, said Jordi Gómez.

Skipper Luis Enrique welcomed them in a typically light-hearted and jokey manner to break the ice and calm nerves.

- Lads, don't forget these! shouted Luis Enrique. He was pointing to some bags belonging to the first team players that the youngsters had been asked to drag around. Cheers, lads!

The other familiar faces (Rafa Márquez, Luis García and Xavi, who is the only one still at Barcelona) and other, more experienced academy players (Jorquera, Navarro, Oleguer, Oscar López, Ros and Santamaría) made sure that the kids didn't get split up from the group, telling them where to go and what to do. All the boys wanted was to get to the dressing room that they would all be sharing. On that day Leo, Oriol, Jordi and Xavier were just names that no one was going to remember. Names that surely no one would even try to remember.

With the team alongside Frank Rijkaard was director of football Txiki Beguiristain.

- It's a good game for the youngsters.
- Have you seen Leo? asked Frank.
- They've spoken to me about him. We passed in the lift the day he arrived at Barcelona. The one who plays for the Juniors, no? Great footballer, isn't he?
- We will see.
- He seems very small, a bit fragile. Perhaps it's all a bit too early for him? I hope they don't hurt him.
- Let's try him out, see what's what.
- You're one brave feller, quipped Beguiristain.
- There is a very small lad in the group, who is he? asked Henk ten Cate, Rijkaard's assistant.
- Lionel Messi, replied the sporting director.

Travelling with them on the charter flight were Jorge Messi, Celia and his brother Rodrigo. Leo was going to pull on the first-team shirt two years and nine months after that first uncertain family trip to Barcelona.

The flight was short, the team ate in the hotel, there was time for a rest and, when it was getting dark, they were taken to the new Estádio do Dragão in Porto. Nobody remembers anything that Messi did in the usual pre-game stroll around the pitch, damp and uneven. It still looked impressive, however, with 50,000 seats and a roof encircling the stands. A section of floodlighting had already been switched on. The opponents were José Mourinho's Porto.

Back in the dressing room, Frank gave his team talk without confirming whether or not the youngsters would play. 'Maybe' was the only thing he would say to them in the stadium.

And then he named his line-up:

Jorquera; Oscar, Ros, Oleguer, Fernando Navarro; Márquez; Gabri, Xavi, Santamaria, Luis Enrique; Luis García.

Porto were playing with some well-known names: Vitor Baía, Secretario, Carvalho, Maniche, Thiago.

During the game, with a fired-up Porto and a Barcelona who allowed themselves to be dominated, Oriol Riera was brought on for Ros, Tiago for Gabri, Jordi Gómez for Santamaria and Exposito for Luis García. There were 25 minutes of the friendly remaining. 'Right, let's put the boy on as well,' said Frank to Ten Cate. 'Warm up, son,' said Rijkaard with his hand on his shoulder. Leo was nervous, his heart pumping hard, but he wanted to play.

He was 16 years and 145 days old, and he could wait no longer. He wore Johan Cruyff's number 14.

He warmed up for ten minutes. 'Son,' shouted Ten Cate. It was his turn.

He came on in the seventy-fifth minute, replacing another academy player, Fernando Navarro. The shirt looked big on him.

In the stand, Jorge and Celia were in tears.

'The truth is that we did cry. For us this was a dream come true, because we never believed that he would make his debut on that day,' remembered Jorge Messi on *Informe Robinson*. 'We thought he was joining to make up the numbers. And then they call him up to warm up. No, surely not. And when he came on, well, yes, the truth is that we wept. I believe it was a reward, the reward for the sacrifices he had made.'

Fernando Navarro, who left the pitch with a very serious expression on his face and hardly looking at the debutant, made history without really wanting to: 'When I see the pictures on the telly, when Messi replaces me ... I was actually quite pissed off. I had been out for a year with an injury and I was upset about coming off. But, okay, with hindsight Leo is now, what, the best player in the world or the best ever? And he came on for me! But, remember, at that point I was being replaced by a Junior.'

Leo could have scored two goals. Shortly after coming on he had his first chance, a loose ball that the goalkeeper got to first, but the second one was a much clearer opportunity: he stole the ball off the keeper, and with an open goal he thought he had less space than he actually did and passed the ball to Oriol. He should have shot.

'Of course I remember that pass; what he did that day he used to do in the youth teams. Some of us weren't surprised,' points out Oriol Riera.

A bit later he tussled for the ball with a defender, lost control on a pitch that wasn't smooth and 'the Flea' fell over.

'It seemed as if he had been playing with us all of his life, his movement was so natural. The first time the ball came to him he created a scoring chance. The second time, he nearly scored,' remembers Ten Cate. 'If you are fifteen or sixteen years old in a game like this against Porto, at the opening of a new stadium full of people, and you do all that, it's because you are something special. Frank and I looked at each other. "What the fuck? Did you see that?"'

'Yes, he did two or three good things,' confirms Txiki Beguiristain.

'I was nervous, I spent the whole match on the bench, I thought Rijkaard would give me a debut of about ten minutes,' says Ginard, the only one of the four Juniors not to play.

On the bench, Leo was the talking point, as Fernando Navarro recalls: 'We were amazed by his personality, his dribbling, his maturity. He was sixteen and I don't know anybody who doesn't get nervous on his debut with the first team. But the guy took the game as if he was in the youth ranks, as if the Juniors were playing.'

Barcelona lost 2–0 but Rijkaard approached the youngsters to congratulate them on their debuts. So did Navarro and the senior players. 'Do you know what? I never again mentioned to him that I was the guy who came off when he made his debut – and I have played against him a few times with Mallorca and now Sevilla. It is ten years since that day. On the anniversary I will be in all the news bulletins – I will have to ask for copyright!' Leo commented to Jordi Gómez and Oriol Riera that he would have preferred to have celebrated his debut with a victory. 'Shame about that first chance,' he told them.

At the press conference, Rijkaard mentioned him: 'He created two chances and nearly scored. He's got a lot of talent and a very promising future.'

'I remember that when he went past the press area he went with his head bowed, crouched, almost too embarrassed to look you in the eye,' says journalist Cristina Cubero. 'I have always said that he has all the strength he needs on the pitch, but off it he shrinks.'

This is what he said to the journalists: 'I always wanted to make my debut for the first team and now my dream has been realised, I hope that in the future I will be able to carry on playing for the first team ... All of a sudden I've been given the opportunity I've been waiting for for so long ...'

'Mourinho? No, he said nothing, he knew nothing about the lad,' says Ten Cate today about that long-ago game.

After the match, there was a certain euphoria among the technical staff. Henk, Txiki and Frank talked about Leo.

– Look what's coming, Frank.
– We'll have to put him with Ronaldinho.
– He's coming like a bullet.

'Did I think he'd get where he is?' asks Oriol Riera. 'This is a question they have asked me lots of times over the past years. No one could have imagined that he would get to where he is now, even less so in such a short time.'

Gio van Bronckhorst, at the time with his national side, Holland, received a phone call that night. 'I've seen a player ... he's incredible, a colossal talent. He will be the new Ronaldinho.' It was Ten Cate. 'I hadn't seen him play, but when Henk told me how good he was I had a look at videos on YouTube. Just watching him run with the ball you knew that he had something special.'

It was a happy Leo who returned home with his parents and Rodrigo. They arrived at Via Gran Carles III at five in the morning.

Messi gave that light-brown number 14 shirt to his mum. Now framed, it hangs in her house in Rosario.

Monday, 17 November 2003

The family woke up late the following day, but they sat down together to eat. The Milanese was seasoned with happiness. Before lunch Leo sent a few emails to various friends. 'I'm really happy how everything went, everyone treated me really well, but now I just hate it that people have started talking about me. I hope they do talk less. Even though everything was really good.'

Tuesday, 18 November 2003

Pere Gratacós got together with Frank Rijkaard, as he usually did on Tuesdays.

– We drew two-all with Novelda. It wasn't bad, considering you left us short of players, Gratacós told him.
– We lost 2-0. Let's see how the internationals come back, we need to win, the league is getting complicated.
– Yes.
– Ronaldinho's been here since Sunday and he's training well.
– Yes. Listen, Frank, what about Messi?
– Ah, Pere. A player who comes on and in sixteen minutes creates one chance, nearly scores and is the man of the match, this boy has got to be with us.
– What shall we do?
– Let him carry on playing with the Junior team, or, better, your B side, but have him train one day a week with the first team. Later, two days, then three. Let's see how he copes with it.

Xavier Ginard spent three years playing in the lower ranks of the Barcelona side before returning to his native Mallorca. He now plays in Spain's second division B. Jordi Gómez is at Wigan. Oriol Riera is now at Osasuna, having scored a hatful of goals in Spain's second division.

And about Leo, Barcelona coaches agreed there was no way of

stopping this little bull. The time had come to put him permanently in the ring. In the hundred years of FC Barcelona's history only two footballers had made their debuts younger than Messi: Paulino Alcantara in 1912 and the Nigerian Haruna Babangida, who played at the end of the Nineties under Louis Van Gaal.

Leo started training daily with Barcelona B and sometimes he joined the first team. In the positional plays and the *rondos* he was not scared of facing older players. Leo was settling in, finding his feet, and, what's more, in a confident and bold manner. There are few things that determine a footballer's place in the game's hierarchy better than the *rondo*. The manner in which they demand the ball, if they return it quicker than the rest, if they keep themselves out of the middle, if they show their talent or not, if they try hard to get control of a tricky ball – all these things define their position in the group. Sixteen-year-old Leo had just two weeks to demonstrate exactly who he was. In the event, he became one of the 'bosses' of the *rondo*, according to his coaches.

In any case, Gratacós knew that Leo had a particular style of playing, and felt that he carried the ball too much. And he tried to correct it, just as others in Barcelona's lower teams had. 'It's a team game, Leo. When you have the ball, look for the pass; when you don't have it, make yourself available so you can also participate ...' his coach would shout at him. 'And then, suddenly, he'd go round three of them, dribble the ball past the goalkeeper and score and so ... what could I say?' admits Gratacós. 'There were training sessions that made my jaw drop. He always wanted to win, during training, in the short games. His motivation was extraordinary. I sometimes said to him: "if you have the same passion in the matches as you do in the training sessions, then no one can beat us."'

On 5 March 2004 he was called up for the Barcelona B squad to play against Mataró. Pere Gratacós takes up the story.

'We'd gone to train at the park next to the Diagonal and we were walking down towards the Mini Stadium. I walked next to Messi. I looked at him and said, "Leo, how are you?"

'"Fine, fine, Boss."

'"You're playing on Sunday." He just looked at me. "You're playing, and don't worry, you just have to play the same way as you do in training."

'"Okay, okay, Boss."

'"And don't worry if for whatever reason you don't play well or things don't work out, don't worry about it. The following Sunday you're still going to start. And if you don't play well in the next game, no problem. But if, after four games, you haven't improved on your first game then I'll send you back to the Junior team."

'"Okay, agreed, Boss, thanks a lot."

'"You're much stronger, I see you now almost at the same physical level as the rest, which was the thing that was worrying me most. Play just the way you're training."

'"Okay."

'Of course, he was used to playing with the under-16 or under-17 side and scoring three or four goals a game,' Pere Gratacós remembers. 'With Pep Boada's third division Barcelona C side he'd score one or two, which is already quite a feat. And when he started to play for us it raised the bar even more, it's another division higher, bigger people, more experienced. Messi began to acquire more physical attributes to get away from defenders, but he still lacked something to be able to compete on an equal footing. So then ... The first game came, against Mataró, and he was so-so; he probably touched the ball twice, not much more.' It was the twenty-eighth weekend of the season, he started, played for most of the game and was substituted in the ninety-first minute, replaced by Sancho, and he also received a yellow card. Barcelona won 1–0.

The following game was away to Nàstic of Tarragona. From the stands, a member of both clubs, Alfred 'Chip' remembers:

'Messi was very well known in the lower ranks of Barcelona FC at that time. Like Gerard Deulofeu most recently, for example. That season I only went to see one of Gimnàstic de Tarragona's games. On television I had just seen a young Argentinian boy make his debut with the B side, who looked to me to be technically gifted and very classy. If I remember correctly he had gone through loads of stages in a very short space of time. I had a lot of fun at that game: to all the people who asked in the Tribune [VIP] section of the New Stadium [at Gimnàstic] why I had come that day I gave the same answer: "Leo Messi: remember his name, because he is going to play for the Barcelona first team, and he is going to be a star." Leo only played the first half because Pere Gratacós substituted him at half-time. Someone was sent off and the game became very aggressive. Despite having quite a good first half, with flashes of class, I think Gratacós subbed him to protect him, because Leo was only sixteen years old.'

And that is true: that game against Nàstic was eight days after his Mataró debut and Leo did not play the second half of a match that finished o–o. Gratacós continues: 'The second game was a bit better, but only a bit. The third game, he improved but didn't score and Leo normally made the difference when he scored. At the moment he was neither making the difference, nor scoring goals. And he was anxious, accustomed to making his mark wherever he went. With us he wanted to, but couldn't.'

Leo felt that he was not passing the test, that things weren't going well; he came onto the pitch anxious and returned to the dressing room disheartened.

'Leo, don't worry, play the way you train, don't worry, the goals will come,' Gratacós said to him.

'We got to the fourth game, against Girona. And Messi scored. He was the best player on the pitch. We went down to the dressing rooms, we looked at each other, we hugged. And I told him, "I will see you tomorrow in training",' remembers Gratacós. 'He played with us five games that season.'

Or that is what has been said up to now, but it is not exactly what happened. As so often occurs, legend rewrites history. That game was won by Girona 1–o. The following season, in the second league game, Barcelona B met Girona away and Leo's team won 2–1, with Leo scoring his first goal with that side, after having played a total of seven games.

Gratacós did not make anything up. The shadow of a legend clouded his memory and, recalling those days years after they took place, a new, more rounded story took root. Memories acquire a life of their own sometimes. I am sure we prefer the made-up version of his first goal for Barcelona B. It's not what happened, but the choice is yours.

Gratacós soon realised that Leo's performances would improve or not, depending upon who was playing alongside him in attack. Towards the end of that season, but especially the following one, when Leo played 17 games for the B team, always in the starting eleven, Pere was clear in his own mind that, in order to get the best out of Leo, rather than matching him up with forwards who were hell-bent on scoring, it would be better to place him with quality players like Joan Verdú and Sergio García who enjoyed playing with mobile forwards such as Leo. He may have been four years younger than them but already the three spoke the same footballing language. And so, gradually, Gratacós began to adjust the team, very much with Leo in mind.

As part of the planning for Messi's season, the coaches of the various sides that he represented would meet every Thursday and decide which team needed him most. And so he ended up as part of the under-16 side in the last three league games of the season, helping them win the title, despite having problems with his groin which meant he couldn't train. 'Anyone else would have got cross,' explained Juan Carlos Rojo. In truth, that year Leo never completely left the Juniors: he would often pass by to see his team-mates, boys of his own age, play, and he would even join in the technical team talks at half-time.

In the 2003–03 campaign, Messi scored in four of the five teams he played for: a total of 35 goals in official games, more than 50 in all competitions.

'Suddenly we went from nothing, to everything we'd dreamed of,' recalls Jorge Messi speaking to the Argentinian press. 'It was so fast that we seemed to have neither the time nor the place to digest it, to celebrate it, to enjoy it.' Pere Gratacós likes to say that year Leo had 10 fathers and 75 brothers, as many as coaches and team-mates.

One doubt remains, though. Was it advisable to ask so much of a boy of just 16 years old? Would it not have been better for him to have gone through every stage of the process? Were Barcelona thinking of the footballer himself when they made him go through so many stages so quickly? Or were they merely focused on winning competitions and avoiding relegation? What are the priorities with a player of only 16? What are the physical and psychological effects on a footballer, or, indeed, on anybody, when they are identified as the winner in the team, the special player, when demands are placed upon them to achieve victory regardless of which level they play at?

Eleven months after his debut in Porto, seven months before his first match with Barcelona B, Leo was going to walk onto the pitch at Camp Nou with the first team for an official competition.

At the same time he recorded the following commercial while he was still with Nike:

http://www.youtube.com/watch?v=youtu.be/8eZCvsv_LkM

In it you see Messi and other promising Barcelona youth players (Jonathan dos Santos, Ricardo, Isma) playing on the beach, in the street, in the Boqueria Market in Barcelona, in the dressing room. You hear the Barcelona anthem being played by a discordant electric guitar, in the style of Jimi Hendrix. At the end the boys turn to the camera. The last one to come out after scoring a goal from a free-kick is the Argentinian.

'Remember my name: Leo Messi.'

The world, Leo, was beginning to take note.

3

Becoming a Champion

There's been an earthquake. Where? In La Plata, Argentina. Are you sure? That's what it looks like. That's how it registered at the Seismographic Department of Weather Information at the La Plata Astronomical Observatory. Confirmed. An earthquake. Registering more than point six on the Richter scale.

It was 5 April 1992. A football match was under way. A goal would move the earth, literally.

In the general scheme of things it had been a game like any other. Gimnasia, the visitors, were playing a *clásico* at the Estudiantes ground in La Plata. There was nothing particularly memorable about it. It was a local derby and, yes, tensions and rivalries were at maximum levels, as usual, but there was certainly no league or title at stake, just the seventh weekend in the Clausura tournament.

The game had developed into a tight physical contest. With 54 minutes played, the Uruguayan winger José Perdomo was about to earn himself the nickname that would stick with him for ever. There was a free-kick against the home side, Estudiantes. Perdomo placed the ball, focused on the opposing goal some 35 metres away. Marcelo Yomo, the goalkeeper, prepared to defend his six-yard box.

Perdomo moved forward, summoning up all the power and accuracy he could muster.

And the keeper could only look on as the ball flew like a rocket, just inside the right-hand post.

Goaaaal!!!!

And in the stands the thousands of *triperos* (Gimnasia supporters) rose as one and celebrated with such joy and passion that La Plata literally shook. It had never happened before, and it would never happen again. Anywhere in the world.

The game, the 113th *clásico* between the two sides, ended in victory for the visitors, thanks to the only goal of the game scored by the newly christened 'Earthquake' Perdomo.

Football creates passion wherever it spreads its roots, but in Argentina it literally shakes the ground. But how is this so? Like everywhere else, football is a mirror of society, but in Argentina it seems to be a reflection from a distorted looking-glass: everything from enthusiasm to legend multiplies dramatically. That's its appeal … and its danger.

The commentator on foreign policy and economics Enrico Udenio paints a pessimistic picture in his book *La Hipocresia Argentina* (2008) in which he says, 'Argentina is comprised of a neurotic society in which its inhabitants feel unfulfilled and compelled to act in a self-destructive manner. It's about a society which in the past longed for greatness but in reality found itself unable to provide for its basic needs, such as housing, food, health, education and security, right up to the most elevated of demands, especially the spiritual and intellectual aspirations of its members.' Within this framework you find the roots of an overheated passion.

'It's a society in which its participants are not only unable to achieve wellbeing, but one where they experience permanent sensations of being threatened' continues Udenio. 'This situation creates a chronic stress whose symptoms are usually seen in the form of tiredness, feelings of impotence, depression, sleeplessness and a failure to respond to stimuli. It's a society that builds up dreams and, when they aren't realised, looks outside itself for explanations and to apportion blame.' They very easily find things and people to blame for their stagnation, 'diabolical figures' as Udenio calls them, and these frustrations become a 'psychological irrationality' and a tendency to see everything in black and white together with an 'accentuated emotional compulsion. This helps raise some of their representatives to the level of gods, with the same speed and facility as it can convert them into demons,' concludes the Italian-born writer who has lived in Latin America since childhood.

The Spanish philosopher José Ortega y Gasset saw it the same way a hundred years ago: 'the Argentinian is a frenetic idealist: he positions his life in a place that, in reality, doesn't exist, in search of an idea or an ideal that he has of himself. The Argentinian is, in fact, what he imagines himself to be.'

Everything had started so well: the country, a fountain of wealth and the destination for waves of immigrants, became, in the early years, the 'El Dorado of half of Europe', in the words of the writer Marcos Aguinis in his essay 'El Atroz Encanto de Ser Argentinos'('The Terrible Delight of Being Argentinian'). Fifty years ago it was still one of the richest countries in the world, one that produced artists, scientists, politicians and writers.

And as Argentina drifted further away from that 'grand destination', one that remained just over the horizon, football became the repository of all the hopes and frustrations of a disillusioned nation. 'I think we are a country that believed itself to be destined for great achievements, great successes, but something went wrong,' reflects the writer Eduardo Sacheri, whose novella *La pregunta de sus ojos* was turned into the Oscar-winning film *El secreto de sus ojos* ('The Secret in Their Eyes'). 'It's very difficult for us to reconcile ourselves with this. We weren't that good, we were not destined for greatness, but none the less, we play football well, strikingly well. Remember that there aren't that many of us. We say that in Brazil they play fantastic football but there are 190 million of them; here we are forty million at the most, and we can still take them on, and hold our heads high as one of the best football teams in the world.'

But this extreme passion for football means that Argentinians are blinded by successes (believing that they have finally arrived at the Promised Land) and also by defeats. And they believe that the good and the bad only happen to them. 'Our "destiny of greatness" is pure fiction, God isn't Argentinian and it's nonsense to claim that Argentina is the best place in the world ... At least now we can laugh at ourselves, and that wasn't always the case when we were locked into a parochial sense of nationalism,' insists Marcos Aguinis.

'Argentina has been in ruins for a generation and a half, and we still haven't reached rock bottom,' confirms Liliana Grabín. 'When you can't feel Argentinian for any other reason, when your country's identity begins to fail, you adapt to whatever idea gives you hope. Football gives us an identity, one that allows us to feel established, rooted. You say "I am Argentinian" and you hear "Maradona" and now "Messi" and the Pope. Yes, this is Argentina.'

Ironically, two of Argentina's most recent exiles have become two of the most famous people in the world: Pope Francis and Leo Messi. Queen Maxima of the Netherlands is another, albeit on a rather more rarefied level. And many more native Argentinians have died abroad after achieving worldwide fame: Che Guevara, José de San Martín, Jorge Luis Borges, Julio Cortázar, Carlos Gardel. Argentina punches well above its weight and yet, as Liliana explains, 'It would seem that you can achieve a greater sense of Argentinian identity by living outside the country rather than inside. Those of us who live here are forced to accept the grim realities of corruption, disenchantment, the fact that people no longer sing the national anthem. Those who leave carry with them an ideal of Homeland which makes a sense of patriotism easier to maintain.'

But there's always football, that substitute for organised religion. In an otherwise grey world of poor economic performance, unemployment, mistrust and general disillusionment, football provides the colour that brightens peoples' lives. In a country failing in virtually every area of growth, it is football alone that produces positive weekly results. As Sergio Levinsky comments, 'Many go so far as to maintain that the national anthem should be replaced by the Argentinian football shirt, because it represents more of what Argentina is than all the rest put together. It's the only thing that wins.'

And although football is also the perfect breeding ground for frustration, unfulfilled dreams, demons, gods, the entire gamut of human emotion, good and bad, it also unites. Sacheri adds, 'In a land where we are accustomed to being divided, on just about every issue, where we have a fervent individualism, the national team is the only thing that unites us, because not even having an Argentinian pope can unite us. An Argentinian pope was elected, and the following week we were fighting to the death over whether he was a good person or a bad one.'

What's at stake in an Argentinian match? Values, pride, a way of understanding the world? Or is it just points, titles? 'Football allows, and continues to allow, any guy from a poor neighbourhood the right to have what has been snatched from him from the cradle: pride.' This is the belief of football coach and intellectual Ángel Cappa. 'That's to say that in football terms I can be somebody, in the deepest sense of the word. I earn self-respect and the respect of the people. In the neighbourhoods the one that earned the most respect was the one who was best at football. What other means does he have, not just to be known, but also to establish his identity? Only the ball. Playing well has an enormous significance.'

A game on a pitch is played for points but also for the chance of gaining a sense of self-importance, admiration. And just about the entire male population and a large percentage of the female one either play, or are involved, in the organisation of these competitions. 'In the neighbourhood the person who didn't play football was a rare bird. From that point on, life codes are formed,' continues Cappa. 'Football shows you how to be brave, to conquer the fear of defeat, the fear of screwing up, of losing the ball. It also teaches you to maintain that balance between success and failure, because you know when you are walking on a narrow ledge where sometimes the difference between success and failure can depend on stupid little things. As a result you become wiser. At the core of it all you know that you can be successful in a game or that you can lose, because sometimes you hit the ball well and it hits the post and then you mishit the ball and it goes in anyway. This to me is fundamental. But above all it's about respect.'

But now, as happens everywhere, the Argentinian footballer has become an employee, a guy with a job. 'After the massive industrialisation of the Sixties the "factory ethic" was transferred to football, which obscured the sheer joy of the game and destroyed that sense of pride we were talking about earlier,' analyses Cappa. 'Consequently what we are creating are production-line players. In general, the footballer produced by this process earns more and more money, as the big capitalists were quick to seize on football as a huge business opportunity, with sportswear, television, radio, etc. What they have achieved is the transformation of twenty-year-olds, kids like Ronaldo [Nazario] and Raúl, into sad youngsters with pots of money'.

In addition to being a worker, the Argentinian footballer is, as has been said, just another emigrant: between 2009 and 2010 Argentina 'exported' close to 1,800 footballers; Brazil, 1,440. 'The very good, the good and the average, they all go,' adds Ángel Cappa. 'In effect everybody goes. And here in Argentina the only ones who play are those who are about to leave and those who have returned late in their careers.'

The good footballer leaves, everybody plays all over the place, the fan, frustrated for six days of the week, allows himself to be carried along on a wave of passion inside the stadium ... and that is how we get to an earthquake! This is football in Argentina. Sacheri encapsulates it best in two scenarios. 'For me football is about two images. On the one side what we call a *campito* [a mini pitch], a barren piece of wasteland without goals, where kids gather to play football. They're normally a long way out of the city. And the other scenario is of another group of blokes jumping about in the stands, which is how we watch football here. This thing about remaining in our seat ... it's very difficult. I go with my son to watch Independiente. And me, at my age I'd say: "... best I go to watch the game in the box and sit down." And I can't because my son says to me, "no, let's go to that place where we've got a bad view, the sun's beating down on us, and where we're squashed for the entire game ... but where we shout, jump, and where everyone is around us." That way we are in a permanent collective conversation, where someone makes a comment, someone else makes fun of somebody, then someone else answers back ... And then you sagely analyse a match with a bloke you can't even see because he is two steps up from you and you can't even turn around and look at him.'

The tango, now enjoying a renaissance in the world of dance, despite not being as popular as it was decades ago, tells us much about what it is to be Argentinian: 'it expresses resentment, fear, sadness and cunning,' explains Marcos Aguinis. Is this the Argentinian gene? *Is* there an Argentinian gene? Is there one in football? And if not, how to explain that three of the top five or six players in the history of the game, three players who marked the age in which they were playing – namely, Alfredo Di Stéfano, Maradona and Messi – have been Argentinian. And, yes, Di Stéfano must be included. Those who don't know him should listen to Jorge Valdano talking to Clarín. 'He directed games, he was someone who broke all the rules in his time. He was the director: the king of the castle, the destabiliser, powerful, brimming with talent. He was not the typical Argentinian footballer of his era. His was a freak talent.'

Those three were born in a country with a smaller population than many of the other world champions (Brazil, England, France, Spain, Germany, Italy). Is it because they play in the streets or on bumpy pitches? 'Technique is improved on good pitches, not bad ones,' says the ex-Real Madrid footballer Santiago Solari. Is it because in Argentina there is more emphasis on individual strength and dribbling skills ahead of the team collective? Is football felt and played as much in other countries as it is in Argentina? Ángel Cappa likes to define the Argentinian footballer as the bearer of historic genes. 'There were, and I say there were, not there are, basic concepts that were learned listening, looking, even before you could walk. And a modesty that obliged you to search for perfection. To put it another way: if I can't create it for myself, if I don't have the skill or the talent, then at least I can give the ball to my companion. The most respected in the neighbourhood was never the bully, but the one who could play with the most skill.'

Cappa and other coaches believe that things are changing, that now anything goes, that everything is good as long as victory is achieved; this is the new mantra, perhaps also the new gene. But there are things that remain even with the passing of time. 'The Argentinian footballer has a personality that is produced from a high level of self-esteem, that helps him excel at the most difficult times,' the veteran coach explains. 'What is very bad in life can be very good for competition – I'm referring to the fact that Argentinian footballers believe themselves to be much better than they really are.'

And the style? Is there an Argentinian style of play? In 1912, the *Standard*, one of the three English-language newspapers in Buenos Aires, was surprised that football and rugby, imported from the British Isles, had been adopted with such enthusiasm in Argentina, even though in practice it was 'not very scientific'. The temperament of the young natives was described as 'vehement and impulsive'. The English insisted that the game had to be enjoyed in a spirit of 'fair play' and promoted this ethos throughout the colonial schooling system, seeking to instil a sense of 'gentlemanly conduct'. Overflowing emotions had to be controlled.

But, just as happened in every country of the world that adopted football as the people's game, the indigenous population would eventually make it their own. In Argentina the driving force behind this new sport would be Spanish and Italian immigrants who, together with locally based Creoles from the main central urban area, Buenos Aires, were determined to create a distance between themselves and the British. A sense of national consciousness was growing among these 'new' Argentinians and their newfound passion would be played their way, according to their rules. And hang 'fair play'. When you've left your country to make a new life in a foreign land you want to succeed. You want to win. Fairness is for those who enjoy the luxury of leisure time and privilege. The Argentinian game would be motivated by the desire to win. It was what drove the immigrants in their daily struggle to survive.

The anthropologist Eduardo Archetti established in his book *El potrero, la pista y el ring: Las patrias del deporto argentino* (2001) (roughly translated as 'The Pitch, the Track and the Ring: The Birthplace of Argentinian Sport') a fascinating relationship between football and the tango in the development of Argentinian masculinity. The first recognition of Argentinian footballers in the twentieth century coincided with the consolidation of the tango as music and an erotic dance, whose difficult choreographed movements served to identify it as an example of Argentinian cultural creativity. Similarly, Argentinian football began to dismiss the British emphasis on physical strength and discipline, and to focus instead on the Creole qualities of 'agility and virtuosity of movement' – especially with dribbling, or *gambeta* as it is known. The dribble is a deception, and, for the Argentinian, whether he likes it or not, deception forms part of his culture.

The international achievements of the national side (runners-up in the 1928 Olympics and in the World Cup of 1930) and a European tour by Boca Juniors in 1925, with the aid of a few other Argentinian clubs, confirmed Argentinian virtuosity in European eyes and hallmarked the dribble, pass and touch as characteristic elements of their style of play. The Europeans, it could be read in *El Gráfico*, were of the belief that the Argentinians 'played football as if they were dealing with a melody'. And later the River Plate side of the 1940s, known as 'the machine', built up a collective strength and understanding of the game: suddenly, beauty could be synchronised.

Alfredo Di Stéfano played in that same River side, if only as a replacement for Adolfo Pedernera. 'The Blond Arrow' (as he is known in Spain) took this style of play wherever he went, both as a player and a coach. On the bench at Espanyol, and tired of seeing the ball flying over the heads of the players, he stopped a training session. 'What is the ball made out of?' he asked the young players. 'Leather,' they answered. 'Where do you get leather from?' 'From a cow,' they said. 'And what does a cow eat?' 'Grass,' they said. To which Di Stéfano replied: 'Right, so … play it on the grass then!'

Argentinian football was born and developed in the fields, or *potreros*. On these uneven pieces of ground, extensions of land that was being built upon, the kids would learn the art of dominating the ball and copying the techniques of their sporting heroes. It is said that, just as the Brazilians learned their shooting and controlling skills from playing barefoot in the sand, so the wastelands of Argentina provided the training ground for the dribbling and passing skills that would become uniquely Argentinian.

All of it creates '*la Nuestra*' as they refer to it. Our Way.

And just as the *potreros* have 'given birth' to some of the world's greatest footballers, including Messi, so their lure continues to draw them back, not just in geographical terms but also in spirit. The Argentinian footballer, often an immigrant, has a constant need to return home, to distance himself from the pressures of professional football. 'I have listened to a lot of first division footballers say that it is a shame that they are not allowed to go out and play on the rough pitches, the *campitos*, the *potreros*,' says Liliana Grabín. 'They have to come out of the city because there are few spaces left in the centre of towns. A lot of people tell them not to do it because the "man of the hour" who comes along for a game will suddenly want to make a name for himself by having marked a famous player: and that's how legs get broken, they say. But the pull is stronger than them, irresistible. They go out, into their neighbourhood, their small city, and smell the earth, and they can't avoid it. They start to play with a friend they grew up with, one who stayed in the neighbourhood.'

For them it is a return to basics.

Ángel Cappa tells in his marvellous book *La intimidad del fúbol* ('The Intimacy of Football') how, one day, René Houseman, star of César Luis Menotti's Huracán, vanished from the training camp the day before the game. The coach couldn't believe it. Then the penny dropped. Menotti asked his assistant Poncini to accompany him to Houseman's poor *villa*, the Bajo Belgrano. When they arrived they were enjoying the usual end-of-the-week kickabout. Houseman was not involved in it. A relieved Menotti thought about returning to the hotel before his eyes were drawn to the bench. There he saw Houseman. 'What are you doing here,' the coach asked. Houseman answered: 'Can't you see how that number eleven is playing!' That anonymous winger had taken his place in the most important game of the week.

There are numerous examples of this inherent appreciation of the value of football to the Argentinian psyche. Newell's Old Boys is but one. Gradually reorganising itself, it still has a way to go but with a new board since 2008 and more popular support, it's getting there. They recently won the 2013 Torneo Final. However, financial constraints continue to hinder progress. Leo Messi donated €22,000 to improve the Malvinas Complex where the youngsters play. It is said that he also paid for the first team's gymnasium in the sports city on the outskirts of Rosario, and that one way or another he is laying the groundwork for his eventual return in the years to come.

It is an anonymous gesture that few know about, but there are many others, less well known, who continue to contribute their time and talents to raising revenue for better sports facilities. A new *pensión* was built for the players in the lower levels and Dr Schwarzstein took it upon himself to collect some of the money needed to buy 40 mattresses at €50 apiece. Recently the first team organised a raffle for the supporters in which the winners would play a game against the professionals, share the dressing rooms, and for one day live the life of a footballer. The money raised helped to build the gymnasium for the lower levels at the club.

Football is life in Argentina, and life is football. And that explains why, at the very apex of the vast mountain of footballers of any age and level, officials, coaches and commentators, you see the names Di Stéfano, Maradona and Messi. 'Leo could not have been born in Syria,' said César Luis Menotti. Without Di Stéfano (or Charro Moreno or Mario Kempes), Maradona would never have risen. Without Maradona, or if Leo's father and brothers had not been footballers, we would not have the Messi we know.

This is Leo. The very synthesis of the Argentinian gene.

Journalist: How did you react when Argentina were eliminated from the last World Cup? [2002].

Messi: I was here, in Barcelona. I watched after playing for the lower side with all the other lads. I felt bad, like all of Argentina. And what's more I had all the other kids around me making fun.

Journalist: And you, you kept quiet? Or did you get into an argument? You don't look like a fighter.

Messi: No, no. The game ended and I went home... normally I'd stay there all day, but on that day I went home.

(Conversation taken from the Argentinian documentary *The Flea Dossier*)

The defeat of your country is even more painful when you are far away from it. The mini drama of the immigrant is that, when things go well for him away from home, his triumphs are of no particular interest to those who live near him. The immigrant footballer likes to return to his neighbourhood so it can be seen that he is doing well. But on his first holidays, back to his home at Las Heras after he had signed for Barcelona, even after he had debuted for the first team, hardly anyone in Rosario was particularly interested in Leo. It was much later, years later, that the teachers, the organisers, the team-mates, began to recall him almost like a divine apparition, a halo of light, a grand presence that changed their very reason for being. The 'I saw him, I touched him, I was there', that says as much about the individuals themselves as it does about Messi, came much later.

In Argentina footballers are distinguished according to the contractual relationship they have with the club: the fans most value those who have won titles and have spent most years at home; it's the same all over the world. But the second type is something very Argentinian: you're a hero if you have been sold after having played for the first team. The third type borders on treason: those who have left without having played in the first division. Or, more than treason, they are never totally accepted by the fans as one of theirs. Like Leo at Newell's. But Messi never stopped being an Argentinian.

But Spain fought to get him to wear the red shirt of Spain.

The coach of the Juniors at Barcelona, Alex García, mentioned to the Under 16 Spanish selector Ginés Menéndez that he had an excellent youngster who, to date, had not played for his country. Ginés went to see him. Leo impressed him and during the Spanish championship that Leo was unable to play in because he was a foreigner, Ginés approached him: 'Would you come with us? If they don't call you up for Argentina, remember us.' The Under 17 tournament was about to take place in Finland and the Spanish side consisted of players like David Silva and Cesc, among others. 'Are you coming?' was the question asked of both him and his father. He had been at Barcelona for two years.

'No thanks,' they both answered.

Leo would never have played for Spain. Messi is Argentinian, from Rosario and a *Leproso*, as he has said on numerous occasions. But, following that offer from Menéndez, several months went by before he received his first call from a member of the Argentinian Federation (AFA) and a year before he got his first official invitation to join the Argentinian squad. The AFA required the presence of 'Lionel Mecci' (sic) at a training camp to be held in the middle of June 2004. Barcelona said they would be delighted to release him, but not immediately, because they were involved in the Copa del Rey Youth Cup.

Until he travelled to Buenos Aires for his first call-up with the national youth team, there would be a series of meetings, coincidences and the odd misunderstanding before Spain would finally abandon its plans to try to convince the youngster to join La Roja.

And the transatlantic journey of a video tape.

Claudio Vivas, Marcelo Bielsa's assistant with Argentina and Athletic Bilbao, is also from Rosario and knew the Messi family, before even Leo started playing. His father, José Vivas, founded the Newell's Old Boys football academy. A certain Rodrigo Messi was shining in his division alongside the *Negro* Sebastián Domínguez who eventually became an international. It was with the young sides at Newell's that Claudio began as a coach. In the club's '87 category there was a 'dwarf' whom everyone was talking about and, during the time that Leo was being coached by Claudio's friend Gabriel Digerolamo, these days a kinesiologist, the young coach would go down to the Malvinas to see their games that featured the up-and-coming star. 'It was a pleasure to watch him,' says Vivas today.

The years passed and Marcelo Bielsa called Vivas to ask him to accompany him on his adventure with the national side, and, after having renewed his contract with the AFA in 2002, both set out in October on a tour of Europe to speak with all the international players they would be counting on. Marcelo wanted to explain to them why he had renewed his contract and what his plans were. In Barcelona he met up with the Barcelona goalkeeper Roberto Bonano and Espanyol's central defender, Mauricio Pochettino, and Claudio asked them, in passing, how Leo Messi was getting on.

'He's murdering them in the Youths, Claudio,' said Bonano.

Vivas wanted to know more. Marcelo and his assistant were staying at the Princesa Sofia hotel close to the Camp Nou and when their presence became known a number of friends and agents came by in search of a few moments of their time. Such as a certain gentleman called Jorge, an Argentinian who worked in the office of Josep María Minguella. The stranger asked for Vivas at reception and he came down to meet him, although the conversation was at first cold and stilted. Jorge was an agent, the type of person the Bielsa team would normally avoid.

– There is an Argentinian kid you need to watch, said the stranger.
– Why is that?
– Well, as you're not doing anything about it, the boy is about to play for the Spanish Under 17 side, insisted Jorge with that level of urgency often employed by agents.
– Have you got any information on the boy?
– By coincidence I just happen to have a video with me.
– Get me five complete games as well.

The video was 12 minutes long and showed the best of Messi playing for Barcelona in a level against boys two years older than himself. Vivas wanted to analyse everything, the good, the bad and the indifferent, his positioning on the pitch, the quality of his rivals and his team-mates, if he was selfless, if he was a long-distance or short-burst player, what he did with the ball, and what he did without it. He needed a wider context and he got this when he saw all the games on the tapes that arrived at his hotel a few hours later.

Vivas put on the first tape. A few seconds passed. 'This ... this ... this is the *dwarf* from the '87 generation that Gabriel used to run!'

Jorge explained to him that the Spanish selectors were prepared to give Leo's father money so that he would play for Spain, but his family only wanted him to play for Argentina, as did the boy himself.

– Tell the father not to worry, that I am going to try to arrange something, suggested Claudio.

Up to that point Marcelo Bielsa had no idea what moves Vivas had initiated, but his assistant felt that the matter was now sufficiently important to be shared with his boss. 'Go ahead, Claudio, don't waste any time. But let me see something,' said Bielsa. He was surprised. 'We can't lose this boy,' was the conclusion.

From his Barcelona hotel room, Vivas phoned Hugo Tocalli who worked with junior Argentina players and at that time ran the under-17 side.

– It's difficult to bring the boy out. But when you return to Argentina come and see me and bring the tapes with you, Tocalli told him.

Vivas could not understand his reticence. He was sure of Messi's extraordinary talent, but he didn't insist. There were other important matters pending for him and Marcelo. On his return to Buenos Aires on 22 November, Vivas turned up at the under-17 training camp and gave Tocalli the evidence.

– Please don't let this opportunity slip.
– We'll analyse it.
– If we don't act quickly – not because of Lionel, not because of his father, but, rather, because of the pressure being put on by Spain – we are going to lose a great player.

Vivas insisted, so much so Tocalli thought, incorrectly, that he had some vested interest in the matter. Vivas was hurt: he was only defending the interests of the national side; what were they thinking? Round about the same time, Carles Rexach, the football director at Barcelona, had called the Spanish Federation to push the possibility that Leo might play for La Roja.

Tocalli continued to delay his analysis. In addition to any

suspicions he might have (all totally unfounded) he wasn't sure that it was necessary to bring a 16-year-old boy from the other side of the ocean with all the costs, doubts, acclimatisation issues and numerous other inconveniences that it entailed.

Vivas felt frustrated. Marcelo knew Claudio well so when he saw him unsettled he felt they needed to chat.

– What's the matter?
– Look, I've had a confrontation over this boy, Messi, and I believe that Argentina could end up losing a great deal in this situation.
– Let me go and talk with Tocalli.
– It might be worth taking the kid training with us, he said. The national side would often bring the youths along to train so they became accustomed to the dynamic that they would encounter later in their careers.

A bit later, Hugo Tocalli received 'advice' from those above him in the federation that he should have a look at the tapes. And act upon what he saw.

Tocalli was just about to leave for Finland to take part in the Under 17 World Championships with some of the players who would later win the Under 20 World Championships (Biglia, Ustari, Garay). He had a look at the tape. 'The video was only five or six plays on synthetic pitches and you could see that he was a special boy with a tremendous change of rhythm and the ball stuck to his body. He went from zero to 100 metres in three seconds. I was surprised by the way he took off,' remembers Tocalli.

Tocalli called the Argentinian coach José Pekerman, at that time sporting director of Leganés in Spain, and asked him for information about Leo. 'A genius,' was the answer. At the same time Tocalli met up with Julio Grondona, the president of the AFA, to whom they had already spoken about the boy. It wasn't necessary to call Leo along to train with Bielsa's side. Grondona and Tocalli decided to organise immediately two friendly internationals, against Paraguay and Uruguay, so he could put on the Argentina shirt, both matches with international referees, so that they could sign an official form that would then be sent to FIFA, thereby preventing Spain from taking Messi from them. They had to make discreet and urgent contact with the Messis.

– Right, lads, you find a place for him or I will, but one way or
  another we are going to sort this out, said Grondona.

An administrator at the AFA started to look for Jorge Messi's telephone number. He tried ten numbers before he got the right one.

– Are you Jorge Messi, Leo's father?
– Yes, that's right.

Found him. Tocalli spoke with his father, and then with Leo. They
both said yes in seconds; there was no question, Leo wanted to play
for Argentina. Thanks for the call, you have made us very happy.
Tocalli explained that he couldn't call him up for the 2003 Under
17 tournament because he had already named his squad, but that he
could count on playing for the Under 20s very soon.

Leo wrote about the episode in a letter to a friend on 17 November 2003: 'Hi, Fabi. I'm writing to you because I told you when
I heard from the national side I would let you know. A couple of
hours ago, Tocalli called me and my old man and he congratulated
me for everything that had happened so far and that they were
going to call me up for training with the kids from the '85 and '84
generation. For the next South American tournament. He told my
dad that he had seen many videos of me but he hadn't called me for
the Under 17 World Cup because he thought I was too small (so he
said). But he said that he saw me recently and now he thinks I'm
okay. Okay, Fabi, I send you a big kiss. Ciao.'

In the Finland Under 17 tournament, which took place in August
2003, Argentina lost in the semi-finals to Spain, for whom Leo's
team-mates in the junior Barcelona side were playing, with Fàbregas scoring twice in a 3–2 win. The two sides were sharing a hotel
and after the match Tocalli asked Cesc about the 'dwarf'. 'Leo? He's
a monster. Extraordinary. They wanted to put him in our side,' said
the Catalan midfielder. 'If he had played today, you would have
scored loads of goals against us and come out as champions. We
wanted him to play for Spain, but he says he wants to go with you.'

Claudio Vivas never mentioned anything to Leo about his battle,
the video, the doubts. He didn't think it was right to. Messi, Vivas
believes, would have played for the national side, sooner or later.
Maybe it would have been delayed a bit, but …

He would never have looked good in a Spanish shirt ... or happy.

'Hello, Fabi, how are you? Well, I'm writing to you to answer all you asked me. The truth is at first I was very happy, appearing in the paper and having the radio call me. But now they're breaking my balls. I can't wait for when all this is over and they're not talking about me all the time. Anyway as far as this dressing room is concerned, I can tell you that everything is really "super-cool" and I have loads of things to tell you, but I'll tell you them when I'm over. I'll explain how everything has gone, step by step. I think everything has gone really well, but now I'm thinking about the next match on Saturday, hoping that I play well and we win. That's what my old man and Coloma tell me.'

(Email sent by Lionel Messi after his debut for Barcelona against Porto, dated 20 November 2003)

He was coping with a season in which he was achieving all his objectives well ahead of schedule. He made his debut for the Barcelona first team after changing his levels no fewer than five times. He was called up by the Argentina national squad for a couple of friendlies. And he was making friends in Barcelona, if only a few.

The 17-year-old Leo travelled to Buenos Aires a week before the first friendly, against Paraguay, and was presented to the group before the first training session.

– Lads, this is Lionel Messi who has come over from Barcelona, said Tocalli.

Leo stood to one side, head bowed.

This is how Pablo Zabaleta remembers it: 'We started to warm up, a little game on a small pitch and you could see it. This bloke is different.' The truth is, Leo was skinning all of them. 'In the first session he left us all with our jaws dropping. With his change of pace he left all of us defenders nailed to the floor.'

Leo was one of only two foreigners in the group along with Mauro Andrés Zanotti, who played with Ternara in Italy. And just as with that first trial organised by Charly Rexach, his team-mates were a couple of years older than him. In addition to Zabaleta, in a team hastily thrown together so that he could put on the Argentina shirt, there were also Ezequiel Lavezzi from Estudiantes of Buenos Aires and recently signed by Genoa, and Ezequiel Garay. The players had no inkling of the reason for the friendlies.

'When he walked on for the warm-up, he did so with the usual humility that characterises him,' says Gerardo Salorio, the team's physical coach known as 'the Professor'. 'And the first thing I said to him was: "if you want to play here the first thing you're going to have to do is take off your ring and get your hair cut, maestro." He half looked at me ... he didn't say anything.' At that time Salorio was working with the senior teams and was asked to help out with the new technical staff of the Under 20 side. He wanted to set the ground rules from the first day, what he called *bajado de linea dura-dura*, which effectively translates as 'my way or the highway'. Leo was irritated.

'I went in too hard, as if they were senior players. I shouldn't have,' Salorio remembers now. 'A few minutes later, I looked at him and said in front of the whole group: "Leo, I need to apologise to you in front of everyone, I went too far with you, I was out of order. I shouldn't have done it, you didn't know the rules, I apologise in front of everyone." And then he looked at me and smiled as if to say: "he's human, this bloke." And that was my first meeting with him. He isn't one to talk much.'

The 29th of June, the day of the friendly against Paraguay, arrived. It was a cold night at the recently revamped Argentina Juniors stadium, renamed the Diego Maradona after the famous number 10 who had made his debut there in 1976 against Talleres. The admission charge for the game, of little interest to fans, was a newspaper, and it would finish up at the Garrahan Children's Hospital that was collecting paper to raise funds. Only 300 people were present to see Messi's debut.

'Now, you would think that the whole world was at the stadium that night if you believe everybody who says they were there,' says Salorio.

Argentina's starting line-up was:

Nereo Champagne; Ricardo Villalba, Ezequiel Garay, Lautaro Formica; Pablo Zabaleta, René Lima, Juan Manuel Torres, Matías Abelairas; Pablo Barrientos; Pablo Vitti, Ezequiel Lavezzi.

Manager: Hugo Tocalli.

Before the game it started to drizzle and in the first half Argentina were an overwhelming 4–0 ahead. It was time to bring on the boy.

'He was a few metres away and I said to him: "Let's go,"' Salorio recalls. 'He is sitting looking at me, as if to say: "Is it my turn then?" And I said. "What? Don't you want to play, then?" He warmed up and started the second half.'

At half-time, Lavezzi and Abelairas came off, and Franco Miranda and Leo, with number 17 on his back, came onto the pitch.

'They couldn't stop him,' Zabaleta says today. Leo made two assists. In the eightieth minute, with the score 6–0, he picked up the ball unmarked on the edge of the centre circle, in the opposition's half. 'It was an extraordinary piece of play, then and now,' 'the Professor' recalls. 'He dribbled past everyone. And I said: "we've got a star here."'

Messi had set off in double-quick time, then, face to face with the keeper, wrong-footed him with a feint and found himself in front of an open goal. His first goal for Argentina.

In the end it was a convincing 8–0 victory. The match was shown on TyC Sports, but the recording was lost for many years. It was recently found and returned to the Argentine federation:

http://www.youtube.com/watch?v=vyrEF6Gnjgs

From that starting eleven, Ricardo Villalba was to make his debut for River Plate's first team but he only played once for them. He tried his luck in the second division (with Rafaela, Defensa and Justicia) and later lower down (with Defensores de Belgrano in the Metropolitan B), before returning to the second division (with Aldosivi). René Lima, who came out of the junior ranks at River, went to Israel for a few months, and then jumped from club to club in the first and second divisions in Argentina before moving to Chile, where he now plays at Cobreloa. Franco Miranda played in Sweden and Scotland (with St Mirren) and now plays for Sportivo Belgrano. Matías Abelairas, who was replaced by Leo, plays for Puebla de Mexico, having moved there from Vasco de Gama. He was rejected by Glasgow Rangers after failing a trial with them. The road to the summit is littered with obstacles; for some, they are insurmountable.

The team then travelled to the Estádio Suppici in Colonia for the next friendly, this time against Uruguay. Leo came on at the start of the second half with the score at 1–1, thanks to a goal from Pablo Vitti. Messi scored twice (47th and 56th minutes) and played a big part in the fourth goal, as Salorio explains. 'The keeper gave the ball to the left-back, Leo was about ten metres way. He got there first! Then he went past one, past the goalkeeper and he was left with a tiny space between the post and the goal line and so he just touched it back so Lavezzi could come in and stick it in. I said: "Whoa, we've got something amazing here …"'

The final 1–4 scoreline reflected the difference between the two sides. 'This Messi is something special' read the headlines on the sports paper *Olé*. 'When we returned on the Buquebus to Argentina, I said to Leo that in December we would take him to train with us because we wanted to take him to the Sudamericano Championships in Colombia in 2005,' says Tocalli.

That cold summer, Leo returned to Rosario to spend the rest of his holidays. He walked the streets without being recognised. They would be his last days of anonymity.

The Sudamericano Championships began on 13 January 2005 and the top four teams would compete in the following summer's World Cup in Holland, and after those two friendlies, Messi was included in the final squad. He arrived in December to join up with the group with Barcelona's permission (it was being played in the middle of the season), despite the fact that he had already made his debut with the first team two months earlier in a match against Espanyol. Zabaleta, captaining the side, was two years his senior and he soon got close to the new arrival, as it was his duty. 'I sat down with him on one occasion to discuss what we had in mind, to ask him what he needed, to tell him that we were with him. And it was all short answers, he was the boy of the group.'

Pancho Ferraro, the coach of Gimnasia de Jujuy, took charge of the Under 20s from January after answering the call from José Pekerman, the new coach of the full side. In January he travelled to Colombia where he shared the bench with Tocalli, who continued as coach of the Under 20s before becoming Pekerman's assistant. 'That's where I first saw Messi,' says Ferraro. 'In the first two

South American games against Venezuela and Bolivia, he was on the bench. The team was playing badly in the first halves but things changed in the second because Leo came on.'

'The Flea' did not have the same physique as the rest of them, they said. But he came on in the sixtieth minute against Venezuela and made it 2–0 (the final score was 3–0), winning the man of the match award. 'But I never got hold of the ball,' he was heard to say; he would have voted for Garay. Against Bolivia he came on at half-time for Barrientos. Five minutes into the second half he made a run from midfield going past everyone before scoring. Thirteen minutes later he scored again to make it 3–0 at the finish.

He was in the starting line-up for the next match against Peru, although this was the exception rather than the rule: he only featured from the start in three of the nine games. 'He lacked intensity, the games were very demanding, some of the stadiums were at quite high altitude, and we realised that he was tiring a bit,' remembers Tocalli. 'Coming out for the second half, he caused havoc,' Ferraro points out. Since he did not perform as well if he played from the start, Tocalli and Ferraro considered putting him back on the bench:

- Pancho, we should speak to Leo.
- About what? Ferraro and Tocalli talked as they drank *mate* [a kind of tea], an Argentinian custom, and sat on the side of the blackboard moving counters around.
- We need to speak to him because he doesn't seem to play as well as when he was coming off the bench. What about if we do it as before, put him on the bench and play him in the second half?
- Okay, Hugo, could be. Let's speak to him.

'We went to get him. He was rooming with Lavezzi,' remembers Pancho Ferraro. 'In the room, Hugo told him what we had in mind and Messi thought it was a good idea. It didn't upset him. On the contrary. "I planned to say the same thing to you", he said. Sometimes you ask yourself how this type of player will take it. And it depends on how you speak to them. It depends how you sit them down, how you look them in the eye, and the words you use. Leo understood.'

The competition continued. Argentina had won four games and

drawn four. They had to play the last game against Brazil on 6 February. Victory would guarantee third place and qualification for the world championships in Holland. Leo came on for Neri Cardozo in the sixty-fifth minute with the sides level at 1–1. Barrientos put in a cross that Leo finished to make it 2–1, the winning goal, his first against a Brazil side that were going to finish top in any case. Colombia, with leading goal scorer Hugo Rodallega, were second and Argentina third.

Leo confirmed that he was now at the level that everyone thought he would be. He never doubted it but the impact he had made on the tournament made him want more. He was aware, though, that his body was putting limitations on him so he listened to the advice of Tocalli: 'work with a personal trainer, like Ronaldinho's.'

And he did exactly that on his return to Barcelona, sometimes in double sessions. Three months after becoming one of the movers and shakers of the Under 20 side, Leo scored his first goal for Barcelona in one of the nine games he played for the first team that season. The season was becoming one full of memorable events.

Before flying to the Netherlands for the world championships, Leo passed through Rosario and returned to the Newell's ground for the first time in five years. Some people greeted him; not all of them knew him but those who did passed the word – 'this is the kid who had to leave, the one from Barcelona'. They asked him about his new home, how were things going for him and about the national team. The Under 20 world championship had grabbed the attention of the Argentinian public. The team, which historically had performed well at this level with three victories in the last five competitions, were very powerful. They were going to Holland to win the title.

The competition actually has a very long and interesting tradition; it is the most important of all the tournaments for the younger ranks of international sides and a window on a host of new faces. It is hard to predict what will happen there: a substitute in a first game can very quickly become an automatic starter and end up the tournament's best player, in what is often the best launching pad for great careers.

At the age of 18, Maradona led his Argentina side to its first world Under 20 title in Japan. In Chile in 1987, Yugoslavia called upon the services of the likes of Robert Prosinecki, Zvonimir Boban and Davor Šuker. Portugal had the golden generation of Luis Figo, João Pinto and Rui Costa who were champions in 1991. And in 1997 France prepared for its attack on the World Cup with the launch of David Trezeguet and Thierry Henry, even though Pablo Aimar's Argentina won the tournament. In 1999, the Spain of Xavi Hernández and Iker Casillas won the title: it was the sign of things to come. In 2001 Argentina won (with Javier Saviola starring) and Dani Alvés faced Andrés Iniesta in the final of 2003.

The fifteenth edition of the tournament was to take place in Holland between 10 June and 2 July. Spain had brought with them players like Fernando Llorente, Cesc, Albiol, José Enrique; Colombia had brought Falcao. Brazil had Rafinha (now with Bayern Munich) and a host of players who still play in their country's domestic leagues.

Argentina gave Leo a few more days' holiday because he was the only player coming from Europe, but he preferred to meet up with the group when the squad was called together. It may have seemed a minor detail but it was one, none the less, that was appreciated by his team-mates: the 'we're all the same' approach is one of the best types of calling cards.

When Tocalli, Ferraro and Zabaleta saw Leo in the meeting prior to the side's departure for Holland, they discovered a new Messi compared to the one of four months earlier. 'We noticed a huge development in those months,' remembers Pancho Ferraro, who would be the only coach of the Under 20s. 'We noticed a Leo in much better physical shape,' recalls Hugo Tocalli. 'He was better armed. He was more resilient. We couldn't forget that he was at Barcelona and he came to us with evidence of all the work he had done there on his physique, tactics and technique.'

He had taken another great leap forward, this time physically. At almost 18, he was 1.69 metres tall and weighed 64 kilos.

This was the Argentina squad for that tournament:

Goalkeepers: Oscar Ustari, Nicolas Navarro, Nereo Champagne
Defenders: Lautaro Formica, Gustavo Cabral, Julio Barroso, Ezequiel Garay, David Abraham
Midfielders: Juan Manuel Torres, Gabriel Paletta, Lucas Biglia,

Pablo Zabaleta, Patricio Pérez, Emiliano Armenteros, Rodrigo
Archubi, Fernando Gago, Neri Cardozo
Forwards: Sergio Agüero, Gustavo Oberman, Pablo Vitti, Lionel
Messi

'I like watching European football very much,' remembers Gustavo
Oberman. 'Leo had made his debut with the Barcelona first team
but he didn't play a lot. I knew that. We'd seen him in the Sudamericano tournament, even though he'd had a lot of physical problems
during that time, but the truth is, in the games he appeared in he
earned the admiration of everyone: team-mates, press ... They all
said: is this the successor to Diego? Because at that time everyone
was waiting for a successor to Maradona, someone that would fight
him for his crown. We spoke about this among ourselves.'

Forty days of planning took place under the aegis of 'Professor'
Salorio. He brought along books and films, invented new educational games and tried to spring surprises on his team every day to
keep them motivated. But Salorio knew that the first hours were
crucial; that's when the pieces begin to fall into place, when personalities are studied, when people recognise each other, choose each
other's company.

Sergio Agüero, '*el Kun*', the same age as Leo and from Independiente, wasn't one for watching television or watching league matches
that weren't Argentinian, or for getting involved on the internet. He
hadn't paid much attention when Leo was being spoken of as the
great prospect from Barcelona. During that first morning the group
were at table having a meal together. Messi to the right of Agüero,
and to the left of him Formica. Garay was facing them. They began
to talk about football boots and Leo commented that a new boot
had just come out in the USA, and stuff like that. Kun looked at
him. And then he looked at him again. He asked himself, who is he?
He had to find out.

– What's your name?

'I said this to Leo,' Agüero recalls now, 'and Leo remembers, eh!!
He pisses himself laughing now. So ... he looked at me and said
"Lionel", "Oh – I said – almost like me. And your surname?"
"Messi," he said. And of course I thought, "fine", and then Formica

looks at me. "What?" I say. "What?? You don't know who that is?" Afterwards I began to realise that I had heard about some player from Barcelona and thought to myself, "Oh, it's him."

'Of course that was when we were eating,' remembers Agüero laughing. 'Later, when we were training, I said, "this guy flies". And after that we used to piss ourselves laughing together, we got on really well and ended up sharing a room.'

Yes, they shared a room in that tournament. 'I created the Kun–Messi mini society,' explains Gerardo Salorio. 'Why? For two reasons: they were the youngest with similar tastes (they were both brilliant at PlayStation) and also I thought I could prepare a double act for the future of Argentinian football.'

Marcelo Roffé, the Argentinian youth squad's psychologist, agreed with Salorio's decision because Messi and Agüero, who had not been at the Sudamericano, found themselves in very similar situations. José Pekerman and the federation saw the need for someone to get close to the boys and help them to express their feelings at an age when everything was quite confusing for them, hence the presence of a psychologist from that tournament onwards. 'Afterwards, some of them had to improve their concentration, the way they handled pressure, made decisions, their feelings of anxiety before the game,' says Roffé. 'There is always prejudice about my job. But they realised that this could be useful to them and so it turned out.'

Leo and Kun became everyone's kids, principally because they were the smallest. And sometimes, with their physical size and that look of innocence, despite the fact that they were both 17 they seemed much more childlike than they really were. 'I remember the first night we heard strange noises, it was half past four in the morning, I was half asleep when the telephone rang,' Salorio remembers. 'I told them that I did not want them to receive any calls in the room from anybody, family or press, that all calls should come through me. I picked up the phone and it was Kun: "I'm scared, I can hear noises …" And I said, "Go to sleep, you pain in the arse, nothing's happening!" Of course, he was a baby, he heard noises and he was frightened.'

Oberman, who hadn't considered himself a starter, is another of those reserved footballers who finds it difficult to open up to people he doesn't know, something typical of those early days in the team gatherings. 'I think Leo is the same,' says the forward, now at Quilmes. 'I was new and it was difficult for me to approach him or ask him about his life, because I didn't know him, but day by day you saw that he was just a normal lad, who didn't try to stick out, didn't raise his voice, minded his own business, didn't boast or make fun of you. A very normal boy managing, what for us, or for anyone, would be something very difficult to cope with – he was playing for the best team in the world but was happy to step down and play at Under 20 level. That is not something just anyone can do, it isn't easy to go down a level.'

Leo wanted to win games with Argentina. Now that he was immersed in the dynamic of the national team, he wasn't about to let anyone take him away from it. He felt that, after the early gift of a place in the Sudamericano, he was where he ought to be, that this was his level. So the earlier he could make his mark, the better.

The first game to be played was against the USA. With the group in the Arke Stadium's dressing room, Pancho Ferraro, having covered the blackboard with numbers, began to call out the names: 'number one Ustari, two Cabral, three … and the forwards Vitti and Oberman.'

Messi was left on the bench.

Group stage
Argentina vs USA
11 June 2005, Arke Stadium, Enschede
Attendance: 10,500
Referee: Terje Hauge (Norway)

Three days before the start of the championship, it became clear that José Sosa was going to start up front with Vitti. Then, in training, he took a pass and as he struggled to control the ball he lost his balance and fell awkwardly, his arm twisting painfully. He was clearly injured and as the shocked team came to terms with his injury, Ferraro decided to abandon the session. Walking towards the dressing rooms Daniel Martínez, the team doctor, approached him. 'Pancho, keep an eye on Leo, he has a slight hamstring strain but nothing to be too concerned about.'

Shortly afterwards, everyone's worst fears were confirmed. Sosa's wrist was fractured. Patricio Pérez of Vélez was called up to the squad. The press screamed that Leo was going to replace Sosa as *enganche*, in the hole behind the striker. Despite his age, Messi was, they said, along with Zabaleta, Gago and Biglia, one of the best players in the squad.

'I thought, "he will play Messi with Vitti",' says Oberman. 'I wasn't playing much in the youth teams, I'd only been involved in three friendlies. I'd had a good championship in the first division, and I thought that I'd be included in the list of 21, and once that was confirmed I was pleased. I never thought I'd be a starter. Afterwards, when we arrived at the world championships and I saw my team-mates, I thought it was going to be it was going to be hard to be in the line-up.'

'I thought about it,' says Pancho Ferraro, 'and I said, "Leo can go on the bench and if I need him, I'll put him on in the second half".' As in the Sudamericano. Vitti was one of the stars at Rosario Central and it was rumoured that he was about to sign for Atlético de Madrid. He was the first-choice striker and Oberman, Messi and Agüero had to fight it out among themselves to catch the eye of the selector for the other attacking role. In the end Vitti played just three matches in those championships and spent one more year at Central, before joining Club Atlético Banfield, where he never really took off. Nor did he blossom when he moved to one of the Argentinian giants, Independiente. He went to Ukraine, then Canada, before making the transition to Peruvian football where he was a championship winner with Universidad de San Martín of Lima. He was then transferred to Universidad de Deportes in the same league. At the age of 18 or 19 the margin between success and failure is extremely narrow and ultimately only time will tell.

In that world championship Vitti was to start ahead of Messi and alongside Oberman. 'I felt a bit strange while Pancho was reading out the names of the starting line-up,' remembers Gustavo Oberman. 'Everyone was looking at each other, in that way that speaks a thousand words,' adds Zabaleta. It seemed strange that the player many considered to be the best was not playing. Leo said nothing; he just looked down at the ground. On the way to the pitch his absence from the line-up was the main topic of conversation. 'He had problems in the Sudamericano,' some of them said. 'Maybe Pancho was frightened of pushing him too hard,' others added. A serious looking Leo sat on the bench. No one spoke to him.

'It was tremendous for me, because I played that game, I did well and after the coaches made some more changes in the line-up, I kept being selected ... I was part of it!' Oberman explains, still with a sense of surprise. For the first match Argentina lined up as follows:

Oscar Ustari; Julio Barroso, Gustavo Cabral, Gabriel Paletta, Lautaro Formica; Pablo Zabaleta, Lucas Biglia, Fernando Gago, Emiliano Armenteros; Pablo Vitti and Gustavo Oberman.

It didn't even occur to Ferraro to glance at the bench during the first half and notice Leo's frustration: 'I was involved with the game.' Ferraro needed more speed and flow up front because the USA were defending very deep. Six minutes before half-time, Chad Barrett put them ahead. Ferraro told Leo to get warmed up because he was coming on for Armenteros, but the change made no difference. Defeat for Argentina 1–0.

It was a grim-faced Leo who returned to the dressing room.

Group stage
Argentina vs Egypt
14 June 2005, Arke Stadium, Enschede
Attendance: 8,500
Referee: Massimo Busacca (Switzerland)

At the end of the game against the USA the senior players met in the dressing room (Biglia, Zabaleta ...). The decision had been made even before discussions were under way. Leo had to play; he was the best. Even though it hadn't been reflected in the score, he had come on for half of the game and had made the difference in terms of speed and boldness. Half a dozen times he had got the ball in the middle of the pitch and moved it forward. Messi made them better and that was why it was worth fighting to have him included. They asked for a meeting with Ferraro and it was Zabaleta who told him what the players had decided. Nothing else needed to be said. The coach agreed.

'Whenever you build a team, you always protect the best player because in the end what you are doing is protecting yourself,' Oberman recognises. 'If someone gives me solutions, then I have to help that person, look after him, give him the ball, make him feel comfortable. This happens in every team in the world.'

Ferraro made changes against Egypt. 'With Messi in the starting line-up, I put Neri Cardozo from Boca on the wing. I didn't touch the defence. The back four, apart from Cabral, who made way for Garay because of two yellow cards in the final, were always the same: Ustari; Barroso, Cabral, Paletta and Formica. After that there was Zabaleta, Gago, '*el Chaco*' (Juan Manuel) Torres and later Neri, or Archubi or Armentero, the three attacking half-backs.' Oberman got the nod to play with Messi. Vitti was on the bench. For Kun Agüero the world championships would come a bit too soon.

It was against Egypt that the group began to see Leo's competitive character. 'In the Under 20 he showed that he had personality,' says Oberman. 'Against Egypt they gave him one hell of a kicking. I'm not sure I'd have got up again. But Leo just got up and carried on, he didn't protest to the referee, I probably protested more than him, because I'm more like that. I can't hold back. I took responsibility for the protesting. For us as long as he had the ball and did what he knew what to do, then we were happy.'

Messi scored in the forty-sixth minute, Zabaleta in the ninety-first. Argentina won 2–0.

Defeat in the first match against the USA meant that the team were now playing for a place in the next stage against Germany, who were also looking for a result. Argentina needed to win, but a draw would be enough to see the Germans through.

Group stage
Argentina vs Germany
18 June 2005, Unive Stadium, Emmen
Attendance: 8,800
Referee: Benito Archundia (Mexico)

Leo played as second striker in a 4-4-2 system even though he spent much of the match on the wing. He was following his gut instinct. 'You could never say to Messi "stay here" because it didn't work. You just let him play and got used to making the most of the space he used to create,' says Gustavo Oberman. Ferraro was beginning to realise that he had to create conditions that would give free rein to Leo's natural style, so that everyone else could reap the benefits. As his partner up front admits: 'They would ask me to make diagonal runs to help Messi, so he could find me, or to open up the way.' The team started to support Leo and give him more and more responsibilities. He took them naturally.

'Messi was just one in the squad, but as the games came and went he got better,' says Ferraro. 'I knew his characteristics, I'd seen all the videos from Barcelona, and I said to everyone else: "we have to be on our guard with him. Sometimes he'll give you the ball, sometimes he won't. Watch out because he may need you to act as a wall to pass back, or as a dummy and then carry on. Make the most of the spaces he creates for you." At that time I used him in central positions but starting either on the right or the left, with Oberman. And I asked the boys to stay alert: if we were pressing three-quarters in of the pitch and there were spaces we could hurt any side because we were very fast, not just the frontmen but also the midfielders who scored goals as well, Zabaleta, Barroso ...' Leo readily accepted one of the obligations of a modern forward: he would be the first line of defence.

The game began. Just before half-time Messi started off from the middle of the pitch, skinned his opponents, before moving wide and putting a precise cross into the area. Oberman let the ball go and Cardozo was there to make it 1–0. It was the forty-third minute, just before the interval.

In the second half, 'Chaco' Torres received a yellow card. Agüero came on for Oberman. Torres got the ball, fell and caught it with his arm. Second yellow: he was sent off, with ten minutes remaining. A decision had to be made. Pancho Ferraro takes up the story.

'[My assistant, Miguel Ángel] Tojo said to me "who do we take off?" I asked Biglia, who was already warming up, to come over. Tojo asked me who I was taking off, I said "Messi". Messi was forty metres away. He came over for the substitution, went past me, and I always gave them a pat on the back, and he sat down. We were winning 1–0. When we left the stadium, as usual they gave us a video of the game. If we had time before supper we would sit down with Tojo and watch it. That's when I saw the face that Messi pulled when I replaced him – I had missed it during the game, but the camera had picked it up. I said to Tojo, "stop, stop, Miguel Ángel, rewind it", which he did. I told him that I hadn't seen that, a strange look on Leo's face.'

Leo had not won a place in the team by pulling faces, but it was hard for him to hide his feelings when things didn't work out for him as he wanted. Leo had given what one of his team-mates described as a *cara de culo*, literally an arse-face.

'He just never wanted to be substituted,' remembers Salorio. 'Leo is someone who doesn't want to come off, even if he's just playing marbles. We had a chat, I went to see him and I think I said: "you are showing disrespect not only to your coach, but you are also being disrespectful to the player who is coming on. He wants to play as well, and he doesn't come on because he asks to, but because he is put on."'

Ferraro continues: 'We watched the video of the game, went for supper and after we'd finished eating, the squad got up and "the Professor", Salorio, came to me and said: "Pancho, Leo would like to speak to you." I said to him, "okay, tell him to wait for me. I'll come now and we can talk."'

– Hello, Leo.
– Hello, Pancho, I wanted to speak to you.
– Fine, what's the matter?
– I was wrong today.
– Why's that then? I said, pretending I didn't know anything.
– No, well … I pulled a face at you and I was wrong. It's just that, Pancho, I want to play.
– That's okay. Don't worry about it, okay? But I'll tell you what – don't do it to Rijkaard, or Pancho, or to any coach. Did you want to play at number five, defensive midfield? No, of course you didn't. After the sending-off, I had to take someone off and Kun Agüero had only just come on. I didn't do it on a whim. I needed to bring on Biglia because he is a number five, a defensive midfielder. But don't worry, there's no problem.
– That's good, Leo said and then returned to the room he was sharing with Kun.

Argentina had qualified for the next round, albeit as runners-up. In any case qualification had relaxed the group. Leo spent his time with Kun on PlayStation (taking turns to be either Barcelona or Argentina). And it was not always that amicable. 'Once we really fought, a proper fight,' Leo remembered in an interview on Mundo Leo TV. 'And we decided there was a long way to go before the end of the tournament, so it was best if we played without trying to kill each other afterwards. A healthier solution.' There was a lot of time to listen to Cumbia music with Ustari or just hang out with the others. 'He felt comfortable with Kun Agüero, and it had been a wise move to put the two of them in the same room,' remembers Ferraro. 'Leo played with the boys, he laughed, always laughing. Kun was more jovial, but Leo was always laughing about what the others did, in particular what Kun did.'

'They're different. Leo is introverted, Kun is an extrovert. But the way they talk is similar, they're a good combination,' says Salorio. 'And Leo waits to see what Kun is doing, it amuses him. And it amuses Kun that he makes Leo laugh.' Agüero performed the task of making Messi's little world a happier place. 'Yes ... Leo would walk around the training camp looking for situations that would make him happy.'

One of Salorio's additional responsibilities on the technical staff was that of imposing discipline and control on the players. After getting off on the wrong foot with Messi at the Sudamericano tournament, he made sure he was a bit more subtle in establishing the ground rules. One day he found Kun and Leo with bags of crisps.

'I slept in the same room as Kun, and there were various meetings that we had to attend at specific times,' Leo remembered in an excellent interview by Martín Souto of TyC Sports where it seems that Leo forgot that the cameras were rolling. 'If you were late, you were fined. Downstairs in the hotel there was a machine that sold sweets and snacks. Everything: chewing gum, sweets, crisps. We were forbidden from buying any of this stuff and at nine o'clock everyone had to be in their room. Downstairs there was also a computer, which was the only one there was, so we used to go down to play on it for a while before curfew time. We went down together and Kun said, "shall we buy something from the machine?" We did and hid what we bought under our shirts. It was three minutes past nine, the door of the lift opens, and it's "the Professor" ...and Kun's there trying to make sure the crisps don't fall out.'

– Nice, are they? asked Salorio.
– Yes.

– Good, let's agree on something then. Eat them, because it's not nice to get food and throw it away, but they will be the last ones you'll be having. Okay? Enjoy them.

Salorio had defused the situation. 'Sometimes bars of chocolate would arrive for the players and I would confiscate them. Then they'd win a game and I'd say to them: "Right, let's have some chocolate." And I'd give every member of the group a bar. I used to carry them around with me in a bag and during the tour I'd be there with my bag, and right up to the last match we would be eating chocolate, sweets, biscuits …'

As he had done on previous occasions, Salorio decided to form a 'government' of players, in which ministers were appointed. The players would be divided into seven departments: cleaning, order and tidiness, economics, the ministry for buying birthday presents, the ministry of fines, special orders and the ministry of entertainment that would put on a different film every night at seven o'clock and also distribute books. 'The Professor' then asked for each ministry to name its leader. Inevitably the players would pick those with the biggest personality so that they could fight their corner for them against Salorio; and those with lesser personalities would inevitably end up in the departments considered of lesser importance. This way the squad would begin to evolve more naturally. The tougher departments were the ones that imposed laws and punishments. And there were stiff fines. With the money raised (it amounted to between $600 and $700) they bought presents for any birthdays being celebrated that month. With anything left they acquired a computer as a reward for the person who won the most competitions. And they would play until ten or eleven at night, either individually or in group competitions. They were slowly coming together.

'The Professor was a star,' Leo told Martín Souto. 'The truth is they would come down hard on us, but they were veteran coaches, they knew what they were doing, and I laugh about it now because I know just how many bollockings I've had from them.'

Leo was not one of the main men in any of the 'ministries' and that perhaps is proof positive of the mark he initially made on the squad: as a footballer he was considered 'relevant', but off the pitch he was small in more than one sense of the word. 'He didn't drink *mate*,' remembers

Salorio. 'Later he got used to it but at that time he didn't drink it like most of them did. He didn't participate. On the pitch, he was an assassin, off the pitch, no. When we were playing darts, I found out who could take the fifth penalty. If someone came along and scored three hundred points, give him the fifth penalty, coach.'

Leo built his small and manageable world within the group: he looked to Kun Agüero for the laughter and, as big groups always put him on the back foot, he looked to Ustari the rest of the time. And that was a lot of time: during meals, going in and out of training sessions, walking about. His team-mates used to joke about the 'couple'. 'Osky, they say we're an item. Does it bother you? Does it bother you? Tell me,' Leo asked Ustari. 'Because if it bothers you, I'll go and say something to them right now!'

He wasn't always so brave, as the goalkeeper recalls. 'He made me go and ask the Professor if he could stay a while longer in our room. And I said to him: "why don't you go?" And he said: "no, because he listens to you, and ..." He was a boy, a boy. We used to put the beds together in my room so Messi could sleep in the middle. That's how he was.'

But as soon as he crossed the white line onto the field of play, Leo became that competitive person with no need of friends. 'In one training session we played a short game,' remembers Ustari. 'There was a shot from about a metre and a half and he whacked it like he wanted to take my head off! And he hit me and I said to him: "What are you doing?" and he looked at me like ... he was the keeper killer, transformed. One day we were doing some dead-ball work and we were laughing and then suddenly the game started and ... well, he was another person. And this was just a training session.'

Ustari found his weak point, how to get to him, to make up for all the goals he used to score against him (a goalkeeper has few ways of getting at a striker, he will invariably lose the footballing challenges). 'You never score from a free-kick, I said to him.' And it was true. Actually, Ustari thought it was something he should improve on, so he discussed it with him. 'You don't score from free-kicks, because you don't want to, because if you were to practise ...' And that's what Leo did. And he started to score from set pieces in training sessions.

'It's only because I started to practise them,' he told Osky.

Finishing second in the group put Argentina in the most difficult part of the draw with their next opponents, a strong Colombia with players like Radamel Falcao, Freddy Guarín and Hugo Rodallega.

Last 16
Argentina vs Colombia
22 June 2005, Unive Stadium, Emmen
Attendance: 8,000
Referee: Claus Bo Larsen (Denmark)

Before the game, Salorio set out to 'make mischief'. He looked for an enemy he could focus on and found him in the opposing coach. A group of players and Argentinian coaches were drinking *mate* when they saw Eduardo Lara, the Colombia coach, coming down the stairs. 'He came down like one of those typical Buenos Aires men, as if he was about to dance a tango, clutching his small bag tightly, and I said to them: "Look at him, he's already winding us up, he already thinks he's beaten us",' said Salorio with a half-smile. 'It wasn't true! The poor bloke was just wandering around the place, much as we were! And they, of course, joined in and said: "You're right, look at him, the son of a bitch!"'

That night 'the Professor' came up with another of his games: with your wrong foot you had to try and score with a plastic ball in a small goal about 20 metres away.

During the match itself, six minutes after Colombia's goal (Otalvaro, 52nd minute), Messi played a one-two with Cardozo who returned it to him inside the area. His angle was getting narrower and so 'the Flea' decided to shoot. 'The feller remembered the game we had played,' 'the Professor' recalls today. 'As everything started to close in, he thought: "If I hit it well last night, why shouldn't I hit it well now?" And he scored from a narrow angle.' He ran back and celebrated with all the rejoicing normally reserved for your first goals. Barroso scored in injury time and Argentina were in the quarter-finals.

That was the first full game that Leo had played for the Argentinian side and put an end to any arguments about whether or not he was worthy of a place. 'There are players who are fast and others who have great technique,' analyses Oberman. 'Riquelme is a great technical player. Jesús Navas of Spain is really fast, but doesn't have Messi's control. Riquelme has fantastic control but doesn't have the speed of Messi. Messi has both things. And that is very difficult to find.'

Quarter-final
Argentina vs Spain
25 June 2005, Arke Stadium, Enschede
Attendance: 11,200
Referee: Benito Archundia (Mexico)

In the next match Argentina had to face the European champions and big favourites who could rely on players like David Silva, Fernando Llorente, José Enrique, Alexis and Cesc Fàbregas, with whom Leo had been reunited after two seasons in London with Arsenal. The night before, Messi met up with Cesc at the hotel where the squads were staying on the day of the game. The last time they had seen each other was with the under-16 side at Barcelona and both had gone on to make their debuts for their respective senior international sides. Cesc only knew it was Leo's birthday when one of his Argentinian team-mates shouted across the room, 'Leo, happy birthday, mate!' Nothing to make a big fuss about, Leo thought.

'And the night before the game my two strikers had a fight!' Salorio remembers. 'I was giving one of my motivational talks, playing a film, and in a flash Messi is fighting with Oberman. A ruckus that no one knew anything about, not even the coach. And all about something really stupid, I'm moving this way, you're moving that way, a push, things get a bit heated, the other gets angry, he throws a punch, he gets one back ... stupid! And we've got Spain the following day. I got the two of them together: "What's going on?" They half explained it to me, shook hands ... and off to bed! It couldn't be solved, and when something can't be sorted out, everyone to bed and we'll try to sort it out in the morning. Recently a friend had given me a very good book – to this day I still have it on my bedside table – called *Why Do People Do Such Stupid Things?*, or something like that. And they had done something stupid. It was four in the morning, I was looking at the book for something that I could read to them about it but couldn't find it ... until I started reading the chapter on adolescence. In the morning they both woke up with faces like smacked arses ... And I said: "Before we start we're going to talk a bit." I read the chapter and I called the two of them. I passed them the book and said: "put your hand here. Do you swear by St Evangelio not to repeat any of these stupidities because the truth is we need you to stop trying to break each other's balls; if we are going to get past Spain we need all the balls we have. And the rest of the group were laughing. And they embraced and everything was forgotten.'

With one problem solved, Salorio needed a new hook to make the next game more of a challenge. 'And I asked myself, how can I get under these guys' skins? So I told them a story: "during the days of Peronism we were a very rich country and Spain was very poor. We got into the habit of sending them three boatloads of grain … These are the great-grandchildren of those we saved from starving. What I mean is that they wouldn't even be here if we hadn't fed them. And so, for that, today we have got to kill them." As you can tell, the story was historically and factually slightly inaccurate. The first ball that their number 9, Llorente, got, Cabral went and killed him, he kicked man and ball and then he pointed his finger upwards. Pancho said to me. "What the fuck did you say to him?" "Nothing, Pancho, I didn't say anything to him." "What the fuck is he saying to him?" "How do I know what they're talking about!" Then the player came up to me and said: "You know what I said to him? I told him about the boats!" And Llorente looked at him with a look as if to say … "what *is* this bloke going on about?"'

Spain were not only the favourites, they were also playing the best football and Pancho Ferraro changed the formation to defend deeper. The match was tied at 1-1 until the seventieth minute, but Leo was getting more and more into the game as it went on. His precise pass from deep infield found Oberman who lifted the ball over the keeper as he came out. The two, involved in the dispute the night before, had united on the football field to score a crucial goal at a key moment.

'It was the only game I did not play as one of the starting eleven,' Oberman remembers. 'It was super-complicated, a hard game. Up until then I hadn't scored goals, and I came on in a bad mood: there were goal-line clearances, I'd hit the post, and smashed the goalkeeper in the face with a shot … and when I scored the first person to come up and congratulate me was Leo. "See, I told you you'd score."'

Two minutes later, a rebound fell to Messi and without it touching the ground he chipped it over the first defender, carried on, and then with the lightest of touches did three more things: rounded another defender before trapping the ball and then hitting it home with his left foot to make it 3–1.

At the end of the game Leo celebrated with the rest of the team on the way to the dressing room and sang as the boys liked to before and after games, at least when they won … 'Ole, ole, ole/ ole, ole, ole, ola/ole. Ole, ole/ every day I love you more/oooooh, Argentina/it's a feeling/ I can't stop', swinging their sweatshirts and football shirts around their heads. And 'Argentina are going to be champions/ Argentina are going to be champions / and we dedicate it to all those fucking mothers who bore you'. Suddenly there was a knock on the changing-room door. It was the chairman of the Spanish Football Federation, Ángel María Villar.

– Lads, quiet, shouted Salorio.
– No, no, for fuck's sake, insisted Villar. My guys have rings, long hair, the latest mobile phones. Yours don't have a pot to piss in, they don't have hair, they run, they give their all, they play, they have balls this big. Let them shout! Viva Argentina!

All of a sudden Leo's life was on fast forward. Any number of things were going on at the same time and Leo was taking them all in his stride. Called up for the national side. Tick. In the starting line-up. Tick. Scoring. Tick. The team's problem solver. Tick. And now, as he entered the final phase of his progression, Barcelona added another box to be ticked. Before the semi-finals against the Brazil of Rafinha, Felipe Luis, Renan and Diego Souza, Leo signed his first professional contract with the FC Barcelona first team. It was the third one he had signed with the club, only this time it came with a buyout clause of €150 million. Box ticked. 'In Holland? Not even I knew about it,' Pancho Ferraro says today. 'But he didn't seem any different. He'd been somewhere with some guys, Barcelona club directors, but I didn't find it strange …' Once again, he was taking steps down a path already trodden, and doing it with his usual lack of emotion.

Obviously, Messi's focus was on the job in hand, specifically the forthcoming test that the national side were facing: the semi-finals of the world championships. Two hours before the game he had to listen to three of his seniors, all of whom had looked after him, had helped him make the most of his talent, had helped him along the road to his first tournament with Argentina.

First, Pancho Ferraro. 'I said to them, "you can make a mistake against Colombia, or Bolivia, but you can't make a mistake against Brazil because if you do they'll kill you". I put the video on for a while, switched it off and then started to talk about what Brazil was and about what we were going to do. And then suddenly, Leo said halfway through the conversation, "Don't worry, we're going to win tomorrow." He addressed it to me but you got the feeling that he was talking to everyone.'

The captain, Pablo Zabaleta, had taken part in the previous Under 20 World Cup finals that had seen Argentina knocked out in the semi-finals, again against Brazil. In Holland the two rivals were now meeting again at the same stage. And in the same hotel. 'Remember, we don't want to look at the Brazilians if we lose, they will be with us if we lose, and we will have to deal with their happiness when we're eating, training ... Better win!' Zabaleta reminded them, too, of the unusual situation that they were facing. 'When it came to me to speak as captain, I said I was being presented with the opportunity to play my last Under 20 World Cup final. I did not want to let that pass. And on top of that they had eliminated us two years earlier. For that reason we had to do everything in our power to win.'

Before going out to warm up, Salorio had prepared a message. 'Emiliano Molina, one of Kun Agüero's best friends and one of Independiente's goalkeepers, had just died. The internet had been banned, so I gave them the news a few days earlier. And ... we were in the semis, we were facing Brazil. This is what I said to them: "lads, on Sunday we're going to have a special advantage in this game because we are going to take them on with three goalkeepers. We are using Ustari, Lucas Molina and another Molina, Emiliano, also of Independiente, who have both died in a six-month period, from heaven they will be battling with us, we cannot lose this game. Let's get out there." Everybody was shocked and emotional, and I walked off. They all followed me to training.'

Semi-final
Argentina vs Brazil
28 June 2005, Galgenwaard Stadium, Utrecht
Attendance: 16,500
Referee: Massimo Busacca (Switzerland)

'Don't worry,' Leo had said. Seventh minute. He collects the ball on the left wing and after a couple of touches senses that the moment is right to launch a rocket from outside the area that flies into the net. 'He nailed it from an angle,' remembers Ferraro.

There was still much to do, much to give. Zabaleta controls the ball, he goes past a Brazilian defender into the penalty area. He loses the ball. Out comes the Brazilian central defender to recover it and the Argentinian captain falls to the ground. The ball goes loose. The defender's foot is raised and Pablo's head is between the ball and the Brazilian's foot. 'One of their defenders wanted to recover the ball and I just blocked it with my head. It was an instinctive reaction,' says Zabaleta. Ferraro made a mental note of this valiant deed.

Brazil equalise through a Renato header following a seventy-fifth-minute free-kick. The game, dramatic, evenly matched, is heading for extra-time but the Argentinian game is now concentrated entirely on the side on which Leo is playing. He is the star and they look to him for the answers.

With 93 minutes gone, Leo receives the ball on the left and after a quick run down the wing he finds himself on the side of the penalty area, one-on-one against a central defender who has come out to block him. Leaving him in his wake, he gets to the by-line before putting in a cross towards the penalty spot. Kun Agüero fails to get to the ball, but the clearance falls short and to the feet of Zabaleta who hits the ball with his left foot. It strikes two defenders before finding its way into the net.

Goal. GOAAAAAAL!

Behind, Pablo, going absolutely nuts, comes running to Leo, flapping his arms as if he were about to take off. A lap to the right, and Pablo follows him, then to the left, at top speed. Leo joins the group hug, shouting and jumping. A few seconds later, the same thing happens all over again when the referee blows his whistle to bring the game to an end. Argentina have made it to the final.

*

– *But is it true that when you spoke on the telephone to Diego you
promised him the cup?*
– *[Laughing loudly] It was incredible. That the best player in the
world should have bothered to speak to me. It's too much. He
asked me to bring the cup back to Argentina. And I cheekily said
that I would! I had already spoken to him after I scored the first
goal of my career against Albacete in the Spanish League. But
every meeting with the greatest is unique.*

(Gente magazine, July 2005)

Final
Argentina vs Nigeria
2 July 2005, Galgenwaard Stadium, Utrecht
Attendance: 24,500
Referee: Terje Hauge (Norway)

Diego Armando Maradona made contact by phone with the side
via a journalist friend. He had a moment with Leo. 'Bring home the
cup,' he said. Nigeria had beaten Morocco and the day before the
final Leo had been awarded the Ballon d'Or for player of the tournament; behind him were two Nigerian players, the midfielder John
Obi Mikel and the left-sided defender Taye Taiwo. After receiving
the prize, Leo prepared a T-shirt that he would wear under his white
and blue international vest.

Pancho Ferraro prepared a video for the boys. And with his finger
on the remote he said: 'Look, I love to see the chip over, the beautiful
game, the nutmegs, but look at this'. He pressed Play. They saw the
incident where Zabaleta had stuck his head between the ball and his
opponent's foot. 'This is what your captain did.' Leo laughed. So did
the rest of them. And Ferraro added: 'If we keep that sort of attitude
tomorrow, we will come out champions.'

'Many of us were going to be leaving the Under 20s. That's the
beauty of this level, that it can generally only be enjoyed once. Let's
not let this chance slip.' That was the message of the captain.

Pancho Ferraro's line-up was: Oscar Ustari; Lautaro Formica,
Gabriel Paletta, Ezequiel Garay, Julio Barroso; Pablo Zabaleta,
Fernando Gago, Juan Manuel Torres, Rodrigo Archubi; Lionel

Messi and Gustavo Oberman. Coming on later were Kun Agüero (for Oberman, 57th minute), Emiliano Armenteros (for Archubi, 61st minute) and Lucas Biglia (for Gago, 72nd minute).

Leo had walked through the hotel on his way to the coach and through the corridors of Utrecht's Galgenwaard Stadium fairly unexcited. He said nothing that anyone remembers. He cannot remember saying anything of note either. 'His personality is calm, very calm,' says Zabaleta. 'Notice when he takes penalties, with an icy coldness.'

Thirty-eighth minute. Leo controls the ball on the left wing and goes off on one of his runs, this time for about 40 metres, going past various players. He gets into the box. Dele Adeleye tries to get the ball back, he can't, he puts one leg in, then the other. He pole-axes him with a tackle born of frustration. A clear penalty. Leo gets up, no hurry, showing no emotion, and walks to the penalty spot.

As captain it fell to Zabaleta to take the penalty, or at the very least to decide who should. 'The person who had to take it was the one who had the most confidence,' Pablo says today. After the foul, Messi, who had spent months practising penalties at the request of his old coach Guillermo Hoyos, picked the ball up, a serious look on his face. Looked at it and with hardly any run-up, one, two, three …

Arsène Wenger says: 'to get to the very highest level, you need to believe in yourself to a greater degree than can be logically justified. All great sportsmen have this capacity for illogical optimism. Not a single athlete has ever reached his maximum potential without the ability to eliminate from his mind any shadow of a doubt.'

… four, five short steps …

The squad had seen a clear change in Leo's personality during these 40 days at training camp. Especially so during the final. The emotion of the group (having come so far, having spoken to Maradona, having taken the lead) was in direct contrast to the cold-blooded calm of Messi that was already making the difference on the pitch and turning him into a strong, silent leader of the group.

… he puts the ball with a light touch to the right of the goal-keeper …

'He hit it with a simplicity, an inner calm, like it was nothing' (Zabaleta).

'It was known that he would be one of the penalty takers, but what we didn't know was how calm he would be about it, and that he would just roll it into one side, slowly' (Oberman).

… and the ball rolls in gently, far from the goalkeeper, Vanzekin, who has launched himself in the opposite direction.

He barely smiles, with a look that says, 'Of course I scored.' He lifts his shirt to reveal a T-shirt with the words which read, For Mari, Bruno, Tomi, Agus. A dedication to his sister, his nephews, Agustín and Tomás, and his cousin, Bruno.

Nigeria equalise in the fifty-second minute and, 20 minutes later, Kun Agüero is brought down in the area. Again a clear foul. And once again Leo picks up the ball.

If the first penalty is something that a left-footed player doesn't usually do (namely, aim his shot to the left), then the second, after three steps, and with the most delicate of touches, sends the ball towards the other post with the keeper hurling himself in the wrong direction.

'He didn't get fazed, not even in the World Cup final. He took the penalty as if he was taking it in his backyard at home. And both of them totally different, in different places' (Pancho Ferraro).

Leo lifts his shirt. Slightly less exuberantly on this occasion.

And the game is over.

There it was. Argentina's fifth Under 20 world championship. And then the jumping began, the jokes and a huge, everlasting smile that became fixed on Leo's face. On their way to pick up their medals they talked about the tight dresses worn by the hostesses, greeting all the visiting dignitaries, before running out again for more leaping around before receiving the final prize, the World Cup.

Cometh the hour, cometh the man: champion and best player of the tournament, just as Maradona had been in 1979, and winner of the Golden Boot as top goalscorer (with one more goal than Fernando Llorente and the Ukrainian Oleksandr Aliiev). Zabaleta teased him, reminding him that if he had not taken the two penalties he would not have won the Golden Boot. And, ecstatic, they both posed alongside Prince William-Alexander, husband of the Argentinian-born Máxima Zorreguieta, today the Queen of the Netherlands.

The team returned to the hotel and 'the Professor' insisted that the group show respect for the other teams that were also spending another night there. So, no party, nothing; just a long celebratory supper, that was it.

And what was Leo thinking? Messi remembered that championship as one of the best experiences of his life. Even after everything that he has achieved in his career, that period was, for him, one of the many 'firsts' in his life (national side, world championship, new group). He came from another country; he wanted to be recognised in his own. In the group phases he was one of many, but his consistency was in question, as was his physical strength. In the crucial knockout stages, he was a determining factor – with his equaliser against Colombia; two minutes of magic for one assist and a goal against Spain; an early strike against Brazil. Even though he had already made his debut in the league and even scored for Barcelona on one occasion that same season, it was in Holland that Leo Messi really took off.

'What did we say to him to give him that extra push?' Salorio was asked. 'We made him a competitive animal, almost evil – the Argentinian always wants to win. We said to him: "Look, if we lose we're out of here, because they're going to beat us to death." I hadn't been able to go with Pancho and Leo to the Sudamericano because of stress. But I enjoyed the World Cup very much. There is one unforgettable memory that I will take with me to my grave: the players, me in a corner, came to get me and picked me up and threw me in the air three times. And I said: "Heck, I must have done a lot for this group that they come to get me while I am just sitting in a corner, clapping …"'

'Kun was, like, crazy, we were all very happy,' adds Oberman. 'I remember that after singing, partying, and when we were all a bit calmer, I went up to Leo and said to him: "truly, I will tell my children one day that I played football with you, because you will become one of the greats." I remember this, and he laughed, and then shyly touched my shoulder. The truth is that I believed he was going to be great, but not that much. He exceeded my expectations. It's what we jokingly said: now Pekerman isn't going to have any problems picking his team for the 2006 World Cup because he's going to have to take him.'

Oberman was from Argentina Juniors and, celebrating after the final, a thought crossed his mind. 'We were playing with a kid who was at one of the most important clubs in the world and he treated us as if he had come from any team from the same level as us, always with humility; with frustration as well, because he would become annoyed during games sometimes, or he would moan when you wouldn't pass to him or something ... I always tried to follow his instinct, and always with the greatest of respect. It was a great pleasure to play with him.'

Gustavo Oberman would not play for his country again. His son is five years old and a fanatical supporter of Messi, Neymar and Ronaldo. When he told his son that he had played with Messi, the kid wouldn't believe him:

– When he played for Barcelona?
– Nooo, in Argentina.
– And when did you play for Argentina?

And Oberman would put on the video of the goal that he scored against Spain after a pass from Leo, just at the point where the commentator begins to pick up the pace: '... Gago, Messi, Oberman ... goaaaaaal!!'

– Look, look Dad!! Mum, Mum!! Dad's playing with Messi!!

– *Did you dream about that moment?*
– *I won't lie to you: I always dreamed about playing and being champions with the national side, but until it happened I wasn't aware of just how beautiful it is to do a lap of honour wearing your country's shirt.*
– *Were you aware that you were inspiring the whole of Argentina?*
– *It was incredible the reception we got, I couldn't believe that it was happening. Now I just want to be with family, enjoy myself with my mum and dad [Jorge, 46 and Celia, 44], my brothers and sister [María Sol, 11, Matías, 22 – who has a greengrocer's and a kiosk in the centre of Rosario – and Rodrigo, 25, who lives with Leo and Jorge in Barcelona, where he is studying to become a chef and with my nephews].*
– *The whole world is comparing you to Maradona. How do you*

manage to keep your feet on the ground?

– [He blushes, and doesn't answer] …With my family we went through many bad times. But as they say, this has been like a dream for me. I still haven't come down to earth. It's something unique that I will never forget. Winning the World Cup has been the happiest moment of my life.

(*Gente* magazine, July 2005)

Leo emailed his mother after winning the title. 'Mama, I can't believe what is happening to me. I have to pinch myself to make sure that I am awake.' He returned to Argentina a hero, the footballer the nation had been waiting for. His name appeared the following day in *L'Équipe*, *La Gazzetta dello Sport*, *El Mundo Deportivo* and *AS*.

'I learned to love the national side when I was sixty years old. When you hear the national anthem, it kills you. It was a great source of pride to be able to have coached all of the side to victory, not just Messi and Sergio Agüero,' says Ferraro today. 'It was the high-point of my career. Only five coaches in the history of Argentina can say, "I was champion of the world": Menotti, Bilardo, Pekerman, Tocalli and me. There is a poster in Ezeiza aiport where you can see all the coaches who were champions of the world and you can see my photo there hugging Messi and Ustari. It was the best moment of my life.'

The idea was to return to Buenos Aires, each to their own homes and their own battles. When they arrived at Ezeiza the players were surprised to see hundreds of supporters waiting to greet them. And television cameras, radio microphones, photographers. As they came out of the arrivals hall everyone was looking for Leo, drowning in a sea of journalists. His uncle, Claudio, and his father, Jorge, had come to pick him up in the van and decided to accept an invitation from a well-known television programme. After it, by which time it was the early hours of the morning, Leo fell asleep in the car taking him to Rosario along with Formica and Garay, who were playing for Newell's at the time.

What happened next is well documented by Toni Frieros in his biography of Messi. Cintia Arellano, Leo's school friend, had alerted the young people in the neighbourhood to prepare something, to collect some money to decorate the streets with bunting and paint. 'Leo, Our Nation's Pride' was daubed in white paint on the front door of Cintia's house. A banner from one side of the street to another said simply, 'Welcome, Champion'. They waited until midnight for him to arrive, with drums and fire crackers at the ready. Along with three television cameras. The cold was getting to them and the wait was becoming longer and longer. Most people eventually went to bed.

At about five in the morning they heard the van approaching. The camera lights were switched on. Confetti was thrown across the van. There was shouting: 'Leo's coming, Leo's coming.' What was arriving was in fact a tired, cold, young man. He wanted to go to bed. But he reacted immediately: greeted everybody, kissed everyone, gave interviews.

The boy who had left five years earlier in tears had returned, champion of the world.

4

Frank Rijkaard. The Rise

'We knew that Messi was going to be better than Ronaldinho. I remember sitting in my office and reading in the paper that we were looking to buy Rafael van der Vaart. I looked at Frank. We'd just seen Barcelona B with Messi starring. Frank said: "Nah, we don't need van der Vaart."'

(Henk ten Cate)

During the 2004–05 season Barcelona continued the necessary restructuring that would ensure that the ball would inexorably find its way into the path of Ronaldinho. Frank Rijkaard approved the departure of Edgar Davids, Patrick Kluivert, Michael Reiziger and Phillip Cocu, while Luis Enrique and Marc Overmars decided to retire. It was the end of an era, and the youthful push of Joan Laporta's board brought with it a return to general optimism at the club. With the money recouped from transfers out, players of great quality and personality arrived: Deco (from a Porto side that had just won the Champions League), Ludovic Giuly (Monaco), Belletti (Villarreal), Edmilson (Lyon), Henrik Larsson (Celtic), Sylvinho (Celta) and Samuel Eto'o, for whom Barcelona had to pay €12 million to Mallorca and the same amount to Real Madrid. In this list you could see the nucleus of a new Barcelona which, from that moment on, looked to a midfield combination of Rafa Márquez, Xavi and Deco (Iniesta was at the time the fresh pair of legs), and a skilful and productive front line in the shape of Eto'o, Giuly and Ronaldinho. Good results and the extensive makeover were also celebrated when

Ronaldinho was named FIFA Player of the Year in December 2004. But what was still lacking was a title that would rubber-stamp the certain feeling that, at long last, Barcelona was emerging from five years in the wilderness.

Leo Messi had made his first-team debut in the friendly against Porto in November 2003, but since that heady opener the doors of the Camp Nou had remained closed to him. Was that talented 16- or 17-year-old kid of no use to Frank Rijkaard despite the fact that he seemed to be progressing very fast? Doubts were being heard from the club and also from the player's family – why was he not playing? How was he taking the lack of chances in the first team? In what would have been a confusing time for any adolescent, never mind one on the fringes of the elite squad, the club proposed that Leo should be examined by an Argentinian psychologist picked by Josep Colomer, the director of the academy at the club.

The role of a sports psychologist is a difficult one; he is seen by the players as a 'grass' and yet some of them take on that role as part and parcel of belonging to such a prestigious institution. The foot-baller is promised total discretion, but the enduring suspicion that any work done begins from a skewed standpoint is never far from the player's thoughts. Colomer's proposal was initially accepted by Leo, but it wasn't long before he told the club that he had no wish to carry on talking with somebody whom he did not trust. And that trust was well and truly broken when the doctor brought in a group of psychology students to see how well he was working with the player. All that was serving no purpose for Leo, who stopped attending the meetings. He believed he could cope with all the pressure that came from being just a step away from the first team – mostly because he did not feel it.

His physical development continued: from August 2003 to April 2004 Leo put on 3.7 kilograms, primarily in muscle. The diminutive Leo was now a thing of the past. It was a growth strengthened not so much in the gym, but, rather, in the coaching sessions and his continued presence in the starting line-up of Barcelona B. The faith shown by Josep Colomer and the insistence of other coaches such as Guillermo Hoyos, Alex García, Tito Vilanova and Pere Gratacós was giving him confidence, too, the most important vitamin in a player's development. 'When he stops progressing, we'll stop him there, whatever level he's at. But why stop him before he's reached that level?' the director of youth football told Leo's dad.

Those were the days when, it seemed, if a footballer did not sport a beard and a moustache, he didn't play in the first team. What had happened in Porto was a product of necessity rather than clear strategy; it was almost impossible for a youngster of his age to make it into Rijkaard's team. So, Messi thought, perhaps they think I have reached my limit. For now, he had to carry on working hard in the B team run by Gratacós.

Gratacós knew that Frank Rijkaard relied on players in his squad who were tried and tested and of great quality and who were blocking Messi's path, but none the less, in his side, Leo was a budding star and he began to pick him regularly. Thus a chink of light began to appear through the cracks of the Camp Nou gates. In exceptional circumstances, they prepared a training regime specifically designed with his physical characteristics in mind and he began to combine his training sessions with the B team and with Rijkaard's side. The Dutchman told the player's family that he saw in Leo some 'extraordinary characteristics' but insisted in 'going bit by bit to exploit them at the appropriate time'.

Gratacós also knew that his obligation was to instil in the player certain things he had not yet incorporated into his game and that were necessary to enable him to fit in with the second division B side. But it wasn't that easy to make him change some of his worst football habits. On more than one occasion the veterans of the side (rarely older than 21) would moan at the coach that Messi lacked the defensive work required of him. 'He doesn't press,' they said to him. Pere was well aware of it and would remind the Argentinian in training sessions that the game still went on even after he'd lost the ball; but he also told his charges, in private, that they should not forget what he brought to the team: 'No, he doesn't press, but what about what he does when he's got the ball? Don't worry, lads, we'll work on it.'

The leap for the 17-year-old was proving arduous. Compared with his stellar rise in the junior ranks, Leo seemed baulked in the first months of this new campaign with the B team. Despite playing every minute, in the first 12 games Leo scored on only five occasions, including one against Girona in the second game. He was finding it hard to get away from defenders, to make a difference.

The team was also spluttering. In September, the Barcelona B side went to play against Zaragoza B. Technical staff thought they had given the right instructions to ensure a positive outcome, only to finish the wrong side of a convincing 3–0 scoreline. Leo left the pitch upset and as soon as he was back in the changing room he began to cry. His reaction surprised Pere Gratacós: 'Bear in mind that he had played well! We had to cheer him up, we told him that he had to persist, to get better, and that we had to convert this defeat into something positive.' He was the only *blaugrana* who did cry in that fifth league match of group three of the Second Division B. For most of them, it was a game just like any other.

Messi trained every day with Gratacós, apart from once a week when he joined up with the first-team squad. This one day a week became two, and then three. The doubts expressed by Rijkaard's technical staff began to disappear, although the Dutchman was still reticent. 'He's going well, he's good, but certain aspects of his play must be improved,' he answered when asked about Leo. He didn't want to rush things. Rijkaard's assistant, Henk ten Cate, thought he was ready. And then one day in October, Ronaldinho and Deco said to both of them that they were wasting time: 'Gaffer, he should be here, playing with us.'

Ten Cate, the 'bad cop' to Rijkaard's good, was responsible for keeping Ronaldinho on the straight and narrow. In other words, it was a stick-and-carrot approach and where broadly speaking his analytical descision-making boss gave the carrot, he was responsible for offering the stick in the form of strong words.

When Barcelona were looking for full-backs with the ability to go up and down the pitch, with personality and understanding of the football style needed, Gio van Bronckhorst fitted the mould admirably and was signed from Arsenal after an initial loan spell. Dutch footballers were all the rage at the time, being of similar upbringing to that of Barcelona youth players. Gio, today assistant manager to Ronald Koeman at Feyenoord, and Henk, whose last job was as coach at Dutch side Sparta Rotterdam, met in the summer of 2013 in a restaurant in Rotterdam to reminisce about the arrival of Leo Messi into the first team.

Gio still talks about Leo with the smile of one who knows he has shared a changing room with perhaps the best ever representative of his profession. Ten Cate says that in 20 years' time he will look back on his career not just as 'the coach who had Messi'. No way. Henk was just a coach. Period.

HTC: We gave him his debut against Porto in the 2003–04 season when he was a teenager, even before he had trained with us. I got to know him for the first time at the airport on the way to Portugal. They had told us that he was very good and on that day we were very short of players. We said, why not? Later we invited him to train with us on a more regular basis.

GVB: Ronaldinho said in the first training session with Leo that this youngster was going to be better than him. And people laughed. 'Yeah, right!!' they replied. More than details, the only memory I have of his first session with us is a general feeling of being pleasantly surprised. And you?

HTC: I remember one thing. From the first minutes the Brazilians took him away and got him under their wing. Before starting training we used to do the *rondos*. You had a group of Spanish players (Puyol, Oleguer, Xavi, Iniesta) with you; then there was a second group of Brazilians with people like Eto'o and Rafa Márquez. It was Sylvinho who said to him, 'come over here, son'. And he joined up in the *rondo* with the Brazilians. Sylvinho embraced him, not literally, but from that moment onwards he became like a father to him.

GVB: If you see a footballer who shines on television, you can shout out, 'what a great player he is!' But you only really know how good someone is when you train with them. It happened to me with Bergkamp, Henry and Ronaldinho. If you are playing with them every day, you discover just how special they are. With Messi, after the first training session you could already see it – I had never come to that conclusion so quickly before! Not even with the other three, even though they are superstars.

HTC: At the time there was an enormous difference between the first team and the young lads in the B side who played two divisions lower. Occasionally we relied on players like Joan Verdú, perhaps the best of the reserves, but not good enough to take the place of the bigger players. But Leo ...

GVB: Some weeks later, we were playing a training match between the B side and the first team. Messi used to play down the middle with the B and that area was being protected by Thiago Motta as defensive midfielder. And Messi was getting the better of him throughout.

HTC: Despite having played well at Porto, despite his self-confidence and quality surprising us, some time went past before we were convinced that he was ready to make his debut in an official match. About a year, in fact. Why? We had a lot of quality in that squad. Giuly on the right, Eto'o as a striker, Deco as leader in midfield and Ronaldinho on the left because we had to put him somewhere. We signed him as *mediapunta* (from PSG), but he kills you when we haven't got the ball because he just doesn't defend – so we stuck him on the wing. Xavi didn't play every game, Iniesta even less, imagine the quality we had. Leo started to get called into the squad in the 2004–05 season, but he spent a lot of matches sitting on the bench.

GVB: The B side and the lower teams played a 3-4-3 and he was the *enganche*, the number 10, just behind the striker. So in the 4-3-3 system that we were using there was no place for him in the position he normally played.

HTC: With the reserves he was almost like a second striker. But the system isn't important, it's the position he naturally takes up when he's on the pitch. And he couldn't play in the middle. Our front target man had to be strong, playing with his back to the goal, able to receive the ball and turn. He wasn't any good for that position.

GVB: What did the coaches say among themselves about all that, about his evolution?

HTC: Frank was a bit sceptical about his possibilities so early in his career. We had to wait, he said. We had a problem because he was very good, but there just weren't many opportunities for him. He carried on training with us, more and more, but we didn't play him. Who would we take off? His time hadn't come.

GVB: Being a left-back, it often fell to me to mark him in training, because you put him on the right of the attack. Let me tell you, thanks! And you saw that for him every ball would be his last one, he had great motivation for every training session. For every attack. It was like Ronaldinho when he turned up wanting to train: you could see they were happy, smiling. And of course there was no way of stopping them.

HTC: They would kill anyone who crossed their path. Leo showed himself to be strong whenever he had the ball. Sometimes you have players who you push to do a bit more. With him you had to put a rope around his neck to pull him back.

GVB: I remember them as good training sessions because we had some really great players. Sometimes we would warm up in the changing room before going out onto the pitch and me, just by seeing Ronnie, or Deco, or Leo do such wonderful things with a ball, I felt ready to train. What a pleasure! Did you have to give Leo lots of instructions? I don't remember you being on top of him all the time.

HTC: Not many, and that's the truth. These people are so talented and so intelligent – two things that usually go hand in hand. With just one word they would understand what we wanted from them on the pitch. Most of what he did on the pitch he carried inside him. What we tried to do was to teach him to become a professional. How to look after himself, how to train ... Sometimes there were three games a week and if he trained like mad, he couldn't play three games in the week, not even two. He needed to match his enthusiasm with his physical capabilities. When he started to play, his level of achievement would go up and down, but that didn't worry us because you could see that here was a young boy who had extraordinary qualities. It's logical that a player of 17 should lack consistency.

GVB: I used to love it when the day before the games we used to have a really good training session, it was a good sign. We'd start with a *rondo* then would come an exercise, depending on who your opposition was, and finally 11 vs 11 on a small pitch. And Leo would play as if his life depended on it. It was impossible not to give him his chance sooner or later.

HTC: Sometimes I would say to Frank, 'Did you see that?' He would get in between two or three [players] where no gap existed. And his shot had such power. With a normal player you can see what his intention is, the movement of the leg, the moment that he pulls his leg back and shoots, all in a split second but with sufficient time so a defender can block it. With him, the leg doesn't appear to move and yet the ball still leaves his foot with enormous power.

GVB: He seems to think before the rest of us. Or he sees a pattern in front of his eyes that allows him to understand exactly what play and movement is required. It's like something from science fiction. All I see is the ball and a lot of legs. He sees the solution.

In the lower teams Leo would not accept playing on the wing, because there he had to wait for the ball to come to him, he didn't get enough of it. But coaches often made him play wide, often on the right. It's common practice: a right-back struggles defending a left-footed player, and Leo could cut inside and shoot often if used on the right wing. But bit by bit he would come out of his position and appear in the *mediapunta* zone. That is where he enjoyed himself more, where he felt he was giving more to the side. In any case, he knew that to go up into the first team he would have to accept the conditions imposed on him. He could not play as a *mediapunta*, because the weight of attack fell upon Ronaldinho who played out on the left. Neither had he sufficient status yet to make demands: the thing at that moment was to get up there with the big boys and stay there. But 11 months after his debut in Porto, and after dozens of coaching sessions with Frank Rijkaard and Henk ten Cate, Leo believed he was ready to make the great leap forward, to make his debut.

So did Rijkaard.

After six games unbeaten, Barcelona found themselves leaders on 16 points, thanks to a solid defence, Eto'o's goals and Ronaldinho's magic. The next game was on 16 October, the derby at Montjuïc, the then home of Espanyol. Leo came on for Deco with eight minutes left to play in a match that was still very much alive, with the *blaugranas* just 1–0 ahead despite having dominated most of the game; it was not a substitution made simply to appease the fans. 'Get yourself on the right wing and look for the break, son,' said Ten Cate. 'Look to use your speed between the full-back and the central defender.' There was no real time for him to make any kind of impact. Barcelona won by the only goal of the game.

At 17 years and four months Messi had become the youngest ever player to represent the club in an official competition.

His father took him back to his flat at Gran Via Carles III, just three streets away from the Camp Nou. As the journalist Roberto Martínez asserts, 'He grew up just three streets from the hue and cry of the stadium, how's he going to get stage fright? He plays at the Camp Nou as if he was playing in his own backyard, except that there are 100,000 people there.'

That night Leo didn't talk about his debut, or about the game, in fact about anything in particular. He didn't have any special celebrations: this was just the beginning. He hadn't reached anywhere yet, he was just starting on the road. In his room, however, although the silence was deafening, the audible memory of a Camp Nou applauding as he stepped on the pitch remained etched on his mind.

After playing 20 minutes in the next game against Osasuna, he spent the next seven games on the bench, including one spectacular 3–0 victory over Real Madrid.

Sitting behind Rijkaard, Leo looked on as Ronaldinho, at the peak of his powers, celebrated, often with his trademark surfing gesture.

> 'Rijkaard, the way he took me step by step, without any real pressure ... I sometimes didn't understand why I hadn't been called into the squad or wasn't playing. Now I look at it dispassionately, and I realise that he brought me along very well, without any rush. I am very grateful to him because he always knew what was best for me.'

(Leo Messi on Barça TV, 2013)

'The fact that Leo had Rijkaard as his first coach at the top level was of tremendous benefit to him,' explains Sylvinho. 'Rijkaard was always the big-hearted type, a true gentleman who always showed concern for everyone.' It's difficult to find anyone who has a bad word to say about the Dutch coach on a personal level.

Frank is from the school of thought that believes a coach should only spend about 20 per cent of his time coaching. The rest of the time is taken up quietly doing whatever is necessary at that particular moment: sometimes he becomes a big brother, or a father, or a colleague. 'I think he's unhappy, let's go and see what the problem is' he might say to one of his assistants. Footballers can sometimes be very cruel, constantly looking for weaknesses in those who coach them, but they are more disposed to being managed when they see the coach has affection for them. And also when he shows he has the same touch with the ball as they have, that he has experienced the same doubts, jealousies and joy as them. In that sense, it suited Rijkaard to have been an altar boy before he became a priest.

He quickly applied this paternalism to Leo. With a hug, a show of interest in his life off the pitch, a joke just before going out to train, Rijkaard was getting closer to the Argentinian. Messi felt comfortable with him. And was eternally thankful. A young player might impress in the lower ranks, but one day a manager gives him the opportunity to play – footballers never forget the man who takes that big step. 'It doesn't matter if you make mistakes', Rijkaard told him. 'You will play again'. That faith in him helped Leo. Their connection was not just a professional one. Frank was born in Amsterdam but is the son of immigrants (his father is from Surinam) and he was the best player in the district, at school, in the junior sides at Ajax. He had empathy with those players who were 'different', including Ronaldinho, because he too had suffered the same stigma. And he also knew that football belonged to the footballers. He reminded them constantly, with every gesture, in every conversation, that he was there to help them. This shrewd tactic, coupled with his honesty, meant Frank got what he wanted out of the players.

Rijkaard spoke more with the other players, especially Ronaldinho, but he made a conscious effort to get Leo, who remained as reserved as ever, to trust him. Ronnie, Eto'o and Sylvinho invariably took the lead in the usual team meetings, while Leo rarely said a word. Only if he was asked. And then his reply would be monosyllabic. The Leo whom Rijkaard had in those first few years was one who wanted only to follow orders, and the Dutchman used the close harmony he was creating to ease the Argentinian's progress into the club elite.

Messi left his apartment in Gran Via Carles III the morning of the match against Albacete, the thirty-fourth match in the league in that 2004–05 season. Since his debut against Espanyol he had played just five games with the first team in the domestic league but only for a few minutes, as well as nine with the Barcelona B side, plus one cup and one Champions League match. When Rijkaard called him up for a home game, Leo knew the routine: he had to get to the Camp Nou at 11 a.m. Those who wanted to could do a bit of gym work or get a massage. If there was time Leo used to play football tennis inside the changing room.

It all began with Sylvinho and Ronaldinho, who would often apply himself more to this pastime than to the training itself. The Brazilians would make the most of a wide rectangular space with three walls in the players' space, between the gym area and where they got changed. They would mark lines on the floor with sticky tape and stretch a bandage across as a net. They played one against one, one bounce, a maximum of three touches before the ball was returned, with the first to reach 11 points the winner. Sylvinho considered himself sufficiently skilful to challenge Ronaldinho; sometimes he did look better than him and he often won. In fact, he ended up beating everybody. Sylvinho became the king of football tennis. Until Leo arrived.

Messi saw football tennis as another challenge. It was just a game, but there was more at stake than a victory in some minor sporting diversion: there was prestige in the game, even within the hierarchy of the squad.

Messi waited his turn to play at the beginning, but before long he was actively seeking opponents. He was the best. And the most consistent, always ready to play a match, a tournament.

'We played before games or especially after training,' remembers former Barcelona left-back Fernando Navarro. 'In the end they put in glass walls, as if it were a cage, and a real net, quite high; the matches became quite explosive and very intense. But it was also good because it meant we got better technically. Messi was the best, the bloke always used to put it by the column; there was a column on one of the sides and he would always put it there, where you couldn't get to it.' Gio tried to beat Leo: 'We would finish training at one and could spend the afternoon playing, even up to six o'clock. But it was unfair if you had to face Messi. He was a monster.'

Even though it was just a space for the players, a bit of fun away from the daily grind, the coaches kept an eye on the football tennis matches: they demonstrated the competitiveness of a player, his character. If a player always played at the same level, it spoke volumes about his ambition. You could test the technical skill of the participant, and as his pulse rate increased, his mental state: see if he was switched on, detached, angry ...

After training, on match days, the team would retire to the nearby Princesa Sofia hotel to eat and rest.

The match against Albacete was played in May. There were four games remaining in the league, and even if the opposition were at the foot of the table Rijkaard called for organisation and concentration. Madrid, with goalkeeper Casillas saving goals at one end and the Brazilian Ronaldo scoring them at the other, had had six wins on the trot, and they were getting close to Barcelona, who had taken up residence at the top for most of the season. The game proved to be more difficult than had been expected: Albacete held off a Barcelona, who, without a recently suspended Xavi, were finding it difficult to get into their rhythm. Iniesta had come on in his place but was unable to give the team the necessary fluidity to break down a packed defence. A couple of diagonal efforts from Giuly, a fluffed shot from Eto'o and an excessive display of overelaboration from Ronaldinho, who kept coming inside and narrowing the game, defined a tense Barcelona. Then, with an hour gone, Eto'o hit a shot from the edge of the area that Raúl Valbuena, having played with assurance all night, was unable to reach.

With seven minutes remaining, and with a tight 1–0 lead, Ten Cate asked Leo to warm up. Eto'o looked to the bench and made a gesture that he was not ready to come off. But he was the one replaced. Messi went up to Rijkaard who spoke to him casually, as if he had played in a hundred games: 'Play how you know. Stick yourself on the right.' Leo looked at his coach, waiting for further instructions. There was nothing else. That's it.

In the eighty-seventh minute an angry Eto'o walked off the pitch, shaking hands with Leo without so much as looking at him, the words of Ten Cate, reprimanding him for his behaviour, ringing in his ears as he headed for the tunnel. He went into the changing room and started kicking things. No one likes to be substituted, least of all by a youngster. Rijkaard said afterwards that he hadn't seen his anger: 'We thought it was an opportune moment to put on a youngster like Messi.'

The game had to be won. The 1–0 scoreline demanded concentration. There were three minutes remaining until the final whistle, plus any added-on time. Ronaldinho went up to Leo. 'I'm going to give you a pass for you to score. Tomorrow it will be you on the front pages,' he said to him. From an attacking right-hand-side position the Brazilian found Messi, who was by himself, and Leo, with one smooth lob, beat the goalkeeper. Valbuena appealed for offside and the referee gave it. It wasn't. The goalkeeper knew it and ruffled Leo's mane by way of apology.

'I'm going to give it to you again,' insisted Ronnie.

With normal time completed, Ronnie, in the position of *media-punta*, used his instep to place a ball over the backs of the Albacete's defenders. Messi let the ball bounce once, and with another delicate touch put the ball over Valbuena. His first goal for the FC Barcelona first team.

And then something extraordinary took place.

Leo ran off with his arms stretched out, shaking his hands. He stopped and turned in search of the collective hug. Ronnie came up to him, bent over and Leo jumped onto his back. The Brazilian was carrying the boy on his back. The kid had scored. The league was just a step away.

The group celebrated the goal and the victory on the pitch. So did the fans. In the changing room the euphoria was palpable. Victory in the next game, with a defeat for Real Madrid, would bring the title back to the Camp Nou for the first time in five years. The whole world wanted to touch the goalscorer: 'congratulations, son,' they said. And: 'careful with this one, Ronnie. He's going to be taking your place. He's even scoring now.'

Leo moved across to the press area. 'Everyone in the changing room treats me very well, but with Ronnie I have a special relationship, hence the celebration. I would like to dedicate this goal to my family. To my mother, who is travelling at the moment, and to a nephew who is on the way.' Rodrigo's wife was pregnant and was due to give birth shortly.

His father Jorge still gets goosebumps when he thinks about that day: 'You hear the people singing Messi, Messi, Messi. It's the biggest thing that can ever happen to anybody.' His son had become the youngest player in the history of the club to score. 'I am very

happy for him,' said Rijkaard in the press conference. 'With that
goal he showed how talented he is.'

Albecete's goalkeeper Valbuena was teased by his team-mates:
'You stop Ronaldinho and then you end up copping it from the little feller.' He kept the ball from that game – he had a premonition.
Today he says he wouldn't swap or sell it for anything. The ball
that featured in the first major goal scored by the best player in the
world is at Raúl Valbuena's home.

Leo Messi returned home. They laughed about the fact that in
three minutes he had scored two goals from almost identical plays.
He had supper and went to bed.

The next day he got a call at lunchtime as he was eating with
the family in the flat. It was Maradona. The first time they
had spoken. Diego congratulated him. Messi was going to hear
from him again a couple of months later in the Under 20 World
Cup Championship.

> *'I always said that from the first moment I came into the chang-
> ing room, Ronaldinho and all the other Brazilians – Deco, Syl-
> vinho and Motta – accepted me and made things easier for me.
> But especially him [Ronaldinho] because he was the star of
> the team. I learned a lot at his side. I'm grateful for the way he
> treated me from the first moment, he was a great help to me
> because I had never been into a changing room like that, and
> with me being the way I am, well, it made everything much
> easier for me.*
>
> *Ronaldinho was the man responsible for the change in Bar-
> celona. It was a bad time for the team and the changes that
> were tried after his arrival were massive. In the first year we
> didn't win anything but people fell in love with him. After that
> the titles came and he made all those people very happy. I think
> Barcelona should always be grateful for everything he did for
> them.'*
>
> (Leo Messi in an interview with Barça TV on the tenth
> anniversary of Ronaldinho joining the club)

'How you doing, bro!' Ronnie said to Leo the first time their paths
crossed in the club's car park. The Brazilian had already heard people talking about 'the Flea'. A few days later, after his first training

session with the first team, Ronaldinho rang his friend, the journalist Cristina Cubero: 'I've just finished training with someone who is going to be better than me,' he told her. 'Don't exaggerate,' replied Cristina.

'The first training session! I remember it perfectly,' Cubero recalls. 'He called me just to tell me that. Lots of times he used to say, "you don't know what he does in training, he is so good". And this is what Ronaldinho, World Cup winner and at the time the best in the world was saying! Deco, too.'

It wasn't Sylvinho, as Ten Cate recalls, but Deco on one of Messi's first trips with the first team, who said, 'hey you! Come here. You are the only Argentinian who's going to sit at our table.' They made space for Leo, the foreigner, at the foreigners' table. Messi, aware of the unwritten codes within the group, was conscious of what a privilege this was: Ronaldinho was the new leader of Barcelona, of the Brazilian side, the best in the world, or so FIFA and anyone who knew anything about football said. He was going to sit at the same table as him! And once you've picked your table, you don't change it: that's how it goes in football. 'Leo used to spend time with the Catalans at La Masía, but he is Argentinian and he felt at home with us, Latin Americans like Márquez, Ronnie, Deco, Edmilson and me,' explains Sylvinho. 'I think he felt more comfortable sitting at a table where he didn't have to talk or anything. He just sat, looked, laughed shyly. He picked up everything very quickly, he enjoyed himself.'

All that helps to explain the gesture of Ronaldinho, his 'guardian', carrying him on his back after that goal against Albacete. 'When he arrived at Barcelona, he had the advantage of being able to grow with a Ronaldinho who was at his best,' explains former director Joan Lacueva. 'He was like a mushroom in the shade of that tree that was Ronaldinho. He toughened up. While people paid more attention to the great things that the great Ronaldinho was doing, Messi was turning himself into a first-team player.'

Ronaldinho showed him the reality of competitive football, of life with the elite, the mechanics to apply on the field of play. Ronnie knew how to use the press so he made sure that they did not turn their attention to the young Argentinian too soon. If Leo had played a poor game, Ronaldinho would come out into the press area to distract the media. And if someone was overaggressive towards him on the pitch, there was the Brazilian or Deco to look after the kid. 'Ronaldinho used to talk football a lot with him,' recalls Cristina Cubero. 'He'd say things like, "hide on the wing and come out when I tell you to". He taught him to follow the NBA, and to learn from the NBA, something he is now obsessed with, and to apply certain things from it to football. The assists from Ronnie have something of the NBA about them. He taught him to understand about blocking, and about reading the game. He educated him a lot more about football than people think.'

'It's clear that Ronaldinho did many good things for him and also some bad ones,' comments Henk ten Cate. 'But if you balance them out, I think it was the correct combination for Leo. He was a good example of what to do. And what not to do.'

In Spanish football there is an expression '*cuidado con los padrinos*', 'careful with the godfathers'. You have to go easy on the 'I'm looking after the boy' approach, because it is just another way of imposing limitations. On the pitch there is only one ball and normally it has only one boss. When team-mates look up, they look for one player, a single point of reference, not two. If you have to pick one out of two, that's when there is conflict. At that time, everyone, including Leo, was only looking for Ronnie.

The great player quickly identifies who is ultimately going to take his place and reacts in one of two ways: either he isn't very supportive of who is up and coming (it's said that Juan Román Riquelme typified that particular approach) or he looks after him and encourages him, as Ronaldinho did with Messi. But with one tacit proviso: don't jump into my seat; remember that you owe me for what I am doing for you. The protection offered in this somewhat perverse parental-type control allowed Leo to shine, but also served as a way of controlling him.

Ronaldinho also did a lot to show Leo all the possibilities off the field. Ronnie, Motta and Deco were the leading social members of this group of greatly talented footballers. Once a month the squad went out together for dinner and Leo joined them, although his voice was rarely heard above the raucous conversation, 'not even when he was speaking,' says van Bronckhorst. But the 17-year-old became hypnotised by what he soon saw as the advantages of being recognised, of being a star. Ronaldinho lived life to the full and showed the adolescent Leo, who up until then had spent his life either on the football field or at home, how to live life in the fast lane.

It was easy to fall under Ronnie's spell, but the first signs that the Brazilian was living too close to the edge were beginning to appear. At the weekly sporting meetings in which select directors and the technical staff met, Messi was mentioned infrequently. It was Ronaldinho who dominated most of their conversations.

Barcelona won the league for the first time in five years, and Leo, who had only played 77 minutes for the first team, including his debut in the Champions League against Shakhtar Donetsk, celebrated next to Thiago Motta, as the victory bus made its way across the city to the Camp Nou. He was the little kid, jumping around with the Brazilians, who had named him *irmão* (little brother), the group's mascot. He danced around with a permanent smile on his face. He was celebrating for many reasons: for the season, for everything he had achieved so far. In the stadium they told him that his brother and his sister-in-law, Florencia, had had to leave the stands at the Camp Nou because she had gone into labour. Leo quickly left the celebrations: his sister-in-law was about to present him with a nephew. That day, Augustín was born.

And after all that he returned to Rosario for a break.

In the balmy first days of the holiday season, Rijkaard insisted that, yes, Leo was special, competitive, but he needed to mature, he was not yet fully formed. He wanted to keep protecting him. For his part, Messi understood that he had finally arrived at the level at which he belonged and under no circumstances should they consider demoting him. Age meant nothing to him. He was 17 years old, but he knew he could bring something to the table, that his rightful place was with Ronnie, with Deco, with Xavi. In the recent campaign he had also played 17 matches with a Barcelona B side that finally finished in seventh place, four points shy of a total that would have seen them promoted to the Second division A. They would be his last games for the second team.

After resting, and with the satisfaction of having made his debut, scoring his first goal, winning the league title and becoming an uncle, Leo Messi set off for Holland for the World Cup Under 20 championships.

He won the title and was voted best player in the tournament.

Suddenly, everything in his world started to speed up.

Those few months in the summer of 2005 were possibly the most frenetic of his whole career. In addition to the impact he had made internationally, Leo Messi was able to celebrate a new contract with Barcelona, his third, signed on his birthday in Holland during the Under 20 World Cup.

The first contract came in the shape of the infamous 'napkin agreement'. The second was agreed on 4 February 2004: it contained a buyout clause of €30 million if he played with Barcelona C, €80 million if he went up to the B team and €150 million if he made it to the first team. It was, despite the fact that he was a youth player, the contract of a Barcelona B player, and lasted until 2012: the first year he would earn €50,000 a year plus €1,600 per game; and the last year, €450,000 and €9,000 per game. It contained an interesting clause: in his first year he was paid €5,500 by way of compensation if he was made to play out of his normal position, a sum that would reach €50,000 in the last season. Barcelona paid for four flights between Argentina and Barcelona, a yearly housing allowance of €9,000 and wrote off a loan of €120,000, which had been given to Messi in his first contract to compensate for the many difficulties he encountered in those early years. In hindsight, members of his entourage describe that Leo as a *mendigo*, someone who goes 'cap in hand'. Essentially he was happy to accept whatever Joan Gaspart offered.

The new management of Joan Laporta, conscious of the difficulties that Leo had experienced, and his bravery and fortitude in the face of so many trials, were firmly on his side. But, as with all new relationships, they had to lay firm foundations based on communication and trust. 'We tried to act as intermediaries between the various groups of people who claimed to represent Leo, some of whom had been involved in his sporting career since he was twelve years old,' remembers ex-president Laporta. 'Additionally, a number of bureaucratic problems emerged which we dealt with competently, and this helped to calm the father's fears – that Leo's right to play football would be somehow compromised. In this way we managed to build up a mutual trust. What we were doing, of course, was defending the interests of one of our players, which, naturally, also served the interests of Barcelona. That's how we began our relationship with Leo, by giving him the priority that he deserved.'

The result was that Barcelona began to structure its financial agreements with Leo in such a way that Leo's qualities as a player would be suitably recognised and rewarded. 'From the point of view of Leo's management, we decided to make his contract much more proactive,' explains the then sporting vice-president Ferran Soriano. 'We thought: every year we'll sit down and talk about how much more we're going to pay him. We didn't tell Jorge that we would increase his son's salary almost every year, but both he and Leo were aware that the matter would be discussed at the beginning of every season. We knew the value of the player, we were aware of his value on the football pitch, and we were conscious, too, that he had never asked for anything. We were moving him up the various levels, setting tasks that became increasingly difficult, but we wanted to send a clear message: "Don't worry about the money. We'll take care of you."'

The third contract was signed in Utrecht during the Under 20 World Cup. Director of football Txiki Beguiristain travelled to Holland and met up with Leo and his father before the semi-final against Brazil. Messi had reached the age of majority and his working contract signed by his father could now be replaced by one signed by the player himself. But it was put together with a degree of haste. It made him a Barcelona player until 2010, two years less than the previous contract, but with much greater financial remuneration. He would be paid as a first-team player; he was never again to be demoted to Barcelona B. His earnings were €90,000 a year in 2004, €110,000 in 2005, and in the last year €450,000; if he played 25 games, he would receive a further million, and an additional million if he got to 45 games; he would also receive a bonus of €225,000 in October 2005. The buyout clause remained at €150 million.

'We have great confidence in the player: we are convinced that his participation in the first team would be very important from this moment on,' said Txiki Beguiristain at the time. He believed Leo could 'alter the rhythm and dynamic of many games'.

This contract would be rendered invalid before it even came into force, and three months later he signed a new one. Such was the speed at which the 'Messi effect' was moving.

From the beginning, Sylvinho happily adopted the roles of confidant, best friend, guide and protector that others, namely Grighini, Ustari and Víctor Vázquez had fulfilled in his previous sides. 'We spoke a lot about football, Leo's not the sort of bloke to tell you a lot, he's more of a listener. And I always liked talking a lot, about life, about what was going on, everything,' says the now retired Brazilian. 'Leo's not one for talking much, nor for jokes, but he's fast, he'll come back at you with a quip very quickly. He always says he is no Sylvinho … He always used to say to me: "okay, Silvi, go out there and tell the press everything you've got to say and then I'll go out there when there's nothing left to say".'

'Messi knew that Sylvinho was very fond of him, that he enjoyed watching over him, he was a father figure,' adds Eidur Gudjohnsen, the Icelandic player signed from Chelsea in 2006. If Ronaldinho was the fallen angel on Leo's left shoulder, then Sylvi, a profoundly committed Christian, was the good one on his right. 'Sylvinho is a good man, there's no side to him. He laughs a lot, makes jokes, but he is very religious, very much a family man, a home lover, and he had a very clear idea of where he was going in life.'

'At the age of seventeen Leo already knew what he wanted, and had very fixed opinions on a number of issues,' insists Sylvinho. 'You'd go up to him to give him some advice, to explain something that had happened and he would tell you that he was aware of it, he knew what was happening. How Barcelona were faring, what was happening in the football world, stories in the media …' The relationship was strengthened on a Barcelona tour in the summer of 2005 to Korea, China and Japan.

Leo went on the promotional tour as world champion, league winner and with his first professional contract. He was, for the first time, a fully recognised member of the first team, with all the security and prestige that such a position affords. And he could begin to enjoy the experience of being an equal member of the group. He followed the Brazilians everywhere. 'He didn't speak a single word of English, so he came with us,' said Sylvinho who spent two years at Arsenal and one at Manchester City. 'I knew enough to be able to change currency, stuff like that, and I used to do it for him. One day I brought the money up to his room and as I went along the hall I could hear shouting from Leo's room, "Go, go, no, leave it. Just go." It was Leo, very agitated. And I thought, "what's going on here?" So I went in and there was a Chinese guy trying to clean the room who didn't understand a word that Leo was saying.

'I was killing myself laughing: "Come on, Silvi, tell him that's enough, that'll do, tell him to go." And I said to him: "I'm not going to tell him anything, leave him." And I thought to myself, "I wonder how this is going to end up?" and there's Leo, with his strong Argentinian accent saying, "Go, go." How was the Chinese guy going to understand him?'

That summer, Leo also found himself a mother figure. 'When we went to China I was pregnant and my maternal instincts were well and truly developed,' recalls Cristina Cubero. 'On those trips, Leo used to spend a lot of time with me, and later Rijkaard would ask me, "what does he talk to you about?" About his home, Rosario, the River Turbio, his friends ... we talked about normal things, he was still a boy. And Rijkaard used to say to me: "He doesn't talk to us." He had problems expressing himself. One day I asked him, "why don't you talk more?" And he said to me, "because I prefer to listen; if I have nothing to say why talk?" On that trip I discovered something: when he trusts you, he looks you in the eye.'

The telltale sign that you have been accepted into his private world.

'I'd be happy to play for even a second,' said 'the Flea' the evening before his debut for the full national side. José Pekerman wanted to reward Leo for his spectacular performance with the Under 20s two months earlier by calling him up for a friendly Argentina were playing against Hungary at the Ferenc Puskás Stadium in Budapest.

With 11 minutes played of the second half, the Argentinian manager asked physical coach Eduardo Urtasún to explain to Leo what was tactically required of him. Urtasún asked him to warm up, whispered a couple of things in his ear and gave him a kiss. In the sixty-fourth minute, Pekerman called him over. Gabriel Milito went over to Leo to encourage him. He wore the number 18 on his back, coincidentally his age. Lisandro López would be the man replaced, the first Argentinian substitution of the game.

Leo's first possession, following a pass from Scaloni, saw him increase the speed of the game. The second time he got the ball he went on a run along the centre of the pitch. He had been on the pitch for 92 seconds. The Hungarian defender Vilmos Vanczák went in with a hefty tackle, at the same time grabbing Leo's shirt, and 'the Flea' reacted by swinging his arm in the air in an effort to shake off his opponent's hand. But his flailing arm struck Vanczák's throat and he fell to the ground, his hands covering his face.

'Leo Messi will take a long time to forget the face of Markus Merk, the German referee in that Hungary–Argentina game which was his debut with the full international side,' wrote Cristina Cubero in *El Mundo Deportivo*, witnessing the events of that day, 17 August 2005. Juan Pablo Sorín, Lionel Scaloni, Gabriel Heinze and Robero Ayala all approached the referee and tried to persuade him that Leo's action was purely defensive and didn't merit a card. Merk disagreed and, with an exaggerated flourish, held aloft the red. Vanczák received a yellow card.

Leo could not believe it and walked off, glancing briefly up at the stands, nervously fiddling with the waistband on his shorts and finally leaving the field with his head bowed. Hugo Tocalli, assistant to Pekerman, reminded him that there would be other games, other days to wear the shirt. 'Messi was crushed at that moment,' writes Cubero. 'He couldn't even remember that Scaloni had come up to embrace him, or that Hernán Crespo had approached him. He didn't hear the stadium beginning to chant his name. He went off in tears, crying like a child, tears of frustration, rage and bitterness. The team's masseur stayed with him in the dressing room.'

'Do you know who was in the crowd?' Cristina Cubero remembers. 'José Mourinho, who had come to see one of his players. After the sending-off, I saw Mourinho in the stand and asked him, "José, what are you doing here? What do you think of what's just happened?" And he answered: "crazy, the referees are mad, how could they have done that to the boy, when he's such a nice lad? Tell him not to worry, tell him from me to cheer up, stay calm."'

When the players arrived back in the dressing room after a 2–1 victory, they saw Messi in a corner, still crying. Alone. His head bowed. 'They all went over to him to cheer him up,' continues Cubero. 'They all assured him that he was now one of them. He had made his debut in the sky-blue and white of his country, and they had smashed his dream into pieces. But he had to understand that these things happen.'

He walked through the press area accompanied by Pablo Zabaleta, who that day also made his debut with the national side, and Hugo Tocalli. The coaching staff told him not to say anything. He looked at the gathered journalists and gave them a rueful glance.

There was little to say. 'Would Merk have had the same courage to send off a revered player like Riquelme for the same reason?' both the Argentinian and Catalan press asked. 'Merk wanted to be famous,' it was said. Hernán Crespo had some harsh words for the referee: 'He took no account of the systematic fouling of the Hungarian, but confined himself to sending Messi off ... I don't know if it was because their coach was a fellow countryman [Lothar Matthäus] or whatever the reason was. An eighteen-year-old kid, fulfilling a dream and making his debut for his country cannot be punished like this. The referee should have been more understanding.'

Markus Merk, now retired and named by the International Federation of Football History and Statistics (IFFHS) as the best referee of the first ten years of the twenty-first century, did not want to talk about it. 'I never make comments after games,' he said. He was questioned further in the press area, but his look said it all.

Curiously, Merk doesn't even mention the incident in his autobiography. The co-author of the book, Oliver Trust, says, 'I remember that he told me from a very young age that he was very clear – he wanted to be strict with fouls, whenever they occurred. No matter who and how famous the player was. He wanted his work as a referee to have a "structure", to be consistent, it was one of the most important things for him. He had to show Messi the red card even though he was sorry for the youngster. He felt and still feels a deep respect for Messi's skill.'

On the way back to the hotel a singing Scaloni attempted to cheer the group up, but Leo sat alone, staring out of the window. Leo Franco ruffled his hair, trying to drag him out of the dark tunnel that he was in. Without success.

'That night I spent six hours with Leo, and he was crying, crying, crying,' remembered Cubero. 'To calm him down I said: it's the first game, you'll have thousands more.'

On his arrival at Barcelona airport he opened up and spoke into the microphones of RAC1: 'I dodged past the Hungarian, who was trying to grab me by the shirt. I got myself free the best way that I could and the referee interpreted it as an elbow. It left me really angry. I had minutes to play, but whatever happened, it was not how I had dreamed it.' He left the airport with his brother Rodrigo and Pablo Zabaleta.

Zabaleta hardly heard a single word from Leo on the way back.

With barely time to dry his tears, the summer would bring another unpleasant surprise. Messi would once again fall victim to bureaucracy. Following on from the delay of his transfer to Barcelona some years before, this time it was a question of passports. He was a spectator for the traditional curtain raiser to the season, the away leg of the Spanish Supercopa final, this time against Betis at the Benito Villamarín Stadium. And in the return leg he was not even called up into the squad. What was going on? The Catalan newspaper *Sport* exposed the 'Messi case'. Leo was classified as a foreign player and in Ronaldinho, Rafa Márquez and Samuel Eto'o Barcelona already had three, the maximum permitted. How then was it possible that he had played seven games the previous year?

Barcelona argued that Messi was an 'assimilated' player, a figure created by the Spanish Football Federation: a footballer born outside the European Union with five seasons in the lower ranks of the club. The federation was not so sure; the regulation was ambiguous. Leo only had an Argentinian passport and after his goal against Albacete did not play again, because Barcelona suspected clubs might consider him an inellegible player and would contest the validity of matches. Barcelona preferred to take him away from the field until this legal grey area had been sorted out definitively.

Curiously, UEFA had no problem with him playing. He had already played in a Champions League match the previous season, but when Barcelona checked that he could still be fielded in Europe, UEFA gave the go-ahead three days later – common sense told them that if he had played once he could do so again.

Leo meanwhile continued to train as if he was going to play in the next game, with a resolve that surprised those who were only just getting to know him. But the uncertainty demanded that the people in the club responsible for such issues sorted out this new problem as quickly as possible. In case there was no quick resolution, loaning the player out was mooted as a possibility.

The season began and behind the scenes discussions were held to discuss Leo's future. If he could not be called upon because of bureaucratic hold-ups, then should he be allowed to grow and develop with another team? This, at least, was the suggestion of those close to Leo and, surprisingly, Barcelona's technical staff concurred. The coaches were actively seeking a solution that would avoid conflict: the young Argentinian was strong, his game deserved more playing time, but Ronaldinho *had* the ball. 'Why don't we loan him out for a year?' it was suggested in Rijkaard's office. Jorge Messi received calls from Spanish clubs (Lleida, Zaragoza ...) and from all over Europe. The most attractive came from Italy (Inter Milan were the most insistent), but also from other leagues (Glasgow Rangers, for example, but curiously not a single offer from an English club).

This is how ex-president of PSV Rob Westerhof explained it: 'It was 2005. I had a good relationship with the president, Laporta, and he said to me, halfway through a G14 meeting, that he had a young lad who was very good and he wanted to loan him out because he couldn't play in Spain. We had a great reputation, Guus Hiddink was our coach, we had just won the league and were into the semi-finals of the Champions League.' Espanyol also tried, trying to take advantage of the closeness of Leo with Pablo Zabaleta, their right-back. 'Our coach, Miguel Ángel Lotina, kept going on about how I should convince him,' the defender remembers. Clubs got as far as negotiating the loan. 'We're going to Espanyol' was heard in the Leo home.

But something changed the perception that the club and world football had of 'the Flea' that would ultimately change FC Barcelona's plans.

The Joan Gamper trophy at the Camp Nou.

*

On that 24 August the traditional Joan Gamper pre-season summer trophy, the team presentation to the fans, was being played at the Camp Nou against the Juventus of Fabio Capello, with del Piero and Ibrahimović up front. It was the first view of a side almost complete with the addition of just two new signings, Mark Van Bommel (from PSV) and Santi Ezquerro (from Athletic de Bilbao). Rijkaard decided to give Leo a place in his starting line-up, a sign of affection and a demonstration of support after a hectic summer. Larsson and Ronaldinho were the other two forwards. Thuram was missing from the Juve defence, but there was still plenty of quality there in the shape of Zebina, Kovač, Cannavaro and Chiellini. And from the first minute…

Leo asked for the ball.

Appeared on both flanks and through the middle.

Started runs from midfield.

Dribbled in the box.

He nutmegged Fabio Cannavaro.

Took possession from Patrick Vieira who, on losing the ball, turned around and aimed a kick at his ankle. Yellow card, one of three earned by the Italian side trying to stop Leo.

Played fearlessly despite Juventus's aggression.

Provided the assist for the first goal.

Dribbled. Shot at goal.

Passed the ball with his chest.

You can see it all here:

http://www.youtube.com/watch?v=RIJBMMADPTs

'I kept asking Zebina, "This kid, who is he?" And we started going in hard on him.' (Patrick Vieira)

The Juve manager Fabio Capello, standing on the touchline next to Rijkaard, had a word with the Dutchman during the game. 'You can't play that guy. Let me have him. For a year, on loan. In any other side he would be an automatic starter with the first team.' The answer was a polite no: 'I think we will sort out the passport problems in three or four months, Fabio.'

'He spoke with Frank, because Frank and Capello got on very well together,' remembers Henk ten Cate. 'Not just to loan him. To buy him, perhaps.'

The Italian coach confesses now: 'When I saw him he dazzled me. As he was legally prevented from playing for Barcelona, I seized the opportunity to ask my friend Frank if we could have him, even on loan. But he told me, no, no way, and that Messi would end up playing that same year for Barcelona. Messi is a genius, someone who can win any game. For me he is among the greats in the history of football alongside Pelé, Cruyff, Di Stéfano or Maradona, even though he has not yet won a World Cup.'

Rijkaard thought he deserved an ovation from the 91,000 spectators present so he substituted Leo in the eighty-ninth minute. On came Giuly who, from that day onwards, recognised that his days as an automatic starter were over.

After a 2–2 draw, Juventus took the cup on penalties.

Leo was named man of the match.

Fabio Capello spoke about Messi at the press conference. 'I've never seen a player with so much quality at that age, and with such personality, wearing such an important shirt. Messi is a great champion and he can do what he likes with the ball. I am pleased that a boy so young does something so beautiful for football. Because these aren't things you see every day. It's an advertisement for the game.'

'Cristiano and Leo have created an era, their styles might differ, but they have a lot in common – the Italian manager continues – they're both trying to be the best, score goals and help their team win. There is more imagination from Messi, his passing and assists are great, but Ronaldo is stronger and faster, and his ability to shoot from long distances, better. Possibly Cristiano Ronaldo plays more to score goals and for himself, Messi, too, scores a lot, but he plays for the team.' At that time nobody was talking of Leo in those terms yet, but Capello saw it coming.

Rexach adds: 'At the end of the game, Capello comes out and says, "today a star was born". The star had been with us for five years, but what happened was that Capello's words crossed borders, and from then on everyone was talking about Messi. And even here everyone sat up and took note. Capello's words, so full of enthusiasm about one of our players, did not fall on deaf ears.'

The journalist Ramón Besa remembers that night: 'Until then no one had pointed him out. Now everyone tells a different history, the easiest thing to do in journalism: I knew him, I discovered him, I had *already written about him ... But I got the feeling that when Capello announced: "this is the one ..." is when people said: "bloody hell, if Capello says it ..." This is such a typical* culé *phenomenon – until someone from outside makes us see what we have, we can't spot it. I have the impression that up to that point, not everyone at the club was supporting Messi. There is a problem with the management of talent at Barcelona. Deep down, however well you have everything organised, or however much you know what has to be done, at some stage someone needs to say: "now, this is the moment".'*

During those days, Txiki Beguiristain called José Pekerman. This is how 'the Professor', Salorio, recalls it: 'The director of Barcelona telephoned us one day and said: "What have you done with Leo? You've changed his attitude." This is what he told Pekerman. "He's a different Leo, he's not the one we sent to the World Cup." What we gave him was a certain type of aggression, not to hit anyone, but just to fear defeat: in the Spanish second division B Barcelona lose, lose, win, draw, draw. Here we have to win or we're all out. There's a queue of twenty people looking to tear us to pieces.'

Juventus put money on the table, but it was Inter Milan who made an astronomical bid for the player. The message received by Beguiristain and Laporta from those close to the player was loud and clear: 'If Leo cannot play in the Spanish league, if the red tape is not sorted out, then he's off to Italy.'

'The only time that there was a real risk of Leo leaving Barcelona was when the offer from Inter came in.' So remembers Joan Laporta, who had to use all his powers of persuasion and diplomacy, and make full use of the bond of trust he had built up with Leo's father, to prevent Leo from playing in Serie A.

Inter understood that this was their opportunity to link up with a footballer whom they had been following for the past three years. This is how Ferran Soriano recalls it. 'There had been moments of crisis with various offers, I remember one from Inter, one from Real Madrid ... but the father always had the confidence that we would back Leo, always call him up in time to offer him a new contract, which was the stability they were looking for.'

No question about that, but in September 2005 things became so complicated that a great deal of tact was required.

'Jorge called me and asked to come by the office,' Laporta explains. The president of Barcelona did not know what it was about. 'I've got something very serious to tell you, I want to share this with you,' Jorge Messi began. Leo's father was asking the opinion of a friend as well as that of the president of Barcelona, a sharing of views and thoughts with Laporta.

Jorge told him that Inter wanted to sign Leo, that they had offered him three times as much money in wages, and weren't put off in the slightest by the €150 million buyout clause.

Joan Laporta spoke to him as club president and as a friend: 'The first thing I told him was that we were not thinking of selling him; secondly, I put myself in the position of the father: "look, you want money for your son, obviously, and they will guarantee his future; but his career here will be assured from a financial point of view, too, and what's more, he will also get the glory." I was taking a bit of a gamble because at that time we'd only had a few good results. We had a team that half the world loved and were beginning to be seen as a point of reference for other clubs. But we had not reached glory yet.'

Jorge Messi knew there was some truth in what Laporta was saying. Leo now considered himself to be part of the first team, and his sporting prospects looked good. And he appreciated Laporta's obvious affection for his young player. The conversation about Leo's future was left hanging in the air.

Around that time, at a supper in Madrid, Massimo Moratti, the owner and president of Inter, told Joan Laporta that he wanted Leo in Italy, that he was in love with left-footed players and that Messi was special. The Barcelona chief told him that, with all due respect, the Barcelona side had no intention of letting him go.

Laporta may have thought that that was the end of the matter, but, with all the cards on the table, everything might easily have been turned upside down in three tense autumn days.

Barcelona travelled to Germany to play Werder Bremen, the strongest team they would face in the Champions League group in which they had been drawn. UEFA had given Lionel permission to play, despite the fact that he was unable to do so in the Spanish league, but Rijkaard took an extra player along just in case there were any problems.

On 14 September, the morning of the match, Jorge Messi got together with Txiki Beguiristain to talk about Inter's interest. The meeting did not go particularly well. It was firstly agreed to keep him at the club until December and, if the bureaucratic problems continued, 'all Spain and the whole of Europe wants him, so loaning him out won't be a problem,' Beguiristain told him.

But then a sticking point was mentioned. The club, conscious of the fact that just three months earlier he had signed a new contract, were in no rush to renew it, despite the pressure being put on them by Inter Milan and the extraordinary summer Messi was having. Barcelona's position was unequivocal: wait and see if Messi is allowed to play, analyse his performances then and after that maybe a new agreement could be negotiated. The lack of sensitivity shown by the club in view of the progress made by Leo, now a full international and an Under 20s World Cup winner, and with regard to the patience shown by him as he continued to train with the same intensity despite being unable to play, exasperated his father. He expected a proposal to renew his contract.

That morning he said, 'we're off'. The road to Inter now looked more likely than ever and the Italians were beginning to talk numbers and promising to have the transfer sorted out for the following season. It looked as though matters were coming to a head. Ferran Soriano received a call from Messi's inner circle and was told that he was thinking of leaving Barcelona.

The day of the Werder Bremen match, Rijkaard decided to include Messi among the substitutes, with Sylvinho left in the stands. Leo came on in the sixty-fifth minute in place of Giuly, stuck himself on the right wing and on the few occasions that he got into the game he made a difference: a couple of dribbles, a couple of runs with Christian Schulz, his opposing full-back, who lost both duels. After an inside pass from Ronaldinho, Leo found himself facing the opposition keeper, only for Schulz to grab him by the shirt in the penalty area. Penalty. Ronaldinho converted it for the final 2–0 Barcelona victory.

'Messi was important to us,' declared Rijkaard after the game. 'Of course I am keen that the bureaucratic problems should be sorted out so I can play in the league but I'm calm,' said Messi. In the stands Ferran Soriano and other members of the board, once again impressed by the reaction of the Argentinian on the pitch, were close to a nervous breakdown. We've got to sort out his future, and now, was the unanimous verdict. 'Can we meet tomorrow?' they asked Jorge Messi.

At ten o'clock the following morning in an office at the Camp Nou, a nervous Joan Laporta, Soriano, Txiki Beguiristain, Alejandro Etxebarria (one of the movers and shakers at the club who was much respected by Leo and all the footballers), and Jorge Messi, all met.

The president repeated in public what he had told Leo's father in private: yes, Inter had put an astronomical offer on the table, but in Milan he would only earn money; at Barcelona he would have both money and glory. 'Jorge believed what I told him,' remembers Laporta. 'Leo wanted to stay, his father wanted him to stay, but we couldn't match Inter's offer, who looked as if they were prepared to pay the €150 million buyout, in addition to paying him two or three times the salary. I wanted to raise his money because he deserved it. Money always helps, but it isn't what makes you happy, I said to Jorge: if he went to Italy it would be a different way of playing, he is used to playing here ... and so on. I was coming out with just about anything I could think of at the time.'

Jorge Messi was told that Leo would play more than Giuly. What's more, at that meeting, Leo gained something else: a direct link to the president. 'For us Leo's case was a very sensitive and special situation,' reiterates Laporta.

Barcelona managed to prevent Leo from going to Inter.

The Italians did not want to pay the buyout clause; instead they intended to challenge in the courts the disproportionate amounts between what he was earning and what the Italians were being asked to pay for him. 'But I had a very good relationship with Moratti and he saw that there was no way that I was going to sell Messi, and it wasn't worth two clubs like Inter and Barcelona facing up to each other on a matter like this,' confirms Laporta. 'And he was told soon after that meeting that Leo and Jorge had decided to stay at Barcelona. I think that's what put an end to Moratti's intentions. Every year there's been an offer, or some kind of movement. But this was the only time I thought there was a real risk of him leaving us.'

After that meeting work began in earnest to draw up a new contract.

Leo's growing celebrity made living at the Gran Via Carles III apartment increasingly awkward. One day as he left his apartment someone threw himself on top of his car, demanding an autograph and refusing to move until he had it. He had neither pen nor paper, and he had to get both from one of the people who was travelling with Messi in the car. The new contract therefore had to include a bonus for renewing the contract that would pay for a new house and garden. In Castelldefels.

Leo and Jorge wanted the contract to run until 2013, a year before the World Cup. That way, if he wasn't playing he could move to another club on a free transfer and still be in good enough shape so as not to miss out on it. That is why the 2014 tournament has always been considered in the Messi household the most important one for Leo – he will be 27 when it takes place, in theory at the height of his career. A further example of the family's vision and careful planning for the future.

Jorge Messi rejected Barcelona's first offer, but when the club altered a few clauses and numbers, agreement was finally reached, just two days before Leo had planned to join Inter. It was his third contract in 18 months.

Barcelona managed to add one more year to the contract than the Messis wanted, up to 2014, but as far as everything else was concerned Leo's new financial position would place him at the level of a medium-class player in the first team. In his first year he would earn €900,000 and by the end of 2014 he would be earning €3.5 million, including all image rights. He would receive a bonus in his first season of €250,000, which would go towards buying the new house. If he played at least 45 minutes in 60 per cent of the games he would receive a further bonus of €280,000 in his first year, going up progressively to €800,000 in the last year. Furthermore, he also received a one-off payment for the renewal of his contract of €2 million. The buyout clause was maintained at €150 million. The contract drawn up in September would come into force in January 2006.

Jorge Messi had asked the club to push for a settling of all the bureaucratic issues as soon as possible, and was told that it was only a matter of days before they would be resolved. On the one hand the Spanish football authorities looked as if they were on the verge of reaching a favourable verdict for Messi and Barcelona, but the

Catalan club also had an ace up its sleeve; the definitive solution.

Running parallel with the process that was grinding along at the football league with exasperating slowness, a similar problem had begun two years earlier, when Jorge Messi had sworn allegiance to the Spanish constitution. A little later, Jorge and his wife asked for Spanish nationality for their son, who was still a minor. Finally, on 26 September 2005, Leo Messi acquired Spanish nationality in the Civil Register Office. He was no longer a foreign player. After missing out on six league games, Leo Messi was available for the seventh match of the season.

'Throughout that whole summer, I never saw my son nervous once,' said his father.

What I'm not saying, or suggesting, or agreeing with, is the statement that we have before us the new Maradona. I prefer to say that we have before us the new Messi. He has a very long road ahead of him. And he can grow as a footballer. He has an innate class that allows him to play in a number of positions even though he believes that ultimately he will play as mediapunta, *in the hole. We have to be grateful that he can assume responsibility to play in whatever position we ask him to, always for the benefit of the team.*

(Frank Rijkaard in 2005)

That 2005–06 season saw the climax of Frank Rijkaard's team. With the arrival of Van Bommel and Ezquerro, and the departure of Gerard López at the end of his contract, the squad had been finely tuned with the same core players as in the previous league-winning season. Positions were doubled up and the collective synchronisation that had started the previous season continued in the new campaign.

Real Madrid, who hadn't won anything relevant in the past two years, added Robinho to their list of *galácticos* – which already included Roberto Carlos, David Beckham, Ronaldo and Zinedine Zidane, who was once asked by Messi if they could swap shirts. Leo would only do that with Gago, Aimar or some friends, he was too embarrassed to ask anybody else. Zidane, who happily complied, was the exception.

Ronaldinho confirmed his status as the great new star of football when in December 2005 he was named as FIFA World Player of the Year for the second year running.

Around that time the ex-Barcelona player Ronald de Boer was having breakfast with Frank Rijkaard when he dared to analyse the Argentinian. He'd only ever seen him on television. 'I've seen this boy, Messi, but truthfully he doesn't impress me.' Rijkaard looked at him in astonishment. 'You need to see him in training, Ronald. He does things that nobody else can do. We don't even need to put ideas in his head. We can just leave him to do what he does. Instinctively.'

But Rijkaard only wanted to say that in private. At the end of one training session, Ten Cate stopped the journalist Roberto Martínez who followed Leo closely and wrote about him in *El Mundo Deportivo*. 'Listen, Roberto, easy with the boy,' Ten Cate said, hoping to calm things down. 'He's good, but not as good as some of the things that you are writing.'

But the brake that the coaches were trying to apply did not correspond to the opportunities that were presenting themselves: with the number 19 on his back Leo's appearances meant that Giuly was no longer first choice. The Barcelona players received a bonus for playing 60 per cent of all matches and they all counted their appearances. 'Sometimes one of the players would tell me: "Boss, I'm at 58 per cent, I need two more games, play me!"' recalls Ten Cate. It became a joke asking Giuly what percentage he had played. 'Forty-eight per cent!' he told van Bronckhorst. 'Lionel is playing.'

'Then,' Gio would add, 'you're twelve per cent short. Leo!! Leo!!! Giuly says he needs twelve per cent! Help him!' the full-back and others used to shout at the Argentinian, laughing.

Ten days after signing his new contract, Messi was in the starting line-up to face Udinese in the second match of the Champions League group phase. Leo, following the performances against Juventus in the Gamper and Werder Bremen, had another storming game. This is how Ramón Besa in *El País* described it: 'Shaken by Messi, the man of the match, Barcelona battered a Udinese side with the trigger of Ronaldinho in his role as chief sniper. The Argentinian dismantled the Italians' plan with a supreme performance.' Barcelona won by a convincing 4–1 scoreline.

In November he scored his first goal in the competition against

Panathinaikos. Rijkaard particularly liked the pressure he exerted to provoke a goalkeeping error: Leo stole the ball, then lifted it over the keeper before rounding him and scoring. It was the third goal in a convincing 5–0 victory.

Barcelona were now in the last 16 where they would face José Mourinho's Chelsea.

But before that, his first appearance in the line-up of a *clásico* at the Bernabéu. So far that season he had only played two full matches, against Osasuna and Panathinaikos, and Rijkaard was trying to protect him and respect the status quo of each player within the squad. His assistants weren't so sure any more that that was the right response to the appetite and quality he offered, and they told the Dutchman so: he was ready to start, even against Madrid, and it was time to forget the old order – Giuly was certainly a step down from Leo. Against his instincts and following the advice of his staff, Rijkaard decided to include him in the starting eleven against Real Madrid, although he didn't tell him until two hours before the game, so as not to put too much pressure on him. Leo had thought he was going to be a substitute. 'It was a surprise,' he said afterwards.

All the *galácticos* were on display but Barcelona confirmed, in one of the greatest of all football settings, that they truly were the team of the moment. All eyes were on Ronaldinho who scored two goals and then received an unexpected present: a standing ovation from the Bernabéu. Barcelona's frontmen of Ronnie, Eto'o and Messi were unstoppable, and the Argentinian, from the right wing, won his personal battle with Roberto Carlos. No longer would they debate who was the better among the new faces, Leo or Robinho. The 3–0 win put an end to all the verbal battles. In the fifty-ninth minute Iniesta came on as substitute for him. Yes, Leo was ready for the big matches.

On 13 December, in the Camp Nou, he received the Golden Boy award given out by Tuttosport to the best Under 21 player. Wayne Rooney was well behind in second place. Ronnie went up to Leo after he received the trophy to tell him that one day, in the not too distant future, they would be giving him the Ballon d'Or, the very trophy that just a few days later the Brazilian himself would receive.

It had been a triumphant year.

*

Leo had played one game at number 10, behind the striker, with Frank Rijkaard. Three months after his debut against Porto, a Barcelona, full of substitutes and youngsters from the B team, organised a friendly behind closed doors against Bernd Schuster's Shakhtar Donetsk. Leo replaced Luis García, and Ten Cate suggested letting him play a free role. Aged just 16, he obliged. But he went back to Barcelona's second team and when, months later, he returned to the first team, he did so to play on the wing. It was designed to get him away from the maelstrom in the centre of the pitch, and they were also looking to make the most of his speed when faced by the full-backs, to make diagonal runs cutting inside, which drew defenders to him and created more space for others. But even Rijkaard knew that his time spent on the wing would only be temporary.

And that his position on the wing was not just a tactical move.

Leo's transition into the Barcelona first team had gone through various stages of evolution: one was tactical and the other was to do with his role within the squad. The two go hand in hand. When Rijkaard began to allow him his passage into the elite, the starting eleven was full of stars. The nucleus was formed by Ronaldinho, Deco and Eto'o. Leo added his own quality to this group. Rijkaard was not prepared to change the established order, those invisible and yet so powerful and essential checks and balances that govern a team. One that was clearly lighting up the world. Messi played on the right wing and, like all youngsters who reach the top, he was prepared to obey orders, did as he was told with the same level of commitment he showed at all levels of La Masía. Without being a typical winger, and despite being left-footed, he immediately showed his value. And the weakest link was sacrificed – Ludovic Giuly.

Leo was growing into his small role on the confines of the wings, but very soon he began to look for more space, to attempt moves more suited to his understanding of the game, away from the flanks. The second stage of his tactical evolution was beginning to take shape.

Good coaches know that if a player keeps on knocking at the door, demanding more space, you're going to have to open it and let him in. But in that eco-system that is a group of footballers, if a new boy wants to invade others' territory, he might well find that those who might be affected are not about to let him demonstrate his superiority, or the coach might decide to clip his wings, because he doesn't want to destabilise the overall collective.

Rijkaard had promised Messi that he would eventually let him play in the centre, but in the first years with the first team he was not given that opportunity. In fact, he had to wait for the arrival of Pep Guardiola before that second tactical evolution took place properly.

The game most representative of the Rijkaard era involving Leo Messi in a starting role but on the flank was the Chelsea–Barcelona Champions League fixture played in February and March 2006.

The year before, Chelsea had eliminated Barcelona at the start of hostilities between the two clubs who ended up facing each other three times in three consecutive seasons. On that occasion, the blaugranas had won the first leg 2-1 but Chelsea manager José Mourinho accused Frank Rijkaard of speaking to the referee, Anders Frisk, at the interval. The death threats that followed Frisk sending off Didier Drogba compelled Frisk to terminate his refereeing career. Mourinho was suspended for two games. In the return leg at Stamford Bridge, Chelsea beat the Catalans 4–2, after a spectacular start that saw the Londoners go into a 3–0 lead. Terry's goal in the last seconds of the game, despite a foul on Víctor Valdés by Ricardo Carvalho that was not acknowledged by the referee, decided the game. 'Barcelona is a great club, but it's only won one Champions League in a hundred years,' said Mourinho, raising the stakes for any future encounters. 'I've only spent a few years coaching, and I've already won it.'

On 22 February 2006, in the first leg of the last 16, there was talk of revenge in the match between possibly the two best teams in Europe at the time, both of whom had two distinct ways of playing and two very different types of coaches. 'There was a tense atmosphere. Everybody felt it,' remembers Asier del Horno, the Chelsea left-back at that time. The Portuguese manager, as usual, laid down the conditions as to how the game should be played: the sprinklers left the pitch like a mudbath, the ball hardly rolled at all and the teams seemed prepared to cancel each other out. Perhaps for that reason Iniesta was left on the bench and the Barcelona midfield contained a lot of muscle: Deco, Edmilson and Motta. The three forwards were as expected. Ronaldinho on the left but with licence to move around, Eto'o would be the striker and Leo Messi on the right wing.

That game was the perfect, graphic example of the Argentinian's game under Rijkaard. From the very first minute he showed himself to be on the offensive, looking for the one vs ones, very wide. And the team were looking for him even though, with him being only just 18, others should have taken more responsibility. Messi, wearing the number 31 on his back, responded with the first shot at goal, creating the first moment of danger for Chelsea, and pressing whenever he lost possession, as he converted himself into public enemy number one for the Chelsea defence.

Del Horno knew from the very beginning that he was facing a fast running and bold opponent.

'Tactically we were well-organised,' explains del Horno. 'Mourinho had prepared the match in detail, with the intention of blocking the movement of Barcelona. In midfield there were people like Makelele, Lampard and Essien who covered the defence, but Messi still got through. He faced up to me two or three times and I tried to stop him with my experience and whatever resources I had.'

On one occasion, Leo got past him and the following time del Horno stopped him with a brutal knee-high tackle that left his stud marks on the Argentinian's right leg. The referee did not caution the defender.

'He didn't retaliate. He said nothing. There is retaliation in football between defenders and forwards but not in this case,' confirms del Horno.

And then came the event that the whole world remembers. The one that marked the whole encounter.

Thirty-sixth minute.

Leo received the ball on the right-hand side around halfway. A heavy touch made Robben think that the ball would go over the line. But Messi had other ideas.

'The Flea' set off at speed to fight for the ball about three metres from the corner flag. Where wingers live and die. Robben was protecting it while Leo tried to get through on Robben's right, then on his left. The Dutch winger attempted a badly miscalculated shoulder charge and lost his balance and Leo took advantage to outrun him on the left.

Leo regained the ball in the quarter circle of the corner.

Robben dived in with two feet, but a smooth touch from the

Argentinian turned the manoeuvre into a nutmeg. With the Chelsea player on the floor, Leo hurried after the ball when ...

'I saw the defender coming towards me, aggressively, with bad intentions...' (Leo)

'I tried to stop him ...' (del Horno)

'...and I jumped ...' (Leo)

'... and he went past me ...' (del Horno)

'... and that's why he didn't get me ...' (Leo)

'He started to roll around the ground and I was sent off' (del Horno).

A melee ensued and with Puyol and Robben unable to understand what the other was saying, plus the tension, they almost came to blows. After a few seconds the referee, Terje Hauge, showed a red card to the Chelsea full-back.

'Messi was clever, he was intelligent, it looked like it had been a terrible tackle but in reality it was nothing ... Lionel exaggerated, without doubt.'

'The saddest thing about the game is that they said that it wasn't a foul,' says Sylvinho. 'It's quite clear, del Horno had lost the plot and was going for Leo at full pelt. It was a red card.'

'It was lunacy' is how Henk ten Cate described it.

'But Leo behaved impeccably,' remembers Sylvinho. 'If it's a foul, it's a foul, if it's red, it's red and that's it.'

'I didn't say anything to the defender. Him to me neither. It was all part of the game, that is football. He tried to do the best for his team,' Messi explains now. 'It was that incident where it all took off but after that the match continued normally.'

Yes. The game continued.

Leo didn't hide after the incident, despite being booed by the Stamford Bridge crowd every time he touched the ball. He hadn't said a word during that clash, or throughout the game. The atmosphere, electric after half an hour's play, was feeding him. He wanted the ball. He went in search of his new rival, Paulo Ferreira, who had moved over onto the left of the defence, with Geremi, who had replaced Joe Cole, on the other side.

The sending-off had given Mourinho the necessary excuse to defend deep in search of a goalless draw. Messi wanted to change the plan but his team was not with him.

Lampard hit a free-kick, Valdés made a mistake in coming out and the ball hit Motta. Own goal. The game was turning Chelsea's way.

Leo carried on demanding the ball. He was the most dominant of all the forwards, continuing to look for the weaknesses in the opposition so as to turn the tie around, giving depth and bravery to the team. The referee ignored a penalty for a foul on 'the Flea'.

Twenty minutes from the end, a free kick from Ronaldinho was deflected off the head of John Terry, under pressure from Rafa Márquez, into his own goal. The sides were level at 1–1.

And eight minutes later, the Mexican central defender took the ball from his own half before putting in a cross to the far post that was met by the head of Eto'o to secure a 2–1 win. José Mourinho's first defeat at home in 49 matches.

'We got our revenge for the previous year,' says a smiling Ten Cate as he recalls the game.

Leo had had five shots on goal, one of which struck the crossbar. He was involved in the sending-off and added intensity to the play of the brilliant but inconsistent Ronaldinho.

No, it wasn't a game for Messi. In theory. But the Argentinian showed up at the Bridge before Barcelona did. He was born a star in that most decisive of scenarios. 'The best appearance in world football for many a year,' wrote Santiago Segurola in El País. The crowning moment in a game for grown-ups.

His performance made such an impact that Ronaldinho and Eto'o, voted FIFA's first and third best players of the year respectively, were treated as secondary actors He had climbed not one but two steps up the hierarchical ladder. After his display against Udinese, and the excellent game at the Bernabéu, his performance at Stamford Bridge was to have a universal impact. And not surprisingly at home as well: no one was going to take his starting place now. Giuly began to appear only occasionally in the team after that match.

José Mourinho started to play the second leg at the press conference. 'It's easier for you to see it than me,' he responded to the journalists when they asked him about del Horno's sending-off, 'because you have monitors. I think it's better if you say what happened, because I don't want to find myself in a difficult situation. The result is 1–2. What can we do? Are we going to suspend Messi for being theatrical? Yes, he was theatrical. Catalonia is a place of *culture and they [referring to the Catalan media] know what theatre is. Theatre is good.'*

The Camp Nou would receive Mourinho two weeks later with a bit of cultural advice: 'Go to the theatre, Mourinho, go to the theatre.'

In the return leg, Leo began the match stuck on the left-hand touchline, but just a few minutes into the game he began to make his way from the left into a more central position; he could stand the heat and he wanted to get into the kitchen, where the goals were created.

Then, suddenly, with 25 minutes played, he collapsed on the pitch. He was injured. A pulled muscle.

He beat the ground in frustration. His fragile body was going to keep him out of the game again.

Rijkaard went over to Leo on his way to the dressing room. And he gave him a hug. Leo's right hand went around the waist of his coach and he buried his head in the Dutchman's coat. He wanted that embrace. Needed it.

Barcelona drew 1–1. But qualification for the quarter-finals [where they would meet Benfica] had come at a cost: Messi's progress had been stalled once again.

Messi had felt a sharp pain when he collided with William Gallas, but he carried on, hoping it was nothing. There was no contact with any other player at the moment he fell to the ground, just the realisation that he was injured and it wasn't just a spasm. When in 2010 Goal.com asked Leo Messi to identify the two key moments in his career, what came to mind was that night in the Camp Nou: 'My first major injury.'

A torn muscle at the top of the femoral bicep in the right leg, the muscle that sprinters depend on to give them an explosive start and one with which Messi will become very familiar. A four-centimetre tear, said Barcelona. Five, said the press. It was the second injury in the same muscle that he had suffered in a month. The first one had kept him out of action for twelve days, following a return to fitness which, with hindsight, had been a little too accelerated. This time he would be out for between four and six weeks. A month and a half later he was still not ready. Leo, who had played 25 games that season, in the end spent 79 days away from the training ground.

They say in football that muscular injuries do not occur by chance, that they are all avoidable. If a muscle gives way it is because something has gone wrong in the warm-up; or it's down to a player's lifestyle, or the lack of attention he pays to his body. Perhaps Messi, despite being rested the previous Sunday for the game against Depor, arrived with accumulated muscular fatigue. Perhaps he had not recovered sufficiently from the previous muscle injury. Some say he had not warmed up properly. The clash with Gallas might have affected it.

But the fact is there are no definitive scientific tests that can explain muscular injuries. Only suspicions and fears, and the need for some precautionary measures. The club has to take some of the blame because at that time they didn't monitor the condition of the players as exhaustively as they do nowadays: they had accumulated twenty similar muscular injuries in three seasons with twelve different players affected.

When he was appealing for calm over Leo, Frank Rijkaard had all this in mind.

Certainly Messi did not know his body's limitations then as well as he does today. It didn't bother him if he finished a game with his ankles and legs scarred, with his feet covered in bruises or with cuts, blisters and grazes. It was the life he had chosen, all part of the game. But two injuries in a month suggested that something else was going on. It didn't sound alarm bells but Leo did begin to ask where all this was coming from.

The answer wasn't simple, but Messi did not have to look very far to discover it. When he arrived in the first team, still an adolescent, in his life off the field he began to relax.

It wasn't a case of too much partying, rather one of order. Or lack of it. In his eating, in his personal timetable.

Also, Leo climbed the ladder of success too quickly; everything had got faster and this distracted him. Maybe he was mentally prepared to move forward more quickly than the majority of players of his age, but sudden changes in physical demands, and the new strains imposed by playing in an elite team, were difficult to assimilate. Every few months at a new level brought new challenges; the game became faster as he progressed, the battles harder, the tempo higher; there was more public attention, a greater need to win, an increasing response to greater expectations. And the first team was a place where to survive as a professional it was essential to take special care of yourself, to keep regular hours, to eat healthily. Vital requirements if he really wanted to shine.

Sometimes you have to make mistakes to find out what your limitations are.

Sometimes Leo would eat at La Masía with Barcelona B and then later on again in one of the Argentinian restaurants. The usual menu there would consist of a couple of *empanadas* (pies), always meat. And then a Scaloppe Milanese. He was so fond of the 200 grams of meat dipped in egg and breadcrumbs with tomato sauce, with ham and cheese, cooked in the oven, always with chips and always without salad, that in the restaurants he frequented it was known as 'la Milamessi'. And, to finish, ice cream made with sweetened milk and chocolate. Occasionally he would vary the *empanadas* and Milanese with a plate of meat ravioli. Always washed down with water or Coca-Cola. He did not touch alcohol.

The waiters used to joke with him about it: 'a bit of fish would do you good.' To which he would answer. 'Yuk! Fish is for the water.' If fish or meat wholesalers happened to offer him a case of Argentinian king prawns as a gift, Leo insisted that they give them to his father – but they should bring some Argentinian meat next time. On occasions he would go to the restaurants to eat on Sunday at midday and go on from there to the ground, especially when Rijkaard in his last months at the club allowed players to arrive at the stadium just before the games. And after the *empanadas*, the Milanese or the pasta, off to play. 'By the time I get there I'll have digested this,' Leo would say.

If there wasn't a game, after training he would have a long siesta, wake up at about four and eat a pizza. Then some *conguitos*, peanuts covered with chocolate. And if he was thirsty he would drink a litre and a half of Coca-Cola. A complete lack of nutritional control. He lived the life of a student.

Leo resembled a luxury car that ran on petrol but consumed diesel. Occasionally you can get away with it, but eventually the engine will seize up.

The irregularity of this lifestyle came to the attention of the board who considered watching over his growth, making sure he ate better, became stronger. 'You should be able to plant this guy in the ground so no one can pull him up' was a comment heard in the boardroom. But, despite the concern, during this period nothing special was done to make Leo change his habits. In fact, both the club and the player waited at least a couple of years before making the decisions that would prompt him to face up to the importance of nutritional and dietary control.

While he was recuperating, the year that could have been Messi's was becoming Barcelona's: Benfica had been eliminated in the quarter-finals, so they faced Milan in the semi-finals and the league was in their pocket.

Leo was now facing a race against time to be fit for the Champions League final. It was to be played on 17 May, ten weeks after his injury. If everything went according to plan, he would be fit.

5

Frank Rijkaard. The Decline

Leo believed he would be fit for the Champions League final.

> *'Playing in a final is always a wonderful experience, and more so in this competition, one of the most important after the World Cup, if not the most important of all. It would be really amazing to play in it and win.'*

(Leo Messi, 2006)

'The two of us would train together, morning and afternoon,' Juanjo Brau, Leo's personal physical trainer, explains. 'Physical work and physiotherapy in the mornings, gym in the afternoons. Every day.' And he would swim. And the rest of the time he would spend at home, resting, sleeping. For one month, every day. He had to be fit. He could not miss the big date in Paris. And on top of that it was World Cup year.

On 10 April, one week before the first leg of the semi-final against Milan, and five before the final, Leo Messi was finally ready to rejoin the group training sessions. He had missed the previous six league matches and both legs of the Champions League quarter-final. If he responded well, Rijkaard intended to take him to Italy but leave him on the bench, only using him to stir things up in the second half. Leo felt ready for anything.

Ten Cate was not as clear on the matter. Before the first group session, he asked the medical team about 'the Flea'. The player had the medical all-clear but doctors recommended that Messi should do individual work. Messi insisted that he was up for training as normal. Ten Cate took him to one side.

'Leo, I've spoken to the doctor and you're still not 100 per cent. You run the risk of missing more matches.'

'No, I feel fine!'

Coaches will always say that, ultimately, it is the footballer who has responsibility for his own body, that he decides if he is fit for training or not. Only they know what they feel inside. Fifteen minutes into that session, Leo felt comfortable and decided to take a free-kick.

Ten Cate called out to him not to. 'Leave it, Leo. Just in case it gets any worse ...'

Leo launched the ball over the bar. And he felt the muscle go again.

A new tear in the same place.

In his leg and in his heart.

The club said that Leo could play again before the end of the league season, as it was not a tear, but nobody risked a prediction on his precise return. The injury to the femoral bicep of his right leg, they explained, needed more oxygen than it was receiving.

The official statement read: 'During the last phase of treatment he has experienced discomfort in the scarred area and significant muscular fatigue. Therefore it has been decided to continue with the treatment guidelines and muscular reconditioning which will last until the player can resume training without symptoms. As things stand he is out of the next game.'

To get the true gist of the medical report you had to read between the lines. What the doctors meant was that Leo was inexperienced with such muscular injuries. His desire to play was akin to punishing himself. Leo had come back earlier because he wanted to get back on the pitch as soon as possible. His sprinting muscles required lots of oxygen and the healing was a slow process. At his age, they concluded, it was only natural that he did not know how to read his body, and that he imagined that he was better than he really was.

Leo did not want to speak to anyone when he got home. Something had failed once again. The latest tests confirmed that it was a new rupture, even though the club wanted to hide it. So it meant restarting the recovery. With Juanjo Brau. Physical work and physiotherapy in the mornings. Gym in the afternoons ... the same routine.

Leo and Brau went to Rosario, well away from those who wanted to get him back onto the pitch too soon, away from distractions. In Argentina they watched Giuly's goal against Milan, which put Barça through to the final. He celebrated it only with a muted 'Goal!' He could be fit for the final, perhaps on the bench. He would definitely make it. He carried on working hard to do so.

Time was ticking away fast; there was not long to go. The final was on 17 May, five weeks after his last setback, three after the semi-final.

In early May, Leo felt well enough. Juanjo Brau told him to be patient.

Messi asked Rijkaard to include him in the squad, and started training with everybody three days before the final against Arsenal in Saint-Denis, Paris. Leo trained with the first-team squad on Sunday at the Camp Nou. And again on Monday. Two days before the final.

On the Tuesday Frank Rijkaard attended the pre-final press conference. As well as saying it would be wrong to make Barcelona favourites against an Arsenal team containing Thierry Henry, Robert Pirès, Ashley Cole and Cesc, he did not want to give any clues about Leo's physical condition. He had taken the whole squad with him to Paris but had to leave two players out. 'I will not decide anything until tomorrow,' said the Dutchman. The journalists kept on probing. 'In terms of emotions, the team is fine. Messi? We will see what happens tomorrow. We are pleased that Leo is recovering, but let's see, because there's another training session and he has only had two with the team. You never know.'

And after the press conference, Rijkaard joined the squad. That Tuesday afternoon, in the French stadium, 'the Flea' was combative, fired up, sharp. He took a powerful shot which Eto'o blocked, leaving him groggy. His muscle was strong.

But Rijkaard and Ten Cate had already made their decision, and they revealed it to him after the training session the day before the final, privately, in an empty dressing room next to the one the players used.

The two men were waiting for him when Leo joined them.

Frank told him that he was not fit and that he was not going to include him in the final squad. Ten Cate nodded in agreement.

Henk had taken the training sessions and had not seen his usual explosive side. He did not think that Leo could handle the pressure and rhythm of a final.

They both knew they were taking him out of the club's most important match. But then again, he was only 18 years old. 'I'm sure you're going to play in many more finals, but this one has come too soon', Ten Cate told him.

Leo became angry. Furious. Not with Rijkaard, but with Ten Cate. It was written all over his face, his emotions evident in his trembling lips.

His eyes started filling up with tears.

His head dropped. Not a sound. His silence was as smooth and still as glass. He breathed in, then out, and was silent again. That was how he cried 'Can you imagine it?' Ten Cate said of that day. 'An eighteen-year-old kid who cannot play because of his own miscalculations?'

According to the technical staff, Leo had made a serious mistake back in April. He failed to read the messages his body was sending him. A lesson for the future, they thought, because if he had not suffered that setback he would have been an important part of the Barcelona team that was preparing to play its fifth European Cup final, in search of its second trophy in Europe's biggest competition.

'These are the most difficult moments for a coach,' insists Henk ten Cate. Xavi was already a mature player and knew what he could and could not do. He had had an operation on a ligament injury and returned to training with the squad, but he realised that he was not at the right level. The centre midfielder had been out of the team for five months and he knew that he was not fully fit for the final. He was going to stay on the bench, accept it. As he was not an explosive player, Rijkaard thought he could be useful in controlling the game if they needed to. That problem was easily resolved. Leo, on the other hand, was much more complicated.

'Tears were filling his eyes and running down his cheeks', remembers an emotional Ten Cate.

Frank got up and hugged him.

Xavi Hernández did not play a single minute of the final. Andrés Iniesta's fitness was also discussed by the coaching staff. He started the game on the bench because Rijkaard and Ten Cate preferred a more physical midfield with Van Bommel, Deco and Edmilson. 'Be careful, Frank,' his assistant said to him. 'Talk to Andrés for a moment, he is about to explode, he expected to play.' The rest of the team was typical of the sort of gamble Rijkaard took in big games: instead of attacking full-backs, the more defensive Oleguer Presas and Gio van Bronckhorst played, tasked with not pushing too far forward and with protecting the backs of Giuly and Ronaldinho.

As far as Leo was concerned, the coaches thought his absence served as a lesson to him: he would learn to listen now, to others, and to his body.

Messi couldn't enjoy the final. He was bitterly disappointed. He vaguely remembers a strange start to the game, with the very early sending-off of Arsenal goalkeeper Jens Lehmann (in the eighteenth minute), Sol Campbell's headed goal, which put Arsenal ahead, and the introduction of Henrik Larsson, who assisted Eto'o and Belletti for the win, and began what seemed an inevitable period of glory and European titles.

In the stands Leo did not feel any personal pleasure in the victory; he did not feel he deserved to be part of the celebration. So he went to the dressing room as soon as he heard the final whistle.

Ten Cate was having a cigarette in the tunnel just after the match, before the celebrations. Leo walked past him with his head down. At a steady pace.

And there he remained, preferring to distance himself from the team, to hide how upset he was. As Juanjo Brau says: 'if he says no, it's no, and if he says yes, it's yes. There is no ambiguity with him.'

Leo does not appear in a single photo from Saint-Denis. He did not want to touch the cup. Nor even pick up his medal. He cried alone in a corner of the locker room.

Amid the jubilation, Brau went to look for Messi. And said to him:

'Leo, in the Chelsea game ... with that infamous tackle, the sending-off... if you had not been fit, we would not have gone through.'

'And suddenly a light bulb went on in my head,' remembers Sylvinho.

'We were all celebrating winning the Champions League and

suddenly, hang on a second, I realise Leo is not with us. I went to the dressing room and there he was. Wearing a Barcelona tracksuit, with the kitman and Juanjo Brau. I went up to him, we spoke. "Come on, let's go onto the pitch." He was down, really down. Rijkaard thought the same as me; "let's go and get him", and the three of us found ourselves in the dressing room. After a while Rijkaard went back to the pitch, but I stayed there for a few minutes talking to him and said: "don't worry, you'll understand soon, we will speak about what is happening here and you will see it in a different light. And there will be many other important matches; calm down." I understood him. He did not need to say a single word to me, I understood perfectly what was happening. And I left him to it. I went back to the pitch to celebrate.'

'How come I missed a Champions League final like this one? I don't know if I will be able to experience another day like today … some footballers wait ten years for a game like this one,' Leo kept repeating.

The childish side of Leo seemed to have taken over.

Sylvinho, though, does not agree that it was the reaction of a child, but that of a young adult who knew that the opportunity of playing in a final might not come again. 'He thought he could have helped us,' says Sylvinho. 'He was missing out on a very special moment, an unforgettable match and party. During the rest of the night, and the following day, I tried to make him see that it was not the end of the world.

'I think he learned a lot that day.' This comes from Sylvinho, but everyone who saw him that day agrees.

Other Barcelona players were slightly less understanding of his reaction. 'Your team has just won, you are eighteen years old, things have gone well for you, the squad wins the cup, you go to the World Cup … It was strange for him to react like that,' said Maxi López in the press area. For those who do not think like Leo, this was just a minor setback. Nothing to get worked up about. Many footballers, on getting back to the dressing room, told him that he was as much a champion as they were.

Deco, who had picked up his medal, hung it around his neck in the dressing room. 'Someday you will see how big a night this has been,' he told Messi.

But Leo did not want to listen. He was in a dark place and wanted to remain there.

Slowly, though, thanks to his team-mates' infectious joy, he began to emerge. Some of them took the cup to the dressing room so that he could finally touch it and have his picture taken with it.

'I realise now that I should have enjoyed that final much more, more than I did, for the moment that it was. I don't think many players get the chance to be able to win the Champions League. I was very young and didn't want to celebrate it. Then Ronaldinho, Deco and Motta brought me the cup, and that is a very beautiful memory. Today I regret not enjoying it more on the pitch, although afterwards I did. I was there, and it is something very special.' So said Leo four years later.

He left the dressing room and on the way to the coach he ran into Ten Cate. 'I think he jumped on my back or something of the sort,' Henk remembers. 'His face had changed, he was now smiling. Everyone was all over him, he felt loved, I imagine. And then I remember the flight back home, he grabbed the microphone. We were sitting on the upper deck of the plane with the players and the directors, the families were sitting on the lower deck. But the whole plane could hear everything through the speakers. So he grabbed the microphone and said: "Mr President, please, I don't want another watch, I want a car." Messi had passed his driving test just before the final, two weeks earlier, and he already had a watch for winning the league, so that is why he said it. They gave us all an Audi. An S3, I think.'

The 'negotiations' for the bonuses did not end there. Laporta bumped into a happier Leo: 'And I said to him, "So, Leo. Happy?" He was sitting in one of the last rows, and he said to me, "I've already looked at a few flats." He was joking. We all laughed. And he continued with the joke: "with a garage to park the car."'

'In the end he came out of his shell and everything was perfect,' insists Sylvinho. 'I remember how we celebrated that final like crazy when we got back to Barcelona, the streets packed with people, unforgettable.'

The season ended with victory in Europe and in the league, Real Madrid's *galácticos* finishing twelve points behind. Samuel Eto'o was the top scorer with 26 goals, and both the Cameroonian and

Ronaldinho were chosen in the best XI of FIFPRO, the footballers' union team of the season.

In 2012 in *El País* Leo Messi analysed that period with a more reflective appreciation: 'Rijkaard is a person to whom I owe practically everything, it was he who had faith in me, it was he who gave me my debut as a kid. It was he who knew how to handle me, he knew to leave me out at that time, when I didn't understand and didn't like it, he knew why he did it and the truth is that everything that came after that, came thanks to him.'

The team was destined for great things, but what no one knew at the time was that that Paris final was as good as it got.

'It was fascinating to see how, before our very eyes, the kid was becoming the best player in the world. And this in only a few months.' Eidur Gudjohnsen, who arrived the following season, along with Thuram and Zambrotta, did, of course, have a privileged view of Leo's progress. But his comment has an added depth. Eidur and Leo recognised each other as outsiders in that small world of the Barcelona squad. The Viking and the Argentinian communicated without understanding a word of what the other was saying: 'I didn't understand Leo: he spoke very quietly or very quickly or with that thick Argentine accent. I would just keep saying, "what has he just said?" I think that made him laugh. And, despite not understanding each other, we got on really well, we would laugh at each other's jokes. Or what we thought were jokes.

'I thought it was an interesting exercise seeing his impressive progression, game by game, and trying to get inside his head,' continues the Icelandic forward. 'And it was not at all easy, because what you see from the outside, even for his team-mates, is a guy who is passionate about football, who lives and breathes football, who spends the rest of his time at home, or sleeping, or playing a bit of PlayStation, and that's it. But I always knew that, behind all that, there was much more, there had to be more.'

The former Chelsea footballer immediately recognised the ascendancy of the group that had just won the two big competitions: the squad revolved around Ronaldinho's eternal smile. 'When Ronnie spoke about football, and he did so often, you could see a very attentive Messi, with the adoring look of a fan. We went to the

United States in pre-season and, when Ronnie got off the coach, it was as if a film star had arrived. He was a real man; and Leo, a boy who admired the best player in the world, and who played in the same team as him,' remembers Gudjohnsen, who is still surprised that they invited him to join their table. 'It was the jokers' table. Sylvinho was my translator, he would explain all the rubbish they used to say.'

After the year of success, Barcelona lost a certain competitiveness in the 2006–07 season. At the start it was unnoticeable, but the departure of Larsson, Gabri and Van Bommel and a reduction in the performance levels of the dressing-room leaders (especially Ronaldinho and Deco) had an effect. Henk ten Cate leaving for Ajax also contributed to the team's gradual break-up.

Rijkaard's assistant's influence was crucial. The league title that had just been won was the result of talent, most certainly, but measures had also been taken early to prevent the team declining. 'If you want the key to that league title and what came after, study the match against Betis at the Benito Villamarín Stadium closely': that was the challenge launched by Ten Cate in the conversation with Gio van Bronckhorst. 'You will see the reason why we won the league and the Champions League. Do you remember, mate?'

Barcelona had made a lacklustre start to the season, drawing against Alavés and Valencia, losing against Atlético de Madrid, and the only win so far had been against Mallorca. Just before they then went to Seville for the encounter Ten Cate talks about, Frank Rijkaard trained behind closed doors with his best eleven. Ronaldinho and Deco wore first XI bibs. But in the end he did not pick either of them to travel.

Until that moment, the two stars had only been out of the team because of injury. The dressing room shook.

Officially Rijkaard spoke about rotation: 'Ronaldinho and Deco have played four games in ten days and I've thought about giving them a rest, because there is a crucial match on Tuesday [Udinese at the Camp Nou] and they are very important players. I want them to relax and then, on Sunday, train again.'

The real reason was different: signs that part of the dressing room resented the two players' behaviour had been brought to Rijkaard's attention. Deco would fly to Brazil frequently and was often absent from training. Ronaldinho was not as professional as he should have been. Some of the players got annoyed, and the group comprising the Dutch, the Catalans and Eto'o made Ten Cate aware of their discontent. They had just won the first of two league titles and it was necessary to rectify the situation and set an example, or 'the group will split up', Rijkaard was told. He responded immediately by leaving the two players out of the Betis match.

Henk ten Cate stated the obvious to the group on the way to Seville: 'Guys, we have to win whatever happens.' Rijkaard had never before taken such momentous disciplinary action, and he had to be backed up by a win. In that match, Eto'o missed a penalty. It was 1–1 for the best part of an hour, but then the Cameroonian scored twice, the second time nicking the ball from Maxi López and shooting. 'You have to think quickly in the six-yard box,' Eto'o told him. Messi did not play in that match.

The season ended well, with the two big titles in the bag, but the negative dynamic of the 'stars' continued on into the new one. Messi was the only light at the end of a tunnel getting darker by the day: he was the only player who had improved from the previous season and who continued his rise in the team. He was suffering fewer injuries, and only missed a week following an ankle strain suffered during Real Madrid's 2–0 win in the *clásico* at the Bernabéu, a defeat that began to suggest that Barcelona, also annihilated 3–0 by Sevilla in the European Super Cup in August, did not fare well in the important matches.

But in November, against Zaragoza, Messi fractured the fifth metatarsal in his left foot. This time it was not a question of lifestyle. Broken bones are down to bad luck: he was out of action for just over two and a half months.

'Not being able to help the team is infuriating. You're in the dressing room with them, you share the time before the match but you know they will go out to play and you won't,' he said to Ramiro Martín in December 2006.

Leo went back to a Barcelona team that kept failing in the big games. They lost against Rafa Benítez's Liverpool in the last sixteen of the Champions League. In that European duel, Benítez knew that he had to cut out Messi's diagonal runs and put Alvaro Arbeloa at left-back precisely because he was right-footed, as well as a good defender. A clever move. Leo was efficiently marked out of the game.

There then followed the return *clásico* league fixture, on 10 March 2007 at the Camp Nou, another opportunity to recover from their European hangover. A long-haired Messi, who had played impressively in various matches since coming back from his metatarsal injury but found it hard to score, took the reins, while Ronaldinho was gradually fading into the background.

It showed the Argentinian's willingness to take responsibility as he outshone even Eto'o, who usually demanded all the attention against Real Madrid. Ronnie was insignificant and the Cameroonian was replaced at half-time when Rijkaard decided to shuffle the team as a result of Oleguer's sending-off in the first half.

He decided that 'the Flea', hogging the touchline, was creating enough danger. He did not do anything wrong: he was choosing the right diagonal runs, he destabilised the right-back, Miguel Torres, with threatening duels on the wing, and he knew when to wait for the ball, as he did for the first goal to equalise after Ruud van Nistelrooy's opener.

Eto'o had released the ball to the left where Leo found himself alone, with sufficient space to manoeuvre, and his shot flew into the far corner, beating Iker Casillas.

Leo raised his shirt. Underneath he wore a T-shirt with the message '*Fuerza, tío*' (strength, uncle). 'I dedicated it to my uncle who has lost his father. He is my godfather, my second father, and I wanted to send him all my support from here,' he explained after the match.

Van Nistelrooy put Real Madrid back in front with a penalty, but Leo continued to shine as the team pushed over to his side. The equaliser began with some classic play by Ronaldinho down the left; moving into the penalty area, he played a one-two with Eto'o, but the Brazilian's shot was turned away by Casillas. The ball fell at Messi's feet and he smashed it home with aplomb: 2–2, 27 minutes into the game.

The sending-off of the Catalan defender Oleguer occurred in one of the most electrifying first halves of a *clásico*. Valdés extraordinarily denied Van Nistelrooy his hat-trick, but Sergio Ramos put Real Madrid in front for the third time and 90 minutes were up.

In stoppage time, a Ronaldinho pass found Messi in the hole, but surrounded by opposition players. With his first touch he started a diagonal run and centre-back Iván Helguera tried to halt his progress by throwing himself to the ground. Messi explained the rest in the press area:

– It all happened very quickly. Helguera was in my way, I tried to get past him, I did so and found myself one on one with Casillas …

He shot across the goal, beating the Real Madrid keeper.

– What did you think when you saw the ball go in?
– We had enough time to win the game, but in the end it was not possible. It was a shame because we had the strength to do it after the final equaliser.
– What did you say to each other as you celebrated?
– We said we had a bit more time to try to win it. We were at the Camp Nou so we had to win.
– Did you think at any point that the match was lost?
– It was complicated. On top of that, we had just played Liverpool and were tired.
– Why did you repeatedly kiss the badge after scoring your third goal?
– Because I owe Barcelona a lot for everything they did for me at the time.

'The Messi match I remember best was the *clásico* at the Camp Nou,' recalls Sylvinho. 'We celebrated the last goal together, because when he scored I was the closest to him, and we celebrated it without words. I mean, we yelled, but there were no words.'

'For me, today, Messi is above any other player. He has an extra gear,' acknowledged Eto'o on a night when he took a step down from the pedestal.

Gudjohnsen tells his own story from another perspective and with affection: 'without the run I made down the right, he wouldn't have had as much space for the third goal, eh!' That match witnessed the beginning of Leo's transition from adolescence to maturity. 'In that season Messi played without pressure,' says Gudjohnsen. 'All the critics were looking the other way, at other players. The easiest thing in football is to be a talented player whereas the most complicated is reaffirming that talent with the passing of time. When a player like that appears, there are always excuses if things do not go well for him in a match or for a month. The difficult part is for that talent to manifest itself regularly. Leo seemed to be ready to take on that responsibility.'

'Great players show it in the important matches,' says ex-president Joan Laporta. 'And Leo has never hidden, especially against Real Madrid. His two big rivalries have always been with Espanyol in the youth team and with Real Madrid in the first team. He knows that those matches are beautiful to play in and what is expected of him. And he is delighted when they come round.'

'Losing against Real Madrid is a fucker. I remember that game, which we were losing and I scored the equalising third goal,' Leo told Luis Martín in *El País* at the end of 2007. 'As a *culé* I always want to beat Real Madrid. On top of that, that match marked my career. I had just come back from injury, I wasn't putting away chances but from that day on more and more went in and I played more regularly.'

Messi scored seven goals in his first eight games against Real Madrid. And some years later, in March 2013, he managed to equalise Alfredo Di Stéfano's record as top scorer in matches between the two big rivals with 18 goals. Leo gradually confirmed himself as a *clásico* specialist as time went on, which equates to being a big-game player.

The draw left Barcelona above Real Madrid and Sevilla who had started the matchday as table-toppers. Nineteen-year-old Leo had forgotten the sour taste of the Champions League final in which he had been unable to feature, and the injury which prevented him from going to the World Cup in Germany in his best shape. He was all over the front pages.

The Messi era was beginning.

I wait for the defender's movement, I play with him. Once I see what he does, I feint to go one way then go the other. I keep looking at my opponent's feet, not the ball. I know where the ball is. I know it is there …

(Leo Messi, 2007)

The club rewarded his progress with a new seven-year contract in March 2007. The financial remuneration was considerable. He went from €1.8 million a year to €6.5 in 2006–07, although part of the increase corresponded to payments from the previous season which had run over into the new campaign. The following season he would earn €4.5 million and it would rise progressively to €6.2 million in 2014, with the same €150 million release clause.

His impact on the pitch was being reflected in the figures.

In the closing stages of what was a mixed season, Barcelona reached the Coppe del Rey semi-final against a modest Getafe team. The result in the first leg (a spectacular 5–2) left Barcelona on the brink of the final, but that encounter will be remembered for the Maradona-like goal scored by Leo Messi, twelve seconds of skill, bursting pace, trickery, five defenders left in his wake, seventy yards that would lead to a moment of posterity.

It is the twenty-ninth minute, Messi gets the ball in midfield in his own half near the centre circle. He moves away from Paredes and Nacho and starts running towards goal.

'I am on the centre line, I dribble past the first defender. I don't nutmeg him even if it looks as if I do. I *do* nutmeg the second one, though,' Leo Messi explained in 2007 in the Argentinian TV programme *Sin Cassette*.

The run continues.

'I see Eto'o opening up the pitch ...'

Centre-back Alexis cannot stop him, Belenguer closes in on him, but before he can stop him Leo gets away. He continues his run between the two of them.

'When I get to the edge of the box, I feint to go to my left, the defender falls for it and I go between both centre-backs as they leave a little space between them.'

Now the goalkeeper, Luis García.

His friend, Roberto 'the Duck' Abbondanzieri, former Boca Juniors keeper, was on the bench and a few days later he said to Leo. 'Thank God it wasn't me!'

He goes round him to the right and, from an almost impossible angle, lifts the ball over Cotelo with the last of his thirteen touches.

'The ball ended up in front of me, in the right place and I dummied as if to put it into the goal, but I took it on my left, the touch was a bit too heavy and the ball went away from me. I thought, "it is going out". I was about to hit it with my right foot when I saw a player going to ground so I lifted the ball slightly.'

Maradona, World Cup '86, against England. Messi scores.

'When I was a kid, I scored a couple of goals like that, but perhaps that was my best yet.' Leo scored his best goal with his right foot.

Sylvinho: 'I was in the stands for that game. Bernd Schuster was the Getafe coach. Him running away with his long hair, dribbling, and running and getting close to the box ...'

Gudjohnsen: 'I put my hands on my head. You can see it on television. There was a moment on the pitch where I thought, "God, I'm on the pitch when a goal that's going to be talked about forever has just been scored. It is Maradona against England all over again!"'

Sylvinho: '... an amazing goal. The Camp Nou was on its feet, and, well ... I was dumbstruck.'

Gudjohnsen: 'And the guy starts celebrating as if it was nothing, and on the pitch we were all speechless. Us and our opponents. I started shouting at him, "incredible, incredible!!!"'

Juanjo Brau: 'You see Xavi or Ronaldinho take a tenth of a second longer to do things because they are thinking. Messi doesn't think about what he is going to do. He just does it.'

Andrés Iniesta: 'It was a spectacular goal, the perfect combination of dribbling, driving at players, skipping past rivals and the final dummy is very complicated. It reminds you of the Maradona goal mainly because of his starting position.'

Deco: 'As soon as we went into the dressing room I told him that his goal was like Maradona's.

Juanjo Brau: 'He used to say to me that he didn't want to copy Maradona, that he doesn't think about what he is going to do, it comes to him naturally.'

Deco: 'These are the goals that go down in history. It is the most beautiful goal I've ever seen, and, don't forget, I've seen Ronaldo, Maradona and Ronaldinho score live. Today's goal is perfect. I thought he would try a one-two when he got close to the area, but ...'

Sylvinho: 'In the dressing room he didn't joke about it, he didn't say, "okay, I've done the Maradona goal, what's next?" Nothing of the sort. Leo respects his rivals, his team-mates, he's not one for poking fun or boasting. He follows his own very strict code of conduct. Not even once in five years did he say, "Ah! Did you see how I dribbled past that one? Look at the screamer I scored ...", never, ever. We did though!'

Juanjo Brau: 'And when he ends up scoring he doesn't think it was like Maradona's. It comes later, when they all tell him that, and they call him from Argentina saying, "what a commotion you've caused". But he still doesn't attach much importance to it.'

Sylvinho: 'We would shout at him, trying to sound like a television commentator, "what a goal, what an *amazing* goal", and he would laugh.'

Deco: 'I was so happy for him. He is incredibly humble and oozes quality. At eighteen he was at Barcelona and at nineteen he scores goals like that. That's impressive.'

Gudjohnsen: 'It was a complicated period but Messi appeared at various stages in the season to our benefit. People started to look at him through different eyes after that goal against Getafe. Ah, so he does this with the big boys! He has dribbled past five or six top division professionals! It had yet to be seen if he could transfer those moments of individual brilliance, that only he could perform, into a full ninety-minute game, but the doubts were gradually disappearing. Can we live without Ronaldinho? Well, yes, they started to say. And he started to accept everything that lay before him, as though it was all perfectly natural. And to grow, to grow, to grow.'

Carlos Salvador Bilardo (coach of the 1986 Argentina World Cup-winning squad): 'I still think the Maradona goal is the best one. Players were continuously coming at him, and the centre-backs were ranked like steps on a ladder: first Butcher and then Fenwick. Messi runs for thirty-five yards and no one gets near him. That is why he touches the ball more with his right foot, his weaker one. He toe-pokes it, and dribbles with his left foot. It is very difficult for the defenders to kick him or stop him because he is almost jumping and running very fast at the same time. In the end, the centre-backs prefer to hold their line and wait for him, which makes it easier for Leo.'

Maradona: 'I'd say that Messi is a phenomenon, who has no limits, but the goal that I scored, apart from being more beautiful,
was against England in the quarter-finals of a World Cup. Messi
scored his against Getafe, who were playing the *offside* rule. It
was an incredible goal, but let's not go overboard.'

Schuster: 'We should have kicked him, even if it had cost us a card.
You can't be that noble.'

And Leo? What did he say?

'Rijkaard congratulated me. I had seen the Maradona goal a million times but I did not think of copying it at any stage. I didn't
think of it after the Getafe goal either. I realised when Deco told me.
I saw both goals, Diego's and mine, played at the same time in a TV
programme. I heard what people were saying, but I didn't stop for a
second to think if it was the best one in history or not. After the goal
and some banter after, it was not mentioned again in the dressing
room. We didn't even talk about it with the family after that day.'

He dedicated the goal to Maradona, who had just been admitted
to a psychiatric clinic.

Since that day Leo has been marked more tightly by defenders.

That goal would never be repeated.

Partly because defences have become more alert to his runs, and
partly because that goal also reflected a series of Barcelona mistakes
that had to be corrected. You cannot prepare such a piece of play on
the training ground, but you can avoid it being necessary: there are
more collective and easier ways to score goals.

This is what Rijkaard said to Messi some time after. According
to the Dutchman, it was the best piece of advice he ever gave him:
'Finish the play: shoot or play the final ball but don't carry on
dribbling.' He wanted to stop Messi from constantly looking to
slalom, dribbling too much and getting into duels with every player
he faced. It could happen once or twice a season, but not in every
game. Rijkaard advised him not to tire himself out so much, but,
rather, to pace himself in order to make the difference in the final
third. He asked him to get closer to the box.

Although that goal is remembered as a piece of genius from Leo,
the sort he had scored many times in the youth teams, in professional football it ended up being the exception that proved the rule.

Pep Guardiola also considered that goal to be an accumulation of mistakes in attack (too much driving forward, a lack of collaboration with team-mates, too deep a starting point, poor team positioning), which, in many ways typified the problems that affected Rijkaard's team.

Leo had dinner with his father and Pablo Zabaleta that evening. And he repeated several times: 'But I was looking for Eto'o to pass him the ball.'

Rijkaard thought Barcelona would get into the final after that and left Messi out of the squad for the return leg. However, they lost 4–0 at Getafe, beaten 6–5 on aggregate, in the most humiliating elimination of the recent history of the club.

There was still the league to be won. It was in their hands; a few straightforward results would give them the title, and could confirm that, despite the disciplinarian problems, they were still aiming to make history. But that was the year of the Tamudazo: Espanyol striker Raúl Tamudo's equalising goal at the Camp Nou in the dying moments of the game and Betis's last-gasp equaliser, both clear lapses of concentration. They handed the league to Real Madrid, who were level on points with the *culés* but won on goal average.

'I watched the Espanyol game from the stands,' says Henk ten Cate. 'Messi has learned many lessons in his professional life. One of those was losing the championship in the game against Espanyol. Leo lost possession and didn't track back to recover the ball. He doesn't make that mistake any more.'

In that Barcelona derby, Leo scored both goals in the 2–2 draw, including one with his hand to make it 1–1. He jumped to head the ball and beat the goalkeeper to it by using his left hand. Moral judgement of the goal draws different conclusions depending on which hemisphere you come from. For better or for worse, guile is considered part of the Latin gene, something that will never be understood by Anglo-Saxon sensibilities.

As someone who knows both worlds, Eidur Gudjohnsen tries to assess it from a footballer's perspective. 'I have played with some South American players and it seems to be a part of their culture: they would do anything to put the ball between the sticks. The truth is that it is hard to celebrate such a goal, but we were losing 1–0, we needed the win, so we did celebrate it.'

Maybe the ends justify the means in football. Cheating exists in both the Latin and Anglo-Saxon worlds (isn't it cheating to raise your hand, telling the referee it should be your throw-in, when you were the last person to touch the ball?). But Leo regretted scoring that goal and has never done anything like it again.

Apart from winning the Spanish Super Cup at the start of the season, Barcelona went off on their summer holidays without any important titles. And with the feeling that a cycle had come to an end.

Sacking Rijkaard and getting rid of Ronaldinho were both considered. In a meeting between Beguiristain, Ferran Soriano, Joan Laporta and Rijkaard himself, the coach spoke categorically: 'I know what needs to be done, we will do it properly next season, it will go well.' Having said that, he got up and left. The meeting continued without him: 'What should we do? Should we back him for another year?' Laporta insisted that the team, and Frank, deserved it. Out of respect for the heights of the previous year, it was decided not to change anything, although they all knew Rijkaard had lost the dressing room.

But the following season, the faith shown by Laporta and the board of directors was not rewarded.

'One day Messi scored one of those amazing goals after drib-bling past about two hundred players and when he came back to his own half, he looked at me: "Hey, don't get all cocky," I said. "I've scored loads like that." He made a face as if to say: "what an arsehole."'

(Eduardo Iturralde González, former international referee)

'The thing is … [he smiles] I've played with loads of players and Leo is something … very strange, isn't he?'

(Thierry Henry)

The 2007–08 season was the one of second chances. Ronaldinho intended to contribute more, having begged Laporta to give him one more year at the club. Frank Rijkaard insisted he was committed to halting the team's downward spiral. The club restored excitement with the signing of a star, Thierry Henry, from Arsenal. Imagine: Ronaldinho, Messi, Henry and Eto'o in the same team. However, they did not play a single minute together.

Other arrivals included Eric Abidal (Lyon), Gabi Milito (Zaragoza) and Yaya Touré (Monaco), who would go on to become one of the main players in another dismal season. In search of a response, the club got rid of Giuly, Belletti, Motta, Saviola and van Bronckhorst.

Gio sent a farewell message to Messi's BlackBerry. Leo had a photo of himself taken in Times Square, New York, on his profile. Just him, alone. After seeing the photo, van Bronckhorst added a question: 'isn't it nice being able to take a photo without anyone around for once in your life?' Such luxuries would soon be a thing of the past for the Argentinian.

Rijkaard was unable to change the dynamic that year in spite of his assurances. The team went to pieces as early as December, confirmed by defeat against Real Madrid at the Camp Nou by a single goal scored by Júlio Baptista. 'The coach was too good for that dressing room,' revealed Edmilson some years later. Frank kept the team as it was, despite the fact that Leo Messi had just about knocked the door down from beating on it so much. He had so much more to offer but was asked to be patient and to continue causing damage on the wing.

Meanwhile, he was starting to become an idol in the stands. 'It didn't seem real when we were on our way into the ground and we saw people with his name on the back of their shirts.' It was like a dream,' his mother Celia used to say.

'That was the season when we became really close, lots of confidence in each other. We even had enough privacy to talk about serious things,' says Sylvinho. 'I was very comfortable, I saw him as an adult and could even speak to him about my frustrations, things I didn't like, what was happening to me, how I was having a hard time. So I found someone in him who would listen to everything I had to say.'

The boy was becoming a man. But, in the process, he oscillated between the responsibilities of being an adult and the changing physique of a youth. And his body was rebelling.

2007–08 season medical report

14/09/07. Australia vs Argentina. Muscle niggle in right hamstring.

Five days out.

> *'I remember when he came to Argentina to recover from a tear,' says Pancho Ferraro. 'He went to Rosario. I was still with the national team. He arrived on a morning flight and we were having breakfast with the boys, the technical staff, Tojo, Fillol, the doctors, and there were six Under 17 players who Tojo managed. The door opened and we saw Messi, his dad and the doctor, who had come from Barcelona. We got up to say hello to them. Messi must have been twenty years old. He sits next to me, I ask him what he wants, "café con leche", we both order from the waiter. They had everything: pastries, biscuits, jam, dulce de leche. They bring him his café con leche, but we were talking and talking, and he sat there silent. He wasn't drinking it. I said to him "Leo, drink it" and he said to me "yes, yes", but he wasn't drinking it. We were all speaking except him. And a moment later, the second time, I say to him "Leo, what's wrong?" and he says "may I go and have this with the boys?" I said to him "go, Leo, go". He got up and went to the other table. It was beautiful. He felt closer to the kids, he was still one himself.'*

15/12/07. Valencia vs Barcelona. A femoral bicep tendon tear in his left leg, not the one he injured against Chelsea the season before. Just under five weeks out. He missed, among other games, the *clásico* at the Camp Nou, which was played a week later.

> *'I remember his injury against Valencia,' says Gudjohnsen. 'It gave me a very strange feeling. Suddenly it came into my head that he played like a man but was still a boy. He cried in the dressing room. There I saw a boy who could not bear the shock of an injury, who could not live away from the ball.'*

04/03/08. Barcelona vs Celtic. A femoral bicep tear of his third proximal in his left leg. Six weeks out.

> *Gordon Strachan (Celtic coach 2005–09): 'The scouts had warned us that the lad was a bit special. A bit special, eh? He scored twice in the first leg, one was a beauty, he did a drag back in the area to make an opening, and goal. They beat us 3–2. In the return leg, almost at the end of the first half, he*

got injured. He was running with two of my players and must
have noticed a shooting pain. It happened right in front of
me. I saw him crying. I didn't cry, I can assure you of that.
I thought, "thank God, now we can relax slightly, because
whoever they bring on won't be as good as him!"'

Leo left the Camp Nou in tears that night. It was his third big
injury in two years. What was happening? Why so many injuries?
Was his body changing? Was it something to do with his diet?
They told him that it was to do with the shape of his foot. Maybe
he was not warming up properly. But no comprehensive study
of the situation had yet been carried out, even though the club
wanted to protect him and look for the causes. Lots of nonsense
was spouted, such as the suggestion that the problem was linked
to his hormonal treatment. Puyol reacted by making accusations
against the press: 'You put pressure on Messi to play and now he
is injured, but what you have to do is show greater respect for
the coach and doctors' decisions,' he said in a press conference.
The captain was responding to the heavy criticism that Rijkaard
received after resting him in the previous match against Atlético de
Madrid at the Calderón.

Commitment and discipline were becoming rare commodities in
the Barcelona dressing room. Attempts were made to preserve unity,
exemplified by Puyol's attack on the press, but a player doesn't get
injured just because of what is written in the media. Many other
factors were at play, which went some way to explaining these sudden and frequent lay-offs.

Joan Laporta received medical reports dismissing the likelihood
of hormonal treatment being a cause. This is how former club doctor Josep Borrell explains it: 'When he arrived at Barcelona we took
him for a private consultation with an endocrinologist, and together
we decided to gradually lower and then take him off the hormonal treatment. His muscular injuries had nothing to do with that.
Messi's muscular morphology is what it is: short muscles and, based
on that, we have to work with him very thoroughly every day, to
prevent him from getting constantly injured.'

Leo had spent many seasons in the lower ranks without suffering injuries. His torn muscles and ligaments were a new develop-

ment, and clearly demonstrated that his body was rebelling, caused by his inability to understand his limitations. The main risk factor with these injuries was the possibility of a setback, and Messi often returned too soon, delaying or even impeding the healing process his body required. Horacio D'Agostino, head doctor of the Argentinian national team, added a factor that everybody preferred to ignore: 'The question of why Messi's injuries recur so frequently has a complicated explanation, but for me the key lies in the demands he imposes on himself. More is demanded than he can physically give, he runs more than his body can handle. He's driven by an obsession to score goals. But how are you going to make a boy of his age understand all this?'

Around that time Jordi Desola, a medical expert in sports injuries, made an interesting analogy on the Catalan radio station RAC1: 'Messi is an athlete at an extremely high level who keeps putting too much pressure on his body. Anyone who drove their car at 120mph in first gear would see how the engine suffers, but the car does not break down and can be used the day after. If something similar is done with a very sophisticated engine such as one used in Formula One, it would break down. Messi is similar to a Formula One car and, even though he has extraordinary stamina, he pushes it beyond its limits. A bad diet or bad habits could affect his injuries, but that is difficult to determine. The muscles that perform such colossal tasks are very vulnerable.'

Barcelona formed a committee made up of Txiki Beguiristain and vice-presidents Marc Ingla and Ferran Soriano, who tried to find a solution. They told Leo that his muscle mass was formed of explosive fibres similar to those of a sprinter: they give him speed but there is always a risk that they will snap. He had to look after himself, and properly, if it was not to become a chronic problem. Marc Ingla says: 'The problem is that we could not get him to stabilise, he always had that recurring muscle injury, so we approached the matter in a comprehensive manner. In order to monitor him we developed a personalised stretching routine and asked him to bulk up his muscles. He had to do it every day and be extremely disciplined, so that we could outline a plan to get the most out of him.'

The club was clearly responding to a widespread concern, but its answer was a somewhat conventional one. The club had a nutritionist, who would prepare him a milkshake full of vitamins after training. He hated the milkshake. Juanjo Brau became his personal physiotherapist and also joined him with the national team. He would have a massage before training and the care would continue after training and matches. He gradually learned how to reduce his participation during training in order to be ready for the matches, to avoid new injuries. 'We would get to the training ground and they would often already be treating him,' remembers Gudjohnsen. 'He reminded me of Michael Jordan: if you have a player like him, you have to look after him at all times because you're going to need him. Nobody had the feeling that it was unfair to treat him differently. Other footballers had their own helpers.'

In any case, muscular injuries are not just coincidence. Twenty-year-old Leo was a youngster who had a fairly unhealthy diet: pizzas and hamburgers, escalopes, too much Coca-Cola, at any time of day. But the feeling in the dressing room was that almost everything was allowed as long as you played well. That was one of the lessons learned from Deco and, especially, Ronaldinho.

> *Why did you choose to live in Castelldefels?*
>
> *After visiting a number of places we decided on Castellde-fels. Both me and my family were convinced by it. Peace and quiet, the beach, mountains, everything. It's also close to Barcelona and the Camp Nou, where I go to train every day.*
>
> *What do you know about Castelldefels and where do you go to shop and to eat?*
>
> *I know Castelldefels football pitch. I went the day they were playing against Club Vilanova in the third division, an Argentinian friend of mine plays there. I went with Zabaleta from Espanyol. When I go out to eat I go to La Pampa, Ushuaia or some other Argentine restaurant. I love meat. What's more, my family is able to buy Argentinian produce in the town shops, even though I would like to find out where I can buy sweet 'medias lunas' [Argentinian sweet cake].*
>
> (Interview with Messi for La Voz, independent newspaper of
Castelldefels, 28 May 2008)

After signing a new contract in 2005, Messi moved with his father to a house in Castelldefels, next to his team-mate Ronaldinho, while Rodrigo stayed in Barcelona with his family. Jorge started coming and going to Argentina, so Zabaleta often kept Leo company in the big house that tended to dwarf him when he was alone. In hot weather they would swim in the pool. When it was dark or it was cold, he would suggest, 'Come and play on my PlayStation.' So Zabaleta, often accompanied by other friends, would spend four hours at a time in front of the screen playing. Leo would win by a mile. On one occasion, Zabaleta arrived at the seaside house and saw by the front door eight cases of new Xboxes that the manufacturers had sent to him. 'Take one,' he told his friend. His house was invariably stuffed with boxes containing all kinds of items sent to him by other manufacturers, all of which he willingly shared with his friends.

'Come round and we'll do a barbecue,' he might say to Zabaleta on another day. And everyone at Leo's house soon discovered that he didn't know where the plates were, or the cutlery, or anything in fact, but none the less they still had a fun *asado*. Or if they didn't feel like making a mess, they'd spend the afternoon at La Pampa, another local Argentinian restaurant.

'We shared a lot,' says Zabaleta today, who was also his travelling companion on flights to Argentina when they were called up to the national squad, a journey that Leo soon started making regularly and one that allowed him to maintain ties with his own country. 'I always lived in Barcelona, and he lived thirty kilometres away. Once we were coming out of a bar and he fell asleep in the car while I was driving. I assumed I was taking him home. Perfect. When we got there after about half an hour he said he was going to his brother's house, next to mine. I could've killed him. So we turned round.' Pablo and Argentinian frontman Martín Posse, also from rivals Espanyol, used to watch Messi at the Camp Nou and they often ended up dining together. 'I used to tell him to calm down when I played him, so that he wouldn't start running around in all directions,' remembers Zabaleta. 'You could see him getting annoyed with himself sometimes. Perhaps something didn't turn out like he wanted in a game and he used to get angry, like everyone.'

Leo's path to adulthood on and off the pitch was being mapped out by Ronaldinho. The Brazilian star had also made his debut in the first division as a 17-year-old, so, as Messi says, 'He knew what I was going through.' But he learnt all types of lessons, good and bad.

Ronnie was teaching him what he should and shouldn't do as a professional. 'He was the best coach for Messi,' says Ten Cate today, who tried to prevent him from messing around with the wrong crowd. 'The Ronaldinho group had a different life philosophy.' It was not a good one for Leo, and Ten Cate told him as much on various occasions. Sylvinho would remind him that there were more important things in life and that he was coming off the rails. Leo would listen and assume the look of an innocent child.

Suddenly all the discipline, effort and sacrifice that had driven him to the top was forgotten as Ronnie's world opened up new and exciting possibilities and sensations. Leo would meet up with Deco, Thiago Motta and Ronaldinho in Castelldefels or in Barcelona. And off to training the day after.

And they would all meet in the rondo. 'We would do rondos to start the sessions, ten on one side and ten on the other,' recalls Ten Cate. Leo usually joined the Brazilian group, which on one occasion was made up of eleven players, leaving nine in the other. One of the coaching staff asked Messi, as the youngest, to even up the numbers. Many times he asked him: four, five, six times. Messi ignored him; he felt a part of that rondo. In the end, Sylvinho asked him to move to the other group. 'Well, if he is like that so young ...' was the view of one of the coaches.

Suddenly Leo began to see some of the consequences of his new lifestyle. He had an accident with a van in Barcelona. Having crashed, he faced the indignant owner who, fortunately, was a fan and was happy to reach an agreement. There were stories of incidents in Barcelona nightclubs.

From the centre of the whirlwind that was his new life, Leo faced up to his father. Rebellion, finally. He had the exuberance of an 18-year-old boy who was starting to understand life and was looking for new emotions.

'Leo was a teenager,' comments Joan Laporta, 'who was playing alongside the best player in the world. Just imagine that. They promote you to the first team and the best player in the world realises that you, the new boy, are actually the best player in the world. You, the one promoted at sixteen. He was a teenager spellbound, of course he was, by Ronnie's way of life. I prefer to remember the positives. Ronnie welcomed him instead of isolating him. We are all human and we can all make mistakes, but I think the way he welcomed Leo on the pitch was very positive, and, on top of that, Ronnie integrated him into his group of friends. Leo was a boy at the time, with twenty-seven and twenty-eight-year-old men. I believe that real-life experiences are incredibly important, to know what suits you and what doesn't, and Leo learned a lot from Ronnie, and he definitely learned in every sense of the word.'

Everyone who was a witness of that tight relationship agrees, although the Brazilian was not always a good example for *la Pulga*.

But the law of football is implacable. One day you are good, the next you are past it. A star player's response before the inevitable decline often defines his personality. The coach bides his time and encourages the player's defiant side in order to squeeze the last drop of blood out of him. But Ronaldinho was not responding to that.

'There came a day when Ronaldinho, he of the eternal smile, the player who had given Barcelona the self-esteem they had lost after five dark seasons, allowed himself to be consumed by long nights of partying, with the corresponding hangovers that were slept off on a massage bed in the changing-room gym. It was free fall without return,' explains the highly-regarded Catalan journalist Lluis Canut in *El Mundo Deportivo*.

In any case, his decline was not normal. And it was accelerating at an alarming rate. What was happening to Ronaldinho? Just a year after being named the best footballer in the world for the second successive season, he had lost his love of the sport. Which is another way of losing self-respect.

But everything has to start somewhere.

Something broke in Ronaldinho's mind at the 2006 World Cup in Germany. Brazil arrived as massive favourites after triumphing in Korea four years earlier and taking away the 2004 Copa America and also the 2005 Confederations Cup. They won their qualifying group, which included Croatia, Japan and Australia, with nine points. But the team (with stars such as Ronaldo, Kaká, Cafu, Roberto Carlos, Lucio and Ronaldinho) was not playing well.

Ronaldinho, a big child, extremely innocent and an eternal pleasure seeker, felt victimised. On some occasions he would call a friend and ask them to visit. He needed to clear his head but he couldn't go out because of the paparazzi. The Brazil squad used the World Cup as an excuse to get away from the routine, to remove the constraints of the many demands put upon them, but it was the new global star who got the stick, despite Brazil qualifying. They annihilated Ghana in the last 16 but did not correct the imbalances that prevented them from beating France in the quarter-finals. It was a huge disappointment in a country in which coming second is regarded as a failure.

And that is where Ronaldinho's love of the game died. The pressure had been excessive. He appeared to lose his enthusiasm for a sport he had started playing for personal enjoyment. He went back to Barcelona weighed down by this. Friends who really loved Ronaldinho saw him sad and depressed from that summer onwards. That often is the sporting tragedy in the elite: one is very alone at the very top. The harder and longer the journey is, the more complicated it is to maintain the balance, because there comes a point when, after so many sacrifices, sportsmen have to make up for lost time, they must relax, they must let themselves go. Ronnie had become tired of fighting to stay at the very top after the World Cup in Germany.

In order to stop the rot, he was asked to train in the afternoons with his own personal trainer. During matches, if he felt worn out but thought he had done enough, Ronnie would tell Rijkaard that he had a muscle problem so that the coach would substitute him. The message being given to the rest of the squad was a dangerous one. He was not the only one who went off the road. The *blaugrana* squad became complacent, something which Joan Laporta spoke about subsequently. In the two years following the World Cup in Germany, the Barcelona back room was transformed into a drifting, rudderless boat. The dressing room was full of black sheep, but Ronaldinho was more conspicuous because of who he was. 'The rest, except Puyol, who was on top form because he tried to get everyone back and was fighting for everyone, had let themselves go,' says prestigious Catalan journalist Cristian Cubero.

Barcelona suffered ten divorces or separations in those seasons of descent into hell. Frank Rijkaard was of the opinion that when a player starts to grow, to lead, score, win, fill the front pages of the sports newspapers, he should not be given more than a three-year contract. And when he is at the crest of the wave, contracts should be renewed year on year, out of respect for the player. And when he starts on the downward curve, he should be transferred, despite pressure from media and fans, who probably see him as an untouchable idol. Such a move extends his career and protects him from the often unbearable pressure of maintaining his god-like status. Moving to a club one step below with fewer demands and expectations would allow him to be welcomed and treated like a hero, and the drop in level would be less noticeable. That's the way to bring the career of an idol to a close, was the Dutch coach's belief; however, the landing could often be a bumpy one.

Rijkaard had the theory, but at Barcelona he was not involved in contracts. And you have to be very brave to make those decisions, both the club which lets a player go and the professional himself.

Besides, he was the type of person who felt obliged, grateful, to the players who had provided the opportunity for him to excel as coach. He was willing to compromise instead of dealing with and halting the slackers, something that had to be done at that time.

Samuel Eto'o preferred to keep his distance from the most unruly group and his enmity with Ronaldinho gradually divided the squad and the club. The two stars continually made gibes at each other in the media until Eto'o exploded at one famous press conference soon after returning from injury

'What you have to remember is I have always trained even when injured and with a few knocks,' Eto'o said, tired of the unprofessional behaviour of many of his peers. Rijkaard had publicly accused him of not wanting to play the last five minutes in the previous match against Racing Santander and Ronaldinho had continued the criticism of the Cameroonian in the pressroom. Eto'o could not control himself any longer: 'If a team-mate says that you have to think about the group, I agree. You do have to think about the group. But I always think about the group first, and then about the money.'

The Ronaldinho problem was a double-edged sword: on the one hand his productivity on the pitch had gone down and on the other, as a dressing-room leader, his wayward behaviour was dragging others down. The directors were asking themselves if he was the best role model for Messi, who was, without doubt, the Brazilian's heir. 'He has to go, he is influencing this boy, he is seeing how a football star behaves. He must never fall into that trap,' explained one of the key executives on the board.

Leo would listen to Ronaldinho and could see he was suffering. The bond between them continued to be essential to both, even though the balance was changing imperceptibly. Ronaldinho now needed Leo more than Leo needed Ronnie. Any unity disappeared completely. Leo continued to allow himself to be influenced by the Brazilian 'godfathers' and any player who elected not to do the same was 'eaten' by the leaders – Bojan would be one such example.

The growing and deserved criticism which the Brazilian was receiving hurt Leo. 'What Ronaldinho has to put up with is not normal,' Leo said back then. 'The best thing we could do would be to leave him in peace. Much is spoken about Ronnie and it isn't always about what happens on the pitch. I don't like that. We all have ups and downs, many matches are played, many minutes. Ronnie is an example to everyone, it is not easy to be the best player in the world and to stay in such high spirits as he does.'

On one occasion, when they were leaving the Camp Nou car park, a group of fans were seen waiting for the stars to come out. Ronaldinho sped past. Next came Leo, with Jorge beside him, and he too accelerated. His father told him to turn round at the next roundabout and go back to the fans, roll his window down and sign autographs for everyone who wanted one.

Who would speak like that, a father or a manager?

The Messi family would frequently go to the Argentinian restaurant Las Cuartetas in Barcelona where Leo's fame would attract attention. On one occasion, having finished his meal, Jorge left first, leaving his son to brave fellow diners demanding autographs and photographs. 'Should I rescue him?' asked one of the waiters. 'No, no, let him get used to it. In situations like this he must not forget who he is, he has to learn to live with this,' answered Jorge.

What his father represented was a way of being.

Leo Messi, just like all footballers, had his adolescence stolen from him by his dream of being a footballer. Or, to phrase it slightly better, he had a very brief adolescence: the time he was with Ron-aldinho. But the muscular injuries, a consequence of his disorderly lifestyle, demanded different behaviour from him. In the 2007–08 season, one that was full of collective failure and disappointment, he had to recognise that he could not carry on the way he was going.

'They were enjoying themselves,' says Joan Laporta. 'They loved being together, the style of play. There was a lot of happiness, but, as they say, what goes up must come down. And that year it all came crashing down. We can find a thousand and one reasons, but everything was part of normal evolution. And Leo learned plenty, because he tasted glory, even though he did not play in the final in Paris, and the pain of the injuries made him realise a great number of things about himself. I have never seen any bad intentions from Ronnie; on the contrary, he was a really genuine guy. And he also liked enjoying himself, it is true, and whether you like it or not that is not incompatible with being a footballer because first and fore-most they are human beings.

'Afterwards,' concludes Laporta, 'your own life puts you in your place. Leo reacted in time. He had the time and enough natural intelligence to say, "Now I need to correct this." And he stopped getting injured.'

The very public changing of the guard was unfolding. The arrival of someone new and a clean start was also needed in order to make Leo Messi the best player that he could become.

He had to free himself of the ties, and friends, that distracted him.

After the World Cup in Germany, in the midst of disciplinary chaos, they managed to fight for the league, but in the following season (2007–08), the points difference with Real Madrid, champions in both seasons, was becoming greater by the month. The team had qualified for the Champions League semi-finals, where they would face Sir Alex Ferguson's Manchester United with Cristiano Ronaldo, Paul Scholes and Carlos Tévez. But in Catalonia that knock-out game was interpreted as the end of an era that might even change the board of directors. 'You do realise that if you don't win today, it will be very difficult to continue, don't you?' Txiki Beguiristain was asked on a programme on TV3, a channel usually friendly towards the club.

The club was going through a very tense political phase at the same time as the sporting hiatus was occurring. Sandro Rosell, vice-president from the first few years of the Joan Laporta era, resigned over a clash about how the club should be run. He had been working in the shadows, preparing a vote of no confidence against the president.

'The opposition had been capable of generating such a level of stress and tension, with the press firmly on their side, leaking rumours and creating needless distractions. It led to hysteria in the club,' remembers Ferran Soriano. The tension was not just one man's perception either: two weeks before the first leg, while the team was playing at the Camp Nou, thieves broke into the offices and stole Laporta's computer, and the same thing happened later on with the database containing club membership information. Laporta was being attacked from all sides.

And the Champions League semi-final arrived.

After a 0–0 draw in the first leg, and without Ronaldinho who had mysteriously disappeared from Rijkaard's squad, the second leg was played in Manchester. At Old Trafford, on the way to the board of directors' lunch, Joan Laporta had a premonition: 'I have a feeling that our necks are on the line, today is going to be dramatic, today is the end.' That day the president betrayed his emotions in the VIP box during the game in a way he had never done before.

That fixture saw the first duel between Leo and a shy Ronaldo, who, having disappointed so far in the big games, was required to play number 9 against his will. Messi was the better player at Old Trafford, orchestrating Barcelona's dangerous attacks. Paul Scholes scored against the run of play and Leo could have equalised, but Van der Sar thwarted him. The match was very even, but there was the inescapable impression that the team was just a shadow of what it had been and would soon be broken up. 1–0 was the final score.

Duly eliminated by Manchester United, the year ended very badly. Third in the league, Barcelona finished 18 points behind Real Madrid and had to perform a guard of honour for the champions at the Santiago Bernabeu; they therefore had to play in the Champions League qualifying round the following season. In the Copa del Rey semi-finals they were eliminated by Ronald Koeman's Valencia, who would go on to win it.

Rather than consider 'how we should look after Messi', the board of directors had to decide what to do with Frank Rijkaard and how to overcome the growing number of enemies. But the changing cycle clearly had to be enacted through the Argentine, as Joan Laporta recognised in an exclusive conversation with the author for this book:

– I have noticed many times that when you make a comment to him, or give him some advice, Leo thinks, he assimilates. There was a moment when he was already the best player in the world and was not awarded the individual accolades that he deserved. Kaká won the Ballon d'Or in December 2007, and Leo came third. Ronaldo second. I remember that we spoke on a plane, and I said to him, 'Leo, you are already the best player in the world. You will start winning individual titles the day the team starts winning.' Ronnie was still at the club, but even Ronaldinho himself realised from day one that we were seeing someone exceptional. We had not won anything for two years and that was reflected in the vote for player of the year. And I said that to him. I think he made that reflection his own.

– **It had been a frustrating season.**

– And we did have to make big decisions. We concluded, together with the board and director of football, that the team had to be freshened up. And the leadership, too: I spoke with the home-grown players (Xavi, Iniesta, Puyol, Víctor Valdés) who had already matured thanks to what they had learned from Deco and company. They had to become the dressing-room leaders. And evidently, Leo would be the leader par excellence. From then on, nobody did anything without Leo's approval or acquiescence, which he always gives in his own way.

– **And the board decided that the next coach had to be José Mourinho or Pep Guardiola. You chose Pep because of his relationship with and knowledge of the club. At the famous meal after the Champions League semi-finals where Pep said to you, 'No tindrás collons' [Catalan for 'You won't have the balls'] to choose him as Rijkaard's replacement, was Leo spoken about?**

– Definitely. We spoke about players, those he wanted and didn't want. And about Leo, Pep kept repeating, 'A machine, he is a machine.' Pep, when he spoke about him, always said that he was the best, a machine. The subject of Ronnie and Deco came up. At the time we discussed whether Eto'o should stay. I think we were right to hold onto him. And Henry was almost fully settled in and on form. Of course Leo was spoken about. He was going to be the focal point.

Pep Guardiola had told the president that he wished he could have changed Ronaldinho back into the player he once was but did not believe it was possible.

As soon as that season ended, Joan Laporta drove to Castellde-fels. To Ronaldinho's house. Ronnie knew what it was about; the president had already told him that changes were planned if the team did not win anything. Laporta considered it the president's duty to communicate the decision, face to face, to the player who had changed the history of the club. 'Ronnie, we think the moment has come for you to end your time here at Barça.' The conversation between the player and the president was an emotional one. Ron-aldinho's sister was also present.

The World Cup two years earlier was discussed. Joan knew that it had touched him deep down and that he had never understood why people reacted so negatively towards him after Brazil's failure. The three of them viewed the situation as unfair, the criticism over the top, but Ronaldinho had not recovered from that. 'Ronnie, our expectations have not been met and, as I told you, we can no longer remain together. Milan want you, Manchester City want you, you have to make up your mind,' Laporta told him.

Ronnie told Laporta that he understood. He would choose a team. He was happy Laporta had come to tell him personally. He could not forget how, at Christmas time, many people, in and outside the club, wanted to get rid of him, but Laporta had convinced them to let him finish the season. Out of respect and gratitude, Ronnie deserved it. That is what the president thought and he said goodbye with a hug that made him cry. And Ronaldinho, too.

Laporta had already spoken to Roberto de Assis, Ronaldinho's brother and agent, in case Barcelona reached this decision. The most interesting deal in financial terms was the City one, but the club that attracted the player more was AC Milan, who ended up signing him for €25 million.

When Joan Laporta left Ronaldinho's house, he gave a big sigh, a combination of sadness and relief. He took his phone out and dialled a familiar number. 'Listen, are you at home? I'm coming round. I want you all to be the first ones to know something.' He had called Jorge Messi who was at home with his son in the house next door to Ronaldinho's. Another decision had been reached by the board and he wanted to inform them.

Laporta knew that the relationship between Leo and Ronnie was special, and had decided to tell the Argentinian first-hand that his friend was not going to stay at the club. And that the board wanted Leo to become the focal point of the team.

'Leo must take the lead, take over from Ronaldinho,' said Laporta with all the gravitas the occasion demanded. 'Accept responsibility. The number ten shirt is all yours.'

Leo lowered his head while they spoke about his friend, but he accepted the challenge. He knew it was what he had to do in professional terms. Laporta understood that he had to generate some enthusiasm with his new star: if he could manage it, he would win him over to the cause. He told him the home-grown players were going to be given more important roles and he also shared with him the technical staff's plans. The coach would be Pep Guardiola. 'Pep is going to understand you, he knows the club inside out and thinks you are a machine,' said Laporta. Dani Alvés and Eric Abidal had signed and Gerard Piqué was close to joining them.

'Sign Piqué, Mr President, sign him, he used to protect me when we played together as teenagers,' said Leo.

A question became inevitable now that he was going to become the new solitary figurehead. 'Who else would you bring in?' Laporta remembers asking Leo. Deco and Motta were to be sold: two more friends going. Maybe Eto'o, too. The team that was forming was, in theory, solid, but needed the approval of the new focal point. Leo's family also participated in the conversation; it was a moment of mixed feelings. They saw the sadness the inevitable transfers of his friends caused Leo. They remembered a particular game in which their son scored while Ronaldinho was recovering from another injury, and he raised both hands, displaying all ten digits as a celebration. It was for the departing number 10, for his mate. But they also wanted to make Leo see that it was in his best interests that Ronaldinho should leave. And that the new acquisitions and decisions on the group dynamic were going to help him.

Leo saw it that way, too.

'In the end Frank could not be angry with the guys. When he should have got angry, he couldn't, because he adored them, he ended up winning two leagues and the Champions League with them ...'

(Txiki Beguiristain)

Frank Rijkaard and Ronaldinho arrived at the club at one of the most difficult moments in its history, and managed to bring FC Barcelona back to the position and standing they deserved. The people in charge of the team, management included, opted for a long-lasting football model and the final downward spiral, led by a number of bad decisions, was, ultimately, the consequence of success. Often, sadly, that is more difficult to digest than failure.

Both Frank and Ronaldinho accompanied Leo on his journey through adolescence, both showed him ways to be professional, new codes, but also one-way paths from which Leo managed to find his way back. 'When I arrived he was a boy,' says Eidur Gudjohnsen. 'Two years later he was a man. The number ten fitted him like a glove. You won't see him training in the gym, or doing many extra hours. But he carried with him the one thing that is so hard to obtain: he knew that it was his time. And he grabbed it with both hands.'

But there remained one thing for Leo Messi to do.

Today Ronaldinho regrets not having been able to be at Barcelona a few more years to enjoy the growth of 'the Flea'. But it was perhaps his very absence that allowed Messi to prosper.

When they were parted that summer, both knew they would not see each other again as regularly, or in the same circumstances. Distance cools everything.

And, sure enough, after a few exchanges between Barcelona and Milan soon after the Brazilian left Barcelona, the two friends lost contact.

At the Beijing Workers' Stadium on 19 August the summer of 2008, Brazil faced Argentina in the semi-finals of the Olympics. Ronaldinho in the *canarinha*, Messi in sky-blue and white. Argentina won 3–0.

At the end of the match, Messi sought out the figure of a disappointed Ronaldinho.

And the hug they gave each other lasts to this day.

6

Leo Is Not a Natural-born Genius. Nobody Is

– Diego, Diego, it's an honour to welcome the best player in the world to our city.
– The best player has already played in Rosario! His name is Carlovich.

That was Maradona's response when he arrived in Rosario in 1993, at the start of his brief stay at Newell's. Carlovich. As it stands it might sound like any other Yugoslavian name – an immigrant's name. And so it is. In the streets of Rosario people fill in the gaps: Carlovich!? A football legend, the king of the double nutmeg. The man who, stepping on the ball, made time stand still. One day he escaped a defensive trap with a single backheel that lobbed three of his opponents. There was no other like him. What Messi does, what Redondo did, what Maradona did, was in his DNA. Not Diego, not Leo, it was Carlovich. He was the greatest.

So they say.

There is not a single piece of film of the man they call *Trinche* Carlovich, an Argentinian footballer of the 1970s. You can find newspaper cuttings and the odd photo that will show the footballer with long legs and long sideburns. Hands firmly planted on his hips. Huge. A footballer from the neighbourhood. Those articles talk about individual moments of brilliance that grow with time and the telling. And also of one legendary game in particular.

Not long ago they asked *Trinche*, no longer physically able to do what he once did with the ball, what he felt when he heard these things, when he remembered how they used to sing his name from the stands and how they came from all over Santa Fe province to see him. 'Tell us,' they said, 'turn back the clock. Would you have done anything differently?' At the end of the day, he played only two games in the first division. Carlovich's lip tightened. 'Nooo.' He turned his head. 'Noo, sir, don't ask me that …' He bit his lip. His face contorted. 'No, not that.' And he wept.

As the twentieth century dawned, immigrants from all over Europe flooded into Argentina eager to take advantage of the country's economic boom. One of these was Mario Carlovich, a Yugoslav, who, like so many of his countrymen, was fleeing the continuing upheaval in the Balkans. He settled in the area of Belgrano, in the west of Rosario, and there he raised his family. Seven sons. The youngest, Tomás Felipe, was born in 1948. He would later acquire the nickname *el Trinche*, 'the Fork', presumably because he was tall with thin legs – even though he himself ignores the meaning and origin of the nickname. Like virtually everyone else in the neighbourhood, football was his passion. He was invited to join the junior ranks of Rosario Central when he was 15, and ended up making his debut for the first team some five years later. He played a second time in the first division. And that was it.

Carlovich was what the Argentinians call a *volante*, a left-footed defensive midfielder. He had class and vision but lacked speed. His technical brilliance failed to impress the coaches of the day, Carlos Grignol among them, who looked for physical presence rather than technical skill. But despite being six foot, he wasn't built for contesting high balls. He wasn't your 'standard type'.

There was nothing standard about him.

On the day of one particular game, the team was getting ready to leave Rosario for Buenos Aires. 'He arrived with a small bag, climbed onto the bus, nodded to the driver, ignored everyone else and made his way to the back,' remembers the well-known Santa Fe journalist Eduardo Amez de Paz, who described that era so emotively in his book *La vida por el fútbol* ('Life for Football'). 'Ten or fifteen minutes later, when no other players had turned up, he went to the front and asked the driver what time they were leaving. "As always, son, we're leaving at half past two, quarter to three." Bored with waiting, he got off the bus, never to return. Days later it was discovered that he had gone to play for the Rio Negro club in the Belgrano neighbourhood, in an amateur tournament.'

'There were some circumstances,' he explains enigmatically now, 'a few things that I didn't like at Central, and made me feel alienated. So I left.' A few months later he reappeared at Central Córdoba, Rosario's third club, his 'home' for more than a decade, an institution that was always in the shadow of the *canallas* and the *leprosos*, and where he won the championship in division C and promotion to the division B in 1973. He donned the *charrúa* shirt over four different periods, playing a total of 236 games and scoring 28 goals. His style and his magic, similar to that of Juan Román Riquelme, remained for ever engraved in the memories of the inhabitants of the Belgrano neighbourhood, and those of La Tablada, where Central Córdoba's modest Gabino Sosa Stadium is situated. It was to here that Marcelo Bielsa, the former Athletic Bilbao trainer, would make frequent pilgrimages over a four-year period, with the sole intention of watching *Trinche* play. The stadium now has a mural of Carlovich at the entrance, painted at the request of those at Canal + who travelled from Madrid a few years ago to make a documentary about him.

During those years at Central Córdoba, his legend spread throughout the pampas. One afternoon before a game against Los Andes, a club in Buenos Aires province, Carlovich realised that he didn't have the necessary document that players had to give to referees in order to take part in the game. The paperwork had been left in Rosario. A local director who had heard of him but had not seen him (division B matches weren't televised) approached one of the officials with a simple request: 'Let him play. I know this person with the long hair and the moustache. It's *Trinche*. Let him play because we'll probably never see anyone like him around these parts again.'

The legend of *Trinche* Carlovich acquired national status and eternal historical importance one night on 17 April 1974 at the Newell's ground. The Argentinian squad of Vladislao Cap was preparing to travel to West Germany for the World Cup. They were looking for a side to play a friendly for the Sports Journalists' Circle charity and picked a Rosario Select XI. Ten first division footballers were called up (five each from the two main Rosario sides, Newell's and Rosario Central) and one from the second division, Córdoba's number 5, Carlovich. They had never trained together and arrived at the ground about two hours before kick-off.

The stadium filled up. There were no television cameras and nobody filmed it, but those present (footballers, coaches, fans), plus a memorable radio commentary by Oscar Vidana on LT8, all spoke of 'the dance of the Rosarinos'. In all its glory. No one could stop Carlovich. *Trinche* himself explains. 'I nutmegged a defender, and by the time he'd turned around, I'd done it again. It's the way I play, but on that day the stadium went crazy.' The double nutmeg wasn't performed on just any player but on Pancho Sa, the defender with the most Copa Libertadores trophies in the history of the game. Eventually, as their frustration grew, the internationals resorted to insults when they realised that things weren't going their way. At half-time it was 3–0. In the dressing room Vladislao Cap approached the Rosario management to ask them to take 'that number 5 off'. And he wasn't joking. Carlovich started the second half, though.

It finished in an unforgettable 3-1 win for the Rosario side and the national side were jeered by a celebrating stadium that, for once, didn't make any distinction between *canallas* and *leprosos*. Here was glory and sublime football in its purest form. It could have meant a new contract or a new club among the elite for *Trinche*, but Carlovich always returned to what Amez de Paz describes as his 'first love', 'the neighbourhood, his friends and the amateur tournaments where his status was assured, where he had nothing to prove and could just enjoy the sheer thrill of the game. When he played in those, he never failed to turn it on, never failed to compete or enjoy himself, as he did, on occasion, in the more important Rio Negro tournaments.' His neighbours at his Belgrano home remember that *Trinche*, after training or after a game, would carry on playing with the boys in the street, of whatever age, at whatever time, and on whatever field happened to be available for a game.

'I love the way the youngsters play, I love the *potreros*,' recalls *Trinche*. 'Today there are very few of them left, they all begin with synthetic surfaces but before it was grass, and more grass. What's more – there's no more space. It's shrinking by the day in Rosario.'

Before there were lots of pitches, now there are no more pitches. I tell you why I like to play in the streets – a player who goes onto the pitch and looks up into the stands where there are 60,000, 100,000 people, how is he going to enjoy the game? He can't play, ever. Those people in the stands, their demands, their insults ...'

In 1976 he signed for Independiente Rivadavia, a club in the city of Mendoza. One Saturday he got himself sent off just before the interval. He had to: if he hadn't he would have missed the bus back to Rosario; Sunday was Mother's Day. On another occasion, on a very hot day, one of those sultry days when you'd rather be at home doing nothing, *Trinche* and a couple of his companions worked the ball across to an area that was shaded by some trees. They were just touching the ball to each other; no one could get it off them. And after ten minutes or so the referee stopped the game. 'Come on, lads, play football!' *Trinche* answered: 'It's too hot in the sun, ref!'

'*Trinche* was a footballing anarchist, something that stopped him making his first division debut much earlier,' writes Amez de Paz. 'It didn't really happen for him until he was about twenty-one. They say that he only played when he wanted to, when he felt like it. I don't think that's strictly true. He enjoyed playing. It was in his blood. But he never looked on football as a way of life, nor was he interested in negotiating a contract. He wanted to play and for him that was all that mattered. The sheer enjoyment of playing.'

He only spent one year in Mendoza before returning to the province of Santa Fe, this time with Colón, but he only played two official games: muscle injuries were beginning to dictate his career. He returned to Central Córdoba where he achieved his second promotion. He began to be known for his lack of appetite for training, a lack of ambition. It is said that at one of the many clubs that he played for, outside Rosario, he asked for a car as part of his contract. When they gave it to him, he got into it and drove home to Belgrano, never to return.

One morning on the day of a game, the Central Córdoba squad got together at the Gabino Sol to head off to Buenos Aires. *Trinche* hadn't arrived: he had overslept. They went to look for him and he came downstairs in his underpants, hair uncombed, and that, more or less, is how they took him to the capital. Nobody remembers who they were playing, maybe it was Almagro, but that day Central

Córdoba won. 1–0. Goal from *Trinche*. We all want the stories to be true. Someone tells them so they must be true. Mustn't they?

Trinche retired, but after three years of inactivity he returned to the field of play. It was 1986. He used to walk through matches but he could anticipate a pass long before anyone else. It was just one last season. For a few years he could be seen in the neighbourhood launching 40 yard passes and doing the occasional dribble.

Carlovich remains the antithesis of Leo Messi: his fame and the best of his career stayed in Santa Fe and because of this he is adored. His legend is commonplace in Rosario. One of those lyrical, almost poetic players who no longer exist. And that's how legends and winners in Argentinian football, like César Luis Menotti, José Pekerman, Carlos Grignol, Aldo Poy, Marcelo Bielsa, Enrique Wolff, Carlos Aimar and Mario Killer, tell his story. 'Remember I was just a young boy when *Trinche*, the likes of whom we no longer have, was playing,' confirms Tata Martino, a native of Rosario, now at Barcelona. 'He'd do nutmegs backwards and forwards, people used to rave about him, above all for his incredible amateur spirit and that Rosario trademark: his unique passion for football. He would play a World Cup game or a match with mates with the same conviction. He had almost everything you need to become one of the greats.' The emphasis is on the word 'almost'.

'What does "getting to the top" mean?' asks *Trinche*. 'The truth is that I never had any other ambition than to play football. And above all I never wanted to distance myself from my neighbourhood, from my parents' house, where I go nearly every afternoon, to stay with Vasco Artola, one of my oldest friends. On the other hand I'm a very solitary person. When I played for Central Córdoba, if I could, I preferred to get changed alone, in the utility room instead of the changing room. I like to be calm, it's not from any ill will.'

After leaving football he worked as a bricklayer, but life dealt him a terrible blow. Amez de Paz explains. 'I didn't know that *Triche* was suffering from a terrible osteoporosis, which had destroyed his hips and practically made him an invalid.' *Trinche* had knocked on various doors seeking assistance, but with little success. 'The first thing I did was speak to my friend, the well-known traumatology doctor and former footballer, Carlos Lancellotti,' adds Amez de Paz who decided to resolve the situation. 'He told me that he would operate on him free of charge, including taking care of the costs of the operation and the post-operative care, but that he needed a prosthetic. At first the request was refused due to lack of funds reserved for such cases. But an appeal was made to the Public Health secretary. Finally, in the first days of September, the order to acquire the prosthetic arrived.'

A tribute evening with two benefit matches was held, organised by Amez de Paz, together with friends, his own children and even the Maradonian Church. The cost of entrance was the equivalent of just one euro. 'We were utterly astounded. A host of great footballers turned up to participate in those games,' recalls the veteran journalist.

That day, Tomás Felipe, *el Trinche*, Carlovich wept. As he did years later when they asked him what he would have changed about his professional career. 'Noo, don't ask me that ...'

The only thing that interested Carlovich was the ball, and he never felt comfortable with commitment. He had all the attributes to build a great career, but lacked the character needed to maintain the discipline. 'It was as if the ball took Carlovich, an intelligent ball, that enjoyed doing artistic things, and meanwhile dragging behind it a footballer,' says Menotti. An amateur one.

It's said that *Trinche* arrived on the scene around the same time as coaches obsessed with physical prowess, who sought to convert football from an art form into something entirely different. It was, they say, an ugly period for the game in Argentina, though that has a slightly hollow ring. 'Perhaps what he lacked was the professionalism needed to compete in football at this level,' confirms former footballer and coach Carlos Aimar.

Menotti adds: 'He never found physical reserves that supported his technical abilities. What's more, he never had anyone who accompanied or understood him. It was a shame because Carlovich should have been one of the most important players in the history of Argentinian football. I don't know what happened to him. Maybe he became bored with professional football. He just enjoyed having a good time.'

Being number one, being the one everybody looks up to, is not for everyone. 'Messi confronts each situation as it's presented to him.

But prior to that he has gone through a great deal, he's suffered, and yet he's come through it,' says Pancho Ferraro. 'He doesn't throw in the towel. There are some for whom life becomes foggy and they can't see the way forward. There are others who find themselves in the middle of hailstorms, and still come through it. Why do so many youngsters fail to make it? Carlovich, a great player. Rodas is a great player, but for some reason neither of them made it. And for me, it annoys me when people say "he didn't have any luck". The fact is they didn't look hard enough for it. They didn't go out and fight for it. That's why the player who gets to the top and stays there should be applauded. Players like the Zanettis, Batistutas, Samuels, Crespos ... these I applaud. Those who come and go ... no!'

Here's another perspective. In an interview on the Argentinian TV channel *TyC*, given from the comfort of his sofa in his Barcelona home, Leo opened up:

– Have you at any time told yourself 'I'm a failure, I'm no good, I'm not going to get anywhere, I'm not going to become a professional footballer'?
– No. There have been games where I didn't score or play well and I'm my own worst critic, so I know when I play well and when I play badly.
– But did you ever, in a rash moment, think that you might not want to be a footballer any more?
– No. To throw it all away? No. I knew that my dream was to play in the first division, and that I was going to fight for that. There were games where I didn't achieve anything and I criticised myself strongly then. But give up? No.
– Did you ever prepare yourself in a special way? Like talking to a psychologist, because the pressures are so great, it isn't for everyone, is it?
– No, I don't talk a lot, I don't like to talk about personal things. It's very difficult to get personal stuff out of me. I have to be with my family or a very close friend to feel comfortable talking about myself, and even then I tend to hold back on any bad things I'm feeling. As I got older I shared more with my family, but at the beginning, not even with them.
– But, never, even with the team psychologist for a chat?

– No, no, I don't like that for the reasons I've just given. I don't like discussing my personal stuff and I thought that if I went it would be a waste of time because I would have nothing to say.

Josep María Minguella says, with a degree of certainty, that Leo 'comes from a marvellous planet, the one from which only the most exceptional come, where architects, doctors, violinists are created. The chosen ones.' Interestingly Jorge Messi never called his son a 'genius'. Many others have, but, in truth, to place him in such a category is to somehow diminish the sacrifice and hard work that have taken him to where he is. The very word 'genius' suggests that his rise was inevitable. But *is* he a genius? He's certainly unique, but, in a way, aren't we all? Our fingerprints alone bear testimony to that fact. What separates Leo from the herd? Or, rather, why do we choose to remain with the herd while those with a supreme talent drift away? And where does the talent come from? Is it genetics, passion, environment? How many hours do you have to devote to football to become a Lionel Messi?

His talent is undoubtedly unique. It differs dramatically from the talents of Maradona or Ronaldo. But over and above his skill with the ball, what drives him to want to be better every day? And is it this drive, constant and relentless, that has raised him to the pinnacle of his profession? And can such drive be taught? Is it inherent or something that can be acquired?

In *Outliers: The Story of Success*, his brilliant study of talent and success, Malcolm Gladwell says that biologists frequently talk about the 'ecology' of an organism: 'the tallest oak in the forest is so because there aren't any other trees that block the sun, because the ground in which it is planted is deep and rich, because there haven't been rabbits eating at its bark and because a woodcutter hasn't cut it down before it has grown'. Successful people have resistant seeds but still need the help of a fertile soil, distracted rabbits, and woodcutters with eyes on other trees.

Pedro Gómez, coach, blogger, physical instructor and sports psychologist, has prepared for this book a list of ten skills that those who excel in a particular field have in common; in this case ten characteristics that help to make Leo unique. The necessary sacrifices have been discussed. It serves as a point of reference for those who wish to get to the very top of their profession, in football, or any field, as much as for those who are contemplating with hope (or otherwise) the development of a child. Is my offspring suitable for this? Could he go far? Should I lead him along this road?

The late actor Christopher Reeve, who knew more than most about the highs and lows, the triumphs and the pain, said that 'many dreams appear impossible at first, later improbable, and finally, when we set our minds to it, they become inevitable'.

Leo had set his mind on becoming one of the greats. Irredeemably. This is how I think he did it.

SKILLS NEEDED TO 'BE ABLE TO LEARN'

1. Family and footballing context

> '*I never played well enough for my old man. As a youngster I'd score four goals, but, for him, it was never good enough. He always had some criticism that made me want to succeed more and more every time in the hope that he'd say "you played well". There were very few times when he said to me "you played well".*'

(Leo Messi)

> '*He plays, we take care of everything else. I live in Spain and Matías in Argentina. Me and my old man manage his affairs … A star like Leo is high-maintenance. He needs a firm support system because the only thing that interests him is playing football. When someone like my brother achieves such fame and prominence in the footballing world, he leaves himself open to all sorts of rumour and false reporting. People talk about his income, they say that he has alienated himself from his people, that he cares about nothing other than football and fame. The fact is that those close to Leo know that none of this stuff is true.*'

(Rodrigo Messi)

From the start, the family closed ranks and set out to build a wall of protection around Leo. He was still growing and it soon became apparent that he needed a shield from various interested parties who would seek to exploit and profit from him. Some had been trusted associates who later proved to be motivated by greed and self-interest. Contracts had been hastily signed and surprise clauses emerged that were not in Leo's best interest. The Messis still have various court actions in process with individuals who they thought were friends.

'The family have had some very bad experiences with agents and the result is that they now function as a family firm whose sole aim is to guarantee Leo's future as a footballer,' explains Carles Folguera, director of La Masía. 'Their aim is to guarantee that no one takes the Messi money that quite rightly belongs to Leo. Messi has become a brand, and a significant brand at that. They all work together as a close-knit clan, but in the best sense of the word.'

As already discussed, having your father as your manager creates a dynamic that is very different from the normal father/son relationship. In the last few years, Leo's father has decided to charge Leo a commission, as any other agent would, drawing a definitive line between his money and that of his son, and trying to overcome the potential difficulties of their bond. They think having a wage is better than not having any money at all, or waiting for your son to pay you something, and prevents money from becoming a divisive issue.

So essentially Leo lives in a world of his own creation, and he does it precisely because it is in his interest to do so. It is a sign of practical intelligence. 'He knows that he is very good at football, and that in this world the fewer entanglements he is involved with, the better,' insists Folguera. 'Some say that as a person he has limitations, but in fact he is conscious that doing anything out of the ordinary can create problems. So he doesn't. He is advised by his family, [in his day] by Guardiola, and by very few people who are close to them. At the end of the day Messi is very much a family man.'

'Away from football he is a sentimental man', says the physiotherapist Juanjo Brau, one of the people who understands Messi best of all. He knew him when he went up to the first team with Frank Rijkaard and for six years has accompanied him everywhere, be it with the Catalan club or the national side, even on his holidays. He instructs him on his body, helps him recover from his injuries, teaches him how to prevent them. They spend hundreds of hours every year together, and he has seen his evolution from close up. 'I feel part of "his people", a very small group of people, but he might never ask me if I am okay or not. If he sees that I am fucked, if there is something troubling me, he will try to find a solution. He would just say, "and why are you like that?" He has that perception, that way of looking after his people.'

Having a familiar, demanding and understanding entourage is the necessary foundation of a great sportsman. But, perhaps more importantly, it was the family approach to his playing (particularly the positive reaction during a *rondo* at the Estado de Israel when he was four) that motivated him and compelled him to work hard to achieve success. If the person watching you, your father, or grandmother or any family member, treats you like a god, then you want to make sure you come up to scratch to please them. His play was brilliant and spontaneous, but in order to rise above the others of his generation who played with equal zeal and fervour, Leo realised he needed to acquire skill and, through skill, recognition.

Football was a prize of great value in the Messi household, and, naturally, children are conditioned by the likes and dislikes of their parents. If you hear at home 'so and so is a great writer' or you visit a friend's house and see the family reading, you will, in a moment of reflection, think to yourself, 'I'd like to do that too.' And if you enjoy it, you end up making it part of your life. The desire to emulate and achieve recognition is part of the drive that makes us human. Leo's desires were formed by the fantasies of his father and wider family. All the men wanted to become professional footballers. Hand in hand they travelled that road of dreams together.

Nothing is accidental. Two of Rafa Nadal's uncles played tennis while he was growing up. In fact, one of them, Miguel Ángel Nadal, the former Barcelona and Spain central defender, had to choose between football and tennis. Aged just three, Rafa was already playing on a tennis court. His grandmother remembered later that she had heard he was quite good and went to watch him on a number of occasions to confirm that the boy had talent – once again evidence of the family eye. Manel Estiarte, considered to be the greatest water polo player in history, had an older brother who practised the sport and even though Manel started off wanting to become a swimmer, he changed direction when he reached adolescence.

What's more, Leo was very thin, almost a dwarf, and the recognition within his small world of his demonstrable footballing talent was compensation for his physical limitations.

How a footballer's ability is viewed and critiqued by those closest to him, his parents, his coach, other players and employees of the club, will ultimately determine how he defines his success. To be constantly told 'you're the best' suggests a particular description of success that is linked to victory and superiority over others. If, on the other hand, he is encouraged to concentrate on the 'struggle' and the desire to get better all the time (the philosophy of Jorge Messi), then the person is inspired to be the best they can be, irrespective of defeat or victory. How many times have we heard Leo say, 'I still have a lot of room for improvement'?

Before the financial crisis hit Argentina, his family were relatively comfortable. This enabled them to become part of the Football Academy world with all the necessary expenses that that entailed. In truth, in the last four decades there have been very few Argentinian footballers from poor backgrounds. Such relative financial stability has formed part of the network of protection that surrounds Leo.

In this he is not dissimilar to the vast majority of those who make it to the first division. Being freed from many of the hazards of normal life, the footballer is free to pursue his dream.

There's more: in Grandoli, as at Newell's, in the trials at River and at Barcelona, he was made to play against older boys, the best in the school. Similarly in the street, against his older brothers. Having the shit kicked out of him, without complaint and always accepting apologies, strengthened his character and his resolve. And made his learning process more difficult – in his training sessions, Tiger Woods would deliberately hit his ball into the sand to make his day more demanding. Players of a high standard, or even players who are older, all help to improve the quality of the practice sessions and help to intensify and promote the winning mentality, the ambition. Quality coaching is key, too: excellence comes from the constant search for the grand objective which is sometimes identified by the coach, the only one capable of seeing whether or not it is obtainable.

It's said that one of the reasons for Brazil's footballing success is because its players have passed through small indoor pitches, similar to those at the Malvinas where Leo played until he was 11. A smaller ball demands more precision, encourages more passes; a smaller space multiplies the contact you have with the ball. At Newell's Leo found a club that was looking for footballers with co-ordination and technique and what the coach, Quique Domínguez, calls 'a continuity of enjoyment'. A great mixture.

Shortly after marrying, Jorge and Celia considered moving to Australia. Leo might have been born in Sydney, without the support of the passionate football infrastructure and the institutions that picked him out because of his co-ordination and technique. That helped him grow, also because of the competition with other good players and the experience of his veteran coaches. The Argentinian gene would have been a long way away, represented only by his father. Insufficient data for the creation of a member of the football-ing elite.

Here's an example: the high altitude region of Nandi in Kenya has produced more marathon runners than anywhere else in the world. It isn't just that the conditions help the development of the body to cope with the rigorous demands of the race: the area is so poor that the children regularly run to school, which can be as far as 20 kilometres away. Success depends on social and geographical conditions, thus it is much easier to be an elite footballer in Argen-tina than it is in Australia. Compare the number of professional footballers from both countries who play in the world's top leagues.

As part of the footballing context, you also have to include the great rivals that Messi has come up against, especially his relation-ship with Cristiano Ronaldo, with whom he constantly competes for ownership of football's throne, a rivalry that has undoubtedly made them both better players.

And what about FC Barcelona?

Maradona says: 'I think Messi makes Barcelona play the way he wants them to.'

Barcelona has added practically nothing to his football idea, to his style. Leo Messi continues to be the 12-year-old boy who always looked for the goal and who considers football to be an individual battle between himself and the defence.

When they asked Leo if he was a son of Argentinian or Spanish football his answer was clear: 'Argentinian, because despite the fact that I have grown here and learned a lot in Spain, I never changed the way that I play, the way I have done since I was very small.'

When he was a small boy, recently arrived in Barcelona, Rodolfo Borrell asked him to play on the wing and Leo answered with a categorical no. 'I'm an *enganche*.' That was his way of asking for permission to play as he wanted. His team-mates from his time at La Masía recalled how, during exercises in possession, it was difficult for him to pair up, and how he enjoyed much more the one on ones with a shot at the end or the challenges where he could exploit his speed. 'For me it was difficult to pass the ball, I kept forgetting to do it,' Leo told *El Gráfico* a few years ago.

In his first years at Barcelona Leo insisted on being Lio, the kid who left Rosario.

'Absolutely everything he does now on the pitch, the moves, the strikes of the ball, the lowering of the head, the intelligence to put the ball between the lines, he has been doing since he was twelve years old, thirty centimetres shorter and twenty kilos lighter.' So says his former coach at Newell's, Adrián Coria.

'Leo had something that I didn't see in many boys,' says Xavi Llorenç, who had him in his first campaign at La Masía. 'When he got here the idea of tracking back hadn't even entered his head and here the direct game doesn't exist. The norm is to attack from the back with the ball, looking for the horizontal pass, going from side to side. "If the goal's over there and I want to score, why do I have to go backwards, if it's easier to go forward?" That's how he thought.'

Leo Messi's footballing mindset, his concept of football, is encapsulated in the now famous Maradona-type goal he scored against Getafe. He made this play, obviously not always with the same success, hundreds of times in the lower ranks. In Barcelona B's youth side he did the same: he would pick the ball up in the middle of the pitch and the only idea that he had in his head was to attempt to dribble past whoever came into his path up to and including the goalkeeper. Later on, in the first team, he got the ball just behind the main striker, playing as the false number 10, and ended up scoring lots of goals breaking from deep. The concept is the same. The only difference is the distance to goal.

Leo is a finisher; very fast with the ball at his feet, like few others in history. Cristiano Ronaldo is fast with space in front of him but he doesn't have Leo's skill in full flight. Hardly anyone in the world could link together three dribbles without falling, and no one is capable of mixing up this power, speed and body movement. Only Maradona, who was slower, can be compared to him on a technical level.

Leo always wanted to play like this, and Barcelona provided him with the platform to exploit his talent.

'Gradually I managed to play more for the team. I didn't make it easy for them, because I have always been very stubborn. Barcelona showed me lots of things, but they never tried to change my style.'

(Leo Messi in *El Gráfico*, 2009)

Messi 'is a fruit from an Argentinian field,' insists Adrián Coria. The last time he said it coincided with the four goals Leo scored against Arsenal in the Champions League. Around about then, April 2010, it was being said that Barcelona was collectively the best team in the world. But most of the offensive moves that night were the product of individual play, especially the fourth goal that he created from nothing, running at the Arsenal defence from deep. It is not a trivial detail. The Barcelona/Messi marriage is, without doubt, a perfect union between a young, quality, direct player and a team style that needs this direct approach because it often overeggs the pudding.

But who needs who more?

Xavi Llorenç, who was an attacking footballer, tried to transmit to the very young players in his charge some bold tactics but without the tactical restrictions of the following years. The following year, Alex García, a former defender, set out to establish certain tactical parameters and positional strategies under the 3-4-3 system that was used throughout the whole academy. It allowed for freedom in attack but demanded the return to the original position when possession was lost. He also forced changes of positions on players so they would understand the feelings and obligations of those who played on other parts of the pitch. 'But you can't put a brake on talent,' says Alex García today. 'You can say to Leo: don't dribble so much. But then he dribbles past two, and then he's gone. At the end of the day, that wins you games.' After Alex, Tito Vilanova, who understood Leo's silent rebellion against certain instructions, insisted on a possession game, but was the first to play him as second striker, where he would always end up anyway, whatever the technical instructions might have been.

The coaches who had him did not demand that he was more disciplined, because they thought he would become more organised with the passing of time and at different levels. Someone else would show him the way. In the meantime they were winning matches, mostly thanks to him.

The junior sides at Barcelona are full of footballers who are the best from their zone, neighbourhood, town, village or wherever. They bring quality together. But when it comes to the best of the best (Messi, for example) demands are not made because, quite simply, the main preoccupation of the coach is to win. Victory makes the coach look good, and continued success means he isn't about to change anything in a footballer that helps him win. In Messi's case it didn't create any great problem because his talent was such that he would win with either more or less tactical knowledge. But there have been other cases, less successful, such as that of Giovanni dos Santos, now at Villarreal, a player of great quality whose talent did not develop at the same rate as Leo's and whose faults became greater than his virtues. He failed to make the first team because, in his day, being the most talented of his generation, he was not made to defend, work and assume responsibilities. He played as he wanted while his coaches passed the responsibility from one to another: someone else will put you right.

With the same neglectful attitude, Leo Messi continued his formative years doing exactly the same as he had done as a 12-year-old in Rosario.

Bit by bit he began to develop muscular definition following a special diet, gym sessions and training. But his footballing concept did not vary and that created new doubts at La Masía. It was understood that, generally speaking, as a footballer grows so does his talent until such a time as that quality stops. No one knows why. Messi was progressing physically, he was getting bigger but some of the coaches at La Masía believed that his style of play would not succeed in the first team because at some point the overflowing nature of his game would be brought to a standstill, as always happened, and would also become limited because of the presence of larger defenders and a collective defensive game that would be difficult to break down. Leo insisted too much on playing his way, it was said, dribbling past one, two, four players, and, when it didn't work out, it became a fault. But Leo felt so capable, so superior, that he carried on trying to score every time he got the ball. And his talent continued to develop, to the astonishment of many.

And he was also acquiring the support of the group because he understood that relying on his companions would make it easier for him to do what he wanted on the pitch, and with greater effect. 'Messi,' explains Charly Rexach, 'is a bloke who, before he got to Barcelona, played well, had intuition, got into good positions: if there was a rebound the ball fell to him, and you'd say "isn't he lucky". But it wasn't luck; he would see a fraction of a second before anyone else where the ball was going, it was intuition. But Messi has evolved. Before he got the ball, and every time he wanted to do a brilliant move, he'd dribble past three or four blokes and score. There were injuries, comings together and everything. Now he has discovered that he knows when to pick the moment to make the play or not. He has evolved, has learned to play his football within the framework of a team.' Rexach has nailed it: 'his football'.

The theory is that La Masía counts on a structure and development of talent that is responsible for the recent success of the first team, but it's difficult to match this philosophy with Leo's performance in the 2003–04 season, when he played for five teams.

'Leo toughened up his personality partly because he was getting older, and as a result of the level of responsibility put upon him,' says Juanjo Brau. 'I remember when he was a kid, always laughing, and he had a certain aura about him. That character became harder, we hardened it up, football did, Barça did. There was a period when they always made him play with the team that needed to win. He trained from Monday to Friday and on Thursday they would tell him which team he would be playing in that weekend. What does that tell you? These teams were dependent on him to win. We have formed this winning player, decisive, determined, necessary.'

Barcelona fed his craving to win that he had brought with him from Rosario, and helped to create the competitive monster that he carried inside and was unleashed as the seasons passed. It hardened the boy.

Fernando Signorini, the former trainer of the Argentinian national side, picks up this line of thought: 'His development exploded so quickly and he was such a highly prized gem, you have to understand that no one dared to say no to him. And a lot of times I think that to do something good from a sporting point of view is quite harmful from a human point of view – it doesn't prepare players for life. In the development we shouldn't worry so much about the body or about victories – we should be thinking about human beings, because there is no guarantee that they are going to become great stars, even though finally some do.'

Leo was always asked to win at all times and in 2013, with the arrival of Neymar, another footballer who likes to play his game in a way that does not automatically fit in with the scheme of play that has brought so much success to Barcelona, he has now been asked to share his level of influence with the new arrival. For a person who is a competitive animal and has, since infancy, shouldered this responsibility, it must be difficult to get his head round this notion. He wants the responsibility, he needs it.

The problem with youth development is that with success comes confusion: Barcelona identified the work they had done at La Masía in the previous decades as the principal reasons for success during the Guardiola era. Perhaps the most sensible interpretation would be the assumption that the titles were won by a cocktail of talent from an extraordinary generation that learned from the youth system things like control of the game, positioning, the importance of technique, and so on, but that clearly benefited from a unique talent led by a coach who knew how to blend everything together, after offering the team to Leo, the special individual.

During the magnificent era of Pep Guardiola, Barcelona went in search of a way to find the La Masía formula, looking to bottle success and to discover new jewels, more titles. But a poor harvest from the academy, following the arrival of Pedro and Sergio Busquets in 2008 (only Thiago has got close to becoming a regular), suggests that perhaps what occurred between 2008 and 2011 was unique and unrepeatable.

Trying to structure success is an intangible, opportunistic job: the function of La Masía is to provide a good base for a football philosophy, but to explain success in a successful era, to try to codify it and repeat it, forgetting the spontaneity of where it all came from, is to ignore its elusive essence. Football is not mathematics.

So, on the pitch, what has been the main contribution of FC Barcelona to Leo? The placing around the Argentinian of some extraordinary players (eight world champions) who have matured and worked around Leo, especially Xavi Hernández and Andrés Iniesta, the three of them peaking at the same time. In the past few years, Barcelona has had players who have kept possession close to their opponents' area giving more options to release the talent of the Argentinian, and who have known how to return the ball to him. If Messi had not played for a team of the standard of Barcelona, especially in the midfield, he would not have become the team player that he is, because the ball would not have come back to him with the ease and quality with which it is returned, nor with the specific tactics needed to allow him to play his game.

'Leo happened upon a spontaneous generation with Xavi, Iniesta, Puyol, Busquets, Piqué, as did the famous Santos in Brazil, or the Ajax of Holland,' Fernando Signorini adds. 'And it is highly unlikely that it will ever be repeated. Some players, very good players, are products of apprenticeships, but he is pure instinct. And after that, yes, almost certainly with the help of Guardiola he began to read games better and to make fewer errors. And nearly all his interventions have resulted in favour of the efficiency of the team: as an individual he makes his contribution to the team, and that's rare these days. Players like him, in this atrocious era of the cult of the individual, with this iniquitous system that we have been plunged into, do not understand what it means to form part of a group, they fail to realise that they are one more brick in the pyramid that has to be built to make a great team.'

And what would Xavi or Iniesta be without Messi? The three of them have respected each other from the very first day because they knew that together they would be able to win more than they would apart.

Over many years, Messi did not have the same facilities with the Argentinian national side that he enjoyed with Barcelona: at

Barcelona he was considered a great player from the start, as well as an idol of the masses, but in his own country he was not considered to be the most important element of the team, nor was he installed as leader till recently. So when the ball left Messi it did not return to him, and it was the others who determined the play. Finally, with Alejandro Sabella in charge, the side has learned to return the ball to him and let him express himself.

After some years of uncertainty, Barcelona's greatest assistance came from off the pitch rather than on it, with the arrival of Joan Laporta. As Messi grew as a player, the club looked to help him financially, to give him security, a crucial requirement for elite footballers, not just from the financial aspect but also for the status and sense of hierarchy that the contracts offer them. 'When he became a professional,' confirms ex-vice-president Ferran Soriano, 'we improved his contract many times without him asking, to match his contributions on the pitch, but also so that he could feel relaxed and be sure that we were always going to value him.'

This is a great achievement for a club that has in the past crushed some of its greatest players: after five years, Johan Cruyff left Barcelona in 1978 by the back door following a misunderstanding with the board. Diego Maradona moved to Napoli after two seasons having failed to produce what had been expected of him. The Brazilian Ronaldo was there for just one year. Ronaldinho, so successful at one point, went into freefall, so much so that he left the club with no wish to carry on playing professionally. 'Barcelona has been intelligent enough always to come forward and say to Messi, "don't suffer, we'll sort things out",' insists Soriano. 'I think he gets the money he could have earned somewhere else. And that doesn't always happen, especially with a player from the lower ranks, who usually earns less than one who has been brought in.'

The hypothesis of a Leo playing somewhere else is an attractive one – after all, Leo did not spring from La Masía: he is an adopted talent who did not want to change his style. Leo has had offers, or, at the very least, close encounters with clubs like Arsenal, Juventus, Inter and Real Madrid. And his talent, despite injuries, probably would have exploded wherever he went. Every conversation for this book that has finished with the question 'would Leo have triumphed away from Barcelona?' has been answered affirmatively, albeit with different emphases. 'Yes, he would have,' confirms Charly Rexach. 'But maybe not to the same extent, because here he touches the ball much more than he would have in another team.'

Jorge Messi, interviewed by *Kicker*, is of a similar mind. 'Maybe it would have been a little bit more difficult [to go so far as a footballer], but I think yes, bearing in mind the attributes he has. With his technique, he'd go boom, boom, boom and the ball would be in the net. But in Barcelona he faced a tactical plan, a different way of playing and a different philosophy.' The former president of Barcelona Joan Gaspart concurs: 'Messi on his own is already an exceptional player. If in addition to that, timewise, he coincides with a Xavi, an Iniesta, a fundamental part of his game, this adds up to much more. But on his own he would still have triumphed with any team in the world.'

'Ah, he would also have triumphed in Argentina!' adds coach Claudio Vivas, but Signorini disagrees: 'It was definitely better for him that he ended up at Barcelona, because he could have been harassed by the *barras bravas* [the organised, fervent and sometimes virulent set of Argentinian supporters]. I can picture it – "dwarf, I'm going to cut your throat, son of a whore ..." every name under the sun, spit at him, break the windows of the team bus ... Can you imagine what would have happened to him?'

When Leo was reminded that in England some say that it remains to be seen whether or not he would be capable of doing it on a cold, rainy Wednesday night in Stoke, he laughed. If you had given Picasso another pencil he would have been just as creative. 'Messi is first and foremost an extraordinary talent, practically unrivalled. He would have developed anywhere, but he planted himself on fertile soil, within a system, where he was cared for and nurtured with affection,' adds Ferran Soriano.

Pep Guardiola designed a dressing room made to measure for Leo and he looked for allies to play the way he likes to. But in Pep's last year, and with Tito Vilanova, it became more difficult to maintain the balance of a group that on occasions appeared overcommitted to Leo, with players, as well as coaches, distancing themselves from their responsibilities, the most worrying consequence of the formation and protection he received at Barcelona.

'He came with a very individual game to which Barcelona added the team game, which helped him with the possession game played at a very fast pace, which suited him,' explained Gerard Piqué during the summer of 2013, before the arrival of Tata Martino and Neymar. 'But it's true that in the past few years the attacks always finish with Leo. We play in a way that we have got used to and that always finishes with him. I think that's good because we use it to maximise the skills of the best player in the world. But to be honest, when he isn't there we get badly penalised.'

SKILLS NECESSARY TO 'WANT TO LEARN'

2. Restlessness/motivation

'I admire his capacity to keep on learning. I don't know anyone who produces so many solutions to so many problems in something as variable as football.'

(Andoni Zubizarreta, sports director of Barcelona)

'We live trying to improve all of our ambitions and with football I am no exception. My objective is to grow, not to remain with what I have. I always say it. I have to get better in everything.'

(Leo Messi after receiving his fourth Ballon d'Or, January 2013)

Leo is a clever bloke. That's how Charly Rexach defines him. He has learned how to play. He knows how to pick what he has to do at every moment. He speaks little but listens a lot. And that triumph is just another event, another step. Without realising, he does precisely what Rudyard Kipling counselled in his poem 'If' – he meets 'with triumph and disaster and treats those two impostors just the same'.

He keeps his eyes wide open and his mind constantly absorbs knowledge. Among the elite it is much easier to get to the top than to continue improving, and only the chosen few are capable of maintaining the motivation after having triumphed – Leo knows that if he doesn't try to get better, he gets worse.

'Without challenges to face, you will stop giving your best, you will get comfortable and the inertia that keeps you successful will begin to make you weaker,' explains Pedro Gómez. 'Your output will diminish without you really noticing. One day you'll wake up and you will realise that you are becoming unfit to stay with the elite.' Messi has no doubts: 'I am my fiercest critic.'

To keep going forward once you have reached such heights you have to have a love, a passion for the game unlike any other. As the producer of massive film successes *The Sting* and *Jaws*, David Brown said: 'success isn't so much about doing what you want, as it is liking what you're doing.' When someone is motivated principally for themselves, rather than financial rewards or social standing, they acquire a long list of psychological benefits: the struggle is less hard, persistence is a pleasure.

Leo's motivation also comes to him from an extremely powerful source. Messi is a Christian, although not an actively practising one. And he is convinced that there is another life after this one. That's why every time he scores he thanks his grandmother for what she did for him. Celia is with him at the most intimate of moments. She continues to inspire him.

3. Ambition, competitiveness and focus

'He has three Champions Leagues but he wants four.'

(Sylvinho)

'As painful as it was [the injection of hormones], he did it because he wanted to become better. He wanted to be the best!'

(Víctor Vázquez)

'I'm sorry for those who want to occupy his throne. He is among the greatest in every sense of the word. He is capable of doing what he does every three days.'

(Pep Guardiola)

'I am very happy. Now I want to keep on getting better, carry on winning things so I can have even more memories. I want to keep on achieving things that I will always remember.'

(Leo Messi at the Ballon d'Or gala, 2012)

'I am used to being the last person to leave; I like being in the dressing room. What's more, I don't have anything better to *do. I love football and training sessions are part of football.'*

(Leo Messi at the same gala)

In the Seventies Gordon Training International published some theories that time has diminished somewhat, but can still help us to understand four basic types of footballer. They called it the 'four phases of apprenticeship'. The kid, when he strikes the ball against the wall or in the schoolyard, isn't aware of how little he knows, how good or bad he is (unconscious incompetence). When he sees someone doing things with the ball that he can't, he recognises his incompetence and consciously learns new skills in an academy to improve his performance (conscious incompetence). Finally, after a lot of practice, footballers are able to understand their ability and carry it out at a high level. They acquire the level of competence that permits them to become professional, a state in which the majority of footballers lead a comfortable life (conscious competence). There is one final, higher level, a group of malcontents who don't believe they've made it merely because they have become professionals, and in this group you'll find Lionel Messi.

This final group, the privileged few, are those who never have enough, who don't believe that they're the best, who want to keep on working to reach the maximum level. They have practised so much that their abilities have become instinctive reaction and the practice of them easy (unconscious competence).

'Leo used to say with confidence that he wanted to be the best. And he didn't say it with any arrogance, rather as something that was going to happen in the future,' explains Víctor Vázquez. 'Cesc, Piqué or I could say it, but we had the fear of knowing that there were players in our position who played our type of game, but not with Messi, because with Messi there is no other like him. They are special players.'

Having clear aims and objectives helps you go far: if you don't know precisely where you want to go, you're never going to get there. And Messi had it clear. He didn't want to be famous, a star. He wanted to be the best footballer he could be. 'We all want to win,' reflects Gustavo Oberman. 'But certainly he, with the qualities he has, will want to win more than the others. A half-good player will want to win a game; he wants to win the tournament, the Ballon d'Or. If I was Messi I'd also want to win it, but I'm not as good as that, so I limit myself to what I can win.'

Oberman continues: 'He also wanted to win during practice, when playing the mini games, and he'd battle for dead balls as if it was a match. Perhaps another type of player, with the same qualities as him, will play more calmly in training because he doesn't have to demonstrate it, but he, like Kun Agüero and many others, obliges us to play to our maximum, because if you don't play to your maximum with players like this it is very difficult to stand out: he clearly has all that deep inside.'

'What?!' adds the Manchester City defender Martín Demichelis. 'He's competitive even in the Friends of Messi against the Rest of the World! In one of the games he said to us, "come on now, let's play seriously, I'm getting bored".'

This highly competitive nature, this winning mentality, this search for all-conquering new achievements creates such an excitement in him that on occasions he has vomited minutes before the start. It's almost like filling a car with petrol before the start of a race. Or like the singer who, before going on stage, before the applause, feels his temperature rising, his nerves jangling. But after that brief moment, as soon as he walks onto the pitch, he resets his body to neutral, his objectives become crystal clear.

His focus, the sports psychologists say, is absolute, centred. It is neither wide nor diffuse, but, rather, reduced. Many of those who stand out in science, culture or sport have the same vision. They say that Archimedes remained focused on an experiment, while Syracuse, the city he lived in, was being invaded. The order had been given that the inventor and astronomer should not be harmed, but he sat concentrating on what he was doing until he noticed the soldier. '*Noli turbare circulos meos*!' – 'Don't mess up my circles,' he told him, as he sat drawing in the sand. The Roman killed him with a single blow.

Those who live in the rarefied realms of the elite, create and dwell in their own world, which, by its very nature, cannot be shared with lesser mortals. Every now and then they emerge from their cocoon and share our world with us. Like actors they need to learn how to come out of character, something that Leo does in private. Jean-Paul Sartre wrote about an actor who played the part of William Shakespeare for 15 years, and at a given moment, when he wanted to date a girl, he wooed her as if he was actually the real Shakespeare. He'd forgotten how to be himself. The elite footballer runs the risk of finishing up locked away in his own private world. Leo tries to ensure that his contact with his nephews, his wife and son, Thiago, his dogs, help him to open up the windows of his life and remind him that there are other worlds beside the rectangle of the football pitch.

But to conclude, as ex-footballer Romario has recently, that his reduced vision and world is proof that Messi has Asperger's syndrome, a form of autism, is very simplistic. In fact it's false – not only is it extremely complicated to diagnose Asperger's, the fact is that it has never been diagnosed. The superficial use of medical terminology is dangerous.

It's a fact, though, that Messi can become so focused, so centred on his own affairs, that his reactions can appear strange. At the end of the Peru vs Argentina game in the quarter-finals of the Copa América in 2007, and just before entering the tunnel to go to the dressing room, a female fan leapt from high up in the stands so that she could get a hug from the star. In the television footage you see Messi looking up, urging the girl not to jump, while he carries on walking. Suddenly a body falls to the ground from at least four metres up, bends double before getting up and embracing the footballer who waits there briefly before carrying on towards the dressing room. Someone asks him for his shirt and you see him debating whether or not to give it. Almost as if nothing had happened seconds earlier.

That's how it appeared from the outside. And Messi explains what he felt inside: 'Wow, it was incredible. I was making signs to her not to jump, but she jumped anyway. I swear to you, I didn't know what to do. It was from at least four metres up. She nearly killed herself, and what's worse they just got the poor kid out of the way as quickly as possible without making sure whether she was okay or not.'

And when he cries after a game? How can you explain both extremes in the same person, the coolness before taking a penalty and the tears? A football match is not for crying, they say in Argentina. If someone does, it's because it is more than just a game of football. What has he played in 90 minutes that has made him cry? A defeat for Leo is not just anything: until he calms down, say the psycholo-

gists, immersed in his own world, focused to the extreme, he feels as
if he has lost his life. Viewed like that, crying would seem appropriate.

'Leo is very special,' says Piqué. 'When he loses a game, you think,
whoa, I wouldn't like to be his wife, or girlfriend. You can imagine
that he goes home and spends the rest of the day without saying
a word. And that is what happens – he doesn't talk to anyone, he
locks himself in his room and he might even arrive late for training
the next day, or not even appear. Not winning, not scoring, hurts
him that badly. It will take him a day or two or three to get over this
wall of silence, but he can't help it. And the next time he loses, the
same thing again.'

Winning is something he has to do. After a victory Leo is left
with the feeling of a job well done. They say that the great wins are
accompanied minutes afterwards by a type of depression, a drop
in physical and mental wellbeing caused by the great effort. 'Is that
it? All that effort for this?' top sportsmen ask at that point. Normally it lasts only a few minutes. Leo feels satisfaction from having
achieved his objective, and he knows how to celebrate. But before
he has a chance to suffer any kind of attack of 'champion's depression', he has already found new challenges. 'The great geniuses are
different from the rest of us,' says Sylvinho. 'Sometimes they don't
seem human. They want more and more … I love this, because if I
see a person, a player, who can do more, who has the talent to do
better, but doesn't do it … yuk. It's painful. Leo doesn't need money,
he doesn't want beautiful things … he's just looking for more successes, to win more.'

Attaining this level of focus is key to advancement. 'Publicity very
often confuses a player,' writes *El País* journalist Santiago Segurola.
'It obliges him to be the best in the world in every move. And that
cannot be. I don't believe players are prepared for the extreme pressure that journalism, critics, success, fame, celebrity, travel, continual sponsorship demands, put on them. They are things that can
distract, that can slow you down.'

But nothing distracts Leo. Ex-Real Madrid and Rosario-born
Santi Solari told his pupils during his first experience as a coach
with a *blancos* youth team not to waste their time, to make the most
of their football education, and not to be distracted by adolescent
things, by going out and partying. He was saying this to 15-year-old

boys, who were at an age when wasting their time was precisely what they should be thinking about. Those who understood what Solari was talking about, those who were mad enough to recognise and follow what he was saying, those are the ones that have the footballing gene. Nothing will distract them.

While Leo was with Tito Vilanova's youth team, Barcelona received an offer from Juventus for him. Messi did not want to go: he had marked out his road and his ambition was to triumph at Barcelona. 'Leo lives, thinks, enjoys, or is saddened by, or whatever, with football,' points out Ferran Soriano, the former vice-president of Barcelona and now executive director at Manchester City. 'It is clear that he thinks that to be the best in the world he has to have a special type of focus: he plays football, trains, even plays football on PlayStation. I remember dining with Fernando Alonso a few years ago. I left with the same impression that I have of Messi: all he talks about is races and cars, nothing else. What will occupy them when they finish their careers?'

SKILLS NECESSARY TO 'KNOW HOW TO LEARN'

4. Constancy

'From what my mum and dad tell me, by the time I was two or three I already had a football. Since I was small I knew that I liked it and that it was what I wanted to do. And as I grew I became more aware of everything ... I wanted it even more.'

(Leo Messi in an Audemars Piguet commercial, 'Defining Moment')

'Messi understands football as if he'd been playing for a hundred years.'

(Santi Solari)

'I have never seen a better footballer than Leo; one who can surpass him in effectiveness. He dedicates himself to winning games with an amazing continuity, and he will always surprise us with something different, like a new brilliant rewarding brushstroke.'

(Jorge Valdano)

'He has been gifted with a great talent, but if it wasn't for an almost insane willpower to give everything and to progress it would have served him nothing.'

(Rodrigo Messi in *France Football*)

'People buy tickets just to see him play and he is leaving something unique. Tell me another player who has kept this level up for four years. Who else has this tremendous physical capacity, who fights like he does? I have never seen anyone who is so consistent ... perhaps I am too young but I have never seen a team-mate like this or, as a coach, had a player like this. He is superior to the rest, he has a special gift.'

(Pep Guardiola in 2011)

There are no short cuts on the path to the summit. You have to learn by trial and error. When it looks like you can't make it, you have to think that you still can. And when you get there, you have to be clear that you haven't arrived, you have merely advanced. A graphic and imaginative example of this is the advertisement in which Cristiano Ronaldo is tormented by his alter ego. 'He appears at the end of every game,' Ronaldo says. 'He follows me. He stalks me. Even if I have scored and had a great game. He always has something to say. He's a pain. I should have got to that pass, I should have controlled that ball, every free-kick should be a goal. His favourite expression? If you think you're already perfect, then you never will be. And he goes on, and on, and on ... every flaming day. Seven days a week. But you know what? I love the bloke.'

We have already seen that is how the greats think. Without this mentality they would not achieve their great objectives. But what else makes them achieve such heights? What path do they take? Can it be taught? Can it be repeated?

For centuries we have believed that success is linked with talent and genetics. 'I became the British table tennis champion, and the number one in 1995,' explains Matthew Syed, Commonwealth table tennis champion and journalist with *The Times* who explores the subject of success in his extraordinary book *Bounce*. 'It was a huge surprise for the sports community in Great Britain. I was very young and not many people thought I would get to the top so quickly. I grew up in Silverdale Road in Reading, in a pretty yet unremarkable street except for one thing: this little community produced more great players of table tennis in the 1980s than the rest of the country put together. Now if you think this is all created because of genetics, then why was just one specific street affected?'

Syed adds another fact: Spartak Moscow, a poor tennis club on the outskirts of the Russian capital, produces more top tennis players than the whole of the United States. Our inclination to think of success purely in genetic terms needs to be revised.

Matthew Syed rejects the use of words like 'genius', 'prodigy' or 'natural talent' when referring to Leo Messi because he believes that excellence is due principally (though not totally) to continual and deliberate practice. The author challenges the cultural belief that a genius is born and not made: with effort comes excellence and, through that, often comes success. So what needs to be applauded is hard work, not talent.

Leo has certainly always played with a ball and at all times. Remember the four games in one day with Quique Domínguez as his coach? Or those extra hours he used to put in at La Masía when the other boys had gone home? There are many more examples.

In a scientific attempt to explain just how those like Messi, Ronaldo and Maradona manage to perform the way they do, various studies have explored the possibility that perhaps they have a wider picture of the field of play than a normal footballer, and that this allows them to see more areas of the pitch, more team-mates and more rivals. But, no, there is no evidence whatsoever to back that theory.

What happens is that the best footballers collect more information in a single look. Syed says that the best chess players remember a board not as 32 individual pieces but in groups of five or six pieces. They already have in their heads between ten and a hundred times more combinations for these groups than lesser players. What's more, the grand masters access this long-term memory in a much faster and more reliable way.

When Messi runs or receives the ball he sees patterns where everyone else sees just players or a ball, in a similar way to the film *The Matrix*. In the film Neo sees ones and twos in place of bullets and this allows him to dodge them. It isn't that Leo spots anything before anyone else; it's that he sees what others don't. When Roger Federer plays tennis, explains Syed in his book, he doesn't pick his best shot from a sensorial information warehouse selected at that moment, but, rather, he sees and hears the world 'in a completely different way', the same way, in fact, that the Eskimos are able to see more variations of white than the rest of us, because of their experiences in Arctic conditions.

'You'd be surprised at the level of information he can gather with one 360-degree look around,' adds Juanjo Brau. 'He's able to tell you where everything is, he's a person with a visual recall that captures everything.' So the extraordinary sportsmen develop an expert intuition, an instinctive subconscious method of solving problems. The creation of these patterns allow them to anticipate and resolve complex problems in the best way possible.

'Leo has a perceptive intelligence, in that he knows at all times what he has to do, his natural habitat is the field of play,' explains Juanjo Brau. 'He is an enormously intelligent player in his profession, as all the maestros are. He is able to see what no one else can. He shoots for goal, not at the target – it's very different. There are other players who get to the goal area, they see three pieces of wood and shoot. He sees the three pieces of wood, the goalkeeper and calculates the right time to get around him ... all in tenths of seconds.'

And if he is waiting in the place he considers appropriate and does not get the ball, he gets cross. He doesn't have time to think that the target of his anger has just come back from injury or is just a youngster. At that moment it's just someone, normally a fellow forward or a winger, the provider of the final pass, who is at fault for not agreeing with him. Manel Estiarte, the water polo star, also saw the move and used to scream at anyone who did not do what he considered to be the right thing, the appropriate thing, the best. As Pep Guardiola has said to him on many occasions, 'You forget that the other players are not as good as you are.' What he probably means is that they do not see what he sees.

And how much effort is needed to reach this extraordinary capacity? Ten thousand hours of deliberate practice. Syed agrees with the assertion of Malcolm Gladwell in *Outliers* that a basic constituent, although not the only one, of sporting excellence is sustained training for a level of at least 10,000 hours. This represents 2.7 hours of training every day for 10 years, although it isn't just a matter of the quantity, but also the quality of the effort made, and that requires a high level of coaching skill and observations from the coach.

Syed and Gladwell thus reclaim the theory of psychologist Anders Ericsson, who, at the beginning of the Nineties, analysed students at the East Berlin Musical Academy. He separated them into three groups from the most skilled to the least. His conclusions were definitive: the only difference was the number of hours of practice (10,000 the best, 6,000 the worst).

'The difference between the musical experts and normal adults is a consequence of their persistence throughout their lives to deliberately strive to improve their level,' wrote Ericsson. Another study confirmed that a group of British musicians of high standing would not necessarily learn faster than those of lower attainment, but they had spent more hours with their instruments.

Mozart, explains Syed, had 3,500 hours of practice by the time he was six, and studied music for 18 years before writing his first great work, his Piano Concerto No. 9, at the age of 21. He is remembered as a prodigy, but the quality of his musical ability came about after more than 10,000 hours of practice. Tiger Woods started to hit a golf ball when he was two years old. Serena Williams started her career when she was three; her sister Venus when she was four. Messi at the age of three was already kicking a ball that was almost bigger than him.

As Janet Starkes, Professor of Kinesiology at Canada's McMaster University in Hamilton, Ontario, explains in *Bounce*, 'the exploitation of advanced information results in the time paradox where skilled performers seem to have all the time in the world. The recognition of family scenarios and the grouping of perceptual information into meaningful wholes and patterns speeds up processes.' And not all of this is innate, but the consequence of deliberate practice and constant competition.

But there's more: experience alone is not enough. What is needed is maximum concentration. 'Every second of every minute of every hour, the objective is to expand the mind and the body as one, to push yourself above and beyond ones limits, immerse yourself so deep into your work so that by the end of your training session you literally feel like a new player,' Syed writes.

These new theories are laying to rest various myths. On the fortieth anniversary of the Van Gogh Museum in Amsterdam, in the summer of 2013, the curators revealed the results of an eight-year investigation into the intimate life of the artist. The show ('Van Gogh at Work') overturns previously held ideas: the artist did not isolate himself from his colleagues. True, he wasn't overendowed with social skills when it came to maintaining amorous relationships, but he did have regular and productive contact with other artists, particularly the Impressionists. Neither did he have an innate gift for painting. He was not an instant genius, but a tireless technician who, to learn his craft, to understand the mechanics and use of colour, copied out the 197 illustrations from a drawing manual by Charles Bargue that was considered to be a classic of its type. Not once, but three times!

For that reason we need to proceed with care: to classify a youngster as a 'natural talent' is to potentially overshadow the struggle and sacrifices he needs to make to develop that talent further; if he thinks he is born like this, he can begin to think that he has no need to put in any effort.

Not even the talented are aware of the gradual process that makes the better than most, so, as a result, the teaching of it in schools is impossible. Collecting and explaining all this information is difficult to grasp because it is so subtle and includes various modes of physical interaction, and a psychology so complex, that it would take an eternity just to codify it. Ten thousand hours of class, therefore, don't necessarily lead to mastery. You can direct the interest of the students and the players, you can suggest what to do and what to avoid. But little more than that.

Paradoxically, failure (or the way great sportsmen deal with it) is part of the consequence of excellence. 'I am my number one critic. I am fanatical. I get angry if I play badly, because I never want to lose,' Leo Messi has said. He learns from his mistakes, from an extraordinary capacity to control his own behaviour. He doesn't just establish his targets and monitor his progress, he also objectively evaluates his aims.

What is it that drives certain people, especially great sportsmen, to pursue excellence relentlessly and tirelessly? Having scaled one peak, why do they set out to scale another with barely a moment's pause? Where does this ambition come from? Matthew Syed thinks he has found an answer: 'their ability to experience the feeling of anti-climax is much faster and to a much deeper extent than the rest of us. All of us have experienced anti-climax, but it is incredible the speed at which the best players come down to earth after winning a big title: almost as if they were distancing themselves from a particular goal that they may have spent years trying to achieve. Emptied out, they have to fill up as quickly as possible with achieving the next goal, and the one after, and on and on ...'

Closely related to this, Leo has a tolerance to pain that makes him get up as soon as he has been kicked. This is something he has had since he was very small: be it through intuition or training, he has the capacity to deal with the pain of a kick in the shortest time possible. Even though the rival has probably done it on purpose to stop him, his only thought is of the next move.

Clearly Leo, like all number ones, has an approach to the world very different from the rest of us.

5. Commitment and sacrifice

'I always want to demonstrate my commitment for the club. At first it was more noticeable. Now it's something more common. This is my home, my club. I owe everything to Barcelona. I've always said it, I'm happy here.'

(Leo Messi in *El País*, 2012)

'He has played many times with his ankle fucked. I know this because many times Juanjo Brau says that it's impossible, and then Leo goes and plays.'

(Gerard Piqué)

The strength of feeling that a footballer has for his club goes a long way to determine his performance. Playing just for the money will be manifestly different from playing with real commitment to a club, particularly one, as in Leo's case, with a protective president and a sympathetic coach. 'This commitment and enthusiasm that Leo demonstrates to the game and to the club that gave him the chance to grow is the energy that supports him and gives him the strength to carry on, to push himself to the limit, to battle against adversity,' says Pedro Gómez. Leo feels a great debt to Charly Rexach and to the president, Joan Laporta, who understood his needs, made efforts to help him and kept their promises through different phases of his *blaugrana* journey.

The ex-president of Barcelona improved Leo's contract on a regular basis and was the first to make him the best paid player in the club. And at a moment of crisis, the president turned the club around (and not only with the first team) so that Leo could triumph and become the leader. Barcelona 'will always do whatever is necessary to ensure that Messi is happy at the club, and we know that Messi has a total commitment to Barca,' said Laporta in 2009. This explains why, in his first years with the first team, he would kiss the badge when he scored: he did it with particular enthusiasm after scoring a hat-trick against Real Madrid in 2007. He wanted the world to identify him with the club whose shirt he was wearing.

His commitment is for the institution, but also, given his history, to those who are close to him: he never forgets where he is from.

'From a very early age I wanted to be a professional, and I dreamt of playing in the first division. Yes, I had to make many sacrifices. The first was to leave Argentina when I was just thirteen years old and start again from zero, make new friends in a city where I knew no one.'

(Leo talking to Audemars Piguet)

The commitment he made stemmed from a basic need to move his dream forward, so that the boy who wanted to be a footballer was not left in the gutter, disillusioned and unfulfilled. Nor was he prepared to allow the same fate to befall his family and those who depended upon him. The sacrifices he made were nothing less than the price he had to pay to reach his destination.

6. Humility

'My first objective is to appear on the list of players pre-selected to compete in the World Cup.'

(Leo Messi upon arriving in Argentina preparing for the World Cup in South Africa, 2010)

'No, I don't believe that this has been my best year. I am more interested in prizes on a team level, rather than personal awards for breaking records or individual performances. There have been years when we won many more things and were better.'

(Leo Messi after winning his fourth Ballon d'Or)

'I love Messi, not only for the pleasure of seeing him when he plays, but also because, despite being the best player in the world, it's almost as though he hasn't realised it. Messi doesn't seem to believe he's Messi!'

(Eduardo Galeano, writer)

'If he has already overcome the phase of believing he is Maradona, then he won't have a problem overcoming the phase of believing he is Messi. And then he can become a footballer the likes of which we have never seen, one so great that he won't even need a name.'

(Martín Caparros, Argentinian writer)

The first awakening of humility is the acknowledgement of one's strengths and weaknesses, a recognition of one's limitations. This is Leo. Listen to his friend Oscar Ustari explain how his companions view him.

'Something that comes as a surprise, above and beyond his footballing skills, is how he presents himself. He is very natural, very unpretentious. And this in professional football where a player's ego is usually all-pervasive. But this doesn't happen with Leo. Today he can have whatever he wants, just by raising his hand: often a footballer measures his success by his possessions. He is not like that at all. So many times we have gone to restaurants in Barcelona or here in Buenos Aires, and he is always the same, unassuming Leo. He surprises me still, even when I see him frequently. We have all had friends who have become famous or important, and have suddenly behaved differently. But Leo remains Leo. And that is truly admirable.

'The Argentina federation wanted to give him some kind of recognition for having played a hundred times for his country, but he said no. In a friendly maybe he would accept it, but not in an official match with the national side. He doesn't like that, he doesn't need it, he doesn't like exposing himself to things like that.

'The other day I disturbed him – I don't like to bother him at all – because the club in my town, where I first started, was celebrating its centenary and I wanted him to send them a message, because today all the little kids want to be like Messi. I asked him if he could do me a favour and send a greeting. He was in Bolivia, the day before a game. And he said to me, "okay, what do you want me to say?" and I said, "I don't know, anything! Send a greeting, they're a hundred years old!" He sat on a bench, it looked like a recording studio, he crossed his legs and began, "well I'm Leo Messi ..." and he sent it straightaway. Incredible, not everyone does that.'

'He would never say "thanks to me ..."' Juanjo Brau explains. 'Leo never asked me for anything but he offered me everything. He's a person who always wants to give, he prefers it. Then it's up to you if you take or not. He is a man of few words, but of great feelings. I get choked up speaking about him like this but I would like people to know him as he really is, people don't know what he is like.'

As Jorge Valdano says, 'He seems like a normal bloke. But he's an alien on the pitch. Or to put it another way, Leo Messi is a genie in the shape of a normal person.'

The writer Eduardo Sacheri believes that if you look at Messi from an emotional viewpoint you cannot detect the various strands that enrich his play: 'You're not going to notice how he scores, or what obstacles he has to overcome. For example, what does he do after he scores a goal? And this is one of the things that I like most about Messi. He always looks for the team-mate who gave him the ball. He isn't the type of person who runs around on his own, taking himself into the corner, making sure he's getting the best camera shot while he beats his breast and runs towards the full-back. He runs ten metres and then turns so his colleagues can catch up with him, and then looks for the one who gave him the ball. And when he assists for somebody else's goal, he celebrates that, too. This kid understands about football. Notice that he has the humility, despite being the best, to know that football is a game played by eleven people, not just one. The man's got an ethic and an aesthetic for playing football. And an ethic is not the same as passion. An ethic is an intellectual construction. He has that understanding in his head and his heart.'

SKILLS NECESSARY TO 'DEMONSTRATE WHAT'S BEEN LEARNED'

7. Self-confidence and leadership

'I've always been the smallest. I don't give orders on the pitch. If I have something to say I do it with the ball. I'm not a great talker.'

(Leo Messi)

'Messi influenced me, what he does is staggering. I copy his moves.'

(Neymar)

'Leo has learned that he should control the game and not that the game should control him. The rest of us are controlled by the game, and we make decisions according to how the game is going. I don't often take the decision I want to or the correct one, but take the one that I can take at that particular moment. Sometimes I'm wrong. Leo has got to the point that it is he who decides when he takes the ball, when not to, when to dribble past three players, and when not to, when to make the goal-scoring pass or when to score himself ... He controls everything, it's what makes the difference, and he decides when to be part of the play and when not to be.'

(Javier Mascherano)

If someone is aspiring to be the best, to reach the summit, it's exactly at that moment that they begin to create the conditions that will make it a reality. The power of positive thinking is strange: we are capable through innate and internal processes to create optimistic scenarios that we can fervently believe in. Leo is positive, has a totally excessive belief in the effectiveness of his talent and has eliminated from his mind the slightest trace of doubt, that most dangerous of elements for any elite sportsman: doubt attracts the fear of defeat, paralyses and scatters itself around at the speed of light. That's probably another reason why Leo cries when he loses: it's pure frustration; it never enters his head that defeat is even a possibility.

This certainty in his ability helps him to look for the second dribble, the third. The second title, the third. The belief in his own abilities permits him to look relaxed, masterful, almost subconsciously, thereby preventing the fascinating (and, when it happens to you, deeply depressing) psychological block known as choking.

Perhaps the most famous example of this was the French golfer Jean van de Velde who suffered the yips at the British Open in 1999. By the time he got to the eighteenth tee it looked like the only decision he had left to make was whether to drink his victory champagne in the Jacuzzi or with his friends. Even with a double bogey, he was guaranteed the trophy, the highest level for a modest golfer. Van de Velde began to walk around the hole, touch the sand, look at the lake, spend too long looking at the grass, change his club, test for wind, try to control the noise of the crowd. He had lost his safety net; the pressure had got to him. He finished the hole on a triple bogey which meant he had to play off against Paul Lawrie. He lost. His descent into mediocrity continued long after the Open.

This mental block, suffered by sportsmen at the peak of their careers, often caused by external pressure, possibly a family problem, occurs when they suddenly become conscious of a skill that they have been nurturing and perfecting, subconsciously, for years. An elite sportsman computes his performance as he advances through his profession, which results, ultimately, in a matrix of millions of complex details, stored subconsciously in his brain. All goes well until the sportsman attempts to consciously unravel the matrix, becomes conscious of what he has been doing subconsciously for years. At this stage he experiences the fears that he had in childhood; that he might not succeed, that he might not run fast enough or hit the ball, or score the goal. He regresses.

There are no known blocks in Leo's case, even though he has been known to miss the odd penalty at moments that mattered. That's just bad luck. On the other hand, his self-confidence at the highest level of football and his repeated appearances at the great moments explain the leadership that he exercises over the club, the city, the country. He is followed by millions of 'hopeful chasers of the dream', as Pedro Gómez says. Or as the writer Juan Mateo and the coach Juanma Lillo put it in their book *Liderar en tempos difíciles* ('Leading in Difficult Times'): 'The true leader helps to magnify the members of his team. He doesn't bring light into the darkness, but what he does do is find places that no one knew existed. He is a factory of ideas. In his head he unleashes an explosion of unedited images. Impulsive and inventive possibilities. He enthuses and is involuntarily converted into an antidote to idleness, that parasite that multiplies at every chance it gets.'

In other words, he inspires.

Leo has the world at his feet because we all want to be in that place that he inhabits – a peaceful environment and an example to all that, with effort, it is possible to achieve anything.

8. Emotional intelligence and its benefits (adaptation, control of emotions)

'I visualise the games moments before I step out onto the pitch. I don't think about any of this during the week. Beforehand I warm up in the dressing room. I don't get nervous. Well, not often.'

'I don't think on the pitch. Well, I only think about getting the ball – to have it and be able to play. When I have it, I play.'

'I don't plan any of the dribbling I do. It just comes out. I work during the week only to keep fit and to follow what my coach asks me to do, but I don't really care who my opponent is. I'm not bothered.'

'The stadiums I like the most are the ones where they get at me and at my team. They motivate me. They make me want to give of my best. For example, when we're playing Real Madrid, I prefer to play in Madrid. I like the rivalry.'

(Leo Messi at the Ballon d'Or gala, 2012)

In one of the first Ballon d'Or galas that Leo attended he was approached by one of the organisers and told that he should say something in English. 'No, no, I don't speak English. And they suggested, "well, just say 'thank you'".' Leo was clear. 'No. If I have to speak English, then I'm not going out.' In the end he did come out, but he didn't speak any English. If they take Leo off the football pitch he will do everything he can not to be messed about, so as not to feel out of his comfort zone. It's nothing to do with shyness. It's about self-protection, reserve. He needs to have everything under control.

Everything is football and the greatest fear is of burnout. His limited world (the club, his shirt, his boots, the ball) limits his association with the wider world. His Dolce & Gabbana polka-dot suit that he wore to the 2012 gala suggests that he is beginning to feel more comfortable away from the ball, but it won't be in interviews or in front of an audience, other than in a football stadium, that we'll be allowed to see the real Leo. Interviews are non-productive in attempting to plumb the depths of his personality. 'It's better that others should speak about me' is his customary response.

When Leo leaves football he will retire, but he will carry on living in this world of the round-ball game. It's the one he knows best, where he recognises himself. This obsession with the game means that a superficial analysis might suggest that off the field of play Messi is an uncomplicated soul. The different levels of intelligence that we have talked about confirm something completely different.

Leo has to co-exist with anxiety, nerves, mistrust, mood, security, motivation, distress, and his handling of them can increase or decrease his performance levels. Well managed, they bring with them wisdom; out of control, they ensure chaos. Emotional intelligence is an essential complement to making good decisions.

In the early Nineties, psychology professor Mihaly Csikszentmihalyi created his theory about what he called the 'flow state'. 'His proposal,' Pedro Gómez explains, 'concerns the existence of something at the highest level of performance called "flow", in which certain individuals display a superior level of control over their emotions to the point where they can activate and apply that control to the job in hand. So effective is this ability to block out everything else and focus entirely on what they are doing that, effectively, time flies. Their actions are seen with great clarity, despite the rivals' attempt to interrupt their concentration. The individual doesn't decide, he anticipates. He doesn't play, he enjoys. He is effectively working on automatic pilot. The player and the game become one, an inseparable reality. In other words, and so you understand it better ... What Messi does game after game in a natural way!'

This doesn't sound like an 'uncomplicated soul'. Rafa Nadal has admitted that he has trained his mind since he was four years old. Leo's mastery of what he does comes partly from that control he has exercised over his emotions from an early age.

Messi also comes from a culture that is aligned to another type of intelligence: craftiness. 'For me, what I like most is his craftiness. He makes the difference because he is so cunning,' says Alfredo Di Stéfano. Espanyol fans still remember that goal he scored with his hand the same season as the famous slalom goal against Getafe.

Leo, in another show of guile, learned how to defend himself against the kicks they would give him from the outset of a match. 'When he takes the ball with his left, notice how as soon as they are about to come into him from the right he lifts his foot [so that the defender crashes into his studs],' discovered José María Cuartetas, eponymous owner of one of Leo's favourite restaurants in Barcelona. 'Pelé used to do that a lot, and Maradona: it's so that the first person to be hurt will be the other guy. And then the next time the defender thinks twice, or decides to go in much harder, which makes it easier for the referee to give a decision.'

9. Enjoyment

> *'My intention is to come onto the pitch and enjoy myself as I did when I was a boy. I know that I have a responsibility and today I play to win to achieve things, but at the same time I enjoy myself, always.'*
>
> (Messi, in the Audemars Piguet commercial)

> *'I don't know what I would have been without football. If I could I'd like to play a game every day.'*
>
> (Leo Messi)

> *'There's a feeling that both Maradona and Messi transmit: the pleasure of playing. They are two people who have fun with the ball ... And say, "let's go and play".'*
>
> (Frank Rijkaard)

'It's like that trick they do with the three coins. The hand is quicker than the eye. The charm of it is that he does with the feet what others do with their hands. The skill comes from time immemorial and is accompanied with a passion and a pleasure for what is football, which means that every time you see him with a ball it's like watching a boy with a chocolate treat.'

(Fernando Signorini, physical coach of Club Deportivo Universidad de San Martín de Porres (Lima) and ex-member of the technical staff of the Argentinian national side)

'When he cries it's because he knows he won't be able to play. When he hurts himself he thinks "Sunday I won't be able to play", he doesn't think of anything else.'

(Juanjo Brau, Barcelona physiotherapist)

'Leo loves football, because he was born to play football. We went somewhere and he asked for a ball. There wasn't one, so he asked for something, anything round that he could have at his feet. Leo's capable of controlling just about anything with his feet. If you were to pass him a slipper he'd do keepy-uppies with that.'

(Juan Cruz Leguizamón, ex-team-mate of Leo in the lower grades at Newell's Old Boys)

When he was a kid, Leo never did any special training. He just played for the pleasure of it. I have asked hundreds of footballers what they would do if they were walking in the park and the ball from a game that some youngsters were playing fell at their feet. Surprisingly the vast majority of them say they would not get involved in the kickabout. David Beckham would certainly start to play with the kids. Leo as well. They love the sport that has made them rich and famous. There are many (Batistuta has even stated it publicly) who don't even like football.

Leo is conspicuously a football man. He knows just about everything about the game; you can ask him about players from wherever, statistics, histories, he remembers results, who scored, who won, with a retentive memory that is surprising. Not only, but predominantly Argentinian football. 'He is joyful with football, or, rather, he treats football with some innocence,' analyses Eduardo Sacheri. 'You see him and what you are watching is a kid in the park, totally unaware of what is happening anywhere else. When something doesn't work out he gets cross. When it comes out right, he's happy. When they kick him his way of getting his own back is to snub whoever is kicking him. These are the football codes he follows.'

Like all elite footballers, although his adolescence was snatched away from him he kept the creative energy and outbursts of a kid, and from this also comes the essence of his art and the attraction of his leadership.

Hernán Casciari, an Argentinian writer resident in Barcelona, has a telling piece in *Revista Orsai* that sums up this essence of his character. 'It all began this morning: I am looking non-stop at Messi goals on YouTube, rather guiltily because I'm in the middle of finishing magazine number six. By chance I click on a compilation of clips that I haven't seen before. It's a strange compilation: the video shows hundreds of images – of about two or three seconds each – in which Messi is fouled really badly but doesn't fall. He neither throws himself to the ground, nor moans. In every frame he follows the ball with his eyes while he regains his balance. He makes superhuman efforts to try to ensure that what is done is not a foul, nor a yellow card for the opposing defender. Suddenly, I'm stunned, because I see something familiar in these images. I put each frame in slow motion and I notice that Messi's eyes are always concentrated on the ball, but I don't remember it in a footballing context. Where have I seen that look before? In whom? I paused the video. Zoomed in on his eyes. And then I remembered it: they were Totín's eyes when he lost all sense of reason for anything except the sponge he was chasing. When I was young I had a dog called Totín. Nothing moved him. He wasn't an intelligent dog. Burglars would come in and he'd watch them steal my television. The doorbell would ring and it seemed that he didn't hear it.' Messi, says Casciari, was effectively the same as his dog, he with the ball, Totín with the sponge. At that point there was nothing else and you could see it in the eyes of both of them. 'This is my theory and I'm sorry if you've got this far expecting more. When football began it was like this. Before, football was played like Messi and Totín play. Everyone just went after the ball and nothing more.' Messi, he adds, is effectively from that era and, to continue the canine analogy, like a dog with a bone. He continues: 'He smashed records from other eras because up to the Fifties football was played by man-dogs. After that FIFA invited everyone to talk about laws and articles and we forgot that what was important was "the sponge".'

'Technique has its limits, and that is given by co-ordination,' says Quique Domínguez. 'Everything else can be taught, everything can be learned, but you need to go beyond the technical level to be a great: Leo gives you a handshake and talks to you, but you can see that, secretly, he is looking for the ball. You have to have that passion, you have to have that commitment.'

10. Genes

'He can score goals, assists, destabilise defences on his own, run with the ball at a hundred miles an hour and change direction. This isn't easy to do. You try it! Then come back and tell me how you got on.'

(Arsène Wenger, Arsenal manager)

'Okay ...Seriously now, someone's got to test Messi's genes ... I'm beginning to firmly believe that Messi is the child of Clark Kent [Superman].'

(Bar Rafaeli, model)

'His physical virtues are something completely natural, but it's curious that they should all come out of him because out of all the brothers the only one with these characteristics is Leo.'

(Fernando Signorini)

There is no gene that makes a child a genius. No one is born a genius. There's a lot of training and some innate properties that help you rise to the giddy heights. Perhaps, as some scientists suggest, the relevant genetic connection is the compulsion to achieve those goals.

'Who are these people who leave their footprint on humanity, in football, science, the arts, culture?' asks sports psychologist Liliana

Grabín. 'They are unique personalities, unrepeatable, they leave a legacy behind, there's no doubt about it. They did not mean to lead anything and that's why they leave a legacy. They are maestros. Science, historically, still doesn't know where it all comes from.'

Leo Messi has a unique mixture of gestural speed (that's to say, the speed of his movements) and skill. There are a few in the world with his characteristics. Marco Reus of Borussia Dortmund, for example, is fast with the ball at his feet and very skilful with the same gestural speed as Leo, but with a larger stride. But he is worse in the overall calculations, because he has difficulty in stringing together successive dribbles, while the Argentinian can put together three, four or more if he comes out from the last one with the ball under control. Messi's legs move faster than any other footballer and this gives him an advantage: the rhythm in his stride, which is essentially natural, is also unique: 4.5 strides per second, better than the 4.4 strides of Asafa Powell, the Jamaican sprinter who broke the 100 metres world record in 2007. The skill to carry out the smoothest of touches, one after the other, assisted by this gestural speed, gives him another advantage. And the ability to turn at full speed (a mixture of co-ordination and speed) is another physical attribute that helps him shake off his opponents.

'This is natural,' says Fernando Signorini. 'You won't achieve this even if you invent 800,000 different co-ordination exercises because, as Panceri [Armando Panceri, Argentinian footballer] says, the unexpected doesn't arrive as a result of specific planning.'

Leo arrived at Barcelona where they look for a profile of a footballer different from that of their rivals (Espanyol, Real Madrid): technical ability. Often those players (at 10, 11, 12 years old) are technically able but with a much better co-ordination than their tallest companions, and shine out because they are able to keep the ball and dribble better than the rest, proof of good co-ordination. The small boys therefore mature and evolve quicker and are more technically competent. Along the way 'the Flea' developed body strategies and rapid movements to compensate for his physical shortcomings, and to avoid an opponent bringing him down, to be able to nullify the advantage that a bigger boy, who was able to cover the same distance but in fewer strides, would have.

Or put another way, while gestural speed has its origins in genetics, it is improved and expanded with practice. In the street, in the football school.

With the passing of the years, many, tall or small, get to the same level from the point of view of co-ordination and technique. In Leo's case he has added a new dimension to an extraordinary level of excellence. And that isn't genetic; rather, it is the product of passion and perseverance.

Leo has always considered himself so superior in these actions of speed, skill and dribbling that he always wanted to do them in every move, every game. The best way to triumph in life is by concentrating on your strengths and for that reason Messi understands the game as a succession of dribbles, one versus one, the essence of football.

Add his intense desire to come out on top and you are getting close to what Leo Messi is about.

Let me add one more thing to the list proposed by Pedro Gómez.

11. Serendipity, luck and opportunity

It has been said that the greatest player of that famous generation of '87, the one who really excelled at Barcelona, was Víctor Vázquez, a comment that has both something a bit too clever about it while also having an element of truth. He could have been better, but it did not happen. Let him explain:

– Víctor, who makes it, and who doesn't?
– I think the good players make it, but luck also plays a part. You can have a lot of injuries, or come across a coach who doesn't like your style. It isn't that Messi was lucky, it's that he was the best, and he had it easy because he was always able to do what he does very well. The others, me for example, needed to have some luck. I had an injury, that if only I hadn't got, but anyway, what can I do? I made my debut in the league with Rijkaard. Later with Pep Guardiola I played a number of games. The last one alongside Leo was against Rubin Kazan at the Camp Nou, which we won 2-0 and I scored the second goal. Pep put me in the side for the match against Shakhtar Donetsk. Two weeks later I injured my knee against Villarreal and I was out of action for 14 months.

And obviously I couldn't get back to the same level. Also, there were many better players in my position than me. Xavi, Iniesta …

Today, Víctor Vázquez plays at Club Brugge, in Belgium. Quique Domínguez agrees with Víctor: 'For me when they ask what a player needs to become successful I say that it is like the three legs of a table: ability, dedication and luck.' A blend of luck and the circumstances generally under the direct control of the sportsman can help him triumph.

Even a thousand interviews with Leo Messi would fail to go any way towards explaining what it was that drove that ambition, the perseverance, the search for more achievements, the understanding of where to go with the ball. He has no idea how to explain it.

One thing is certain. As Jorge Valdano says, we never expected to see a player like Lionel in the twenty-first century. 'We were waiting to see a footballer with more of the characteristics of someone like Cristiano Ronaldo with his natural physique built up with lots of exercise and emphasis on gym work.' Maybe. In any case, Messi is the result of a bunch of circumstances and coincidences that enabled him to exploit his talent. A combination, that in its supreme expression, is seldom experienced. A perfect storm.

In our society we enjoy the success of the individual, men and women who have triumphed on their own, who have achieved their own particular 'American dream'. But those who have arrived at the highest level, as Malcolm Gladwell says, 'are invariably the beneficiaries of hidden advantages, extraordinary opportunities and cultural inheritances that allow them to work hard and make sense of the world in a way that others can't'.

Could there have been other Messis? Perhaps, but those who had the chance to one be might not have been lucky enough to get there. Or, more likely, couldn't see the opportunity. Or were born in the wrong country.

One final point. Leo has always been aware of the baggage he is carrying, and he will be a happy man in old age, simply because he is doing everything he can to be the best that he can possibly be. Not like *Trinche*. Being *Trinche* is easier.

What's difficult is to be Leo Messi.

7

Dealing with Maradona

'*I already knew he would be representing the national side during the World Cup in Holland, although he could have played with the Under 20 side for another year. I arranged a meeting with him in my room and I told him the news: "The teacher called me." He looked at me. "Pekerman is the teacher. You are going to be called up for the next full international. This is a secret between you and me, okay? And if the coach knows I'm telling you this, he'll kill me." He smiled and left. He is a man of few words. I used to communicate a lot using drawings. I remember drawing him a Formula One car in the 2006 World Cup. He still had many laps to complete. It wasn't his time to win the race. That is what the drawing represented.*

'*He didn't accept it, but he listened and kept the drawing.*'

(Gerardo 'the Professor' Salorio)

Messi's uncles would often say to him jokingly that he would play in the 2006 World Cup in Germany. 'They mentioned the date, but only as a joke. I never imagined I was going to play in one, never mind one that was fast approaching,' Leo recalled years later. But his life with the national team had a rocky start.

The Argentinian journalist Luis Calvano remembers walking behind Leo on the way to the meeting point of the national squad in Budapest, at the Ferenc Puskás Stadium. It was Leo's first call-up and he did not know what to do. Other players started arriving from the airport in different groups and some of them walked past the new kid, thinking he was a kitman's assistant. Messi was waiting for instructions standing by the wall, head down, fiddling nervously with the cord of his shorts. The first to recognise him was Luciano Figueroa. He took hold of him and began introducing him to the squad.

He made his debut two days later. And was sent off after 90 seconds. After that game, played in the summer of 2005, 'the Flea' was a regular in José Pekerman's squads during the months leading up to Germany. Away from the pitch, in the background, all but invisible to the rest of the group. He knew that, just as had happened in the Barcelona dressing room, he had to go through the same stages with the national side of gaining approval and acceptance. The leap forward he had taken at Barcelona had become, at least for the moment, a step backwards under Pekerman. He realised he was in two different worlds.

Messi usually sat with Oscar Ustari or Pablo Zabaleta, from the Under 20 World Cup squad, and later with Javier Mascherano, with whom he bonded instantly. 'The first time I saw him was just before the World Cup,' says Mascherano. Despite him being injured, Pekerman, who was relying on the midfielder for Germany, asked Mascherano to join the group in Switzerland where Argentina were to play a friendly against England. 'On that trip we spent a few days together. We first met in his room, he wasn't one for leaving his room much. In those days he was really quiet, very introverted … We had friends in common and obviously that helped with the conversation. But when you come to a new place you have a certain shyness and it's difficult until you begin to open up, isn't it? And even more so when you're just a boy.' Leo felt embarrassed; he didn't want to interrupt the camaraderie. So he spent most of the time in the hotel room. 'I was also young, I was twenty-two years old, he was eighteen, so, in a sense, we grew up together and became friends.'

From very early on the president of the federation, Julio Grondona, recognised that 'the Flea's' talent would make him one of the national side's leading lights. And, what's more, a leader. All in good time, he thought. The swift organisation of the two Under 20 friendlies had demonstrated the institutional support he was going to receive, and stole a march on Spain in the process. Grondona had to learn to cope with a very unmanageable Diego Armando Maradona, but he would make Leo his favourite son, his creation. 'I want this to be your son's side, and I have mentioned that to him, too,' he told Jorge Messi on one occasion. He was equally frank with Leo: he insisted that Argentina had to be his team and he should be the captain in the future. As is frequently the case in the European footballing culture – and perhaps it is a remnant of that culture – the captain's armband assumes great importance in the Argentine psyche. It represents the beacon of the group.

For the 2006 World Cup, Juan Pablo Sorín was captain. And as long as the captain has the support of the senior players and the most influential ones, the wearer of the armband is the winner in any disputes that may occur. That would explain the absence of Juan Sebastián Verón from the final squad for Germany. 'The fight between Juan Sebastián Verón and Juan Pablo Sorín halfway through the match between Inter and Villarreal, which was witnessed by millions of television viewers throughout the world, was a naked display of a deep internal wound in the Argentina side,' it was reported in *El Clarín* in April 2006. 'One that leaves Sorín in – and as captain – and Verón out. Everyone around the Inter player is convinced that Sorín is the man principally responsible for the non-selection of Verón in the last call-ups …'

Verón had been very influential when Daniel Passarella was coach, and an automatic starter under Marcelo Bielsa, even when the side's captain was the central defender Roberto Ayala. But Verón stopped being called up once Pekerman was appointed coach, and he, unlike Bielsa, who allowed his players to vote, picked Sorín despite pressure from some of his senior players to give the armband to Roberto Ayala. Such are the politics involved.

And the hierarchy is there to be respected. Leo Messi formed part of the 'new boys' group and, along with Oscar Ustari, was the only Under 20-year-old to go to that tournament. They were there to listen and to wait their turn. In the meantime, the final squad was being picked in a very Argentinian way: at a gathering in May, in the Spanish town of Boadilla, Pablo Aimar, who was enjoying a very successful season with Valencia, was missing. Pekerman had no intention of calling him up for the World Cup and justified his absence by citing the player's physical weakness – in April of that year he had suffered an acute form of viral meningitis. The squad leaders, fronted by Juan Román Riquelme, dug their heels in and their 'advice' was finally accepted by the coach. And so Aimar, the only idol recognised by Leo, was called up for the tournament. They would share the same dressing room.

'As I was growing and learning more, I studied his movements, how he played. I followed him,' admitted Leo who has every Pablo Aimar shirt he has been able to get hold of (Benfica, Valencia, Argentina) in his home. 'I should be the one doing the collecting,' says the ex-River player today.

Despite his tender years, Messi, who had just signed up with Adidas after leaving Nike, was one of the stars of the German sportswear company in the World Cup summer. He featured in an award-winning commercial ('History is chasing me but I'm quicker'), in which 'the Flea' draws a small doll playing football with much bigger dolls, and describes his dream of not going unnoticed despite being the weakest. Huge posters showed his face in the biggest footballing cities in the world, and a special pair of boots was designed for him with two stars and the inscription 'The hand of God' and the date 22 June 1986. This marketing approach was not to everybody's taste in the squad – too much noise for a youngster, some felt.

In any case, Leo had only just made the World Cup squad. After injuring himself against Chelsea in March, he suffered another setback in April and Rijkaard did not think he was fit enough to play in the Champions League final in May. He certainly wasn't match fit, but he didn't want to travel to Germany just to make up the numbers. He wanted to help, even offer something that, in truth, he had no right to expect at his age, and with his physical limitations.

Some days before setting off for Germany in a combined match between the national side and Under 20s at the Monumental Stadium, Pekerman played him in the last half hour of the game to see how he performed after his 79 days out. It was a way of loosening him up: the coach could see that anxiety was building up. He finished the match and he seemed okay, the manager thought. Leo quickly made his way to the tunnel with his head down. And he started to cry. 'Have you injured yourself again? What is wrong, Leo?' the medical staff asked him. Messi shook his head – that wasn't it, that wasn't the problem. He hid the tension and remained silent. And then, with a gesture of despair, he came out with it. An inconsolable Leo shouted, 'I'm a disaster, I can't play like this!' It was his pride talking, the need to be on top form before the World Cup. Leo and his eternal discontent.

As part of his baptism, very clear rules as to who was in charge of the squad were established. In a pre-World Cup press conference in Nuremberg with Roberto Ayala and Gabriel Heinze, an innocuous question (How does the group pass the time?) culminated in a diatribe against the new young players. 'They don't say much', 'They don't come and drink *mate*', 'They're always on their PlayStations', 'Our generation has another way of doing things'. The strong group in the dressing room had not readily accepted the call-up of Oscar Ustari, Leo's friend, which had made him the youngest ever Argentinian goalkeeper to be selected for a World Cup. This had been in preference to German Lux, the River Plate goalkeeper who had won the 2004 Olympic title, keeping a clean sheet in the process, resulting in him being called up for every match in the previous three years.

According to the Argentinian press there was an incident before the tournament that, reading between the lines, confirmed Leo would find it difficult to impress his new colleagues so early on in his career. In a training session, Messi nutmegged Heinze. In the unwritten code of Argentinian football, something like that had to be avenged: Heinze continually went in hard on Leo. But he was in for a surprise; rather than apologise, 'the Flea' looked him straight in the eye and gave him a warning: 'Don't do that to me again.'

The 18-year-old boy, who at times seemed 25 on the pitch and 14 off it, was going to be part of a World Cup squad. 'We each had a room with a connecting door in between,' remembers Ustari. 'One day, I went into mine and he followed me in. There were two beds in each room and he said: "you're not going to sleep here on your own and me over there, in another room, on my own." So he slept in my room. And constantly, at all hours of the day, he would play keepy-uppies. With anything. With a tea bag! I would carry *mate* around in little round balls and he would do dozens of kick-ups with them. At three o'clock in the morning! They gave him two little footballs and he was there in bed leaning back against the headboard slowly kicking both the balls in the air, bang, bang, bang. With both footballs at the same time!'

And he would play on the PlayStation every day. 'In the training camp in Germany I saw that he would take all the children of the other players to his room to play on the PlayStation, four- and five-year-olds, Crespo's sons,' remembers 'Professor' Salorio. 'I'd look at him and ... one day I saw that he was giving them sweets, they were all around him.'

And that's how he arrived at the greatest show on earth. The World Cup. The one he had dreamed of winning for Argentina.

Javier Saviola and Hernán Crespo were the two forwards selected to start against the Ivory Coast.

Pekerman did not play him, and a 2–1 win was a good start even though the performance was far from brilliant.

Serbia and Montenegro were up next.

Maradona came down to the dressing room to greet the lads and, taking Leo to one side, said to him, 'have strength, courage and score a goal'.

A packed stadium in Gelsenkirchen saw him come on against Serbia in the seventy-fifth minute in place of Maxi Rodríguez with the scoreboard reading 3–0, already reflecting the superiority of the sky-blue and whites who were making the most of the speed and efficiency of their side. His World Cup debut. And at a younger age than Maradona.

In the 16 minutes that he was on the pitch he provided Crespo with an assist to make it 4–0 before scoring the sixth and final goal himself, to make it 6–0 – the only goal he has so far scored for his country in the World Cup finals. Maradona rose to his feet to give him an emotional salute from the stands.

A draw in their next match saw Argentina, together with Holland, through to the next round. The result benefited both teams, and when things are destined to end a certain way, that's generally what happens. Both sides had made several changes to their starting line-ups. Leo started up front alongside Carlos Tévez. Argentina showed, in the words of ESPN, 'a little bit of Leo, and a lot of Tévez' – occasional sparks from the start, and a smattering of dribbles and daring as the game progressed.

But for last 16 against Mexico, Saviola and Crespo were once again the front two picked by Pekerman. Leo came on in the eighty-fourth minute of a hard game with the score 1-1. Argentina won after extra time. 'With an open heart, with a suffering ravaging their whole bodies, with a soul that was full of hope and expectation, with sparks of intelligence, with other footballing acts of bravado, Argentina continued along the path, and now look ahead to Germany in the quarter-finals,' *El Clarín* reported the following morning in typically gushing style. Leo showed flashes of brilliance with a direct style of play that pushed Mexico onto the back foot.

The match was played on Leo's birthday. And also on Riquelme's, who was nine years older. That night Leo retired to his room but decided to call in on his team-mate's party. He opened his bedroom door, walked in and Riquelme turned around to him, irritated: 'Idiot! Don't you know how to knock! You're going to have to learn how to knock on a door! Who the fuck do you think you are?' A pale Messi lowered his head, turned around and left. And so the learning process continued.

'Look, we all saw him as a player who was already different, let's say.' So says Javier Mascherano. 'You could see him and, of course … He turned nineteen at the World Cup, but you could already see he was a footballer who did things differently.'

Messi wasn't in the starting line-up for the quarter-final against Germany because Saviola and Crespo continued in that role. He sat on the bench with his headphones on.

No one talks about whether Leo should have been in the starting line-up or not. It's what happened during the game that is still talked about today.

Argentina dominated possession during the first half and also for part of the second without really creating any great danger.

Until Ayala put his side ahead with a header from a corner.

The host nation had to push up and by pressuring high up the pitch hoped to regain possession and hurt Argentina. As a result there was a great deal of space behind their four defenders who were not especially fast.

And then, suddenly, over a nine-minute period, a World Cup was lost.

The goalkeeper Roberto Abbondanzieri got injured. Pekerman was forced to make a change. On came Leo Franco.

Cambiasso replaced an angry Riquelme.

Pekerman apologised to Juan Román. He was looking to refresh the midfield.

There was one change left. A quick player could do a lot of damage. That's what they're all saying now. Hindsight is a wonderful thing.

Pekerman thought that at that moment what was needed was a tall striker, one who could complement Tévez and hold the ball up, a very useful recourse when a team is under the sort of pressure that Germany were applying. And his presence would also work as a weapon to defend, to avoid the greatest German danger: set pieces.

There were 11 minutes remaining.

Julio Cruz, a physically imposing forward, came on for Hernán Crespo.

Messi stayed on the bench. Recognising that he wasn't going to get on, he removed his boots. He was criticised for that.

It is said, and written, that it will never really be understood why Pekerman chose not to bring him on. There's talk about group dynamic and hierarchies. That it was a divided squad. That Julio Cruz carried more weight in the squad at the time, and that he was part of the group who were in charge in the dressing room. Even that it is a secret the coach will take to his grave.

It seems that, in truth, people don't want to listen to Pekerman. As always happens, defeat removed his right to an audience.

Such decisions are not taken for one reason only, and neither are they made because of political considerations. Would it have been talked about if Klose hadn't scored a minute after Crespo had been substituted, to make it 1–1, or if, after extra time, Ayala and Cambiasso hadn't missed their penalties in the shoot-out? Would Messi removing his boots have been talked about? Do you see how defeat causes confusion, how thin the line is separating victory from failure?

'They all criticise us for the substitution – we were winning 1–0 and we didn't put Leo on,' says Hugo Tocalli, Pekerman's assistant. 'If the match were to be repeated, we would do exactly the same. Let's not forget that in the previous game we were drawing 1–1 and Messi and Aimar came on. That's to say we were neither capricious nor anti-Messi.'

With hindsight, the decision can be seen as an injustice, overlooking the fact that here was a 19-year-old boy who had only played 122 minutes in the World Cup and had only recently returned from injury. Hindsight forgets that he was not then the same Messi that he is today.

'These are decisions that coaches make, but there was a lot of debate in Argentina,' Mascherano explains. 'That is the typical debate generated by sportsmen as great as Messi. But after that World Cup the debate ended. Leo was unquestionably an automatic starter after that.'

Gerardo Salorio was a member of Pekerman's technical team at that World Cup and he has no doubts: 'He didn't play because the coach, in the tenth of a second that he has to decide, stuck with the conviction that he had from the first twenty minutes of the game: that the only way they were going to score against us was with a header. And that's why he put Cruz on, mostly to defend. The injury to our goalkeeper killed us, otherwise Leo would have come on and possibly affected the game in the last fifteen minutes. The Germans were physically dead ...but anyway ... it wasn't our destiny.'

Back in the dressing room, Leo cried. He wasn't the only one. Argentina seemed to have the look of champions, but ... With these 'buts' are written the histories of all the world's national teams.

And the boots? 'I'm strange, sometimes I prefer being alone ... I do stupid things, but I don't handle my pain depending on whether I play or not. Sometimes I'm fucked. I suffer as a footballer. I know that they were saying that I didn't feel the pain of our elimination. It looks like I don't feel anything, that I'm made of stone and that I don't have the right to suffer in my own way' [Leo, July, 2006].

Afterwards, Messi would not watch any more games in the tournament.

But he was grateful. He did not forget that Claudio Vivas, coach Pekerman and his assistant Hugo Tocalli had launched a plan some two years earlier for him to play in the sky-blue and white of his country. 'I thought I was going to play more. I lost ground with my injury and got there just in time. I will always be thankful to Pekerman for taking me [Leo in 2009].'

He had just made his debut in the World Cup and he took that home with him. That and the pain of a national defeat that, thirteen years after the last major title, the Copa América of 1993, still left an open wound.

Argentina arrived at the Copa América the following year in Venezuela as favourites with Leo Messi as a fixture in the starting line-up. He played all 90 minutes of the opening match against the United States (4–1) alongside an in-form Crespo, who scored a brace. The Flea's' spark and quality were acknowledged by reporters. In the second match against Colombia he once again started, was fouled for a penalty which was converted to make it 1–1, and helped create the second (scored by Riquelme) in an emphatic *albiceleste* 4–2 victory. With passage to the next round secured, Leo was rested from the start and Paraguay were narrowly beaten; he played the last 25 minutes.

Messi scored the second goal in the quarter-final against Peru which ended in a convincing 4–0 win. He scored against Mexico in the semi-finals (3–0) and it was not just any goal.

He picked the ball up in the right-hand corner of the penalty area where the centre-back was waiting for him, and as soon as he entered the box he chipped the ball over the waiting goalkeeper in the six-yard box. He had no right to invent that finish; the conditions were not suited to that goal.

'Only geniuses are capable of finishing as Messi did. They should have had to close the stadium after that,' coach Coco Basile, who had replaced Pekerman, said that day.

In the space of two years, Messi was an Under 20 World Cup winner, a World Cup debutant and Copa América finalist against a Brazil side that had arrived at the competition with many second-string players (Ronaldinho and Kaká stayed at home) and Robinho as their star player. The *cariocas* had reached the final thanks to individual brilliance and despite uninspired collective performances, and almost nobody backed them. After an almost 15-year drought, it seemed that the *albiceleste* could win a title.

But Argentina were comprehensively beaten 3–0.

Olé summed up the country's feelings in four sentences: 'We did not deserve an end like that. Everyone had fallen in love with our team but they broke our hearts against Brazil. After the shock, Basile must shuffle things around and start over. A cycle was ended in Venezuela.'

The team, lacking in cohesion, lived off its leading figures but had died with them. But, as the Argentinian newspaper stated, it was damaged by expectations that bordered on excessive: 'Riquelme was not Zidane; nor was Messi Maradonita'. Leo was forgiven because of his age and rank, but harsh criticism was aimed at Riquelme, who some included in the resultant criticism.

Juan Román Riquelme, leader of the generation that won the Under 20 World Cup in 1997, had been entrusted with the task of being the saviour of the homeland. But he started to decline fatally in that Copa América. Riquelme was known as '*Tristelme*' (a play on his name and *triste*, meaning sad). He fought, on and off the pitch, to maintain his status and quit his role as protector of the new star, Leo. If, in truth, he ever had been: the central midfielder is of the opinion that you have to pay your dues, you have to start very close to the bottom, no matter how much Julio Grondona hugs you, as he used to hug Leo – Riquelme himself only ever received a handshake from the president of the federation. On speaking about Barcelona, Riquelme always mentioned the importance of Xavi and especially Iniesta, 'the genius'. Note the lack of recognition for Leo. Riquelme was suffering with the rise of 'the Flea'.

Messi felt that the path to leadership was narrow and Riquelme was blocking his way. But he did not demand anything: and things were going to get much worse before he put all his efforts into creating a more harmonious national team.

Riquelme was given his last chance at the Beijing Olympics the following year.

In Argentina the period that started in 2008 with the defeat against Chile in the World Cup 2010 qualifying stage, and left the *albiceleste* seven points behind leaders Paraguay, is known as 'the decline'. Something broke at that time and the gold medal at the Beijing Olympics with an Under 23 team was no compensation.

Summer 2008 was extremely tense in the Messi household. Leo wanted to go to the Olympics but Barcelona tried, initially, to deny him that opportunity, because it clashed with the Champions League qualifying round that the club had to win, thanks to their disastrous third-place finish the previous season. The Court of Arbitration for Sport (CAS) granted Barça legal authority to decide Leo's future with regard to the Games and Joan Laporta wanted Messi, who had joined the national team to prepare for the tournament, to return to the club tour in the United States and not miss the vital match against Wisła Kraków: one slip and Barcelona would be out of the main European competition.

'People were saying that he was not going to come with us,' remembers Oscar Ustari, reserve goalkeeper in that Under 23 team. 'He said to me: "don't worry, I'm going to do everything possible to come."'

Guardiola, having just arrived as coach at Barcelona, had, with the departure of Ronaldinho and Deco, decided to make Leo Messi the focal point of the team, but during a phone call with him from his New York hotel he realised just how complicated a month 'the Flea' had had. Up to that point, Leo had always made himself available to the club, but in that conversation Messi, who was relying on the fact that Pep had been a player himself, and would understand him, asked him not to insist on his return. 'Play in the Olympics and win the gold medal,' Pep told him. In the ensuing press conference, Guardiola admitted to having noticed 'a lot of emotional tension. I saw that he was very uncomfortable with the situation – it was not a good idea to bring him back, his head was in Beijing.'

Argentina, with Mascherano, Leo, Kun Agüero, and Riquelme as one of the over 23-year-olds allowed to play, were defending their gold medal won at Athens, and they did so successfully. And with Messi as the first name on the team sheet. They won every single game (1–0 in the final against Nigeria) without conceding a goal. Messi scored twice and was involved in five of the others.

That Olympic tournament is remembered for three things.

For something that was witnessed: a very public hug between Ronaldinho, with socks rolled down and a vacant gaze, and Leo, which lasted more than 30 seconds after the historic 3–0 *albiceleste* victory over Brazil in the semi-finals. It was the symbolic representation of the passing over of the baton at Barcelona.

Also for something that was not widely witnessed, but remained etched in the memory of those who did see it. Ustari explains: 'It was amazing to see Kobe Bryant going to say hello to my friend, not to the famous Lionel Messi, but to my friend Leo! "Kobe Bryant is going up to that lucky sod!" I was saying. This is what happened: we went into the dining hall, I was filming and saying: "well, we have one or two of the best players in the world", and just then Román [Riquelme] and Leo came out, and I filmed them. And I continued, "we can also see the world's best in basketball". Kobe was still a fair few feet away and I was pointing the camera at him. And I saw him walking towards us, and my hand and camera start shaking! Leo took everything calmly, well, in reality he didn't know what to do. He seemed embarrassed about him [Bryant] coming over, he couldn't believe it. And we took a photo with him, of course.'

And, thirdly, for something that was not seen, but felt. 'There was a momentous change from the Under 20 World Cup to the Olympics, with the World Cup in between,' continues Ustari. 'Everyone our age changed. Given Leo's trustworthy and likeable nature, he was already becoming a leader.' So, what was going to happen to Riquelme?

The transition towards Leo's Argentina began that year. 'The Flea' would return to Barcelona grateful to his new coach, and with the boost of new success with the national team.

He was now on the springboard.

The 'decline' of the national team would continue in 2008, and put Coco Basile's position in danger. In a calculated initiative to pile pressure on the coach, Maradona singled Leo out as the culprit for the team's poor performances. With the attitude of those who believe they are always right, he created a general mistrust of Messi in the minds of the average Argentine fans, who took Maradona's word as gospel.

Argentina had just drawn 1–1 with Peru and Maradona had something to say about that. 'Sometimes, Messi plays for Messi. He has so much arrogance that he forgets about his team-mates,' he said in a telephone conversation on Fox Sports. 'It is FC Messi. If he were to play more with Agüero or Riquelme, opposition defenders would have more to worry about. Matches are not won by attacking every time you have the ball, but by knowing how to attack. And you have to work on that.'

However, other players, argued Diego, deserved the fans' affection. 'I hope he is better than me, but just now Mascherano is more important to Argentina than Riquelme and Lionel. And the team has to look after Tévez much more – all he is asking for is security. Not the captaincy or anything extraordinary. That insecurity leads him to do more than he actually can manage and he is all over the place.'

'Leo lacks character,' he had said previously, suggesting that Messi had not put up enough of a fight against Barcelona in their pre-Olympics conflict with the Argentine Football Association. In reality, Messi had fought, but without announcing it openly to the media. What was Maradona up to? Surely he was only too aware of the pressure associated with wearing the sky-blue and white shirt and conscious that Messi was only 21 at the time?

These were Maradona's thoughts at the start of the close season: Messi would be subject to criticism, even before maturing in the national team. A negative image of Messi was now being created and as far as most critics were concerned it would only become positive if he won matches on his own. And a World Cup, if possible. Just as Maradona had done. An enormous task.

Leo and his family were hurt by those words. After another long journey from Buenos Aires, where he had played for the national side, Leo answered in his own way on his arrival at Barcelona airport: 'I'm used to Diego speaking out. We all know what he is like.'

There was a theory doing the rounds at the Argentine Football Association: some day, so as to silence Maradona's continual criticism, the best thing to do would be to make him coach of the *albiceleste*. If he was successful, fantastic. If he wasn't, he would have nothing more to say. The mistakes and bad results in the 2010 World Cup qualifying campaign caused Basile to resign from the national team after a defeat against Chile, and in autumn 2008 *el Pelusa*, Maradona, was appointed coach of Argentina.

Little more than a year after the Maradona-esque goals (the one against Getafe, of course, but also that handball against Espanyol), Maradona himself, having acquired no coaching badges and with a grand total of three victories in his two stints as manager with Mandiyú and Racing Club in the Nineties, was about to find himself on the same pitch as his heir apparent.

One of the new coach's first tasks was to try to fit Messi's talent into the squad, something he had never previously considered when criticising him from the sidelines. Some aspects of his game were certainly starting to cause concern: his disconnection with the midfield, his lack of alternatives for releasing the ball, the few passes that he received and his insistence on making an individual run when there was a lack of support. The team had to improve, but so did Messi's decisions and performances.

Maradona, who needed some good results and as quickly as possible in order to get Argentina's qualifying campaign back on track, had one thing in his favour: Leo, now free of those who, consciously or otherwise, had prevented him from blossoming at Barcelona, was playing his best football under the team's new coach, Pep Guardiola. Maradona's job was to create the right sort of atmosphere with Argentina so that Messi could make a similar impact with the national team.

They had two years together, Diego and Leo, to get it right, with all eyes on the World Cup in South Africa in 2010.

So began Leo's trial before the Argentine public. Although Carlitos Tévez was the 'village player', more popular than Leo at home in Argentina, Messi had officially become the saviour of the homeland.

– *Pelé and Maradona were the best footballers in history. When you see them play, is there anything that makes you say 'Wow! he does this or that so well'?*

– *The thing is they were good at everything. I haven't seen many videos of Pelé, Di Stéfano or Cruyff. On the other hand I've seen everything Maradona did, I even managed to see him play live when I was a kid.*

– *Seriously?*

– *Yes, as a kid. I don't remember any of it, but I have been told I saw him on his Newell's debut against Emelec.*

– *Of course, it was in 1993, you were six.*

– *Yes.*

(A video of Maradona looking at the camera appears and he says: 'Leo, you know that I love you a lot, let the others do the talking, you're going to be the best player in history. We will decide that when you hang up your boots. Today carry on doing what you're doing and I hope you're happy with your family. I love you a lot, Leo')

– *It's good, isn't it? That you have the relationship you have with*

Diego. Because everyone wants to believe you don't get on.

– *We do, and when he was the national coach, we were the clos-est we have ever been. I saw him after the match against Real Madrid. I was in a bad state after the way the match had gone, but seeing him was a joy. I really cheered him up, too. I hadn't seen him in a long time. But you won't hear me say anything against him.*

– *He watched the game in Cristiano's box, a bit strange, but know-ing what Diego is like …*

– *I found out afterwards, I read it somewhere, but it doesn't matter.*

(Leo Messi, interview with Martín Souto, TyC Sports, March 2013)

Leo's father took his six-year-old son to the Newell's Old Boys stadium to enjoy the performance of a declining Diego Maradona who was preparing for the 1994 World Cup. The club organised a friendly against Emelec of Ecuador and, as on other occasions, Leo was asked to come onto the pitch to do keepy-uppies with a ball that seemed twice the size of the one the adults were using. 'No problem, I would love to do it,' he told his father when he suggested it to him. He did not feel nervous or under pressure. People were shouting at him 'Maradooo, Maradooo'.

But Leo does not remember any of that. He remembers scoring goals for Grandoli at the age of four. But nothing about the Emelec day. Maradona was Jorge Messi's idol (he kept videos of him, which he would play now and then) and that of his generation, a venera-tion which continued with the next generation of supporters. And the next, and the next.

'Leo told me a story which explains everything,' Cristina Cubero says. 'I asked him about Diego and he told me: "I get it that you don't understand the Maradona phenomenon. For Argentines he is much more than a footballer, and since I was little, I would go to my cousins' on both sides of the family and the first thing we would do would be to sit down and watch the goals against England. I have grown up watching his goals on tape. Our greeting to each other would be: let's go and watch Maradona's goals."'

So, from an early age, Messi was introduced to the football world of heroes and villains and epic victories.

And of legendary goals that were recorded on old video tapes.

Just like the dribble through the English defence at the World Cup in Mexico which, as sociologist Eduardo Archetti says, was the perfect Argentinian goal, with the mixture of park pitches (the freedom to create) and the audacity of kids: 'It was an unusual goal, almost romantic, which does not belong to our much more rational era.'

'When the ball went in I instantly knew that it would be a case of before that goal and after that goal for Maradona,' Jorge Valdano told the magazine *Jotdown*. 'And I actually told him in the shower: "That's it, you are now occupying the same throne as Pelé." And then he started explaining some of the play. I always say, jokingly, that it was me who retrieved the ball from the back of the net. Nobody thinks anything of that. I ran to give him the ball; after the goal I felt I had to do something useful rather than just hug him.'

Valdano, a sharp observer and analyst, believes that Maradona solved a problem for Argentina in what was one of their worst performances, 'the only one that, without doubt, we would not have won without Diego'. It was also a symbolically charged match due to the proximity, time-wise, to the Falklands War. 'That day Maradona, through strength of personality and his footballing genius, became the new General San Martín,' concludes Valdano, in reference to one of the liberators of Spanish South America.

Argentinians had found their hero, albeit one who would later be revealed as a tragic figure, full of imperfections, all of them shown on television. And they loved it. Without knowing it, Leo Messi, while he was doing little tricks on the pitch, was setting out on the road towards the same footballing destiny as Maradona, who would become, at different points, his travelling companion, his nemesis, a mirror, a demanding voice, light and shadow on his path.

The first time Leo and Diego spoke was in 2005, the first big year of Messi's career, just after his first goal against Albacete. Leo was at home having lunch when he received that call on his mobile phone. 'Congratulations,' Diego had said to him. He told him that he had been following him for a few games, that he looked good, had a bright future, and that he should continue scoring.

There was another chat on the phone soon after: following Brazil's elimination from the Under 20 World Cup, a journalist from *La Gazzetta dello Sport* who was in Holland passed him his mobile.

'What are you doing, monster?' Diego said to him. Leo made a request: 'I hope we can meet face-to-face one day.'

Diego and Leo arranged to meet in August, to take part in *La Noche del 10*, the television programme that Maradona presented on Canal 13.

Messi arrived at the studio very early and sat in a room with his father, uncle and a cousin.

'It was the first time in my life that I was nervous,' he said some years after. 'That night I had my head in the clouds, my hands were sweating. Suddenly the door opened and Diego appeared. He said a couple of things to me. My chest felt like it would explode.'

Leo told Diego that his mother's dream was that he would one day manage her son. 'The number ten will come to you naturally,' Maradona told him.

On his programme, Diego used to play football tennis. On that occasion, it would be an encounter of four of the best Latin American players ever. On one side the old guard, represented by Francescoli and Maradona. On the other, the heirs to the throne: Messi and Tévez. The first to ten were the winners.

It started out as a friendly game, but the tension and tempo soon increased. Leo's hands were no longer sweating, he was competing. A point was argued over, the rules were debated. By Tévez and Diego. Leo and Francescoli watched it from a distance, not getting involved.

Not a single point was given away. Nobody wanted to lose. But one team had to.

When the score was level at seven all, Tévez complained that the opposition had stolen a point. The score was changed. The youngsters were ahead.

Everyone made mistakes; something much more than a game of football tennis was at stake.

In the end, Leo and Tévez beat Maradona and Francescoli 10–6. Diego's only loss in the whole series.

On returning to Barcelona, Messi could not stop talking about it. 'Yeeees! For me, when I saw him, wow, the best, it was a dream come true. Really amazing,' he kept repeating.

'Messi always has to be Messi,' said Maradona at the time. But not everybody was prepared to let that happen.

When Leo heard that he had been anointed 'the Successor' (with a capital S) he would say: 'It is an honour for me to hear that, but I have only just started out. There is only one Diego and there will never be another, and I try to mark my path and keep on growing.' However, footballing opinion all over the world differed as to how good Messi really was in comparison to Maradona. Many journalists, some of them with considerable influence on the choice of internationals and on public opinion, could not accept the existence of a new god. 'Ah, in Europe they don't hit him, they don't go hard in on him,' some would say. The doubts about Leo gradually increased, in parallel with poor performances from Maradona's Argentina team, which was struggling to qualify for the World Cup in South Africa.

As has been explained, it is no coincidence that a player who could rival Maradona in terms of hero-worship emerged in Argentina. For that to happen a decade after his retirement sounds like a Hollywood movie, but you had to choose between one and the other – that is how Argentinian society works. 'We Argentines are fanatical about countless things,' says Quique Domínguez. 'If it is about one club, we do not accept anything from the others. We are fanatical about a religion and do not tolerate others, we are fanatical about our city, and so on ... And we have to decide to be with Leo or with Diego.'

Instead of enjoying two extraordinary talents, the country started to squabble about who was the best. To be honest, though, it is not just an Argentinian thing: there really does not seem to be room in the world for more than one legend.

'If it is all about success, Di Stéfano never won a World Cup. Nor did Cruyff, and then you have Pelé, who never played [club football] in Europe. If Maradona had been Brazilian and Pelé had been Argentinian, who would have been considered the best in the world in Argentina?'

(Fernando Signorini)

It is obvious that when people talk about who is the best footballer in history, they are not really talking about football – or not just about football. Leo and Diego, debutants for their respective clubs at a very young age, both with scintillating left feet, are two number

1os who have worn the captain's armband for the national team. They are footballers who have defined their eras and on whom Argentinians have pinned their hopes of World Cup success. They are also an excuse for a debate, Argentinians' main preoccupation. Every country needs its stars but the first problem arises with the definition of the word 'star': a brilliant player, for Argentinians, is more attractive if he possesses an 'innate talent', one that emerges as if by magic and which he uses to reach 'impossible' targets that, tragically, will end up condemning him. Messi represents hard work, sacrifice and compromise with his profession and his body; but it is difficult for him to be accepted as a star because, as well as all this, he has a public image (the one he has chosen) that offers little evidence of verbal imagination and a private life that is secluded and free from drama.

Being the best is not enough to be considered the best. 'Messi is a poster, Maradona is a flag,' wrote Argentine writer Hugo Asch in an article ironically entitled 'Messi, the foreigner'.

Maradona displays the characteristics of an astute, streetwise Latin. Messi has also scored a goal with his hand but over 90 minutes, over a season, that Latin guile seldom appears. With the ball, like Diego he always has a trick up his sleeve, but he does not look to bend the rules to his own advantage.

Messi is too correct and proper in a country that is attracted to and even demands the incorrect way. People's fascination with him ends as soon as he crosses the touchline towards the dressing room; he is then no longer a part of their world. While Messi's succinctness makes the majority of his interviews dispensable, Maradona has no filter. He likes to draw a red line under any topic for discussion, to place himself on one side and point out the enemy on the other. He manipulates verbs with mastery and has a dynamic use of the language, drawing expressions from the streets ('suck it', 'the hand of God', 'they chopped me down'). He came out with the line that Sergio Batista (his replacement as national coach) 'will have to dress up as Piñón Fijo [an Argentinian clown and singer-songwriter] to make Messi happy'.

Sometimes his posturing suggests that he needs the media more than they need him. That is why he called up a magazine programme from the United Arab Emirates to clear up a few personal issues. A journalist friend went to see him at the Chenot Clinic (in Switzerland) where he was trying to lose weight. They had been walking in numerous streets without anyone stopping them and the friend remarked about this to him. 'It's marvellous, isn't it?' Maradona's reply sums it all up: 'one more block, and I'll die.'

'Diego was really explosive, and that converted him into an informative, permanent consumer product, on and off the pitch,' Jorge Valdano says in *Jotdown*. 'I went to visit him once in Naples and it was like a non-stop carnival. He would leave his house in his car and twenty or thirty boys on motorbikes were waiting for him downstairs. They would go with him, some would overtake and repeatedly shout '*Arriva Maradona!*', and then the shopkeeper would come out, the guy at the bar, too ... Every day, situations would arise which could only happen to a character like Maradona. I cannot imagine a similar episode with Messi in Barcelona.'

Leo's only remotely political statement was to defend the Catalan language, but Diego showed himself to be anti-authority while he played (with strong words against the Vatican or right-wing politicians). He was the spokesman for the man on the street without a voice, although he later ended up being a friend of the country's then president, Carlos Menem, and of Cuba's Fidel Castro, showing one of his many contradictions that suggest an unstable personality: it is one thing to be a rebel, but another to be constantly searching for a path to follow. It is like being in the middle of everything and a part of nothing.

Maradona's very defects became virtues in the eyes of his adoring fans. 'All that converted him into a terrible, reflective surface of the Argentines; not of what we Argentines are, but of what we want to believe we are: creative in the face of adversity, spontaneous, heroic, passionate ...' says Eduardo Sacheri.

Diego is so Argentinian, typically Argentinian some would say. Messi has been called 'the foreigner' even though, paradoxically, he is, according to Cristina Cubero, the most Argentinian of the Argentinian footballers who have lived in Barcelona. That tends to be the personal drama of every immigrant – unaccepted at home and an alien abroad.

Diego Maradona has said that he went out into the street, he was kicked and taken to the top – and with nobody to tell him what he had to do to live at those heights. Instead of people looking after him, he had to look after lots of them. Leo has always been protected.

Maradona was educated on the street, in Villa Fiorito, surrounded by his brothers, on streets where the one who succeeds is the strongest, the most macho, although the poor districts (*villa miserias*) of the more affluent Seventies were not the abandoned shantytowns of the Nineties, where, for instance, Carlos Tévez grew up to the sounds of gunfire. Still, Messi is a city boy and Maradona, will always be a *villa miseria* boy, a shantytown boy. And the one from a shantytown always carries with him the misunderstood ambition to want to show the world that he was not born in one.

Leo left Argentina not because he wanted to, but because the crisis at the time forced his family to look for a way out. However, young Maradona's Argentina was, as well as being more colourful, fiercely protectionist, and this allowed Diego to stay at home, at Argentinos Juniors and subsequently Boca Juniors until 1982. The player who reaches the top league and then leaves to conquer Europe is admired. But in order to gain the status of national hero, Maradona needed the 1986 World Cup – it was a source of joy for a country waiting for Paradise, scarred by dictatorship and the devalued austral (the former monetary unit of Argentina).

And afterwards Maradona's story was seen as the 'attractive' tragedy of the hero's rise and fall. 'In that sense, for our history and our personality, Maradona represents us better. He doesn't put us in a good light, but he represents us better,' says sociologist Sergio Levinsky. Maradona loves living life on the edge, challenging death. Messi, on the other hand, embraces life, he challenges it.

In an age in which the loudmouths who react to everything are praised and those who sit in the corner patiently doing puzzles are disregarded, it is normal that Diego is spoken about in such laudable terms. And that is why he has a religion – the Church of Maradona. Leo will not have even a small crypt. Let's hear from Jorge Valdano talking to *Jotdown*: 'It is not at all easy being Maradona. I went to Bariloche, Argentina, recently, and I found myself with a flag with Che Guevara, Evita, Gardel and Maradona on it. Of course, if you are dead you get away with it, but being a living legend is a real burden.'

If Messi is *cumbia* (his favourite music), Maradona is Latin rock (Charly García, Javier Calamaro), melancholic and excessively sweet pop (Pimpinela) and *cuartetazo* (Rodrigo) – complex, then, with many faces.

In any case, neither is tango, the glum music of the loss, the absences, often the song of the defeated who wallows in defeat. Although Messi had to create a Rosario in Barcelona to survive, he does not miss a better life or a love. Only a space.

But to go back to the flag Valdano speaks about: that is Argentina for most Argentinians, so Diego does not need to show where he is from. Messi needed to give signs of it; he has been asked to become a bit more like Maradona. But Leo, the Catalan in Argentina and the Argentinian in Catalonia, was not always going to be asking permission to be an Argentinian. In fact, he was getting more and more pissed off with every defeat and piece of personal criticism.

Since Leo burst onto the scene, decades of Argentinian frustration have been thrust upon him. Even though he won trophies with his club and individual titles, he was expected to win a World Cup in order to be accepted by his country. And, if he failed in the attempt, it will forever be said, 'You see, we knew it! He is no Maradona.'

'It is almost impossible to fight a religious icon,' as Jorge Valdano says. Leo, it must be said, has never tried to.

'I've got a theory about him, although it isn't based on any scientific fact. I think Messi is a one-off in the history of humanity, because he is actually capable of having a football inside his foot. They always said that Maradona had the ball stuck to his foot but Messi seems to have it inside his foot and that is scientifically inexplicable, but when you see seven, eleven, twenty-two rivals all trying and failing to get the ball off him, you must admit it has to be because of that.'

(Eduardo Galeano)

'Leo or Diego? They're different eras as well. Diego's was from the era of man-marking.'

(Carlos Bilardo)

'Leo, from a physical point of view, is a model of athleticism with blistering acceleration. He has twists and turns like a Scalextric. He has the latest generation braking system and peripheral vision. I also

*think that through his windscreen he can see behind without even
turning around. So has Diego. They are exceptional cases, rarities.
A doctor friend of mine told me that Diego would have made an
excellent war pilot because of his capacity to see the whole picture.
And what's more, the precision of timing to put time and distance
together. Between the two of them they could have formed a spectacular force. You need to look at their DNA to see if they have the
butterfly gene in their legs because they, like the butterfly, seem to
have the sense of taste in their feet. And a very good taste.*

(Fernando Signorini)

And on the pitch, what unites them and what separates them?

'Football-wise, they have nothing in common,' says Hugo Tocalli.
'Maradona was the conductor. Leo isn't. They played in different
positions – Messi is more of a player for the last third. And they are
from two distinct eras.' The role of the number 10 reflects the differences in football between the Eighties and today and goes a long
way towards explaining what makes them different.

Thirty years ago the number 10 was a symbolic figure, the conductor of the orchestra who gradually disappeared from the centre,
before being seen in the 4-4-2 system that became all the rage, either
situated on the wing, becoming a second forward off the main one,
or dropping back as a defensive midfielder in front of the back four.
It ceased to have the importance that it had had before, and the
game suffered as a result. Then, with Pep Guardiola and the Spanish side, it reappeared but in a position further up the pitch, in its
latest evolution: the target man disappeared and was replaced by a
false nine.

With much tighter, more together and more physical defences,
the Maradona-like player who orchestrated things from the midfield can no longer exist. The centre of the action, the engine room
of the team, moved closer to the box, in that position known as
mediapunta in Spanish, or 'in the hole', from where the major influence on attacking play occurs today. Maradona would have been a
Messi if he were to break through today. We'll have to see if Leo,
when he begins to lose his pace, can drop back and convert himself
into the type of organiser that Maradona was. Many feel that this
might be how he will evolve.

The statistics favour Leo: at the age of 25 he had already won 21 titles compared to Maradona's five (Pelé had won 18, including two World Cups). Leo passed the 311 club appearances and 34 international goals that Maradona scored before retiring at the age of 38, a long time ago. But that is clearly a reflection of the way they play – Leo spends a lot more time in or around the area than Diego did.

In any case the stats count for little in this particular discussion: 'In the confused comparison as to who is the best, Diego or Leo, Messi appears to be the perfect machine, capable of smashing all possible records, although realistically I don't know if he will ever be able to entertain quite like Maradona.' So says well-known *Olé* journalist Luis Calvano.

As for the rest, this footballing tale is full of common myths. In the 1986 World Cup, so it is said, Maradona won the tournament practically single-handedly without playing in a side better than the Argentina of today. It is repeatedly written that he played for everyone in an eleven bursting with destroyers. The fact is that without Bilardo's defensive system they would not have won the World Cup, and without intelligent players it is impossible to mount any sort of decent system. When Diego wasn't playing well, the team supported him. Similarly, at Napoli and at Italia '90, when Argentina were runners-up, Maradona had a good defensive structure protecting him.

It is said that Barcelona play for Messi. They surround him with eight world champions as well as other extraordinary figures (Eto'o, Ronaldinho, Iniesta, Xavi, Busquets, Villa). But Barcelona without Messi would not have won as much, or as consistently: it would have been a great side but lacking its leading light, the killer, the assassin in the box.

Time for a quick game: put a 25-year-old Maradona in Pep's Barcelona team. Where would he play? Xavi or even Messi now occupies the space taken up by the number 10 of yesteryear. Diego had an explosiveness and skill that would allow him to play further up the pitch. He would bang in the goals. But these days players cover many more miles than in his era and, given his tendency to let himself go physically, he could find it difficult to keep up with the demanding rhythm of a whole season. And now imagine Messi in Maradona's Napoli shirt. Up against those tough defences that opted for man-marking, his intelligence and efficiency would make him the star of the side. But the space, the tactics, even the ball is different, heavier; he may well have found it difficult to elude his rival.

An entertaining, if ultimately pointless, exercise.

'Of Pelé it can be said that he played in an era where footballers didn't move and while I hope Messi takes Argentina to victory in the World Cup, it won't be easy because he is known by everybody. In the last game against Milan they built a cage around him. He is a great lad, but I sincerely believe that I have been the greatest player in the history of the game until now.'

Who said that? You got it – Maradona.

With Diego '*el Pelusa*' Maradona in charge of the national side, a cycle came to an end. Four months after his first appearance as coach, Juan Román Riquelme, the then successful leader of Boca Juniors, retired from the national side claiming that he did not have 'the same codes' or 'the same way of thinking' as the coach. They could not carry on working together. Without actually saying as much, Riquelme was criticising the fact that things had been done badly: he found out on the radio that he was not going to be called up for a friendly, learned on television that Maradona was putting his place in the starting line-up in doubt because of the 'physical problems' that he seemed to be having at his club. 'He's of no use to me like that,' Maradona had said publicly. But in his claims Riquelme was referring to something else: a group of players had received calls from the Maradona camp asking them to create a 'difficult climate' for the then Argentina manager Coco Basile, who had always pro-tected Riquelme. If the conspiracy that the Boca footballer suspected was true, it had worked and now it was affecting him.

The leadership was changing.

With the World Cup a year away, Maradona stopped criticising 'the Flea' and turned his team's attention to the Barcelona star to try to make the most of his talent. Maradona, a man prone to mak-ing public gestures, symbolically offered Leo the number 10 shirt for his first official game as coach against Venezuela, where victory was essential, not just for the purposes of classification but also to give credit to the new order. Leo wanted the emblematic number, but had not asked for it. When he accepted it, he already knew that Maradona had spoken to the captain Javier Mascherano and the veteran Verón about it. Both gave him the okay. 'It would be an honour,' he said in answer to Diego's proposal.

People were dreaming of and speculating about how the two of them would work together and things did indeed start well. 'Seeing Messi like this every day is a pleasure. We should all leave the ground, pay again and come back in,' said Maradona after a convincing 4–0 victory over Venezuela that saw a 21-year-old Messi at the centre of operations: he scored the first goal, provided the assist for the second and made the difference in an attack that included Carlos Tévez and Sergio Agüero. The number 10 shirt that had weighed so heavily on the shoulders of Ariel Ortega, Marcelo Gallardo, Pablo Aimar, Andrés D'Alessandro and Riquelme had a new owner. 'It made me very happy that Diego gave me the number ten. The two shirts that I wore will be for my mother and my brother,' explained Messi at the end of the game. The one that finished up in the hands of Matías Messi is now part of the museum that the city of Rosario is designing in homage to Leo and other sporting stars from the city.

'Román is dead, long live Lionel,' proclaimed the newspaper *El Comercio*.

Long may he live and long may he survive. 'Diego was worried that Leo would get kicked around, it's the biggest worry you have with these kids who are crucial for the team,' explains Signorini. 'Because if you don't have a figure like that in your squad, but rely on six or seven players who play more or less the same, well, one of them gets kicked, you stick on another. But Diego thought, whoa, if they break Leo then you're left with nothing.'

'In August 2009 we went to play a friendly in Russia,' remembers Mascherano, 'and Leo got injured the day before ... and it was like someone had hit Diego over the head with a hammer. Maradona loved Leo. I think more than just love, it was almost like he had been rejuvenated, gone back thirty years, he could see himself in Leo. And anyway, on that day, he was dead. Diego went off by himself to the middle of the pitch while the doctors were checking Leo. And it was only a friendly! Maradona needed Leo.'

After winning the first three games, including the one in Moscow (2–3) that Leo played no part in, Maradona's side was humiliated 6–1 in La Paz by Bolivia which was explained in no small part by the altitude sickness that caused Leo to vomit. Maradona had taken part a year before in a match organised by the Bolivian president, Evo Morales, to call upon FIFA to end a ban on any match played at an altitude of more than 2,750 metres. He therefore let coach Fernando Signorini ('It's like an external doping') and Leo ('Personally, I think it's impossible to play here, even though other players come here and play. Equally this can't be used an excuse for the defeat') explain the difficult conditions the team had faced.

As early in his tenure as then, criticism of the Maradona regime was running deep. 'Never before had he been so associated with football mistakes. He got it grossly wrong in the game plan,' wrote Juan Pablo Varsky in Canchallena.com.

Argentina were not playing well, but the confusing coaching was not helping either. 'Maradona's way was a total mess,' says Cristina Cubero, who regularly attended Argentina matches. 'Maradona was a great footballer but an appalling manager: tactics were never worked on, it was total anarchy. Training sessions were terrible, kickabouts without any corrections, order or organisation. A bit like touchy-touchy; you've seen how I touch the ball, no? Well, do the same.'

Messi was not at his best either. Having been given the responsibility of leading the team, he kept trying too hard, looking too often for the individual move, appearing in the wrong part of the pitch. But not all was lost yet – qualification was still in Argentina's hands.

They scraped past Colombia and lost away to Ecuador, before facing Brazil in Rosario, a request by Messi that was respected. There were four games left and they had to win at least two of them. It was at the Rosario Central ground, the Gigante de Arroyito Stadium, and all his friends and family were there to see him. Brazil won by a comfortable 3–1 scoreline, a result that guaranteed their passage to the South Africa World Cup. The subsequent disapproval that followed showed no respect for past or present idols. Leo and Maradona both copped it. 'In the battle of the "aces", Kaká enjoyed himself and beat Messi,' was the headline in *El Clarín*.

Olé did not believe the Tévez–Messi partnership was working.

'Tévez runs everywhere and clashes with Messi. That is why the Flea gets close to Verón, in a deeper position. And then Mascherano has got no space to distribute the ball. The team is a mess.' Juan Pablo Varsky reflected on most commentators' opinion of Leo: 'They say he is a problem. He doesn't play with anybody apart from Verón. In Barcelona he simply plays, here he is always expected to score the Getafe goal ... He did not play well against Brazil. He wanted the ball but he rarely did what the move demanded. While the 10 of Argentina was playing for his prestige in every ball, the 10 of Brazil [Kaká] did everything in a simple way.'

Another defeat, this time against Paraguay, left Argentina one place below where they needed to be to qualify. *Olé* had warned before the game that 'so far Maradona has got it all wrong, he has not been able to hide his weaknesses as a national coach'. The same mistakes had been appearing regularly and were repeated against Paraguay (wrong tactics, too many players called up, wrong substitutions, inexplicable absences), but the sports newspaper also put the finger of blame on the players: 'It is they who have to help Maradona.'

Messi tried to run at defenders where he didn't have to, didn't keep the ball when it was the best option, was not sure what his role was, and, the worse the team played, the more he got it wrong in his search for the heroic series of dribbles. Leo was evidence that the team was less than the sum of its parts. In Guardiola's historic Barcelona he had a team that strengthened his potential; in Argentina he had to save the side. 'He plays everywhere and plays at nothing. Tévez and him don't pass to each other,' Mdzol.com wrote at the time.

Former national coach César Luis Menotti was more understanding: 'He is not a strategist, he finishes off the strategy. In Argentina, everything is confusion and he is caged in it. Messi, at Barcelona, plays; with the national team, he runs.' Maradona asked him to play as he wanted, but did not create the necessary conditions for Leo's football to shine; in any case, 'the Flea' knew he was failing to help and felt responsible for what was unfolding.

But there was something that was hurting Leo and his family, to the extent that he was losing the hunger to play for his national team – the personal attacks. The online magazine 'Minutouno.com' published an article in October 2009 that explored the reasons for his bad performances and came to some astonishing conclusions. 'The answer could be found in the emotional conflicts in the head of the player. Having left Argentina as a kid, psychologists believe he might feel a possible uprooting and resentment towards his country of origin. "Instead of getting upset with his parents, he takes the distress out on his nation," the psychoanalyst Cristina Carrillo explains. "It is difficult for a child who grew up away from his country to connect amicably with it."' It was 'difficult to defend the *albiceleste* shirt' due to that 'unresolved situation of his childhood'.

Leo knew about what was being written, about these doubts. And they were making him irritable. He felt not just Argentinian, but *very* Argentinian. And yet playing for his country was becoming painful – there was no pleasure in it, only sacrifice as he was being punished by the press and fans, who identified the national team he was leading with failure.

El Clarín's headline after the Paraguay match was excruciating: 'You cannot play any worse, Argentina'. The defeat meant Maradona's cycle was defined by two victories and four defeats, the most negative stats in 25 years. There was only one way out of this mess: they had to beat Peru and Uruguay in the last two qualifying matches.

Martín Palermo scored in injury time, and from an offside position, in torrential rain, when it looked as if Argentina might be out of the World Cup. The referee gave the goal and Maradona threw himself to the ground and slid along the grass on his knees in celebration.

The sky-blue and whites also beat Uruguay. On the pitch of the Centenario Stadium in Montevideo, with a place in South Africa now assured, a completely wired Maradona screamed in the pouring rain 'suck it, and keep on sucking!!' at the press while he hugged technical coach Carlos Bilardo.

The coach wanted his survival to be seen as a job well done, but the media preferred to focus instead on the poor play, the lack of a system, the unjustified changes in the starting eleven that were never repeated, and also on the revolving squad (55 players called up for 13 games). On this occasion Messi was not only criticised for his performance – he was taken to task by fans for not joining in the celebration of Mario Bolatti's winning goal against Uruguay.

In the Messi entourage none of that was easy to deal with. Why so much criticism, so much impatience? It was not just him who had played badly. Was it the challenge to the footballing legend that was Maradona's? Jorge and Celia witnessed a morose 22-year-old Leo days after every call-up to the national squad. He hardly spoke, his conversations with his mother over the internet when he was back in Barcelona were monosyllabic and his father too failed to lift him from his melancholy. At times he walked like an old man, with his shoulders hunched. 'If they carry on busting his balls, we're not going back,' a family member said at one point. No one likes to see their son suffer.

Maradona was very aware of the situation and used press conferences to defend Leo. But he had to go further. Before getting to the World Cup, he needed to speak to Leo alone, to make him feel his support, his love. *El Pelusa* liked to say in his usual witty way that talking to Messi on the phone was 'harder than speaking to Obama', which he later changed to 'harder than speaking to Cristina [Kirchner, Argentina's president]'. Finally he decided to go to Barcelona.

He did so at the end of March 2010, a few months before the start of the World Cup.

Maradona made his way to the training ground to say hello to Pep Guardiola, and later met up with Messi on his own at the Majestic Hotel. Leo listened to Diego and his manager, worried about how the team was playing, took a piece of paper and asked Messi to sketch out a system in which he would feel more comfortable playing. Leo, initially surprised, did nothing at first but Maradona insisted.

Messi, who loves attacking teams, thought he knew what was going wrong with the national side. With the abundance of talent in the forward line, it was a question of getting the right mix to guarantee the best performance. And he could play in a position whereby he was instrumental in the creation of the play, but could also affect the result and score.

Leo suggested dispensing with the 4-4-2 system that Maradona employed more often than not, with two wingers (Ángel Di María and Jonás Gutiérrez), two centre-midfielders (Mascherano and

Verón) and two forwards (Messi and Higuaín). Instead, he suggested a 4-3-1-2 or a 3-4-1-2 system – effectively three up front, but with enough players to defend. Someone with lots of running in him, such as Jonás or Di María could be one of the wingers, going up and down to defend and to attack. Carlos Tévez and Gonzalo Higuaín could be the forwards. Leo would mix with the two up front, and the three or four midfielders who were protecting him. That way, he would always be close to the ball.

Maradona agreed.

Suddenly, Leo felt positive about the World Cup. Despite the difficulties of qualifying, he thought he and Diego had found some common ground. After Barcelona won the 2009–10 league title, the team went to celebrate with the fans at the Camp Nou. As tradition dictates, the players got hold of the microphone on the pitch to send the supporters a message. '*Bona nit*,' Leo started his brief discourse in Catalan as the stands were chanting his name. 'I am not going to say anything strange this year. Simply, thanks to everybody, *visca el Barça, visca Catalunya,* and *¡aguante Argentina, la concha de tu madre!*'(Keep at it, Argentina, you bastard!), a war cry for his nation.

The World Cup was a month away.

This is how *El País*, from the other side of the ocean and with the impartiality that geographical distance gives you, analysed the Argentina team that was arriving in South Africa:

Maradona waits for Messi.

The coach entrusts the forward with the leadership of the albiceleste *just like at Barça. Until now, the Flea has felt like a stranger in his national team.*

Will it be Maradona's Argentina? Will it be Messi's Argentina? Or maybe the magic of the World Cup will make the Argentine god and the best player in the world put aside their differences and triumph together. Their coexistence has gone down a rocky path until now. Argentina suffered like never before in the qualifying stage to get to the World Cup. The team was contorted and disorientated by Maradona's changing and strange blackboard. His players saw him more as a reverential figure, the untouchable idol from their youth, than as a coach from whom they could learn tactics. Always

crammed into his tracksuit, Maradona has previously shown him-
self to be brazenly headstrong in front of the microphones through
his verbosity. A combination of his decisions from the bench, and
the general chaos which the albiceleste's *style of play has become,*
has cost Messi more than anyone else. He is a superstar at Barcelona
and a shadow of his usual self in the national team, because nobody
plays the Barça symphony around him. There is no orchestra, only
a group of soloists instead. They are always different because Mara-
dona has moved heaven and earth from one call-up to another (even
calling up players who were unable to play or injured).

The Flea has even been attacked from home. The jeering has esca-
lated because of the supposed lack of importance he attaches to his
country since he packed his bags for the Camp Nou as a boy. While
he is a symbol at Barça, Messi feels like a stranger with his national
team. Maradona has not exactly made his life easier. Guardiola has
freed Leo from all the chains and the little forward has erupted: 47
goals over the season, from the Ballon d'Or to the Golden Boot,
squaring the circle. Maradona says that he will now copy the blaugrana *model in search of the key to solve all his selection headaches.*
Argentina have played until now without style at Verón's elephant
pace. The list of attackers is scary, given that Agüero, Higuaín, Tévez,
Diego Milito and even Palermo (included because of his miracu-
lous goal against Peru) all appear alongside Messi. Two Champions
League winners (Cambiasso and Zanetti) and Real Madrid's Gago
have fallen out of favour. Riquelme is nowhere to be seen either;
he was the heart of the team until he got into a fight with el Pelusa
which was never resolved.

Maradona's eagerness to be the protagonist threatens to eat Messi
alive. The former likes to speak and wants to have the spotlights
shine on him, whereas the latter is quiet off the pitch, but a beast
on it. The country forgives Maradona's faults in the same way that
it demands more bite from Messi, as if the coach were the good
guy and the forward the bad guy. Classes in school were suspended
as televisions were switched on during the World Cup so that students could watch. On one side of the touchline is Maradona, on
the other Messi. It has yet to be seen if they will share a victorious
hug. It seems as if Maradona doesn't want Messi to take his place

on the altar of the supporters, as if his ego were still more important than the ball.

Argentina hopes that the past and present will triumph together in South Africa.

The first World Cup match was against Nigeria in a group that also included South Korea and Greece. In the pre-match press conference Maradona had said: 'Argentina is still a Rolls-Royce but now it is driven by Messi.'

The team had Leo behind Tévez and Higuaín, with the latter regularly floating out on the wing, with Verón, Mascherano and Di María protecting the back four and creating. Jonás Gutiérrez, an attacking wing-back, started at right-back.

Very soon the best player in the world justified that title – Leo was without doubt the shining light, the best player on the pitch, perhaps, along with the Nigerian goalkeeper Vincent Enyeama who stopped everything except Gabriel Heinze's header in the sixth minute. 'The Flea' was linking, shooting, crossing. He got past players, put pressure on Nigeria and managed to get eight shots in. He made more passes than any other player, but the two strikers had an off day.

Maradona's substitutions created confusion and suffering towards the end, the team fragmented and did not seem defensively solid. Everything was disguised, however, by the result, and the hug and handshake between Maradona and Leo at the end: Diego lifted him off the ground. He also kissed him twice.

In the post-match press conference, Leo expressed his happiness: 'It was a good match. I had a lot of freedom to move around and was very well supported by my team-mates. I had more touches of the ball. I dropped off a bit more than usual and I like that, because I have to participate in the build-up.' Maradona enjoyed Leo's happiness: 'Leo enjoys himself with the ball at his feet, and as long as he enjoys himself, we all enjoy ourselves.'

Against South Korea, Maradona took a further step towards making the most of Leo's stupendous form. Javier Mascherano was asked to plug the gaps, with Leo positioned in front of him. Four players would feed off his inspiration: Maxi, Tévez, Di María and Higuaín, who scored a hat-trick. Leo was involved in all the goals in an emphatic 4–1 win, although the decision to move him further away from the box would have consequences after the end of tournament.

Argentina had qualified for the last sixteen. A couple of matches would not suffice to bury the hatchet, but it did disarm many. When Leo was asked about what had happened during the previous months, he did not hide his feelings: 'In the national team I was not the same, I was not who I was at Barcelona and I felt I had to do more. But I've always had Diego's support and I changed all of that thanks to my team-mates' confidence in me.'

That support from Diego, logical in sporting terms, needs some clarification. Julio Grondona, who always believed in Messi, often reminded Maradona that he had to do with Leo what Bilardo did with him at the 1986 World Cup: make him feel number one, give him the captain's armband. Of course, *el Pelusa* saw his new number 10 as a great footballer but he never dared state unequivocally that he was heading for a unique, insuperable status in history. That position was already occupied. Maybe he was the best in the world. At that point in time. And as a consequence he was making him the focal point of the team. But he was not willing to go any further.

For whatever reason, and as early as 2008, Maradona had always preferred to highlight Messi's defects, as when he said that Messi had to 'decide for himself before the Olympics. It is time to become more of a man. It is a great opportunity to grow.' Shortly after he was complaining about how Messi was still not the obvious leader: 'I hope Leo changes his temperament, because I do not see him ready to go and fight for honours, to tell a team-mate something and moti-vate him or say to him "give it to me": I hope that over time he gradually becomes more of a footballer, I hope that in two or three years we are able to say that Leo is the leader.' In the midst of that verbal thrashing, Maradona went to the Olympics in Beijing as a spectator and visited his son-in-law, Sergio Agüero, who was sharing a room with Leo. Messi was never around whenever Diego arrived.

Messages from Maradona came in the form of public gestures. In January 2009, in his first few months in charge of the national team, he went to the Calderón to see Atlético de Madrid vs Barce-lona, a game in which Messi excelled. Maradona, in the stands, did not rise to applaud Leo's stunning goal, a swift shimmy past the goalkeeper after starting with his back to goal and finishing with his right foot. Maradona then travelled to Portugal to see Benfica's

Ángel Di María. The winger also scored, a goal of less beauty than Leo's, and the Argentine press pointed out *el Pelusa*'s reaction: he was photographed getting up to applaud when no one else did.

After he was named national coach, Maradona gradually began admiring on the inside what he could not see on the outside. He started to discover that Leo was an ambitious player, with football-ing knowledge, who was anxious to be part of a national team, and that he wanted to offer the team everything he had – but he did not need to be a big mouth. Diego, remembering Grondona's words, decided to reward Leo's attitude now that he understood his personality a bit more.

The day before the match against Greece that brought the group stage to a close, Maradona showed up in Leo's room. He wanted to offer a helping hand to the group's positive, mental state and offered Messi the captaincy. Emotional, even embarrassed, Leo accepted it.

And he asked Juan Sebastián Verón, with whom 'the Flea' shared a room and who could not sleep because of Leo's snoring, for advice. 'I only saw him nervous once,' remembers the veteran midfielder. 'It was the day before the Greece match, when Maradona offered him the captain's armband. But it was not the responsibility of leader-ship that made him uncomfortable; what kept him up was having to make a speech in front of his team-mates.' As for the snoring, there was a solution according to Verón: 'a few thumps with a pillow and job done.'

It was cold the next morning. When the starting eleven formed a circle to listen to the new captain's words just before the Greece game, Leo could not string a sentence together. Juan Sebastián shouted a few things out and the team jumped onto the pitch. Argentina, with a midfield of Bolatti, Verón, in his last game as a starter, and Messi, did not have to go into fifth gear to defeat a Greece team that tried to combat Maradona's team physically. The final result was 2–0: Argentina went to the next round as group winners. Without setting the world alight but none the less operat-ing effectively, the *albiceleste* were now to face Mexico, three days after Leo's twenty-third birthday. Everybody celebrated his birthday but, to the chagrin of Carlos Tévez, nobody had remembered team-mate Javier Pastore's four days earlier.

It was time to loosen up the squad, a job belonging to the fitness coach and official loosen-upper, Fernando Signorini. He decided to hand out books. 'Some looked at them, because obviously they are not the biggest readers. Mascherano would walk around with *Why I Am Not a Christian* by Bertrand Russell, for example. And the *gringo* Heinze had grabbed hold of *La sociedad de la nieve*, the story of the Uruguayan boys who went down in a plane accident in the Andes. I gave Carlitos Tévez *Las fuerzas morales* by José Ingenieros as a present; he would walk around Ezeiza with the book under his arm.' And Leo? 'He was with Verón in their room, so they must have shared something or other.' Messi has only ever opened two books in his life, the Bible, or so he said when he was 12, and Maradona's biography, which he started but did not finish.

What Signorini did discover was that Lionel was completely focused, despite the noise surrounding him. 'I have a habit of doing the following: you go on the pitch and see a player coming towards you with the ball, calm, walking, and bam! I take it off him, or I feign to take the ball off him, and say: "You have to pay attention on the pitch." One day training had finished and Leo was coming towards me with the ball. Walking straight at me, about thirty centimetres away. He started to look away and I moved quickly towards him, and bam! But Leo took the ball past me to one side before I got close to it! I didn't say anything to him, but he had done me! Of course I wanted to get the ball off him. But I couldn't; he was wide awake.'

The last 16, Argentina vs Mexico.

Maradona had split the team in two with Mascherano as the only pivot. It had worked till then, but the next opponents would be a greater challenge. The difficulties of creating chances started to become obvious with a constantly outnumbered midfield. Leo, again in that strange position as a midfielder in front of Mascherano, did what you tend to do in such cases: too much. Away from the box, he took charge of everything, he dropped too deep to look for the ball, and that damaged him physically and tactically. The Mexican coach Javier Aguirre managed to stop him and the team was running out of ideas. Leo looked to individual brilliance for the goal which still would not come but that did not work either.

Argentina's 3–1 victory had much to do with an error by referee Roberto Rosetti, who failed to see that Tévez was clearly offside for the first goal, and a Mexican defensive error for the second.

Verón, who did not appear in the starting line-up, came on in the sixty-ninth minute at 3–0. He had fallen out of the team while *el Pelusa* accommodated Leo in the new game plan: the idea of having two strikers in front of him, which had been discussed in Barcelona, had become four. Instead of making the most of Leo's speed in the final third, Diego wanted to convert him into a little Maradona. And in that equation Verón was superfluous.

That night, Verón and Leo chatted in the hotel room. Now it was 'the Flea' who had to listen to his friend who felt distanced from the team's centre of operations for no apparent reason.

Practically none of the players left the Mexico game convinced of the merits of the system. It was said in the dressing room that things would have to improve against Germany.

Fernando Signorini: 'I remember that just before the start of the quarter-final against Germany, I went up to Leo and took his face in both my hands. I said to him: "Little Leo, don't worry, you're on the way to becoming the greatest of all time. Today the only thing that is asked of you is that you give your all and nothing else, because you're incredibly young and you're going to have other World Cups, so don't worry about anything. And, as always, those outside are there and have to stay there, on the outside. Just focus on pleasing that group of seven or eight people who are the ones who will never fail you; play for them and play, especially, to have fun. Be happy, because if you're not happy, if you don't enjoy it, you can't entertain anyone and it means you're playing badly." He had just turned twenty-three. We used to say with Diego that if our team started winning, it was very difficult for any team to come back. The problem would be if we went a goal down, because many of the lads were in great shape, but they lacked experience. We had Di María at twenty-one, Agüero at twenty-one, Higuaín at twenty-two, the same with Javier Pastore, Nicolás Otamendi …'

The game was a disaster. Argentina were humiliated.

Four years later, history would repeat itself against the same adversary. Germany had a new generation (Müller, Özil, Khedira) who were following Lahm, Podolski, Schweinsteiger and Klose's lead. In the previous round, they knocked England out with an emphatic 4–1 win and in the quarter-finals they demolished the *albiceleste* with some electric play.

A goal by Thomas Müller in the opening stages put Argentina in exactly the situation Diego feared. And where was Leo?

Messi, who once again played with four target men in front of him and Mascherano protecting him, hardly got a kick in the first quarter of an hour. As he had been instructed, he went back to the centre circle to pick the ball up, and he was supposed to finish the move, too. He got lost in the dribble and the confusion, and the Germans did not even feel the need to foul him to stop him. He lost the ball twelve times and did not win it back once. An intelligent player, he found and created space but his team-mates did not see him.

The German steamroller was unstoppable in the second half. Miroslav Klose and Arne Friedrich put the game out of reach for Maradona's men after some great play by Schweinsteiger. They did not know how to respond to the challenges of the games. Messi was sent into a more attacking position right at the end. To see how it went. Too little, too late.

Eighty-ninth minute. Klose finished off a counter-attack to make it 4–0. Messi, sunk, with his head down and a vacant stare, walked into the goalscorer's path; it was his turn to be on the losing side once again.

In the first big game at the World Cup, Argentina collapsed like the house of cards that it was.

Barcelona's 47-goal Messi ended up without a single goal in his five games. Despite being the player with the most shots, 30, and hitting the woodwork twice. In that World Cup, which belonged to Spain, to Iniesta, other big names disappointed, too: Wayne Rooney, Franck Ribéry, Cristiano Ronaldo, Kaká.

Leo was inconsolable. Rage, frustration and pain all started to boil up inside him as soon as the game finished. Maradona kissed and hugged him in front of the cameras on the pitch. Leo just stared into space.

Seconds later, Fernando Signorini saw him collapse in the dressing room: 'He died. He died. He wasn't crying; he was shouting, hopeless.'

'He was shouting, yes, yes, yes. It came out like … it was something he couldn't avoid; it came from within him … I got hold of him, many times, but there was no way to stop it. He was like …

in the dressing room, the benches were fixed to the wall, with gaps between them, and he was sitting in that gap, on the floor, with both legs together and flexed, not in the foetal position, slightly more stretched out, and shouting ... he was almost convulsing.'

'The atmosphere was dreadful ... I said to them, "Nooo, that's it, it's over ... Now go, meet your families and children, everything is okay, everything is wonderful, you gave it your all, don't be too down about it."'

But Leo had died. Every defeat is a little death for him.

An emotional Maradona told the press conference how Leo was crying disconsolately in the dressing room.

'Bad, he was bad,' remembers Bilardo. 'I saw him cry. He was crying, he cries because he feels it. They say that this kid, with everything that he has, with the fame he has, doesn't feel it. But that is not the case. Maradona, who had everything he had, always wanted to win. Leo, too.'

That World Cup started with Maradona shouting in Montevideo ('Suck it!'). A coach with a more serious attitude, wearing a grey suit, with a groomed beard, went to South Africa. He ended up sunk but defiant, with doubts about his future.

Maradona left the *albiceleste* that summer. The eternal number 10 would have tried to make the final victory his, but he allowed the defeat to have other authors.

With Maradona, Leo had his worst ever goalscoring return: three goals in sixteen games. He had got almost nothing out of Messi, and exposed his inadequacies as a coach on the greatest stage of all. But this latest failure of the national team was interpreted as a general one: 'Hang on, wasn't Messi supposed to be a genius?'

The analysis was insulting and opportunistic. It was written and said that Leo should have lifted an average team to the category of world champions, but he was not capable of doing it, of repeating what Maradona had done.

Many in Argentina actually asked themselves if Maradona had wanted Messi to have a good World Cup. What a load of codswallop. Saying that ignores what these sportsmen are made of. But it is true that, having been able to study the way Leo was handled by Guardiola, and even Coco Basile or Pancho Ferraro, and how he worked with them, *el Pelusa* had still preferred Leo to triumph à la

Maradona, eventually making him play as an all-round midfielder, something Messi was not, and forgetting that conversation they'd had in Barcelona where the team for the World Cup was designed. A historic opportunity wasted.

'Argentina was a little team from a city park,' Goal.com wrote. 'The stupidities of Maradona were more powerful than the team. The stubbornness of Maradona not to recognise his mistakes took Argentina to the debacle.' *El Clarín* pursued the same idea: 'Maradona never found the team. All the responsibility fell on Messi and he is not Maradona. The coach was inept. He didn't put Messi on the box in South Africa, where he can hurt. The players discovered Father Christmas doesn't exist – Maradona is not what they thought he was.'

Analysing the World Cup for *El País*, Leo bade farewell to the tournament in Germany: '[That was] something ugly that happened because of the way things turned out, the aim was to go further and we had the team to do it. We arrived at the World Cup in a bad state after qualifying by the skin of our teeth. In the World Cup I think that we had done things well until the Germany match. That was another kettle of fish. They were deserved winners given the way the game panned out; they scored very early and dominated the whole match: the truth is that it was a disappointment not to get further.'

The two World Cups and even the 2007 Copa América saw an inconsistent Leo. It would have been worse without him but clearly they had not managed to build a team that could get the most out of the most talented footballer of his generation. Messi instigated a footballing debate even before it became known that Maradona was not continuing as coach. 'We have to start again from zero,' he said. That might have been a prudent analysis of the situation but what really happened was that the World Cup in South Africa saw an increase in the split between the Argentine fans and Messi. And nobody was going to shut up about it: the flow of accusations continued, universal, unstinting. Leo did not stand up to be counted after the Germany defeat. If he had been earning euros, he would have played better. He did not celebrate goals with enough passion. He was arrogant. Cold-hearted. Protected by Grondona. Even autistic. All these things were said and written.

And hearing all that was killing Leo. He still did not understand the reasons. Fellow professionals defended him, Maradona
included. 'I think that the press had a lot to do with putting ideas in
people's heads, Leo this, Leo that, and remember he is twenty-four,
twenty-five years old! I won the World Cup at twenty-six! He is at
the right age to be a fully rounded player and show the Argentine
public that they are completely wrong.'

But, tired of being misunderstood, Leo was close to giving up. He
decided that he was either going to be accepted as he was, or he was
not going to be accepted at all – whatever the consequences. 'Society doesn't understand him because he doesn't sing the national
anthem,' says Gerardo Salorio. 'Because he is a guy who shows little
emotion. Here we like *bread and circuses*, that is how we are, that
is how we like it. Serious people do not triumph in our country, you
have to be a bit of a puppet. That is why Bielsa's seriousness fitted
so well in Bilbao. Such a serious Argentinian cannot exist in our
homeland, as is the case with José Pekerman himself, Pancho Ferraro, Hugo Tocalli …'

'I would ask Leo, because it would also be beautiful to help him
think, what does the national anthem have to do with a football
match?' Signorini suggests. 'What does the national anthem have
to do with anything? Because when you think about any national
anthem, it brings to mind epic battles. You always think about the
nastiness of war.'

You could write calmly against Messi: it became fashionable.
The problem was that his personal life continued to be mixed up
with his footballing life. The prize-winning writer Martín Caparrós
launched into a diatribe against Leo in October 2011, which was
widely read. 'He tries to be Argentine, three billion reaffirm that he
is; only his supposed compatriots doubt him. He still hasn't aroused
affection or a sense of closeness within us: Messi is a guy who does
incredible pirouettes with a ball on the other side of the world and
who, luckily, belongs to us for World Cups. Of course it makes us
proud – pride comes easily to us Argentines, as easily as a plaintive
cry – but it is slightly artificial: as if we feared that the trick would
be discovered at any moment.'

Without the media support that Riquelme (who helped certain
journalists climb the ladder on television) or Maradona received,

Leo was more and more a stranger in his own land. It is a very typical type of Argentine jealousy. Messi left and triumphed; during the crisis, he packed his bags, electing not to stay and put up with it like the rest of them. 'It may not be just an Argentine thing, but it is prominent here,' Sergio Levinsky explains. 'There has been a long-standing tradition of not selecting players for the World Cup if they plied their trade in Europe. Argentina went to Sweden in 1958 and failed miserably; neither Alfredo Di Stéfano nor Enrique Omar Sívori were there. They were the best players in the world, but, as they played in Europe, they were deemed superfluous to requirements.' Even Maradona, between 1982 and 1985, had a spell in which he was not called up, because he was playing in Europe.

Leo describes his house in Castelldefels as a 'normal' home. He has many items of sentimental value in Rosario, in his house, his mother's or his brother's. It is where his roots are. However, there is hardly any trace of him in his city. It was not until 2013 that the local tourist board published a leaflet with a 'Messi route' on it for the first time. Plans for a sports museum are being drawn up. Messi insists that he will retire at Newell's: 'I don't know when it will be, but it is what I want. I want to play in Argentine football because of everything it means.' There is sincerity in his words, but they often sound like an appeal for acceptance.

But, as Eduardo Sacheri said in *El Gráfico*, 'It isn't Messi's fault that we Argentines are incapable of ending our mourning for Diego.'

'I have always said it: Argentina has treated him unfairly. We are very bad at that, aren't we? When things don't go well for us ... We players always used to say it: Leo does not have to save us, we have to help him so that he can really do everything he is used to doing. If a team doesn't support him, it is very difficult. And I felt that the team was not managing to give him everything he needed to really prosper. He has always played really well for Argentina; at some points he has not shone as he has at Barcelona, but nor has he played badly. It is very difficult to see Leo play badly, because the decisions that he takes are usually the right ones.'

(Javier Mascherano)

'Di Stéfano, Garrincha, Pelé, Cruyff or Maradona, Platini or
Zidane, did they need so much pampering to play? Didn't
they play as well for their teams as for the national team, with
different journeys and coaches and team-mates thrown into
the mix? Did they ever need the coaches to build the team
around them so they could shine? Or be captains? Or wear the
number ten? Or have their families jump to defend them? Has
anyone, in any national team, ever been given five years and
fifty matches? Is he, in some way, responsible for what happens to the national team, or, as his advocates say, is the world
to blame, the surroundings? Silence.'

(Fernando Araújo Vélez, journalist with *El Magazín*)

Argentina have not won a major tournament since 1993. Looking back at Leo's first 50 caps, there were important goals, beautiful
ones, too, but still no afternoon of glory in the latter stages of a tournament. Sergio Batista replaced Maradona and wanted to replicate
history, which is why he decided to use the system that Guardiola had
mastered at Barcelona, giving Leo freedom. But it was neither Xavi
nor Iniesta who helped him, nor was the team built from the back
with the efficiency of Puyol and Piqué. The new coach was building a
house from the roof down, imposing the formation, before creating
the conditions to make the most of the talent at his disposal, but the
nature of international duty offers little alternative or time.

He also repeated what Pep had done with Ronaldinho and Deco:
Batista confronted Tévez, who subsequently disappeared from
the scene. There are numerous theories: *el Apache* was one of the
few who, after the Germany failure, backed Maradona, long-term
enemy of Batista. In a friendly against Brazil in Doha, Tévez did
not travel because of a supposed muscular injury, but he played for
Manchester City days later. 'That shows a lack of loyalty' was the
message coming from Batista's camp.

Another more football-related example can be added: Batista
announced that he was going to build a team around Messi. The style
had to be chosen. Tévez offered fight and battling spirit, but that came
at a price; he was more comfortable playing the lone striker.

The coach travelled to England to see some of his players and did
not even call Tévez. His future seemed to be clear, but there was a

problem. It was 2011, the year of the Copa América, which was to be held in Argentina. Tévez, from a humble background and baptised by Maradona as the 'people's player', had at the time greater marketing power than Leo: his face was in TV commercials and on posters all over the country. There was enormous pressure from the companies sponsoring the national team to keep *el Apache* in the squad. Some days before the beginning of the tournament, Batista phoned Tévez. He was going to be called up.

As always happens, cliques started forming around the leaders. Leo shared tables, time, games and chats with Pablo Zabaleta, Mascherano and both Gabriel and Diego Milito. They had already been known since South Africa as the *Ferran Adriàs,* in honour of the famous Catalan chef. The name would be abandoned as it gradually became the most relevant group.

For that tournament, Checho Batista featured in a 4-3-3 system with Esteban Cambiasso, Javier Mascherano and Ever Banega as the three central midfielders, although two of them had to play more of a box-to-box role and wider than usual. Ezequiel Lavezzi joined the Tévez/Messi duo up front.

The problems were obvious from the first minute against Bolivia, in the opening game. Messi and Tévez were making the same runs, they were using similar spaces, they did not fit. And as the game continued all square, both dropped deep to help the build-up. The same thing happened in the following match, against Colombia. Two draws to start with. And the public made itself heard: they preferred Tévez. The chants and insults were aimed at Leo, who would leave the pitch with a vacant stare. And also the boos, the first he had heard since his *albiceleste* debut five years earlier.

The press did not let it go.

'You only fall in love with Argentina at the beginning, when you land at the airport or when the national anthem is sung.'
(El Clarín)

'The 11 nutcases. This is not Messi.'
(Olé)

Jorge Messi spoke on Radio 10. Leo 'is having a very hard time. It is the very first time that he has been booed, it is something he didn't expect. It is really tough … People are free to think whatever they want. What is irritating is what the press says, they create situations that are unfair. They are adding fuel to the fire. The Argentine press can criticise, because it is their job. Argentina are playing badly, but they should look after their team a bit more.'

The media was creating opinion, but Jorge could see something more than an innocent footballing debate: 'I don't understand the envy. Beyond that there are people who are opinion formers and speak about someone's personal life. That hurts and annoys. Lionel is in a bad state because when he arrived in the country a few days ago, people were rallying around him.' The rift that the federation created between the squad and the fans, who were denied the opportunity to get photographs signed or to take pictures of their heroes in the hotels, did little to create a sympathetic atmosphere.

Leo had to respond in his own way, on the pitch. Victory against Costa Rica was essential. It was in Córdoba, in the Mario Kempes Stadium, and for once the fans did not give anyone stick: they got behind the team and Leo felt their appreciation. In return, Leo played a blinder. It went well for him alongside Kun Agüero, Di María and Higuaín, who waited for his or Fernando Gago's passes. The latter felt at ease controlling the tempo of the game, waiting for the moment when Leo could make the difference. Tévez stayed on the bench. Messi provided an assist for one of Agüero's two goals and also made the pass for Di María's. The final score was 3–0.

'*You had to pamper and look after Leo. That is how the Mario Kempes crowd understood it as they chanted his name. Before the game. During. And immediately after every involvement (brilliant or not) by the world's best player.*'

(*Olé*)

'*Messi was colossal … He bewildered the Costa Ricans who could never stop him, but he also drove the Córdoba, Corrientes and Santa Fe people crazy.*'

(*El Clarín*)

At the end of the game the Costa Rica players queued up to get Leo to sign their shirts.

In the quarter-finals, the Río de la Plata *clásico*. Argentina fielded the same team but Uruguay, who played with a man less for 48 minutes, won on penalties. Tévez, who missed one in the shoot-out, would not wear the *albiceleste* shirt again. Messi's sojourn with the national team was broken once again. The criticism was aimed at Batista.

'National Failure.'

(Olé)

'It cannot go on like this. Without heart, without defence, without a tactical idea, without support for Messi's football.'

(Olé)

'Lionel Messi, the best in the world, the ace of spades, the Sword of Damocles.'

(Daniel Arcucci)

But as soon as the lights went out on the tournament after Uruguay's deserved triumph, the old personal accusations against Messi started flying again. Fans were annoyed that he seemed to prefer to defend himself with silence. That lack of response to public criticism was, however, adding fuel to the fire: and that criticism was even harsher than before. It was unbearable.

Leo Messi thought of quitting the national team for good.

– *The man on the street was questioning you, with the whole 'he isn't Argentine' thing and that rubbish. There are Argentine players that you've seen go to Italy and speak Italian within a few months. How did you find it out there in Barcelona?*

– *I came from Rosario and every time I spoke, they would say to me, 'What? What are you saying?' And I would make an effort to speak like them to avoid having to repeat myself until I got to the first division where there were various languages spoken and everyone spoke as they wished.*

– *But you did the best you could ...*

– *Yes. I still go out for some food and order chicken (pronounced 'posho' in Argentinian Spanish) and they say to me 'poio' (in a Spanish accent).*

– *A couple of times I've seen that the national anthem was playing and you weren't singing it so I tweeted: 'I like the way Messi doesn't sing the national anthem' and the question is: is it to do with 'get off my back, I'm not going to sing it'?*

– *Yes, because I thought what they said was ridiculous. I was upset and I reacted that way after I heard all that. They would say all sorts of nonsense.*

– *They did not like you not singing it.*

– *Of course not. They would criticise me for everything and for*

that too – since 2006 when they started with a chant against
me. They don't sing it any more, but, apart from that, there were
moments of rage because of the crap people used to say.
– *But jeers are also a driving force.*
– *Yes, I've been on the receiving end of so many bad, ugly ones with*
the national team, I've heard it all. People I hear today who speak
so well about me, oh well …
– *What is the worst you've heard?*
– *I already knew that I wasn't performing well with the national*
team but I wasn't the only one. The team wasn't performing. Peo-
ple, or should I say the press, expected me to join the national
team and win matches singlehandedly. That doesn't happen either
in the national team or in any team. I knew I was not on top form
but I didn't want that. I'm the first person who wants to play well
for my club and country.
– *Do you believe things were said in bad faith?*
– *Yes. Things were said that had nothing to do with playing well or*
badly. That was what hurt me, because I am used to being criti-
cised for what I do on the pitch. I play football and am used to
people having nice and not so nice things to say.
– *What should we do, should we sing the national anthem? I'll tell*
you another thing. I even heard: he doesn't know it!
– *As I've told you, so many things were said …*
– *Are you going to sing it now? Or should we leave it for a later*
date?
– *Let's leave it for a later date, for a special occasion.*

(Leo Messi, interview with Martín Souto on TyC Sports, March 2013)

Oscar Ustari: When he was criticised for not feeling Argentinian, I
went to see him during the Copa América, in 2011. I had had a
knee operation and I was not playing. I went to say hello to my
team-mates and to him, and I stayed in the same room as Leo
for a while. He eventually calmed down and that, but seeing him
with tears in his eyes shocks you.

Pablo Zabaleta: He had a really hard time of it when so much drivel
was said, especially after the 2011 Copa América, where we saw
how fed up he was with football and Argentina.

Juanjo Brau: When your country treats you badly, it leaves some sort of mark ... but I would say to him, 'Don't worry, you're going to turn this around.' I know who he is, I know him better than he knows himself. And I could see he was capable of turning it around.

Pablo Zabaleta: It all comes from the fact that he left and had success abroad, without doing so beforehand at home. On top of that the results in the major tournaments were not good.

Javier Mascherano: Losing really hurts him, it hurts his soul. And I think that it hurt more with the national team, not so much because of what they said, but because of how he felt towards his country and his responsibilities with the team. And the drivel that he has had to listen to, when his behaviour was completely the opposite ...

Juanjo Brau: It is clear that there is a moment when cheering someone up who is in this state is complicated. You have to make him see who he is, the best in the world...

Carlos Bilardo: It was the same with Diego, they didn't love him that much, they said no, yes, he was this, his club was one thing and his country was another. And I was saying Diego was going to be my captain, and they got really angry. If you read the magazines and newspapers from the time, you'll put your head in your hands. Many youngsters read that stuff now and they say to me: 'Did they really say that?' And I say, 'Yes, they did say that about Maradona.'

Juanjo Brau: I always travel with him, and I think that I have to be in a certain place so that when he turns his head, he sees me. And when he says to me: 'Juanjo' I reply saying: 'What?' so that he doesn't have to say it twice.

Javier Mascherano: The reaction on the return flights would vary. A bad result, a bad performance, would affect him, and he would consequently stay silent all the way.

Juanjo Brau: On returning to Barcelona he had to flick the switch. He had his rucksack with him and every single thing that was going badly would go in his rucksack. There was a time when it was full.

Eidur Gudjohnsen: I saw how relieved he was to be back, although somewhat quieter than normal. He was back in an environment where he wasn't criticised, where he was loved, where he could be himself. We would watch the matches and Leo was a shadow of himself with the national team. We would talk about it among ourselves, we would say there were two Messis.

Juanjo Brau: On his first day back on the training pitch having been in Argentina, we usually spoke about how things had to go from now on, trying to move him on. And his team-mates would arrive, and, off to work! Were there jokes made about Argentina's results in the dressing room? Nobody dared ... maybe in little groups. Leo is a highly respected person.

Carlos Bilardo: Two years ago I made some announcements: do not say anything else to him, do not criticise Messi any more because he is going to get angry and will not come, he will not want to come. Because he is an idol over there, and he comes home and gets insulted, he will stop coming, and twenty-five million of us will have to go to Barcelona to see him.

At home, Leo was asking himself, why is this happening to me? What have I done to them? He felt rage and a lack of understanding because he knew that, in the right circumstances he could be an asset to the national team. The years between 2005 and 2011 were tough for the Messi family. And the possibility of not returning to the national team was discussed on more than one occasion. Maybe others should be allowed to go, maybe the coaches should build the team for other stars.

In fact, Leo, in the weeks after the Copa América 2011, seriously considered not going back to the national team.

But, as the days passed, the conclusion he came to was always the same: you have to live with it; you have to learn to live with it. It is the price you pay for being the best. The thing he had aimed for all his career.

It helped him that, as he left Argentina behind, he was also going back to a Barcelona where Pep Guardiola was waiting for him. Full of expectations.

Part Three

At the Peak

1

Breaking Records

'Guardiola gradually transmitted the huge excitement that he had generated on arriving at Barcelona, and over time he gained everyone's trust. As time went on, everyone became happier at work and there was a new enthusiasm. We could see that things were going well. Guardiola knows an incredible amount about football and he shared his wisdom, so that everything would be easier for us on the pitch.'

(Leo Messi on Uefa.com, 2009)

'Guardiola arrived at a time when we hadn't won anything for the past two years. We were in a bad state mentally. He found a broken dressing room. It was his way of working, transmitting his message, and the trust he built up, that helped change everything. His personality allows him to challenge anyone with clear and concise ideas.'

(Leo Messi interview with Martín Souto, TyC Sports, March 2013)

'**N**ow I live in Munich. I will be there if you need me.'

That is how Pep Guardiola let me know he would be available to discuss his years with Messi, in his own words, for this book. A unique era that lasted four seasons, with all the records and the six titles (in one year) that launched Leo into the footballing stratosphere. Football evolved in that period.

That period began with Leo isolated from his good friends and his 'adopted' father, and with Pep unable to connect with his big star. It finally ended with a heartfelt hug at the Camp Nou after he scored the fourth goal against Espanyol at the end of Guardiola's final season. What was the process of synchronisation? What relationship did they have? Was it the usual coach/player one? Who helped who?

I met Guardiola in Munich at the beginning of September 2013. The season had just started, his reputation was still assured in the eyes of his new audience, the Bayern Munich fans, the German press and the management of his new club. In fact, Pep was altogether in fashion: his first international biography was all over the main bookshops in the city, it was the topic of conversation among the few fans who went to the training ground that day to see a team decimated by the absence of internationals, who were off playing for their national sides. Everyone was scrambling for his attention (Pep, Pep ... hello, photo, wave!). They discussed what Guardiola wanted, what had changed and how complicated it was to improve a team that had already won everything.

At the time Pep was hoping for a game in which the team could show harmony. That match would come soon after, on 2 October 2013, in Manchester against City in the Champions League group stage; it ended in a 3–1 win and confirmed Pep had managed to give his players conviction. Not only did they win, but they played as Guardiola had instructed. That is how his new adventure took off.

On the way to his office, a modern, high-ceilinged room with a large stained-glass window opposite his desk, a whiteboard, board pens and carefully arranged DVDs, Guardiola said 'hello' in German to everybody he saw and had little chats with the kitman, with a player, with his secretary. Nobody had to correct his new language. His immersion in the club was beginning.

Seated on one of those rather generic high-backed swivel chairs, Guardiola took a deep breath. As he exhaled, you could almost hear doors closing somewhere in the building. Shut away from the outside world, Pep started trawling through the Leo period once again, through those years of victories and anxiety.

Hearing Guardiola speak, it seemed as if his time at Barcelona was like one of those memorable summers: intense, fruitful, one that is remembered with profound melancholy as something irreplaceable that can never be forgotten. But as our conversation ended it became clear that the relationships created during that period belong solely to that period; they are impossible to recover now that they have been left behind.

Leo and Pep have only seen each other once since they went their separate ways. A brief greeting and an exchange of pleasantries at the Ballon d'Or gala in early 2013. And that was it.

Leo Messi is a footballer. Pep Guardiola was his coach. Pep did everything for Leo. Leo will be eternally grateful to Pep. But Messi is now on another planet. And maybe Pep is, too.

Not even when Barcelona played a pre-season friendly at the Allianz Arena against Bayern did the two of them cross paths. 'I have not seen him' is what Leo said at the time.

It is perhaps more painful for those on the outside looking in, and discovering the distance between them, than it is for the main protagonists themselves. They will see each other one day, but there doesn't seem to be any rush. But why do these things happen? Has football made Leo so much tougher that he does not feel the need to share anything with the coach who looked after him so well? Or does Guardiola's intense hands-on style require a cooling-off period before relations can be resumed, even personal ones?

In order to understand it all and to try to find a response, you have to start at the beginning.

Pep Guardiola: The first time I saw him I was with Nike, where my brother Pere used to work. Leo was signed to them, too. We happened to meet in a shop. His father was there as well, and I was introduced to him. He said hello to me, I saw he was shy, we said goodbye: that was the first point of contact. Sometime after, chatting with Tito [Vilanova], he told me he had a fantastic player who was going to break through. Then I found out about his quality. And I started following him on television. He was spot-on. Tito was spot-on.

Another key player in the team Guardiola has outlined, Messi will finally know today if he is to make the journey to Argentina to join the national side, which will play in the Olympic Games from 8 to 24 August. The Catalan club has moved heaven and earth in an attempt to prevent that journey. Barcelona's management claims that Messi is a very important player and that it cannot allow the luxury of releasing him to the national team with such a crucial fixture coming up. The Champions League qualifying matches will be played on 12 or 13 and 26 or 27 August (against Wisła Kraków).

After defeating Scottish team Hibernian by six goals (one by Messi), the conflict of interests surrounding Messi persists ... 'Leo's right to go to the Games is non-negotiable,' declared Jorge Messi, his father, the previous week. From the dressing room they say that the player's head is in Beijing ... 'If the Players' Status Committee concluded that we must release Messi, we will go to the CAS,' announced Joan Laporta, Barcelona president, who heads a revolution of European clubs – the Bundesliga has supported him publicly and the club offices have received supportive faxes from Italian and Serbian organisations – regarding FIFA's ruling.

El País, 21 July 2008

1. THE DISAGREEMENT AT ST ANDREWS, SCOTLAND. PRE-SEASON, SUMMER 2008

In the first days of pre-season at St Andrews, Pep Guardiola had introduced himself to the squad, had demanded discipline and promised them hard work. Leo Messi had said goodbye to the friends with whom he had grown up. Out of the group that had looked after him, 'only José Manuel Pinto, Rafa Márquez and I remained,' remembers Silvinho. 'It was the first time Leo had gone through a squad overhaul. I was used to it, of course. But he lived through the changes with a certain sadness.' And a coach with only a year's experience, with Barcelona B in the third division, had been placed at the helm of the ship. Leo had heard very good things about him, he knew that he was a legendary Barcelona captain, but every coach in every dressing room in the world is welcomed with a degree of suspicion.

Jordi Quixano wrote something in *El País* that describes the moment: 'Rather unresponsive to Pep Guardiola's chats about tactical positioning, Messi even sneered on a couple of occasions during the meet-up in Scotland.' Frank Rijkaard had promised him that, when the time was right, he was going to play him up front, down the middle, which was like telling him that the team was going to look for him, pass him the ball and look to him to lead the side. This had eventually not happened under the Dutchman, but the tactical evolution was underway. That is what Leo thought, in fact what everyone assumed, after Ronaldinho's departure. 'The Flea' was simply waiting for confirmation.

Pep knew that he had an excellent group of players, although they were low in self-esteem after two years in the wilderness. Leo was the player who would make the difference: in the coach's eyes, already the best footballer in the world. Leo did not know if Pep was the best coach in the world, so Guardiola's first job was to convince him that he was going to make him the best. Pep anticipated making a series of conditions and decisions that he would apply no matter what, things necessary for Leo's growth. Ronaldinho and Deco left, Eto'o was also to be allowed to leave: in Guardiola's opinion, he was a leader who did not willingly accept sharing that role with anyone. Thierry Henry did not pose such a problem because, although he did require special treatment, he did not carry enough weight in the dressing room to demand a leadership role which, in any case, he did not seek. Instead of Daddy Eto'o, Pep thought Leo needed a father who would make a real effort to get to know him properly, to look after him, someone who would always know what he needed. The coach put himself forward for that role.

As Joan Laporta recalls, Eto'o surprised Pep in training: he showed himself to be humble, hardworking and willing to fight for his place. Messi realised that Ronaldinho had been the best player in the world thanks in large part to Eto'o making the most of his passes. 'Leo told us that he wanted to play with Eto'o that season,' remembers Laporta, 'which made me very happy because I also wanted Eto'o to stay.' The senior players suggested to Guardiola that Eto'o could be very useful if he was handled properly. In the first two friendlies (against Hibernian and Dundee United), an outstanding Leo scored four goals. In the second match, Messi and

Eto'o played together in the second half and scored four between them. The combination appeared to be working.

But, speaking of necessities, Leo still wanted to go to the Olympics that summer. His story with the Argentina team had started very well and he wanted to add to the gold medal his country had obtained four years earlier. Barcelona decided to oppose him going. 'On the one hand we thought: we have no reason to let him go,' explains Txiki Beguiristain, the director of football at the time. 'We had got rid of Ronnie and Deco, and the national team then wanted our best player. At that time, the most important match in the history of the club was the Champions League qualifier which was to be played around the same dates. But on the other hand, we knew that he would be happier if he went to Beijing. There was a great deal of tension.' The issue dragged on for weeks.

Leo did not feel comfortable with the situation. And when that sort of thing happens, it is impossible for him to hide his feelings.

In the first training session, Pep discovered that he had made the right decision to select Leo as the team's centre of operations: he had a special spark, was effective in front of goal, displaying the same form that he had shown the previous season, when Ronaldinho had given up being professional. But away from the training pitch, Leo was distant and Guardiola feared that without winning him over, by contradicting him and not having him on board, life at the club was going to be much more complicated. He took him by the arm at the end of a training session and asked him what was going on, but Leo did not respond. Guardiola witnessed for the first time the hostile stare of the boy from Rosario.

Pep was making attempts to penetrate Leo's armour during those early days in Scotland, but the Argentinian preferred to avoid his gaze and refused to speak openly about what was troubling him. He remained taciturn and would not even discuss the subject with his team-mates, even though everyone knew what it was about – he was desperate to go to the Olympics. 'The club is not talking to him about the case, it is a negotiation between Barcelona and the Argentinian federation,' his mother Celia said at the time. 'And Leo doesn't talk, doesn't ask. He is just waiting to be told what to do.'

The days went by without any resolution and he began to look tense in training. During one session, Rafa Márquez tackled him from behind with surprising force, uncommon in practice matches. Leo bounced off him, got up, faced up to him and said a few angry words. Under normal circumstances a dirty look would have sufficed, and then, back to the game. But Leo was angry. He got to the showers before anyone else that day.

'There is a clear conflict of interests and my son is right in the middle,' Jorge Messi declared at the time. 'They are using my kid as cannon fodder. You cannot and should not put a twenty-one-year-old footballer in that situation because it can create all sorts of problems. It is crazy that a player has to take a decision. It's ridiculous that the powers that be can't agree among themselves. We don't know what to do.'

Pep Guardiola's right-hand man, Manel Estiarte, called Jorge on various occasions. 'Look, Jorge, this is not a good situation. Your son is not okay. What can we do?' Estiarte, who had years earlier been the best water-polo player in history, realised that Leo was very similar to himself: if he wanted to win him over, Pep had to make an effort to show him, subtly, that he was on his side, that he supported him and that he was going to help him. Pep and Manel conversed at length on the subject, while plans were laid to find a satisfactory answer.

Tito Vilanova, who had coached him as a teenager, got the ball rolling by telling him that both Pep and he were there to look after him. If he wanted Juanjo Brau, his personal trainer, to travel with him, it would be arranged. But Vilanova knew that it was not just about that. 'What else do you need?' he asked him. 'Whenever you want anything, come to see me and you'll have it.'

During those first few days during pre-season, Leo noticed that Pep was a demanding, meticulous coach with very clear ideas of who was going to help them win. But it was necessary for Pep to intervene in the Olympic Games issue, in order to convince Leo that he was indeed, as he said he was, 'on his side'.

Messi hardly ever made public statements about his situation, but without revealing too much he had made it very clear what he wanted. He joined the Argentina squad in China waiting for news. Barcelona were continuing the fight to keep him, but in the meantime they let him go: 'If we get what we want, you'll have to come back.' Leo accepted the conditions.

Barcelona, meanwhile, left on tour to the United States while Argentina prepared for the imminent Olympic tournament in Beijing.

'Jorge, I have to speak to your son and I can't find him anywhere.' Guardiola had made the decision but wanted to tell Leo first. 'He is at the training camp in Shanghai,' Leo's father told him. 'Get him on the phone for me,' the coach asked him. Pep organised a meeting in his New York hotel room. President Joan Laporta, Txiki Beguiristain and Rafa Yusté, the sporting vice-president, were called in.

Guardiola had convinced Laporta that the best option was to let Messi play in the Beijing Games.

Pep dialled the number that Jorge Messi had given him and he and those present heard Leo's emotional request for the first time. He definitely did not want to come back. They all sensed in his words the tension that he had lived through that summer.

Pep told him of his decision: 'Play in the Olympics and win the gold medal,' he told his player.

GB: At St Andrews you and Leo had to adapt.
PG: He already seemed to me to be a different footballer just from watching him on television. This type of player always observes you on the pitch, he observes you, to see what you do and what you don't do, to see if what you do is good for him ... They are different from us. You have to adapt to this type of player, history turns up very few of them and you have to adapt to understand, more than the other way round. They are not stupid; they are more intelligent than your average Joe. Maybe intelligent is not the word, but more intuitive than average. We noticed that he was a bit depressed at the start, but you tried to understand him and talk to him ... I spoke to everyone a lot in the first few days at St Andrews, not just to him. You had to meet the people, discover what had happened to them in previous years. And I also talked to him a lot, but to the others, too.
GB: During that time you also got rid of three of his adopted 'brothers'. And his sporting 'father' is suddenly not there either. And after, there was the whole Olympics saga. I don't know if Leo's mind was on training.
PG: I remember that he always trained really well in the early days.

We always aimed to make him comfortable. If we could not manage that with a player of his quality, then he would be better off being coached by someone else – if it didn't work, I would have to go or he would. Faced with that prospect, we decided that we had to give him that comfort, we had to give him what he needed. He had to enjoy himself, that was key. This is more or less the idea I've always had, since I started with the reserves, up to my present position in Germany, too: it only makes sense if you always enjoy yourself. If you only enjoy it when you win a match, this job doesn't make sense. But the club, Txiki, myself, decided to let him go to Beijing. We were clear that we had to take his discontentment seriously because we knew we had a very special player in our hands.

GB: How do you speak to Leo? Is he one of those you can ask, 'What's wrong?' and who replies, 'Well, look, x, y and z'?

PG: Some days, yes. It depends on the day. He always says, 'when I shut myself away, I shut myself away and don't speak to anyone, and have to get better alone', and it must be respected. At the start I found it hard to understand him but you gradually get to know him better over time. You realise he is a different person. Just like everyone, he has his private moments and on those days you leave him alone, and when you notice he wants you to speak to him, you go and speak to him. As for the Olympics: Laporta was the key. Naturally I had the last word, but he knew Leo much better than I did at the time. I remember that he said to me: 'We will make a mistake if we make him come back. If he wants to go to the Olympics, he must be allowed to.' I already knew what the Olympics meant; I knew what that event signified. At that moment you think, 'We will play the Champions League qualifier, we are new here, without the best player we have, let's see how it goes.' But at the end of the day, what use is a player who wants to be at the Olympics to me? If his mind is at the Olympic Games and not here, why do I want him to be here for the Champions League qualifier in our first season? I have never believed in impositions in football. That is to say, however much we say play this way, if I don't convince them, it will not work. Then we spoke to him on the phone and, with president Laporta, we decided that it was best to let him go to the Olympics.

GB: And that was one of those 'you owe me one' decisions.

PG: No, no. At that time, I understood that it was best for him to be able to go and enjoy it; going to the Olympics is something that happens once in a lifetime. That was the only argument and the only reason behind the decision. Evidently, it could also have gone wrong, and if we had not got enough out of him it wouldn't have worked. Nor do I think he is like that. I thought that when he got back, he would try to play well today, tomorrow and the day after tomorrow. But not because he had to give anything back to me.

Leo Messi will always be grateful to him: 'Guardiola always tells me that I don't have to thank him for that, but it was his decision, he thought it was best for me,' he explained that summer. The first match in the Olympic tournament was on 7 August. Ivory Coast were the opponents. Leo scored the first goal of the game and assisted Lautaro for the second in a tight 2–1 victory. Three days later, Argentina scraped past Australia. Having already qualified, Sergio Batista left Leo on the bench in the third game so that he would be fresh for the quarter-finals against Holland. He scored the first goal in that round but Holland equalised and the team needed one of his assists so that Di María could score the winning goal. In the semi-finals, Argentina would face Ronaldinho's Brazil.

Ronnie had already sealed his transfer to Milan, and Messi insisted in a press conference that his former team-mate was the best footballer with whom he had ever played, that he would always be the best. 'It is perfectly natural that he missed such an outstanding presence,' admits Barcelona winger Pedro Rodríguez. 'When you have very strong support, as Ronaldinho provided for Leo, and he leaves, you end up a little bit alone. But he found himself with players who had been here for many years, such as Víctor Valdés, Andrés, Xavi and Puyol, who were prepared to shield and protect him.' Players with the club's DNA running through their veins would be positioned around Leo. And so with those players the Guardiola era began: or the Messi era. Call it what you will.

Argentina convincingly beat their eternal rivals 3–0 in the semi-finals, and the much-remembered hug that marked the handing over of the baton from Ronaldinho to Messi. Messi had accepted the challenge to replace him and, regardless of the reluctance he would show in public, privately he felt himself capable of it. 'He wanted to succeed at Barça,' says Cristina Cubero, who would keep Messi informed about how things were going in Barcelona and with whom he spent many hours in Beijing. 'He said to me: well, I want to succeed and I'm going to win the medal, and then we're going to win everything with Barcelona, I want to be the leader of the team.' Thus spoke a 21-year-old-boy who had grown up before his time and who thought he had achieved his first triumph: the fact that Barcelona, in search of glory, had chosen him to show them the way.

'I think he was very clear about it in his head: "I know what I want, I want the Champions League, I want the World Cup, I want titles, I want records … I want all of this because I can achieve it",' explains Ferran Soriano, financial vice-president who resigned that summer, disillusioned with Joan Laporta's style of leadership. 'I've always seen very clearly that, without saying a single word about these things, Leo had no doubts about it: because of his attitude and behaviour, he was convinced he could go far and reach the heights. Things would happen to him and he was still up for everything.'

Argentina played in the Olympic tournament final on 23 August. The 1–0 win over Nigeria saw the gold medals hung around their necks. 'It was an incomparable prize,' declared 'the Flea', who returned to Barcelona soon after. The club had all but secured qualification to the Champions League group stage following a 4–0 win over Wisła Kraków. The return leg, played three days after the final in Beijing and watched on TV by Leo at his home in Castelldefels, ended in an irrelevant 1–0 defeat.

Leo joined up with the squad when they got back from Poland. The Spanish league was about to start and the foundations upon which the group would work had been laid. Messi had worn the number 30 in his first games with the Barcelona first team, and later the number 19. From that summer, the number 10 shirt became his. 'When they gave me the number ten, obviously I felt very proud and happy to be able to wear it,' he explained in the Audemars Piguet advertisement. 'It is a shirt that many great players have worn at this club, Ronaldinho used to wear it, a man who has done so many things for this club. It was a fantastic responsibility for me.'

But if Leo now had the ball, as it were, what was to be done about

Samuel Eto'o? While Messi was taking Beijing by storm and having heard what 'the Flea' thought of him, Pep Guardiola and Txiki Beguiristain decided one morning that the Cameroonian was going to stay at the club: his attitude was admirable. Although they suspected that Eto'o wanted to be the boss, he seemed to have accepted the Argentinian's lead. Furthermore, Leo and the senior players felt comfortable with him and he was one of the greatest goalscorers in the world. If he played in the Champions League qualifier, he would be cup-tied and so could no longer be sold, so at breakfast on the morning of the first leg against Wisła it was decided that he would start and they duly informed Eto'o and president Joan Laporta. 'Awesome,' thought Leo, conscious of his role, and, back in Barcelona with his gold medal, he endorsed Pep's decision to the press.

Intelligence is measured by the ability to recognise and adapt to new opportunities. Seizing and making the most of them is the mark of bravery and ambition. Leo showed that he had all these qualities during a trying summer. He also revealed a more complex side to his nature: he has a clear idea of his path and demands that his trajectory be followed, and the presiding coach, in order to get the best out of him, must know how to manage him.

Pep only had a few days before the start of the season to get his ideas across while trying to find the right equilibrium for the squad. From the start, winning would be vital in order to put in place the first few bricks of the building he was constructing.

Guardiola took advantage of Messi's absence to reflect on his relationship with 'the Flea', and he realised there was a particular way of handling him: you could not meet him head-on, the train-crash approach was not to be recommended. Pep blended tactical discussions alone with Messi in his office with indirect instructions in front of the group: 'Today the forwards are going to press high up, because Leo is going to do it, too, and we cannot leave him on his own.' So he was ordering Messi without exactly doing that. Yes, he was going to be treated differently, with respect, because the player felt more encouraged that way.

After the initial reservations, Leo would enjoy the sessions that always involved ballwork. Pep knew that players got bored with tactical meetings. That is why, when he sat them down, his speeches were short and sweet.

'I remember pre-season was full of little details and tactical adjustments,' explains Eidur Gudjohnsen. 'He would not bore us because he would very intelligently mix the tactical part with games, challenges and explanations. He would leave us in peace while we implemented what he would ask of us, but suddenly he would demand that we concentrate on two or three details that he had prepared for that particular day. He wanted us to end up doing those things subconsciously and that is why the first sessions were somewhat repetitive: about the positions we had to take up, or, if the opponents had the ball, how the attackers had to press ... lots of little things. Suddenly, after two or three weeks, he no longer had to shout, we knew instinctively what was expected of us.'

He would sometimes ask Leo, as he did other important players, what he thought of the last session, how he felt. But he needed to do it less and less: Messi understood what was being asked of him and would smile. He was clearly ready for the upcoming season.

'That pre-season was spectacular, really spectacular,' says Txiki Beguiristain. 'They were all ten out of tens, in intensity, desire, commitment, explanations, details. It was a bloody brilliant pre-season.'

And then Barcelona lost their first league match against lowly Numancia.

'This season we will have many matches and it is good that the whole squad is ready to play at any time. It [the rotation system] motivates everyone, because you never know who will play. There are always new team-mates coming in, which focuses you and helps you to concentrate on the next game if it's your turn to play. Guardiola is very close to the players and seems like another member of the squad, another player. He is very committed to us, constantly giving us instructions and teaching us what he wants us to do. In the meantime, we are trying to soak up a bit of everything so we can do the best we can. He asks the same from me as he does from the rest of the lads: high pressing, in a group and well-organised, but, when it's time to play, he gives me a lot of freedom, although always with structure. I hope we can win a title this year, and if possible more!'

(Leo Messi on the club website, October 2008)

Martín Souto: 'Did he [Guardiola] get on your nerves in the beginning?'

Leo Messi: 'No, because you could see straightaway that the guy knew his stuff. In pre-season he did drills that we didn't do again for the rest of the year. He prepared us pre-season and then we all knew how he wanted to play, what movement he wanted in defence, midfield and up front. A few details remained but he had already taught us everything.'

Martín Souto: 'Who taught you more? Don't say "everyone" because not everyone can teach.'

Leo Messi: 'Well, the man from whom I learned the most was Guardiola. Not only because he knew so much, but because he took me under his wing during a stage when I was developing, the stage at which I grew and learned the most.'

(Leo Messi, interview with Martín Souto, TyC Sports, March 2013)

2. MATCH AGAINST SPORTING GIJÓN AFTER ONE POINT FROM SIX

Barcelona's loss against Numancia 1–0 did not reflect the Catalan team's dominance or their persistent pressure. 'We were going through a transitional period, a bit like the one I experienced with José Mourinho at Chelsea,' remembers Eidur Gudjohnsen. 'The foundations were there, the quality was tangible, the house just had to be rebuilt. And we lost the first game against one of the smallest teams. Guardiola was furious. He told us that we had forgotten everything we had done pre-season and had disappointed him. Leo was staring at the floor, he knew that he was right.'

Leo Messi, on the wing with Eto'o in the centre and Henry on the left of the attack, hit the post.

As Luis Martín wrote in *El País*, 'the Flea' and Barcelona were certainly missing 'a pinch of salt and a few minutes' cooking time'. But as well as the positional errors and the result, something else annoyed Pep. Samuel Eto'o, following on from previous seasons, had called a meeting with the players before the game and left Guardiola and the entire technical team outside the dressing room. He gave a team talk, a clear threat to the authority of the coach who anyway was suspicious of the Cameroonian's apparent acquiescence. The squad's willingness to adapt to new leadership was going to lead to a bumpy ride.

While new rules were established, Leo distanced himself from everything and everyone; he was, as one player who saw him up close, states, 'waiting to see what unfolded'.

After the defeat by Numancia, players joined their national teams and, following that, Messi – having just returned from Buenos Aires – was left on the bench until the last half-hour against Racing Santander at the Camp Nou so he would be fresh for the Sporting Lisbon match four days later. But Barcelona could only draw – one point out of six in the league.

'There was uncertainty, people were nervous,' remembers Sylvinho. 'They would say: "well, what is this new Barcelona doing, and what is Guardiola doing to Barcelona? He is not right for the first team, he isn't tough enough." But from the inside, working there, I knew we had chosen the right path.'

PG: *The week after the Numancia defeat was a long one.*

GB: *After the draw with Racing, you had one point from six and were in the bottom half of the table.*

PG: *After the international break, we played Racing and drew. Following that was Sporting Lisbon in the Champions League, who we beat 3–1, and then we played Sporting Gijón.*

GB: *Did you have any doubts at the time? Did you receive any messages of support from the squad or were they all convinced you were on the right path?*

PG: *We knew we were on the right path. The only one I heard from was Andrés Iniesta. He came to my office. He said: 'don't worry, everything is going bloody well, we are doing everything well and it will be fine.' I don't think many people had much faith in us those first few days after the defeat against Numancia. Nor after the draw with Racing at home. But that was normal. We were at a low, and very few believed in us from the beginning anyway. I always thought: 'It's better that way.' You disappoint fewer when there are so few who think it will go well. They weren't easy days but I remember I said to myself one day: 'Look, we will do what we think we have to do, we will keep going. We will play as I like my team to play. And that's that.' Txiki was on my side back then.*

I felt him, that's the right word, very close to me. He had more faith in me than I had in myself.

Football is not a process where I can just come along with an idea and carry it out in a short time. No, the process involves trying a player out here, another one there ... and you need time for that, in a world where time is at a premium.

Barcelona travelled to Gijón with a certain amount of apprehension.

Matchday 3 (21 September 2008) Sporting Gijón 1–6 Barcelona

Barcelona: Valdés; Alvés, Márquez, Puyol, Abidal; Xavi, Busquets (Cáceres, 81st minute), Keita (Gudjohnsen, 71st minute); Messi, Eto'o (Bojan, 67th minute) and Iniesta. Subs not used: Pinto; Piqué, Pedro and Touré.

Sporting Gijón: Sergio Sánchez; Sastre, Gerard Autet, Jorge, Canella; Andreu, Matabuena (Michel, 45th minute); Maldonado (Kike Mateo, 62nd minute), Carmelo, Castro; and Bilic (Barral, 59th minute). Subs not used: Pichu Cuéllar; Colin, Iván Hernández and Camacho.

Goals: 0–1. 26th minute: Xavi puts away an Iniesta cross. 0–2. 32nd minute: Eto'o heads home a Puyol header on the goal-line from a corner. 0–3. 48th minute: Jorge, own goal. 1–3. 50th minute: Maldonado finishes in the area. 56th minute: Gerard Autet sent off for fouling Messi.

Gerard Autet, former Barcelona youth player, was making his league debut for Sporting that day. At the age of 30. A dream come true for the centre-back, a mere detail in the context of the game. Sporting were aware of the pressure on Barcelona and tried to take advantage of it. Autet and the other centre-back and the full-back tried to come up with a plan to stop Messi: we will have to try to put two men on him and keep an eye open to give support. But Barcelona were on fire from the start of the match, especially Iniesta on the left wing, and Leo, who was everywhere up front. It was impossible to keep two men on him; when he received the ball he would turn and face the opposition without the defenders having had much time to react. Autet and Messi had crossed paths on a couple of occasions in the first half, but, with the score 3–1, a long but imprecise goal kick by the Sporting goalkeeper ended up at Messi's feet. He was facing the debutant centre-back. An ominous one on one for the defender.

Autet had thought about just such a moment. What to do? He came to an interesting conclusion: it is Messi, therefore you have to accept the challenge with as much focus as possible, but also without extra pressure as the normal outcome would be for Leo to go past him. Problem is at 3–1 down, Sporting still had a chance. As is so often the case, the theory for such a moment was easier said than done. The foul Autet committed deserved a red card. And Barcelona were not in a forgiving mood.

1–4. 70th minute: Iniesta makes the most of a chipped Messi through ball after an exquisite piece of play. 1–5. 85th minute: Messi hammers home a deflected Iniesta cross on the volley. 1–6. 89th minute: Messi heads home.

El País: Barça played the whole game in opposition territory. 'It was crucial to press high,' explained Guardiola, 'because, thanks to the pressing of the attackers, many balls were recovered.' Messi agreed with him: 'We played with a very fast tempo from the start. This is the current Barça, this is how we want to play, although we must keep growing.'

That emphatic victory marked the point of no return for Pep Guardiola's Barcelona. 'We really started to click when we beat Sporting Lisbon in the Champions League and then Gijón. Leo felt at ease, was enjoying himself,' remembers Gerard Piqué. The criticism disappeared, Samuel Eto'o stopped playing leader off the pitch (he was not even captain) and he focused on linking up with Leo and giving the team depth. And Messi started to establish himself as the focal point of the team, although at the time it was from the right wing. There was no let-up from the ever meticulous Pep, who stuck to his guns and asked him to perform a series of defensive duties, which he did – at least to begin with.

GB: You all decided that the leader on the pitch had to be Leo but at the time he is still on the right wing. Were you already planning on pushing him into the middle?

PG: No, no, no. Not at that time. We had Eto'o, who is the best centre-forward I've ever coached. No, I didn't put him on the wing to then bring him into the middle. That was a different process. What I learned from Leo at that time was that he would vindicate himself on the pitch. That's where he did the talking. He does it through actions, when he gets on the pitch it is as if he were saying 'now I speak', scoring two or three goals, every single day. This is something important he has learned as a sportsman: with all the noise in football, we all speak more than usual; the place where Leo talks is on the pitch. This is what he teaches us, this is his great value: he demonstrates that he doesn't have to be anything else apart from a footballer. Unfinished business is settled there, on the pitch. I get the impression that is how the greats are, they don't look for excuses: whether the coach has done it better or worse … Leo doesn't play to please you. Leo won't say to you 'it's your fault' when things go really badly: the greats don't look for excuses such as the coach played him out of position or it didn't work out for me here or there. The perception I've always had of Leo is that he thinks: organise a team for me so I can get on the ball a lot and I'll take care of the rest. Others would ask for that place, the one Leo has earned on the pitch for being important in the key, decisive moments; but then, unlike Leo, the moment of truth arrives and they fail. And they fail over and over again. And then make excuses. Leo doesn't, you give Leo the ball, he takes a risk and wins you the match. That could be the clearest definition of what this guy is. He thinks: 'If you don't organise the team well, it's your fault. If we have to get angry, we will, because I'm here to become known, to reach a much higher status, a status that only the greats from history reach. Therefore I don't play to please you, nor do I play to please the fans, nor do I play for anybody ... I play to improve every day. I will do it, but you have to give me the raw materials, you have to create the perfect situation for me to succeed. I'll take care of the rest.'

Pep Guardiola described how the relationship between footballers and coaches is built to Albert Puig in his book *La fuerza de un sueño* ('The Strength of a Dream'). 'However professional they are, they are also scared of losing, and look for a figure to give them the key, to say to them: "Listen! Come this way ..." This is what we coaches have to do. We have to transmit confidence and assurance through our decisions.' Messi recognised that the new coach was not only demanding, but also capable of finding solutions that not even the players were capable of seeing. Guardiola was creating the conditions in which he could be at ease, and Leo was willing to be taken down that path.

But Pep had not arrived alone: he introduced dieticians and nutritionists to the first team to change the squad's habits. The objective was to improve output and prevent muscular injuries by eating well. In a nutshell it was also to modernise training, at a time when more and more work was being put into the personal analysis of footballers.

Messi's tears after tearing his femoral biceps against Celtic had been imprinted on Guardiola's memory. The injury to the muscle that enables an individual to sprint was the Argentinian's eighth in two years with the first team, more than half of them affecting that same muscle: in Rijkaard's last season he was out for a total of two and a half months because of physical problems.

'At a certain time eating habits change,' says Juanjo Brau. 'As you increase the demands, the fuel must be equally refined. As he grew both physically and as a footballer, he gradually had to make a few adjustments to his life. To go at fifty miles an hour, a normal lifestyle suffices; but to go quicker you need to function perfectly, and that requires refinements in your lifestyle.'

A holistic, global study of Messi's physical condition was conducted, and deficiencies were revealed. 'Leo started to see that Pep worried about improving his output, his nutrition,' remembers Joan Laporta. 'Back then he was still a boy who ate, as youngsters do, frankfurters, Coca-Cola, McDonald's and the like. We detected it and assigned him a nutritionist who did a spectacular job, and remember that Leo hardly got injured during the Guardiola era. I'm of the opinion that Leo really valued that.'

Guardiola made all the players eat together at the training ground, breakfast before training and then lunch before going home. It was as much to do with the need to build a team spirit as it was about controlling their diets: out of three meals, the club provided two.

For Leo, that was the end of his favourite sweets, the end of fizzy drinks, Argentinian barbecues, pizzas, the Milaneses from Las Cuartetas, which he stopped going to after Pep's arrival. He discovered fish, which he had always refused up to that point. Almost nothing fatty, lots of glucose, fruit, vegetables ... Pep applied the tactics he'd learned earlier to communicate with Leo: he 'recommended' Leo follow the instructions. 'From what I can see, this would be good for you ...' And Leo accepted with a certain 'reluctance', because of the obligation to vary his routine: we know that man is an animal of habit. But the results were decisive: free from injury, Messi saw the benefit of those strict changes and they ended up becoming a lifestyle. Leo gradually learned how to look after and listen to his body, as Frank Rijkaard had asked him to do years earlier.

Leo would hydrate himself and tone up as requested, he would rest as much as demanded – he was always a fan of the siesta but they were going to be taken at a regular time and not for long periods; one hour would do. With Juanjo Brau he would follow a personal training routine that he had already started under Rijkaard. 'At the end of the day he is a different player and different players must be treated differently,' insists Brau. 'As long as it doesn't affect the stability of the group, of course.' The group accepted the difference: they knew it was going to help them win.

Since then, Brau has been with Leo before matches to do specific warming-up exercises and stretches, so that he can then join his team-mates on the pitch for some group work. Juanjo hardly speaks to him during these sessions. He just gives him short, snappy orders: 'Control this. Pay attention.' If there's danger of injury but it's an important match, one of those in which it is necessary to play, Brau will remind him that he must be aware of how his body is feeling. 'Don't drive yourself mad, only make the necessary runs, listen to yourself, your body will tell you, if you notice anything, raise your hand ...' Footballers have to follow much more than tactical instructions.

At the end of training or a match, Brau goes up to him again and asks him about his muscular requirements. 'Should we do anything today? We should warm down your legs.' It is a question of asking him for a translation of what his muscles demand from him and working the miracle of readjusting his body to prime settings on the treatment table. If strength and speed are worked on with the team, injury prevention is in the hands of Brau and down to Leo's lifestyle. Those are the keys to physical preparation.

The study of Messi's morphology also produced a change on the pitch. He is often accused of resting during matches, of not pressing and of drifting. There was a scientific explanation for this that Pep asked him to apply to his game after a particular condition was identified. Leo has a muscle typology with a very high energy consumption; his muscles empty themselves of energy very quickly and recover almost as swiftly. But the gap is extreme and that means a period of rest before another effort. 'He can't be up and down all the time because his muscular typology is not suited to such physical demands,' explains Juanjo Brau.

Messi was asked to expend his energies more sparingly. It was explained to him that, as they are all so finely tuned and so physically demanding, he could not permanently be looking for excellence in every passage of play. Not that he would be unable to find it, but it was better for his body for him to choose the moments. 'Leo has a professional and footballing maturity level which helps him make his efforts fruitful,' concludes Brau.

And so a fragile body gradually became a top athlete's physique. From that injury against Celtic in March 2008 until Guardiola's departure four years later, 'the Flea' was only out from injury for ten days. He played 219 games in those seasons. Guardiola, almost like a sergeant major on such issues, was constantly monitoring him so that his good habits were maintained.

If the youth team gave Leo collective mentality and formation, and Rijkaard gave him confidence, Pep Guardiola added order to his life. When he arrived in Barcelona, Leo was 1.43 metres tall and weighed 35 kilos. With Pep he stabilised at 1.69 metres and 69 kilos, but, more importantly, he discovered body language.

'There is one thing that I've repeated many times in the conferences I've given on leadership,' adds Ferran Soriano. 'Messi described Pep Guardiola to me in one short sentence: "He's awesome, because he's strict but fair" He added work to the group following a period when nobody worked much.'

After the win over Sporting Gijón, a cycle began which required all the elements of the Camp Nou dressing room: the local hero, Pep, who found footballers who were fed up with the best players' poor discipline, a group of home-grown players who established very high standards, and Messi, who was reaching his peak.

The perfect storm was brewing.

3. 4–0 VICTORY OVER BAYERN MUNICH. BUT ISSUES REMAIN

Martín Souto: Why do you never get taken off? Why never? There are games that you're winning 3–0 and it's clear that you don't stay on just so you can score goals, but if they want to take you off, you get angry.

Leo Messi: Because I don't like going off. I like finishing games, no matter how they are going. I prefer coming on to going off. I want to play. I don't like the idea of things happening while I'm stuck on the bench.

Martín Souto: And one day you got angry, is that right? You were taken off, you didn't like it and didn't go to the following training session supposedly because you had a temperature but you were really irritated about being taken off, in the Pep era, right?

Leo Messi: Yes, against Valencia. We were 4–0 up.

Martín Souto: 4–0? You're nuts!

Leo Messi: Yes, it was stupid. I got over it afterwards.

(Leo Messi interview with Martín Souto, TyC Sports, March 2013)

Pep Guardiola discovered one of Leo's pressure points early on in his tenure. As he admitted to Martín Souto, Messi got annoyed because he was replaced in the eighty-first minute by Pedro. With the match already wrapped up with an emphatic 4–0 lead, Pep wanted to give him a rest in preparation for the Real Madrid match seven days later. Thierry Henry had scored a hat-trick but Leo was quiet. According to Catalan radio station RAC1, 'the Flea' turned up at the training ground the following day but did not get changed and was clearly mad about the match and substitution.

Messi gets angry when he is replaced and also when he is not given the ball when he thinks he should get it. But, as Estiarte once said to Leo, other footballers simply do not see the game as he does: 'I used to be like you. I would see it clearly, but the thing is it is not that obvious to the others. They aren't as good as you.'

'Look, I also get annoyed when they don't pass it to me, if I see an opening and I don't get the ball,' explains Gustavo Oberman, the Argentine international who won the Under 20 World Cup alongside Messi. 'Maybe his anger is more noticeable with so many cameras on him. But it is something that every player does, from the best in the world to the village boys having a kickabout with friends. I do it because I think the best option is down my side and there are times when I don't pass because I can't see the other openings. It isn't out of selfishness or personal ambition, because he provides many assists, too, he doesn't just score.'

That was the same Leo whom Pep discovered to be competitive to the extreme, even in friendlies. Diego Milito tells of how Messi used to shout: 'Pass to me, I'll sort it out' if his team was losing in a kickabout in training. He also followed football codes that he had learned in Argentina: in the book *When We Never Lost* Juan Villoro tells of a training session in which Sergio Busquets went hard in on the ball and gashed Messi's leg. The session continued and in the dressing room the midfielder went to apologise to him. 'The victim answered in a measured voice,' Villoro continues, 'pointing to the wound: "it says Sergio Busquets here".' Leo was not going to forget that; he owed him one. 'Days later, the incident apparently forgotten, he tackled Busquets very hard and smiled with almost childish glee: it had been payback time.' Villoro explains that in a game against Espanyol, the city rivals, at their stadium in Cornella, he celebrated the 5–1 victory by patrolling the wing nearest to the benches, occasionally throwing sidelong glances at the rival coach, fellow Argentinian Mauricio Pochettino.

And every now and then if a winger or forward, those around him, didn't pass him the ball, he would also show his disgust. Guardiola understood that those were two faces of the same coin. And he was learning how to handle it.

Since starting his career in the game, Pep has always known there are footballers who have to be treated differently. He saw it in the Barcelona dressing room as a player with Hristo Stoichkov and Romario. When he started to think as a coach, he reflected on how such supposed favouritism could be applied without affecting the group. While at Brescia in 2003, he decided to call the Argentina volleyball coach Julio Velasco, a two-time world champion, for advice.

'There is an Argentine coach, Julio Velasco, who revolutionised volleyball in Italy and won absolutely everything,' explained Guardiola in a Banco de Sabadell interview. 'One day I was very keen to meet him, and when I did he told me that he had always got other coaches to repeat to him: "all players are the same, for me you are all the same." That is the biggest lie in the sport, Velasco told me. They are not all the same, nor do they all have to be treated the same; with the same respect, yes ... To get the best out of someone, you might have to invite him out to eat away from the workplace; or you might have to summon him to your office; or maybe you should never speak to him about tactics; or you might speak to him about what he does in his free time all day long. You have to find the way with each one, that is the fascinating part of our job; what to say to him, or what to do to him, or how to trick him or how to seduce him to bring him to your field and get the best out of him. We appear to be above them, that is how they see us. In reality we are below, because we depend on them and we want to "trick them" to get the best out of them, to get what we hope for.'

'He told me he had seen me speak on television and wanted to chat to me. We ended up meeting in Rome,' remembers Velasco on the website canchallena.com. 'He asked me loads of questions and I understood, because I also developed like that. He especially wanted to know how to manage groups and I told him what I've always professed, that not everyone should be treated in the same way, because every man has different psychological characteristics. Managing a group is an art and I see that he applies these key principles.'

Juanjo Brau knows how to handle Leo's less diplomatic side. He does not impose anything on him, he merely suggests. 'He knows what I am to him, so at the very least he will pay attention,' says the physiotherapist. Leo gets the message. And if something has to be negotiated one day, perhaps about exercises, massages or whatever, Brau allows Leo to make the choice: 'When does it suit you to do it?' he will ask. By putting him in charge of his own decisions, Brau makes work seem less like an imposition; he makes it more easygoing.

Pep found out quickly that, in fact, the best way to deal with Leo was to manage his silences. Some players express themselves very openly, but Messi is a man of few words. If he is angry, it is the coach's job to find out why. Messi rarely says what is wrong, what he is thinking, it has to be drawn out of him; his attitude, behaviour and moods need to be interpreted. You have to get it right in order to be able to apply the solution. That is what Pep refers to when he speaks of understanding all his players: each one is a world unto himself.

Guardiola took Thierry Henry out to dinner to ask him to make an effort to connect with the team: he seemed faraway, emotionally distant from the changes that were taking place. Henry responded to that invitation by scoring a hat-trick against Valencia. But Pep never thought about taking Leo out for a meal: conversations between them were always going to take place at the training ground.

Following Velasco's advice, during his first Christmas holidays with the first team, Pep would give Messi and the rest of the South American players more holiday time so they could be with their families. Leo, though, came back before he was asked, because he was bored and he missed the football and the squad. He wanted to get back to training.

In a demonstration of affection towards the new leader of the team, in press conferences Guardiola would refer to Leo as the best player in the world. Over and over again. He had come to the conclusion that, despite being shielded by a loving family, Leo needed that affection. As you would do with a needy child, Guardiola opened the doors of his house to him, so that he could come and go as he pleased. Pep suggested less an adult dialogue than a pupil/teacher one.

Having established a way of communicating, Guardiola had to continue trying to convince Leo that what he proposed in terms of football would make him a better player.

From day one, he had imposed a very rigid tactical system, in which everyone had to carry out their roles and responsibilities. And Messi? Senior players such as Xavi and Iniesta bore more responsibility than they had in the previous regime. Leo had to help the team on the pitch from the demanding and not always rewarding space that is the wing. And Pep's wingers were expected to hog the touchline, to make defenders ask whether they should close them down or try to prevent the midfield trio from pushing forward. Messi was a very important player, a key one, but in the beginning the team revolved around Xavi, who communicated effortlessly with the coach. Both the central midfielder and the other players from the youth team gave their blessing to Pep's tactical plan, and Messi had to accept his roles and duties: stretch the play, defend against the winger, join in pressing the opposition and supporting Eto'o, who was to be the central striker.

But Leo was no longer the same winger who had duelled with Del Horno at Chelsea. Then he had dutifully accepted his role in a team in which he had only just arrived, and whose undoubted centre of attention was Ronaldinho. With Pep, however, he gradually abandoned the wing and began to appear more down the middle: he was asking to be the main protagonist.

Pep kept insisting on Messi following the strict tactical instructions and he wanted the Argentinian to be more proactive when the team lost the ball. But, when he lost possession, Messi often lost concentration and teams attacked freely down his flank. Guardiola began to realise that it was going to be difficult to maroon him on one side of the pitch, and that doing so would in fact be damaging to the team.

'A "Guardiolina" is a telling-off, but Guardiola-style. In his gentle voice, no shouting, straight to the point but without pointing a finger or offending anyone: looking to convince the player with constructive arguments,' wrote analyst Martí Perarnau. 'On one occasion, earlier in his first season, two players were recipients of the message, but, to sweeten the telling-off, they were accompanied by another three so that it would not get out of hand. Needless to say those two recipients were Messi and Henry. They received the "Guardiolina". They were the ones who failed to obey the ground rules on which this Barça was based. Against Espanyol and Lyon. Other players made more calamitous mistakes ... But those mistakes were not responsible for the sinking of Barcelona's collective team plan in both matches.'

Leo and Thierry had neglected to press the defenders and to tighten up when possession was lost. They were happy to participate when the ball was at their feet, but would drift out the game when it was time to defend. Against Lyon, the French side controlled the middle of the pitch with ease. 'This is the match from which we can gain more pointers for the future,' said Guardiola. 'It will be used to illustrate to the players very clearly what is expected of them and, if they understand that, we can fight for everything.' According to Perarnau, Pep had a meeting with both Messi and Henry, in the presence of Iniesta, Hleb and Pedro, and told them, in Perarnau's words, 'no more slacking'.

GB: *Was there any match in particular when you said: we have to change this?*

PG: *The Lyon game in the first year and Stuttgart in the second, in the knockout stages of the Champions League, were good lessons for me. Their left-wingers caused us many problems. Not only because Leo wasn't doing his defensive duties ... It also happened that Leo was not very often part of the build-up. You could tell this guy needed to play in a position where he would see more of the ball. That is what we wanted in the end.*

GB: *In the 4–0 win against Bayern in your first year, he was still on the wing ...*

PG: *In the first year when we won every title, Leo played on the wing in 95 per cent of the games. That is to say, it's good to have a system, but sometimes the analysis is simple: as simple as realising that this guy would do something each time he touched the ball, that something would happen. And if you put him in the middle, he would touch it more than on the wing. I mean: if he is convinced he has to play in the centre of midfield in the future he will become an amazing midfielder.*

And so the first tactical modification designed to make the most of 'the Flea's' unstoppable growth was gradually being conceived: during that first Pep season he played mainly on the wing, a 'false' winger, who was more often than not cutting inside and roaming in the middle and when he had the ball lots of good things happened.

He had scored 30 goals by April (in the previous season, under Rijkaard, he had scored 17), with a dozen extraordinary performances, and another dozen very good ones. Barcelona were playing in the league with a level of efficiency that surprised even the coach. They were heading for the title.

But it was not always a smooth ride.

Before the return leg of the Lyon fixture, in the last 16 of the Champions League, Guardiola realised the team was going through a difficult patch, something confirmed not only by the statistics (one victory and two defeats in six matches, including a hard-fought 1–1 draw in the first leg against the French team) but that was also apparent to the naked eye. The team needed a psychological boost, a hug, some sort of reactivating. It is one of those downers every side goes through once or twice a season, a mixture of physical and mental tiredness creeps in.

Guardiola asked for a video to be compiled in which he could show everything they had been doing, what they had been building up the whole season. All the goals were included in it, set to a soundtrack of The Killers' song 'Human', which, as Ricard Torquemada explains in his book *Fórmula Barça*, 'became the hymn of the squad in that last part of the campaign'. Lyon were comprehensively beaten 5–2 and Messi asked for a copy of the DVD of the match.

Having eliminated the French team, they faced Bayern Munich over two legs in the quarter-finals, two games that were regarded as being evenly balanced. The first leg was played in Barcelona. Bayern had just lost 5–1 to Wolfsburg, who ended up winning the Bundesliga that season, but Bayern could not have imagined what lay in wait for them at the Camp Nou.

8 April 2009. Champions League quarter-final first leg. Barcelona 4–0 Bayern Munich

Barcelona: Valdés; Alvés, Márquez, Piqué, Puyol; Xavi, Touré (Busquets, 81st minute), Iniesta; Messi, Eto'o (Bojan, 89th minute) and Henry (Keita, 74th minute). Subs not used: Pinto; Cáceres, Gudjohnsen and Sylvinho.

Bayern Munich: Butt; Oddo, Demichelis, Breno, Lell; Sch-weinsteiger, Van Bommel, Zé Roberto (Sosa, 77th minute); Altintop (Ottl, 46th minute), Ribéry; and Toni. Subs not used: Rensing; Podolski, Lahm, Borowski and Badstuber.

Goals: 1–0. 9th minute: Messi, Eto'o assist. 2–0. 12th minute: Eto'o, from a Messi assist. 3–0. 38th minute: Messi puts away a Henry cross. 4–0. 43rd minute: Henry, from a Van Bommel pass.

El País: Messi had three shots on goal, scored twice and hit the woodwork. He has scored eight in eight in the Champions League this season – he is the top scorer in Europe and, with another two last night, now has 32 since the start of the season. He also provided two assists, one for Eto'o and one for Henry, his tireless team-mates up front.

The referee booked Messi after Lell stuck a leg out for what seemed to be a penalty. He infuriated the stadium by booking the Argentinian for simulation. Even Guardiola ended up getting sent off.

Messi resurfaced to link up with Henry after combining well with Eto'o. The Argentinian applied a striker's finish to a splendid cross by the Frenchman before the roles were reversed. He finished off a move involving some Argentinian wizardry. One half was enough for Barça to annihilate Bayern: 4–0.

The four goals were scored in a first half defined by Laporta as the 'best forty-five minutes in the history of the club'. The team were on a roll, and were enjoying every minute of it.

The president's words would soon be out of date.

4. THE 6–2 VICTORY AT THE BERNABÉU

El País: Are the matches against Mourinho's Real Madrid especially tough?

Leo Messi: All matches are tough but those against Real are even more so because of the significance and the ability of their players.

El País: What do you admire about Real Madrid?

Leo Messi: I really like playing at the Bernabéu. It is a great club with great history.

El País: And about Mourinho's team?

Leo Messi: Real can kill you on the counter. They have incredibly fast attackers and they break from defence in five seconds and it's a goal. They don't need to play well to score three goals. They create many situations for their players, who are very good. I am lucky enough to know Higuaín and Di María well. El Pipa [Higuaín] doesn't turn up, he touches the ball twice and scores two goals against you. Real can score out of the blue.

El País: What do you think of Mourinho?

Leo Messi: I can't say. I don't know him; I've never spoken to him. I can only speak about what he has achieved, which is many, many titles. I know his players speak highly of him, but I don't know him.

El País: Which match against Real Madrid is the most memorable for you?

Leo Messi: I remember all the ones we won. That is the best, beating Real, because of its importance.

(Leo Messi interview with Ramón Besa and Luis Martín, *El País*,
30 September 2012)

Leo Messi was eating with a fellow team-member when he received a call from Guardiola. He had something to show him. Pep asked him to go to the training centre where he had been studying how to beat Madrid, the first *clásico* of the young coach at the Bernabéu. The game fell between the first and second legs of the Champions League semi-final against Chelsea, and it demanded total concentration from Barcelona – the crucial two weeks of the season, the ones that would determine the success of the new era. The league was coming to a close and Juande Ramos' Madrid had won seven straight games and were four points behind the *culés* with five games remaining. Guardiola stated that he was going to Madrid to win and believed he had discovered how to do that. He had prepared some videos and he wanted to convince Leo to apply a tactical change which could create doubts in the Real defence.

GB: *The 6–2. Did you prepare his position as a consequence of his progression and influence in the team, or did it just materialise with the realisation that their two centre-backs were slow or they preferred to deal with a target man?*

PG: *We looked at some images together and we studied how they moved, and that if Leo moved infield he could get on the ball frequently. That was important and was always our main objective: him being very involved in our play.*

GB: *And how did you do it? Did you show him videos?*

PG: *Yes, we found some images and …*

GG: *Just you two?*

PG: *Yes, I called him and said: 'come here and take a look at this.' He was looking at it and laughing. And that's it.*

GB: *He was laughing because it was so obvious!*

PG: *I imagine he thought, 'I'm going to be all by myself in that position!' I imagine that's what he thought. But that is the easy bit, of course. The other, more important, bit remains. 'I have space but now I need to cover those last fifteen or twenty yards and score.' Of course there is no video, or any particular image that solves that problem for you. When we speak about tactics, we always speak about players. Without them tactics wouldn't make sense. At the end of the day, coaches are here only to be at the disposal of the best players. I have always tried to make the best ones play in their best positions, to get them on the ball in the right areas.*

GB: *Leo brought his style of play with him from Rosario. Barcelona have given him security, helped him to be professional, made him understand his body. You improve the team but he has essentially always played in the same way. Do you agree?*

PG: *He's a purely intuitive player, which is why you have to give him freedom. Some players ask for freedom without really knowing what to do with it once they've got it. You can give it to him. But Barcelona have given him the ability to understand the game, from such a young age, to understand where you have to position yourself, to get into space, and the explanation as to why you've played better or worse in this or that position. So I guess that, within his ideas and footballing intelligence, he will have reached his own conclusions: 'bloody hell, it's true, doing that suits me better, doing that isn't as good for me.' And little by little that education will have helped him find his way of playing.*

After Pep and Leo's conversations in front of a computer screen, the idea was clear: it was the ideal tactical solution to that match. 'In a chat before the game, Pep told us how Leo was going to play,' remembers Piqué. 'I don't think we even managed to practise during the week. Leo was going to play as a false number nine, and Samuel [Eto'o] on the wing.'

Pep Guardiola did not invent the concept of the false number 9, nor did he ever claim to have done so. It was born in the famous Hungary team of the Fifties with Nándor Hidegkuti. Alfredo Di Stéfano was the complete player who also caused damage from a false striker's position (he was also a false central midfielder, a false winger ...). Rinus Michels occasionally gave Johan Cruyff that role in the Seventies and it was brought back by Michael Laudrup in the Dream Team with Johan Cruyff on the bench and a young Pep Guardiola at number 4.

Sylvinho remembers that many things were worked on in the days leading up to the match: 'There was a strategy, play down the wing with Thierry, Samuel's movement. All of us – and I mean Guardiola, the squad, the group – outlined a great match. We went 1–0 down and it seemed that everything was going down the drain ...'

And there was an extra factor to be considered: before the game the senior players reminded Leo and the squad not to seek revenge for the guard of honour they had been obliged to form for the new champions at the Bernabéu the previous season. But Leo and those who had played that day could not hide the festering wound. 'It was a thorn in our sides,' Messi told *La Gazzetta dello Sport*. 'In fact, more so for the poor result and the way we lost, than for the humiliation of the guard of honour.' That night Barcelona lost 4–1 to the league champions. The thorn was about to be extracted.

In the idea that Pep had with Leo, the coach explained to him that placing him in the centre would create doubts among the central defenders. If one of them pressured him there the chance would always remain for a one on one with the other defender, either from the forwards or from Leo himself should he be able to get past the

Matchday 34 (2 May 2009) Real Madrid 2–6 Barcelona

Barcelona: Valdés; Alvés, Puyol, Piqué, Abidal; Touré (Busquets, 85th minute), Xavi, Iniesta (Bojan, 85th minute); Messi, Eto'o and Henry (Keita, 62nd minute). Subs not used: Jorquera; Cáceres, Sylvinho, Gudjohnsen and Hleb.

Real Madrid: Casillas; Sergio Ramos (Van der Vaart, 71st minute), Cannavaro, Metzelder, Heinze; Gago, Lass; Robben (Javi García, 79th minute), Raúl, Marcelo (Huntelaar, 59th minute); and Higuaín. Subs not used: Dudek; Torres, Drenthe, Faubert and Saviola.

Goals: 1–0. 13th minute: Higuaín. 1–1. 17th minute: Henry. 1–2. 19th minute: Puyol. 1–3. 35th minute: Messi. 2–3. 56th minute: Ramos. 2–4. 58th minute: Henry. 2–5. 75th minute: Messi. 2–6. 82nd minute: Piqué.

El País: Messi scored his first goal at the Bernabéu. Guardiola moved him off the wing so that he could take on Madrid's two centre-backs Cannavaro and Metzelder as much as possible. He massacred them. Not just them, but also the two central midfielders, given that Messi was dropping deep into midfield. Messi gathered the ball alongside Xavi, with brief exchanges with Henry. One of them, a chip, left Henry one on one with Casillas, resulting in the first *blaugrana* goal.

Piqué/Xavi/Iniesta/Messi – they were the core on a memorable night for Barcelonism.

Ramón Besa, *El País*. The key to the *clásico* is called Messi. The key was in moving Messi from his usual position on the right into the centre line as a false number 9 or fourth midfielder. 'The Flea' moved between the lines to link with Xavi and Iniesta, even to the point of creating three-on-two situations against Gago and Lass – man-markers of the two *blaugrana* midfielders – and tempting the two central defenders out, much further forward than usual, confused by the depth of Henry and Eto'o, who were always in line. The Barcelona coaches wanted to prevent their opponents from playing an 'anti-Messi' game and convinced the Argentinian that he should play as he had done for a short period in Seville and against Valencia at the Camp Nou. The *blaugrana* won the game through the middle with Xavi/Messi and Iniesta and on the wings with Henry and Eto'o, who was sacrificed out wide, seemingly isolated but still involved in moves like the sixth goal. Even Eto'o admitted: 'The boss was very clever when he put me on the wing while putting Messi through the middle.' Once egos had been put aside for the good of the team, the triumph became simpler for a historic Barça ...

In the press conference, Pep said: 'Messi, Xavi and Iniesta can make any idea a good one.'

first centre-back. 'The plan worked brilliantly,' remembers Piqué. 'Madrid never considered this possibility, the defenders couldn't come out, and didn't know what to do, and as a result Leo had masses of space to turn into and run at them.'

'The dressing room was like a madhouse,' remembers Sylvinho. 'I celebrated as much as those who had played. It was enormously satisfying for the whole team. What we had worked for, studied, talked about, had all been achieved in ninety minutes of perfect football.'

The tactical change had come off. Leo went back to the wing and his position as a false number 9 would not reappear until the Champions League final against Manchester United.

Alex Ferguson prepared himself to face the usual Barcelona precisely at the moment when they had decided to stop being the usual Barcelona.

5. CHAMPIONS LEAGUE FINAL AGAINST MANCHESTER UNITED AND THE 2009 FIFA CLUB WORLD CUP. SIX OUT OF SIX

In the second leg of the Champions League semi-final against Chelsea, Barcelona employed an attack with Iniesta on the left, Eto'o down the middle and Leo starting wide right but moving with freedom, the focal point of the attacks. The 0–0 draw in the first leg at the Camp Nou made the match at Stamford Bridge even more difficult when Michael Essien scored after eight minutes and Éric Abidal was sent off after sixty-six. Guus Hiddink probably sent out the wrong message when he replaced Didier Drogba with defender Juliano Belletti twenty minutes from the end. The initiative was with Barcelona in any case, even though they were not creating chances. It was a very tense encounter. In the ninety-third minute, with time almost up, Messi passed to Iniesta who, with a stunning strike from outside the box that finally beat Chelsea's formidable defence, added another page to the club's history.

Barcelona had to play the Copa del Rey final against Athletic de Bilbao before the Champions League final. They were en route for glory, three steps away from the extraordinary feat of winning everything that season. 'On Wednesday 13 May,' explains Luis Martín in *El País*, 'when the team was leaving the ground to catch a plane to Valencia, where the Copa del Rey final would be played that night, Iniesta, who had remained in Barcelona recovering from an injury, went up to Messi and said: "Bring me the cup and I will get you the Ballon d'Or in Rome."'

It was the first final with Leo in the line-up since breaking into the first team. Barcelona won by an emphatic 4–1, but Athletic opened the scoring. Leo was involved in three of the four goals, scoring one himself to make it 2–1 in a piece of play that would be repeated many times thereafter. On the ball in the area, he dummied and kept possession until finding the gap between dozens of legs to get it past the opposition's defence.

Three days later, Barcelona were crowned league champions without even touching a ball against Mallorca. Real Madrid had lost at Villarreal and were eight points behind the leaders with two games left to play: the eternal rivals had surrendered following that *blaugrana* masterclass at the Bernabéu. Barça won the fifth double of their history.

Cristiano Ronaldo's Manchester United awaited them in the Champions League final in Rome.

Two main things were said about that match. Manchester United were clear favourites (according to the English press) and the two best players in the world were going to go head-to-head. 'Without doubt the best two at the moment, they've had fantastic seasons,' said Sir Alex Ferguson. 'Alex prefers Ronaldo, we prefer Leo,' added Pep. 'How interesting to have both in a final,' concluded the Scot.

The public and especially the media have since decided that the only possible relationship between Leo and Cristiano is one of hatred. In a Twitter-obsessed, 140-character long, black and white world, there is hardly room for anyone else. Whenever they crossed paths that night in Rome, however, they showed that mixture of feelings that exist between nemeses, those rivals you have to overcome but who make you improve. There is no affection, but neither is there contempt. Arrogant and barbed comments about one another are all part of the performance, but their private relationship is one of mutual respect.

In *El País* Luis Martín recalls an anecdote that took place twenty-four hours before the game. 'Messi couldn't believe what he saw when he arrived at the hotel on Tuesday. He phoned Estiarte. "Can you come to my room? I have a problem." Guardiola's guardian angel has spread his wings to protect all his friend's pupils in any way possible. So he rushed there at once, anxious, fearing that something had happened that he would be unable to deal with, because Messi never complains. "Look, Manel, there's no bed," Leo told him. Estiarte breathed a sigh of relief: the problem had a solution. Player liaison man Carlos Naval took care of the matter.'

Otherwise, Leo was walking up and down the corridors of the team's hotel with his ticket for the final booked as if nothing unusual was occurring. 'In reality everything was normal as usual, up until the match, a day like any other. We were very calm and confident in our own ability,' Messi said days after. He knew that people were saying he had not yet been able to score against an English team. He accepted the challenge.

'We tried out the false number nine option in training the days before the final,' remembers Pedro. 'Pep told us it was the best way to beat them because they had two very tall centre-backs who didn't come out to press very much. In that central space, Leo could pick up the ball and create danger.'

Leo, noticing his family and best friends sitting next to the rest of the relatives of the squad, commented that the final was like being at the Camp Nou. He was enjoying the electrifying atmosphere in the Italian stadium.

27 May 2009. Champions League final. Barcelona 2–0 Manchester United. Olympic Stadium, Rome

Barcelona: Víctor Valdés; Puyol, Touré, Piqué, Sylvinho; Xavi, Busquets, Iniesta (Pedro, 90th minute); Messi, Eto'o and Henry (Keita, 70th minute). Subs not used: Pinto; Cáceres, Gudjohnsen, Bojan and Muniesa.

Manchester United: Van der Sar; O'Shea, Ferdinand, Vidić, Evra; Park (Berbatov, 65th minute), Anderson (Tévez, 46th minute), Carrick, Rooney; Giggs (Scholes, 74th minute); and Ronaldo. Subs not used: Kuszczak; Rafael, Evans and Nani.

Goals: 1–0. 9th minute: Iniesta passes to Eto'o, who dribbles past Vidić and beats Van der Sar with a toe-poke. 2–0. 70th minute: Messi heads a Xavi cross into the far corner.

El País: 'Messi is the best.' 'The Flea' scores with a header and demonstrates to Cristiano Ronaldo, who was not himself, who the real king is.

Luis Martín, *El País:* Messi, who didn't even get a glimpse of Evra because he never attacked down the left wing, did not have his finest day, but, as Guardiola usually says, he never plays badly. It was his night, he had to turn up and he did. He almost always made the United centre-backs come out and found a path through a forest of white shirts a couple of times, without causing Van der Sar any problems until creeping in between defenders to head home a Xavi cross for the second goal. Guardiola had warned about it in a press conference when he was asked if Leo needed to score headers to be the best in the world. 'I recommend you don't test him because one day he will score a header and shut you all up,' prophesied the man from Santpedor ... And at the Olympic Stadium 20,000 *culés* were heard chanting Messi's name, 'the Flea'. With 12 Champions League goals and every title in the bag, there can no longer be any doubt. Iniesta kept his word [about the Ballon d'Or] and there is effectively no doubt: Messi is the best.

Martí Perarnau, *Sport*: As yet nobody has found the words to do Messi justice, an unforgettable man with the ball stuck to his foot, the pilot of a glider, always finding the net at the right time. In slow motion, like a colossus, defining the age, bringing eternal delight to the *blaugrana* faithful, the master of his own destiny. Messi exemplifies all the values that bring this team together: humility and commitment, sacrifice and solidarity, effort and happiness, freshness and talent, youth and ambition.

GB: *The Champions League final arrives. And the pattern of the game changes after ten minutes.*

PG: *We had tried it against Madrid. We played differently against Chelsea; we didn't go back to the false number 9 until the final. We said: in the first ten minutes we will start as I imagine they think we will play, and after ten minutes …*

GB: *So it was planned.*

PG: *Yes, after ten minutes Samuel goes on the wing, and Leo down the middle. But Leo doesn't track Evra in the first minute and a moment of danger is created, which is what I was telling you about the European games. And then there is the free-kick which Cristiano takes and Víctor saves a clear chance. Samuel deserves a lot of credit as he adapted to what we asked of him … I remember very well that when we had so many problems against Lyon he also adapted. I put him on the wing for 35 or 40 minutes and Leo down the middle so that the eleven was more balanced and we could tighten up defensively. Samuel could also help us going forward because he has the perfect qualities to make excellent diagonal runs from the wing. Without Samuel we wouldn't have been able to do all of that in my first season, nor in that match. He is another big player for the big games. He very rarely disappoints in the big moments.*

GB: *The tactical change was a surprise to Manchester United, the English hadn't studied the Real Madrid match.*

PG: *Even if they had studied it, it is difficult to stop. Because you force the centre-back to move out of his normal position, they don't like that. Centre-backs in England, and almost the rest of*

*the world, are used to taking on tall, strong centre-forwards, and
that is when they feel comfortable. And if they have to defend
against players of different profiles, small, dynamic, if they feel
forced to come out of position, even if it's ten metres, they find it
a bit tougher.*

Leo had not only carried out his defensive duties, following Pep's
instructions and his own intuition, but he had scored, too. And after
jumping to intercept the perfectly placed ball from Xavi, he sent a
looping header over the keeper to score – a goal that Van der Sar
has since consistently refused to discuss, either in public or in private. In the process, his boot came off. It was as if Leo had needed to
stretch so much to reach the right height that his foot was suddenly
too small for him. It was an Adidas boot. The best publicity they
could have hoped for.

'Pep liked being on top of his players, knowing their mood, when
they are fine, when they are not,' says Pedro. 'It is very important
for us to have someone who sees you and understands you with all
the days we spend training and all the matches we play. No two
days are the same; one day you might be in high spirits in training
or in a match, but down in the next. You need to have someone
who makes demands on you but is also around when you need him,
someone who knows what you're feeling almost without speaking.
Pep demanded plenty from Leo, but he knew that the boss was there
in the good times and the bad, that he was by his side, and Messi
responded to that.

'So when Guardiola made changes, it was so that Leo could shine
and Messi knew that,' continues Pedro. 'And when things went well,
in this case the final in Rome, you could see there was a special connection between the two of them, like saying "just as we planned it".'

Leo and Pep hugged each other the first time they met up again in
the privacy of the Rome dressing room. They did not say anything.
There was no need to. It was their way of saying 'we've done it'.

'Yes, it was a beautiful thing, it is always incredible to score goals
and even more so in that match, in that final, it was something incon-
ceivable, like a dream, so it was amazing. It was all happiness after
that, lots of partying, lots of joy,' recalled Messi some years later. He
explained to *El País* what was behind all the rejoicing, over and above

the level of celebration that such a victory always brings. 'There had been the 2006 Champions League final which I was unfortunately unable to play in, because of the injury against Chelsea in the last sixteen which I didn't recover from. I had said I wanted to win the Champions League as a participant and that was really beautiful.'

'It was a really happy, and, at the same time, complicated match for me,' remembers Sylvinho. The full-back knew his time at Barcelona was coming to an end; the club had still not offered him a contract extension and ultimately never would. He was 35 years old and had played in almost all the cup games and many league ones, too, due to injuries to Puyol and Abidal, which forced Pep to reshuffle the defence. He also started the Champions League final at left-back after Abidal's suspension and Keita telling Guardiola not to select him out of position, as the coach had planned: Keita told him the team would suffer if he did so.

While Sylvinho walked around the Olympic Stadium pitch after the victory, he thought back to journeys with Ronaldinho, conversations with Rijkaard, the day Deco invited Leo to sit at the Brazilian table, the Argentinian's rant at the Chinese cleaner in the hotel. He asked Messi for a photo with him. 'While celebrating on the pitch, I was aware that it wasn't just a friendship coming to an end, but an important part of my life. It was an ending. And I knew that Leo would be one of those people with whom I would find it hard to stay in contact, and it would hurt me not to have him by my side, as a team-mate, as a friend. It was a very difficult night. He didn't understand it at the time, but I gave him a big hug on the pitch and cried quite a bit … I gave him a big hug because I wasn't going to have him by my side as much as I wanted. And in my head, I kept saying to myself: "it's ending for me."'

Leo was hugging him happily, but Sylvinho was deeply sad. 'I started the final: what a way to end a career. And while I was with him I was saying goodbye without saying anything to him. It was a night of mixed feelings.' Sylvinho recently sent him the photo of them hugging. 'Bloody hell, Sylvio, what an amazing photo,' Leo replied to him. 'You don't remember, do you?' Sylvinho prompted him. 'Yes, I do,' said Messi. And then it finally hit Leo: he at last discovered the reason for that emotional hug.

'I remember that when we were having dinner with our families after the Rome final, the fans were going up to him and he received them with calmness and humility,' recalls Pedro.

In fact, the evening turned into a nightmare for 'the Flea'. Barcelona had organised a celebration in a castle near Rome, in theory a private do, but it became a parade of hangers-on. 'Even the cats got in,' one Barcelona player says. It was a struggle getting through the throng and, as a result, the players spent hardly any time with their families. The harassment was such that it became impossible to enjoy the evening. Not an appropriate celebration for such a historic night.

The mood changed in the morning, on the plane, as Juanjo Brau remembers: 'On the flight home, he grabbed the microphone and did a few turns. He couldn't stop laughing, making jokes about his team-mates with fine Argentinian irony.'

'Leo demonstrated that he was the best player in the world,' concludes Piqué. 'We had already said it but nobody believed it. After that night, the order of things was pretty clear.' Messi had become the top goalscorer in the competition with nine goals, two more than Steven Gerrard of Liverpool and Bayern Munich's Miroslav Klose. Also, in the eyes of most commentators, the best player in the world.

At the Camp Nou while celebrating the treble after a bus ride through the streets of Barcelona, Leo, wearing a scarf and Catalan cap, grabbed the microphone and shouted, slightly the worse for wear from alcohol, his voice a little hoarse: 'Next year we are going to carry on and win everything, and we are going to celebrate it all over again. *¡Visca el Barça i visca Catalunya!*' Jorge Messi watched this with a mixture of embarrassment and pride.

Goals in the 2008–09 season

Messi: League, 23; Copa del Rey, 6; 9 in six Champions League games: total = 38.

Henry: League, 19; Copa del Rey, 1; 6 in five Champions League games: total = 25.

Eto'o: League, 30; 6 in five Champions League games: total = 36.

The following season Pep Guardiola decided to dispense with the services of Samuel Eto'o. He spoke of 'feeling' (using the English word at a press conference), to avoid having to explain that Eto'o had no wish to continue playing second fiddle to the new star. In one training session he had shouted at Guardiola, reminding him that he was a forward and that Guardiola had never been one; that he knew what he was doing. At the end of that campaign there was no longer any understanding, or patience. Pep was conscious of the enormous effort that Eto'o had made that year, but they had reached an impasse. The coach's decision was inevitable: the development of 'the Flea' required he be given all the leeway that Eto'o was demanding.

GB: How do you explain the departure of Samuel Eto'o?

PG: It was a tactical decision, a purely tactical choice, nothing else. No other reason. It would have been impossible to win everything we won that first year without Samuel, absolutely impossible. He adapted to Leo when I told him to do so, and to the tactical plans at the Bernabéu and also in Rome. But I decided Leo was going to play regularly down the middle and I thought it would be unfair to ask Samuel to play every game on the wing. I did not think it was right to ask him to adapt to Leo eighty games a season, it was not the correct thing to do. Pedro, Jeffrén, Bojan … they could; not Samuel.

'Ronaldinho brought hope to the "Barcelonistas" back to the club and Eto'o helped immensely with the victories that came as a consequence,' explains Joan Laporta. 'I assumed the responsibility of telling Samuel that he would not be continuing at the club. For a player as temperamental as him, it is difficult to take on board that concept of "feeling" that Pep mentioned, even though he knew that he could have done more to please the coach. This was not a whim of Pep's, rather a decision that was very difficult for us to take. That year we wanted to sign Villa, or Forlán or Ibrahimović. We tried Villa first of all, but financially it was impossible. Finally was Ibra. We needed Eto'o to agree to the deal before we could bring in his replacement, but Samuel did not want to go on loan to Valencia, although he said yes to Inter Milan. What's more, Ibra was the technical staff's preference. Manchester City offered us €32 million for Eto'o, but he did

Man of the match, goalscorer of the 2–1 . . . at Wembley Leo Messi
helped Barcelona win another Champions League.

His third Champions
League win, but he
only celebrated two.

In 2011, at Wembley, the world recognised he was not just something special. He was probably the best ever. Sir Alex Ferguson went out of his way to shake his hand.

Pep had to understand how to talk to Leo.
At first, fluent communication was not easy.

The 2011 Club World Cup against Santos was the consecration of the Barcelona style.

On that day, Leo Messi asked Neymar to join Barcelona.

Lionel with his mother Celia (right) and Monica Fein, mayor of Messi's home town Rosario, after being made Honorary Citizen on 30 December 2011. He is finally recognised at home.

Third Ballon d'Or. He wanted more.

On the pitch at the last game with Pep Guardiola at the Camp Nou. Messi scored four goals and said goodbye to him on the pitch. 'Thank you for everything, Leo,' Pep told him.

Tito Vilanova was the first coach at the Barcelona academy to make him play in his current position. They met again in the first team and Leo backed him when he became first-team coach. Seeing Vilanova getting ill was very hard for him.

Leo and a ball.
A special relationship.

With Jose Manuel Pinto,
a close friend who knows
how to look after him.

He works with the Leo Messi Foundation to help children. He started it after a visit to a ward with kids suffering from cancer which made him cry.

Nobody got this far.

not want to go there either because they still had not qualified for the Champions League.' Zlatan cost the €20 million at which Eto'o was valued plus €46 million more, making him the most expensive player in the history of the club.

The new tactical approach offered the possibility of implementing the classic Dutch 4-3-3 formation with a forward in Ibra capable of holding the ball and playing with his back to goal, something that gave the option of using the long ball more often, but also someone with the talent to drive at goal and to score. Pep had played in such a formation under Louis Van Gaal, with Patrick Kluivert the player up front.

But for that to work a fruitful relationship had to be established between Zlatan and his colleagues up front, especially Leo, who would often come inside with dangerous diagonal runs. That was the challenge for the coming season and it would reach its peak in December when the club hoped to consolidate all that it had set out to do a year and a half earlier. To do so they had to win the sixth title out of six, the FIFA Club World Cup in Abu Dhabi.

Leo had a minor ankle injury and had some recuperative sessions with Juanjo Brau on the beach at Abu Dhabi. He was not yet ready to start the semi-final against the Mexican club Atlante, and stayed on the bench. The game became an uphill battle after Barcelona conceded a goal in the fourth minute. Not even Atlante were ready for that: they knew they were up against the best team of the year and felt they didn't stand a chance. 'Boys, we'll defend deep and let's hope we don't concede five,' said one of the senior players before taking to the field. But, given the chance, the Mexicans were not going to give anything away. Busquets equalised in the thirty-fifth minute, but it was difficult to create chances against the defensiveness of Atlante. In the fifty-fourth minute, Ibrahimović placed the ball into space for Leo, who had just come on, to run on to and he scored to make it 2–1. Pedro scored the final goal to make it 3–1, becoming at that moment the only player to score in all competitions in a single year.

Before the final against the Argentinian team Estudiantes de la Plata, Messi witnessed one of the most memorable speeches Pep Guardiola ever gave his team. He ended it with the words: 'If we lose today, we will still be the best team in the world. If we win, we will be eternal.'

But Estudiantes scored the first goal and then dropped deep to defend their advantage.

*19 December 2009. FIFA Club World Cup Championship. Estudiantes
1–2 Barcelona. Abu Dhabi*

*Barcelona: Valdés; Alvés, Puyol, Piqué, Abidal; Xavi, Busquets
(Touré, 79th minute), Keita (Pedro, 46th minute); Messi, Ibra
and Henry (Jeffrén, 82nd minute).*

*Estudiantes: Albil; Rodríguez, Cellay, Desábato, Ré (Rojo,
90th+1 minute); Díaz, Benítez (Sánchez, 76th minute), Verón,
Braña; Enzo Pérez (Máxi Núñez, 79th minute) and Boselli.*

*Goals: 1–0, 37th minute: Boselli. 1–1, 89th minute: Pedro.
1–2, 110th minute; Messi.*

Ramón Besa, *El País*. Messi doesn't just have feet and a head,
although he probably has the best ones in the world, but he is
also very good with his chest. And he scores goals with a heart
that wins titles as he did yesterday in Abu Dhabi. Such are the
subtleties of football. Something so serious, a title as grand
as the World Club Championship ends up being child's play,
Messi's chest, Jeffrén's legs, Pedro's head … Pedro forced extra
time in the penultimate minute. He scored following a Barcelona attack, and once Albil was beaten it was only a matter
of Messi putting the ball into the net with his chest following
a cross from Dani Alvés. The best *pibe* [little kid] ended up
confirming the defeat of his Argentinian compatriots.

Luis Martín, *El País*: The ball came to him following the slightest of deflections, perfect for finishing off and anyone else
would have looked to meet it with their head. Not Messi; he'd
shown what he could do with his head in Rome, the day his
boot came off and Barcelona won the Champions League and
with it the treble. Yesterday he invented a goal with his chest.
Or was it his heart? He showed his back to Verón and Cellay
and his chest to the ball. And Albil was left there looking at the
ball as it went in. 'I stayed up there because I wanted to make
sure, that's all. I hit it with my chest and my heart,' the Argentine explained. And then, Messi ran off with his face burst-

ing with happiness. His colleagues embraced him, and when he emerged from that cluster he raised his arms to the sky in tribute to his late grandmother, Celia. And it was over. What no one had ever managed to do before, Guardiola's Barcelona did yesterday: in one year, six titles. The lot. And Messi was in all of them. He celebrated on and off the pitch, where he was prompted to say: 'A lot of time is going to have to pass by for us to appreciate what we have achieved but it is great. Today we don't realise it. It's going to be very difficult for anyone to repeat it because no other side has ever managed it.' Leo's words.

'I felt more confident doing it like that because I was too close to the goalkeeper to try a header. The ball came to me at a strange angle, we'd been practising a lot and as I was so close I thought about guiding it more than just hitting it with my head,' he told Martín Souto in the interview for TyC. Leo explained in *El País* that 'I tried to guide the ball. I saw the goalkeeper going in one direction and I thought I would send it the other way.'

It was the day that Pep Guardiola cried on the pitch, the culmination of an extraordinary year and a half of pressure, pleasure and results. Leo was the first to hug him, grateful, before going to shake the hand of all his rivals, all defeated Argentinians.

'This group and Barcelona owe a great deal to Pep for everything that he has done,' explained Leo after the title had been won. 'He arrived when we had gone through two bad years, where we had failed to meet our objectives, and he changed the mentality of the dressing room.'

Leo was now undoubtedly one of the main protagonists in a side that had entered the history books, part of a collective that identified him as a beacon, that vital piece among a group of people who understood a type of football that would survive football's normally limited memory span.

The players took photos in the dressing room with the latest trophy and then there was a party. Together and apart. Ibrahimović with his people, Leo with his brothers.

'The thing is,' recalls Joan Laporta, 'I remember him dancing when we were celebrating winning the title in Abu Dhabi in 2009. And he was messing around as usual when the senior players (Xavi, Puyol, Iniesta, Valdés) came up to me and asked me for their bonuses. When that happened, Leo was always there, watching, because they would share the final decision with him simply with a look.'

Ibrahimović never did understand the senior players' acquiescent nature.

6. FOUR GOALS IN THE CHAMPIONS LEAGUE QUARTER-FINALS AGAINST ARSENAL, 2010

In fourteen months, Leo Messi had signed two new contracts: one in July 2008 on an annual salary of €7.8 million with a €1.5 million bonus for matches played; his release clause stood at €150 million. But in September 2009, Barcelona offered him a new deal which reflected the success in Guardiola's first season: his salary reached €12 million. If the team won the league or Champions League and he played 60 per cent of the games, bonuses of up to €2 million would be added as a fixed wage the following season. The contract expired in 2016 and also had a release clause. If someone wanted to sign Leo without negotiating with Barcelona, his price was now €250 million.

After victory in the FIFA Club World Cup the players left for their holidays. On their return they were to face Villarreal. Those Christmas holidays, unlike the previous year, were used to the last day, and Leo returned the day before the match. Guardiola wanted to save him for a cup match against Sevilla three days later. The player said he was available for the league match but Pep stuck to his guns. After the 1–1 draw with Villarreal, the coach mixed some fringe players (Pinto, Chigrinski, Maxwell, Thiago and Bojan, who played as a number 9) with first team players against Sevilla. In fact, the bench, with the exception of Ibra, had played in both the Champions League final and the Club World Cup final. Messi started on the wing.

Sevilla applied a simple but effective tactic: they defended very deep and launched long balls in behind the defence. On seeing the disillusionment within the squad after the defeat, Pep felt he had disap-

5 January 2010. First leg. Barcelona 1–2 Sevilla

Barcelona: Pinto; Alvés, Milito (Busquets, 66th minute), Chi-grinski, Maxwell; Thiago (Xavi, 71st minute), Márquez, Ini-esta; Messi, Bojan and Pedro (Ibrahimović, 46th minute). Subs not used: Valdés, Henry, Puyol and Piqué.

Sevilla: Palop; Konko, Escudé, Dragutinović, Navarro; Romarić, Lolo (Duscher, 81st minute); Capel, Navas (Renato, 46th minute), Perotti and Koné (Negredo, 69th minute). Subs not used: Dani Jiménez, Cala, José Carlos and Redondo.

Goals: 0–1. 60th minute: Capel puts away a Perotti cross which Renato dummies. 1–1. 73rd minute: Ibrahimović, from a Márquez pass. 1–2. 75th minute: Negredo penalty.

Jordi Quixano, *El País*: Messi returned from Argentina bringing back with him fantasy football. Two bursts from the wing were the highlights of the duel. After one, he fired in a venomous shot which Palop diverted round the post. Then in a brilliant move, with almost no space for the shot, the genius curled an effort against the woodwork.

pointed them and determined to reward their ambition by fielding the strongest possible team for the return leg, except for Pinto in goal, the cup goalkeeper.

In eighteen months Guardiola's Barcelona had still not lost a single knockout match.

His players' response in Sevilla was magnificent, in a real cup tie played in torrential rain which added an epic touch: the raids on goal, defended by an extraordinary Palop, were incessant, especially in the second half.

'He was burning with rage,' remembers Gerard Piqué. He was crying silently, with his shirt covering his face, discreetly, crestfallen. Away from everyone. 'If you didn't look carefully, you wouldn't even realise.' In those circumstances, it's better to leave him alone, which is what most of his team-mates did that night.

---

13 January 2010. Second leg. Sevilla 0–1 Barcelona

Barcelona: Pinto; Alvés (Pedro, 84th minute), Piqué, Puyol, Abidal; Xavi, Busquets, Iniesta; Messi, Ibrahimović (Bojan, 84th minute) and Henry. Subs not used: Valdés; Milito, Chigrinski, Maxwell and Jonathan.

Sevilla: Palop; Konkó, Escudé, Dragutinović, Navarro; Navas, Duscher (Lolo, 58th minute), Romarić (Cala, 92nd minute), Adriano (Capel, 64th minute); Renato and Negredo. Subs not used: Javi Varas; Koné, José Carlos and Stankevicius.

Goal: 0–1. 63rd minute: Xavi slots a well-placed shot just inside the post from the edge of the area.

Martí Perarnau, *Sport*: José Manuel Pinto and Leo Messi already have something else in common, apart from belonging to the same club and winning six cups in one year: they cried disconsolately on that early Wednesday morning in full view of all of their team-mates in the Sánchez Pizjuán dressing room. Compatriot Gabi Milito, the man who acts as a bodyguard for the *blaugrana* forward, tried to console Messi … The example of the man who fights to the limit of his sporting ability transcends a timely triumph, or a bitter defeat, in a society all too accustomed to throwing in the towel in the face of the slightest difficulty. Today's world no longer needs stars, but examples.

It was the first title that Guardiola had failed to win.

Pep went to console Leo. The Argentinian felt guilty about the elimination and told the coach as much. 'Nobody is guilty here,' Guardiola told him. 'And if the finger should be pointed at anyone it should be at me for not knowing how to lead you into the next round.'

GB: *What do you say to Leo when he is crying? Or is it better to leave him to weep?*

PG: *It is best to let him be. You see him and you think, 'He will be okay'. You realise that it is best, as a coach, to have this kind of player rather than those who, after a defeat, start playing poker and laughing on the team bus home. You prefer a guy who, yes, can play poker at the end, but he has also expressed clearly that he hates losing.*

GB: *In Argentina, there is a saying: a game shouldn't make you cry. But if you do cry after a defeat it must be because somehow you are playing for your life.*

PG: *Maybe it is what you say. That love to win, the passion, the competitiveness ... he is an animal, as Tiger Woods is, or Michael Jordan, or Rafa Nadal. Those athletes are unique and all you have to do when you meet them is try to understand them. You cannot say, 'I am the coach, I have the moral authority because the club has put me here and we are going to do what I want you to do.' They are a rare species that you have to make the effort to understand. You have to get inside their heads. Manel Estiarte was key for that learning process, having been the best ever at his sport. At the start of Manel's career he wanted the ball all the time, he wanted everything his own way, he had days where he did not want to talk to anybody. When Leo got like that, Manel would say, 'let him be. In a few days try to approach him again and chat again.' But what you cannot do is let him do everything he wants; you have to demand a series of things from him, always trying to synchronise with the way he thinks. His mind is that of a privileged player, unique. And as such you have to try to understand how he thinks.*

GB: *What do you think motivates him?*

PG: *Leo's facial expression and body language tell you how he feels, how he is. And going by that, it is evident that he doesn't compete to have a fantastic girlfriend perhaps, or to be in magazines or in the press, or to film an advertisement. He competes to win in those 90 minutes, the rest doesn't interest him. He is like Cristiano Ronaldo, decisive and imperious. Coaches have to give him all the elements so that he can express himself near the area and be happy. He does the rest, he has that special gift. He's at his happiest when he's on the pitch.*

And if he wins, of course. And scores. In three consecutive matches in February, luck was not on Messi's side and he was less prominent than usual. The third of those was the first leg of the last 16 against Stuttgart in the Champions League, a match which had consequences for Guardiola's future plans. Barcelona drew 1–1 in Germany and Leo was unnoteworthy. What was happening? Any other coach would have sat the footballer down, given him a break and allowed him to reflect. Pep reacted in another way. He blamed himself for not managing to get the best out of Leo and studied the reasons for such a poor Messi, together with assistant Tito Vilanova. The conclusion was not surprising: his talent was being wasted on the wing.

With Ibrahimović in the centre of the attack in the usual 4-3-3, Pep told Messi to start on the wing but play inside as often as he wanted. But Leo did not touch the ball often enough in those circumstances.

And, in addition, Leo no longer ran down the touchline. Those diagonal runs inside caused a serious problem to his own team: the team suffered defensively. 'They murdered us down that flank,' it was said privately after the match in Germany. Cristian Molinaro, the left-back, pushed forward with total freedom as Leo did not track back. Pep, who remembered similar problems against Lyon, admitted after the match that Leo was no longer going to play on the wing, he clearly didn't want to and shouldn't: the risk was too great and that could be very costly in Europe.

Pep knew that Messi did his talking on the pitch and those constant diagonal bursts sent out a clear message: 'This is my game.' And not only that, but his habitat, the area in which he wanted to be most influential, was the space between defenders and central midfielders.

There was an added problem: when he made those runs, the presence of other attackers, his own team-mates, literally blocked his route to goal; they were in his way. Something had to be done. The tactical evolution of Leo and, therefore the side, was irresistible from then on.

When Pep found the time, when he saw Leo was willing to discuss the subject, the conversation was as he imagined it would be: he did not feel comfortable; he liked playing in a different way. Leo never told him that Ibrahimović had to go, but as the season went on, Guardiola realised that the two of them were tactically incompatible, and there were too many weaknesses without the ball.

He knew Leo could be more effective if he was surrounded by a clearly defined organisational structure – he was going to be the unstable element and there had to be stable elements at his side, players who would give offensive organisation to the team. If everyone knew what Messi was going to do, they could apply themselves to offering him the solutions that would allow him to make the most of his creative talent. This would make another vital requirement easier: getting the ball back. If they attacked in a disciplined way, each man in his position except Leo, it would be easier to initiate the pressing. Guardiola wanted to control where the opposition danger came from, and he preferred it to be down the middle; Keita and Pedro, with greater defensive discipline and happy to track back, were going to play out wide in the big games.

Guardiola said to Leo: 'You're going to play down the middle from now on. And you're going to score a bucketload of goals, three or four per game.' Four days after the draw in Germany, Pep tried a 4-2-3-1 with Ibra up top and Messi behind him. 'He was not contributing much. We needed him to get more involved,' Pep explained the change in a press conference. 'He is capable of playing very well in all positions. Last year he played on the right wing 90 per cent of the time. He knows that, even if he plays there, he can drift inside whenever he wants to. But if he plays as a winger, we are more predictable.'

With Ibra on the bench, Messi moved into the middle in the return leg against Stuttgart at the Camp Nou: 4–0 to Barcelona with two goals from 'the Flea', who was also involved in the third. The dip in form was forgotten; he had scored seven goals in three matches. His goalscoring rate would shoot up from that moment. He would not have been able to do it from the wing. Nor as a classic number 9; centre-backs would have eaten him up.

Did Guardiola find him his position or did Leo keep knocking on the door until he got what he wanted? A close look at the evolution of the process suggests that it was surely a bit of both.

At a press conference in Buenos Aires in summer 2013, Pep explained in detail: 'When I started at Barcelona, Laudrup would appear down the middle and I, the midfielder, could pass the ball everywhere; there was one more of us in midfield, we outnumbered our opponents. And I would say, bloody hell, I like this. Leo understood what playing down the middle was all about very quickly. He would have picked it up if I told him to go and play at left-back. Ah, and you will say, well, you have that monster of a player, and that makes everything easy. Would you have done it without Leo? Well, maybe not.'

Everything that Pep decided at Barcelona was for Leo, so that Leo would score goals and the team, and Guardiola, win matches. It is therefore a selfish decision by the coach: that is how Guardiola understands it himself. Or, put another way, Pep's generosity towards Messi's wishes was not the only factor. But it got to a point where he had to take the decision, and in his second season in charge he effectively gave the team to Leo.

GB: *When he arrives at La Masía and Rodolfo Borrell says to him: 'Okay, you start on the wing', Leo answered him: 'No, no, I play in the hole.' Subsequent coaches, with the exception of Tito, ask him to do the same, despite his natural habitat being down the middle. He finally ends up playing regularly as a second striker with Gratacós at Barça B. Rijkaard puts him back on the wing and, when you arrive, I imagine that Leo was hoping to move to a position where he could see more of the ball. Is his impatience or need to be the centre of operations noticeable?*

PG: *No. It is true that you get more of the ball down the middle than on the wing. You have to be more patient on the wing. In reality, teams were gradually learning how to silence the danger that Dani Alvés and he brought down the wing and in the end you reach the conclusion that this guy has not touched the ball in twenty minutes. And he's the best we've got; we have to do something so he gets on the ball more. It's as simple as that. I realised that, especially when we played in Europe, where it's a more physically demanding game where you have to be more rigorous defensively and sometimes Leo wasn't involved in the play, he would disappear from the match which would create problems. It is all a learning process, how you get to know the players.*

GB: *Leo has felt very comfortable playing down the middle since he was a boy. Why did it take so long for him to be played in his natural position then?*

PG: *The questions you ask yourself are: where do I want to go with these players, how do I want to play, what do I need? And you gradually adapt the tactics. It's difficult for the players to understand because they never put themselves in the coach's head to have a global vision, they have a biased one, their one. You try to make them understand why such decisions are made and why they benefit everyone, through talks or explaining the reasons for victories or defeats. Some accept them and others don't. The coach's big challenge is to make them understand what is good for them and the team, and to make them see that they each have a role.*

Barcelona travelled to London to face Cesc Fàbregas' Arsenal in the first leg of the Champions League quarter-final. Thierry Henry was suffering the consequences of the tactical change and stayed on the bench. The Frenchman never fully accepted the situation and explained to other players years later: 'One day I asked for a pass, and never started a game again.' For Henry, his demotion was a mystery.

Víctor Vázquez, who played with Leo in the lower ranks, explains it differently: 'When I started to see Leo down the middle, it reminded me of our youth team. One player had to be sacrificed. At that time it was Songo'o, he used to play at centre-forward because of his physical presence, not his quality. Songo'o was a beast, a real powerhouse who would knock people over, like a game of bowling. And when Leo arrived, Songo'o had to move over towards the right wing with Toni Calvo, and they both had to vie for the same spot: Messi was the number ten, he needed the space left by Songo'o to grow.'

A strange situation occurred during that match in London: Barcelona at their best, as they were in the first half, had a clumsy Ibrahimović trying to force play up front, more distant than ever from the *culé* style. But he scored two great goals after half-time to put the team in the driving seat, although the game finished in an intriguing 2–2. It was the peak at the club for the Swede who so far had scored 15 league goals and four in Europe, two more than Eto'o at that stage the previous season. Leo was playing behind Ibra and was very quiet. Xavi and Iniesta told him as much bluntly: they needed more from him; he seemed uninterested and did not get involved.

Leo listened to Xavi and Iniesta. He was aware that not only were they both supreme central midfielders, but they were helping him grow, he needed them. They did not really show their emotions on the pitch, but they had taken on great responsibility and power in the dressing room. Around that time, a kitman from the Argentina national team, who everyone knows as Marito, went to Barcelona to follow Guardiola's training sessions. Messi introduced him to the players in the dressing room. When 'the Flea' was busy sorting out his kit, Marito decided to wind him up for a laugh. He shouted in Messi's direction: 'Leo, listen to what they're saying about you. You only play well because of this guy [Iniesta].' To which Messi responded amid laughter: 'They are right.'

If Xavi and Iniesta were his partners on the pitch, those who gave him the ball in the best situations so they could play his game, Pinto, Dani Alvés and Gabi Milito had become his Praetorian Guard. The latter filled the gap that Sylvinho had left. If anyone kicked him in training, Milito would lose his temper: 'Oi, careful!'

Leo knew that he had played badly against Arsenal and deserved a telling-off from his team-mates: he had to respond in the return leg.

PG: *That knockout game against Arsenal was really beauti-*
    ful. Arsenal play good football, the matches in England have
    always been spectacular. We played well in the first leg, but they
    have always caused us problems because they are quick on the
    counter-attack. They have always caused us problems at our sta-
    dium, too. The thing is we had some players who ...wow ...

During that season of collective tweaks, Messi had already scored three hat-tricks before his display against Arsenal. As Ramón Besa says, a more childlike Leo went out to play that night. Watch the goal celebrations:

http://www.youtube.com/watch?v=r6BHyv6nkAs

After the second goal, sitting with legs and arms stretched out with a child's smile, he seems to be saying 'look at what I've done' rather than 'I've done it'. A subtle gesture follows the fourth goal as he moves his head from one side to the other while running to celebrate. You can almost hear the childish chant coming from him:

---

6 April 2010. Champions League quarter-final second leg. Barcelona 4–1 Arsenal

Barcelona: Valdés; Alvés, Márquez, Milito, Abidal (Maxwell, 53rd minute); Xavi, Busquets; Messi; Pedro (Iniesta, 86th minute), Bojan (Touré, 56th minute) and Keita. Subs not used substitutes: Pinto; Fontàs, Henry and Jeffrén.

Arsenal: Almunia; Sagna, Vermaelen, Silvestre (Eboué, 63rd minute), Clichy; Denilson, Diaby; Walcott, Nasri, Rosicky (Eduardo, 73rd minute); and Bendtner. Subs not used: Fabiański; Traoré, Mérida, Campbell and Eastmond.

Goals: 0–1. 18th minute: Bendtner. 1–1. 21st minute: Messi. 2–1. 37th minute. Messi: 3–1. 42nd minute. Messi. 4–1. 88th minute: Messi.

Marca (Madrid-based newspaper): Outstanding performance by Leo to take Barcelona to the semi-finals. Messi fell from heaven to put things in their place. Bendtner scored the first goal of the game, but that was the beginning of the end for Arsenal, victims of another superhuman game by Leo Messi, scorer of four goals. The keys – Leo is unique, a one-off. He doesn't play football, he practises another sport unachievable for the rest. He joins a select group of players who have scored four goals in a Champions League game, alongside Van Basten, Simone Inzaghi, Prso, Van Nistelrooy and Shevchenko.

Luis Martín, *El País*: Leo knows that in another team, under another coach, it would be difficult for him to enjoy his football as much as he is right now at the Camp Nou. Because with other players, another coach and at another club, the ball would be with the opposition.

'lalalalala-la, the fourth goal against Arsenal, in the Champions League …'

The British press admitted that there was no longer any doubt about who the best player of that generation was: they had just seen one of his great individual performances in a European competition.

PG: *Tito would always say to me: you can organise your part of the game, put the players in position, but later, the last 15 metres ... bloody hell, the ability to dribble, shoot and score a goal ... you either have it or you don't. And Leo has that ease with which he can win you a game in 15 or 20 minutes like he did that day.*

GB: *He scored four goals against Arsenal, it was a great day, you can see how happy he is ... Does he switch off when he goes into the dressing room or does he continue celebrating?*

PG: *No, he is happy, of course: he takes his time, has a relaxing shower, stays longer at dinner. Just like everyone: when I give a press conference after we win, I am happier than when we lose. That is normal.*

GB: *I'm writing about his first goal against Albacete and, just like against Arsenal, you see one of these childlike Leo situations: Ronnie – another kid – gives him a piggy-back ride. But he doesn't do a special celebration at the end of the match, because he thinks it is the first goal of many. I don't know if you know many players with this mentality, so conscious that the target is much further away.*

PG: *These processes that would be almost definitive for anyone else are not a big deal to him. This is what I was saying to you, he thinks: 'I come here to win the league, to win titles. I win the league, great, but I've scored 40 goals, if not, the league matters very little to me.' He always wants more. And you are lucky enough, as am I, to meet him one day on the path in your professional career. And I'm sure the only thing running through his head now is the World Cup, I mean, everything else is going really well, but he will be prepared for this World Cup, I know it. If he and Argentina arrive in good shape, anything can happen: if he arrives in good shape, consider Argentina favourites.*

After the Arsenal game, Leo kept the ball as a souvenir. It was the trophy from that night. He did not do it for superstitious reasons (there are strikers who say keeping such things brings luck to the home and their careers). Leo neither has nor wants lucky charms: 'No, I haven't got any superstitions. I just think about my family before playing,' he said on the UEFA website.

In the semi-finals, Barcelona faced José Mourinho's Inter Milan.

20 April 2010. Champions League semi-final first leg. Inter Milan 3–1 Barcelona

Inter: Julio César; Maicon (Chivu, 72nd minute), Lucio, Samuel, Zanetti; Motta, Cambiasso; Eto'o, Sneijder, Pandev (Stankovic, 55th minute); and Diego Milito (Balotelli, 75th minute). Subs not used: Orlandoni; Córdoba, Muntari and Materazzi.

Barcelona: Valdés; Alvés, Piqué, Puyol, Maxwell; Xavi, Busquets; Pedro, Messi, Keita; and Ibrahimović (Abidal, 61st minute). Subs not used: Pinto; Márquez, Bojan, Henry, G. Milito and Touré.

Goals: 0–1. 18th minute: Pedro, from a Maxwell pull-back. 1–1. 30th minute: Sneijder scores from a Milito assist. 2–1. 48th minute: Maicon, from a Milito pass. 3–1. 61st minute: Milito, header.

ESPN Deportes: The *blaugrana* team had yet another one of those games where they lacked effectiveness up front, the same as the Saturday game against Espanyol (0–0). Ibrahimović was again in the line-up. The Swede did not receive clear passes but nor did he move around with intelligence so Messi, Xavi or Busquets could find him (…) Guardiola took off a useless Ibrahimović and asked Abidal to move to the left-back position with Maxwell in front of him, and also he moved Messi to the centre to fight it out with the two big centre-backs, Samuel and Lucio.

Pablo Egea, *Marca:* For the first time since Guardiola took over the first team, the coach has looked inferior to his rival and has not won the game on the blackboard. On this occasion, Mourinho beat him with a well-researched performance and managed to nullify all the weapons from the last Champions League winners. Also, for the first time, the best coach of last year failed in his substitutions and gave the impression of not being in control of the game.

The Portuguese coach had spoken about his opponents' 'obsession' with wanting to reach the final at the Santiago Bernabéu. Once again, he was laying down an emotive challenge in this match. It was the knockout game in which Guardiola betrayed himself and the tactical evolution he had decided to apply to the side. He might have lost the connection he had developed with Leo. In the first leg in Milan, Pep once again used Ibrahimović as a number 9, which even went against his intuition.

Pep, who replaced Ibrahimović early on in the second half, in the only change he made all game, stuck to the idea of using the Swede as the reference point up front in the return leg, but corrected it after wasting an hour. At the Camp Nou, Plan Ibrahimović definitively came to an end.

GB: *When you decide that Ibra is an option, as happened against Arsenal, Leo seems to turn into a tortoise: he withdraws inside himself, he finds it hard to communicate, he puts up a barrier which all of his coaches have encountered, it appears when things don't go the way his talent desires. How is that situation dealt with?*

PG: *Trying to convince him over and over again. And at the right moment, grabbing him and explaining why you've thought about doing it that way, the benefits this has, the benefits that has. That year we won the league with 99 points and we didn't win the Champions League semi-final because Inter probably were better or probably because I didn't interpret the second leg correctly. These things happen, because we did everything so that he could be comfortable. That season we even played with a double pivot so that he could play in the hole behind Ibra and the Swede could work his magic down the middle. But decisions are always made thinking about the best for everyone. Am I wrong? Yes, of course. Two hundred times. But I don't look for excuses. You move on. It is pointless to look for them.*

Ibrahimović, sensing that the rise of a hungry 22-year-old Leo was blocking his own ascendancy, asked Pep many times that season what he should do to help more. In some way, Pep had nothing else to say to him, the team was going in another direction and the coach had to make decisions.

*28 April 2010. Champions League semi-final second leg. Barcelona
1–0 Inter Milan*

*Barcelona: Valdés; Piqué, Touré, Gaby Milito (Maxwell, 46th
minute); Alvés, Xavi, Busquets (Jeffrén, 63rd minute), Keita;
Messi, Ibrahimović (Bojan, 63rd minute) and Pedro. Subs not
used: Pinto; Márquez, Henry and Thiago.*

*Inter: Julio César; Maicon, Lucio, Samuel, Zanetti; Cambiasso,
Motta; Eto'o (Mariga, 85th minute), Sneijder (Muntari, 66th
minute), Chivu; and Diego Milito (Córdoba, 81st minute).
Subs not used: Toldo, Materazzi, Arnautović and Balotelli.*

*Goals: 1–0. 84th minute: Piqué receives the ball from Xavi in
the area, turns and scores.*

Marca: So much hard work but the team died just before
reaching port. The wonderful story of the last year and a half
did not have a good ending, Barcelona has had to wake up
from the dream unexpectedly. Pep started with three centre-
backs with freedom to go forward and used Alvés in the midfield as another offensive weapon, but not everything came
off. Without spaces and with Ibra too static, they lacked ideas.
Messi was too far away from the box. He wanted to sort out
all the problems of the team by himself, but in football you
have to remember that, no matter how good your players are,
it is always 11 vs 11.

'The "conductor of the orchestra" or the most influential player
has always conditioned the team's formation in football,' explains
Josep María Minguella who was Vic Buckingham and Rinus
Michels' assistant at Barcelona for six seasons, as well as an agent.
'Di Stéfano used to do it, or Cruyff, who had total control at Ajax.
When there are players who bother the top guy in some way, the
coach looks for a way to make it easier for him so he is relaxed. It's
not about discussing the quality of Eto'o or Ibrahimović, two sensational players, but if you want to look for a game style that suits the

top man better, you don't play them. On top of that, it helps having excellent, educated players who keep a low profile in the dressing room instead of those with strong personalities, like those two.'

What broke the Pep–Zlatan relationship? Was it the tactical evolution of Messi asking for space or the character of a player who does not accept change for the benefit of the team? Ibra had been the protagonist at all his clubs, it is what he asked for, so he was not willing to make space for Leo. In part because it went against his style of play to create space for 'the Flea'. And when a player of that level is required to do things that do not fit with his natural style, the relationship with the one who forces him always snaps.

Ibra told the story in his own way in his autobiography, *I Am Zlatan*. And his own way, even though couched in the language of the street, does not differ much from Leo and Pep's version. Sometimes he seems to understand the motives, but resented the way issues were handled. At other times he seems to understand nothing.

'Everything started well but then Messi started speaking. Messi is remarkable. Fucking incredible. I don't know him very well. We are very different. He arrived at Barça at 13 and grew up in the culture. He has no problem with all that school bollocks. The game revolves around him in the team, which is natural. He shines, but I had arrived, and I was scoring more than him. So he went to Guardiola and said to him: "I don't want to play on the right wing any more. I want to be in the middle." That is where I was. But Guardiola didn't give a shit. He changed tactics. He went from 4-3-3 to 4-5-1 with me up top and Messi behind, and he left me in the wilderness. Every ball went through Messi and I couldn't play my game. I have to be free like a bird on the pitch. I'm the guy who wants to make the difference at every level. But Guardiola sacrificed me. That is the truth. He trapped me up there. Well, I can understand his situation. Messi was the star. Guardiola had to listen to him. But come on! I had scored goal after goal at Barça, I was lethal too. He could not adapt the team just for one man. I mean: why the hell did they sign me then? Nobody pays that amount of money just to strangle me as a player. Guardiola had to think about both of us and, of course, the atmosphere at board level changed slightly. I was their biggest investment and didn't feel right in the new formation. I was too expensive not to feel right.

Sporting director Txiki Beguiristain was pushing me, he was telling me I had to speak to the coach. "Resolve it!"

'So I addressed the coach. I went up to him on the pitch during training, and I was careful about one thing. I didn't want a fight, and I told him:

'"I don't want to fight. I don't want a war. I just want to discuss things."

'He nodded his head. But he seemed a little scared, so I repeated: "If you think I want a fight, we will leave it. I just want to speak."

'"Good! I like speaking to my players."

'"Listen!" I continued. "You are not using my ability. If I was not the goalscorer you wanted, you should have bought Inzaghi or someone else. I need space, and to be free. I can't go up and down constantly. I weigh 98 kilos. I don't have the physique for it." He stood there thinking. He often did that. "I think we can play this way. And if we cannot ... Well, then it is better if you leave me on the bench. With all due respect, I understand you, but I am being sacrificed for other players. This is not working. It is like you bought a Ferrari, but you are driving it as if it were a Fiat."

'He carried on thinking: "Okay, maybe it was a mistake. This is my problem. I'm going to work on it."

'I felt happy. He was going to work on it. ... The conversation seemed to go well, but suddenly Guardiola started to ignore me.'

After the book was published, Zlatan explained it all with this sentence: 'Guardiola sacrificed me for Messi and didn't have the decency to tell me.' What Ibrahimović doesn't say is that he demanded the coach make a change that would benefit him: 'The midget has to be dropped.'

'Leo never asked for Zlatan to leave,' assures ex-director of football Txiki Beguiristain. 'His football demanded his coach make a decision. And it was not in Barcelona's interests to stop that process.' The proposal was clear: the individual had to be sacrificed for the benefit of the group and the Swede did not want to do it. In his book *El largo viaje de Pep* ('Pep's Long Journey'), Martí Perarnau quotes anonymously from a first-team player: 'At Barça, when the ball is in one part of the pitch, the team knows that it must have a concrete formation. If the ball moves into another area, everyone's obligations change. There are some established criteria and we all follow them. Nobody is excluded, but Ibra excluded himself from them, he didn't want to participate. When he didn't have the ball, he didn't follow instructions. And when he had the ball, he did his pirouettes and didn't co-operate with the others.'

But Ibrahimović, who had taken a pay cut to go to Barcelona, is right about a number of things: Pep realised he had made a mistake by signing him and he took Leo's side. Since then the Swede has insisted on one thing: Leo is the best in the world and he did not have a bad relationship with him. 'That is gossip that someone spreads. I never had any sort of conflict with him,' he explained in Swedish newspaper *Fotbollskanalen*.

So at the end of that season, Ibra was going to be sacrificed.

In Guardiola's second year, Barcelona won the league with 99 points, three more than Real Madrid and with only one defeat. Leo scored 34 goals in domestic competition, a number that used to belong to another era; in fact the closest to him was Real's Gonzalo Higuaín, the second highest scorer with 27. After Zlatan's loan move to AC Milan the following season, David Villa arrived. He was told to forget about being the team's top scorer and was asked always to run into space and give depth.

Villa, who thought he was signing as a number 9, understood the situation soon after arriving and accepted the conditions.

7. THE 5–0 AGAINST MOURINHO'S MADRID AND THE FOUR CLÁSICOS IN TWO WEEKS

(The interview with Martín Souto on TyC from 2013 shows a video of Messi's altercation with Marcelo in a *clásico* against Real Madrid):

– *You're a hothead, aren't you?*
– *Yes.*
– *A bastard.*
– *Yes, I'm a hothead. More so when I'm playing for something important. I don't like to lose and I get agitated if I think I might.*

After two consecutive league titles, the 2010–11 season arrived in an air of optimism. Yaya Touré, Dmytro Chigrinski, Thierry Henry, Hleb, Rafa Márquez and Zlatan had all left the club. The message had to be reaffirmed: the side had to keep one step ahead of its rivals' defences who now recognised Barcelona as the greatest side in the world, and Leo as the greatest player of his generation. In addition to David Villa, versatile Brazilian Adriano and winger Ibrahim Afellay both arrived.

Leo was coming from another disappointment with the national side – Argentina had gone down in the quarter-finals of the World Cup against the hosts, Germany – and was now hoping that the following 2011 Copa América that was being played in Argentina would help repair the damage caused by the World Cup defeat.

At the World Cup, Leo had found himself a new friend. Javier Mascherano, the central midfielder from Liverpool, had spent the summer filling his head with the idea that he should convince Guardiola: he wanted to come to Barcelona, for whom he had been close to signing twelve months earlier. 'At the World Cup Leo had told me that Pep was looking for a central midfielder now that Yaya Touré had gone, and so I said to him, "Go on, speak to him, please ..." and he would answer me, "Yes, I'll mention it". "Tell him I'm not going to be one of those bad Argentines",' the 'little boss' Mascherano explained jokingly. 'When you've got someone like Leo at your club and he gives you a good reference, this helps you a great deal. Both he and Gabi Milito helped me. A big part of the reason I am here and have been able to live all of this is because of Leo.'

Mascherano arrived at a club that had finally mapped out the route it intended to take, and also knew those they needed to help them reach their destination. 'I arrived there halfway through that journey, and, from what I could see, Leo had a special bond with Pep because of all the things he did. How do you see that? Well, you notice it when a coach is surprised by some of the things that a player can do and shows that surprise, and also in the way Pep talked about Leo, with admiration, awe. It's very unusual to find that.'

When the signing was confirmed and Mascherano flew to Barcelona, Leo waited to see him, once all the necessary protocol had been completed. Mascherano had his photograph taken with the club badge at the Camp Nou, gave a press conference and Messi, waiting alone, embraced him in the room where families wait at the end of a game. 'Welcome,' he said.

The 'little boss' found that, on the pitch, his team-mates looked to Leo because the team had been built around his qualities, and also so they could benefit from the ease with which he understood the game. 'Leo reads games very well and knows how to adapt to any particular situation,' explains Pedro Rodríguez. 'If an opponent plays very forward, he always looks for the back of the defence; if he is back, he tries to come behind to get the ball to help us create space, to create the play. It sounds simple to know what's going on at every moment of a game and to know where to go, but it's not.'

The connection with Pedro and the players who surrounded 'the Flea' (Xavi, Iniesta, Busquets) reached a point where words were no longer necessary. 'There are always moments on the pitch, where we have to correct ourselves,' explains Pedro. '"Listen, close down more here", or "close down deeper", but they are unusual. In this team everything runs like clockwork, we know one another very well, we have spent a lot of time playing like this, and it all comes naturally, we hardly ever need to speak. There are times when I can play a whole game without saying a word to Leo.'

Martín Souto: With Barcelona's game, there are moments when the team brings the ball from one side to the other and you're stopped for something like a minute, and then suddenly they pass you the ball and 'goal'. In these situations is it like you're taking a breather so later on you can trick them, or is it something natural?

Lionel Messi: No, it's natural, because I know what our players are like. I know that at one time or another, the ball is going to come to me. I don't have to drive myself mad and where I'm stopped I know I can hurt my opponent. I wait for the moment because I know, because of the players we have, that it will come to me. We have become used to having the ball practically throughout the game.

(Leo Messi with Martín Souto on TyC)

It is clear that Leo Messi and Barcelona had developed what seemed to be an eternally symbiotic relationship. Eternal? Leo had been close to going to Inter and Real Madrid 'came looking for him every year,' according to Joan Laporta.

Since the time when Jorge Valdano was director of the *blancos*,

Real Madrid never closed the door on Leo. No one ever contacted Barcelona directly, but various intermediaries close to president Florentino Pérez kept in permanent contact with all those in Leo's entourage. 'I don't blame him, because he is the best player in the world and it's normal that a club like Madrid, like Milan, like Inter, like Juve, like Chelsea … should want him,' reflects Laporta. 'Madrid have people who can get into Leo's entourage, but Leo has always rejected their advances outright.' Approaches have also come from London and Manchester, but have always been ignored.

The Real Madrid president's admiration for Leo is well known. In the summer of 2012, Cristiano Ronaldo announced in the press room at the Bernabéu that he was so 'sad' when he scored two goals against Granada that he chose not to celebrate. He confirmed that this was for 'professional' reasons and those 'within the club' knew why. Ronaldo had met the previous day with the president to tell him that he did not feel valued at the club and that he wanted to leave. According to the journalist Javier Matallanas, Florentino Pérez answered him, 'If you want to go, bring me the money so I can sign Messi.'

Inevitably, the matches against Madrid are marked in red on Leo's calendar. And that 2010–11 season saw the first *clásico* with José Mourinho in charge of Real. He had been appointed from Inter with a brief to halt the *blaugrana* advance and modernise the historic club. In a preview of the game, Mourinho had insisted that football was a 'box of surprises' and he wasn't sure how his troops would respond. That night at the Camp Nou there followed an extraordinary meeting of minds between players, fans and a coach, between an ideal and its practical execution.

GB: Is a match against Real Madrid like any other match for Leo?
PG: Leo doesn't do what he does for me, he does it for himself. There are players who will do anything to gain their coach's love, so their colleagues will sing their praises, so they will be spoken of well in public. He competes against himself as well as against his rivals. And, of course, against his most direct rivals, as Cristiano does and by the same token Ronaldo competes against Messi, Barcelona vs Real Madrid…And not only does he compete against himself, he is also the most demanding player of all, much

more demanding of himself than I ever could be of him. He's unhappy when he does not play well and he feels that he is letting people down or letting himself down, not giving everything he could give. That's why he has achieved what he has and why he can maintain this extraordinarily high standard and that's why the team continues to support him.

Matchday 13 (29 November 2010) Barcelona 5–0 Real Madrid

Barcelona: Valdés; Alvés, Puyol, Piqué, Abidal; Xavi (Keita, 86th minute), Busquets, Iniesta; Messi, Villa (Bojan, 76th minute) and Pedro (Jeffrén, 86th minute). Subs not used: Pinto; Adriano, Maxwell, Thiago and Mascherano.

Real Madrid: Casillas; Ramos, Pepe, Carvalho, Marcelo (Arbeloa, 60th minute); Khedira, Xabi Alonso; Di María, Özil (Lass, 46th minute), Ronaldo; and Benzema. Subs not used: Dudek; Albiol, Granero, Pedro León and Higuaín.

Goals: 1–0. 10th minute: Xavi. 2–0. 18th minute: Pedro. 3–0. 55th minute: Villa. 4–0. 58th minute: Villa. 5–0. 90th minute: Jeffrén.

Santiago Siguero, *Marca*: One more season, and counting, Barcelona showed Real Madrid the huge gap that separates them. Away from the impressive score, five goals that could have significant repercussions for both teams, the game reflected again the differences between a unit that knows what it wants, and another one that needs to be built, yet … Messi again. He didn't score but destroyed Madrid once again. The white team suffers like no other from the Argentinian's talent. Guardiola placed him few metres deeper than usual. From a position in the hole, in the second part he could not stop passing balls in behind the Real defenders.

Conscious of the fact that his side contained more quality than he had ever had before, Mourinho looked to face Barcelona head-on. But he made various errors. He asked the physically fragile Özil to cover too much space in defence, including when Leo had the ball. The *merengues* should have kept a very tight central pressing line but ended up being an unresponsive unit with lines set too far apart with plenty of gaps to attack: a joy for Leo. The central defenders had no point of reference because 'the Flea' was moving around all of the attacking zone and Khedira and Xabi Alonso were always outnumbered. In the second half Mourinho brought on Lass Diarra as a third central midfielder, a precursor to what he would do in future encounters.

GB: What do you remember about the 5–0, what did you ask Leo to do?

PG: We adapted ourselves to Cristiano's counter-attacks. Based on where Cristiano was, our full-back had to go forward or come back. That was the defensive question; we knew from experience that, being a Mourinho side, they would attack the spaces. I was clear that they would wait for us to lose the ball to attack us as quickly as possible in behind our defenders, especially through Cristiano, who was always more isolated waiting for the counter. And when in attack, we should look for Leo. We had to find him in positions where he could be in space, and move freely and score. Curiously, he didn't score, but he did set up a few goals. We played well.

GB: In that season there was another Leo moment that had nothing to do with scoring. I remember him doing an incredibly long run after he had lost the ball in his opponent's half, to get it back off Kun Agüero. Have you ever used him to say, 'look, if a player like this does it …'?

PG: Yes, sometimes we have used our forwards who have made an enormous effort in defence to say: that's how we are as a team, it's not just the defenders that run, that's how we are as a team, don't ever forget it. That particular incident has become famous. Leo constantly needs challenges and at that particular time there were debates as to whether Kun was better than Leo. It was then a personal duel: now I'm going to run and take the ball off you. It's probably all about personal challenges, when he has them there are no problems.

It's worth taking a look at: http://www.youtube.com/watch?v=3YxOSDgrPzI JzBvB5TcdQ

GB: *From 17 April to 3 May those four famous and controversial* clásicos *were played. Firstly in the league, the Copa del Rey final, and then the Champions League semi-final. How was Leo during those days with tension at an all-time high?*

PG: *Well, the pressure he carries inside. Sometimes we forget he carries the weight of being the best player in the world, of all time, that he has a whole country behind him and a club that hopes he can win them games. And this on a daily basis. I always think that he is the best in history for that reason, for the continuity of things that he has done. I am convinced that Cruyff changed football, Pelé, of course, Maradona, but they were from another era. It's true that there are more cameras and for that reason less aggression than before. Before, so they say, there was a lot more kicking and the game was much harder than it is now. But it is also true that today everybody is physically much better prepared. Bear in mind that this bloke has the ability in this day and age to score 50, 60 goals and appear in every game, every day. It's very difficult for a youngster to be able to do this over such a long period of time. More than just the titles he has won, no one will change my opinion of him whether he wins a World Cup or not. If he does, congratulations to him, but if he doesn't my opinion won't change. He is a unique player and his challenge now is the World Cup, we'll see. In those days of the* clásicos *he probably felt the pressure but I thought he looked okay, as always. I was probably more occupied looking to find a way of winning rather than concerning myself with how the others were. I spent days thinking and studying what both we and our rivals had done and what we had to do to win, who we had available ...the day of the semi-final of the Champions League, Iniesta injured himself and we had to put in Keita ...you are always occupied with matters like this.*

GB: *At any time has he come up to you and said: Calm down, we're going to win. That's what he said to the Under 20 World Cup coach Pancho Ferraro and to some of the trainers at La Masía.*

PG: No. *He never said it to me, certainly not to me directly. But there have been moments or certain gestures that have made me think: this bloke's going to win it for us today. You catch a look, you look at him and then you say to yourself: he's going to win it. He has to be convinced that we're going well to feel like this.*

The first *clásico* in those two weeks was in the league, at the Bernabéu. Madrid were eight points adrift of Barcelona with seven games to go, but José Mourinho used it as a way of initiating hostilities with his sights set on winning the cup, but above all the Champions League. The grass was left long and dry to impede good passing of the ball, and Madrid played with a defensive midfield trio, one of which was the centre-back Pepe. The objective was to kill the spaces in which Leo operated. Both sides shared control of the game and both were content with a 1–1 draw; the league title was now destined for the Barcelona trophy cabinet for the third year running.

But it had been a tense affair: seven yellow cards, a red for Albiol and two penalties. The Madrid fans insulted Leo every time he touched the ball, and from the stands a laser pen was directed at his eyes while he took the penalty from which he scored. Mourinho's efforts to emotionally destabilise Barcelona were beginning to work. With the match just about finished Leo went chasing after a ball that he just failed to reach. He then decided to whack it into the stands, narrowly missing former Madrid coach John Toshack and a Sky Sports correspondent, who were sitting at pitch level.

The game carried on in the press conference afterwards and in the coaching sessions: Mourinho wanted to keep the tension cranked up, reminding his Spanish players that they shouldn't regard their colleagues in the national side as friends, players he accused of being 'actors' who constantly tried to influence the referee. What's more, he asked the directors at Madrid to try to stop the watering of the Mestalla pitch where the final of the Copa del Rey was to be played. But they failed to carry out his request.

The defeat hit the squad hard. Leo felt he had not done enough: he had been unable to find a solution to the tactical plan set up by Madrid. It was a double disappointment.

> **20 April 2011. Copa del Rey final. Barcelona 0–1 Real Madrid. Mestalla Stadium**
>
> *FC Barcelona: Pinto; Alvés, Piqué, Mascherano, Adriano (Maxwell, 118th minute): Busquets (Keita, 107th minute), Xavi, Iniesta; Pedro, Messi and Villa (Afellay, 105th minute). Subs not used: Pinto; Adriano, Maxwell, Thiago and Mascherano.*
>
> *Real Madrid: Casillas; Arbeloa, Ramos, Carvalho (Garay, 118th minute), Marcelo; Pepe, Xabi Alonso, Khedira (Granero, 103rd minute); Di María, Ronaldo and Özil (Adebayor, 69th minute). Subs not used: Dudek; Albiol, Granero, León and Higuaín.*
>
> *Goals: 0–1, 103rd minute: cross from Di María finished by Cristiano Ronaldo header beyond the reach of Pinto.*
>
> Cayetano Ros, *El País*: [Messi] desperate, tried from just about every position possible dropping deep and wide, without success. His zigzagging invariably ended in the snares of the Madrid defence. 'The Flea' controlled less, because his team was passing the ball less than ever in the first half. After the interval everything changed and his deep pass to Pedrito was excellent despite the fact that the linesman disallowed the goal for offside. Messi drifted towards the right-hand side, leaving the centre of the park less crowded and gaps started appearing which the *blaugrana* penetrated. And with Villa as a centre-forward the team found a point of reference they had not had until then.

Off the pitch, Mourinho was interpreting Barcelona's game and the danger of Messi well. In bringing in a third midfielder, Messi had found himself coming across another obstacle in his path. Pepe could take charge of stopping the inside diagonal runs that the Argentinian would frequently make, and that was going to be the big gamble that Mourinho would take when the two sides met in the Champions League semi-finals.

The tension continued. Pep Guardiola saw his side so downcast that he decided to take the bull by the horns. His motivational team talk was going to take place in Madrid in a deliberate move, at a press conference before the match. The Barcelona coach said that Mourinho was '*el puto amo*' (the 'fucking guv'nor') of the press conferences. This title, he said, he would give him, the other one they would contest on the pitch. For the first leg, Mourinho called for more pressure on their opponents, on the referee, more committed tackling and counter-attacks but without risk: winner takes all at the return leg at the Camp Nou. But the plan went wrong because Pepe put in a tackle with his studs showing on Dani Alvés who made the most of the challenge: the result was a red card for the defensive pivot. Mourinho was also sent off. It was a moment of highly charged emotional intensity, just half an hour from the end of the game. A match that, at that point, needed someone to grab it by the scruff of the neck.

---

27 April 2011. Champions League semi-final first leg. Real Madrid 0–2 Barcelona

Barcelona: Valdés; Alvés; Piqué, Mascherano, Puyol; Xavi, Busquets, Keita; Pedro (Afellay, 71st minute), Messi and Villa (Sergi Roberto, 90th minute). Subs not used: Pinto, Jeffrén, Milito, Fontàs and Thiago Alcántara.

Real Madrid: Casillas; Arbeloa, Ramos, Albiol, Marcelo; Xabi Alonso, Pepe, Lass; Ozil (Adebayor, 46th minute), Di María and Ronaldo. Subs not used: Adán, Kaká, Benzema, Granero, Garay and Higuaín.

Goals: 0–1. 76th minute: Leo Messi finishes after a pass from the right from Ibrahim Afellay. 0–2. 87th minute: Leo Messi, individual effort.

José Sámano, *El Pais*: In another *clásico* of intrigue and excuses for some, the football was about Barcelona and the glory of their greatest ambassador: Messi. Nothing symbolises Barcelona more than 'the Flea'. In front of them, a shutdown by a Madrid side that enjoyed a meagre 26.4 per cent possession. Statistics far more conclusive than a sending-off, however harsh that might have been. Messi, Barcelona, the visitors avoided the miserable o–o that Mourinho was dreaming of … Messi demonstrates more as an illustrious midfielder and the goal may not be as close to him as it was before, but he still appears at the right time. Ubiquitous and omnipresent, 'the Flea' assists and scores.

Jordi Quixano, *El País*: Messi. Two versions, one result. At the start, he was too far from the final metres, from Casillas's goal, he spent too much time on dribbles in unthreatening zones. As soon as Barcelona found themselves playing against ten men, the screw tightened on their opponents and he set the seal on the game. First he successfully met a cross from Afellay and later he scored after a superb mazy dribble. Two plays, two goals.

The most international *clásico* of them all, the one that was talked about most, had finished with a demonstration of quality and emotional stability from Leo in Cristiano Ronaldo's backyard. But also with a torrent of accusations. Tensions boiled over in the tunnel leading to the dressing rooms with both verbal and physical confrontations and with Puyol and Pepe swapping blows. Messi decided to distance himself from the scene. Mourinho was asked why this always happened to him against Barcelona after announcing: 'If I tell the referee and UEFA what I'm thinking, my career finishes today.' Madrid denounced Barcelona for what they said was unsporting behaviour by Guardiola and eight other players (Leo wasn't among them) to UEFA's Discipline and Control Committee, an accusation that was dismissed.

Mourinho watched the return leg at the team hotel in Barcelona. Madrid, for the first time under the Portuguese coach, looked to press higher up the pitch, his players' favoured option.

'We want him to have freedom so he can give full rein to his creative talents,' said Guardiola at the end of the game. 'He is pleased with that, it can be done because he has players who support him, as Pedro and Villa have done. Because if one doesn't have the will,

3 May 2011. Champions League semi-final second leg. Barcelona 1–1 Real Madrid

Barcelona: Valdés; Alvés, Piqué, Mascherano, Puyol (Abidal, 90th minute); Busquets, Xavi, Iniesta; Pedro, Messi and Villa (Keita, 74th minute). Subs not used: Olazábal, Jeffrén, Fontàs and Thiago Alcántara.

Real Madrid: Casillas; Arbeloa, Carvalho, Albiol, Marcelo; Lass Diarra, Xabi Alonso; Di María, Kaká (Özil, 60th minute), Ronaldo; Higuaín (Adebayor, 55th minute). Subs not used: Dudek, Benzema, Granero, Garay and Nacho Fernández.

Goals: 1–0, 54th minute: Pedro. 1–1, 64th minute: Marcelo.

Luis Martín, *El País*: Always Messi, with or without a goal. 'The Flea', who runs in excess of eight kilometres, demonstrated his generosity working like a navvy rather than a star because that is what the game demanded of him. Messi did not score, but his talents are difficult to resist. Yesterday the Argentine from Rosario had an enormous game, but that is hardly news any more. He celebrated the goal as if he had scored it himself. Generous, 'the Flea' jumped for joy in his orange boots for the glory of everyone.

It is hardly a surprise that Messi has been fouled more than anyone else in the Champions League: there are days when the only way he can be stopped is by bending the rules. Often he is left physically drained after 12 or more fouls.

Ever shy, came the moment to celebrate, Messi let himself be carried out by the festive atmosphere inside the Camp Nou, embracing Pedro and Busquets. He was in his glory. Overflowing with emotion. So much so that when it looked like he could not fight back the tears, tears of joy of course, Pep Guardiola, his protector, appeared in order give him a hug.

the desire and the ability to know that what you are doing is for the benefit of the whole group, it is impossible to get to a final as magical as the one we will be competing in on the 28th.'

Mourinho had tried with all the weapons in his arsenal, and his efforts had left a mark. He managed to make sure that in future *clásicos* you had to keep an eye on what was going on away from the game. The Spanish Supercup match the following summer (the one in which Mourinho's finger ended up in Tito Vilanova's eye) was not a peaceful one for Leo. After drawing 2–2 in the away leg, recently back from holiday and against a Madrid side that was ready to win their first trophy of the season, Barcelona had to wait until the final minutes of the second leg at the Camp Nou to take the title.

Near the end of the game, Messi spat close to the Madrid bench and Mourinho raised his finger to his nose suggesting that Leo was dirty. The clincher to make it 3–2 arrived two minutes from the end: a goal from the Argentinian, his second of the day. After scoring it he made a gesture to the Madrid bench, opening and closing his left hand, seemingly inviting them to continue protesting, to continue talking. Shortly after, he clashed strongly with Fabio Coentrao who had not been aware of 'the Flea's' presence. What the cameras had not seen were the little kicks that Messi got and hardly anyone saw, on the ankle, from behind, constantly, the ones that hurt.

'He turns up in his flip-flops and scores three goals against Madrid,' said Xavi after the game.

In the league five months later, Pepe premeditatedly trod on his hand and the Portuguese defender ended up apologising for his actions on the Real Madrid website. He said it had been an involuntary gesture. There were more personal confrontations in the following years, while Mourinho was on the Real bench. It was becoming harder to enjoy the *clásicos*; they had stopped being entertaining games, becoming instead pitched battles and smear campaigns. The constant appearances of Leo, who drew level with Alfredo Di Stéfano on goals scored in matches between the two sides, confirmed that he was a player for the big occasion, but in the last *clásicos* it was becoming clear that Mourinho had become the first to find the antidote to their game, opening the way for others (Chelsea, Bayern Munich) to cast doubt in the following months upon the dominance of their team.

Mourinho, with his constant doubts over the legitimacy of the *blaugranas*' triumphs, contributed something else as well: people became tired of seeing Barcelona win. That's certainly how Leo understands it as he explained in an interview with Martín Souto of TyC.

Martín Souto: Why do you think that people celebrate when Barcelona lose, without necessarily being fans of Madrid. Is it jealousy perhaps?

Lionel Messi: I don't know. One time Guardiola said that this thing about winning everything and so many times means that people tire of it and that's why some want us to lose, but there can be many reasons. With the people of Madrid, it's because they're from Madrid.

Martín Souto: But does the same thing happen in Argentina?

Lionel Messi: No, the truth is that I don't think about it, neither does it interest me. I know that a lot of people are waiting for us to fail and be out of everything, but it doesn't bother me.

8. THE SECOND CHAMPIONS LEAGUE FINAL AGAINST MANCHESTER UNITED, 2011

Picture the scene: Barcelona fly from Valencia where the team had faced Levante and won the league title. In the middle of the flight there's a party, some players are standing up, others applauding from their seats, there are songs. 'Slow down, slow down, slow down … we took their arses down', referring to Real Madrid, of course. And an announcement comes over the tannoy: 'This is your captain speaking. One of the emergency doors has been activated. Please, we are in the critical phase of the flight. I know that you are all very happy, but try to contain it for a moment.' Without realising it, Leo had activated it during the celebration. With a cheeky smirk, he looked behind him, just in case someone had seen him do it. The laughter continued until they reached Ciudad Condal.

It had been a very tough league. The pressure from Madrid was difficult to come to terms with. They had made it uncomfortable for Messi on the pitch, too. Mourinho had found a formula to prevent his diagonal runs and link-up play: a midfielder was waiting for him at the start of each piece of play, aggressive in the tackle and with the intention of not letting him get out of second gear. On top of that, the *merengues* were packing the midfield. And ultimately they even raised the defensive line to reduce the space. The model for stopping Barcelona had been put in place.

But few teams had sufficient numbers of intelligent and capable players who could cause damage on the counter like Real Madrid. Before the Champions League final, Messi had scored 52 goals and provided 24 assists in all competitions. 'How do you stop this guy?' sports newspaper *Marca* asked.

The answer was not clear for the majority of teams. Listen to Atlético de Madrid left-back Mariano Pernía, who told a funny story on the TyC Sports programme *Extra Time* during a televised barbecue with other Argentinian players: 'The worst thing about Messi, the worst … we were losing 3 or 4–1, at the Calderón, and he stopped in the middle of the pitch. He just stopped, completely motionless. Literally. He froze! And I was seven or eight metres away, and I say: "Oh shit …" Well, I go over there … more through obligation than anything else … And … I don't know what he did to me, I just don't know!' Leo had waited for Pernía to arrive and made as if to move, his feet planted firmly on the ground. And then he was off. The defender was left behind. 'I got home and my missus says to me: "What did he do to you?" And I say: "How do I know!? You tell me. You saw it on TV!" I swear I don't know. I went to close him down as he was about to cut in; but he didn't cut in, I don't know what he did.'

To help him prevent defenders overpowering him, Leo built his muscles up. José María Cuartetas noticed the physical change after the 2010 World Cup: 'He went to Argentina and when he came back, the three of us who were working [in the restaurant] that day, said: "he has done something, he has spent the summer in the gym." You could see he was more muscular. Now his legs are more developed, more pronounced, firmer arms, a stronger chest … and we spoke about it with his father, but he told us he hadn't done anything, just trained as normal. You see him now, they barge into him and he handles it.'

So how do you defend against him then? 'Even if you know the move he is going to do, he'll dummy you so quickly and burst with such explosiveness that you lose him,' says Cesc, who marked him while at Arsenal and hundreds of times in training. 'It's like the game in front of a mirror with a person behind who moves to one side and you have to follow him. You never have time to do what he does.'

'Messi combines his perfect touch with an incredible agility and rapid acceleration,' explains coach Henk ten Cate. 'He often changes position over the first couple of yards. As a defender, you lose your courage. The beautiful thing is that he does all of that right on the edge of the box. Therefore, practically every action by Messi creates danger from the moment he receives possession.'

Football is an action-reaction sport and teams therefore gradually changed their strategies as Leo changed his. When he played as a winger, the full-back would take care of him. On top of that, as Pep said at a press conference in Buenos Aires: 'He had the touchline, which is the best defender around.'

'In the Copa del Rey match when they knocked us out, he played mainly down the right,' explains Fernando Navarro, ex-Barcelona and now at Sevilla. 'You always try to show him outside as he is left-footed, that's less dangerous. In the second half, I tried to send him outside but he took a shot which hit the post. And my keeper, Andrés Palop, shouted at me: "show him inside, Fernando." In the next piece of play he ran at me again, went inside and hit the post again. And I say to Palop: "Andrés, don't tell me where to go because he will still dribble past me!"'

'I faced him many times, he wore number thirty for the first few, I remember because I have the shirt safe at home,' explains the Argentinian former Zaragoza player Leonardo Ponzio in *El Gráfico*. 'You went to defend against him knowing what he could do to you. As for precautions. At the Camp Nou you couldn't take any, because the pitch is so big ... But at our stadium, if you gather around him and mark him with two men, and are always close to him, you could keep him under wraps a bit more.'

In his magnificent matches still as a winger, nobody knew how to stop him apart from committing fouls: he would easily get past his man in one on ones, so defensive midfielders started to collaborate. 'Even if you think you know what he is going to do, he is so quick and his timing so good that he becomes almost infallible,' admits

Fernando Navarro. 'He waits for the opportune moment to change direction. How many times has he scored that goal when he starts on the right, and drives inside, further inside, and further inside, almost ending up on the opposite wing and shoots into the far corner? Many times. And it's still hard to stop him.'

'When he was close to me,' remembers Ponzio, 'I wouldn't say to him: "Don't go past me any more, we are both from Newell's." And if they were winning 4–0, I would say: "Take it down a gear, that's enough." He would listen to me, but never took the suggestion on board.'

When he went on his diagonal runs, at the end of the Rijkaard era and in Guardiola's first year, the tactical problem was his own team-mates: he would go past opponents at such speed that his own side would hinder him en route to goal. His team-mates had to learn how to make space for him, and over time the obvious solution was for the number 9, who was in the space that Leo needed, to disappear.

When he finally moved into the middle, the difficulty the opposition had was deciding who would mark him, who would push out to him when he had the ball: the centre-backs preferred to wait for him on the edge of the area but he had already started his run by then, and, with his skill, it was easier for him to get past them: as for the central midfielder, he would be overwhelmed by the presence of more Barcelona players than his own team-mates.

'Speaking about defensive tactics against Messi at his best is of little use,' says ex-Villarreal coach Juan Carlos Garrido. 'They have all been tried out: he has been man-marked, deep defences, a high line ... no tactic has worked against Messi at his best.'

'He is too good to be man-marked,' says Gio van Bronckhorst. 'He always finds an escape route in the one on one.' His compatriot Mark Van Bommel, who shared the dressing room with Messi in the 2005–06 season, has a solution: 'Sometimes, when he gets too cocky, I tackle him fiercely. The little brat likes to nutmeg you. He did it to me twice on one occasion, so I went in on him with a full-blooded tackle. Rijkaard was furious. We can't do that stuff in training. But you can in a match!' Paolo Montero, Uruguay international and ex-Juventus, agrees: 'The only way is the old-school one: kicking him off the park, it's the only way I can see.'

Teams were aware that they could not just mark Messi but had to defend against Barcelona as a whole. They started bunching up down the middle and leaving the wings free for Guardiola's outfit: they could only do damage from there with balls into the box, but the *blaugranas* did not have a striker capable of winning aerial battles.

So, in May 2011, Manchester United had a choice of defensive strategies.

For that final at Wembley, Barcelona were able to count on Éric Abidal, who had played a few minutes of the semi-final against Real Madrid in one of the most emotional moments of the season. The French player had had an operation on a liver tumour in March. He started against Manchester United.

PG: *In the second final against Manchester United we knew one another much better; we had been together for three years and played slightly more aware of the match's relevance: the first was like a present for everyone. Faced with the threat of an ash cloud from an Icelandic volcano which would delay flights, we had to go to London earlier. That provided us with four whole days for ourselves, some time to relax, something which was very rare. We were far from Barcelona and the pressure from fans, friends and family. We were delighted to be able to train at Arsenal's training ground, and we had time to prepare ourselves properly, to think about what we had to do, without leaving any loose ends. In the final, it's more than obvious that we played well and were the better team. The first final in Rome was more even, but in the second at Wembley, we were better.*

GB: *You made another tactical change after ten minutes, by dropping Leo into Xavi's zone in midfield and the latter alongside Busquets to build from the back in superior numbers, always looking to have one Barcelona player more than the rival in each part of the pitch. Or was it the players' decision based on how the match was going?*

PG: *At Wembley, United already knew that we were going to look to dominate midfield, because we always played that way. The thing is it's difficult to stop: you force the centre-back to go out of position into unfamiliar territory.*

GB: *The players understood what was required in the match ...*

PG: *Xavi naturally dropped back when needed. There is little you can teach a player like Xavi. Just whisper things to him. He knows the rest already.*

Guardiola asked the team to be themselves, to be more Barcelona than ever, faithful to the style.

---

28 May 2011. Champions League final. Barcelona 3–1 Manchester United. Wembley Stadium, London

Barcelona: Valdés; Alvés (Puyol, 88th minute), Piqué, Mascherano, Abidal, Busquets, Xavi, Iniesta; Pedro (Afellay, 92nd minute), Messi and Villa (Keita, 86th minute). Subs not used: Olazábal, Bojan, Adriano and Thiago Alcántara.

Manchester United; Van der Sar; Fabio (Nani, 69th minute), Ferdinand, Vidić, Evra; Valencia, Carrick (Scholes, 76th minute), Giggs, Park; Rooney and Javier 'Chicharito' Hernández. Subs not used: Kuszczak, Owen, Anderson, Smalling and Fletcher.

Goals: 1–0, 27th minute: Pedro. 1–1, 34th minute: Rooney. 2–1, 54th minute: Messi. 3–1, 69th minute: Villa.

Luis Martín, *El País*: Generous as always, Messi played for the team rather than himself, he combined well and looked for damaging inside passes. He managed it, it was a nightmare, a devil against the Red Devils. The Manchester United players could not get near him. Leo has goals entrenched within him, so he did not leave without his prize: a rasping strike from outside the box to which Van der Sar could not even react. 'I had the space, the goalie came out and luckily it went in,' described Messi himself. It may not have been the most beautiful goal, but it put Barcelona ahead when they needed it most. He shouted like never before while running to the corner to celebrate. On the way he kicked a microphone and an advertising hoarding as he almost always does. And although he did not jump into the stands to hug the fans, he was close to doing so.

Tweets by Martí Perarnau that day: Shutting down the Divine Trinity was the key for MU. They never managed it. They left the doors open and Xavi, Iniesta and Messi had a stroll in the park ... Quick touches by Xavi, Iniesta and Messi to unsettle the opposition and outnumber them. When they see weakness and tiredness, they strike ... Pep and Xavi are the guardians of the footballing language. Messi and Iniesta, the magic potion. Puyol, the captain of values. The pillars of *blaugrana* territory ... eighty-ninth minute: eight players from the youth team on the pitch, three more on the bench, three more in the stands. La Masía, more than a youth team ... There are question marks over the future, of course. Pep's future is one of them. Messi's hunger is another. Guardiola sent a double message out to the club: don't bring anyone in who will disturb Messi. Bring players in who will support, surround and help Messi to keep growing.

It was the complete match by Messi and by the team. Exquisite in terms of link-up play and with Leo's decisive influence. The Champions League had just been won by possibly the best team in history. And they did it through quality, but also intelligence. 'Based on how the game was going, Pep would say to Leo: "Go down the middle" or whatever,' says Pedro. 'And we would change our shape straightaway, all very quickly. We worked really hard on tactics all that week which is why things came naturally to us.'

At Wembley, it was not about Messi's usual game, diagonal runs or dribbling. His role in that game was to generate a numerical advantage in midfield with him, Xavi, Busquets, Iniesta and Abidal when he pushed up on the wing. Leo helped Barcelona have 68 per cent possession and 22 shots on goal. Manchester United could only muster four. He scored the second goal and was involved in the third. 'We played incredibly well. I don't think we were aware of just what we were achieving today,' said Leo that night.

Sir Alex Ferguson went onto the pitch to congratulate Leo.

'We were never really able to control Messi, it was something we had already been warned about. We did not manage to close them down enough in midfield to neutralise them,' he explained later.

PG: *I have learned over time that the great coaches are people coaches. Tactics are very important, but the Fergusons, Mourinhos, and others are all great at dealing with the personalities they find in the dressing room.*

GB: *Despite two years of saying he knew how to play against Barcelona after the defeat in Rome, Ferguson didn't know how to neutralise your game.*

PG: *They didn't go out there to defend. When we were good, it was difficult to stop us. We would pass the ball around and gradually push them back. They did not decide to defend in their area, but we managed to push them back. Their idea was to press us on the ball which is how it was in the first 10 or 15 minutes both in Rome and London. But we knew how to create superiority and Manchester United, a great team, lost control of the match.*

Guardiola went round hugging everyone and, when he came to Leo, he thanked him.

'He's the best player I've seen and will ever see,' stated Guardiola about Messi in a press conference, repeating a statement which he had made at the Spanish Super Cup in August 2009. 'We could compete at a very high level, but without him we would not make the jump in quality … I hope he doesn't get bored and that we are capable of making him feel comfortable because when that happens, Leo doesn't fail.'

Éric Abidal played the whole match. Carles Puyol lent him the captain's armband so he could lift the European Cup, the fourth in the club's history.

Messi was named man of the match and, after the celebrations on the pitch, he spoke to the press: 'We want to carry on winning things. Today we were much better and deserved to win. Now we're on holiday. Well, I'm going to the Copa América, but first let's celebrate.'

Lionel Messi went to Argentina to rest, and then to suffer in the Copa América.

9. THE FIVE GOALS AGAINST BAYER LEVERKUSEN

A month and a half after Wembley, Leo Messi's Argentina were beaten on penalties in the quarter-finals of the Copa América that took place on his home turf. 'The Flea' had scored 53 goals with Barcelona that season but not a single one with the national side since March 2009, more than two years ago. And the criticism became fierce; even former professionals had a field day with Leo: 'Diego Maradona had a different personality, he was overwhelming, contagious; I can't see that in Leo Messi,' Gabriel Batistuta, Argentina's historic goalscorer declared.

When the dismissal of Sergio Batista and the appointment of Alejandro Sabella were confirmed, the new national coach travelled to Barcelona to chat with Pep Guardiola who advised him to avoid too much conversation with Leo, to surround him with team-mates who respected him and would make his job easier, and to listen to the few words that he did say and never, ever, to substitute him, 'not even to receive a standing ovation'.

Leo returned from his holiday a few days later due to his participation in the Copa América, to a Barcelona who had signed Cesc from Arsenal and Alexis from Udinese, and were to face José Mourinho's Real Madrid, the same day that José decided to point a finger in the wrong place.

---

14 August 2011. Super Cup first leg. Real Madrid 2–2 Barcelona

Barcelona: Valdés; Alvés, Piqué, Abidal, Adriano, Xavi Hernández, Keita, Iniesta, Messi, Villa, Rodríguez.

Real Madrid: Casillas; Ramos, Pepe, Carvalho, Marcelo; Xabi Alonso, Khedira; Özil, Di María, Ronaldo; Benzema.

Goals: 1–0. 13th minute: Özil. 1–1 35th minute: Villa. 1–2. 45th minute: Messi. 2–2. 53rd minute: Xabi Alonso.

Diego Torres, *El País*: The last thing known about Lionel Messi Cuccittini before catching up with the pre-season, on Monday of last week, was that he spent a few days with his girlfriend

Antonella on a yacht anchored in Formentera. Since then, exactly seven days have passed. Five training sessions were more than enough for him to get into shape to come to the Bernabéu and play in the Spanish Super Cup. Forget friendlies. Don't mention summer tours. Let's play proper games. That is exactly what he did.

Messi only did one thing in the first half-hour: a low pass to Villa in behind Ramos. The pass was perfect like a curved missile meeting the attacker who had lost his marker in a made-to-measure coupling. The referee blew the whistle for offside. In the thirty-fifth minute, Messi reloaded his left foot, this time from a more central position.

José Sámano, *El País:* When the omens predicted a storm for Barcelona, the game took an unexpected turn. Messi, until that point, had been invisible. But Messi who never needs much encouragement to play, finally turned up and Villa, with his side's first shot, hit the ball with a banana-shaped trajectory. The ball took an impossible swerve, flying past Casillas, leaving Madrid bewildered and incredulous. Messi, cunning as he is, realised his rivals were tumbling and took advantage of the lack of co-ordination between Khedira and Pepe before scoring.

The matter would be concluded in the second leg.

17 August 2011. Super Cup second leg. Barcelona 3–2 Real Madrid

Barcelona: Valdés; Alvés, Piqué, Mascherano, Abidal, Busquets (Keita, 85th minute), Xavi, Iniesta, Pedro (Cesc, 82nd minute), Villa (Adriano, 73rd minute) and Messi.

Real Madrid: Casillas; Ramos, Pepe, Carvalho, Coentrao; Xabi Alonso, Khedira (Marcelo, 45th minute); Di María (Higuaín, 63rd minute), Özil (Kaká, 78th minute), Ronaldo; and Benzema.

Goals: 1–0, 15th mimute: Iniesta. 1–1, 19th minute: Ronaldo.

2–1, 44th minute: Messi. 2–2, 82nd minute: Benzema. 3–2, 88th minute: Messi.

José Sámano, *El País*: Messi is unique. The Argentinian resolved the Super Cup clash in Barcelona's favour after a fierce duel with Madrid. No Madrid side at the moment can live with Messi, the best finisher in their history. Not even when Mourinho's side apply themselves as never before against a Barcelona that is still a little stiff. But he is unique; with Messi up front, the *blaugrana* side plays with freedom.

Cayetano Ros, *El País*: Messi, angry, edgy, motivated, the Argentinian notched two more goals against his favourite rivals, avoiding extra time against a fresher Real Madrid. Seeing himself shackled by a man-marking exercise by Pepe, he dropped into midfield where he could take in some air. There he disengaged himself from Khedira before sending a pass to Iniesta who opened the game up, making it a priceless spectacle. Although not yet match fit, he still managed to find the breath to create another work of art with Piqué: the latter's backheel left him one on one with Casillas. This time he resolved the matter with a neat little dink with his right foot over the outstretched body of the Madrid goalkeeper. Messi finished the job with a volley that is worthy of the Super Cup. Santiago Siguero, *Marca*: Messi beat Real Madrid. Practically on his own, the Argentinian once again destroyed a team that has found Messi to be its curse. The thing is it was a good Real Madrid this time, better collectively than Barcelona, but individually Messi wins the comparison with Cristiano Ronaldo. He is the Di Stéfano of FC Barcelona.

That season that had started so well became a time of bad news that left the squad emotionally exhausted. In November 2011 Tito Vilanova discovered that he had cancer of the parotid gland.

Leo also suffered in silence the news that a close family member had cancer. The contrast between the joy of winning titles and these reality checks was difficult to bear, but Messi did all he could to avoid the setbacks becoming apparent on the training ground. Suddenly the world had become a complex, grown-up place. He gravitated ever closer to his family and distanced himself from anything he considered trivial and unimportant. He also drew apart from some of Pep's collaborators, who attempted to get close to him during that confusing period in his life.

While the tumour was growing inside him, Abidal was named as a starter for the World Club final against the Santos of Neymar Jr, who, it was said, could very soon become one of the greatest players in the world. Messi had another target: to maintain the status quo. Partly because of the arrival of Cesc Fàbregas, Guardiola looked for the maximum expression of his football ideal in putting on five midfielders and Messi, who was becoming a mixture of a number 8 (a creator), a 9 (scorer) and a 10 (assistant). Dani Alvés and Thiago would play as false wingers in a footballing hall of mirrors in which no one was what they seemed to be.

Barcelona had gained their tenth victory in 11 finals. And Messi had equalled Pedro's record set two years earlier of scoring in all competitions: there did not seem to be any record beyond his reach and striving for them also fed his ambitions. He got another: he

---

18 December 2011. FIFA Club World Cup final. Santos 0–4 Barcelona. Yokohama

Barcelona: Valdés; Puyol (Fontás, 85th minute), Piqué (Mascherano, 56th minute), Abidal; Alvés, Busquets, Xavi, Thiago (Pedro, 78th minute); Iniesta, Cesc; and Messi.

Santos: Cabral; Danilo (Elano, 30th minute), Drácena, Rodrigo, Durval, Leo; Henrique, Arouca, Ganso (Ibson, 83rd minute); Borges (Kardec, 78th minute) and Neymar.

Goals: 1–0, 17th minute: Messi. 2–0. 24th minute: Xavi. 3–0, 45th minute: Cesc. 4–0. 82nd minute: Messi.

Luis Martín, *El País*: 'Let history judge him,' pleaded Mascherano when talking about Messi, who yesterday demonstrated once again just why he will surely receive his third consecutive Ballon d'Or on 9 January. Messi, named man of the match and man of the tournament, today has no rival able to match his talent. Neymar did not manage to do it when put face to face with the miracle that is 'the Flea'.

FIFA were cross with Barcelona because Messi did not appear all week to promote the final. He did not go to the press area after victory in the semi-finals nor did he take part in the official press conference on Saturday... He trained, rested, went for a stroll with his family and then went out to supper with them and his girlfriend on days when he had permission. But he didn't speak until yesterday. On the pitch. And in another final. Barcelona won their thirteenth title out of a possible 16 since Pep Guardiola sat himself on the *blaugrana* bench. And Messi once again scored on another big occasion, as always. He's now scored 17 times in finals in all competitions.

Martí Perarnau, *Sport*: The first half-hour of this final was the very apotheosis of the *rondo*, the piggy in the middle concept, the very sublimation of the swapping of roles. A swarm of small wasps took control of the ball, stinging Brazil's Santos, who were a shadow of themselves. Just like someone suffering post-traumatic shock, Neymar summed it up in a simple sentence. 'Today we learned how to play football.'

provided assists in all competitions so it could be said that he had surpassed his team-mate. Leo's successes were heading into the stratosphere.

Messi met Neymar at the award presentation ceremony and they had a conversation around which was formed the basis of their future relationship. Leo, who was aware of Barcelona's interest in the Brazilian, asked him to come to the club. Neymar assured him that was his dream, but the truth was the Brazilian already had an agreement in place with the Catalans.

After the World Club Cup final, Messi went to Rosario for a rest, where among other things, he was updated on the status of the Leo Messi Foundation that has channelled money to promote projects for young children and adolescents at risk since 2007. During that period, when they asked Guardiola why he gave Messi more days holiday, the coach would only give half-answers, conscious of Leo's concerns about the illness of his close family member: 'I decide, they don't. There are reasons. Leo is sensitive about a number of personal issues and I want him to be with his family for the New Year.'

In the new year, the group received another big blow: in March the club announced that Abidal would have to undergo a liver transplant following the return of a carcinogenic tumour. The full-back lost 19 kilos in weight and had to be operated on no fewer than five times. But just a year later he was back on the pitch.

Coming back after Christmas and with the return of the Champions League, Messi continued with his tactical progress and excellent statistics: he scored again for Argentina and in March became, at just 24, the highest goalscorer in Barça's history, overtaking the record of César Rodríguez's 232 goals in an *blaugrana* shirt.

However, some things never change. Before certain games, Leo still suffers from nausea and vomiting. 'It's quite common. There are a lot of players who go through this,' says Pedro. 'Sometimes they start retching. It's the adrenaline, the tension just before a game. From the outside you don't see any of this. We always have the obligation to win and to do well, to be physically well. And it isn't always like that. But that's how it is and you have to be prepared for everything.'

Some footballers say that the feeling you get is like a greyhound before a race, or a car revving up just before the clutch is released. 'When he retches, Leo feels it is a very personal moment and he tries to keep his distance,' says Mascherano. 'It happens to a number of us, me included. For all the experience that you have, the adrenaline doesn't disappear. And before a game with all this nervous tension, sometimes it causes nausea. Once the game starts it disappears.'

'There was one game where he was suffering from flu, against Osasuna,' remembers the 'little boss' Mascherano. Messi was signed off sick in the morning with a slight temperature, flu symptoms and a cold, but three hours before the Copa del Rey game he said to Pep that he was ready to play. 'When he told me that, I put him on the bench,' explained Pep.

'He had a fever. He scored two goals! Seriously, he played with a temperature!' insists Mascherano. 'The doctors had signed him off sick because you couldn't count on him, but he wanted to play. And he came on, and well …' Leo came on half an hour from the end, long enough for him to score twice.

Before the last 16 second-leg Champions League game against Bayer Leverkusen at the Camp Nou, Leo felt unwell. He had a headache. They gave him a paracetamol. 'Really? I've only just found out that he wasn't feeling well,' admits Mascherano.

GB: *In the match against Bayer Leverkusen, Leo had a headache. Have you seen him vomit before any games?*

PG: *I also used to vomit. If you're tense, you have to get rid of the nerves and that's what you do.*

GB: *But you seem to get nervous. And Messi seems to be the calmer type.*

PG: *It's probably all inside him. Let's put ourselves in his place. He has this burden on him to have to do what he does over and over again, and I'm sure that at times this is difficult. Well, I imagine it is, because to tell you the truth I don't know how he carries so much weight on his shoulders.*

GB: *Did he seem quieter on the day of the Leverkusen match?*

PG: *I don't remember anything like that. I don't go into the dressing rooms with the team before a game, I don't want to see them, it's their moment, I was in my office. Just before going out we are together, but that's it.*

GB: *Did you say anything special to him after those five goals?*

PG: *I can't remember. I suppose I congratulated them all. In the Champions League when you go through you always think you still have two more games to enjoy in Europe. You never know when it's going to finish. With the passing of time I find myself congratulating fewer people, it's probably my age. To us, the technical staff, we had our moments of enjoyment and often I would stay in my office to celebrate it between ourselves. At that game I don't remember whether I did or didn't go to congratulate him. Normally in the Champions League I would, because playing in Europe is beautiful.*

7 March 2012. Last 16 of the Champions League second leg. Barcelona 7–1 Bayer Leverkusen

Barcelona: Valdés; Alvés, Piqué, Mascherano, Adriano (Muniesa, 63rd minute); Busquets, Xavi (Keita, 52nd minute), Cesc; Pedro, Messi and Iniesta (Tello, 52nd minute).

Bayer Leverkusen: Leno; Castro, Schwaab, Toprak, Kadlec; Renato Augusto (Oczipka, 67th minute), Reinartz, Rolfes, Bender (Schürrle, 55th minute); Kiessling and Derdiyok (Bellarabi, 55th minute).

Goals: 1–0. 25th minute: Messi. Receives a pass from Xavi in space and chips it over the keeper. 2–0. 42nd minute: Messi. Receives a pass from Iniesta and scores after some individual brilliance. 3–0. 50th minute Messi. Pass from Cesc and scores with another chip. 4–0. 55th minute: Tello: 57th minute: 5–0 Messi. The keeper fails to hold onto the ball and he pounces on the rebound. 6–0. 62nd minute: Tello. 7–0. 84th minute: Messi. Left-foot shot from the edge of the area. 7–1. 90th minute: Bellarabi.

Ramón Besa, *El País*: Hurricane Messi. Messi must be thanked for wanting to play all the time, that he makes no distinction between friendly or official matches, easy or difficult ones, important or banal, and that he does not accept being substituted, even when the result is a foregone conclusion, whether he is on form or not, whether it be hot or cold, home or away, Wednesday or Saturday. There are no formalities for 'the Flea' to adhere to, least of all in the Champions League, a competition in which he has already scored 12 goals in seven games, following his five goals against Bayer, a figure previously unheard of in the tournament's history. No one is more demanding than Messi himself, with each one of his performances converted into a spectacle and he, therefore, accepts the blame for displays that fail to shine. Nobody finds more passing channels better than Piqué, Xavi and Iniesta. The ball always arrives well placed, balanced, perfectly timed at the feet of the genius that is Messi.

Robert Alvarez, *El Pais*: Messi arrived at the Camp Nou with a headache. However, as he didn't want to be sent home he asked Doctor Ricard Pruna for a painkiller. The Barcelona coach who left after the game with the Argentine boss, Alejandro Sabella, explained the virtue of 'the Flea'. 'It makes no difference if it's raining or it's cold, it doesn't matter whether they kick him or not. I would imagine that in the days of Di Stéfano, of Maradona, of Cruyff, of Pelé, they said that they were the best. Now he sits on the throne and only he will decide when he wants to leave it.'

'Was that a game in the Champions League or was that Messi on PlayStation2?' asked Atlético's Falcao ironically. 'Messi is unreal. For me, the best ever,' said Rooney of Manchester United. There are no words to describe the way Barcelona plays. It is at an extraordinary level, without doubt. 'Without Messi, Barcelona are the best team in the world, with him they are from another galaxy,' concluded Bayer coach Robin Dutt.

10. THE FOUR BALLONS D'OR

El País: You say that you are not interested in how many goals you can score, that you prefer titles. What is your motivation?

Leo Messi: I prefer winning titles with the team over individual awards or scoring more goals than anyone else. I am more concerned about being a good person than being the best footballer in the world. On top of that, in the end when all of this finishes, what do you take away from it? My intention, when I retire, is to be remembered for being a good guy. I like scoring goals, but also having friends among the players I've played with. It is good for people to value you as a person and have a good opinion of you.

El País: So you are not too bothered about winning your fourth Ballon d'Or?

Leo Messi: Awards are good. I am thankful for them, of course. But at the end of the day, it interests you guys more, you're always asking if this one is better than that one. Xavi or Iniesta? Who knows? …The team definitely makes me better. Without the help of my team-mates, I would be nothing, I would win nothing. No titles, no prizes, nothing.

(Interview with Leo Messi in *El País*, Ramón Besa and Luis Martín, 30 September 2012)

In *El largo viaje de Pep*, Martí Perarnau writes that around October that year Guardiola had a discussion with his players in which he asked them to forget about comparisons and not to speculate over which team was the best. That was the job of journalists and talk shows. 'Look,' he said to them, 'it's not a question of discussing whether we are better than this or that team,' writes Perarnau. 'Some will have one opinion and we will have another. We will only see the true picture, like in good films, as the years pass and you watch them again and speak about them. They become classics. Now we cannot understand everything,' he told them, 'but you will be spoken about in fifteen years. Definitely. You will be spoken about and, then, at that moment, the whole world will recognise that we were a great team.'

GB: Rodrigo Messi tells how Leo, at the age of 13, said he wanted to win the Ballon d'Or.

PG: Did he say that? He wasn't wrong, was he? I was so happy when he won it after the Champions League final in Rome. We said to him on that night: 'The award is yours.' It was clear that it was his. These awards have always made him very happy, he has always taken it like that: something that he wants to win. I imagine that Michael Jordan wanted to be the best defender, top scorer and best rebounder in the NBA ... Well, Leo is the same. And you say, why, is a league, Champions League and Ballon d'Or not enough? Why does he want more? Because that's how they are. They thought Nadal was finished, and he goes and wins everything. And I'm sure Jordan has thought someday, why don't I go back at 50? We are made of different stuff, from another place, different parents; we are competitive, we like to win, but you have another way of thinking, and you say: listen, you've lost today, and you feel bad, but you think, what can you do, that's life. And you know your limitations and say to yourself: I can't do this because I don't know so much. Leo doesn't, he always has the perception that if he's okay, he will win.

First Ballon d'Or, 2009, and FIFA Player of the Year

Leo Messi had been third in the *France Football* magazine's choice for the Ballon d'Or in 2007 (behind Kaká and Ronaldo) and second in 2008 (the Portuguese won it): but in 2009, at 22 years old, not only had he been chosen at the end of the summer as the best player in the Champions League and best striker in the competition, but he also carried away the most prestigious award with a notable statistic: never before had there been such a huge margin between first and second place, between Leo Messi and Cristiano Ronaldo. Xavi Hernández, also representing a Barcelona team that had won everything, came third.

The ceremony took place in Paris and all Leo's family travelled with him. Celia, his mother, attended the event in an elegant red dress, and Jorge looking thinner than usual and slightly under the weather, surveyed the scene and recalled decisions, journeys, tensions, distances. Surrounded by his four children, with Leo holding the Ballon d'Or, while the obligatory photos were taken, Jorge started to cry. 'I have achieved the objective I set myself in life: I have four phenomenal children, their lives are all on track. I've done it.'

At the next match at the Nou Camp against Espanyol, his mother handed him the Ballon d'Or on the pitch while the stadium, his team-mates, the opposition captain and even referee Iturralde González gave him a standing ovation.

FIFA also gave him the award for the Player of the Year in a ceremony that took place in Zurich on 21 December. The Ballon d'Or is voted for by journalists, whereas the FIFA Player of the Year is voted for by international managers and national team captains. Once again he won by the biggest margin in the trophy's history.

Hours before the gala, the Barcelona delegation met in the hotel lobby where they were staying, planning to leave together for the Palace of Congress where the ceremony was being held. Leo was nowhere to be seen. They looked everywhere for him. 'Go up to his room to see if he's there,' said Laporta. And there he was, on the bed, finishing a game on the PlayStation with his brothers Rodrigo and Matias. Hurriedly they tried to put one another's bow ties on, but didn't know how to do it. Father Jorge had to come to the rescue.

Second FIFA Ballon d'Or, 2010

10 January 2011, Messi received the first FIFA Ballon d'Or, the combination of the two awards that had a 450-man jury comprising national coaches, captains and journalists. It was the year of the triple *blaugrana* representation, which rewarded what Barcelona and La Masía had done for football, and also the Spanish national team's first World Cup victory.

Leo did not expect to take the award home; no one was really putting their money on him. Which is probably why he nearly left his black Dolce & Gabbana tuxedo and bow tie at home. On this occasion his parents and sister went to the ceremony with him, as well as an aunt, uncle and cousin. Seven Barcelona players had featured in the team of the year and Pep Guardiola, nominated for coach of the year, also travelled with them. That prize ended up going to Mourinho, Champions League winner with Inter.

For the press, the big favourite was Andrés Iniesta, who had scored the goal that clinched the World Cup for Spain. Nike had prepared 10,000 shirts to celebrate the award. What happened to them is unknown. The world of football, starting with UEFA President Michel Platini, thought it was time to pay homage to Xavi, for his journey, for his titles, for the possession style he advocated.

In Spain they were saying that if Iniesta did not win it, Xavi should take it away. But the two central midfielders were about to discover that the Spanish players did not seem to get the same respect internationally as they got at home.

It was Guardiola's task to announce the winner. 'And the winner is … Ay, ay, ay,' said the coach before reading out Leo Messi's name. 'The Flea's' group observed a certain coldness in Guardiola's expression, something they found hard to ignore.

The usual suspect had won because he was the best. Discussions about Xavi and Iniesta's footballing merits remained just that: words. When it came to voting, someone had to be first, and the man who is the best at this game was chosen by the majority.

Leo had to improvise his speech. He leaned on the microphone stand nervously: 'Good evening and thank you very much for the applause … ehh … The truth is … I didn't expect to win today. It was already enough to be here with my two team-mates, but being able to win it once again, well ... It's a very special day for me. I want to share it and thank my team-mates, as I would obviously not be here without them. I wanted to share it with all my loved ones who have always supported me and been by my side. And I want to share it with all the Barcelonistas and Argentines. Thank you very much.'

Despite the whiff of controversy when his name was read out, Leo, Andrés and Xavi seemed closer than ever on the journey home. Iniesta knew that he wasn't going to have another chance like that; *La Gazzetta dello Sport* had even announced that he would be the winner. He felt somewhat disappointed, but never disguised his admiration for Leo.

'Everyone has the right to an opinion, but there was no problem with the decision, none at all,' says Iniesta. 'We were delighted to be there to see Leo win his second Ballon d'Or. I think that you have to value the nomination, which is very difficult to achieve. We felt the people's huge appreciation, affection and respect. The three of us knew that it was about the team, we were there as individuals, but it was a collective thing, we were all clear about that.'

Xavi did not expect anything; in fact, he said in private that he had been certain about who was going to win the award: Leo, of course, because quite simply ... he was the best. The Catalan central midfielder could not believe that he had been nominated for prizes to which he did not attach a great deal of importance. What worried him more that year was if the *bolets* (mushroom) season would be a good one.

'It would have been a surprise whatever happened,' explains Xavi. 'Leo won and for me it was right; he is an extraordinary footballer and he deserves it. We enjoyed something historic: Barcelona's football and the Barça youth system won, and that made me particularly happy.'

Xavi had been one of those who had smoothed Leo's path upon his arrival in the first team, one of those who had reminded him from the start that if he found himself up against four defenders it would be better to play the ball back; if it was one or two, let the games begin. Xavi and Leo's conversations were generally about football-based issues and, with Pep's arrival, they focused more on the evolution that Messi had to experience. Xavi enjoyed seeing how 'the Flea' started to do things he had not done before Guardiola took over, playing the right pass at the right time and in the right place, gradually shared in the build-up as they'd discussed in training.

Leo felt very grateful towards those who had helped him go so far, his people. And that year he felt he owed a debt to Xavi and Iniesta for furthering his career. On returning from Switzerland he made his gratitude clear both in public and in private.

'Come on, Leo, a toast,' shouted Piqué, often the man in charge of organising photos on such occasions.

On the plane, while sitting next to his mother and with Iniesta in the seat behind him, he was asked to say a few words as the bottles of Cava were opened. 'I want to make a toast to Xavi and Andrés, who deserved the award as much as, if not more than, me, even though I won it.' Group photos were taken, glasses raised, every face wreathed in smiles.

There was one question coming out of the Barcelona dressing room that will probably never be answered. What would have happened if Iniesta or Xavi had won? The players prepared themselves to look after Leo in case of such an eventuality, but in the end it was not necessary.

Leo did not like the Spanish or international press's response, however, pointing the finger at UEFA, FIFA and the rest of the footballing planet for such an unfair result. *La Gaceta* went with the headline 'This Ball Is Not Made of Gold', *ABC* said 'FIFA disregards the world champions' and *La Stampa* claimed that football had lost its way: '[Messi] in the competitions which count he has won nothing.' That is what Leo woke up to the morning after winning the award.

That afternoon, the Barcelona players returned to training and 'the Flea' felt he had a point to make to the football world. His personal standing was being doubted.

Pep Guardiola still remembers that training session.

'He was colossal in training, absolutely incredible,' recalls Txiki Beguiristain. 'Pep told me, "bloody hell, you should have seen him".'

In the six-a-side matches that were organised that day, Messi scored all sorts of goals, five in total; he dribbled, shot, drove forward, assisted and ran more than anyone. That was why he had been awarded the Ballon d'Or. He showered and went home.

Leo had put everyone in their place.

Third FIFA Ballon d'Or, 2011

9 January 2012, Leo Messi received his third FIFA Ballon d'Or, equalling Platini's record as the only man to have won it in consecutive years. Johan Cruyff and Marco Van Basten also had three to their names. Cristiano Ronaldo was second in that vote and Xavi third. Messi was wearing Dolce & Gabbana once again, a dark maroon, velvet suit jacket, white shirt, black tie. His smile was no longer timid, but broad.

Leo had received 47 per cent of the votes. Ronaldo had 21 and Xavi 9. He picked up the award standing between Ronaldo Nazario, Sepp Blatter and Michel Platini. If he had been hesitant at the first award and a bundle of nerves at the second, at the third one he accepted the footballing world's congratulations with grace and confidence.

And his team-mate Xavi was not forgotten in the speech, although Ronaldo, absent that evening, was: he had a Copa del Rey match the following day.

Back then, in the simplistic way with which everything is analysed in football, Ronaldo was cast as the pantomime villain, the villain who is so bad that he is almost charming, the antithesis of Barcelona's success and good deeds. Messi (or any other Barça player) was the knight in shining armour, a classic hero, handsome, educated, with enormous talent and always successful. Naturally, the relationship between Cristiano and Leo is far more complex than such clichés would have us believe as we will see later.

'I especially want to share this Ballon d'Or with my friend Xavi. It's the fourth time we've come to this gala together. You deserve it, too,' he said. 'It's a pleasure to be by your side here and on the pitch.' Xavi was not expecting such recognition. 'We are very good friends. He is a great person,' says Xavi. 'It was a lovely touch. What Leo did was worth more than any award.' Neymar, present because of a spectacular goal he had scored against Flamengo, spent the evening staring at Messi in admiration.

Fourth FIFA Ballon d'Or, 2012

On 7 January 2013, Messi became the first player in the history of football to win a fourth Ballon d'Or. And he celebrated it wearing a polka-dot dinner suit.

Platini, Van Basten and Cruyff won it three times. Beckenbauer, Di Stéfano and Ronaldo twice. Cristiano Ronaldo once. In the previous six years, there had been little rotation, proof of how complicated it is to reach the top: Ronaldo was on the podium on five occasions, Iniesta two, Xavi four. Messi on all of them.

Leo did not vote for Ronaldo (he voted for Iniesta, Xavi and Manchester City striker Kun Agüero) and nor did Ronaldo vote for Leo (his votes were taken by compatriot Bruno Alvés who went for Ronaldo first, followed by Radamel Falcao and Robin van Persie).

While Messi walked to the stage, the cameras cruelly zoomed in on Ronaldo's twisted face, he was finding it hard to project a smile. Messi received 41 per cent of the votes, Ronaldo 23 and Andrés Iniesta 10.

That was the year Rodrigo Messi told *L'Équipe* that his brother had been clear about it from the beginning: 'I still remember when he told me he'd love to win the Ballon d'Or some day. He was thirteen years old.'

Although he was known to be favourite, Leo's words did not flow easily: 'I want to share and thank my Barcelona team-mates, especially Andrés. I am proud to be by your side today and train and play with you every day. To my Argentina team-mates. To those who voted for me, both captains and coaches.' There Leo stopped. 'I don't know … I'm very nervous. Thanks to my family, my friends and lastly and especially my wife and son who is the most beautiful thing God has given me.' Later he explained what had happened: 'I went blank in the middle because of the joy and because of the nerves. The truth is that I'm not used to speaking in front of so many people. I told the truth, but I was nervous.'

Thiago 'doesn't understand anything yet,' he said later in a press conference, but he wanted to name him and his girlfriend Antonella, too. He also wanted to pay tribute to Tito Vilanova and Éric Abidal but the nerves betrayed him: 'Obviously, this one is for Tito, too.

As I said recently, at that moment the words wouldn't come out. It is for Tito and Abidal. It was a tough blow for us but I hope to see them now, it makes us very happy. The biggest prize we can receive is them being here with us.'

2012 was a year of ups and downs for the team, with *only* the Spanish and European Supercup, the Copa del Rey and the FIFA Club World Cup victories, yet Messi still received individual accolades: 'I look at the years in terms of titles won. Unfortunately we couldn't win many, the best years were when we won titles.'

Ex-Real Madrid player and now coach Santi Solari described in *El País* the Argentinian's new achievement: 'No other player has combined the competitiveness of professional football with the spontaneity of street football so naturally. No other player is capable of solving tactical conundrums so frequently, as if he were playing just outside his house. And no other player has connected the quantitative with the qualitative quite so perfectly. Watching Messi play is like taking a trip back through time: when he's on the ball he opens a crack which we can peek through to spy on the essence of football. Each time he drives forward, he takes us on a journey to the village kickabouts, to breaktimes in school playgrounds, to the little pitches in the country. A journey to the very roots of the game, to that childish freedom to play the game just for the sake of the game.'

In a modest celebration, making the most of Málaga's visit to the Camp Nou in the cup, Leo shared with the fans his prize, which was handed to him by first-team liaison man Carlos Naval. Messi, to whom Adidas paid tribute with black boots sporting a serigraph of four golden balls which he wore for the match, had his photograph taken with the four awards. And, while he was at it, he scored against Málaga, too: he stole the ball from Wellington and beat Kameni.

Curiously, while Leo was breaking records (he scored 91 goals in 2012) and winning individual awards, Barcelona were experiencing a few hiccups.

Guardiola wanted to retain the order that had brought them success. But Cesc's arrival that season added another dimension to the team, which gradually affected Pep's idea. The control and balance provided by Xavi and Iniesta, the main advocates of that style, were gradually breaking down. The team was stretching following Cesc's lead and his desire to get to goal as soon as possible.

That also fitted Leo's natural tendency to run at defenders, something that had been somehow tamed by Xavi, Iniesta and later Pep, who insisted that he had to help the moves to develop, be patient, keep the ball.

Pep, now beginning to sense that people were tired of the same old story and the same faces, felt that the team was slipping from his grasp.

11. PEP'S GOODBYE

El País: Did Pep show you the way?
Messi: Yes, Pep showed us the way and we are still going. He made us play with initiative, to always go for goal. He gave us the right attitude, the conviction that we were going to win. He was spectacular, beyond what he knows as a coach. The way he analysed matches, how he prepared for them … I don't think there will ever be another coach like him.

(Interview with Messi, Ramón Besa and Luis Martín, El País,
30 September 2012)

After spending a year playing together on PlayStation online, Cesc Fàbregas in London and Messi in Barcelona, they were now, once again, reunited in the same dressing room. The prospect of returning home after eight years in England and playing under Pep and alongside Leo became irresistible for the central midfielder. Three months after arriving, the best players of that generation of '87 happened to spend 90 minutes on the pitch together. It was against Viktoria Plzeň in the Champions League. The combined talent was electrifying: Messi scored a hat-trick, one of the goals was assisted by Piqué, and Cesc grabbed the other in a clinical 4–0 victory.

The Argentinian was still scoring and generating yet more extraordinary statistics. But the doubts over collective play persisted. The introduction of Cesc added a new passing midfielder to the team and, following the Cruyffist idea that you always have to play your best players, Pep tried to fit him in. But Fàbregas came from many years of being the Messi of his own team (at Arsenal), running freely in the centre of the midfield, and it became difficult to impose on him the positional game and the strict tactical demands that the midfielders required to get the best out of Leo.

Cesc started in splendid form and the team beat Real Madrid and won three titles (Spanish and European Super Cup, World Club Cup). Leo, meanwhile, was playing every minute. Well, almost.

Leo had received precise instructions in Guardiola's first season about nutrition, but the coach gradually accepted that nobody knows their own strength like the footballer himself, always with Juanjo Brau by his side. So if he was okay, he would play. But maybe, three years later, it was now time to review the idea that he could play every game. Pep explained to him on occasions that the team was more protected with him on the pitch, but maybe it would be a good idea to rotate. At times he could be more decisive in 20 minutes than in 90, and Pep wanted to give him a rest. Leo did not accept that.

After being a substitute in a 4–0 win over Sevilla the previous season, he did not turn up for training. *El País* reported that players had not realised his anger and, when they did not see him the next day, they thought he had a cold or something similar. 'When he is that upset, or has lost a game, he doesn't feel like doing anything,' explains Cristina Cubero. 'Basically he no longer gives a damn about going to training, or whatever has to be done the next day.'

In that 2011–12 season, the last time Messi was seen on the bench was against Real Sociedad after a transatlantic flight to play for the national team. Barcelona went 2–0 up but the local team brought it back to 2–2. He went on in the sixty-second minute but the deadlock remained. According to *El País*, Leo did not attend training the following day, disgusted once again at not starting. For reactions like those, some commentators call Messi, a 'child champion'.

If Messi got angry, he could go several days without speaking to Guardiola. It is one of Leo's usual ways of dealing with conflict:

erect a wall. He does it with Pep and even with his mother. Then, a few days later, his mood mellows and the door is once more open: 'Speak to me' his eyes say, or 'I'm back'. Not even Leo can bear himself when he reacts in that way. 'If I shut myself up, I go crazy,' he said in an interview for *El Mundo Deportivo*. It is part of his baggage and that is how it is understood in the dressing room.

But the distance that Leo created during these periods of sulking was difficult for Guardiola to endure.

Guardiola understood that his success as a coach was due in no small part to Messi helping him to reach his peak, in exchange for Pep keeping him happy, for creating a team that would help him to maximise his talent. But he also thought that Messi listened to him and acted upon his advice. In that season, Pep's fourth, the coach began to feel that Leo listened to him less and less. It became increasingly difficult to get his ideas across to him.

Eventually Guardiola gave in: he decided to play him whenever he was fit. If it was what he wanted, if that made him happy, then let him have it.

Messi played every game until Christmas. He was able to rest up in Rosario, ten days during which he slept, forgot about his diet and hardly did any exercise. It was what he needed and on his return he seemed unfit. That confirmed 'the Flea's' suspicions: it was better to carry on playing and not lose that physical sharpness that he needed to make the difference.

GB: *Did you find it hard to explain to him that he could not play in every game? Do you think that he is more aware of his body's limits now?*

PG: *There is a hint of the amateur here. There are people who say: every player wants to play. No, not every player wants to play. There are days when they are happy if they don't play. He doesn't have those days, he always wants to play. I haven't spoken to him in a while and I don't know if he has realised his limits or not. Evidently he knows his body better than anyone else. I did the best I could.*

Despite the years they spent together, Leo Messi, often difficult to interpret, is still something of a mystery to Guardiola. At the start, he found it hard to understand that Leo's mentality was different from his own. 'How is it possible for him to be like that, to go three days without speaking to me?' he would ask himself. But in the end, he discovered that the question was misguided, and that you have to think as Leo, Michael Jordan or Tiger Woods do. He had to make an effort to understand him, instead of forcing or managing him.

He tried to find a balance between making concessions to the star player and taking decisions for the collective good, between the amount of goals and the triumphs. Pep left him to his own devices, he let him play, because it was what he wanted and also because he scored two or three goals for him per match. It was a policy that brought success in its wake.

But at the end of his time in charge, it became clear to Guardiola that coaches are simply instruments used by the greats (be they Michael Jordan, Maradona or Pelé) in order to achieve the maximum expression of their potential. Pep finally understood that Leo was above him, and above Barcelona, in the same way Pelé was above Santos or Maradona was above Napoli. They all construct a building that they use to achieve the goal they set themselves when they were children. And when the coach leaves, another arrives; it is as simple as that. In effect, the coach is superfluous.

Pep accepted all responsibility for the departures of Eto'o, Ibra and Bojan, the young winger from the youth team who felt mistreated by Guardiola because he stopped playing regularly, despite a promising start to his career. But his decisions were taken to create the conditions to benefit Messi's game on the pitch and to make him the best in the world. Messi does not have to ask for other forwards to be removed; the coach does that for him.

And what will go through Leo's head? He must think, of course you have to choose and you have to make those choices that benefit me, because I am the best and because I win matches. Pure logic. Leo must think that the coach would do everything necessary to keep him happy, because that was his duty.

Barcelona, incidentally, had gradually adopted a policy of feeding Leo's ambition and making him feel special. Thus, at 26, with the responsibility of carrying a universally acclaimed club and the hopes of a nation on his shoulders, Leo's life became extremely complicated. How to live a normal life when you are indulged and given anything you want, so long as you continue to win titles? We live in another world, we cannot see what Leo sees, we have no idea what it is to live with those expectations. But it remains clear that it is precisely because of that pressure that he openly demands the ball from David Villa, Cuenca or Tello. Leo thinks that they are making a mistake if a chance of an opening, which he clearly sees, is lost.

Guardiola's success was also down to a phenomenal group of people with whom Leo shares the dressing room. It was almost impossible to combine Pep's vision in the same team, the fourth best player in the world answered to the third, the third to the second, and all of them to Messi. So, who has won 14 out of 19 titles, the extraordinary figure achieved in the Guardiola era? Does the success belong to Leo, his team-mates, the coach? They say that with everything Barcelona has given him, Messi should be eternally grateful to the Catalan club. But Guardiola will add that he has earned everything he got from Barcelona on the pitch.

Guardiola started his career with the idea of dictating the team from the bench, where the players are pieces with specific roles that must adapt to his particular philosophy. But little by little, experience made him give in to the magic of footballers, their role in the game.

The coach's submission to Leo and the team organisation in order to make him feel comfortable was a general plea from the coach to the group to obey the star. And that exercise inevitably leads to unbalances.

It is in these thoughts that the roots of the so-called 'Messidependence' are found, which soon became a topic for discussion that season: team-mates started to avoid taking responsibility and always gave him the ball; Leo always wanted it. It was becoming difficult to balance the team spirit with the Argentinian's needs, something Pep had managed successfully until then.

But something else brought that dependence on the Flea. It was very difficult to arrive from another club and fit into that team straight away. The well-oiled machine that was Barcelona needed players that had enough talent and personality to add when they arrived – and the centre back Chygrinski, Ibrahimović, Afellay or Alexis were not acquisitions that made the team better. With every failed signing, the team looked more and more to Messi for solutions.

As always happens, time gradually erodes dressing-room relationships, and Pep's with Leo was also starting to wear. 'What you cannot hope for is a group of players to last for ever, they are not machines,' explains Josep María Minguella, a man who knows the ins and outs at Barcelona better than most. 'There are ways of being, there is jealousy, different egos, changes in hierarchy, in line-ups, all of that causes tiredness and stress which you have to know how to accept. It has occurred historically: Ajax came and then disappeared, later Bayern, with the same result; Milan ... And Barça's turn came, they had their time with Pep. But, given Pep's personal characteristics, with his hands-on approach which tires players out, and the normal procession of players, it is impossible for that to last indefinitely.'

Pep's exhaustion was clear for everybody to see and even his partner Cristina discussed openly with relatives of the players that the demands of the job were extraordinary and having an adverse effect. But his departure was more complex than just a plea for rest.

Perhaps in the end Guardiola did not have the strength to reinvent the team around Messi. Or did not know how to make Leo happy. There was a falling-out after the Christmas holidays: Messi returned later than scheduled and it was made to look as if he had had permission from the club to do so, although he had not. Manel Estiarte dealt with those issues to avoid the further strain on Guardiola, who was already beginning to lose the enthusiasm to carry on. It bothered Leo that the coach had not spoken to him directly. That's what happens when you are together for a long time: the small things start to get bigger.

Pep thought that the end he feared so much, that he had predicted since that first day in the first-team dressing room, was coming. Relationships with Leo and some of the senior players were gradually breaking down with that degree of impatience that comes from overfamiliarity. Coaches' decisions were questioned; the message was not reaching the players no matter how much effort he put into it. He tried to shield the players by appearing at every press conference that he could, but that created a mythology and adulation around Guardiola that was verging on the religious.

It was Guardiola's team.

And the players? Pep's excessive protagonism in the eyes of fans and commentators made players unhappy and the distance between them and the coach was becoming agonising.

Pep had to take big decisions if he wanted to recapture the magic and authority, to recycle the message and the squad, but preferred not to do so. He no longer wanted, was able to or knew how to put limits on his players. He chose not to correct the situation.

As Guardiola always said, football cycles last two or three years. In fact, his revolutionary era probably lasted a year more than he had expected, but having surrendered to the magic of players and what they had done for the club, he could not find the strength to get rid of some of them and start all over again.

Those are the reasons why Pep left FC Barcelona. He did not do it because of Leo Messi, as it has been so simplistically written.

With the erosion of time, the relaxation after years of winning and the loss of the understanding that had worked so well for three years, the collective organisation disappeared gradually on the pitch, especially without the ball; it is the first thing a team loses when things are not right. Players are inclined towards comfort, like all human beings and in all professions – and comfort means doing what you most fancy, not what you have to do.

The Catalan media preferred to ignore the warning signs. They unanimously backed Guardiola and wanted him to confirm as quickly as possible that he was going to renew his contract again for another year, which would be his fifth. Suggestions started appearing about players having lost the passion or the focus that had taken them so far. But the team was progressing in the competitions, Real Madrid seemed stronger than in previous years and not too far away in the league, and that always hides the cracks.

As journalists do not have access to the training ground, some snippets of information were now used to match certain personal agendas or opinions. An incident took place on the training ground that was taken out of context by those who had decided that there was another 'darker' side to Messi. Leo reacted to a hard tackle from youth player Marc Bartra, which caused bruising on his calf and prevented him from playing in a friendly against Hamburg, with very public recriminations. As had happened in similar situations with Thiago Motta or Sergio Busquets in previous years, nobody likes to be whacked that hard in training. Bartra was trying to make an impact in his first season with the first team, and his understandable enthusiasm made him mistime the tackle from behind, which could have seriously injured Leo. Messi's reaction was, for some outside the club, proof of his new 'boorish' behaviour. For his team-mates, some of whom laid into Bartra, it was just the typical response to an excessive use of force.

In this confusing atmosphere, everything was being weighed up; Guardiola was about to make a decision about his future. 'It would be difficult to find a replacement. Barcelona have been playing like that for four years for him,' said Messi in March of that season. 'For me, he is more important than me at Barcelona. We are the same as all of you, waiting for him to decide whether he stays or not.' And what would happen if Pep decided to leave? 'The club will go on and we will, too. But it will be very different without Guardiola.'

And so April arrived, a key month in a season in which Real Madrid were ahead in the domestic competition and Barcelona were in the Champions League semi-finals. Chelsea were their opponents. The technical staff at Chelsea were surprised by the fact that Messi,

---

18 April 2012. Champions League semi-final first leg. Chelsea 1–0 Barcelona

Chelsea: Cech; Ivanović, Terry, Cahill, Cole; Mikel, Lampard; Mata (Kalou, 74th minute), Meireles, Ramires (Bosingwa, 88th minute); and Drogba. Subs not used: Turnbull; Essien, Torres, Malouda and Sturridge.

Barcelona: Valdés; Alvés, Puyol, Mascherano, Adriano; Xavi (Cuenca, 87th minute), Busquets, Cesc (Thiago, 78th minute); Alexis (Pedro, 66th minute), Messi and Iniesta. Subs not used: Pinto; Piqué, Bartra and Keita.

Goal: 1–0. 45th minute+2: Drogba, from a Ramires pass from the left.

Martí Perarnau on www.martiperarnau.com: Chelsea only wanted to do one thing – steal possession, even just once, and give the ball to Drogba to score. And they only had one chance: precisely the one from which he scored. In a clumsy moment, Messi lost possession, Chelsea took the ball, counter-attacked and a bite ... Drogba in Capital Letters, as he has always been. The man for the big occasions.

The English club closed down all the channels and made an impenetrable net. Terry and Cahill did the 'Levante' tactic of waiting for Messi, not jumping on him. Last Saturday, Levante's defenders only tried to tackle Messi once – and he scored. Today, the two Chelsea centre-backs did not fall into the trap and waited for him, knowing that is what hurts the Argentinian.

caught in the English side's defensive trap, only managed three high-intensity passages of play throughout the whole match. Chelsea didn't play 4-5–1 as suspected, but 4-4–1; Raul Meireles was the eleventh man stuck like a lamppost on the left-hand side of the pitch from where Messi looked to start his runs, and with the sole brief of preventing him from doing so.

Three days later in the *clásico* at the Nou Camp the league was going to be decided. With four games to play, Madrid were four points ahead.

According to Diego Torres in his book *Prepárense para perder*, the Madrid players remarked that they were surprised at how Messi had played, mostly in fits and starts, as if he was protecting an injury. 'The local hero walked about, looked around, pondered the situation. Was he saving himself? For what? Something was amiss in the Guardiola home and Madrid turned up with Cristiano at his peak.' It was Mourinho's second victory in a *clásico*, following his victory in the Copa del Rey final the previous season.

Pep's decision to start Tello and leave Piqué, Cesc, Pedro and Alexis on the bench provoked a discussion in the dressing room. What did Guardiola have in mind with this decision? Was he, as

---

Matchday 35 (21 April 2102) Barcelona 1–2 Real Madrid

Barcelona: Valdés; Puyol, Mascherano, Adriano (Pedro, 74th minute); Thiago, Xavi (Alexis, 69th minute), Busquets, Iniesta; Alvés, Messi and Tello (Cesc, 80th minute). Subs not used: Pinto; Piqué, Keita and Montoya.

Real Madrid: Casillas; Arbeloa, Ramos, Pepe, Coentrão; Khedira, Xabi Alonso; Di María (Granero, 74th minute), Özil (Callejón, 88th minute), Ronaldo; and Benzema (Higuaín, 93rd minute). Subs not useds: Adán; Kaká, Marcelo and Albiol.

Goals: 0–1. 17th minute: Khedira. 1–1. 70th minute: Alexis. 1–2. 73rd minute: Ronaldo.

Santiago Siguero, *Marca*: A Cristiano goal finishing off a counter-attack killed off Barcelona and brought the title closer to Madrid, who did a practical and efficient job at the Camp Nou. Moments after Barcelona equalised, the Portuguese received a precise pass into space from Özil. That goal could mean that, after three years of Barcelona domination, Madrid win La Liga. And maybe it could also be the start of that change of cycle that Madrid fans have been dreaming of for so long.

Olé (Argentina): On this occasion, the duel between Messi and Ronaldo was won by the Portuguese, who got the winning goal at the Camp Nou and also goes ahead of Messi in the goals-scoring tables with 42. Before that, after some good defending, the best player in the world gave the pass of a genius that made the score 1–1.

---

some players suspected, looking to punish someone who wasn't being as obedient as he should have been? Cuenca was in the starting line-up against Chelsea, a decision deemed by many as yet another error of judgement. Look at the bench.

In the dressing room Pedro was in tears, as was Leo, who had already scored 63 goals that season but sent his penalty, which would have made it 3–1, crashing against the woodwork, as well as

25 April 2012. Champions League semi-final second leg. Barcelona 2–2 Chelsea

Barcelona: Valdés; Puyol, Piqué (Alvés, 26th minute), Mascher-ano; Xavi, Busquets, Cesc (Keita, 74th minute); Messi; Cuenca (Tello, 67th minute), Alexis and Iniesta. Subs not used: Pinto; Adriano, Thiago and Pedro.

Chelsea: Cech; Ivanović, Cahill (Bosingwa, 12th minute), Terry, Cole; Lampard, Mikel; Mata (Kalou, 58th minute), Meireles, Ramires; and Drogba (Torres, 80th minute). Subs not used: Turnbull; Essien, Malouda and Sturridge.

Goals: 1–0. 35th minute: Busquets. 2–0. 43rd minute: Iniesta. 2–1. 45th minute+1: Ramires. 2–2. 92nd minute: Torres.

Ramón Besa, *El Pais*: They say that the Lord giveth and the Lord taketh away. But it's not as if Barcelona's titles had all been gifted since the arrival of Pep Guardiola. The football of the *blaugrana* has captivated all those that love the game. Now it seems that the ball that once finished in the back of the net is now crashing against the woodwork, and defeats are now linking up at the same speed as victories used to come along. The same rivals that until now Barcelona would subdue with their own brand of 'jazz' football are making Barcelona pay as they bring with them their 'rock and vengeance' style of play, and strikers, previously made to look small by Messi, are queuing around the Camp Nou seeking their revenge. It had already happened with Madrid on Saturday and it happened yesterday with Chelsea. It occurred with Cristiano Ronaldo and Drogba, even with Torres. Tormented, fragile, and very unlucky, Barcelona now miss out on the Champions League final, just three days after losing the league.

Marti Perarnau on www.martiperarnau.com: Game where history repeats itself. Groundhog Day: Inter 2010; Chelsea 2012. Total domination, a subdued rival, an armed concrete wall, a magnificent exercise in survival from a Chelsea side weakened by an injury to Cahill and the dismissal of Terry following an inexplicable act from an experienced skipper. Guardiola planned the game well. Open up the flanks, place a double false number 9 in the shape of Messi and Cesc and play what looks like a version of handball, passing the ball from side to side as you look to break through the middle.

A mobile defence on top of Messi who tried and tried, with support from Xavi and Busquets, but found himself inexorably crashing against a white wall. This Barcelona, the team that became invincible, probably the most solid, cohesive and competitive team in the history of the game, has discovered its Achilles heel: people have found out the answers, now Barcelona will have to find new questions to ask, new challenges to set.

hitting the post on another occasion. 'It was a final that we wanted to play in and it got away from us,' recalls the Canary Islands-born winger. 'And it was the game where perhaps I saw him most upset and hurt, I don't know, maybe because he missed the penalty or perhaps because he was not going to be in the final. I suppose everything has an effect.'

Pep called a meeting with the president for the following morning. Suspecting that he was leaving, Leo sent various affectionate text messages to his coach trying to persuade him not to. Pep has them to this day.

But the small wounds that had been appearing in the previously thick skin of the squad had become infected.

Two days later, Pep told his players in the training ground that he was leaving.

The players were not sure till that moment if Pep really would go. But, after receiving confirmation while they were already on the training ground, the conversation turned to the future. Who was going to take his place? After the session, the group knew that Tito Vilanova would be taking charge of the side, which came as a relief; the best possible solution. 'After losing the most successful coach in the history of the club, the fact that you have someone so close to the club available was really good for us,' says Mascherano, who remembers the feeling of shock at that very light training session.

After training, Pep accompanied by the president, Sandro Rosell, and the sporting director, Andoni Zubizarreta, announced his decision at a press conference. Leo wasn't there but Puyol, Xavi, Iniesta, Busquets, Valdés, Cesc, Piqué and Pedro all attended.

'Time always wears you out and I am worn out,' said Guardiola. 'I am empty and need to refill. I sincerely believe that the next man can give things that I cannot. To sit here every three days a coach has to be strong, has to have life, passion. I have to get that back and I can only do that by resting, distancing myself, because I believe we would have hurt each other, that is my perception ... I know what I'm leaving behind me but I believe I am doing what is right for me.'

'Leo's here! Leo's here! The demonstrations of affection I have received these past days have been great,' concluded Guardiola when asked about the absence of the Argentinian.

Messi was not sure what was happening after the training session. 'He was furious that Pep was announcing his departure and he wasn't there,' says Piqué. 'There was a breakdown in communication in the dressing room.' The four captains (Valdés, Xavi, Iniesta, Puyol) got the news about the press announcement and started to pass it around but it didn't reach everyone. What's more, it was initially thought that only the four spokesmen of the team would attend. Those who went were surprised not to see him there and that's where the confusion arose. As soon as Leo and Mascherano noted the presence of some players as well as the senior ones, they knew that their absence would cause speculation.

A few hours later, 'the Flea' posted the following message on Facebook. 'I want to thank Pep with all my heart for everything that he has done for my professional career and for my life. Due to how emotional I feel, I preferred not to attend Pep's press conference. I wanted to be far from the press above all, because I know they will be looking for the sadness on the faces of the players, and this is something that I have decided not to show.'

There remained one more thing to do. Barcelona were facing Espanyol in their thirty-seventh league match of the season with everything already decided. The club took the opportunity of guaranteeing that the last match at the Camp Nou would be a homage to Pep. Leo Messi scored all the game's four goals. 'The Flea' pointed towards Guardiola after his first, directly from a free-kick. Two more went in.

Before the game, Leo told his dad that he felt sad about the departure of Pep; 'the Flea' feels every big change like a little mourning. He recognised he had done a lot of good things for him and the side, and was thinking he deserved a little public gesture. Just before the fourth goal, Javier Mascherano told Messi it would be a good idea to approach Pep if he scored again.

And his fourth goal of the game duly arrived. Leo ran towards the bench to embrace his coach.

If the hug he gave Ronaldinho was the embrace of a generational swap and from a boy who wanted to thank his mentor for looking after him, that day at the Camp Nou the fans saw a gesture of gratitude to his boss for having understood his needs. 'Thanks for everything,' Pep told Messi in his ear. 'I did it to thank him and because that's how it came out,' said Leo after the game.

There was still time to win the Copa del Rey, against Athletic de Bilbao, 3–0, with another goal from Messi, the second of the game. After winning the fourteenth title of that era, Pep said again to 'the Flea': 'thanks Leo. We've won loads, but without you we wouldn't have won half of them.'

Leo went off with the national side a few days later and from there had some words to say about Guardiola. 'I was surprised and sad when I found out he was leaving. He will always have my respect and admiration. Now a new stage begins, we hope to continue in the same manner. Guardiola always said that everything he did was together with Tito Vilanova. We hope things go well for Tito for the benefit of everyone.'

Leo Messi and Pep Guardiola did not speak again. They lost contact.

They saw each other briefly at the Ballon d'Or awards ceremony in January 2013. They greeted each other but little more. Nor did they come across one another when Barcelona played against Bayern Munich in a friendly in the late summer of 2013. 'I haven't seen him,' said Leo after the game.

Players and coaches do not have to behave like father and son. They don't even need to love each other.

But Pep probably needs another warm embrace from Leo. He did everything for him. And surely Leo would want to offer him some sign of affection and gratitude.

The distance, the coldness, can only be explained by the need for a period of decompression, of distance, after four intense years. 'A certain amount of time has to pass, don't you think?' suggests Joan Laporta. 'With the benefit of time, you realise just what he has done, the success he has had, who he has had at his side. Top competition brings with it a mental pressure way above what is normal. And at the end of it you need time to see it with new eyes. There's affection from both sides, I'm sure.'

Pep will always remember that he had the best player in history under his guidance. And he knows that Leo loves him.

And that Messi doesn't know how to say it.

Both are conscious of the fact that they have been mutually helpful to each other. And when they retire, or when they meet again, at some time or another they will embrace again. And there will be no need to say anything else.

But with Pep gone, Leo was now mostly worried about how things would go under a new coach.

2

Where Is Leo Heading?

1. Cristiano Ronaldo

– *Friends come and go in life. It is very rare to be able to maintain a thirty-year relationship with anyone, apart from your siblings and parents.*
– *Above everything it is a relationship that you never had with anyone else: going through the same things to reach the same point in your life, but never at the same time. One or the other would win, we were never in the same emotional place, but we did go through the same things. So we can empathise completely.*
– *Even so it is very strange that we are capable of maintaining such respect and intimacy despite trying to beat and annoy each other constantly as much as possible. You were definitely a part of my life every single day, whether I liked it or not, because I had to compete and read about you absolutely every day.*
– *You know? Your image was really funny; I was the tough one. But your image was the tough one, and I laughed, because I knew that I was the toughie. That's the way it was, I'm not saying it to boast or anything.*
– *You were like a meringue with a ball of steel inside, and I was the ball of steel with porridge inside.*
– *You were so smooth inside, so vulnerable, so emotional; and I was the tenacious, stubborn one. People had a different impression of what we were like on the inside.*
– *I think that contrast cements a great rivalry, the ying and the*

yang, the black and the white, as we used to have, you and I. We were polar opposites in the eyes of the public. I was more passive in my game, you were more aggressive, you were emotional, I was cold. What contrast could you see?

– *The most obvious was in style, but the emotional component was even more so, because I simply couldn't keep my feelings locked away in a box. I had to let them out in the matches.*

– *I didn't understand how you could cry on the pitch. I tried to understand why you couldn't control yourself, in front of sixty million people watching you on television, but on the other hand I admired you because you were capable of showing your emotions without limits.*

– *You were one of the best competitors in history.*

– *I was jealous of you for a long time. I didn't want you to win. At other times I would admire your honesty, you spoke with your heart in your hands. I kept everything trapped inside, I wouldn't say anything bad about anyone in a press conference because my mother used to say to me: 'If you don't have anything nice to say about someone, don't say anything.' I always wanted to be like you. I respected you and admired you deeply.*

– *Nobody wants to lose when they play, but my biggest motivation was testing and beating myself. I was competitive with myself.*

– *You were dominant in such a way that I couldn't find a single crack in your armoury which would help me discover how to beat you. I had to make myself stronger mentally.*

– *I would see headlines, the goodie against the baddie, and that killed me. I was the villain and it hurt me. I didn't like it, but what could I do? When your name was spoken, everyone applauded. When they spoke mine, some whistled. I was jealous of you too.*

(Extract from a conversation between tennis players Chris Evert (America's sweetheart) and Martina Navratilova (poker-faced Czech-born player) in a fascinating ESPN documentary, *Unmatched*)

Maybe Ronaldo and Leo will one day have the chance to spend a weekend together as Evert and Navratilova did at the request of ESPN. It would be fascinating to hear the conversation between these two giants, admitting both their admiration for and rage against their nemesis. 'Messi and his poetry should not take anything away from another chosen one, Cristiano Ronaldo, a sublime player who also defines an era,' as journalist José Sámano puts it.

One is tall, good-looking, with a powerful shot, a sprinter's acceleration. The other is small, a dribbler with any number of roles on the pitch; he can be a goalscorer, passer or organiser. Both play for teams that have been constructed to play to their particular strengths. Both have humble origins. Leo does not need external recognition as much as Ronaldo, merely acceptance. The Argentinian has a small posse of protectors, whereas various companies revolve around the Portuguese, looking after his money and his image.

Cristiano exemplifies the stereotypical world-class player we're now so used to seeing: he woos the paparazzi, lives the lifestyle of a Hollywood actor. Messi is the polar opposite, perhaps the first star who just wants to be a footballer. Leo knows that he could have a supermodel by his side, but he prefers his friend's cousin, Antonella, whom he grew up with.

But that is the superficial vision upon which the media feeds. The reality is that they both have as much in common as separates them: they have the same competitive spirit; they have both sacrificed their lives to achieve their dreams. They both share some fundamentals: kicks from opponents, various demands on them, the deep desire to win, the pain of defeat. They appreciate, seek and desire the collective title, but they also want the individual one, and the goals.

Tell me if this story sounds familiar.

Cristiano Ronaldo dos Santo Aveiro was born in February 1985 on the island of Madeira, the fourth child of María Dolores, cook, and José Dinis, gardener, a family with financial difficulties. Not only did José love football, but it was part of his world as a kitman at Andorinha, the village team. Cristiano lived with a ball at his feet and, when he did not have a leather one, he would make himself one out of anything that was lying around. Sporting Lisbon signed him and he left Madeira for the first time in his life at the age of 12. At the club residence they laughed at his Madeira accent, which in Lisbon was considered a poor boy's accent. In one season alone he played at five different levels at Sporting, including the first team.

Cristiano, whose dad passed away in 2006, speaks of Sir Alex Ferguson, his manager at Manchester United, as a second father. Leo has Jorge as a manager and father, two roles which are difficult to combine. Ronaldo's mother mixes her maternal role with that of confidante and protector, and is always ready to help care for her bachelor son's child. Messi's older brother, Rodrigo, often acts as his father. Both men therefore share the same circumstances of close family ties and the presence of trusted confidants, together with the varied and often interchangeable roles that these people are required to adopt.

Both have children, which has been character changing and has matured them. Both have consulted a psychologist at different times in their careers, although each has responded in a different way: Leo did not think it was of much use, whereas Ronaldo has had one at Real Madrid for the past few years now in an effort to change his public image and to help him control his emotions better. And both have fantasised about their futures since they were very young: each told himself that he was going to be the best, as if it were written in the stars.

In 2009, the German magazine *Der Spiegel* confirmed that Ronaldo was the 'fastest footballer on the planet', the result of an extraordinary 'fine tuning of a high output motor': he regularly does 3,000 sit-ups, he systematically gets eight hours' sleep every night and has extraordinary mental strength. His thousands of hours with the ball allow him to make decisions unconsciously and to know the permutations of the game without thinking: he dribbles at full speed looking at his adversary's feet (he can dribble around 13 cones in eight seconds); he anticipates opponents' presence, the amount of available and necessary space; and he senses where the ball is going to fall even in darkness, as he demonstrated in a filmed exercise in which he was asked to shoot with the light switched off just as a cross was put in.

He scored on both occasions: his reaction time was 300 milliseconds. He even scored when the shot left the foot of the crosser after the lights were off. His shot, the famous Tomahawk that sees the ball rise and fall like a missile, is the consequence of practising 25 to 30 free-kicks every day.

But the world has decided that one is the villain, arrogant, stuck-up; that the other is the tireless worker, modest. That is how they are often described in the Latin world anyway. CR7 (Cristiano Ronaldo and his shirt number) often shows his feelings and that is why opposition fans try to put him off with shouts of 'Messi, Messi', whereas Leo keeps his emotions under control most of the time. People feed on rivalries such as this one, and the fact that Ronaldo encourages the comparison does him no favours. But he cannot help it: it is the tragedy of those who are one step behind, yet, in their own way, equally extraordinary.

Pedro Pinto (CNN): We are going to speak about images rather than football. Do you think that you are sometimes a victim of your own persona?

Cristiano Ronaldo: I'm not going to make a thing about that, but sometimes I think so, yes.

Pedro Pinto: Why?

Cristiano Ronaldo: Why? Perhaps ... I never give a 100 per cent correct answer, because sometimes I really don't know. Maybe I agree sometimes, maybe I have a bad image on the pitch, because I'm too serious ... But, if you really know me, if you're my friend, if you come to my house, if you spend the day with me ... you will realise that I hate losing!

Four years after arriving at Real Madrid, *merengue* fans are still not clear about who Cristiano really is. 'People think his life is made up of an undefined succession of daily crises,' writes Diego Torres. 'In reality, they do not know that, apart from when his competitive streak gets the better of him, he is a simple lad, educated, noble, respectful of his opponents, and grateful to be able to live in a city that he appreciates.'

In a memorable scene from the film *Rush*, the story of the rivalry between James Hunt and Nikki Lauda, the then recently married Austrian F1 racing driver admits: 'Happiness is the enemy, it weakens you, suddenly you have something to lose', and that 'having an enemy is a blessing'. The following is no coincidence: on 28 January 2013, Ronaldo celebrated three goals against Getafe. A few hours later, at the Camp Nou, Messi scored four against Osasuna. 'The level they demand from themselves varies and increases as the enemy's achievements increase,' the writer and physical coach Pedro Gómez writes for this book. 'Thinking small makes us grow only a little. If the level we demand from ourselves is not stimulated daily, we stop evolving. If one of them didn't exist, the other would be satisfied with being top scorer with twenty-five goals.' One makes the other better, just as used to be the case with Navratilova and Evert.

But the perception at the moment is that Messi is one step ahead of Ronaldo, as even though Cristiano won his second Ballon d'Or in 2014 and the Champions League, his physique has limited him, and in Brazil Leo showed some of his best form again. In the time they have been together in La Liga (since 2009), Barcelona have won 15 titles, Madrid four. Messi wins the Golden Boot battle 3–1 and according to the CIES Football Observatory, Messi's market value is €250 million, Ronaldo between €102.2 and €118.7 million.

Ronaldo suffers more from the comparison: it must be so painful to be second despite all that effort, sacrifice, ambition and talent. And Messi is something of an obsession for the Portuguese player: he is his point of reference. He demands his club treat him as Barcelona treats Leo, and that they give him the same affection.

For as long as they are in competition their relationship will be marked by their battle for the same space, that small, distant space in which the truly greats live. But how do they get on? What do they say to each other when they meet? And when they are not in the spotlight?

At the 2013 Ballon d'Or gala, Ruud Gullit thought he noticed 'a strange relationship between Cristiano and Messi; they barely say hello to one another'. The relationship, in the presence of others, is cold. It is not bad; it is respectful but distant. They do not hate each other, as some people might believe, say the families of both. Conversation does not usually go beyond 'hello, how are you, everything okay?' At public events, Messi is always surrounded by his own crew, or with Xavi and Iniesta, whereas Ronaldo usually shows up on his own, even though mixing with people he does not know intimidates him.

And it is difficult to break the ice when they see each other in private. In September 2012 the UEFA player of the season was selected. Iniesta, Messi and Ronaldo were waiting in a private room before going onstage. Nobody else was present. According to *El Mundo*, one of the three took the first step. Cristiano looked at Leo and asked him about his summer and about recent matches. Messi answered him and Iniesta brought himself into the conversation, which ended up being friendly and football-related. The two *blaugranas* were surprised to see such a warm Ronaldo for the first time, and this at the height of the José Mourinho era.

Diego Torres relates an anecdote that confirms the two stars' diplomacy in his book *Prepárense para perder* ('Prepare for Defeat'). It happened at the Ballon d'Or 2012, the day Real Madrid President Florentino Pérez feared for the first time, according to Torres, that Ronaldo could end up at Barcelona. Andrés Iniesta, Pep Guardiola and Vicente del Bosque were witnesses to the following:

'On 7 January 2013, the president found himself in an isolated corner of a hall in the Kongresshaus Zürich, keeping an eye on Messi while he was being interviewed on television. Cristiano suddenly appeared at the other side of the hall. Then, exactly what the president had feared occurred. Messi called him over, Cristiano went, and they hugged just like children. Pérez confessed to his friends that he watched the scene in anguish. He felt danger. He could visualise everything. Cristiano would be free in January 2015 and then any club, Barcelona included, would be able to sign him without negotiating with Real Madrid.'

One year earlier, Ronaldo had gone to Pérez's office at the Bernabéu to express his indignation at the club's behaviour, the distance they showed him and the slowness of his contract renewal negotiations. The player threatened to leave Madrid. 'If it's a question of money, I'll come back tomorrow with a hundred million euros,' Ronaldo told the president. Florentino retorted: 'It's not a hundred, your release clause is €1 billion … If you want to go, bring me the money to sign Messi.'

They are not friends but they are polite to one another in public; anything else, those who are close to them insist, is all media-generated.

Messi admires Cristiano's shooting and heading ability but is tired of comparisons between the two of them. He understands that Ronaldo is not comfortable about it either, and has watched without the slightest pleasure his supposed arch-enemy responding with anger to the public pestering from those who like to see them fighting. Ronaldo, who will take part in a commercial with Leo for the first time to promote the Google Nexus 11 tablet, does not think that they can be compared: 'Messi and I are as different as Ferrari and Porsche.'

Ronaldo, perhaps as a symptom of the immaturity that marks so many footballers, thinks it necessary to put on a brave face in front of his team-mates, not be scared of Messi and to rise to the challenge. All very macho; all very false. And that is why, according to some Real Madrid players, CR7 has a nickname for him: 'motherfucker'; and if he sees someone from the club speaking to Leo, he also ends up being baptised 'motherfucker'. In that environment, Ronaldo usually compares their relationship with that between the Republic of Ireland and the United Kingdom. And the Madrid players, with their less than subtle dressing-room sense of humour, have a long list of jokes that include Messi as Ronaldo's dog or puppet, or kept in a designer handbag belonging to the Portuguese player. And much worse.

Ronaldo fits the Real Madrid business plan and their search for *galácticos*. Messi fits the more romantic image that Barcelona portrays. That is why Barça cannot imagine selling their flagship footballer: if the club behaved like a business, Leo would be sold at his peak, when the highest transfer fee could be obtained. If a romantic idea is followed, Messi will not be allowed to leave until he decides to go to Newell's, on his last legs.

Ronaldo was offered to Barcelona by his agent Jorge Mendes before he signed for Manchester United, and in 2010, when already at Madrid, he said, 'You can never say never, you never know what might happen in the future.' Can you imagine Messi, Ronaldo and Neymar together? In any case, both clubs have made sure that both their wages reflect their top-billing, and their contracts have recently taken, or are about to take, a historic leap. Ronaldo renewed his in September 2013 and now receives €21 million net. Barcelona are negotiating Messi's and the aim is to announce a renewal in December, ten months after the last one. Leo could earn, including bonuses, €23 million net.

'Both are really good,' says former Argentina coach Carlos Bilardo. 'Messi comes at you and you don't know where he's going, this way or that way. However, football people know in which direction Ronaldo is shooting. Messi is the best by far.'

'It is dreadfully bad luck for Cristiano to coincide with Messi,' believes the Brazilian Ronaldo. 'The two of them are far superior to the rest, although for me Messi is slightly better.'

'They are different. The only thing they have in common is goals'; 'they have different starting positions'; and 'Cristiano prefers coming in from the wing to look for a goal and Messi moves around wherever he wants,' explains Vicente del Bosque.

'Messi is the most difficult to stop, unpredictable,' says former Valencia coach Miroslav Djukic. 'Cristiano stands out for his shot, he does better with space in front of him. He is also good in the air. He is pure power. Messi is the best team player in all three categories, something not normal in a goalscorer. Very good at one on ones and in confined spaces.'

Gerard Piqué came up with an appropriate sentence with which to compare them: 'Messi is an extra-terrestrial, and Cristiano the best human being.'

At the end of the day this is a pointless debate anyway. There is no precise way of measuring individuals in what is a team game. But one thing seems clear. A champion is not the same as a star. The champion has a very clear mindset: he is harmonious, creative. The star can cave in at any moment because he has a very large and fragile ego. The champion tries harder the more difficult the situation. You cannot put limits on the champion; you cannot hinder his progress, because he brings you goals and titles.

Despite all that, and regardless of the way it looks, both Ronaldo and Messi are unquestionably champions.

2. Tito Vilanova, the New Leader

Martín Souto: Are coaches overrated? Do you say, 'we all know each other already, we don't need coaches'?

Leo Messi: No. I think that the coach is vitally important, perhaps more so than ever. You can know each other, play instinctively, but you need him for a number of details, to prepare for a game. Since Tito has been away, we have missed him. With all due respect to [Jordi] Roura, he is our coach and he is going along the same path as us, trying to help, but at the beginning of the year our coach was Tito and not having him was a severe blow.

Martín Souto: Tito did a lot of work during the Pep era, didn't he?

Leo Messi: Yes, and afterwards he did it in his own way. Tito is a

very intelligent person who knows a lot about football. A differ-
ent type of guy from Guardiola, with a distinct way of getting
his message across. From the very first day, when he was number
two, he was highly respected, and for that reason the change-over
from Pep to Tito was fairly smooth.

(Leo Messi, interview with Martín Souto, TyC Sports, March 2013)

When Leo found out that Vilanova was to be Pep's successor, he smiled broadly. That was just what he needed. Guardiola's former assistant was not only the first coach to play him just behind the main striker in the *Infantiles*, but they had also been together for four years during the Pep era. Messi welcomed the continuity. 'He is a normal, open person. He's straight, tells you things to your face. I like that,' Messi told *El País*. Tito was to be football coach, nothing more; the club had finally assumed some of the responsibilities that it had bestowed on an exhausted Guardiola.

The first summer of the post-Pep era saw very few changes to the squad. Tito Vilanova had been looking for a central defender and a centre midfielder, or preferably someone who could fill both roles: he thought about Javi Martínez, but Alex Song arrived from Arsenal. Jordi Alba, an extremely offensive full-back, was signed from Valencia. Seydou Keita left but, overall, the 2012–13 side was physically not as strong.

Barcelona had only won minor titles the previous season – the Copa del Rey, the World Club Championship and the Spanish Super Cup – but the feeling was that only a little fine-tuning was required – especially in the work without the ball. The team also needed to find new options in attack but Tito thought it could all be sorted with the players he had.

Leo had scored 211 goals in 219 games under Guardiola; or, put another way, 150 in his last 135 matches. His increased goal tally was in direct proportion to the growing influence he was having on games. The mental state of a side can be measured by the distribution of the goals. When it is always the same person scoring, that fragile state of equilibrium that is a football team begins to show cracks.

The challenge was twofold. The new coach had to ensure that no one shirked their responsibilities. At the same time Leo had to allow for the growth of other players around him: the opposition would then have more to worry about.

But Vilanova decided something else altogether: his reign would begin with a pact with the players. The status quo was going to be maintained, the changes in tactics and hierarchy kept to a minimum. He even stopped the requirement that players should eat together, a subtle form of diet control imposed by Guardiola.

The beginning of the season was hopeful. The football was more direct; Leo saw less of the ball than he had done under Pep, but he continued to be crucial. They made the best ever start in the history of La Liga.

Being direct also meant losing control of the game. Leo and Cesc, in keeping with their style, enjoyed trying to finish the play as quickly as possible, and the moves were no longer created by a patient build-up from Xavi and Iniesta.

In Tito's team talks, ball retention was still insisted upon but possession for possession's sake was seen as serving no purpose. The key to the success of Guardiola's Barcelona was an organisational structure that allowed for everyone to be in the right place to apply pressure high up the pitch when they lost possession, with Alexis, Villa and Pedro waiting in the wings, without the ball, while the rest of the team cooked up the game.

There was an order to what they did.

The three of them, Alexis, Pedro and Villa, knew what they had to do and were very aware of what the others were up to. But when that rigorousness and control disappear, teams start depending on individual play rather than team co-ordination – everybody starts applying their own solutions. That problem really started under Pep but was accentuated under the more lenient leadership of Tito.

And then, halfway through that programme, Vilanova's illness returned. From that moment on, an assessment of his work was made on a sentimental rather than a professional basis.

In May 2012 his doctors announced he had made a complete recovery after undergoing an emergency operation for a tumour on the parotid gland. But on 19 December it was announced that Tito would leave the Barcelona bench for another operation, scheduled for the following day.

From then on, Tito came and went from the training ground as he bravely tried to combine his recovery with preparing the team for upcoming matches. In the second week of January 2013 he travelled to New York for a few days to get a second opinion and returned to the United States the following week to undergo radiotherapy and chemotherapy sessions. He wasn't present at the 3–2 defeat at the hands of Real Sociedad, though the team responded with a 5–1 demolition of Osasuna in the next game.

From New York, Tito communicated by telephone to select his side for the games, and during the matches he was in direct contact via Whatsapp with Jordi Roura, who replaced him in his absence. Two months later he rejoined the squad.

On his return, Tito explained to the team how he was getting on. Leo is not one for listening much, or at least that's the impression he gives: during talks his gaze wanders. But in this meeting Leo looked straight into Tito's eyes, hanging onto his every word. Leo, like all of them, was suffering the pain that fate had dealt them.

In November, Eric Abidal had returned to training, even though he did so away from the squad at first, and in December the doctors gave him a clean bill of health so that he could play again: he was involved in five games, including a full match. Players took hope from the Frenchman's recovery every time they saw Tito calmly walking along the touchline wearing a scarf to hide the surgical scars on his neck.

It was a strangely anomalous situation. The directors of the club had gambled on Jordi Roura, who had analysed games and prepared dossiers on rivals for Guardiola. It effectively meant leaving the team to manage itself, affording the peace of mind that there was a committed dressing room capable of dealing with any situation in an intelligent way. The senior players ruled, Leo included.

On a day-to-day basis, however, the situation was complicated. Most of the training sessions lasted 40 minutes – 20 minutes of drills and 20 minutes of possession football. What was missing was the attention to detail. The dynamic initiated at the start of the season – pressuring high up the field – was being lost because of a question of attitude. If you do not make demands of a footballer, the first thing to go is his work off the ball.

In those days of self-management, Messi was at his most proactive, seeking to participate in both the creation and execution of play.

The year 2012 became one of extraordinary achievements, some of which seem almost impossible to better. Not only did he beat Gerd Müller's 40-year-old record for goals in a calendar year with 91, and win his fourth consecutive Ballon d'Or, but his bag was also filled with other achievements that year: (courtesy of @MessiStats) European Cup top scorer four years in a row; the only player to score five goals in a Champions League match (against Bayer Leverkusen); the most La Liga hat-tricks in one season by any player; scorer in the greatest number of consecutive La Liga matches; most goals scored in a year by a player for Argentina (jointly held with Gabriel Batistuta); most goals scored in a single European Cup season; most La Liga hat-tricks by a Barcelona player; most goals scored by a Barcelona player in *clásicos*; most goals scored by a player in a La Liga season; most goals scored in European competition by a Barcelona player. In addition, he scored one goal for every 63 minutes played in 2012 for club and country; the most goals for a Barcelona player in La Liga; and the most goals by a Barcelona player in all competitions, beating César Rodríguez Alvarez's 232 ... And that is just a selection.

And he added another interesting statistic to his growing list of records: he was scoring about 15 per cent of his goals with his right foot, his 'bad foot': the effort to improve had brought with it some reward.

Without a relevant leader of the squad, the team increasingly turned towards Leo, something that had already started under Guardiola. And 'the Flea', as he had always done, wanted more: more of the ball, more goals, more influence.

'Guardiola put everything towards the creation of the Messi system,' writes Martí Perarnau in *Sport* newspaper. 'At the beginning it involved everyone playing for Xavi so that he could activate Messi.' Perarnau alluded to an interview with the Catalan central midfielder in *Süddeutsche Zeitung* which explained the situation graphically. 'If I notice that Messi hasn't touched the ball for about five minutes, I think: "This isn't right. It can't be. Where is he?" So I get hold of him and tell him: "Get closer, let's start playing." Messi is an attacker and attackers go quiet sometimes. As if he were switched off. But when he comes back into midfield, he starts to enjoy himself.'

But when Cesc started by-passing Xavi to get to Messi more quickly, the foundations of Messidependence were being laid.

With a team which now depended upon him more and more, Leo became even more demanding of himself, more concerned lest the team should start to decline, and tougher on anyone who wouldn't respond. His childish personality traits became accentuated, while at the same time he acted very much like an adult who had been around the block, seen it all, done it all.

Such is the conundrum facing great stars, and the difficulty we have in understanding them: men 20 or 30 years older are seldom, if ever, faced with the level of responsibility that Leo took on at the age of 26.

Footballers dare to talk about tactics, as Leo did in February on Barça TV after a difficult comeback against Sevilla at the Camp Nou: 'The team continues to keep the ball without creating the same dangerous situations. We need depth to break down defences.'

He suggested a solution. 'Having a point of reference like *el Guaje* [David Villa] means the central defenders stay in their positions and don't come out. It all helps to create more space for everyone else.' With Villa, Messi played a freer game and *el Guaje* played in the position between the two opposing central defenders so that Leo could have more space, and he himself could be closer to goal – with the result that Villa scored in three games, making him the second highest goalscorer in the squad.

During this campaign the relationship between David Villa and Messi was often discussed, especially after a very public exchange of views that occurred between the two players in the first half of the fifth match of the season between Barcelona and Granada, after Villa had failed to pass the ball to Leo when he was in a scoring position. Canal + broadcast the following transcription:

Messi. '*Play it in front of me, in front! Play it there!*'

Villa: '*But you can't control it! Fucking hell, man. I had one and gave it to you.*'

Messi: '*Over there, for fuck's sake!*' (*pointing to the space where he should have received the ball*).

El Guaje had lost ground in the first team following his serious injury in the World Club Championship in December 2011. Tito considered Alexis the better combination with Leo in attack and Villa, a world champion, is not one of those players who takes being replaced with good grace.

'I have said that you should not look for problems where none exist, look somewhere else,' Leo told *El País* at the time. 'There is nothing here. It's a dressing room that functions above and beyond sport, spectacularly well. We've been together for a long time and we get on very well together at a human level. No one knows how much fun we have. And after so many years that isn't easy.'

In the match against Glasgow Celtic that ended in the club's second defeat of the season, however, Villa opted to shoot for goal when he had the option of passing to Leo. You could have cut the air with a knife.

Even though Leo's suggestion of including Villa in the team was working for the team, it became patently obvious that Messi, like the team itself, needed someone to direct his talent, instincts and needs. Barcelona's football became an exchange of blows with the opposition – goals at both ends, no control. It was to no one's benefit, and it was shortening Leo's football life: with limits, with challenges and targets, Messi can last much longer; his influence is more effective when there are clear parameters and guidelines.

Without clear leadership, lines get blurred and confusion reigns.

In a game before the one against Bayer Leverkusen, Alexis scored twice but also got a mouthful from Leo for not passing when he should have done. The players who got it from Messi were forwards and wingers, those who have to deliver the ball: Leo's demands have their roots in football. But he was also one of the leading figures in the dressing room, just as Ronaldinho had been before him, and only those who dare to challenge the establishment grow, as Leo had done in getting into the first team. Those who cannot meet this challenge fall by the wayside.

Martín Souto: I have to ask you this. Have you ever fought with a team-mate?

Messi: Yes but not to the point that we have come to blows. For me what is in the past stays in the past. It stays on the pitch. I can be cross for a day or two, but then it goes.

Martín Souto: But has it happened with a really close friend?

Messi: Yes. It happened with Pinto in a training session in a short game that they won, and then began to celebrate and we began to argue and fight. And he knows me and came up to me the day after, looked at me and we both started to laugh, and that was it.

(Leo Messi, interview with Martín Souto, TyC Sports, March 2013)

Incidentally, Pinto, Leo's pal and protector, is a goalkeeper, like Oscar Ustari and Juan Cruz Leguizamón, two of his best friends. Leo has always felt at home with them, apparently more so than with the others. Maybe because they are all outsiders, or 'different' (*el distinto*), as he himself was described in the title of a book about Leo published by *Olé* in 2013.

In any case, the tension on the pitch, the footballing disputes, came about once again because of the absence of leadership. The boy who had made such great efforts to get to the highest level now faced another challenge: how to handle success. The struggle hadn't stopped, it had just changed.

The year finished with two great pieces of news for Messi: on 2 November his son Thiago was born, Leo and Antonella's first child. At exactly 17.14, fourteen minutes past five in the afternoon Twitter went nuts: first because of the good news, and because the time of birth, 1714, is the year of the Catalan defeat by the Spanish Bourbons in the War of Spanish Succession, and in honour of which the national day of Catalonia is commemorated.

And, secondly, Leo renewed his contract.

After a telephone call Leo gave the go-ahead for a contract renewal that was announced at the same time as those of Xavi and Puyol, with a view to sending out a message of dressing-room harmony. The two senior players and the star of the side were pledging their futures to the club. Jorge Messi had received – and rejected – a sensational offer from a Russian club willing to pay €400 million for his son; Leo would have received €32 million a year.

He had renewed his contract on two occasions with Guardiola, and now signed a new one with Tito until 2018. The buyout clause of €250 million stayed in place, his fixed wage rose to €13 million net (€22 gross) and he received a bonus of €3.2 million a year for playing 60 per cent of matches.

Barcelona, despite doubts about their style, continued on a steady path in the league, while in Madrid the climate of tension and mistrust grew; the wheels had well and truly come off just a few months after the eternal rivals had won the league.

But, head to head, José Mourinho had evolved a tactical plan for his team that made Leo's contribution more difficult. Leo had equalled Alfredo Di Stéfano's record of 18 goals in *clásicos*, but the *blancos'* high defensive line was choking him and keeping him away from goal. Madrid knocked Barcelona out of the cup after a 1–1 draw at the Bernabéu, followed by a 3–1 victory at the Camp Nou.

According to Diego Torres in his book, Mourinho instructed his players to tap Messi on the face, an action which, the Portuguese had learned, infuriated him. Alvaro Arbeloa and Xabi Alonso did just that, to the astonishment of Leo, who looked to the linesman flabbergasted.

At the end of the game there was the leaking of an alleged incident that took place with Mourinho's loyal assistant, Aitor Karanka (apparently Leo said to him, 'What the f— are you looking at, you Mourinho puppet?'), and also with Arbeloa to whom he crossed over and said, 'What are you looking at, you clown? I'll be waiting for you in Barcelona.'

In a post-match press conference, José Callejón, one of Mourinho's players, explained: 'I saw the thing with Aitor because I was coming up behind him. Maybe it's normal that we're all a bit wound up on the pitch and we say things that we regret later. But a fellow professional waiting an hour, to an hour and a half, to abuse another professional who was with his wife is over the top.'

Barcelona had left the stadium 45 minutes after the end of the game and eyewitnesses claim that Leo was heading for the bus when Arbeloa came out in his car, but that no conversation took place. Paco García Caridad, the prestigious journalist for Madrid newspaper *Marca*, said on air and on Twitter: 'the attempt to discredit Messi leans toward the grotesque. Who leaks these things that Messi is supposed to have done? Mou? His number two? Do we know who the leak is? Now, do we have to besmirch Messi's image?' The object of the exercise was nonetheless clear: to add fuel to a campaign that had begun months earlier, coinciding with Messi's words with Villa, and designed to discredit him even more.

In any case his goals and the consistent performances of Iniesta were disguising the deficiencies that were beginning to threaten the team. Injuries to Xavi and Puyol, two of the senior players, had left them weaker, while another, Víctor Valdés, had told the club in the summer of 2013 that he would be leaving at the end of his contract. Training sessions lacked intensity, players became angrier when not selected. On the pitch the lines weren't coming together and teams were scoring against them too easily. Barcelona conceded goals in thirteen games on the trot. It had all become routine and was lacking precision and tactical cohesion.

Then it was April, the most important stage of the season, the one in which titles are decided. Ramón Besa summed up in *El País* what the team lacked. 'What's needed is to close the gym and the clinic, take the roll call at training and rediscover the culture of trying harder.'

During those weeks Leo did not look happy. 'Day-to-day he looks normal, he looks fine,' said Dani Alvés in *El Mundo* around that time. 'But I'm no hypocrite, I don't paint over things. It's quite clear that in the past few games his morale has been low. Why? I don't know, I haven't tried to find out. I only want to know what people want to share with me. And if someone doesn't want to share their life, or how they are living it, who am I to ask? I respect his space. But I have noticed that he is a bit more down than usual.'

Despite his enormous effectiveness in the league, where he managed to score in 19 consecutive games and 38 times in 25 matches, Messi was invisible in the Cup *clásicos*, and again when they met AC Milan in the away leg in the last 16 of the Champions League, where a 2–0 defeat exposed Barcelona's shortcomings.

Marcelo Sottile, assistant secretary of the newspaper *Olé*, skilfully explained the team mood. 'Barcelona seem to be a depressed team. The mirror doesn't reflect the image of the best, the most beautiful. Now you just see eleven dispirited faces; little individual inspiration; little tactical awareness from the bench, and not even much physicality – a product either of tired legs or tired minds – that can change the rhythm and overcome the strategies of Milan and Madrid, who have both beaten them with organisation and a lot of football.'

Leo exercised his leadership and declared on ESPN: 'The team is a little lacklustre. We've had some bad results and now is the time to pick ourselves up, to believe in ourselves, to do the same things we have been doing for years.'

*12 March 2013. Champions League last 16 second leg. Barcelona
4–0 Milan*

*Barcelona: Valdés; Alvés, Piqué, Mascherano (Puyol, 77th
minute), Alba; Xavi, Busquets, Iniesta; Messi; Pedro (Adriano,
83rd minute) and Villa (Alexis, 75th minute). Subs not used:
Pinto; Cesc, Song and Tello.*

*Milan: Abbiati; Abate, Mexès, Zapata, Constant; Montolivo,
Ambrosini (Muntari, 60th minute), Flamini (Bojan, 75th min-
ute); Boateng, Niang (Robinho, 60th minute) and El Shaarawy.
Subs not used: Amelia; Bonera, De Sciglio and Nocerino.*

*Goals: 1–0. 5th minute: Messi, just inside the area. 2–0. 39th
minute: Messi, from the edge of the area. 3–0. 55th minute:
Villa cross-shot finish from Xavi pass. 4–0. 92 minute: Jordi
Alba after counter-attack following a pass from Alexis.*

Ramón Besa, *El País*: It won't be Milan singing a requiem to
Messi's Barcelona, half-colossus, half-warrior, at times aesthetic, other times epic, always there on an immense night. The
best victories often come after the worst defeats. The number
10 destroyed one of the best organised defences in the world.
Messi's reign is that of a benevolent dictatorship, with gratitude and kindness which was sweeter than ever last night.
Around the number 10, Barcelona played a majestic game,
well organised from both an emotional and tactical point of
view, played with the head and feet, well seen by the coaches
and players, cheered by the enthusiastic faithful. Extraordinary
in their pressure, Barcelona played the game in the Milan half.
Martí Perarnau: Every piece returned to where it should be,
not where they have been finishing up in previous weeks. Each
to his own and no one in anybody's space.

They needed a comeback at the Camp Nou in the return leg.
But it would prove to be the club's swansong.
Around this time Leo was asked on Barça TV if he needed to rest

since he was playing every game. 'It's good for me to accumulate playing time because that way I don't lose my rhythm,' was his reply.

2 February 2013. Next round of the Champions League, quarter-finals against PSG, with Tito Vilanova in the dugout. Messi, who had scored the first goal of the game, feels a pull in his right leg and is substituted at half-time. Juanjo Brau has taught him to listen to his body and he asks to be substituted. Ibrahimović equalises ten minutes from the end. The game finishes 2–2 after Xavi's penalty in the eighty-ninth minute and an error from Valdés in time added on.

3 April 2013. Medical tests reveal a tear of the femoral bicep. The muscle used for sprints and changes of pace once again. Messi is ruled out of the next game against Mallorca.

10 April 2013. Messi is on the bench for the return leg against PSG. The French take the lead with a goal from Pastore: they play with speed and courage and frighten Barcelona. In what looks like a reflex action following the scoring of the goal, Messi pulls his socks up, watching and waiting from the bench: his participation is part of the plan if things are not going well, although, quite clearly, his injury needs far longer to heal.

He comes onto the pitch twelve minutes after the goal.

The technical staff stick their own El Cid on the back of the horse. Frightened, PSG retreat.

'The number 10 eliminated PSG with one play, one touch, one pass and one chance. Imperious for an hour, the French side sur-rendered at the very sight of Messi. Beaten, lost, vanquished, the *blaugrana* felt invincible for half an hour with their number 10,' wrote Ramón Besa.

'It's the Leo effect,' says Cesc Fàbregas. 'He came on for me, and just by him coming onto the pitch the crowd's spirits were lifted.'

'When he came on, we all felt bigger, stronger,' admitted Piqué.

'It's a bit of what Leo creates,' said Mascherano. 'They were dom-inating us, we were about to be eliminated from the competition: and he comes on, on one leg, manages to draw three players and makes the play for Pedro to finish. On one leg!'

The goal from Pedro earns a 1–1 draw and passage into the semi-finals of the Champions League.

11 April 2013. Further tests on Messi reveal that, despite playing

*23 April 2013, Champions League semi-final first leg. Bayern 4–0
Barcelona*

*Bayern: Neuer; Lahm, Boateng, Dante, Alaba; Martínez, Sch-
weinsteiger, Robben; Müller (Pizarro, 82nd minute), Ribéry
(Shaqiri, 89th minute) and Gómez (Luiz Gustavo, 71st minute). Subs not used: Tarke; van Buyten, Rafinha and Tymoshchuk.*

*Barcelona: Valdés; Alvés, Piqué, Bartra, Jordi Alba; Xavi, Bus-
quets, Iniesta; Alexis, Messi and Pedro (Villa, 83rd minute).
Subs not used: Pinto; Montoya, Abidal, Cesc, Thiago and Song.*

*Goals: 1–0. 25th minute: Müller, from a corner. 2–0. 49th min-
ute: Mario Gómez, from another corner. 3–0. 73rd minute:
Robben shoots across Valdés. 4–0. 82nd minute Müller finishes from an Alaba cross.*

Ramón Besa, *El País*: The *blaugrana* Champions League journey has been a 'way of the cross' that has found its salvation at
the Camp Nou, until yesterday when Barcelona were crucified
in Munich. The feeling is that the team has been consuming
itself before falling vanquished, going backwards along Bayern's exuberant road. No club today plays as well as Barcelona
used to. Especially not Barcelona themselves. It's not worth
waiting for Messi to get better and save the situation, so timid
is this Barça. You don't limp to victory against Bayern.

Luis Martín, *El País*: Messi was on the pitch but he didn't play.
The official UEFA statistics show that Messi had one shot
throughout the whole match, but the memory that millions
of people will be left with will be of a night when we saw *la
Pulga* turn up, but not play. Of the 11 occasions he had to go
on runs, only two came off.

against PSG, the injury has not been aggravated.

23 April 2013. Messi rests for three matches and is in the starting
line-up against Bayern (4–0). It's time to find out whether or not the
self-management plan has worked.

Defeat is unavoidable and confirms the team has lost its competitiveness.

27 April 2013. Leo plays for half an hour against Athletic Bilbao, provides an assist for Alexis and scores an extraordinary goal. In the tightest of spaces he gets away from his opponents, who seem to appear from everywhere but are unable to stop him before shooting from the edge of the area with a placed shot, accurate and out of goalkeeper Gorka Iraizoz's reach. 'How did he do that?' asks Athletic's Ander Herrera. 'He had his back to me and he just did a tremendous turn. I was marking him and he just went. Next time I see him I'll ask him to explain it to me properly.' Claudio Vivas, assistant to Marcelo Bielsa with the Basque side, saw something more than just an accurate shot. 'The frustrations of the season were all reflected in that goal.'

Barcelona draw the game 2–2.

But muscular injuries are very delicate, and can be quite treacherous. Was it the correct decision to play against Athletic with the league so close? Wouldn't it have been better to take a chance on a game of greater importance, to save him for the return leg of the Bayern semis? Did he get injured again at the San Mamés? The staff and the player took the decision for him to play to get back to match fitness.

30 April 2013. Leo Messi announces: 'We need the Camp Nou to be a pressure cooker. We will only be able to get close to the comeback if we all believe in it.'

1 May 2013: An hour before kick-off a rumour circulates that Messi will not be in the starting eleven.

Vilanova justifies Leo's absence, explaining that he had felt something strange at the end of the game at Bilbao. 'On Monday he didn't train and this morning, after training, after talking to the doctors and the physios, I spoke with him when he arrived at the hotel. Given how he was, there was a risk that it would break. And he didn't feel comfortable and, in that condition, he was not able to help the team.' Leo sat on the bench just in case Tito needed to risk him for a place in the final.

5 May 2013. Match against Betis. Messi reappears in the hour of need. He comes off the bench in the fifty-sixth minute, with the score at 2–2. He soon makes his presence felt and scores twice on a diffi-

1 May 2013. Champions League semi-final second leg.
Barcelona 0–3 Bayern

Barcelona: Valdés; Alvés, Piqué, Bartra (Montoya, 86th min-
ute), Adriano; Song, Xavi (Alexis, 55th minute), Iniesta (Thi-
ago, 65th minute); Pedro, Cesc and Villa. Subs not used: Pinto;
dos Santos, Messi and Tello.

Bayern Munich: Neuer; Lahm (Rafinha, 76th minute), Boateng,
van Buyten, Alaba; Javi Martínez (Tymoshchuk, 74th minute),
Schweinsteiger (Luiz Gustavo, 66th minute), Müller; Robben,
Ribéry and Mandzukic. Subs not used: Starke, Dante, Shaqiri
and Gómez.

Goals: 0–1. 48th minute: Robben. 0–2. 72nd minute : Piqué
(og). 0–3. 7th minute : Müller.

Ramón Besa, *El País*: Goodbye Europe. Barcelona's departure
from Europe was so humiliating that it will be difficult to raise
spirits high enough to sing the '*alirón*' [the song sung after
winning a major tournament]. So as to give La Liga its due
importance, perhaps even too much, it caused serious weakness in Europe. Uncompetitive from the start and even less
after the changes. Public ridicule has been major from start
to finish, away and at home, with or without Messi. *Barce-*
lonismo accompanied its team en masse up to the gates of
the Camp Nou when they found out that Leo wasn't playing.
Some season ticket holders wanted to go home, feeling surprised, ripped off and deceived. No one believed in the game
or the comeback. Supporters were stunned to see the number
10 on the bench. His injuries have become as big a mystery to
the observer as his play to defences: all that was known up till
this game was that he never hid himself away and was capable
of playing on one leg. The management of Messi's injury is
worrying.

cult night for Barcelona (4–2). This is, without doubt, Messi's league.

12 May 2013 Leo goes off in the sixty-seventh minute of the match against Atlético de Madrid in the Vicente Calderón, after once again feeling a niggle in the femoral bicep of his right leg. Tito has already made three changes so Barcelona play the rest of the game with ten men. Barcelona nonetheless win 2–1.

So what was going on with Messi's injury?

Leo knows his body well and also his Achilles heel – the injury to the femoral bicep. He knew that he was doing something that was working against his recovery, but the team's need made him push himself to the limit. The same injury in a player who doesn't need explosive pace, who has less muscle wear and tear, can clear up in two weeks, but Leo has physical characteristics that rely on a very high usage of muscular energy.

Since tearing the muscle in the away leg at PSG, Messi had undergone treatment with Juanjo Brau that did not correspond to the injury – he should have had different work on it and much more rest. The two of them dedicated between seven and eight hours a day to getting fit for the game that was being played eight days later. They were never in any rush to go home. The objective of the exercise was that he should be able to play at least 15 minutes and 35 in the best-case scenario.

In the match at the Camp Nou against the French side, Leo was told to follow the strictest of instructions to be effective in his contributions: 'Only go for the ball that you can win, pick and choose your runs,' Juanjo Brau told him. The physical coach knew that he could control and advise on instances when he didn't have the ball ('when you don't have the ball, stay up front, don't wear yourself out, because if you do we're not going to be on the pitch for long,' he told him). Juanjo added another piece of advice that he knew was hardly necessary: 'Do what you have to do when you get the ball.' When Leo has the ball he only does what he thinks of at that moment without ever calculating the consequences.

'We were losing and I remember when he came out to warm up, the atmosphere inside the stadium changed as did the emotional state of the fans,' says Brau. 'They were saying to themselves: "now we can win." Sometimes we've got a lot of petrol, but no one else has the spark he adds to it.'

And the treatment worked: he got to play for long enough to change the dynamic of the game.

In the first leg against Bayern Munich, Leo did not break down again as has been stated, but the fact is that there were no miracles. Despite the unorthodox work carried out by the coaching staff in the 21 days since his injury against the French, Leo could not compete at the best level. So, then, why play against Athletic Bilbao between the two semi-final legs?

Coaches will always say that in football you have to win, that you cannot wait for the following week, and getting points at the San Mamés helped them to close in on a league title that was important to everyone: the coaching staff wanted to win the title the year after Guardiola's departure, the players wanted to show that they could win things without Pep and that self-management, over and above being necessary, was also effective.

After the match against Athletic, the third in three weeks when he should have played none, Leo suffered discomfort, one of the usual consequences of a femoral bicep injury. Even though the muscle had healed, the sudden unexpected surge of pain had not disappeared completely.

Tito and Leo had decided that with a 4–0 deficit to make up, the Argentinian, who still had not played a full ninety minutes since the injury, would only come off the bench if really necessary.

'I spoke to him a lot,' explains Cesc. 'You have to heal this type of injury. I had a terrible year at Arsenal, with seven relapses, and when you find yourself in that dynamic, you're lost. I told him that he had to cure himself completely or else. But when you're needed and you play injured but then relapse, you dig yourself into a hole, and the confusion is as mental as it is physical.' Between games Leo used to say he was '*de puta madre*' (fucking great). And he trained without problems. But a training session isn't a match.

'Who's going to tell Messi that he can't play? The coach? I don't think so,' the Argentine national team doctor, Homero de Agostino, explained to the Spanish media. 'Messi has a superlative condition as well as great mental strength that no one can stop. But poor Messi feels obliged to honour all his commitments. He's incapable of saying no.'

Leo's injury was handled this way because of the circumstances of the season; it was full of risks and one of those was far beyond just a muscular injury. When a player has so much responsibility, the environment, the club, the coaches paradoxically wear him out more quickly. 'We cannot allow the situation whereby Leo is always the solution. It isn't about ability, it's about wear and tear, because he is human like the rest of us,' says Juanjo Brau. The whole world thinks itself capable of speaking about Messi, but we often forget that there is another Leo: the one who gets up in the morning. Always to be excellent comes at a huge emotional cost. How long will he last at this level?

Barcelona won their twenty-second league title and Messi's statistics demonstrated that victory was mostly down to him: he scored 40.5 per cent of all goals and was the top scorer with 45, racking up 61 across the three competitions in which the team participated. For the first time a footballer had scored in every single match in the first half of the season. He had gone past the 345 goals scored by Maradona throughout his whole career. At 25 years old.

Speaking on TV Azteca, Leo asked for understanding of a very difficult year: 'When Tito came we felt really good, because practically nothing changed. But when he left we noticed the change; not because Roura or the other people could not do it, but because we were missing our first coach, missing the one who had spoken to us from day one.' Elimination by Bayern, in his opinion, proved that clubs now knew how to play against Barcelona: 'For years we've been playing the same way and the coaches and rival teams study you. But we shouldn't drive ourselves mad because of what's happened this year. We can't change Barcelona's style because that is what has always characterised us.'

Tito Vilanova had said in his first press conference after his return from New York that he felt he had the strength to carry on the following season. What he didn't say was that in January, before travelling to the United States, he had put his future in the hands of the board. If they wanted to look for a replacement he would understand perfectly, he told them. After winning the title, he once again tendered his resignation. President Sandro Rosell insisted on both occasions that if the doctors gave him the all clear, if he wanted to carry on, the job was his.

On Friday, 19 July, Tito Vilanova took training as usual. The players had been called in at half past seven for another one. On that occasion, Tito asked them to gather around before going out onto the pitch. Then he gave them the news: 'This was my life's dream, but now I have to leave.' He thanked them for their work and their help. And then he went home to try to recover from the cancer that assaulted his body once again.

The team's planned trip to Poland, where they were due to play a friendly, was cancelled. The official announcement was made by Rosell and Andoni Zubizarreta. In the first row of the press room, Carles Puyol, Messi, Pinto and Mascherano sat together, united in misery.

Leo had also experienced the worry and anxiety of a close family member suffering from the same disease. And Tito was a trainer whom he could trust, someone who had been with him in his early development in the team. He felt a debt towards him and wanted to give everything back that he had received from him.

It was not to be. Nine months later, Tito Vilanova died at the age of forty-five.

3. Leo's Image

In an effort to make the most of 'the Flea's' international celebrity, Adidas decided to organise a visit to London, one of those ideas that gets marketing executives all excited but invariably suffers in the execution. On 15 September 2010, Messi was scheduled to play a football match with a group of 15-year-old boys on Hackney Marshes, in London's East End. The helicopter would land, Leo would emerge from it and then the coach would bring him on in place of one of the players. The boys had started the game and did not know what was about to happen, but they suspected something was afoot when they saw the Sky Sports cameras arrive.

Leo arrived by helicopter.

He took no more than ten steps before being mobbed by hundreds of fans, who had discovered what was going to happen from the clues that Adidas had given out on their social network channels. Thus Adidas had to extricate him quickly and fly him to the next publicity stunt: giving away football boots at a stall in the famous Brick Lane market, something he did manage to do.

Lastly, he had to go to Tower Hamlets, a multicultural, working-class London borough, where he was to play a five-a-side match with the first nine boys who arrived at the pitch in the shadow of modest tower blocks. Since his security could not be guaranteed, however, it was decided to cancel the final event.

In fact, Leo *had* travelled to Tower Hamlets (his was the van with tinted windows parked near the pitch) but it was soon realised that it would be almost impossible to get him out of there in time to get him back to London City Airport. The cameraman waiting with the Sky correspondent in the centre circle made some clumsy excuse and left the pitch, an act that almost led to an incident. Soon afterwards, on discovering that Leo was leaving London, the youngsters threw bottles, cans and whatever they could find in the direction of the pitch and police had to clear the area.

Leo and the company organising the event were accused of showing a 'lack of respect to the fans'; despite this, Adidas managed to attract the world's attention for an entire day.

It was a risky idea that did not go at all well, and the sponsor learnt from it, albeit after the damage had been done. But what happened in summer 2013 was a series of events that did not exactly go to plan either.

At a time when he had already conquered the hearts of Argentinians, after another year of records, titles and praise, Leo suddenly started to appear on the covers of gossip magazines and in the non-sports sections of newspapers. Let's look at some examples: a man spills the beans on how, supposedly, a few years earlier, Messi had defied Guardiola by drinking a can of some soft drink that had been forbidden, and challenges anyone who doubts his word to take him to court, thereby suggesting that his source was a member of that very squad. Both Leo and Pep, consulted for this book, deny the incident took place, but a denial does fewer rounds than a story about a supposed confrontation between the world's greatest footballer and the world's greatest coach.

Another absurd story came to light: an Argentinian magazine published photos from a party in Las Vegas in which Leo is seen burying his face in the large breasts of a stripper; many are unaware that those images were fake, they only remember Leo's innocent face looking at the camera. That summer a book came out which, according to the Messis, told lies about Pep and Leo, including supposed details over the payment for his hormonal treatment, but with such carefully chosen words that the Messis cannot file a complaint, as they would like to have done.

And then the most serious of all: the Spanish financial authorities accused the family of tax evasion.

Leo's image was being assailed from all sides.

If that were not enough, two of the four friendlies that he planned for that summer (Lima and Los Angeles) represented headaches for Messi. In the first – billed the 'Duel of the Giants' as it pitted Messi against Neymar – there was an incident when some of his and Neymar's friends and family were removed from the bench area by Peruvian police.

Leo did not know about it but it was published that the police had been heavy-handed and that when it had reached Leo's ears, he had decided to ask to be substituted in the second half and left without even taking a shower. Not true, but the denial from the Messi camp did not fill the same newspaper inches.

The following friendly at the Los Angeles Memorial Coliseum was cancelled generating a barrage of accusations. Leo decided not to participate because of the extortionate ticket prices for what was supposed to be a charitable match, but more importantly what was not said is that the promoter, who had organized the travel expenses and fees of the players, did not get enough money from the company that sold the tickets for the event. Somebody tried to be too clever but Messi was blamed after 50,000 tickets had been purchased. Leo expressed on Facebook his 'disappointment with the organization', but his image was tarnished once again.

What was going on? The Madrid press suggested that the real Messi was at last being seen. Some people around Leo also began asking themselves if his support for the Catalan language at a Turkish Airlines event was the 'beginning of the end' of his love affair with the Spanish people.

The world has surely not become tired of always seeing the same face, the same winners, has it? Now, with Neymar at Barcelona, sponsors and public alike have a new option, which is attractive for that very reason – it presents a different face. Furthermore, Nike was looking to make Neymar its ambassador for its Brazil World Cup campaign, and Leo, although he once wore the very same brand, now wears Adidas. Sponsors, especially the big ones, do not forget such disloyalty.

Leo's entourage is small and quite low key with regard to commercial interests. Until now they have considered that this was in the best interests of an individual who only wanted to play football and who was completely disinterested in the world of sponsorship and commerce. Consequently, when Leo felt under fire that summer, those looking after his interests struggled to manage the different crises.

'We have been a family business for some time, but the difference is that the earnings are not for the family, but for Lionel,' explains Jorge Messi in Sique Rodríguez's book *Educados para ganar* ('Educated to Win'). 'It is a way of defending his future. It is his business. Everything revolves around him. Everything is in his name. It is our way of protecting him.' His father is effectively his agent, his brother Rodrigo takes care of his diary and, together with former Barcelona employee Pablo Negre, he organises events and media deals for him. His mother Celia and his brother Matías take care of the Leo Messi Foundation and other personal and professional affairs in Rosario. They have a few lawyers and little else.

'Messi's entourage is much more complex than Ronaldinho or Maradona's in terms of relationships with the press,' says Ramón Besa of *El País*. Messi would speak through his agent, Jorge Cyterszpiler or his assistant, Jorge Blanco. Ronaldinho, who kept a certain level of inaccessibility, had family members working as spokesmen. 'But the people who surround Messi are a mystery, because he is like a child ... Who is Messi? To whom do you have to speak to find out what he thinks? His father? Antonella? Getting to Messi is very complex,' concludes Besa.

Besa recalls that he asked an Italian journalist who interviewed Messi in Barcelona how it had gone: 'badly, because in order to interview Messi you prepare yourself in the same way that a defender prepares to play against him, and you don't know how, but he ends up outwitting you; in other words I didn't get anything out of the ten questions I had asked.' The journalist is referring here to Leo and his family's defensive attitude. Messi doesn't see an interview as a way of connecting with his fans, but a check-up on him as a person. In Messi's world the word 'you already know what Messi is like' is just another way of shutting the door on the interference. His world is a closed one, almost like that of a child, protected by his own family. And he defends that, it suits him, it fits his personality. Furthermore, that mistrust may stem from those people who did get close to him and who ended up trying to take advantage of him. Some of them have been taken to court.

'Javier Marías says in *Salvajes y sentimentales* ['Wild and Sentimental'] that football takes us back to our childhood, but the moment you become a commercial product as an adult, you can no longer carry on behaving as if you were a child,' concludes Besa, the most perceptive of the journalists covering Barcelona. 'Has anyone thought about this, about what the Messi world means? I think that they live off the positive dynamic, off the goals, but maybe one day he will not score as many, maybe one day someone will make him realise that no one is writing his side of the story any more.'

Leo's image is linked solely to his performance, to his results on the pitch. He has never wanted to sell anything that does not fit that *natural* profile. He does not have a marketing policy, like David Beckham for example, who exemplifies the opposite extreme, in which image is everything.

Esteve Calzada, publicity expert and ex-Barcelona marketing director, gives a clear example of the difference in his book *Show Me the Money*: 'When Lionel Messi was called up to the stage to receive his second Ballon d'Or at the FIFA gala in December 2010, he was so surprised that he didn't know what to say or how to appear in front of the microphones, a clear demonstration that he had nothing prepared. Nor did he acknowledge his supporting team-mates from that year, Xavi and Andrés Iniesta. The following year, on winning the prize again on the same stage, it was very clear that he had conferred with his advisers and prepared a speech in which thank-yous and a special trophy dedication to his team-mate Xavi, who had been nominated again, were to the fore.'

Although Leo acts as if he is the best, he never speaks about himself as such; he always refers to the football team. 'They have always wanted to be responsible for Leo's low-profile image, even if they have been able to recruit one of the big advertising agencies,' says ex-Barcelona financial vice-president Ferrán Soriano. 'It is like applying a defence mechanism: it's an "I don't want anything." This has the advantage that nobody screws you; and the disadvantage, you don't maximise the value. He earns twenty something million euros for playing football and for advertising it must be around fifteen or twenty. If you receive forty million a year, why should you want more?'

The Messis are scrupulous with costs. They have a conservative, financial mentality, they don't waste much, and they track every euro that is spent. 'They know they can earn more, but it doesn't interest them,' concludes Soriano.

Until now Leo has been the face of soft drinks, airlines (the advertisement with Kobe Bryant for Turkish Airlines has exceeded 105 million hits on the internet, one of the ten most viewed in 2012), watches, sliced bread, sportswear and even a Japanese cosmetics brand in whose commercial he had to say a few words in Japanese. And according to a *liga* BBVA report carried out by Brand Value Solutions, Messi had an 11 per cent media presence compared to the rest of the players; Ronaldo's was 9.2 per cent. Now that Argentinians have placed him on a pedestal, if he wants to prevent Spanish disapproval from growing, he should focus more on his image. Of course Neymar and Ronaldo have more than twenty professionals looking after their respective images; it is all a system of communication aimed at presenting their best profiles to the world. But is that the solution?

In 2013 the Messi family employed the biggest advertising agency in the world to protect Leo and look for ways of exploiting his personal image.

Another side of this parallel universe to football with which Messi has to fight, whether he likes it or not, is in his dress sense. His friend Domenico Dolce, for whom he has even modelled Dolce & Gabbana clothing, has plenty to say about this. As we have seen, he has worn D&G at the Ballons d'Or and has been a regular customer for some time. Maybe he was chosen as a media icon because he more resembles the man on the street rather than the one with the perfectly toned body typified by many other footballers. Although Leo prefers a casual look, his fashion brand has given him a more sophisticated touch, and the fact that he wore a polka-dot dinner suit to pick up his fourth Ballon d'Or says a lot about the way he has evolved in this regard. Furthermore, if he, with his fairly average physique, was bold enough to wear such clothes, others might be encouraged to do the same. That is what advertising and icons are all about.

What is clear is that Leo has left behind the boy who went on stage on his twentieth birthday, to play instruments and cheer on the public, so that the *cumbia* group that was playing would carry on. Incidentally, it was the same band that composed 'El pibe de oro' ('The Golden Boy') in homage to the Argentinian.

Not only did he leave that period behind, but he was learning to protect himself. And he had to do so swiftly, because that confusing summer of 2013 brought with it serious accusations of fiscal fraud, a complex situation in which the Messis are claiming protection from civil laws which supposedly approve what the tax advisers suggested to them.

When his problems with the taxman surfaced, two situations occurred which reflect the state of our society. On the one hand, a high percentage of Spanish and international (mainly sporting) press decided that he was guilty until proven innocent, and, on the other hand, the news reached non-footballing corners, too.

Nothing quite justifies the innocence with which Leo's family followed the financial and tax advice they were given, but it goes without saying that everything should be put into context.

In 2013, the Agencia Tributaria instructed inspectors to take action against celebrities they believed to be tax-dodging, and thus acquired valuable media coverage. And so the chef Sergi Arola, the heiress Liliana Godia and Leo Messi came under scrutiny and were accused of suspected tax breaches. The objective was to boost the authorities' damaged image; they had been accused of being too lenient with famous people. They tried to make an example of Leo, and the others accused, in a period of financial crisis in which people judged this type of behaviour as reprehensible.

'They did it to me in '79,' explains Johan Cruyff to *La Vanguardia* newspaper. 'When you are a public personality, they use celebrities so that people are scared. And Messi is one of them. I can't imagine Leo is responsible because he knows as much about the tax office as I do, which is zero. Therefore, it is the people around him who manage these things. The press and government use him to say "look who we've caught". They do it to set an example. They also did it to me and I had to wait nine years before they said I was innocent.'

In football, as in all other professions, everyone looks for a way to pay less tax, and the management of image rights is the official method for clubs and footballers to save costs. Elite players, who are in the highest tax bracket, prefer their clubs to convert part of their salaries into image rights, which are then paid to a company set up by the player. The tax liability is lower. That way, taxes are 'avoided' rather than evaded.

In Leo's case, his contract assigns 85 per cent of the money as salary, and the remaining 15 per cent to image rights, which is what Spanish law allows. In general, Barcelona have never wanted to implicate themselves in any business related to his image. According to the club it is a permanent source of conflict since players are usually not very willing to give up part of the money earned for commercial deals. Real Madrid see it differently: they keep 50 per cent of player earnings in this regard. Barcelona demand a percentage of the player's image rights and Leo can do what he wants with the rest.

Going back to the accusations of fraud, the idea of lying to the taxman may seem incomprehensible to northern European, Anglo-Saxon sensibilities, but it seems to be an inherent part of Latin culture, which grew up with reading classics such as *El lazarillo de Tormes* or Quevedo's *El Buscón*. In Spain or Argentina, tax evasion is not as widely frowned upon as in other countries, perhaps because of the lack of confidence in the authorities and the bad example they set, especially in recent years, where corruption cases against political and corporate bodies seem to be multiplying. In other words, 'If they do it, why should I or my cousin or neighbour not do it?'

What does fraud consist of? Footballers are obliged to pay tax from their wages in the country in which they play, but taxes on image rights are paid in the country in which the company that holds them is based. It is common for there to be an almost systematic 'externalisation' from the countries where the tax liability is very high. In other words, the money is declared in countries with much lower tax rates. That capital detour can be fraudulent or not. When ghost companies which do not exist are created in the receiving country, we can then speak of fraud.

Leo and his father are not financial experts. Messi has never dealt with such things; he does not even know how much he has in the bank. His father put the matter into the hands of Rodolfo Schinocca, the family adviser for the last decade, who tried to keep Messi's image rights. Schinocca promised easy money and the Messis fell for it. Then Schinocca ended up creating a system whereby he would keep most of the money. When the Messi family realised this, Schinocca and Leo's parents filed complaints against each other – the lawsuit against the Messis was thrown out by the Argentine Supreme Court, while the one against Schinocca continues.

When the Spanish tax authorities started investigating players with companies overseas, Messi's name was on the list. Leo and Jorge were accused of evading paying tax on more than €4 million relating to image rights between 2007 and 2009. The prosecutor denounced Jorge Messi and Schinocca for creating a web of shell companies with headquarters in tax havens (mainly Belize and Uruguay). Contracts with Danone, Adidas, PepsiCo and Telefónica were invoiced from those countries. Furthermore, it was stated that 'the initiative to defraud came from Jorge Messi' and that in 2006 'Leo Messi ratified his father's fraudulent initiative through a public deed conferred before a notary'.

On 4 September 2013, the Messis handed over €5 million (€4.1 million plus interest) to the court in Gavá to resolve the debt and try to reduce their legal liabilities. Jorge accepted full responsibility for the creation of the web before a judge, but that investigating judge decided in July 2014 that Leo should remain an official suspect as he 'may have been aware of and consented to the creation and preservation of a network of fictitious companies'. In the document presented by Messi's father, not only did he exonerate his son, but he accused his ex-partner Schinocca of deception, accepted responsibility for a lack of control over his financial advisers and expressed his willingness to collaborate with the law. The court case seemed inevitable.

Messi concurrently presented supplementary income statements from 2010 and 2011, and an additional €10 million, which resolved the issue relating to those years.

Of course, nobody is blameless: in England in 2010, dozens of British footballers received letters from the Inland Revenue notifying them that an investigation into tax evasion was being opened. The person who does not try it is rare indeed, and the Messi's have been hunted.

Jorge and Leo declared in the court in Gavá on 27 September. Leo was shaking like a jelly while testifying. Jorge blamed himself. 'My son does not know how the money is generated,' he explained.

The day after, Leo got injured. A small tear in his right hamstring, his perennial Achilles heel, sidelined him for three weeks. Such things almost never happen by chance.

In July he said in a press conference that he was starting the upcoming season 'relaxed, my father is dealing with the matter with the lawyers and advisers, and we trust them as they are the ones who must solve it. I don't understand anything about it.' He promised not to speak any more about the matter. But the case made the Messis feel that the club's support was somewhat lacking: president Sandro Rosell took a whole day to call Jorge when the matter became public knowledge, and other directors privately criticised the way in which the Messis managed Leo's fortune; but nobody offered to help the family clear the matter up.

'Provided that it is legal, we will do everything Messi asks us,' explained Rosell a few weeks later. 'We will help him in any way we can. If he carries on as number one, of course his wages will go up. Because every year he demonstrates that he deserves more and more. For me he is the best player in the club's history and also in football. But it is clear that we will not give him the money to pay for this affair [with the tax authorities].'

What Barcelona did do was support the Leo Messi Foundation from the beginning, an idea which, according to Jorge Messi in Sique Rodríguez's *Educados para ganar*, came up 'after Messi visited a hospital for the terminally ill in the United States'.

Cristina Cubero was present that day. 'We went to a Boston hospital for children with cancer. We were in a room, a mother arrived and said to him: "I'm Argentine, my daughter wants to meet you." And the girl came, bloated, bald ... he was told that the girl was terminally ill. I was already outside, and Messi left in tears, he saw me and hugged me, he clung onto me for four minutes. Crying like a baby. He always tells me that it was as a result of what he saw there that he started to collaborate with bodies battling cancer.'

Leo's father tells in Rodríguez's book how the footballer himself told them that 'part of his earnings had to be reinvested into society. Our foundation works for children who have all sorts of problems. From health problems to social exclusion problems.'

It is not the Rosario-born Messi's only demonstration of social awareness: he is a UNICEF goodwill ambassador; he has assigned his name to a Rosario company so that they can manufacture children's products, sales of which engender a percentage for the Messi Foundation, which will then invest the funds in social projects.

He donated some $790,000 to refurbish a ward at the Rosario Children's Hospital, while the Foundation also has various agreements with Catalan hospitals: he has collaborated with the Can Ruti reform, he has invested in the department for children with oncological problems at the Sant Joan de Déu health centre. He also finances training for Argentinian doctors and awards research grants.

Furthermore, he collaborates with Sarmiento, a football club based in the neighbourhood in which he was born. 'We don't manage the club, we have some players at Boca, River, Newell's, Central,' says Jorge Messi in the magazine *Kicker*. 'It's a wasteland at the moment, but it is going to be expanded; better dressing rooms and all-weather pitches will be put in.'

And some funds have been given to Newell's Old Boys. The club where he plans to end his playing career.

4. The Arrival of Neymar

In the FIFA Club World Cup final when Neymar's Santos met Barcelona, the Brazilian star told Leo Messi that he would like to play with the *blaugrana* club. 'Messi told him that he would be very happy at Barcelona,' says Sandro Rosell. In fact, by that final in 2011 the Brazilian had already agreed to join the *blaugranas*.

From that moment onwards plans for his arrival were underway: 'No one can match Messi,' said the Brazilian, with a nod to Leo rather than to Barcelona.

Before arriving in his new city, Neymar was known for his goals

(172 since his debut in 2009), his explosive speed down the left flank or as a *mediapunta*, for his unbelievable dribbles, and for having led Brazil to victory against an all-conquering Spanish side in the final of the Confederations Cup.

Influenced by indoor football, his style of play was very Brazilian, played with a smile, with a great variety of technical options. But he had above all the soul of a winner and a hunger to win titles: he won the Copa Libertadores in 2011, three consecutive São Paolo regional championships, the Brazilian cup of 2010 and with his country, the Under 20 South American championship.

His story is a familiar one: discovered by Santos at the age of 12, he suffered abuse from parents of other children because of his style of play. Some of the Santos directors did not want to invest in his future, firstly because they regarded him as being almost as small as a table football player and, secondly, because of the jealousy he provoked.

He made his debut with the first team at the age of 17 and opened his scoring account in his third match. Despite his good season in the year of the South African World Cup, and despite media pressure, national team boss Dunga chose not to pick him. He made his debut for Brazil with the next coach, Mano Menezes, in August 2010, scoring against the United States. It was the beginning of his leadership of the *canarinha*.

In the early years, interviews with him gave up precious little information. Neymar was shy and monosyllabic, albeit with a beaming smile. He is 'simple and humble,' says his team-mate Dani Alvés. Since then he has matured, controlling his behaviour on the pitch which at times smacked of insolence. In Brazil he had a reputation for diving too often, a result of his desire to be one of the protagonists, but he started to change his habits at Barcelona.

He has charisma, and, media-wise, is very high-profile. The public love him – they copy his ever-changing hairstyles. And he is addicted to social networks. He earns €22 million a year. His father, who played for clubs in lower divisions, is his agent and carefully controls his image, his money and his diary, especially regular visits to the church. His girlfriend Bruna Marquezine is an actress in Brazilian soaps, and he has a son, David Lucca, who was born in August 2011 from a previous relationship.

The perfect boy for the football fans landed on to the scene.

The world of sponsorship is wide open to Neymar. In May 2013, according to the rankings of the American sports magazine *SportsPro*, Messi and Neymar had the highest commercial value and Cristiano was eighth. 'There is no doubt that Messi is the best player in the world, but we also know that he is not particularly charismatic off the pitch, nor does he look so happy or confident in front of the cameras,' confirmed David Cushnan, the chief editor of *SportsPro*.

The rise of Neymar began just after the biggest statement ever made by the Messi worshippers: the day of the match against Bayern Munich at the Camp Nou when numerous fans, on their way to the stadium, decided to turn around and go home instead when they discovered that Messi wasn't playing. It was a semi-final of the Champions League.

Perhaps for that reason, Neymar's arrival at Barcelona was greeted with mixed feelings in the Catalan press. *Sport* asked if it was a good idea to bring in another 'cockerel': 'His media presence is disproportionate to what he brings onto the pitch and the resentment is alarming: Neymar, because of his price, salary and treatment by the club, has come here to be one of the leading players in the squad. What position in the hierarchy will Xavi, Iniesta and Cesc hold now? Barcelona will find it difficult to justify the fact that Neymar earns more than him[Messi].'

According to Barcelona, who said they had paid €57 million for their new star, Neymar had a wage of seven million, with a bonus of one million for reaching certain objectives. But during the summer another interpretation of the deal surfaced: some €40 million in commission was payable to Neymar's father over a period of five years, the same length of time as his son's contract. If you add this to the wage of the player, it makes him, at €15 million, the highest paid player in the squad, even ahead of Leo at that point.

His arrival therefore destabilised the team, and it was no coincidence that all manner of problems suddenly started to arise. Víctor Valdés announced his imminent departure, David Villa was transferred to Atlético de Madrid and Bayern bought Thiago. The representatives of Cesc Fàbregas, who had gone down a notch in the hierarchy and was still earning €4 million a year net, made contact with the new manager at Manchester United, who were looking to sign him. Andrés Iniesta's agent asked for a new contract.

Barcelona tried to calm the storm created by the arrival of Neymar by initiating talks for a new contract with Messi, just six months after the signing of the last one. Including his fixed salary and bonuses, Leo was going to be offered below the €20 million a year net mark.

All this gave the impression that the club had decided to control the market by buying the best player available (perhaps to support or substitute their star, perhaps to prevent a rival from signing him, as Madrid tried to do right up to the eleventh hour), without thinking about the consequences. Or even whether it was appropriate.

After the departure of Guardiola and Tito Vilanova, after losing their European crown to Bayern, Barcelona were at a crossroads and needed to reinvent themselves somehow. There were debates about the methods, the ideology, the values, because the Barcelonista found himself in an undefined space, without leadership coming from the bench.

And then, while doubts continued, the club decided to demonstrate its power by signing Neymar. Johan Cruyff predicted a storm with the arrival of the Brazilian. 'Two captains on the same ship? We should learn from the past,' he advised, remembering perhaps the time when Maradona and Bernd Schuster were unable to work together. And he gave president Rosell, his arch-enemy, a piece of advice. 'With Neymar signed, I would have taken on board the possibility of selling Messi, and that is something that some people would have been for and others against.'

It wasn't a conflict such as the Ronaldinho–Eto'o one that Cruyff was analysing, when the whole world knew that the Brazilian was number one; more a Lewis Hamilton–Fernando Alonso situation when both parties were fighting for the same crown.

Joan Laporta also expressed doubts: 'He has a lot of talent. And I like the way he has behaved since his arrival, giving support to the team and to Leo. If I put myself in his [Messi's] place, I would not like the fact that one way or another they are looking to dethrone me.'

In the boardroom, some directors wondered how things would go if Neymar passed the whole season stuck on the left wing. 'Neymar was a priority for us, we need him,' says Tito Vilanova who remembered that, during the year of the treble, the forwards were Messi, Eto'o and Henry, and it worked well. Tito, who finally accepted that the team needed new talent upfront, was not unduly worried about the matter because as he often said, Messi was the least demanding of the football geniuses and not difficult to keep happy.

'We are a split personality of a country,' analyses Ramón Besa. We have the *seny i la rauxa* [wisdom and recklessness] and the *blau-grana y blanquiazul* [the claret and blue, and the white and blue], Cruyff and Rexach, Ronaldinho and Messi. Two good friends told me years ago that Ronaldinho was the beach, the Mediterranean, the girls, the sun; and Messi the district, the *barrio*, the one who went about his work, had no time for bullshit. And this analogy, when Ronaldinho was the icon and Messi the apprentice, worked. Now we will have to see, when the roles are switched and the boy of the *barrio* is above the one from the beach, whether or not it works the same way.'

Originally, Rosell, who worked for many years for Nike, considered the signing of Neymar to be one of the great successes of his mandate, effectively another victory over Madrid, while in the dressing room there were doubts over the need to sign another forward like him. Conscious of Messi's leadership and the strong personality of Neymar hidden behind his smile, the senior players in the squad asked what would happen if the Brazilian scored a hat-trick in the Camp Nou and the stadium celebrated. No one wanted to be in the boots of Tata Martino, Tito Vilanova's successor.

And Messi?

His first statement about the whole business, in July, was revealing: 'He is a great player and will have no problem adapting both on and off the pitch. I don't know him well, but he seems like a good lad and he won't have any problems with me. I don't know why you people say these things,' he told the media, making a point to anyone who was in any doubt. 'He is going to bring a lot [to the team] because he can be a key player. We create numerous one-on-one chances and in this Neymar is very strong. Let's hope for his sake and for that of the team that he scores lots of goals, because that's what we have to look for, the best for everybody.'

Leo was asked about the signing of Neymar before the club went ahead with it, as is customary with the leaders in the dressing room.

There was no problem, he told the board. But it must have hurt him when, months later, his last contract was being haggled over, while Neymar, who had yet to prove his worth, became the highest paid player from the moment he arrived at the age of just 21. It's all about footballing etiquette, eternal codes: four Ballons d'Or deserve greater respect.

When *Marca* asked Johan Cruyff if Neymar's might be a case similar to those of Eto'o, Ibrahimović or Bojan, the Dutchman explained a couple of things which you can only understand if you have been inside a dressing room: 'The way some analyse it, it would seem that Messi is a dictator. When you have the chance to be the best player in every game, you *have* to be a bit of a dictator, because it's not just the team you are playing for, but also for your status as number one and your prestige. In that sense the pressure on Messi is enormous because whoever goes to see him at the stadium is hoping to see marvels performed. And for these marvels to appear, everything has to function properly. And if things don't come out well, the first one they'll hit out at is you. That's the problem with being number one, and that's why you have to be very demanding of the whole team. On and off the pitch.'

Including Neymar, Barcelona had spent €205 million on forwards over a period of five years, looking for the right companion for Leo. But the context was different from that of the arrival of Ronaldinho: it was not about activating the virtuous circle, the Laporta policy of the sporting success feeding the economical one and vice versa, as had occurred ten years ago with Ronaldinho, but, rather, the reshaping of a side and a style of play which needed new energy.

Often the new figure arrives as a direct competitor for his place, not as an accompanying player, something that generates tension for those seeking to defend the space they've won for themselves. That convulsive summer of 2013 led to some commentators fearing the repetition of a phenomenon that has occurred at many clubs, including FC Barcelona: stars raised to the highest levels but who are then allowed to fall. It happened with Ronaldinho.

If, what is more, as happened to Leo, he suffers the loss of his coach and friend in Tito, sport psychologists will confirm that it is difficult for the player to be at his best. In fact, all these events coincided with the recurrence of injuries for Leo at the end of the

2011–12 season, plus a new one at the start of the following campaign.

Finally came the day of Neymar's presentation to the Camp Nou. 3 June. News arrived from Brazil that the player was mentally ready for the challenge (the legendary Jairzinho pointed out that 'there exists no pressure greater than that of the Brazilian supporters') and at a huge press conference with 334 journalists from all over the world, Neymar made it quite clear that he knew what the rules were: 'I am not bothered about being the leader of the team, nor of being the best player in the world. The best is here already and he is Messi. It is my good fortune and a tremendous honour to be able to play alongside him and to help him carry on being the best so he can win more Ballons d'Or.'

Barcelona can now count on the best player in the world, and the one they say will one day replace him. And this is an interesting time: Leo Messi has raised his personal records to new heights over the past two years, but at the same time Barcelona have stopped winning the big titles: just one league and one cup in two years. Could it be that what is good for the star isn't necessarily good for the club? At the very least the idea is worthy of reflection.

And from here emerges another question. Did the club discuss sufficiently the significance of the arrival of Neymar to Messi, the leader of the best Barcelona team in history? Have they thought of the consequences of amending the team's eco-system? Ramón Besa suggests a hypothetical scenario with the coach from Santpedor. 'Guardiola, above and beyond the fact that at the end he lived moments of high tension and that he lost sight of the world, would have said: the day Neymar arrives I will receive him, I'll ask him to sit down and tell him what he has to do.' Instead, you get the impression that the Brazilian simply arrived and did not get that pep talk, as if everything was ever so slightly improvised.

But was it Neymar who Leo needed? Or was his signing above all an institutional triumph? Will it create a Brazilian clique with Alvés, Adriano and Neymar, living next door to the Argentinians Messi, Mascherano and Pinto?

All these questions were left for Tata Martino to answer.

At the beginning of the new season everything seemed to be

running smoothly: the team broke winning records in the league and Neymar adapted with ease to playing on the left wing. *El Tata* seemed to have found the key.

Neymar showed his potential, making the most of Leo's absence in a game against Valladolid in October at the Nou Camp (4–0), where he played in the Argentinian's position: he scored just the one goal but the whole team revolved around his game.

A player with his characteristics had not come along in a long time: speed of movement, pace, ability and vision. He showed that he could be a top player if he had continuity, but also that he was intelligent: on Leo's return, he continued with his modest attitude, exquisite, obeying orders, without demanding a leading role.

He knew what he had to do, and he was aware that his moment would come. It was similar to the way Leo conducted himself, the way he lived and breathed, when he initially arrived in the first team.

The headlines in the Catalan newspapers also changed: Neymar was often seen walking through Barcelona, singing a song on You-Tube to his girlfriend, filling more headlines than Messi.

There's a big difference between Neymar and the other players (Eto'o, Bojan, Ibrahimović and Villa) who have failed, or haven't lasted, as forwards alongside Leo. Apart from the Swede, the others did not look like stars; not even Ibrahimović arrived with the aura of Neymar. And when Leo needed the space they took up on the pitch, the coach decided to support 'the Flea'.

But Neymar is not a number 9, so for that reason he does not hurt Leo's runs towards goal, he doesn't take his space. What's more, he has accepted the submissive role he has been offered. Never before has the question been asked so openly – would Leo welcome the new arrival, would Neymar get on with Messi? And Leo has felt obliged to insist that, of course, he has opened all the doors for him, and anything less would have been unacceptable. The world is looking at *la Pulga* to see if he has indeed accepted the presence of another great footballer, if he can live with and survive this new challenge: life at the very top does not end on reaching the summit.

Without cause for complaint, Messi accepted and embraced the arrival of Neymar, and, in the process, silenced all those who doubted it.

But one day Neymar will want his turn.

Maybe then, Messi, five years older than the Brazilian, will be in the next phase, at Newell's. But if he is not, the picture that is emerging is one that is as fascinating as it is difficult to predict.

5. Tata Martino

The Leo Messi whom Gerard Piqué and Cesc Fàbregas met on their arrival at Barcelona was not the reserved boy with whom they had shared the youth-team dressing room. He still fed on victories, but football had made him stronger. 'He has been acquiring responsibility since he played in the youth team,' explained Pedro. 'Now he has the status of the best player in the world, and that is so difficult to maintain because new players who want to achieve great things come along every day. And he continues to display that level and accept that responsibility. The flipside is when he's not there. I miss everything he generates on the pitch ...'

What should be done when one footballer's influence is so great? Carry on creating conditions so that he scores more goals? Or look for a replacement? What do the great coaches say in this regard?

Pep Guardiola has compared Leo Messi's domination in his sport with that of basketball great Michael Jordan. He was the best and had been for many years. The American went through a situation similar to the one in which Messi finds himself now: the team simply could not live without him.

Legendary NBA coach Pat Riley explains 'the disease of more' in his book *Showtime*. For the former Los Angeles Lakers player and coach 'success is often the first step towards disaster' – a process that he experienced with the Lakers after winning the title in 1980. Everyone became more selfish; the players won as a team but wanted individual rewards: more money, more playing time, more recognition. They were spending more hours in Hollywood stars' swimming pools than in training. They lost perspective and stopped doing the little things that helped them win – and carry on winning. The disaster was confirmed by the abysmal results in the season after the 1980 title.

When players get weighed down by the baggage that comes with victory, you stop winning.

Pat Riley thought that the solution was the reinforcement of the authority of the coach – clear ideas and personality as well as no fear of making decisions.

That had been a growing problem at Barcelona in the Vilanova era, but, as has been said, Messi's ambition and Iniesta's great play allowed them to win the league. Instability was evident, though. Too much depended on Leo.

When Phil Jackson became the Chicago Bulls coach in 1989, he inherited a team that included Michael Jordan. Simply, everything went through him. Jordan was the top scorer, assist provider and rebounder, but the Bulls were not winning titles. Although Barcelona have won everything with Leo, the example is still appropriate, because Phil Jackson decided to rebuild the team by rebalancing the relationship that the star had with his team-mates.

Jackson made a conscious effort to knock Michael Jordan off his pedestal by insistently repeating the following mantra: 'No man is an island. No man takes his path alone. What I put into other people's lives will come back to me.' They are not easy words for sportsmen who have joined the elite to comprehend, as they are so used to being told that they are unique, special, the ones responsible for victory. So Jackson, who was asking his star to do less, would often say to the team: 'Do you understand what I'm saying? Nobody goes anywhere alone. We are in this together.'

But Jordan wanted to carry on being the top scorer.

The new coach signed quality players to improve the starting five, but the press kept focusing on the star. Eventually both Jackson and Jordan reached the same conclusion: the player could carry on having the best scoring statistics, even if his points average went down. To allow the players around him to grow, Jordan offered to reduce his influence, reducing the 'me' to obtain a victorious 'us'. This was decided after listening to the coach, although Jordan thought he was offering the concession voluntarily.

What happened to the Chicago Bulls that season required tremendous personal and collective willpower, and it was this philosophy allowed the team to win six NBA titles.

Curiously, Michael Jordan did not win a single championship without Phil Jackson, but the latter did win titles without Michael.

In fact, he did the same again with Kobe Bryant. Even the best players need direction.

'Barça have worked with Romário, Laudrup, Stoichkov, Koeman, Eto'o, Ronaldinho,' explains Charly Rexach, Johan Cruyff's assistant in the victorious *blaugrana* dream team. 'We've always had stars and important players. The problem is knowing how to manage that.' Charly thinks that the coach has to know how to set limits from day one so that everyone gets the best out of themselves.

'The key to everything is having a good, intelligent coach,' reflects Rexach. 'Someone who says, "Messi is good because he does a few things, the other one is good because he does other things ..." And he says to the new guys, "What do you do? Why were you signed? Very well, do what you did in your old team, but as soon as you do something that you're not supposed to, you're out!" That's how it goes.'

'Next year all that is left for you to do is break your own records,' a well-known coach, who wants to remain anonymous, told Leo at the end of the 2012–13 season. Leo laughed. In reality, the challenge for the following campaigns was much greater. The pressures of being the best in the world had to be balanced with the improvement of a team that had lost some of its essence and was suffering the consequences of a lack of leadership.

Ernesto Valverde and Manuel Pellegrini were spoken of as replacements for Vilanova, and Luis Enrique was approached when Tito had to leave the bench. In the end, four days after the announcement of his departure, an ex-Newell's player from Rosario was chosen. He held the record for the most appearances for the Argentinian outfit and, fittingly, a little Leo did kick-ups on the pitch during his testimonial. His only European experience was a short stint for Tenerife.

The reasons for choosing Gerardo 'Tata' Martino were numerous: he had just won the league and reached the semi-final of the Copa Libertadores with a Newell's Old Boys team that favoured high pressing and possession. He did not know Leo Messi personally, but he did know his father Jorge, and the reports that reached Barcelona from different sources were excellent. 'There are no other teams that play like us, but there is a culture of play which we have established and has become universal,' wrote Andoni Zubizarreta in the club magazine.

Sandro Rosell had known Martino for years and they had spoken about football on various occasions when the Barcelona president was working at Nike. He asked a mutual friend, the Paraguay president, for el Tata's phone number, and he called him immediately. 'Let's do it,' answered Martino when he was offered the post.

Leo had said in *Olé* a year earlier that he admired el Tata, in charge of his beloved *Ñuls*: 'I like Martino. He's a really great coach. You could see what he was doing with the team at the Clausura competition – the good results, the good football.'

'I know the Messis spoke to Barça, and I thank them for that,' said the new coach before travelling from Buenos Aires to Barcelona. 'I'm sure Lionel and Jorge have had an influence and have spoken to the Barça management.'

One day later, however, after a friendly against Bayern Munich, Leo declared, 'I haven't anything to do with Martino joining, nor do I have to give explanations. It is between President Rosell and the club.'

El Tata himself had to deny it all in his inaugural press conference at the Camp Nou.

But that Martino was on Leo's wavelength was logical in terms of geography and their feelings about Newell's. Barcelona's success up to that point had occurred because the conditions had been put in place to enable their star to shine at the top level. Bringing in a coach who understood him was therefore a sensible step. And Adrián Coria, Leo's ex-coach in Rosario, was part of the technical team which el Tata took with him to Barcelona. But they say in Rosario that the connection between the Messis and Martino did not go any further than that.

Sandro Rosell also denied the Messis had anything to do with his arrival: 'As for the appointment of our new coach, despite what people might think, Messi had absolutely nothing to do with the selection. They did not even know each other and had never spoken before.'

Bringing in an Argentinian coach who understood Barcelona was a coherent decision, but did Martino have a thorough enough understanding of the club's style from only watching it on television?

Martino's inaugural press conference was dominated by talk of his plans for the Argentinian star: 'I want him to find the same comforts, to feel at ease in the team and allow him to take care of the rest.'

The coach knew that he had taken over a squad with big stars and great footballers, but he wanted to make clear what their job was from day one. And he did it very intelligently: by announcing that he would not change anything. 'Don't get tired of winning,' he told them, and he stated that he wanted to bring back the high pressing from Guardiola's best years.

On their first day together, el Tata followed Leo very closely. The Argentinian had a sensational training session, pressing, scoring goals, stealing the ball. The team seemed focused after Martino's arrival.

Leo and el Tata spoke during training and Martino later had a meeting with captain Carles Puyol, to whom he emphasised the same key points: he told him not to worry, as he did not plan to change the training sessions and would still allow the whole squad to get together on the day of a game, a favourite remnant of the Pep era.

He told them: 'Lads, the status quo remains.'

The first league match, against Levante, marked the new pattern: el Tata substituted Leo in the 71st minute. Messi had not been replaced since May 2010, except for injuries. Neymar went on in the 64th minute – the left winger's integration into the team was going to be gradual.

Martino explained himself in a press conference: 'We reached an agreement very quickly. I spoke to him a few weeks ago about the importance of understanding that it was good to rest. Various parts of various matches where you sit on the bench are like resting for a whole match. I will not replace him in a tight game. I won't, nor will anyone. It would be crazy.' Barcelona had thrashed Levante 7–0.

Clever Martino. In reality he was changing things from day one.

He asked the full-backs to push forward less; the wingers to open play up instead of coming inside; the midfielders to get into the box more, not to come as deep to pick up the ball and to find the forwards quicker; the centre-backs to bring the ball out calmly and to launch diagonal passes to the wingers; the defenders to man-mark on long balls; and the goalkeeper to play it long sometimes. He also demanded a change in attitude to restore pressing high up the field.

Despite what el Tata had said in his first press conference, he discussed with Leo the possibility of playing him in a different position and even using a system similar to the one applied with Argentina, with Leo behind a striker, like Higuaín. Leo agreed that in some games it was a good idea to surprise the opposition by playing him wide or deeper, as he ended up doing in the first *clásico* of the La Liga season at the Camp Nou.

Leo, who felt comfortable with the tactical changes, had already explained in March 2013 (in an interview with Martín Souto on TyC Sports) that he felt the team had to rethink and to look for alternatives.

Leo Messi: *The most difficult matches are those where our opponents sit back and let us attack down the wings. That's how Chelsea and Mourinho's Inter beat us. Real Madrid set out like that against us ...*

Martín Souto: *Yes, but if you stay back and they do the same, the ball remains in midfield, you can't play football ...*

Leo Messi: *We don't really know how to play any other way, and it sometimes costs us big time. We speak about it before important games. In the cup match the same thing happened, too. They had to go out to look for the result and the first goal came from our free-kick, which we had taken quickly. We lost the ball, and the counter comes with Ronaldo one on one with Piqué ...*

Martín Souto: *Yes, and did you speak about it? Did you say, 'Let's take our foot off the accelerator. Let's give them the ball for a bit'?*

Leo Messi: *Yes, but we aren't used to that. We are used to looking to win matches in the same way and playing like that.*

Martino's proposal received general acceptance. 'We have recovered automatism which was lost over time due to Tito's absence,' said Xavi. 'Last year we did very little on tactics in training.' Strong dressing-room figures such as Alvés, Busquets, Piqué (who spoke about being slaves to tiki taka) and Valdés all publicly backed the changes, although the press debated the merits of a style that was moving away from the one which had taken them to footballing heaven, especially when, for the first time in four years, an opponent (the modest Rayo Vallecano) had more possession than Barcelona in a match. Leo joined in with the praise: 'The more variants we have, the better.'

El Tata found himself with another matter which he had to manage in the dressing room to guarantee progress along the right path that season: the leadership transition. Víctor Valdés was leaving the club, Carles Puyol made a titanic effort to recover from his latest knee injury that kept him away from the day-to-day happenings, Xavi could no longer play as often as in previous years, while Iniesta tended to show his influence on the pitch rather than in the dressing room. Gerard Piqué, Javier Mascherano and Cesc Fàbregas were gradually gaining influence as a result of their personalities and performances on the pitch.

Meanwhile, Leo experienced an inconsistent start to the campaign in terms of physical fitness: he suffered an injury on 22 August in the first leg of the Super Cup against Atlético de Madrid, a bruise to the femoral biceps in his left leg. Until that moment he had completed only one match out of 25, the 4–0 loss against Bayern Munich. He was injured once again on 29 September against Almería, a muscle injury to the right thigh, the same one he suffered against PSG.

In a World Cup year, in what he hoped would be his tournament, Leo wanted to reach the end of the season in perfect condition, both physically and mentally. So he reduced his level of intensity in training, following his body's instructions and those of Juanjo Brau. He once again put himself in the hands of a nutritionist, this time one from outside the club, and lost two kilos in September.

Meanwhile, Real Madrid lost points at the start of the league campaign and the team was performing well in Europe, too. In the first *clásico* of the Martino era, at the Camp Nou on 26 October, new variations were introduced: predicting rightly that Real Madrid, to avoid being outnumbered, would play with three midfielders, and one of them, Sergio Ramos, would try to stop Leo's runs from midfield, Martino decided to play Messi on the right-hand side of the attack, which attracted defenders and allowed Neymar on the other side and Cesc as a false nine to have more space. Messi, in his second game in five days after being out for three weeks with his muscle injury, spent some of his energy tracking back and also applying pressure to Madrid defenders when they were in possession, and he carefully chose his runs with the ball as he was not yet physically ready for an intense 90-minute game.

So his influence on the game was reduced and the team looked more for Neymar, as they felt he was sharper than 'the Flea'. The match sent out worrying signals despite the 2–1 victory, with Neymar and Alexis on the score sheet. Barcelona defend much better with the ball, but the insistence of Neymar and Messi on finishing the attacks early, without slowly 'cooking' the moves with Xavi and Iniesta, forced the team to exert much greater physical strain than usual as they were unable to find the right positioning. Player energy levels suffered in the second half as Barcelona dropped very deep. Real deserved a point.

As debate regarding Leo's fitness wore on, it would be just two weeks until his inability to play was making the headlines once again.

6. The Injury and Recuperation

Putting together the media explanations behind Messi's injuries would be reason enough not to step foot outside the house, because we would probably all pull our hamstrings, too. Apparently it was down to playing friendlies during his holidays. Would it not be worse to have a kick-about with some friends on an uneven pitch at the park for hour after hour? There can be no doubt that changes to a player's personal life can be disruptive. But, if becoming a father causes injuries, why did Piqué and Cesc not suffer, too?

Furthermore, it was still yet to be determined whether all the injuries to the same muscle, five in the same year, could be painted with the same brush, because one in the upper part (such as the one against Chelsea) was vastly different from one in the lower part (such as the one against Betis). Some injuries were even added to the list when, in reality, they were not even mini-breaks and others never became anything more than slight irritations (when the muscle wall suffered damage, but not the muscle itself).

The fact that the last one was in a different area from the one against PSG, for example, meant we could have been speaking about the effect of a knock when the player had been running at full pace, meaning the muscle had been contracted, and consequently at greater risk, rather than a repeat of his femoral biceps injury. Messi had received a knee to the leg from a Betis defender that caused him to fall to the ground. What did this have to do with his diet?

The story had been written starting from the end. There was actually no scientific confirmation of where the muscle injuries came from, but dethroning the king was still deemed acceptable. Something else did not help clarify the matter: the silence of the Barcelona medical team.

Leo and the club began to carry out a full-scale investigation into what action could be taken in order to avoid subsequent muscle injuries, something they had successfully achieved five and a half years earlier. Given that the requirements and needs of an athlete's body change over time, it was concluded that individual preparation was needed, as that is what evolution in football dictates.

Juanjo Brau's 'disappearance' was strongly linked to Leo's latest muscle problems and things between them had seemed strained since the previous season. One event suggested that perhaps a change was needed: Barcelona had already been crowned champions ahead of their previous visit to the Calderón eight months earlier. Although Leo was not fully fit on that occasion, he still wanted to play. He was advised not to do so, however, and ended up getting injured. Luis Martín gave his take on the match in *El País*: 'A raging Leo kicked everything he could find on his walk back to the dressing room, blaming everyone and everything for his misfortune. Everything except his stubbornness, of course. Not even Juanjo Brau, his trusted physiotherapist at the time, was able to calm him down and make him see reason. Maybe that was the evening when his friend understood that their relationship had been partially damaged.'

It was considered beneficial to experience a change of routine and scenery. Messi's preparation, as had been the case for several months, consisted of a mix of what the ever-faithful Brau offered alongside the Argentina fitness coach and physiotherapist. Further-more, his compatriot and physiotherapist Luis García, who had already lent a hand during Rijkaard's final year at the helm, was also going to help with the new recovery process.

In any case, Messi's issue was clearly psychological as well as physical: he had not felt like himself for far too long. 'The Flea' was having a hard time, not only with his latest injury against Betis, but also since the one he'd suffered against PSG. Leo sensed that it could all turn against him at any moment, as he felt regular pain and knew his body was not quite right. He gradually adapted to the situation and worked hard in order to be available for the team but never had the feeling deep down that everything was completely resolved. When contact with the Betis defender caused him to stretch his leg, breaking his femoral biceps in the process, Leo felt strange. It was almost predictable, but that did not make it any less painful. Leo was deflated.

Leo wanted to start from scratch by analysing everything in detail. In order to do so, he also needed to relax his mind and remove him-self from the day-to-day stresses of football as a way of keeping his long-term vision clear. He would isolate himself from the press and enclose himself in a bubble. It was decided that he would distance himself from the team, the club and the city by returning home to Argentina. The priority was recovery and getting back to his previous level. Following a two-week rest period which allowed the tear to heal, Leo devoted more than ten hours a day to recovery work at the AFA's fitness facilities in Ezeiza. He would arrive at 8.30 in the morning, have some *mate*, eat breakfast and then jump into his physiotherapy sessions under the supervision of Luis García. Elvio Paolorosso, who works with Martino, and Dady, the national team's fitness coach, also kept an eye on Leo. He would then eat lunch at the sports centre, have an afternoon nap and head out onto the training field for various stop-start drills. That kept him occupied until 7 p.m., when he would return to his flat in Buenos Aires, which was 40 minutes away.

The programme comprised of double sessions Monday to Friday, a five-hour session on Saturday and a deserved day off on Sunday. Leo's routine aimed to strengthen his leg muscles and readjust to the playing surface in what was a type of intense pre-season programme, something which he had not enjoyed in many years. His fears gradually disappeared to the point that he was brimming with confidence once again just before the winter break. He felt ready to do sprint drills. The most important feeling for a footballer is being able to express oneself freely and without pain on the pitch with the sparkle that being physically fit brings. Leo was raring to go, which was also a new feeling.

Coincidentally, Ronaldo also suffered an injury two and a half weeks before the winter break. He missed some league and cup outings due to a few niggles which he wanted to alleviate properly. The injury lay-off combined with the winter break gave the Real Madrid star ample time to fully recharge his batteries. 'He doesn't need to be fit now but in April,' was the word from the coaching staff. Both players, competitive monsters who define the present era, needed time to get back to full fitness before resuming their all-encapsulating duel.

The start of Leo's recovery period was brightened by the award of the Golden Shoe for top goalscorer in Europe in the 2012–13 season, totalling 46 goals in just 32 matches, on top of a 21-game scoring streak and being the top goalscorer in the Champions League for a fourth consecutive season. He also became the first player to win the illustrious award for a third time. 'Now I have to strengthen my whole body so that nothing else happens to me and I can be relaxed when I play, although that depends on Him up there,' he said on the day he received the award.

One sole storm brewed during that Argentinian summer leading up to Christmas in Rosario. Club vice-president Javier Faus declared his reluctance for Leo to be offered another new contract: 'I don't see any reason to improve the contract for a man who had it renewed just two years ago.' It was 10 December. Ten days later, Messi's words reached Catalan radio station RAC1. 'He is someone who doesn't know anything about football and wants to manage Barcelona like a business, which it is not,' exclaimed the player, becoming his own spokesman for the first time in the process when faced with a small crisis. 'Barcelona is the best club in the world and must be represented by the best board members. Besides, I would remind him that neither I nor anyone from my camp has asked for any wage increase and he knows that very well.'

This unexpected, blunt reaction took the Barcelona board by surprise. Rosell did not need reminding that it was the first time that the player had engaged in such controversy, and furthermore, he did so without the interference of his father, as had previously occurred. It was purely Leo's initiative. His father, Jorge, endeavoured to ease the situation a few days later by explaining that nobody had anything against Barcelona. The crux of the matter was the general feeling, which would be confirmed one month later by Rosell's resignation, that the board measured the importance of Neymar and Messi with different financial barometers.

New rumours began doing the rounds regarding interest in Messi from abroad and Real Madrid. There was talk for the first time that maybe Rosell wanted to let him go. The president had to intervene in order to silence them. 'Messi is the best in the world and his wages must reflect that,' the chairman said to the press. Faus himself made those words his own one month later: 'The financial, social and sporting project of Barcelona is incomprehensible without Leo Messi ... The best player in the world deserves the best financial treatment in the world.' Leo deemed the crisis to be over.

After 58 days on the sidelines and a two-kilo drop in weight during his time in Argentina, the scar had disappeared and Leo triumphantly returned to training on 2 January. The flurry of worries over the injury could finally be buried. 'The Flea' participated in an afternoon training session behind closed doors and trained with the group as normal. Xavi was even heard to say, 'The new lad is really good!'

Messi would have to wait until the first leg of the last-16 tie of the Copa del Rey against Getafe on 9 January to take to the pitch once again.

In Leo's absence, the Tata effect was producing results, although doubt lingered over whether the more direct style would prevail in the most important clashes. His squad-rotation policy seemed to be proving successful and the emergence of new talent provided previously unavailable solutions. Neymar stepped up to the plate in December while 'the Flea' journeyed down the road to recovery.

The team had fared relatively well without Messi: seven victories and two defeats kept the side on top of the pile. The cup match with Getafe finally arrived, el Tata gave Leo just under half an hour to ease himself back into first-team action, with one eye on the crucial upcoming league clash with Cholo's second-placed Atlético de Madrid.

That was more than enough time for Messi to make an impact, scoring twice in the convincing 4–0 victory. The second was a neat left-footed finish following a classic pacey run in which he dribbled past all comers, something which had not been seen in months. It was the 70th brace of his Barcelona career, which returned him to the top of the scoring charts with 16 strikes, one ahead of Pedro. 'Leo's career is a film script,' accurately explained Martino, as the forward seemingly immediately returned to his deadly best.

'It was really good for me to get away from everything and be back in my country,' explained Leo. 'I didn't feel any pain. Once the injury cleared up, I worked on my fitness to be able to enjoy myself out on the pitch again.' He also quashed all rumours with his final statement: 'The idea is to stay here and spend my whole career at Barcelona.'

On the way home, Leo hardly spoke about the match. He left that to his father, who could not stop recapturing the hundreds of little details that the match produced. That was, without saying it, his way of expressing both happiness and relief at seeing his son enjoy himself on a pitch again.

Simeone's much-feared Atlético de Madrid side were up next. Messi's growing maturity was evident in an interview about his recovery and possible inclusion in the side for the upcoming battle at the top: 'I shall speak to Martino and the doctor. Now I'm over the injuries, I want to play again. If I can be out there, I will. I always think about the club. Nobody here is indispensable. Whoever plays will do a good job.'

The top-of-the-table clash was finely poised, as Atlético knew that they could overtake their opponents with a victory. Following discussions with el Tata and the medical team, Leo accepted his place on the substitutes' bench alongside Neymar, who had fallen below Pedro and an on-fire Alexis in the pecking order. Martino's authority was on the rise. 'The Flea' showed that he knew how to listen. 'We're in January, not April. There's too long to go for us not to look after him,' announced a cautious Martino before the match.

Leo entered the fray with the score 0–0 in a very tight match with few clear-cut goalscoring opportunities. Messi provided a few glimpses of his brilliance, but the importance of the goalless encounter lay in the dynamics between the coach and his biggest star.

Leo made his first start in two months in the second leg against Getafe. His brace brought his blistering scoring statistics to the fore once again, as he was averaging a goal every forty minutes since his return. His second goal was a mesmerising run in which he escaped from four defenders and eventually the goalkeeper. The burst of pace and sublime nutmeg en route to goal were clear indicators that Messi was back.

'Leo did what he had to do: look after himself, have a good pre-season and come back raring to go,' explained Cesc.

Messi started once again against a resilient Levante side that defended very deep and had already made things difficult for Real Madrid and Atlético. Messi opened them up on three occasions, but their splendid goalkeeper Keylor Navas kept Barça at bay. The *blaugranas* conceded their sixth goal of the season from set pieces meaning the 1–1 draw tightened things up at the top of the table: just one point separated the three title contenders.

Despite Xavi's presence, Leo opted for a deep starting position in midfield that day, an exercise which would be repeated during the remainder of the campaign. 'We expect goals from Messi, and he came back as an organiser on top of that,' accurately explained Jorge Valdano.

Yet several stories would emerge soon after, shaking the foundations of the club: the investigation into Neymar's transfer deal, with allegations of financial irregularities investigated by the State Attorney, Sandro Rosell's resignation and the FIFA sanction for breaching transfer regulations. The off-field problems were coupled with a decline on the pitch which seemingly showed no signs of stopping. The foundations on which the team's previous success had been built were gradually wearing thin: high pressing, movement off the ball, building the play from the back and work ethic. Intensity levels were waning, defensive mistakes were plentiful, possession was being lost too easily and players were often found out of position.

Barcelona's Treble dreams were shattered in a fateful week in April. Defeat against Granada (their fifth of the campaign) was a devastating blow to their title challenge, the Champions League quarter-final defeat against Atlético de Madrid meant the *blaugranas* would not feature in the semi-finals for the first time in seven years and Real Madrid deservedly clinched the Copa del Rey. Leo's performance in the big games was brought into question with statistics showing that he ran only 1.6 kilometres more than goalkeeper Pinto. There was even media talk that Barcelona were assessing a possible post-World Cup transfer.

What was happening to 'the Flea'? Was anything actually happening to him? The statistics did not lie: his passing accuracy was at a similar level to previous years (83.1 per cent this campaign compared with 85.1 per cent in earlier seasons), he was getting a similar number of shots away (3.67 per match with Pep in the dugout compared with 3.47 with el Tata) and he was making a similar number of explosive runs to the norm, with around five per game. His efficiency in front of goal was similar to Cristiano's, who needed 173 attempts to score his first 24 goals of the campaign, while Messi's first 15 league goals came from 101 efforts.

The noticeable difference was that he was running around two kilometres less per match compared with his early years in the first team. This was due to the psychological blow from his latest injury, his age (26) and a more personalised training regime. Yet there is a far more important factor that was being ignored: Messi was running less because there was less reliance on him. He had fewer touches of the ball than in the Guardiola era: he received 68.9 passes per match in 2010–11 compared with 53.5 in 2013–14.

The team was playing down the wings but their overall play was not improving: Dani Alvés's incessant crossing was bearing no fruit. A veteran Xavi Hernández was dropping deeper and rarely found himself on the edge of the penalty area, where he used to cause the most damage, distancing himself from Messi in the process. The full-backs would find themselves bunched up with the forwards who were not making the diagonal runs of previous years that created space for Leo to perform one-twos and wreak havoc in. The full-backs were becoming wingers, meaning their attacking presence was no longer a surprise and, conversely, they took up the space on which Messi thrives.

The word 'mystery' was bandied about when people tried to explain what was happening to Leo. Tata Martino's Barcelona were no longer creating the necessary conditions for 'the Flea' to flourish and have the upper hand over defenders. Consequently, a frustrated Messi would either drop ever deeper to receive the ball or he would simply disappear from games. Pep Guardiola used to say that you had to 'make Leo happy and give him the ball'. However, Barcelona were taking the ball away from their biggest star.

There is no mystery – certain conditions have to be met to get the best out of Messi. That simply did not happen in the 2013–14 season. Simplistic analysis shows that the media hung the player out to dry at a time when he felt exposed. Was the criticism premeditated? Leo was frustrated out on the pitch, but the feeling was rife that there was a campaign against him.

Comparisons with Neymar became inevitable. The Brazilian's inconsistent performances were ignored in spite of him being one of the most expensive players in history. Conversely, the Brazilian starlet seemed to be receiving preferential treatment over Barcelona's most important player, the one that had helped the club win so much. There was talk that Leo would become the world's best-paid player, but the opening contract-renewal offers did not reflect that, because the club planned to keep half of the player's image rights. The subsequent offer failed to acknowledge certain agreements that had already been put in place. Was so much bargaining necessary?

The ball had been put in Messi's court, leaving him exposed to public opinion. With what in mind? It would all be explained by a possible sale, which Sandro Rosell considered before his resignation. You cannot simply sell the world's best player, but you can sell an 'unmanageable player who will never be the same, who prevents others from progressing, who only thinks about the World Cup ...' and other such words which were spoken about 'the Flea'. Manchester United and PSG started to gather information about Leo in case he would be open to an unlikely move.

3

Leo's World Cup

It had to be

1. Before the World Cup. The Foundations

It was going to be the tournament that would see Leo, at the age of 27, at his peak. It was being played in South America, and Argentina have traditionally felt more comfortable on their own continent. The aim was to win it. In their biggest rival's backyard. The team revolved around the Rosario-born star and the necessary conditions had been created to maximise not only his characteristics, but also those of his team-mates in attack: Sergio Agüero, Gonzalo Higuaín, Ángel Di María. They are the Real Madrid of national teams: they enjoy playing on the break, with pace, pressing high without the ball, but keeping possession if required. They knew they had limitations – six had to defend and four to attack, not much football required. It was going to be debated, but it couldn't be any other way: try not to concede and hope that Messi's moments would be decisive.

Leo prepared both mentally and physically to arrive in perfect condition. For Leo, it was his World Cup. All the baggage, everything he had learned and everything he had fought for so his national team understood him was brought to the table in the summer in Brazil.

At last Argentina were contenders for the title. But it needed the arrival of a new national coach. Despite the convincing 4–1 victory in 2010 against recently crowned World Champions Spain, and despite the pleasure Messi experienced from hearing the fans sing his name for the first time, Sergio Batista, the manager at the time, was not able to combine 'the Flea's' footballing growth with a team that worked. He tried Barcelona's 4-3-3 formation and distanced Carlos Tévez from the national team because he understood that he did not fit the group's new dynamics, but the results were dismal: he failed in the Copa América held in Argentina, losing to Uruguay on penalties in the quarter-finals. The opposition goalkeeper, Fernando Muslera, was, without doubt, the man of the match, but that fact did not appease local supporters who showed their impatience with their team. They were Messi's worst moments with the *albiceleste*.

It was Alejandro Sabella's turn to get rid of the deadwood and initiate a new project which had to start with the talented front line at his disposal. At 56, he used his experience not only as a footballer but also as assistant to Daniel Passarella, the coach who had led Argentina to the 1998 World Cup. His low profile helped lift spirits without making too much noise, and his footballing rigorousness helped him make decisions, some of them painful ones: Tévez was not going to return, nor was Riquelme. The call-ups and style gradually became consistent and revolved around the same group. The four forwards (Messi, Di María, Kun Agüero and Higuaín) had been developing an understanding and would be sure starters. And in midfield, a combination of Javier Mascherano's tactical discipline and Fernando Gago's touch, coupled with their experience and balance, made them leaders both on and off the pitch. Messi had Gago behind him and Agüero as his partner up front in both his titles with Argentina (the Under-20 World Cup and the Olympic Games). They were reunited under Sabella. And Leo, alongside team-mates who were on the same wavelength as him, was playing with freedom. In and around the box, he started becoming Barcelona's Messi.

'The only thing I said as soon as I joined the national team was that he had to be left in peace,' explains Alejandro Sabella in the book *El distinto*. 'He once missed a penalty and it was as if an asteroid had struck the earth. Please! Then they started, what if he's depressed, what's happening to Messi ... It turns out that he scored five goals in the following two matches. We have to understand that Messi is a human being.'

Sabella needed Pep Guardiola's advice: 'Protect him with players who make his job simpler ... And make him feel loved.' With that in mind, the new coach flew to Barcelona to give Messi the captaincy.

Javier Mascherano: I was the captain and the one who gave it to him. I spoke to him here, at the Barcelona training ground. I told

him that I would no longer be captain. Obviously, I had not spo-
ken to the coach yet, but I told him that it would no longer be me.
I felt that he had to be the captain because of everything he rep-
resented for us. I had already thought about it before. I wanted
to do it before the Copa América. Well, it didn't happen, and ... a
moment arrived when I said to him, 'Look, Leo, you have to be
the captain for me. I think the best person who represents all of
us here is you.'

Guillem Balague: When exactly was that?

Javier Mascherano: In 2011, after the Copa América. Obviously,
there is a new coach and he chooses. After that, Sabella also said,
'I want Leo to be the captain ...' And he asked him and obviously
he accepted.

Guillem Balague: And what did Leo say when you told him?

Javier Mascherano: He didn't want to at the time. He was saying,
'No! How? You are the captain!' And I was saying to him, 'No,
Leo, it has to be you. The one who represents us in the best way is
you, and I don't think anyone is giving you a gift here. It is right
for it to be you.'

Captaincy suited Leo down to the ground; it filled him with seren-
ity. Well, that is if you ignore his first talk – or, if the one-off against
Greece in the 2010 World Cup is counted, the second one, too. 'He
told me the other day,' explained Gerard Piqué, 'that in Argentina
they have a tradition of captains giving speeches before each match.
When he was given the armband and it was his turn to give one, he
arrived and said, "There is no speech today. Come on, let's get on
the pitch!" That in his first match as captain!'

But he gradually adapted to the responsibilities of the role, including what were for him the least attractive ones. 'At the beginning
he would speak to us on a more individual basis,' recounted Pablo
Zabaleta. 'But now he says, "This is Argentina, let's go for it from
the start, remember the importance to the country." General and
group things, with some individual instructions. He has taken on
the role.' And Pablo stopped giving him tips as he had as a youngster. This Messi was in another dimension.

'They aren't tactical things. That's what the coach's talks in the
hotel are for,' explained Oscar Ustari. 'When we come back in from

the warm-up, we get changed, we all shout, we call out a few things – "Come on lads! We are Argentina! We are going to win!" Then Leo rounds us up in a circle just before we go back out. And he calms us down, or he speaks about the team, the fans who have come to see us. He might say something else in the tunnel. And at half-time, he is doing his boots up, you can hear him saying, "We're going to continue in the same way, we are doing well ..."'

Fernando Signorini, the ex-national team fitness coach, offered a different opinion of who should have had the armband: 'He didn't need it at all [the captaincy]. Besides, I think Mascherano is much more of a captain than Leo, and Leo recognises it himself. He is not stupid. But it is part of the game because this comes from when Bilardo gave it to Diego because it gave Diego a special buzz. But, in this day and age, the captain, the leader, practically no longer exists, times have changed, cultural norms. When society was different, a leader was more contemplative, more respectful in his ways. Today it is all up for debate and it's good that it's like that, because things are going badly, in football and in society. Provided that Leo is happy doing what he does, don't try to give him too many responsibilities as a footballer. Just let him play.'

Maradona was a captain who fought rivals both on and off the pitch, with hints of political leanings, which he demonstrated by criticising the Pope or praising Fidel Castro, whereas Leo just wanted to express his opinion on systems of play. 'He is helped by two positive leaders behind him in Zabaleta and Mascherano,' said 'Professor' Salorio. 'Sometimes it's good to have one leader with two behind. In any case, the Leo that I met in the Under-20 World Cup is not this one. This Leo is a guy who asks, demands in the true sense of the word, eh? When he demands, he demands what he has to demand, and when he asks, he asks for what he has to ask for. He isn't a nonconformist like Diego can be.'

Leo speaks without saying a single word in training – by not complaining about getting fouled again, by constantly wanting the ball so he can assume responsibility, calling his injured team-mates from Barcelona, rejecting special privileges or by participating in the organisation of trips.

The journalist Ezequiel Fernández Moores wrote in *El País* about the first decision Leo made when wearing the captain's armband:

'Dozens of kids jump onto the track at the IBK Stadium in Calcutta. Policemen take photos with Lionel Messi. His presence in India is a success. The promoter of the match happily pays him $200,000 on top. "Lads," says the new Argentina captain while he rounds up his team-mates, "I suffer from the heat like you, I've been on a journey like you and I've had vaccinations like you. This cash is for everyone." It is 2 September 2012, a friendly which Argentina win 1–0 against Venezuela, the debut of new coach, Alejandro Sabella.'

In June 2013, the Guatemalan Football Association agreed to pay a fee of $1 million to the Argentinian federation for a friendly between the countries' national teams. Leo was a doubt because of some trouble that had been dragging on since his injury against PSG. If he played, they would pay another half a million. Leo duly travelled and played in Guatemala, and that extra half a million, which was earned through his appearance, was distributed among the players selected.

'I saw him covering at right-back in Peru, the best in the world,' added Oscar Ustari. 'Dropping back to defend. That was in qualifying. And you say, he's the best of all and he's here, defending. How are you not going to get infected by it if the team-mate who has won it all is here. Of course you have to build the team around that person.'

The points were gradually being amassed during qualification, but the odd slip-up still occurred. Meanwhile, he was filling his own pockets with goals as well. On the back of not scoring at the World Cup in South Africa or at the 2011 Copa América, he averaged almost a goal per game following the arrival of the new coach.

'There is something very interesting about Sabella's Argentina,' said Carlos Bilardo. 'That pressure over three-quarters of the pitch means Leo has to run very little. That is to say, he covers less ground than he did in South Africa. Whenever Leo is around, the opponents have to have at least three players on him. And the others find themselves with space and time to cause damage.'

The ecosystem was finally harmonious, even if the football was not impressive. But every king needs a coronation, and Leo's came on a very hot day in Barranquilla, Colombia. Sabella explained it in the foreword of this book. It was the day everything fell into place. Argentina had just lost against Venezuela, a historic defeat, the first ever against *La Vinotinto* (The Burgundy), and drawn with Bolivia. Colombia opened the scoring in Barranquilla. The heat, another enemy, was unbearable. And Kun showed himself to be the best partner for Messi up front. 'Based on what us Argentinians are like, that qualifying match against Colombia, when we came back with a spectacular second-half performance by Lionel, was key,' remembered Eduardo Sacheri. 'We were destined to lose that match and make qualifying complicated, and he made us win. It was epic: a Messi who can give no more, dying from the heat, on the brink of exhaustion ... and he turned it around in those conditions, against very difficult opposition. We love those stories.'

At that moment Argentinian society became reconciled with Leo. Victories followed for the *albiceleste* in Chile and Paraguay, and they were also unbeaten in Quito and La Paz, four matches which had ended in defeat in qualifying for the World Cup in South Africa. 'Until that moment there was no definition of his role on the pitch,' explained Salorio. 'Now he has a fixed position. I don't like it when he has to go so deep to get the ball. That's why Gago is a great teammate to have. I've always said that the difference between Barcelona and Argentina is that Barcelona have Frank Sinatra with good musicians. Argentina didn't used to have good musicians for Frank Sinatra. But now they are assembling them.'

The year 2012 continued in the same vein. In those 12 months, Leo scored 12 goals, equalling Batistuta's record, although the latter did it in a World Cup year. And he bagged a hat-trick in a friendly against Brazil in June. For the first goal, he finished a counter-attack after Higuaín had stolen the ball, the second was after a one-two with Di María and his hat-trick was completed with a belter from outside the area that made it 4–3, six minutes from the end after a run similar to the one against Getafe but without opposing players in his way. The match against Venezuela, played at River's stadium in March 2013, cleared up any doubts, if there were any left that is. It was a sell-out. There were thousands of number-10 Messi shirts streaming to the stadium in Buenos Aires to celebrate the fact that the national team could call on the best in the world.

In the stands there were banners saluting him: 'Raise hell, Messi', '*Messiento enamorado*' (I feel in love), 'Leo Messi, national pride' and 'God and the Messias'. In order to commemorate his 100th cap,

15 November 2011. Colombia 1–2 Argentina. Roberto Menéndez Stadium, Barranquilla

Colombia: Ospina; Zúñiga, Mosquera, Yepes, Armero; Pabón (D.Moreno, 61st minute), Bolívar, A. Aguilar (Arias, 76th minute), J. Rodríguez; Ramos and J. Martínez (Quintero, 76th minute). Subs not used: Castillo, Zapata, Henríquez, Valencia, Vallejo, Gutiérrez, Marrugo.

Argentina: Romero; Zabaleta, F. Fernández, Burdisso (Desábato, 36th minute), C. Rodríguez; Sosa, Mascherano, Guiñazú (Agüero, 46th minute), Braña; Messi and Higuaín (Gago, 85th minute). Subs not used: Andújar, Orión, Demichelis, Monzón, Álvarez, Gaitán, Pastore, Denis and Lavezzi.

Goals: 1–0. 45th minute: Pabón. 1–1. 61st minute: Messi. 1–2. 84th minute: Agüero.

Cayetano Ros, *El País*: Agüero improves 'the Flea' and their partnership helped Argentina come back against Colombia. El Kun switched Messi on, who started both moves in the comeback. 'The Flea' finished the first himself after a Sosa cross. He played Higuaín in for the second; his shot was pushed away by Ospina, and Agüero hammered home to leave Colombia desolate in the end.

the Argentinian Football Association also set up a tribute that day. It was very discreet: a plaque and applause after the announcement over the Tannoy. Julio Grondona, the 81-year-old president, kissed Leo Messi, the player to whom he offered the national team, or at least that is how he will want the story to be written. And then came the match. La Monumental rose to its feet every time Messi embarked on one of his runs. And suddenly a chant went up that had belonged to Diego Maradona up until that point. 'Come, come, sing with me, you'll find a friend, Lionel Messi, who will hold your hand and we all spin around.' The hand referred to is Maradona's infamous 'hand of God' from the 1986 World Cup match against England.

Leo's name was chanted on four occasions, and the performance was even more convincing than the scoreline suggests, a 3–0 win with a penalty scored by 'the Flea' and a Higuaín brace following two Leo assists, the kind of eye-of-the-needle passes that you need to see on the television replay. At 25 years old, Messi had won the fans' complete and utter admiration.

One small detail that perhaps defined the group was seen on the pitch when they were just about to qualify for the World Cup in Brazil. From time to time, the ball would pass within a few metres of Messi and he would not go for it. He was allowed to do this. He had permission to reserve his energy and focus on his game with the ball, and he could choose when he wanted to press. 'With another technical team or at another time, he would have tried to be Messi for the whole first ten minutes and then he would have burnt out. for good,' said Eduardo Sacheri. 'It seems to me that Messi feels happy in the national team these days, as he has never felt before. And at last we are capable of accepting that we were the problem, not Messi.'

Leo had improved his team contribution under Sabella, although the problem had only really existed previously in the stands, on the bench or in the media. 'I knew that I wasn't performing well for the national team, but I wasn't the only one,' said Leo Messi in March 2013. 'The national team wasn't performing. The people or the press expected me to go and win games single-handedly, and that has never happened in any team. I knew I wasn't at my best and I didn't want that.'

His performances under Sabella (20 goals in 22 games, whereas under previous coaches he had scored 17 in 61) matched those of the team – Leo, Di María, Higuaín and Agüero scored 90 per cent of Argentina's goals in qualifying. The new manager, 'the Flea' confirmed, had helped. It was 'an important change in the way of constructing the team, of positioning ourselves on the pitch and organising the unit tactically'.

And Sabella himself made his own contribution to the folklore by coming up with a new adjective to define the striker: *immessionante*, a combination in Spanish of the words 'Messi' and 'impressive'. It was included in the 2013 edition of the Santillana dictionary.

Qualification for the World Cup was sealed with a 5–2 thrashing of Paraguay, featuring two Messi goals, although the two conceded still left some question marks over the defence's fragility. Despite this, the nation started to imagine a good World Cup. At the back of the dressing room full of ecstatic and expectant Argentinians, a veteran of other battles, Fernando Signorini, was sitting on a chair with his legs crossed. The national team's physical trainer in South Africa had a few words of warning. 'One worry is the large number of matches they make him play because that wears out his system,' he said. 'I hope they leave him in peace so he can go sunbathing with his wife for a week to recharge his batteries, because if not … It's impossible for a thoroughbred to set records at the San Isidro horse racing track every Sunday.'

Signorini told how one day he had convinced Messi not to play a match, a friendly against the Catalonia national team. And that is not easy to do. 'I spoke to Diego and said to him, "Leo must not play in this match. What does he represent to us? Another $200,000 for the Argentinian Football Association? Well, it doesn't come down to the AFA here. We have to think about the human being, too."

'So I said to a member of the technical team, "When Leo arrives, send him to my room." And he came. As soon as he came in, I said to him:

– How are you?
– Fine.
– Your left ankle hurts, doesn't it?
– No, sir.
– Yes, yes, it's swollen, don't give me that. You're not going to play in this match. Do you know what we're going to do? I've already spoken to Diego, you relax, leave, we will sort this out with the Barcelona medical team, catch your flight, fly to Buenos Aires, to Rosario … you're not playing in this match. Agreed? Leave it with me.

'I ruffled his hair, and then he left. Like a little child, Leo!'

The idea of not winning in Brazil did not come into Leo's head; he denied the possibility as he used to deny not getting into the Barcelona first team. It ate away at him that although he felt he was number one, he did not think he had yet made history. And he was possibly still clearing up an old doubt: that of being accepted. 'If we come back after the quarter-finals, they will lambast him again,' reflected Sacheri. 'And if he wins, maybe Diego will move aside for him. Or we put both of them on the altar, father and son. The advantage of Christianity is that way we can love more than one divine personality.'

Now that Messi had gotten used to being Messi, his goal was to win the World Cup.

As if it were written in the stars.

2. The World Cup. In Brazil

Argentina were drawn in a favourable World Cup group from which they were expected to qualify at a canter. Bosnia were making their bow at the tournament, Carlos Queiroz's Iran would be defensively hard to break down and Nigeria were a side that seemed to be at a standstill.

Several other stars had already announced their arrival on the world's biggest stage before Argentina's opener against Bosnia. Neymar, van Persie, Müller and Benzema had all found the back of the net. Not as much was expected from Cristiano Ronaldo, however, whose lingering injury problems over the previous three months had prevented him from performing at his best.

BOSNIA

15 June at the Maracanã. The Argentina supporters generated an electric atmosphere after spending the night on the beach having barbecues. Brazilian taxi drivers were heard complaining that 'it was full of Argentinians'.

Messi was seen chewing gum in the tunnel ahead of the game, exhibiting the assurance of a player who was accustomed to the big occasion, before suddenly bursting into laughter following an exchange with the children accompanying the teams out onto the pitch. But inside he could not wait to start. The recently renovated, iconic stadium erupted as Leo's name was read out. It was time to head out onto the pitch. The greyhound was about to explode out of the traps.

The national anthems were played, with Argentina choosing a shorter instrumental version, thereby avoiding any scrutiny of who did or did not sing along, which typically happens after defeats. The Argentinians crossed themselves ('Oooo, Argentina') as kick-off neared.

Argentina: Romero; Zabaleta, Campagnaro, Fernández, Garay, Rojo; Mascherano, Maxi Rodríguez, Di María; Agüero, Messi.

Bosnia: Begović; Mujdža, Spahić, Kolašinac, Bičakčić; Hajrović, Pjanić, Misimović, Bešić, Lulić; Džeko.

Sabella was aware that his team could be worryingly easy to break down. He was not fully sure of the sharpness of his strikers, so, with all things considered, he opted for three centre-backs in the starting line-up, just as he had done in a friendly against the same team, Bosnia, seven months earlier. His conservative instincts had taken over.

Sead Kolašinac's own goal gave Argentina the advantage in the fifth minute before the game had even taken shape. Leo's first diagonal run was far less fruitful as he lost the ball and ended up committing a foul. His subsequent involvements in the game, far away from the rival box, saw him struggle to control two passes that were fizzed at him. His first touch was rusty. He did not feel comfortable, surrounded by so many opposition players.

'*Oe, oe, somos locales otra vez*' ('Oe, oe, we're the local team again!') chanted 40,000 Argentinians at the Brazilian temple of football. The *cariocas* responded with 'Olés' whenever an increasingly comfortable Bosnia side completed successful passes as the Argentina passes were going astray.

Leo was roaming around the pitch hoping for a break and some space. He was saving energy for his sprints, but the slow build-up play stifled him. Just like the other forwards, he was not pressing the opposition when they brought the ball out from defence. The Argentina defensive line was too deep to try to press high, and without recovering possession in the opposition half, the element of surprise was non-existent. Leo even moved away from the ball in order to surprise Bosnia. It was not working – the team was not creating chances.

And it was becoming impossible to counter against a team that, after losing possession, moved quickly to defend very deep. Messi trudged off the pitch at half-time with a downward stare, reflecting on a half in which he lost the ball on 15 occasions and completed only 12 per cent of his forward passes. The Argentina supporters remained in buoyant mood with chants of 'Brazilians, Brazilians, you look so bitter, compared to Pelé, Maradona was better!' The reception from the locals was thunderous.

A conversation took place in the changing room. Leo told Sabella that the forwards were isolated, that it would be better if they could return to the 4-3-3 that had worked so well since that day in Barranquilla. For the start of the second half, Sabella switched from the frustrating 5-3-2 to the more attacking formation, to the delight of the offense-minded players. Centre-back Campagnaro and Maxi Rodríguez made way for Gago and Higuaín. The team was more balanced, with the midfield protecting the defence. Messi was placed closer to the rival box and with one extra player up front.

The 65th minute arrived; it was Leo's time. He went on a mesmerising diagonal run from right to left, just like in the videos of when he was eight years old, and drilled a left-footed strike home from the edge of the area, via the inside of the post. His second ever World Cup goal.

He celebrated by grabbing hold of his shirt, stretching it out in order to clearly reveal the crest, before raising his arms and pointing towards his family in the directors' box. Ibišević made it 2–1 with seven minutes remaining, bringing everybody back down to earth. Leo woke up again and went on a few more runs in the final ten minutes, finishing the game well as Argentina claimed their first victory of the tournament. Haris Medunjanin asked Leo for his shirt and he complied.

At the press conference, 'The Flea' had to carry out his media responsibilities as man of the match and explained, 'We did things that we're not used to in the first half, giving Bosnia space. I found it hard to get on the ball. I was far from the action and lost the ball quite a few times, which is why I was frustrated. Things weren't coming off for me.'

Higuaín, Agüero, Zabaleta and Mascherano all repeated the same idea. The system used in the second half was the one. It had to be accepted that Leo needed two forwards and a winger beside him, thereby creating more space in attack. Sabella concurred: 'Although we controlled Bosnia, we didn't really get in behind them and threaten. The match had become really flat. You couldn't see where our second goal would come from. Anything could have happened. We had more room to improve. Leo received better service and had more support after the changes.'

'The goal was a weight off all of our shoulders, especially mine,' concluded Leo.

Messi had three efforts on goal, was fouled twice and committed one himself, his passing accuracy was 88 per cent and he made two interceptions. He ran 8.1 kilometres. Six matches remained, if everything went to plan.

IRAN

The Bosnia match had planted a seed of doubt. Argentina had conceded too many chances and, in certain phases, too much possession, but the feeling was that Iran could be in for a hiding six days later. 'As if it was going to be easy,' said Pablo Zabaleta. The coach opted for the trusted 4-3-3 formation, showing his sensitivity to the team's demands. But he had to be convinced of the physical strength of the forwards to run forward and back to defend. Queiroz was aware of Argentina's uneasiness when taking the game to the opposition and consequently set his team up to defend deep, not leave space in behind the defence and hope that Leo would not produce any magic.

Half an hour before kick-off in the Estádio Mineirão in Belo Horizonte, 30,000 Argentinians eagerly awaited the arrival of their troops.

The much-desired and supposedly magic formation did not achieve much against a tactically astute Iran side. The team seemed disjointed and was not recovering possession in opposition territory.

> *Argentina: Romero; Zabaleta, Garay, Fernández, Rojo; Gago, Mascherano, Di María; Messi, Higuaín, Agüero*
>
> *Iran: Haghighi; Montazeri, Hosseini, Sadeghi, Pooladi; Timotian, Nekounam, Dejagah, Shojaei, Haji Safi; Ghoochannejad.*

There was no movement and no surprises. Argentina needed Sergio Romero to make three saves following Iran counter-attacks, which could have silenced the stadium, notably from a Reza Ghoochnannejad header in the 85th minute.

Leo, who was often waiting for the ball on the left of the attack, was creating danger from the odd set-piece. He managed to escape from his marker on a classic run down the middle before his shot grazed the outside of the post and went wide. It was a tough match and Leo threw up once again in the first half. He had to leave the playing field temporarily to refresh himself, have some water and let the retching pass.

According to his family, that bodily reaction is a consequence of unreleased pressure, but also of a small hiatal hernia that causes the reflux of stomach acid, provoking him to retch. Since a gastroenteritis specialist suggested it a few years back, he takes an antacid before going on to the pitch, but it doesn't always work.

Stoppage time arrived. Messi picked up the ball on the right wing, ran infield and aimed for the only place where he could score. His left-footed strike from the edge of the area nestled into the corner of the net, to the goalkeeper's right. The saviour had struck again. The stadium shook with delirium, celebrating it as more than a victory with chants of 'Que de la mano, de Lio Messi, todos la vuelta vamos a dar' ('With Leo Messi's hand, we're all going to Ring Around the Rosie'). It seemed to be the confirmation that something big was brewing. The stars were aligning for Argentina.

1–0.

Leo had not put a foot wrong, but his team-mates' contributions were scrutinised. However, the fact was that Argentina had qualified for the next round after only two games, while Spain and

England had already been eliminated from the World Cup at the same stage. Messi received a gargantuan hug from his coach in the tunnel.

'Thank God the "dwarf" rubbed his magic lamp in the last minute,' said Romero.

'Messi is a game changer. He's different from other players. Everything is possible when he's in your team,' explained Sabella.

'Everyone thought it would be easy, but they were very disciplined,' stated Zabaleta when I stopped him in the press area. 'In the first half, we had more strength to get the ball back high up the pitch, but in the second half, given we'd put so much into getting the first goal, the opposition took advantage, because they were in better physical shape, they'd been waiting for us. We know we run a risk. Playing the way we play, we are more exposed than others. It's difficult for the back four – we have to defend against many one-on-ones – but we have to get through.'

Just then Leo stopped to say hello, having received his second man-of-the-match award. 'How did you feel after the goal? Relieved, happy?' I asked him.

'Very happy.'

His extraordinariness had finished, as usual, with the last whistle.

During the press conference for his award, he added, 'We know that there's much room for improvement. We weren't expecting such a match. Up front we couldn't find any space against a well-armed defence that didn't allow us to play balls in between the defensive lines that cause the opposition so much damage. I don't think the state of the pitch helped us either. It was dry from the heat, which stopped us moving the ball around quickly, which is key when playing against a deep-lying defence.'

Messi ran 7.7 kilometres during the match.

He had scored eight times in his previous seven appearances for his country, and the most recent two meant he had achieved something that the great Diego Armando Maradona never managed: scoring in the first two games at a World Cup.

Incidentally, Diego left his seat at the Mineirão before Leo's strike. 'The bad luck charm left and we won,' said Julio Grondona, president of the Argentinian Federation, in the aftermath of the victory. Maradona used a daily television programme, on which he appeared with Víctor Hugo Morales in Brazil for Venezuelan television (*De Zurda*), to respond to him: 'What a stupid man. This [win] is because of Messi, not because I left.'

After making a quick escape from the press area in the stadium and arriving at the hotel in Belo Horizonte, Leo relaxed with his wife, son, parents and brothers.

The World Cup seemed to belong to either Leo or Neymar, who had also scored two in two. *Olé* ran with the headline 'A different God', but *El Gráfico* told the public, 'Don't let Messi hide the cracks.'

NIGERIA

25 June. Estádio Beira-Rio, Porto Alegre

Nigeria: Enyeama; Omeruo, Yobo, Oboabona, Ambrose; Onazi, Mikel, Odemwingie, Babatunde, Musa; Emenike.

Argentina: Romero; Zabaleta, Fernández, Garay, Rojo; Gago, Mascherano, Di María; Messi, Agüero, Higuaín.

José Sámano's column in *El País*: In order for Argentina to accurately measure their own performance, a clear assessment of Messi is needed. Every second that the star spends on the pitch must be examined: whether he runs or jogs, whether he touches the ball in the middle or runs with it, whether he smiles or raises his eyebrows, whether he disappears or finds himself on the ball frequently, whether a fly distracts him or he bewilders the opposition. Everything must be evaluated, no matter how insignificant it may seem. To the relief of all Argentinians, 'the Flea' was back to his best against Nigeria, and not the stiff player seen in recent times. He simply lit the game up. He went through the gears, unsettled defenders, made assists, found the net and even willingly accepted being substituted by Sabella just after the hour with a smile.

His first goal was a convincing finish after Enyeama parried a Di María effort. Musa levelled to begin a period of dangerous Nigeria counter-attacks as Argentina's midfield struggled to deal with the opposition's energy. Then Leo put his country back in front with a sublime free-kick just before the interval.

Kun had got injured by that point, which, according to Sabella, gave the team greater equilibrium, with Ezequiel Lavezzi coming in: one of the three forwards was no longer a number nine, but a winger aware of his defensive duties. Sabella was addressing the imbalances.

Musa struck again before Marco Rojo's header gave Argentina a 3–2 victory and first place in the group ahead of Nigeria. Messi's previous 24 international appearances had produced 17 victories, seven draws, 24 goals and five assists.

The World Cup in Brazil did not seem to be graced with the same Leo who had scored 91 goals in two and half years. He was more of an attacking midfielder than a striker. He would stamp his own pace on the game; sometimes he would stop the ball dead slowing down the play, at other times he would release it quickly. Messi was not losing his marker, and he would wait for the ball without putting pressure on the opposition.

Was there something going on with him?

The media debate ensued. 'Gago tries to quicken the rhythm with one or two touches,' wrote Jorge Valdano in *El País*. 'If he finds Messi, then great, but he is marked tightly like the genius that he is and furthermore he walks around looking for space. We all know that to lose your marker you have to know how to pull out all the tricks possible in football: accelerating and braking, feigning to go in order to go back, asking for the ball to feet, but also into space ... if you walk, it is impossible for any of this to happen.' Leo needed the ball to be taken wherever he was, cleverly 'at his door' explained Valdano.

Martin Caparrós also noticed a different Leo: 'Nobody doubts that this team should be great. For now, it is a strange network surrounding its sleepy hero. If young Messi showed anything especially surprising, it is that he was Messi all the time. Now he is in infrequent bursts: it is not enough. (When the game ended, I watched some videos of him: if that kid played, everything would be so easy.

The one playing now uses the ball in the same way, but has a third of the speed and a quarter of the drive.)'

'Messi saves the day with staggering, individual brilliance that only he can conjure up,' concluded Valdano.

Matthew Syed offered an alternative perspective from the Anglo-Saxon world: 'He takes the ball and literally stops. He stands there, like a mongoose facing a snake, daring his opponent to take a bite. These are fascinating moments in the game because they demonstrate that almost all the important action is going on not in the feet, but in the brain.'

He was becoming a player who chose his moments. Why?

Argentina entirely depended on those moments, meaning that if everything went well, the tournament would belong to Leo. Just like in 1986 with Diego.

SWITZERLAND. THE LAST SIXTEEN

The team had to travel to Sao Paulo for the last-16 clash with Switzerland. Many of the tournament favourites remained, but Italy had packed their bags, with Costa Rica and Uruguay qualifying from a tricky group. Luis Suárez, however, would play no further part in the competition after biting Italian defender Giorgio Chiellini, which served as an extraordinary reminder of the way in which others cope, or fail to cope, with the pressure.

In a World Cup packed full of goals, Argentina were yet to take off, but they were improving. Sabella thought it opportune to remind his troops that it was not 11 against 11, but 40 million Argentinians against 11. He showed them a motivational video.

'You are the warriors'. 'You are the strength of the country'. 'I hope you play with the excitement I feel right now'. 'Do it for my old man. I don't know how long he has left'. Supporters of all ages were sending in messages of encouragement. 'Strength, guts, heart, soul and life'. 'We're going to win, come on!'

Argentina: Romero; Zabaleta, Fernández, Garay, Rojo; Gago, Mascherano, Di María, Lavezzi; Messi, Higuaín.

Switzerland: Benaglio; Lichtsteiner, Djourou, Schär, Rodríguez; Inler, Behrami; Xhaka, Shaqiri, Mehmedi; Drmic.

Rojo: *Leo is happy and that is reassuring for us. He is the clear leader. Before each game he encourages us to give us confidence. The team spirit is great.*

Messi: *My role? I'm just another player. It's a spectacular group. We all get on very well, and all have the same vision of achieving something fantastic.*

Sabella had included Lavezzi in the line-up but insisted that the defensive line shouldn't be very high. Again that forced the forwards to start their runs deep and stopped any possibility of pressure high up the pitch. Argentina dominated, they had the lion's share of possession and created dangerous openings, but could not make their advantage count. The efforts to break down the Swiss defensive line came more from the heart than from organisation. Di María dilly-dallied on the ball, Lavezzi caused more damage coming off the bench, Rojo was rushing everything and Higuaín left his shooting boots in the dressing room.

Maradona: *I didn't like the set-up. I didn't like the way they built up from the back. Argentina don't have a change in rhythm. They seem weary and predictable.*

They were still two teams in one: up front, the two forwards; the rest of the team defending, but too deep. Mascherano and Gago had similar roles, and the full-backs were too frightened to push up. They were not getting in behind the opposition and were seemingly outnumbered all over the pitch.

Zabaleta: *We haven't hidden the fact that we've never played together as a team. We make the most of our firepower up front. We try to balance it with the six of us behind them so we aren't as exposed, but we know that we take that risk. We like getting in behind the opposition quickly, but the quicker the ball goes forward, the quicker it returns. We tried to be a more compact team against Switzerland.*

When the number ten occasionally got on the ball, it seemed that something was about to happen, although the one-twos were only coming off with Di María. But no danger was created. In fact, Leo was not seeing much of the ball at all, a tactical deficiency that was increasing as the competition was progressing.

The game went to extra time. You could smell penalties.

Mascherano: It was a very tough match. Everything about it was really tough. They were very well set up defensively. In Brazil, the favourites have been suffering in games that were supposed to be easy.

As extra time drew to a close, Switzerland lost the ball in the 118th minute. Rodrigo Palacio picked it up and passed to Leo, who ran towards the opposition penalty area with the ball attached to his foot. He left the first defender for dead.

Messi: I saw the space and started running. I thought about going for it myself ...

He reached the edge of the Swiss penalty area. He could have shot. The defenders awaited his decision. Leo looked right out of the corner of his eye.

Messi: ... then Fideo (Di María) turned up and I decided to give it to him.
Di María: Fer (Fede Fernández) told me during the break in extra time, 'You're going to win this game.'
Zabaleta: He always plays those accurate passes, which are perfect to be hit first time without needing to control the ball.
Di María: I just run forward, that's it. He decides who to give it to. And he gave it to me at just the right moment.

Di María shot on the run.

*Di María: I saw the goalkeeper moving towards one side, and I just
tried to slot it into the other corner.*

The ball nestled in at the far post.

*Di María: Messi is the best in the world. It's his goal, not mine. Only
he can create things like that.*
Messi: Luckily we were able to celebrate.

Delirium on the pitch. Delirium in the stands. In the country.

*Higuaín: It isn't easy to play against two banks of four when they
don't give you any space, but Leo had three or four runs that
made the difference. It's what we expect from a different player:
not quantity, but quality.*
*Zabaleta: What did I say to Leo after the goal? I congratulated him.
Although he didn't score the goal, his brilliance created it. We
shared the joy.*

Leo's last hug before the match resumed was with Di María.
But football is a strategy game. It all comes down to moments.
Things happen that escape logic and explanation. Dzemaili
hit the post just before the end. In a parallel universe, Dzemaili scores instead. It is possible. And Switzerland win the lot-
tery of penalties. It is possible too. How can that be explained?
Where would that have left Sabella? What would Leo be thinking
today?

*Zabaleta: In the dressing room? We sang ... we're a group that
always sings. Before or after, we have a sing-song.*
*Mascherano: I was so tired when I got back that I didn't really feel
like celebrating. I lost my voice because of shouting out on the
pitch.*
*Messi (chosen as man of the match for the fourth consecutive game):
It was really tough. We're tired from the effort we put in. We got
the result we wanted. Let's see what's up next. This World Cup*

*is full of surprises. Teams that nobody expected to perform have
done well.*

*Maradona: We didn't get going. Our team could have played bet-
ter, but we suffered. There are players capable of playing another
[superior] kind of football. We cannot be team Messi. Leo can
do his bit, but if it doesn't come off, let's not blame him for the
Argentinian catastrophe. Messi and Di María are the two keeping
the boat afloat. And the Jefecito [the little boss] Mascherano was
superb. His physicality was crucial.*

Di María had taken eight shots, Leo two (via @argen_stats), but
he created eight chances, more than any other player in one match
over the course of the tournament.

In general, Messi had never reached such a level with the national
team in big competitions, even if it was becoming clear that the
team was not built for him, but rather for a defensive structure that
had only conceded three goals so far and was producing results.

Messi on Instagram: 'Nobody said it would be easy. One more
little step.'

BELGIUM. THE QUARTERS

Light training continued. There was lots of time to kill. Meanwhile,
Sabella's messages insisted on one thing: the group. The strength of
the unit, the need for nobody to doubt themselves, even if the team
did not play well, or, more accurately, if the team did not play as
people liked, including many Argentinians. The group knew that
not everybody supported the style that had been chosen to get the
team to this point in the tournament.

The coach's words would prove to be important in the quarter-
final clash with Belgium, which gave Argentina the chance to reach
a first World Cup semi-final in 24 years. Yet every day the tournament provided a new talking point that dominated conversations
at the Argentina training camp. The Argentinian press had a field
day following Neymar's injury, which left the Brazilian with a fractured vertebra after a knee in the back by Colombian defender
Juan Zúñiga. The front cover of *Olé* arrived in Cidade do Galo:
'We wanted to beat him'. Argentina were only in the quarters! Any

possible clash with Brazil would have taken place in the final. Talk
about confidence.

Argentinians (commentators, supporters, football people) live
in search of a utopia, not a new one where they have never been
and to which they would like to aspire, but one where they believe
they have always been and belonged. Everybody mentions the 1986
World Cup victory as the reference point of footballing paradise.
In other conversations, however, people say that Maradona did it
all himself and it was a poor team. Some members of that squad
even insist that Diego's influence on the whole tournament did not
go beyond those ten minutes and that time creates legends. What
should we go with? Perhaps Sabella was right when he said that
the country believed itself to be more than it really was during a
press conference before the match. Although you can look at it differently: if you aspire for the best, if you dream of the final, you get
there quicker.

Leo sent his club team-mate a message over the social networks.
The dream encounter in the final at the Maracanã was not going
to take place: 'Neymar, I hope you get better very soon, my friend!'

Belgium, on the other hand, were receiving plenty of media hype.
Much was written about the methods used in order to produce a
very talented generation of players, although they had only been
applied seven years previously. In reality, the breakthrough of Hazard, Courtois, Origi, Lukaku and company was probably more a
case of a generation of talented players emerging spontaneously, as
had happened three decades before.

One thing was crucial, however. The weight of Belgium's football
history as a nation that has always respected the ball dictated that
they would not be able to play as Iran had done. Or Bosnia. Or
Switzerland.

The temperature on 5 July in the Estádio Nacional in Brasilia
was not as high as it had been in other stadiums. It was around
17 degrees in the shade, but very warm in the sun, where Belgium
would play in the first half. The dry air was like having cling film
over your face.

Olé reported that Mascherano gave the team-talk before the
game. 'I'm tired of eating shit,' he is reported to have said in reference to the previous two World Cups in which Argentina fell at

the quarter-final stage. 'We have to get over this hurdle for me, the former players and all of us. Come on!'

Argentina lined up in a 4-3-3 formation: Romero; Demichelis, Zabaleta, Garay, Basanta; Mascherano, Biglia, Di María; Higuaín, Lavezzi, Messi, who equalled Maradona's tally of international caps (91).

Belgium started with a 4-4-2 formation: Courtois; Kompany, van Buyten, Vertonghen, Alderweireld; Fellaini, Witsel, Hazard, De Bruyne; Mirallas, Origi.

Once out on the pitch, Leo read out a FIFA statement against racism at the Garrincha stadium, which was booed by the Brazilian supporters. Messi reacted without as much as a flinch, deaf to the outside world.

He was the one remaining superstar in a World Cup already without Cristiano, James Rodríguez (the Colombia attacking-midfielder) and Neymar.

Belgium seemed happy to have reached the latter stages of the tournament and never managed to find any real aggression during their periods of pressure. Argentina, on the other hand, demonstrated their pedigree with real desire to get on the ball, and they dominated the game at the slow pace that suited them. That day they all ran. And they all won the ball back. Messi's pressure on Witsel allowed Mascherano to recover possession in the eighth minute. He passed to Leo, who attracted the attention of De Bruyne and Fellaini before twisting and turning to get away from them. He drove forward and found Di María, who tried to play Zabaleta in down the right. The pass was blocked and fell to Higuaín, who struck it fiercely first time to score his first international goal since August 2013. Goooooooal. Just a few minutes had gone by since 88-year old Alfredo di Stéfano had suffered a heart attack, which would eventually take his life. The footballing world had its eyes on Argentina, for the good and the bad.

It was the match when Messi played *that* pass to Di María. An extraordinary technical moment. Argentina were defending in their area, they recovered possession following another toothless Belgium attack and Messi picked up the ball in the number-four position. Most other players would have given it to Di María, who had started his run in front of Leo, at that moment. Messi, however, feigned to pass but delayed for a tenth of a second so that his teammate's sprint would get him past the three players ahead of him. The pass was then delivered, taking six Belgians out of the game and landing at the winger's feet on the edge of the D, at the right time with the right pace, although Di María's shot was blocked by van Buyten. The Argentina winger got injured in the process and was replaced by central midfielder Enzo Pérez, another step towards the team Sabella was happier with: Argentina moved to deeper positions, gained control and became more organised at the expense of attacking threat. Without the fantastic four (Kun, Di María, Higuaín, Leo), Sabella had to find 'eleven lions' as Martín Mazur appropriately put it.

Marc Wilmot's men only created danger when they crossed the ball in for the target men, but the clock was moving exasperatingly slowly for Argentina, who continued to sing the song of the tournament.

Messi was more of a midfielder than ever. He was running more than ever, taking the free-kicks and dictating the rhythm as usual, although not consistently. He was doing a bit of everything in his most dynamic performance, but as the minutes went by he gradually waned, as did the rest of the team.

The match was coming to an end and Messi's moment arrived, a one-on-one with Courtois, but the Belgian won the duel. 'I was able to stop Messi, but not Higuaín,' complained the goalkeeper.

Messi attempted 21 passes, six in the second half, four misplaced ones, the joint most with Higuaín. He created chances, had one piece of play in the area and committed three fouls, while he was fouled only twice. He had five dribbles and four shots on goal. 'The Flea's' best team performance.

'I was never before asked to play like this. It was a match for running. We knew that we all had to give it our best to get through,' explained Messi. He got his hands dirty. The following day, it was said that he played like Riquelme. He helped his side have 53 per cent of possession. As Argentina were unable to counter-attack in the tournament, apart from a few moments against Nigeria, the team had to reinvent itself. It was becoming Mascherano's team.

Was that the Messi that audiences demanded? The topic was debated the day after the match. 'Against Belgium, Messi was Maradona for the first time in his career,' said *Olé* director Leo Farinella. 'He didn't show off, but he did what he had to. He was only missing a swollen ankle like Diego had.' Daniel Avellaneda from *Clarin* added that, 'When Messi arrived, he questioned Sabella's outline, but then he realised that you win a World Cup differently.' Others, such as Marin Eula, chief writer at *Olé*, and Diego Macías, chief writer on Ole.com, thought that those duties were damaging his already fragile physical state, as was seen with the failed one-on-one. It does say a lot about Argentina that what they expect of their main man is to run a lot.

Sabella fervently defended his star in the subsequent press conference. 'He's like water in the desert. He keeps the ball, he passes, he dribbles. He gives us air each time he's on the ball.'

In a match containing just three shots on target, a tournament low since the 1990 final, the stars on the day were Pipa Higuaín, Garay, Biglia, Demichelis and Mascherano, the last most of all. The World Cup was being defined by the Barcelona midfielder's commitment and work for the team.

Marc Wilmots later complained about the referee's leniency towards Leo after Italian Nicola Rizzoli let him off a yellow card. As for the result, Argentina had fallen in the quarter-finals in 1998, 2006 and 2010, in the last 16 in 1994 and in the group stage in 2002, with the help of a David Beckham penalty, but a solitary goal was enough to seal their progress to the semi-finals this time around.

Messi celebrated like a supporter, joining in the chants. 'It is a [great] feeling, I can't stop,' he sang with the fans. He hugged Higuaín, Maxi Rodríguez and Biglia. A 27-year-old boy whom everyone was trying to hunt down. When they did, he embraced them.

The hug with Kun was one of friendship, relief and extreme happiness, with a semi-final to look forward to. Being able to get over that hurdle [the quarter-finals] is very beautiful,' Leo said. He uttered the same sentiment on Instagram: 'One more little step! Come on Argentina!'

THE NETHERLANDS. THE SEMI-FINAL

On 9 July at the Arena in Sao Paulo, Argentina would try to reach a glorious final in Rio with the footballing foundations that they had established – a solid defensive team. No more, no less. They hoped that the Dutch tactical framework would leave a crack through which Messi's water would flow.

For the first time in World Cup history, Argentina, Brazil and Germany were all in the semi-finals. The outsiders (Belgium, Colombia, Costa Rica) had run out of steam in the quarter-finals. The Netherlands were attempting to reach their fourth final. Argentina, who were fast becoming the disappointment of world football along with England, were after their fifth. They had not won a title since 1993.

The route to the semi-final had been far from a breeze for Argentina, in stark comparison to their qualifying campaign leading to Brazil. They'd had to cope with injuries and had scraped through each match by the odd goal.

In the build-up to the game, Leo sent a message of condolence to Alfredo di Stéfano's family after the 88 year old sadly passed away. The match was for 40 million Argentinians, but also for him. And for Jorge 'Topo' López, a young Argentinian journalist who tragically died in a car crash aged 38 when a stolen car occupied by three men, including two teenagers, crashed into the taxi he was in. López, who was close to the Messi family, was the only victim. All three men were arrested. It was terrible for all of us who knew him. Leo wore two black armbands. One for Alfredo and another for Topo. Rest in peace.

Netherlands: Cillesen; De Vrij, Vlaar, Martins Indi; Kuyt, de Jong, Wijnaldum, Blind; Robben, Sneijder, van Persie.

Argentina: Romero; Zabaleta, Demichelis, Garay, Rojo; Pérez, Mascherano, Biglia, Lavezzi; Messi, Higuaín.

MY NOTES

The Netherlands line up with three centre-backs. It will be interesting to see how wing-backs Kuyt and Blind perform. Will they attack much?

Man-marking is taking place with de Jong tracking Messi and Wijnaldum following Mascherano around whenever he is in the attacking third.

Argentina with the initiative. They are unable to get in behind the opposition. The Dutch are not letting them. The Dutch wing-backs are hardly pushing up.

Nobody is changing the rhythm. Leo's not getting many touches of the ball as the opposition are surrounding him.

The only option: to find space in behind the wing-backs. Lavezzi understands this, generating danger down the right flank.

Garay comes close with a header from a corner in the 24th minute.

Mascherano, groggy from a clash of heads with Wijnaldum. He's recovered now, although he initially struggled, playing two horrible, wayward passes.

Without Di María and without a second striker, Leo finds himself isolated. He has to drop deep.

The whole game is being played within 15 metres either side of the halfway line.

'*Sieeeete, sieeeete, sieeeeete*' ('Seeeeeven, seeeeeven, seeeeeeven'), sing the Argentinian faithful. '*Pentacampeao ... Pentacampeao*' ('Five-time champions ... Five-time champions') retort the Brazilians.

Messi wins back possession and darts past Martins Indi, who is booked for grabbing a handful of his shirt.

A slow-paced, dour first half in which neither team has taken any risks comes to an end. After the first five minutes of the game, you could see extra-time or penalties were on the way.

[Apparently Leo was retching again in the tunnel at half-time.]

'*Brasil decime que se siente, comiste siete de local ...*' ('Brazil, tell me what you feel, you let in seven at home ...')

Both teams are waiting for a mistake or a moment of brilliance by Messi or Robben. The Netherlands have had just one shot on goal in over an hour.

Interesting: Clasie replaces de Jong in the 63rd minute – in theory, an attacking move.

It's been raining for large periods of the second half. The ball's moved quicker but nothing much has changed. Four corners in the first half, none as of yet in the second.

Another Argentina chance: Leo is involved in the build-up in the 75th minute. Enzo Pérez puts in a low cross which Higuaín gets a toe to. The ball deceptively nestled on the outside of the net, although the striker was incorrectly flagged for offside.

Leo finds it hard to get past quick players. The balance that Sabella found in his team does not go hand in hand with Messi's contribution to the team. He's run 7.8 kilometres over the 90 minutes. Robben has run 10, many of them back towards his own goal.

Extra-time looms. Wait a second: Sneijder plays a perfect through ball to Robben, who gets in behind and seems destined to score. Mascherano stretches out a leg and miraculously gets a block in. Yes, we are going to extra-time.

Sabella speaks to the players in the centre circle. Mascherano adds a few words ... Messi closes it off. He speaks with positive body language, moving his head with determination. He does not seem to be a boy.

Must ask Mascherano about what Messi said. [He later told me in the mixed zone: 'Nothing really. Just that he was very proud of what we were doing and that we had the sufficient strengths to go on and win this, that he was very confident and that we could win.']

Extra-time begins: the teams are both playing to stop the opposition playing.

First shot on target for the Dutch. And it is in the 98th minute!

Maxi enters the fray in the 99th minute. Until this point the changes have added nothing.

103rd minute. The stadium chants 'Messi, Messi', demanding a telling contribution, but he is hardly noticeable. The Netherlands are penned in.

The chance of the match arrives! Rodrigo Palacio. With just the keeper to beat, he tries to head the ball over him. The worst possible choice, poorly executed.

Messi dribbles past three players down the right. Is this his moment? He crosses it for Maxi, who cannot apply a fitting finish. That was a moment, but nothing materialised.

Penalties: 60 per cent of teams that take the first kick (Netherlands) progress, which effectively means statistics do not mean anything much when it comes to penalties – 60 per cent is practically a coin toss.

Vlaar goes up first! Romero saves it! But ... the ball bounces back to the goal but stands on the line. Nobody notices how close it was to being a goal.

Leo ... tricks the goalkeeper, who dives to his left with the ball going to his right.

Robben scores.

Garay scores! Messi clenches his fist. His facial expression still shows fear and tension.

Sneijder misses!

Kun, GOAL. Cillesen almost stopped it. Leo celebrates and covers his face with his hands. He jumps out of the group. The players stand in unison. Messi continues to cover his face.

Kuyt scores. 3–2 to Argentina.

Maxi ... If he scores, they go through. AND HE SCORES!

Leo does not run towards Maxi, but to Romero, who made two saves. His face is emotional.

He is crying.

And then decides to avoid the mixed zone by running away from the journalists hiding behind volunteers. Others are going to do the talking.

Leo on Facebook:

I had to have a drugs test and can't be in the dressing room experiencing this moment. I feel very proud to be part of this squad!! They are all phenomenal, what a match they had, it's crazy!!! We're in the final!! Let's enjoy it ... One more little step ...

A big hug to all of Argentina and a special mention for Jorge 'Topo' López, this victory is especially for you, my friend. A huge hug to the family, all the best, LIO.

He signed off with the Argentinian version of his name.

GERMANY. THE FINAL

It is a case of what if, but if you catch a replay of the match at the Maracanã on 13 July and stop seven minutes before the end, I'm sure you would agree with me that the final could have been won by either team. Argentina, in the words of a member of the Messi family on the eve of the game, 'had walked a chosen path, and that road showed them that they had to fight. That is what they did the whole tournament. They are ready for the final.'

In fact, Argentina did more than that – they were about to have their best 90 minutes of the World Cup. Then, with both teams tired in extra time, it was a coin toss.

Argentina: Romero; Zabaleta, Demichelis, Garay, Rojo; Biglia, Mascherano, Enzo Pérez; Lavezzi, Messi, Higuaín.

Germany: Neuer; Lahm, Boateng, Hummels, Höwedes; Kroos, Schweinsteiger, Kramer (a late replacement for Khedira, who was injured in the warm-up); Müller, Özil; Klose.

Messi led the team through the tunnel, and took the side to do a shorter warm-up than the Germans, who had already started. As he used to do when he was ten, he did the first stretches and the other players followed his routine. Muscles were being warmed up, heads relaxed.

In the path chosen by Sabella, the heroes were not the forwards, but Mascherano and three players who were not in the starting line-up against Bosnia in the first game: centre-back Demichelis, and midfielders Enzo Pérez and Lucas Biglia. Balance, coaches call it. Kun Agüero recovered and came on at half-time for Lavezzi in a very controversial decision: both Lavezzi and Enzo Pérez were doing a great job of stopping Lahm and Höwedes down the wings, and Argentina were controlling the game without the ball. The German high line allowed them to counter-attack for the first time in the tournament and they knew they were going to have chances. If they converted them, the job would be done.

And the opportunities came – the two front men found themselves in a two-on-two on a few occasions. Leo had chosen the right wing to attack, as he thought Höwedes had more weaknesses. He beat the full-back twice within ten minutes. His best chance was stopped by Hummels, who touched the ball inside the six-yard box just before Messi could connect. But he had to do much more than just create chances: he ran 30 metres after Schweinsteiger had taken the ball off him and forced a throw-in. He waited for the ball, his distant friend in this World Cup, in the midfield area. He had a chance just before half-time, and after the break a pass into space and a shot close to the post made Argentina fans hope for the best. Two shots on goal, with typical diagonal runs, suggested that he was not as sharp in front of goal as he had been two years previously.

'Messi could walk as the team was keeping the lines together in the defensive phase, so he could have fresh legs and energy to make the difference,' was José Mourinho's analysis later for Yahoo.com.

Higuaín had another big chance after a wayward Kroos header left him on his own with only the goalkeeper to beat, but he looked at the defender and lost sight of the ball before shooting without much power. A correctly disallowed Higuaín goal came next, and a possible penalty by Neuer on the Napoli striker wasn't given. The system was changed with the introduction of Agüero, and the team parted into two, as the front three did not have the legs to pressure the German build-up. Even so, Rodrigo Palacio came close again in extra time.

Meanwhile, Germany had responded well to the injuries of Khedira and Kramer. They moved the ball in clever triangles, forced some saves from Romero and were the sharper side in extra-time as Schürrle created havoc down the left flank against an exhausted side.

Anything could have happened, but, deep into extra time, it was Götze who had the last say with a moment of brilliance. He collected a cross from Schürrle, cushioned it on his chest and volleyed it past Romero. Garay arrived too late to intervene. 'Show the world you are better than Messi,' his coach Löw told him when he had came on for Klose just before the start of extra-time.

History was made. Germany, the best team overall during the previous month, had won the World Cup.

Leo won the award for player of the tournament. He had to collect it just after the game had finished. It was a ridiculous decision to make him do so immediately after such a difficult defeat.

The biggest defeat.

Brazil 2014 had not seen the best of Messi. He had thrown up again in the first half of the final, and various theories, on subjects ranging from his physical state to Argentina's tactics, were aired as being contributing factors for his below-par performances. His walking around the pitch, his deep position and his lack of touches up front in the knockout stages were all analysed in detail. 'He sacrificed himself for the team,' Mourinho said. 'He prefers to win than to be the top goalscorer. I saw him playing in areas that are not his usual ones. Coming deep to get the ball, then having to beat two rival lines, trying to create for his team to score. The Di María goal against Switzerland is a good example. Messi played for his national team and not everybody can say they did that in this World Cup.'

So, what exactly happened to Messi? Why did we not see him at his best?

Nothing happens by chance. *The Godfather Part II* came after *The Godfather*. And *The Godfather Part III* was filmed because Francis Ford Coppola was ruined after the failure of *One from the Heart*.

After every injury, as the tournament progressed, Alejandro Sabella wanted the team not to expose itself, not to concede. Especially after the Switzerland game, he asked the team to drop deeper and wait for counter-attacking chances. As a consequence, it was difficult for Leo to get into the box from his position close to the midfielders and around the halfway line. How did Leo become the best player in the world? By playing around 20 metres from the box. After Pep and Tito, and after a series of injuries, Tata Martino asked him to play in deep positions and with a different footballing concept – no pressure high up the pitch, fast transitions. Everything started to change for Leo.

Messi started walking onto the pitch seemingly with less commitment to el Tata. There was more of the same in Brazil. It coincided, not by chance, with him seeing less of the ball. He tried to create chances, and in some cases, when he got hold of the ball in space, managed to do so, but he was too far away from goal to do it often.

Crucially, his physical preparation had been designed for him to run as little as possible and for the ball to do the work instead. At Barcelona, the training sessions covered many situations in small spaces, including small games, where players did not have to cover long distances to have a goalscoring chance. If they wanted to defend deep, players would have to be prepared differently. Also, automatic reactions to game situations, all based on the idea of controlling games and affecting the play in the final third, had been drilled into Messi's head, via continuous repetitions of exercises since he'd arrived at Barcelona.

It is impossible for a Barcelona player with the physical shape of Messi, Iniesta or Xavi to have the physique to defend near their own box and then to dominate with the ball and create continuous chances in the opposition one. It just does not happen, and that is why Guardiola succeeded – he realised his team had to play in the opposition half as often as possible. To defend and to attack.

With the reduction in possession that Martino and Sabella's teams had enjoyed compared to previous years, Messi's legs suffered immensely, even after only 45 minutes. He was not ready for that kind of game and couldn't still be expected to have bursts of acceleration and pace over 50 metres.

In terms of physical condition, deep positions are demanding in different ways. Neither Xavi, nor Iniesta, nor Messi, nor Pedro, are physically capable of defending 50 metres away from their area and then, a moment later, arriving in opposition territory with the ball under control to score. To do that, you need very high levels of aerobic power (described scientifically as the highest amount of oxygen a person can consume during maximal exercise of several minutes' duration) in order to be able to cover lots of ground and recover quickly. Centre-midfielders consistently exert more energy and they do so more often than forwards or attacking midfielders, who have more time to recover from any explosive runs or sprints.

Players also need to maintain their intensity and repeat it, all of which requires training. Players without that aerobic power who are forced to play deep cannot cope for more than 50 minutes putting in that kind of physical effort. If you throw the Brazilian humidity and high temperatures into the mix, the players needed physical conditioning far superior to the average in Europe. Simply too many factors went against Messi's body. If you also consider that Leo had had years of training and developing with a team whose tendency was very rarely to play on the counter-attack, it becomes clear that it was always very unlikely that we would see the very best from Messi in Brazil.

Hence his walking. In fact, his sprints in the last ten minutes against Iran, Switzerland, Belgium or the Netherlands suggested that he ended the games with enough petrol in the tank to do damage when defenders were more tired.

Also, the fear factor Leo generates meant he was man-marked in certain games and generally defended against zonally by more than one player. An added hurdle.

However, Messi had chances that he could have converted. No doubt about that.

Gabriele Marcotti raised another issue in his column on ESPN. Messi's running in the World Cup (8.15 kilometres on average per game) was similar to the 2012–13 Champions League (8.22). But the pace had changed: 'According to FIFA's numbers, Messi achieved a top speed of 29.6 km/h (18.4 mph) at this World Cup ... it's still somewhat jarring to see Messi clock in at a full 2 km/h less than Mario Yepes, who is more than a decade older. There is not a single forward among the four semi-finalists who reached a lower top speed.' There is something to say about Leo being surrounded by players when he got the ball and being fouled to avoid him gaining an advantage, but the stats could show the effect of a long season too. In any case, nobody could say that Argentina, in the World Cup, were designed for his characteristics or to win in the attacking way they had played in the qualifiers. It was, instead, a very defensive team that exalted another type of player. It took them to the final. But this tournament would not become Leo's World Cup.

The newspapers repeated the same word: *orgullo* (pride). The team had recovered historical lost ground and had shown a way to compete that made Argentinians proud. But there was space for criticism too. 'Maybe more could have been done. Messi was not up for the challenge,' Mario Kempes said. 'I expected more from him.' But he also added, 'I could tell he was not happy on the pitch. He did not have much company around him.'

Maradona also felt that the player of the World Cup award was not deserved: 'I would give heaven and earth to Leo, but when marketing people want him to win something he didn't [deserve to] win, it is unfair. I could see that he didn't want to go up and collect it [the award].'

On television there were also stronger words. 'He is the best in the world but was not the best one in the tournament. It might sound ungracious, but I expected much more from him … it was a good World Cup for Argentina, but not for Leo,' said Diego Díaz of TyC Sport.

Messi would be 31 at the next World Cup. By then, perhaps he would have evolved tactically into a number ten. If he wanted to lengthen his sporting career, he needed to take a step back on the pitch and use other characteristics of his game that do not always require explosiveness and maximum muscular demands. And to change his physical preparation to be able to recover and adapt.

The following season was going to be the first one of the new era. And Leo had, even before travelling to Brazil, discussed his new role with the club. He was happy to accept the changes. In fact, having Luis Suárez and Neymar in front of him, in a similar role to the one he enjoyed with the national team before the World Cup, could only be an exciting project. But first, he had to take the pain away.

4

Thiago: The Definitive 10

This is what Gerardo Martino told Guardiola in a public chat in Buenos Aires in the summer of 2014, a month after he had left the *blaugrana* club: 'Pep's Barcelona were the best team in history. The comparison was never positive. At Barcelona, winning is not enough. If we won, that was down to the players, and if we lost, it was down to me. It made it hard to continue. And it is very pleasing when players publicly back the manager, but only briefly. They had to do it often, which is very tiring.'

The 2013–14 season was a very complicated one. The mysterious resignation of Sandro Rosell in January 2014 set the tone for the rest of the campaign. Under pressure for the contradictory information about the Neymar transfer (with Barcelona eventually admitting that they had paid a third more for him than they had said initially, which had potential implications for the taxman, as some of the money was wrongly accounted), under pressure as well from his own family, especially his influential dad, and with difficulties in his personal business, a feeling of isolation at the club had grown in Rosell, perhaps provoked by the his lack of trust in some of his collaborators.

Rosell had reduced the club's debt by more than €230 million and had won two league titles, one Champions League, a World Club Cup and a Copa del Rey, but the distance between him and Leo Messi had grown with time, culminating in the slowness of the renewal of his contract, a promise Rosell had made to Jorge Messi in August 2013. More than a renewal, it was going to be an 'adjustment' in relation to Neymar's wages and the new Ronaldo contract, which earned the Portuguese star €17 million net. Messi was going to be, Barcelona promised, the best-paid player in the world. But for months the club gave out the impression that they were not in a rush to agree a deal, and that they were willing to sell the player if anybody came in with €250 million to meet his buy-out clause. That possibility was further enhanced by accident in a private email during the negotiations.

There were other situations that went against the idea of a well-run club and with the right values at the forefront of their decisions. The Audiencia Nacional (a national high court) investigated the Neymar transfer. In addition, FIFA punished Barcelona for contravening the rules regarding transfers of players under 16 and 18 years old. They could not sign anybody till June 2015.

The club's image had been tarnished.

In the sporting arena, injuries to Neymar, Piqué, Valdés, Messi and Jordi Alba affected the side well beyond performances on the pitch. The lack of authority on the bench also meant less commitment from the players. As well as Valdés, Puyol announced his departure and eventually said goodbye in a press conference that occurred, strangely, during the last few days of the season, when the team was fighting for the title. Xavi Hernández decided to look for an opportunity abroad and spent the summer looking for a way out of the club, a more difficult exercise than he expected. There was a clear lack of leadership in the squad.

The players did not gladly accept the new methodology brought in by Tata Martino and his physical trainer, Pautasso. Too regimented, too different from what the players were used to. Martino did not understand the criticism because he felt that it came as a result of an agenda, not from a genuine football discussion. He wanted to change the side – Barcelona had to evolve or take a different route. He insisted on that. But he soon realised that not everybody (at the top as well as on the training ground) wanted to change.

The squad, so the players thought, was not designed for double pivots or for the counter-attack. The team was playing less as a unit and only individual talent helped Barcelona continue to challenge for titles. They were on top of the table for 24 weeks. But without doubt the worst news that season was the death of Tito Vilanova, the manager who had started the campaign. The cancer that he had been battling for three years took him at the early age of 45. The coach who had placed Leo in his favourite position, the one who had helped Leo reached unparalleled heights, the one who had spoken about football more than any other with Leo, especially after taking over the team, was gone. The gentleman with the spirit of a man from a countryside village died on 25 April 2014.

El Tata, who had been offered the Argentina national post, as Sabella was thinking of leaving after Brazil, had managed to keep the team unbeaten for 20 weeks, reach the semi-finals of the Copa del Rey, convincingly beat Manchester City in the last-16 of the Champions League and destroy Rayo, who had beaten his team in terms of possession earlier in the season, with an impressive 6–0 scoreline. It had all seemed to be going the right way, but the big nights were approaching. A defeat against Real Sociedad, with Xavi and Cesc surprisingly on the bench, and Busquets and Song as centre-midfielders, cut short the false impression that everything was fine. Not even a Messi hat-trick against Madrid, in a 4–3 victory at the Bernabéu, covered the cracks.

Barcelona were knocked out by Atlético in the quarter-finals of the Champions League, lost the cup final against Real Madrid, and defeat versus the modest Valladolid and Granada handed the impetus in the title race to Real Madrid or Atlético, with the latter side competing with dignity against the winners of the last nine titles. Barcelona were handed one last chance: they had to beat Diego Simeone's team at the Camp Nou in the last game of the season. Xavi was left on the bench.

A basic defensive mistake from a corner meant that Atlético got the point they needed and won the title. Deservedly so. The fans demanded change. So did Leo Messi, unable to rescue a side that had lost their essence: hard work had been replaced by complacency. The team was getting older without grace.

The club managed to get the transfer ban suspended pending an appeal, but the restructuring was agreed by the decision makers. Tata Martino announced his departure the same night as the Atlético draw.

Two days later, Messi, who had scored 41 goals in a season in which nobody had been at the required level, signed his new contract next to the new chairman, Josep Maria Bartomeu, just before flying to Argentina to join the national team. He was going to be the best-paid player in the world, but the buy-out clause was not going to be changed. Strangely, the documents were signed at the airport in Barcelona. The moment required a better stage. And when he landed in Buenos Aires, Leo, who wanted to respond to the whistles he received from certain sections of the Camp Nou in the last game of the season three days earlier, sent a message to the fans: 'The day that I am not wanted, I will not stay. I love the club but if there are people who do not want me, who doubt me and prefer me to go, I have no problem at all. I will go. My choice is to continue, but ...' It sounded like something he wanted to get off his chest. A complaint and an attempt to address the situation: he had heard the fans' discontent; now they were hearing his.

Leo had demanded a competitive team for the next season during the contract negotiations. The restructuring was going to be led by Luis Enrique, announced on 19 May, as the new Barcelona coach for two seasons.

The former Barcelona player promised Leo two things: the team was going to be led by him, and it was going to be a strong squad. Messi found out that Luis Suárez was on his way and was very excited about the idea. His friend Cesc left for Chelsea and Alexis was going to be sold to Arsenal, but he heard Luis Enrique's plans for the team, the formation he wanted to play, and it sounded not only like a new collective challenge but an individual one too for 'the Flea'.

In April 2013, in *Kicker* magazine, Jorge Messi explained the transformation that he imagined his son might eventually have to undergo on the pitch: 'I can see him playing deeper, as a playmaker, something that he already does from time to time at Barça. He starts off many passages of play from deep.' Pep Guardiola trusts Leo's intelligence and intuition to make the next step. 'Central midfielder? No. Well, I don't know. It's an option, I guess. I just know that if he's tip-top, his team will always be the favourite to win any match he plays in until the day he retires. When he is on form. Obviously you can't be at the top level for eleven months a year for fifteen to twenty years of a sporting career. But if he gets it into his head that he is fit enough, no team can stop him.'

The tactical change, his evolution, was also as a result of opposing teams playing with a very compact midfield so that Messi could not cause damage. Traps were being placed in front of him so that he could not develop his game. So it was getting to the point that to make the most of the fear that he generated in his rivals, he was going to have to look for his team-mates, for Neymar and Luis Suárez, for two wing-backs, not just to use them for one-twos and finishing the play: he was going to have to become a number 10 under Luis Enrique, even if that meant going away from the usual 4-3-3. The whole idea, a challenge to the positional game that required tactical discipline from the forwards so that they would be well placed to recover possession when it was lost, was questioned by Johan Cruyff: 'The three of them are individualists. It has become clear that Barcelona prefers individual actions to a team that plays good football.' What a tactical prospect, and one that raised many questions about the group dynamic, ones that only time would answer. Leo relished the possibilities.

Leo ran one risk, said Fernando Signorini: 'Atahualpa Yupanqui used to say, "Vanity is a human weed that poisons every garden."' What he was referring to was that, in Argentina, if you are successful they pump 'vanity into your veins'. Signorini said that Leo could not take that risk: 'In reality, I would like him not to come to Argentina too often, or at least just enough time for him to enjoy it without losing any of his spontaneity and freshness. Look at what Diego is going through, the hell they are forcing him to live through. He is a prisoner of having made so many people happy through his talent.'

Faced with the possibility of winning a World Cup and the pressure of compensating for the many deficiencies in Argentinian life by being the 'star' that the people needed him to be, Signorini offered some advice: 'He has to make the family his rock. Now it is him, his girlfriend, his son and the children to come. Everything else is superficial. He's fantastic, and she is too. I met her and they seem to make a great couple, the type who bring a smile to your face and make you say, "Look at how sweet they are. They get on so well and to think of what they have to deal with ..."'

Would it be Leo or his body that showed the first signs of decline? A new study claimed that a child who specialises in sports before the age of 15 increases the risk of injury and exhaustion by one and a half times. It was an old theory: Adriano, Robinho, Kaka, Owen, Cassano, Ronaldinho ... they were all at the top of the footballing world, but they could not maintain that highly competitive level for very long. They were overwhelmed by the success and proved incapable of living with it. Burnout syndrome, defined initially by Freudenberger during the seventies, is more psychological than physical, an imbalance between perceived demands of the player and his ability to meet them. And the fire that consumes and burns gradually swallows up his motivation.

Messi had always been capable of responding to new challenges and handling what was thrown at him, but at some point he would need to change his thoughts and beliefs about reality. 'His mental training will become more important than physical, technical or tactical training,' explained trainer Pedro Gómez. 'His own motivation will be his real engine. Long may he continue playing as if he were a boy!'

Charly Rexach masterfully explained the footballer's transformation: 'You don't start to dip until twenty-nine or thirty, so he still has a few years left yet, but you suddenly take longer to recover from each match. And there is another effect, which is worse than the physical one: you enjoy yourself less and less – they don't let you enjoy yourself. At twenty years old, you play with freedom. You mess around as much as you want. You are gradually given the responsibility of deciding matches. You have to win them yourself. And then another phase arrives, the one where you're 3–0 up, you've scored one or two, and the coach takes you off in the second half because the match that needs to be won is the next one. Even if you complain and say you want to play more for fun, the coach tells you that you can't, someone else will have fun. So as you get older, you only play to win.'

Then they would start to take the ball off Leo. And then keep him away from it. 'There is more and more responsibility and it is more and more difficult to maintain the level,' said Rexach. 'Messi has taken on that responsibility and embraces it. But he also needs others who can take over, to bag the goals if he isn't there, so that we are ahead when he comes back. These days you suffer three defeats and you can lose a league.'

'I dare say he will have to make a change,' said the former Argentina player. 'Something changed in my head, making me want to be a coach. I see that he's always going to want to play. And he'll be thirty-three, thirty-four and will still want to carry on playing. But he will have to prepare himself for it, over the years, not now, but later on, to see what he likes.' And one day he would go home, to play, to be with his people and to enjoy himself again, his mother included. At Newell's. And he would eventually stop playing. We would no longer see him every weekend. Di Stéfano gave up. Pelé gave up. So did Maradona. And he would have to be well looked after so that the loss would be tolerable. And those whom he loves would also have to be prepared.

'It just so happens I was talking about that with my wife the other day,' explained Jorge Messi in *Kicker*. 'I told her the day Leo stops playing, I think I will lose all the excitement I have for the game and will stop watching it. I love everything about football and imagining that Leo will not play anymore one day distresses me. I don't even want to think about it.'

Martín Souto, asking Messi if he wanted to be a coach one day: Do you like it? In the future do you plan to ...?

Leo Messi: I always say no. As things are today, I'm not going to be a coach, but at some point in the future I don't know what might happen. Maybe I will want to try and give it a go.

Martín Souto: Let's see ... let's pretend, let's play ... how would Messi's team play?

Leo Messi: I have learnt things from all the coaches I've had. During my time at Barça I've been lucky enough to be with Rijkaard, Guardiola. The same ideas, the same game philosophy, but I can tell you: I don't even think about it because I don't think I'll be one.

(Interview with Leo Messi by Martín Souto on TyC, March 2013)

In the same interview, Lionel explained how one day, quite recently, he'd gone to see his brother Matías play in the village, with the boys, with Ever Banega's brother. 'The Flea' had wanted to join in. And they wouldn't let him. He was not on the player list for that amateur league and the opposition would not accept him being added to his brother's team. Obviously.

Martín Souto: When you finish with football, would you like to live
   in Argentina?
Leo Messi: Yes, today I'd say yes. My son is going to be growing up,
   he will definitely go to school here [in Barcelona] so I don't know
   when I'll go back there.

A newborn son often becomes an incentive. Many parents want
to start and finish the training session, dedicate that moment to
football with all the intensity they are capable of, in order to go
back home to play with their sons. Piqué, Cesc and Leo belong to
that group, having all become fathers at around the same time. As
with all changes, there are losses. Leo has grown up with his family
by his side, some closer than others, but only geographically. Emotionally they have been a rock. And now it's his turn to split from
them, and live with his wife and son. When that happens, the player,
who knows his relatives have sacrificed everything for him sometimes feels in debt in some way and something inside him breaks a
little. Newfound independence is sometimes accompanied by other
changes, such as those involving one's house, town and surroundings. This causes tension. And that can also cause injuries. The birth
of a son brings new anxieties with it. Antonella would often tell
Lionel that having a child had to be, was going to be, the most
beautiful thing that can happen to you. 'Until you have one, you
can't appreciate it,' 'the Flea' said on TyC. 'You just can't explain it.'

Thiago was born on the seventh floor of a hospital overlooking
the Camp Nou. The *Nuls* supporters celebrated with the banner
'Welcome Thiago Messi to the *LEPROSO* WORLD . Thiago Messi
Member N. 2.288.152.' An amusing attempt to make him a club
member, but it was not true that he was one. You could imagine
which team he would support one day, but Leo had not registered
him yet. He changed Thiago's nappies. He bathed him. And he said
that the child had only peed on him once ... And, meanwhile, life
changed him. 'You no longer think about yourself. You think about
him, so that he never has any type of problem whatsoever. Yes, it
changes, of course it changes the way you perceive things,' Messi
said in *El País*.

'Leo is a different man,' said Oscar Ustari. 'When I ask him, he
sends me photos. My son is even named Bautista Lionel after him.'

'Thiago comes first, everything else after,' Leo said on ESPN. In his first match after his son was born, he wore boots with Thiago's name on the heels, and a few weeks later he sported a wristband with the words 'I love you, Thiago'. And on Father's Day he tattooed his name on his calf. And almost everything was new: his first Christmas as a father was different. 'Now he's here and he's the one who gets all the cuddles, I'm learning to be a dad,' he confessed to *Olé*.

But not everything changed. Leo still had a reinvigorating siesta on the sofa or in bed. Just before nodding off, he would look at his phone, where his son's face appeared. On finishing training, Leo would go home to Thiago, and if he was asleep, it would be he who would wake him up. He would go for a walk with his wife or drive to his father's house to spend the afternoon there. When Messi travelled with the team, Thiago would look for him without understanding why his dad was not there, and Leo would call him and tell him that he missed him and that he could not wait to get back to be with him. Thiago would listen without understanding yet. It's the same story for parents all over the world.

Leo said that even his nieces and nephews called him Messi: 'I say to them, "You are a Messi too!"' Maybe one day he would have to explain to his son who 'the Flea' was. And one day he would take Thiago to the park to play football. When he was ten years old, Leo would be around 37. And he would pass him the ball.

Dramatis Personae

(Part 1, Chapter 2. Waiting for Leo)

Eduardo Abrahamian: Former River player and then leader of the *Infantiles* section at River.

Leandro Benítez: Defender and left-back, former team-mate of Messi in Newell's 'Machine of '87'. His last club was Quilmes Atletico Club.

Nestor Casal: Former workmate of Jorge Messi.

Franco Casanova: Team-mate of Messi in the 'Machine of '87'.

Adrián Coria: Leo's coach in the lower ranks of NOB (Newell's Old Boys).

Gabriel Digerolamo: Leo Messi's coach at the beginning in the lower ranks of NOB.

Enrique 'Quique' Domínguez: Coach of Leo Messi (1998–99), when he was 11 and 12 years old. His team was known as the 'Machine of '87'. It was his last year at the Newell's school.

Gazzo: Radio host, presenter at the time of the programme *Baby Gol*.

Leandro Giménez: Ex-player.

Liliana Grabín: Specialist in sports psychology.

Gerardo Grighini: Team-mate of Messi in the lower ranks at Newell's in 'the Machine of '87'.

Juan Cruz Leguizamón: Newell's goalkeeper in the 'Machine of '87', and friend of Messi. He currently plays for Central Córdoba.

Sergio Levinsky: Author, sociologist and Argentinian journalist.

Kevin Méndez: The Friendship Cup of 1996 in Peru was organised by Cantolao, the team that Kevin Mendez, son of William Mendez, was playing for and in whose house Leo lodged after asking the NOB coaches who their best player was. Today Kevin is a professional chef, and still has the first shirt Leo ever swapped with another player.

William Méndez: During the summer of 1997, Messi lodged at the house of the Mendez family in Pueblo Libre, Peru, during the celebration of a tournament. William is the father of the boy who played with Messi on that occasion.

Roberto Mensi: Member of the Newell's board, in charge of media. Also a sports reporter. Producer of www.morenoycordoba19hs.com.ar. Columnist on www.elrojinegro.com.

Jorge Messi: Leo Messi's father.

Matías Messi: Older brother of Leo, Rodrigo's younger brother.

Bruno Milanesio: Ex-junior player at NOB.

Diego Rovira: NOB's number 9 and striker during the time Messi was player in '87.

Nestor Rozín: Former director of Newell's; leading businessman in Rosario.

Ángel Ruani: Father of 'Luli' Ruani, team-mate in the 'Machine of '87'.

Roberto Saviano: Italian writer and author of *Gomorra*, and author of a text on Leo Messi.

Lucas Scaglia: Said to be Leo's best friend, team-mate at NOB, and cousin of Messi's wife, Antonella. Now playing with Deportivo Cali in Colombia.

Diego Schwarzstein: Rosario doctor who treated Messi for his hormone growth deficiency.

Federico Vairo: Leading figure in the Fifties and Sixties and then supervisor of the *Infantiles* trials at River Plate.

Jorge Valdano: Ex-footballer and Argentina coach and world champion with Argentina in the 1986 Mexico World Cup. Played up front; his first club was NOB.

Ernesto Vecchio: Technical director who had Lionel Messi for the longest period in the red and black baby section; recognised trainer.

Claudio Vivas: Trainer and co-ordinator of the Malvinas school (his father was the founder), and also the director of the fourth and fifth sides at Newell's. Pitch assistant to Bielsa for the national side. One of the architects, along with Tocalli and Pekerman, who ensured Messi played for the Argentine national side.

Diario Olé: Argentinian sports newspaper.

Kicker: Prestigious German sports magazine.

Additional Sources

Abrahamain, Eduardo and Vairo, Federico: quoted in Martínez, Roberto, *Barcargentinos*, De Vecchi Ediciones, 2013

Benítez, Leandro: article 'Messi, el gen argentino', *Cabal*, Argentina, www.revistacabal.coop

Casanova, Franco: quoted in article by Federico Bassahún, *Perfil*, Argentina, www.perfil.com

Digeralamo, Gabriel: quoted in *Informe Robinson: Messi*, Canal Plus. 2007

Mendes, Kevin and Mendez, William: quoted in article by Javier Saúl, *Canchallena*, Argentina, www. canchallena.lanacion.com.ar

Mensi, Roberto: quoted in article by Maria Julia Andrés, 'El Diego que hizo crecer a Messi', http://florecerdelupines. blogspot.com.es

Messi, Jorge: quoted in Martínez, Roberto, *Barcargentinnos*, De Vecchi Ediciones, 2013; *Kicker*, Germany; *Informe Robinson: Messi*, Canal Plus, 2007

Messi, Matías: quoted in *Informe Robinson: Messi*, Canal Plus, 2007

Rovira, Diego: quoted in article by Ignacio Fusco, *Don Julio 1*, Argentina, www.revistadonjulio.com

Rozín, Nestor: quoted in *Messi, la historia Argentina*, Canal 13, 2013

Valdano, Jorge: interview with Enric Gonzàlez, *JotDown*, www.jotdown.es

Vecchio, Ernesto: quoted in *Canchaallena*, Argentina, www.canchaallena.lanacion.com.ar/www.rosariofutbol.com

Bibliography

(including books, magazines, articles and DVDs/videos consulted)

Books:
Aguinis, Marcos. *The Terrible Charm of Being Argentinian*. Planeta, 2001
Amez de Paz, Eduardo. *Life Through Football*. Rosario: published by the author, 2002
Archetti, Eduardo. *The Paddock, the Track and the Ring*. Cultural Economic Foundation, Buenos Aires, 2001
Calzada, Esteve. *Show Me the Money*. Cabecera Books, 2012
Cubeiro, J. C. and Gallardo, Leonor. *Messi, Falcao and Cristiano Ronaldo*. Alienta Ed., 2013
Diario Sport. *Stars of the Masía*. Diario Sport, 2010
Frieros, Toni. *Leo Messi: The Treasure of Barcelona*. Diario Sport, 2006
García-Otero, J. M. *Dreams of a Little Prince*. Madrid: Al Poste Editions, 2013
Gil, Jordi. *Discovering Cesc Fàbregas*. Diario Sport, 2012
Hunter, Graham. *Barça: The Making of the Greatest Team in the World*. Back-Page Press, 2012
Ibrahimović, Zlatan. *I am Zlatan Ibrahimović*. Albert Bonniers Förlag, 2011
Jackson, Phil and Delehanty, Hugh. *Eleven Rings: The Soul of Success*. Penguin Books, 2013
Martín, Ramiro. *Messi: A Genius in the School of Football*. Lectio Editions, 2013
Martínez, Roberto. *Barçargentinos*. De Vecchi Ediciones, 2013
Mateo, Juan and Lillo, Juan Manuel. *Leading in Difficult Times*. McGraw-Hill/Interamericana de España, SA, 2003
Minguella, J. M. *Almost the Whole Truth*. Base Ed., 2008
Perarnau, Martí. *The Road of Champions*. Columna Editions, 2011
— *Pep's Long Journey*. Madrid, first published, 2012
Pereira, L. M. and Bandeira, J. P. *Messi's Bible*. Prime Books, 2012
Puig, Albert. *The Strength of a Dream. The Roads to Success*. Plataforma, 2010
Rodríguez Gairí, Sique. *Taught to Win*. Now Books, 2011
Syed, Matthew. *Bounce: The Myth of Talent and the Power of Practice*. HarperCollins, 2010
Torquemada, Ricard. *Fórmula Barça*. Lectio Editions, 2012
Torres, Diego. *Preparing to Lose*. Ediciones B, 2013
Udenio, Enrico. *The Argentinian Hypocrisy*. Books on the net, 2007
Villoro, Juan. *When We Never Lost*. Alfaguara Editions, 2011

DVDs/Videos:

Audemars Piguet spot 'Defining Moment'

Baabour, Gustavo. *Messi, The Argentina Story*. Special programme by TN Sports transmitted on 13/01/2013, TN Argentina News Channel

Gok, Guney. *Lionel Messi, World's Greatest Player* [documentary]. ITV 4, 2012

Lax, Lisa and Stern, Nancy. *Unmatched* [DVD]. Hanna Storm, ESPN films, 2010

Leo Messi: The Flea File, the Beginnings [Programa TV]. Expediente Fútbol, Fox Sports, 2012

López, G., Serrat, J. and Represa, R. *Porta 104: Messi, ADN blaugrana* [DVD]. Barça TV, 2009

McDowall, Mike. *Ronaldo, Tested to the Limit* [documentary]. Castrol Edge, 2011

Oliversa, Luciano. *Leo's World* [TV programme]. DeporTV, 2013

Robinson, Michael. *Informe Robinson: Messi*. Canal +, December 2007

— *Informe Robinson: The Legend of Trinche*. Canal +, November 2011

Souto, Martín. *The Private Messi. Especial Líbero* [TV programme]. Líbero, TyC Sports, 2013

Various videos from Punto Pelota, Intereconomía

Varsky, Juan Pablo. *Kun Agüero*. Interview on Direct TV Sports

Articles (specifically ordered for this book or borrowed from other authors):

Gómez Piqueras, Pedro. 'Will Leo's fire at Barcelona be extinguished?'; 'Leo Messi, the X factor of a genius in full flow'; 'The Ten Emotional Strengths of Leo Messi'; 'Messi and "piggy-in-the-middle"'; 'If you reach the finishing line, onward, onward, onward!'; 'Emotional Intelligence and Football'; 'FCB, Quantum Football for a Future Age'

Levinsky, Sergio. 'The Professional Boys' Syndrome'

Articles consulted:

Altman, Daniel. 'Economy and Football. Shared Hardships'. Published on Brando (www.conexionbrando.com)

Asch, Hugo. 'The Fathers of Patriotism'. Published on Perfil.com

Candance, Piette. 'Argentine home city's pride in football star Messi'. Published on BBC News

Caparros, Martín. 'Diatribe against Messi'. Published on SoHo.com.co.

Carlin, John. 'Pep Guardiola: Football's Most Wanted'. Published in the *Financial Times Magazine* (www.ft.com)

Casas, Gabriel. 'Messi, the idol without epic'. Published on Marcha.org.ar

Casciari, Hernan. 'Messi is a dog'. Published in *Orsai*

Daskal, Ouriel. 'Talent is not a gift. It's a skill'. Published on Soccerissue.com

Padilla Castro, Nelson. 'The Capital Sins of Messi'. Published in *El Espectador* (www.elespectador.com)

Saviano, Roberto. 'Little Big Man'. Published in the culture supplement of *El Clarín*, Argentina

Thompson, Wright. 'The idol without a city'. Published on ESPN Sports

Viel, Ricardo. 'Neymar and the Monster'. Published in *El Puercoespín*. (www.elpuercoespin.com.ar)

Magazines:

AuGol, sports magazine, Argentina (www.augol.com)

Canchallena, daily digital sports magazine *La Nación*, Argentina (www.canchallena.lanacion.com.ar)

Digital Cable Magazine (www.revistacabal.coop), Argentina

Don Julio, Eleven Stories of Football, Argentina (www.revistadonjulio.com)

L'Équipe Sport Style, France (www.sportetstyle.fr)

ESPN Sports (http://espndeportes.espn.go.com/la-revista/)

Gente, weekly Argentinian magazine (www.gente.com.ar)

El Gráfico, sports magazine, Argentina (www.elgrafico.com.ar)

JotDown, cultural magazine, Spain (www.jotdown.es)

Kicker, sports magazine, Germany

Negro & White, Argentina (www.negrowhite.net)

Orsai, Argentina (www.editorialorsai.com)

Panenka, football magazine, Spain (www.panenka.org)

Worldsport 360 (www.worldsport360.com)

XL Semanal, Sunday supplement of the Vocento Group, Spain

Newspapers:

AS, Madrid, Spain (www.as.com)

La Capital de Rosario, Argentina (www.lacapital.com.ar)

El Clarín, Argentina (www.clarin.com)

El Comercio de Perú, Peru (www.elcomercio.pe)

Corriere della Sera, Italy (www.corriere.it)

La Gazzetta dello Sport, Italy (www.gazzetta.it)

Marca, Madrid, Spain (www.marca.com)

Mundo D, sports supplement of *La Voz*, Argentina (www.lavoz.com.ar)

El Mundo Deportivo, Barcelona, Spain (www.mundodeportivo.com)

Noticias Hoy, Mexico (www.noticiashoy.com.mx)

El País, Madrid, Spain (www.elpais.com)

Panorama, Venezuela (www.panorama.com.ve)

Perfil, Buenos Aires, Argentina (www.perfil.com)

El Periódico de Catalunya, Spain (www.elperiodico.com)

La Razón, Buenos Aires, Argentina (www.larazon.com.ar)

El Sol, Mendoza, Argentina (www.elsolonline.com)

Sport, Barcelona, Spain, (www.sport.es)

La Vanguardia, Barcelona, Spain (www.lavanguardia.com)

La Voz, independent newspaper from Castelldefels, Barcelona, Spain (www.lavoz.cat)

Blogs:

Alejandro Carnero blog: The Ball Does Not Bend: http://la-pelota-no-dobla.blogspot.com

Roberto Martínez blog: Touch and Dribble: http://toqueygambeta.com

Humberto Perozo blog: From My Arcade http://desdemiarqueriapanorama.blogspot.com.es/

For further resources, please visit my website at www.guillembalague.com

Acknowledgements

Having just finished writing a biography of Pep Guardiola, Alan Samson and David Luxton suggested doing a book on Messi. 'Why not?' I said, not looking at the calendar. It has been a very rewarding and demanding few months, with plenty of trips, reading and conversations to try to get to understand what moves and motivates someone as special as Lionel Messi.

But none of this would have made sense if I had not spoken to the people that love him most. You know who you are and how grateful I am.

Talking of special. This book would not have passed the finish line without the time, effort and love put in it by Maribel Herruzo. Thank you is not enough, so we will have to go to Morocco. And thanks so much to Kike Duce for looking after (and cooking for) Maribel!

Having the manuscript read by Luis Miguel García, my best friend and the most privileged brain I know, is one of the biggest luxuries of this project.

A thousand thanks to Orion and Alan for having giving me the opportunity again to use my time wisely writing, instead of wasting it; I don't know, relaxing or something. Honestly, it is an honour and a privilege to have your confidence. Thanks, David, for listening to me at any time and any day; as you are aware, the concept of time disappeared in my mind. Lucinda McNeile has got the most subtle and charming way to put pressure and give encouragement.

The hard work of Peter Lockyer all summer has helped the book take shape. The injection of enthusiasm of Marc Joss at the end gave me a new push and all that was overseen by the greatest motivator of all, William Glasswell.

Sergio Levinsky was always available and cheerful, and was a needed source of good news in Argentina. He provided contacts and/or interviews with Alejandro Sabella, Professor Salorio, Fernando Signorini, Pancho Ferraro, Liliana Grabín, Carlos Bilardo, Gustavo Oberman, Eduardo Sacheri and Gerardo Grighini. Brent Wilks gave us all support so the whole house didn't collapse.

I have to be eternally grateful again to Pep Guardiola who gave me time to talk about a very unique time in his life. The same has to be said of Esteve Calzada who laid the first brick of this building; I owe you lots, Esteve.

Santi Solari was the perfect guide in Rosario and we started a conversation that continues even when he is not around. Pedro Gómez gave me new angles on this simple but complex world of football. The knowledge and encouragement of Pep Segura, Pako Ayestarán and of Youknowwhoyouare run throughout this book.

While I wrote and travelled, Stevie Rowe and Scott Minto dealt wonderfully with my moods and tiredness. Thanks for being so understanding. Damien O'Brien, James Wheeler (thank you for your stats!) and the rest of the Revista crew (Mark Payne, Luke Arthur, George Lansdale, Adam Chenery, Graham Hunter) have always had a word of support which was a bigger boost than they think. But it would have been very different without the confidence Dave Lawrence and Nigel Dean had in me.

Thank you so much to President Sandro Rosell for taking time from his busy agenda to add his personal touch to this book. And I owe a few meals to Iñigo Juárez – choose the restaurant.

I learned so much about Messi and football (and life) talking and listening to Sir Alex Ferguson, Edwin van der Sar, Míchel Salgado, Steve Clarke, Fabio Capello, Rafa Benítez, Henrik Larsson, Asier del Horno, Patrick Vieira, Claudio Vivas, Pere Gratacós, Henk ten Cate, Xavi Llorenç, Alex García, Quique Domínguez, Juan Carlos Garrido, Rodolfo Borrell, Gerardo 'Tata' Martino, Xavi Hernández, Andrés Iniesta, Pancho Ferraro, Carlos Marconi, Carlos Bilardo, Alejandro Sabella, Fernando Signorini, Gerardo Salorio, Juanjo Brau, Diego Schwarsztein, Liliana Grabín, Cesc Fàbregas, Eiður Guðjohnsen, Javier Mascherano, Pedro Rodríguez, Giovanni van

Bronckhorst, Fernando Navarro, Gerardo Ruben Grighini, Guillermo Amor, Gustavo Oberman, Gerard Piqué, Sylvio Mendes Campos 'Sylvinho', Oscar Ustari, Víctor Vázquez, Pablo Zabaleta, Roberto Martínez, Ramón Besa, Ferran Soriano, Txiqui Begiristain, Joan Gaspart, Joan Laporta, Carles Reixach, José María Cuartetas, Josep Maria Minguella and Professors Andreas Sosa, Diana Torreto, Mónica Domine, Silvana Suárez, Cristina Castañeira.

I needed the help of these friends who always gave me a hand and returned calls straight away: Chemi Teres, Gerard Autet, Nathan Smith, Pedro Pinto, Xavi Alegría, Sergio Alegre, Gabrielle Marcotti, Raphael Honigstein, Hernán Amez, Cristina Cubero, my teacher and friend Moisés Alvarez, Peter Bennett, Gaizka Mendieta, Joey Barton and of course Mark Wright.

Special thanks to the time and work put in by Oscar Elías, Eugenia Vega, my cousin Elena Cruz, Oliver Trust, Mariajo Fernández (for helping Maribel), Magda Gascón (for her help about the politics of the Catalan language), Federico Bassahún and Nacho Fusco (editors of *Don Julio*), Gerard Nus (with a clever transcription of the Guardiola speech in Buenos Aires), Luis Calvano, Coco Ventura, Diego Torres, Javier Sánchez Napal (author of the song 'Mundo Redondo'), Martín Souto (who did the fantastic interview with Leo for TyC Sports) and Brian Zwaschka (with his suggestions about Phil Jackson and Michael Jordan).

My brother Gustavo knows how hard it is to work on deadlines and was always very supportive. My sister Yolanda even transcribed interviews – everybody gave a hand! My mother looked after me even when she struggled to fight off her own headaches, and seeing my dad reading the Pep book, after decades not opening one, and then looking for new ones to read is the biggest reward I got for writing it.

So thank you all.